DRAMA
for Students

Presenting Analysis, Context, and Criticism on Commonly Studied Dramas

Volume 14

Jennifer Smith, Editor

Foreword by Carole L. Hamilton

GALE GROUP

THOMSON LEARNING

Detroit • New York • San Diego • San Francisco
Boston • New Haven, Conn. • Waterville, Maine
London • Munich

DRAMA
for Students

National Advisory Board

Drama for Students

Staff

Editor: Jennifer Smith.

Contributing Editors: Anne Marie Hacht, Michael L. LaBlanc, Ira Mark Milne, Daniel Toronto, Carol Ullmann.

Managing Editor, Content: Dwayne D. Hayes.

Managing Editor, Product: David Galens.

Publisher, Literature Product: Mark Scott.

Literature Content Capture: Joyce Nakamura, *Managing Editor*. Michelle Kazensky, *Associate Editor*.

Research: Victoria B. Cariappa, *Research Manager*. Sarah Genik, Ron Morelli, Tamara Nott, Tracie A. Richardson, *Research Associates*. Nicodemus Ford, *Research Assistant*.

Permissions: Maria L. Franklin, *Permissions Manager*. Kim Davis, *Permissions Associate*.

Manufacturing: Mary Beth Trimper, *Manager, Composition and Electronic Prepress*. Evi Seoud, *Assistant Manager, Composition Purchasing and Electronic Prepress*. Stacy Melson, *Buyer*.

Imaging and Multimedia Content Team: Barbara Yarrow, *Manager*. Randy Bassett, *Imaging Supervisor*. Robert Duncan, Dan Newell, Luke Rademacher, *Imaging Specialists*. Pamela A. Reed, *Imaging Coordinator*. Leitha Etheridge-Sims, Mary Grimes, David G. Oblender, *Image Catalogers*. Robyn V. Young, *Project Manager*. Dean Dauphinais, *Senior Image Editor*. Kelly A. Quin, *Image Editor*.

Product Design Team: Pamela A. E. Galbreath, *Senior Art Director*. Michael Logusz, *Graphic Artist*.

Table of Contents

The Study of Drama

We study drama in order to learn what meaning others have made of life, to comprehend what it takes to produce a work of art, and to glean some understanding of ourselves. Drama produces in a separate, aesthetic world, a moment of being for the audience to experience, while maintaining the detachment of a reflective observer.

Drama is a representational art, a visible and audible narrative presenting virtual, fictional characters within a virtual, fictional universe. Dramatic realizations may pretend to approximate reality or else stubbornly defy, distort, and deform reality into an artistic statement. From this separate universe that is obviously not "real life" we expect a valid reflection upon reality, yet drama never is mistaken for reality—the methods of theater are integral to its form and meaning. Theater is art, and art's appeal lies in its ability both to approximate life and to depart from it. By presenting its distorted version of life to our consciousness, art gives us a new perspective and appreciation of reality. Although, to some extent, all aesthetic experiences perform this service, theater does it most effectively by creating a separate, cohesive universe that freely acknowledges its status as an art form.

And what is the purpose of the aesthetic universe of drama? The potential answers to such a question are nearly as many and varied as there are plays written, performed, and enjoyed. Dramatic texts can be problems posed, answers asserted, or moments portrayed. Dramas (tragedies as well as comedies) may serve strictly "to ease the anguish of a torturing hour" (as stated in William Shakespeare's *A Midsummer Night's Dream*)—to divert and entertain—or aspire to move the viewer to action with social issues. Whether to entertain or to instruct, affirm or influence, pacify or shock, dramatic art wraps us in the spell of its imaginary world for the length of the work and then dispenses us back to the real world, entertained, purged, as Aristotle said, of pity and fear, and edified—or at least weary enough to sleep peacefully.

It is commonly thought that theater, being an art of performance, must be experienced—that is, seen—in order to be appreciated fully. However, to view a production of a dramatic text is to be limited to a single interpretation of that text—all other interpretations are for the moment closed off, inaccessible. In the process of producing a play, the director, stage designer, and performers interpret and transform the script into a work of art that always departs in some measure from the author's original conception. Novelist and critic Umberto Eco, in his *The Role of the Reader: Explorations in the Semiotics of Texts,* explained, "In short, we can say that every performance offers us a complete and satisfying version of the work, but at the same time makes it incomplete for us, because it cannot simultaneously give all the other artistic solutions which the work may admit."

Thus Laurence Olivier's coldly formal and neurotic film presentation of Shakespeare's *Hamlet* (in which he played the title character as well as directed) shows marked differences from subsequent adaptations. While Olivier's Hamlet is clearly entangled in a Freudian relationship with his mother, Gertrude, he would be incapable of shushing her with the impassioned kiss that Mel Gibson's mercurial Hamlet (in director Franco Zeffirelli's 1990 film) does. Although each of the performances rings true to Shakespeare's text, each is also a mutually exclusive work of art. Also important to consider are the time periods in which each of these films were produced: Olivier made his film in 1948, a time in which overt references to sexuality (especially incest) were frowned upon. Gibson and Zeffirelli made their film in a culture more relaxed and comfortable with these issues. Just as actors and directors can influence the presentation of drama, so too can the time period of the production affect what the audience will see.

A play script is an open text from which an infinity of specific realizations may be derived. Dramatic scripts that are more open to interpretive creativity (such as those of Ntozake Shange and Tomson Highway) actually require the creative improvisation of the production troupe in order to complete the text. Even the most prescriptive scripts (those of Neil Simon, Lillian Hellman, and Robert Bolt, for example), can never fully control the actualization of live performance, and circumstantial events, including the attitude and receptivity of the audience, make every performance a unique event. Thus, while it is important to view a production of a dramatic piece, if one wants to understand a drama fully it is equally important to read the original dramatic text.

The reader of a dramatic text or script is not limited by either the specific interpretation of a given production or by the unstoppable action of a moving spectacle. The reader of a dramatic text may discover the nuances of the play's language, structure, and events at their own pace. Yet studied alone, the author's blueprint for artistic production does not tell the whole story of a play's life and significance. One also needs to assess the play's critical reviews to discover how it resonated to cultural themes at the time of its debut and how the shifting tides of cultural interest have revised its interpretation and impact on audiences. And to do this, one needs to know a little about the culture of the times which produced the play as well as the author who penned it.

Drama for Students supplies this material in a useful compendium for the student of dramatic theater. Covering a range of dramatic works that span from the fifth century B.C. to the 1990s, this book focuses on significant theatrical works whose themes and form transcend the uncertainty of dramatic fads. These are plays that have proven to be both memorable and teachable. *Drama for Students* seeks to enhance appreciation of these dramatic texts by providing scholarly materials written with the secondary and college/university student in mind. It provides for each play a concise summary of the plot and characters as well as a detailed explanation of its themes and techniques. In addition, background material on the historical context of the play, its critical reception, and the author's life help the student to understand the work's position in the chronicle of dramatic history. For each play entry a new work of scholarly criticism is also included, as well as segments of other significant critical works for handy reference. A thorough bibliography provides a starting point for further research.

These inaugural two volumes offer comprehensive educational resources for students of drama. *Drama for Students* is a vital book for dramatic interpretation and a valuable addition to any reference library.

Source: Eco, Umberto, *The Role of the Reader: Explorations in the Semiotics of Texts,* Indiana University Press, 1979.

Carole L. Hamilton
Author and Instructor of English
Cary Academy
Cary, North Carolina

Introduction

Purpose of Drama for Students

The purpose of *Drama for Students* (*DfS*) is to provide readers with a guide to understanding, enjoying, and studying dramas by giving them easy access to information about the work. Part of Gale's ''For Students'' literature line, *DfS* is specifically designed to meet the curricular needs of high school and undergraduate college students and their teachers, as well as the interests of general readers and researchers considering specific plays. While each volume contains entries on ''classic'' dramas frequently studied in classrooms, there are also entries containing hard-to-find information on contemporary plays, including works by multicultural, international, and women playwrights.

The information covered in each entry includes an introduction to the play and the work's author; a plot summary, to help readers unravel and understand the events in a drama; descriptions of important characters, including explanation of a given character's role in the drama as well as discussion about that character's relationship to other characters in the play; analysis of important themes in the drama; and an explanation of important literary techniques and movements as they are demonstrated in the play.

In addition to this material, which helps the readers analyze the play itself, students are also provided with important information on the literary and historical background informing each work.

This includes a historical context essay, a box comparing the time or place the drama was written to modern Western culture, a critical overview essay, and excerpts from critical essays on the play. A unique feature of *DfS* is a specially commissioned overview essay on each drama by an academic expert, targeted toward the student reader.

To further aid the student in studying and enjoying each play, information on media adaptations is provided, as well as reading suggestions for works of fiction and nonfiction on similar themes and topics. Classroom aids include ideas for research papers and lists of critical sources that provide additional material on each drama.

Selection Criteria

The titles for each volume of *DfS* were selected by surveying numerous sources on teaching literature and analyzing course curricula for various school districts. Some of the sources surveyed included: literature anthologies; *Reading Lists for College-Bound Students: The Books Most Recommended by America's Top Colleges;* textbooks on teaching dramas; a College Board survey of plays commonly studied in high schools; a National Council of Teachers of English (NCTE) survey of plays commonly studied in high schools; St. James Press's *International Dictionary of Theatre;* and Arthur Applebee's 1993 study *Literature in the Secondary School: Studies of Curriculum and Instruction in the United States.*

Input was also solicited from our expert advisory board (both experienced educators specializing in English), as well as educators from various areas. From these discussions, it was determined that each volume should have a mix of ''classic'' dramas (those works commonly taught in literature classes) and contemporary dramas for which information is often hard to find. Because of the interest in expanding the canon of literature, an emphasis was also placed on including works by international, multicultural, and women playwrights. Our advisory board members—current high school teachers—helped pare down the list for each volume. If a work was not selected for the present volume, it was often noted as a possibility for a future volume. As always, the editor welcomes suggestions for titles to be included in future volumes.

How Each Entry Is Organized

Each entry, or chapter, in *DfS* focuses on one play. Each entry heading lists the full name of the play, the author's name, and the date of the play's first production or publication. The following elements are contained in each entry:

- **Introduction:** a brief overview of the drama which provides information about its first appearance, its literary standing, any controversies surrounding the work, and major conflicts or themes within the work.

- **Author Biography:** this section includes basic facts about the author's life, and focuses on events and times in the author's life that inspired the drama in question.

- **Plot Summary:** a description of the major events in the play, with interpretation of how these events help articulate the play's themes. Subheads demarcate the plays' various acts or scenes.

- **Characters:** an alphabetical listing of major characters in the play. Each character name is followed by a brief to an extensive description of the character's role in the plays, as well as discussion of the character's actions, relationships, and possible motivation.

  Characters are listed alphabetically by last name. If a character is unnamed—for instance, the Stage Manager in *Our Town*—the character is listed as ''The Stage Manager'' and alphabetized as ''Stage Manager.'' If a character's first name

is the only one given, the name will appear alphabetically by the name.

  Variant names are also included for each character. Thus, the nickname ''Babe'' would head the listing for a character in *Crimes of the Heart,* but below that listing would be her less-mentioned married name ''Rebecca Botrelle.''

- **Themes:** a thorough overview of how the major topics, themes, and issues are addressed within the play. Each theme discussed appears in a separate subhead, and is easily accessed through the boldface entries in the Subject/Theme Index.

- **Style:** this section addresses important style elements of the drama, such as setting, point of view, and narration; important literary devices used, such as imagery, foreshadowing, symbolism; and, if applicable, genres to which the work might have belonged, such as Gothicism or Romanticism. Literary terms are explained within the entry, but can also be found in the Glossary.

- **Historical and Cultural Context:** This section outlines the social, political, and cultural climate *in which the author lived and the play was created.* This section may include descriptions of related historical events, pertinent aspects of daily life in the culture, and the artistic and literary sensibilities of the time in which the work was written. If the play is a historical work, information regarding the time in which the play is set is also included. Each section is broken down with helpful subheads.

- **Critical Overview:** this section provides background on the critical reputation of the play, including bannings or any other public controversies surrounding the work. For older plays, this section includes a history of how the drama was first received and how perceptions of it may have changed over the years; for more recent plays, direct quotes from early reviews may also be included.

- **Criticism:** an essay commissioned by *DfS* which specifically deals with the play and is written specifically for the student audience, as well as excerpts from previously published criticism on the work.

- **Sources:** an alphabetical list of critical material quoted in the entry, with full bibliographical information.

- **Further Reading:** an alphabetical list of other critical sources which may prove useful for the student. Includes full bibliographical information and a brief annotation.

In addition, each entry contains the following highlighted sections, set separate from the main text:

- **Media Adaptations:** a list of important film and television adaptations of the play, including source information. The list may also include such variations on the work as audio recordings, musical adaptations, and other stage interpretations.

- **Topics for Further Study:** a list of potential study questions or research topics dealing with the play. This section includes questions related to other disciplines the student may be studying, such as American history, world history, science, math, government, business, geography, economics, psychology, etc.

- **Compare and Contrast Box:** an ''at-a-glance'' comparison of the cultural and historical differences between the author's time and culture and late twentieth-century Western culture. This box includes pertinent parallels between the major scientific, political, and cultural movements of the time or place the drama was written, the time or place the play was set (if a historical work), and modern Western culture. Works written after the mid-1970s may not have this box.

- **What Do I Read Next?:** a list of works that might complement the featured play or serve as a contrast to it. This includes works by the same author and others, works of fiction and nonfiction, and works from various genres, cultures, and eras.

Other Features

DfS includes ''The Study of Drama,'' a foreword by Carole Hamilton, an educator and author who specializes in dramatic works. This essay examines the basis for drama in societies and what drives people to study such work. Hamilton also discusses how *Drama for Students* can help teachers show students how to enrich their own reading/viewing experiences.

A Cumulative Author/Title Index lists the authors and titles covered in each volume of the *DfS* series.

A Cumulative Nationality/Ethnicity Index breaks down the authors and titles covered in each volume of the *DfS* series by nationality and ethnicity.

A Subject/Theme Index, specific to each volume, provides easy reference for users who may be studying a particular subject or theme rather than a single work. Significant subjects from events to broad themes are included, and the entries pointing to the specific theme discussions in each entry are indicated in **boldface.**

Each entry has several illustrations, including photos of the author, stills from stage productions, and stills from film adaptations.

Citing Drama for Students

When writing papers, students who quote directly from any volume of *Drama for Students* may use the following general forms. These examples are based on MLA style; teachers may request that students adhere to a different style, so the following examples may be adapted as needed.

When citing text from *DfS* that is not attributed to a particular author (i.e., the Themes, Style, Historical Context sections, etc.), the following format should be used in the bibliography section:

> ''Our Town,'' *Drama for Students.* Ed. David Galens and Lynn Spampinato. Vol. 1. Detroit: Gale, 1998. 227–30.

When quoting the specially commissioned essay from *DfS* (usually the first piece under the ''Criticism'' subhead), the following format should be used:

> Fiero, John. Essay on ''Twilight: Los Angeles, 1992.'' *Drama for Students.* Ed. David Galens and Lynn Spampinato. Vol. 2. Detroit: Gale, 1998. 247–49.

When quoting a journal or newspaper essay that is reprinted in a volume of *DfS,* the following form may be used:

> Rich, Frank. ''Theatre: A Mamet Play, 'Glengarry Glen Ross'.'' *New York Theatre Critics' Review* Vol. 45, No. 4 (March 5, 1984), 5–7; excerpted and reprinted in *Drama for Students,* Vol. 2, ed. David Galens and Lynn Spampinato (Detroit: Gale, 1998), pp. 51–53.

When quoting material reprinted from a book that appears in a volume of *DfS,* the following form may be used:

> Kerr, Walter. ''The Miracle Worker,'' in *The Theatre in Spite of Itself* (Simon & Schuster), 1963, 255–57; excerpted and reprinted in *Drama for Students,* Vol. 2, ed. Dave Galens and Lynn Spampinato (Detroit: Gale, 1998), pp. 123–24.

We Welcome Your Suggestions

The editor of *Drama for Students* welcomes your comments and ideas. Readers who wish to suggest dramas to appear in future volumes, or who have other suggestions, are cordially invited to contact the editor. You may contact the editor via E-mail at: **ForStudentsEditors@galegroup.com.** Or write to the editor at:

Editor, *Drama for Students*
The Gale Group
27500 Drake Rd.
Farmington Hills, MI 48331-3535

Literary Chronology

1670: William Congreve is born on January 24 in Bardsey, Yorkshire, England.

1695: William Congreve's *Love for Love* is published.

1729: William Congreve dies in January and is buried in Westminster Abbey in London, England.

1732: Pierre-Augustin Caron de Beaumarchais is born on January 24 in Paris, France.

1751: Richard Brinsley Sheridan is born on October 30 in Dublin, Ireland.

1779: Richard Brinsley Sheridan's *The Critic* is first performed at Drury Lane on October 30.

1784: Pierre-Augustin Caron de Beaumarchais's *The Marriage of Figaro* is published.

1799: Pierre-Augustin Caron de Beaumarchais dies on May 18 in Paris, France, from a stroke.

1816: Richard Brinsley Sheridan dies on July 7 and is buried in Poet's Corner in Westminster Abbey in London, England.

1906: Sidney Kingsley is born on October 22 in New York City.

1906: Lillian Hellman is born on June 20 in New Orleans.

1916: Natalia Ginzburg is born.

1920: Alice Childress is born on October 12 in Charleston, South Carolina.

1924: Kobo Abe is born on March 7 in Tokyo.

1928: Edward Albee is born on March 12 in Washington, D.C.

1930: Harold Pinter is born on October 30 in Hackney in East London.

1933: Sidney Kingsley's *Men in White* is published.

1934: Sidney Kingsley wins the 1934 Pultizer Prize for Drama for *Men in White*.

1935: Mart Crowley is born in Vicksburg, Mississippi.

1937: Arthur Kopt is born on May 10 in New York City.

1941: Lillian Hellman's *A Watch on the Rhine* is published.

1941: Lillian Hellman wins the 1941 Drama Critics Circle Award.

1943: Sam Shepard is born on November 5 in Fort Sheridan, Illinois.

1948: Pearl Cleage is born on December 7 in Springfield, Massachusetts.

1951: Paula Vogel is born on November 16 in Washington, D.C.

1956: Alice Childress wins the 1956 Obie Award for Best Original Off-Broadway Play and is the first woman playwright ever to receive this award.

1964: Harold Pinter wins the New York Film Critics Award for *The Servant*. He later wins the British Film Academy Award in 1965 and 1971. He also wins the New York Drama Critics Circle Award for *The Homecoming*.

1964: Kobo Abe wins the 1964 special jury prize from the Cannes Film Festival for the film *Woman in the Dunes*.

1966: Edward Albee's *A Delicate Balance* is published.

1967: Edward Albee wins the Pulitzer Prize for Drama and later wins a Tony Award in 1996 for the best revival play of the year.

1967: Kobo Abe's *The Man Who Turned into a Stick* is published.

1968: Natalia Ginzburg's *The Advertisement* is published.

1968: Mart Crowley's *The Boys in the Band* is published.

1969: Alice Childress's *Wine in the Wilderness* is published.

1977: Sam Shepard's *Curse of the Starving Class* is published.

1984: Lillian Hellman dies from a heart attack on June 30 in Martha's Vineyard, Massachusetts.

1988: Paula Vogel wins the Pulitzer Prize for Drama, as well as the Obie Award, Drama Desk Award, New York Drama Critics Award, Outer Circle Critics Award, and Lucille Lortel Award.

1988: Harold Pinter's *Mountain Language* is published.

1991: Natalia Ginzburg dies from cancer.

1993: Kobo Abe dies of a heart attack on January 22.

1994: Alice Childress dies from cancer on August 14 in New York City.

1995: Pearl Cleage's *Blues for an Alabama Sky* is published.

1995: Sidney Kingsley dies on March 20 in Oakland, New Jersey, after a stroke.

1998: Paula Vogel's *How I Learned to Drive* is published.

1999: Arthur Kopt's *Y2K* is published.

Acknowledgments

The editors wish to thank the copyright holders of the excerpted criticism included in this volume and the permissions managers of many book and magazine publishing companies for assisting us in securing reproduction rights. We are also grateful to the staffs of the Detroit Public Library, the Library of Congress, the University of Detroit Mercy Library, Wayne State University Purdy/Kresge Library Complex, and the University of Michigan Libraries for making their resources available to us. Following is a list of the copyright holders who have granted us permission to reproduce material in this volume of *Drama for Students (DfS)*. Every effort has been made to trace copyright, but if omissions have been made, please let us know.

COPYRIGHTED MATERIALS IN *DfS*, VOLUME 14, WERE REPRODUCED FROM THE FOLLOWING PERIODICALS:

American Journal of Psychotherapy, v. XLIV, October, 1990. Reproduced by permission of the Association for the Advancement of Psychotherapy.—*Contemporary Literature*, v. 9, Spring, 1968. Copyright © 1968 The Board of Regents of the University of Wisconsin System. All rights reserved. Reproduced by permission.—*Essays in Literature*, v. 7, Spring, 1980. Copyright 1980 by Western Illinois University. Reproduced by permission.—*Journal of Popular Film & Television*, v. 23, Summer, 1995. Copyright © 1995 Helen Dwight Reid Educational Foundation. Reproduced with permission of the Helen Dwight Reid Educational Foundation, published by Heldref Publications, 1319 18th Street, NW, Washington, DC 20036–1802.—*Modern Drama*, v. 17, June, 1974; v. 42, Spring, 1999. Copyright © 1974, 1999 University of Toronto, Graduate Centre for Study of Drama. Reproduced by permission.—*The New Leader*, v. LXXX, June 30, 1997. © 1997 by The American Labor Conference on International Affairs, Inc. Reproduced by permission.—*The New York Times*, December 5, 1999 for "Going Online and Finding a Window on the Times" by Katie Hafner. Copyright © 1999 by The New York Times Company. Reproduced by permission.—*The Progressive*, v. 60, August, 1996. Copyright © 1996 by The Progressive, Inc. Reproduced by permission of *The Progressive*, 409 East Main Street, Madison, WI 53703.—*Representations*, v. 61, Winter, 1998 for "Embodying the Public Sphere: Censorship and the Reading Subject in Beaumarchais's *Mariage de Figaro*" by Elizabeth J. MacArthur. Copyright © 1998 by The Regents of the University of California. Reproduced by permission of the publisher and the author.—*Texas Studies in Language and Literature*, v. XIV, Fall, 1972 for "The Philosophical Assumptions of Congreve's *Love for Love*" by F.P. Jarvis. Reproduced by permission of the publisher.

COPYRIGHTED MATERIALS IN *DfS*, VOLUME 14, WERE REPRODUCED FROM THE FOLLOWING BOOKS:

Auburn, Mark S. From *Sheridan's Comedies*. University of Nebraska Press, 1977. Copyright © 1977 by the University of Nebraska Press. Reproduced by permission.—Brown, Janet. From *Feminist Drama: Definition and Critical Analysis*. The Scarecrow Press, Inc., 1979. Copyright ©1979 by Janet Brown. Reproduced by permission.—DeRose, David J. From *Sam Shepard*. Twayne Publishers, 1992. Copyright © 1992 by Twayne Publishers. All rights reserved. The Gale Group.—Griffin, Alice. From *Understanding Lillian Hellman*. University of South Carolina Press. © 1999 University of South Carolina. Reproduced by permission.—Hall, Ann C. From "Voices in the Dark: The Disembodied Voice in Harold Pinter's *Mountain Language*," in *The Pinter Review: Annual Essays 1991*. The University of Tampa Press, 1991. Reproduced by permission of the author.—Jennings, La Vinia Delois. From *Alice Childress*. Twayne Publishers, 1995. Copyright © 1995 by Twayne Publishers. The Gale Group.—Knowles, Ronald. From *Understanding Harold Pinter*. University of South Carolina Press, 1995. © 1995 by the University of South Carolina. Reproduced by permission.—Lederer, Katherine. From *Lillian Hellman*. Twayne Publishers, 1995. The Gale Group.—Love, Harold. From *Congreve*. Rowman and Littlefield, 1975. © Basil Blackwell 1974. Reproduced by permission of Blackwell Publishers.—Lyons, Charles R. From *Rereading Shepard: Contemporary Critical Essays on the Plays of Sam Shepard*. St. Martin's Press, 1993. © The Macmillan Press Ltd 1993. Reproduced by permission of Macmillan, London and Basingstoke.—Prentice, Penelope. From "*Mountain Language*: Torture Revisited," in *The Pinter Ethic*. Garland Publishing, Inc., 1994. Copyright © 1994 Penelope Prentice. All rights reserved. Reproduced by permission of the publisher and the author.—Rex, Walter E. From "The Marriage of Figaro," in *The Attraction of the Contrary: Essays on the Literature of the French Enlightenment*. Cambridge University Press, 1987. © Cambridge University Press, 1987. Reprinted with permission of Cambridge University Press and the author.—Rutenberg, Michael E. From "*A Delicate Balance*," in *Edward Albee: Playwright in Protest*. DBS Publications, Inc., 1969. © Copyright 1969 by Michael E. Rutenberg. All rights reserved under International and Pan-American Copyright Conventions. Reproduced by permission of the author.

PHOTOGRAPHS AND ILLUSTRATIONS APPEARING IN *DfS*, VOLUME 14, WERE RECEIVED FROM THE FOLLOWING SOURCES:

Abe, Kobo, photograph. © Jerry Bauer. Reproduced by permission.—Albee, Edward, photograph by Marc Geller. Reproduced by permission of Marc Geller.—Ashcroft, Peggy as Fanny Farrelly, scene from a 1980 production of *Watch on the Rhine*, written by Lillian Hellman, photograph. © Donald Cooper/Photostage. Reproduced by permission.—Beaumarchais, Pierre August, engraving. The Library of Congress.—Black man running down West 125th Street, in Harlem, as a firefighter attempts to extinguish store on fire after the assassination of Martin Luther King, Jr., photograph. © Bettmann/Crobis. Reproduced by permission.—Buggy, Niall as Scandal (left to right), Tim Curry as Tattle, Stephen Moore as Valentine, and Amanda Redman as Angelica, scene from a 1985 production of *Love for Love*, written by William Congreve © Donald Cooper/Photostage. Reproduced by permission.—Childress, Alice, photograph. © Jerry Bauer. Reproduced by permission.—Cleage, Pearl, photograph. © Barry Forbus. Reproduced by permission of Pearl Cleage.—Congreve, William, print. Archive Photos, Inc. Reoproduced by permission.—Cotton Club, nightclub's name in neon lights, doorman wearing uniform, standing next to double doors, beauty Salon to the left, dress shop to the right, Harlem, New York City, ca. 1920–1940, photograph. Corbis Corporation. Reproduced by permission.—Cover of the Playbill for *Y2K*, written by Arthur Kopit, directed by Bob Balaban, performed by the Manhattan Theatre Club at the Lucille Lortel Theatre, 1999. PLAYBILL is a registered trademark of Playbill Incorporated, N.Y.C. All rights reserved. Reproduced by permission of Richard Stoddard Performing Arts Books.—Credits page from the Playbill for *Y2K*, written by Arthur Kopit, directed by Bob Balaban, 1999. PLAYBILL is a registered trademark of Playbill Incorporated, N.Y.C. All rights reserved. Reproduced by permission of Richard Stoddard Performing Arts Books.—Crowley, Mart, photograph by Donald Cooper. AP/Wide World Photos. Reproduced by permission.—Ginzburg, Natalia, photograph. © Jerry Bauer. Reproduced by permission.—Gordon, C. Henry (left to right) as Dr. Cunningham, Clark Gable as Dr. George Ferguson and Elizabeth Allan as Barbara Denham in the 1934 film production of the play *Men in White*, written by Sidney Kingsley, directed by Richard Boleslawski, photograph. Kobal Collection. Reproduced by permission.—Hellman, Lillian, 1966, photograph. AP/Wide World Photos. Reproduced by permission.—

Hepburn, Katherine and Paul Scofield in the film *A Delicate Balance*, 1973, photograph. The Kobal Collection. Reproduced by permission.—Kingsley, Sidney, 1934, photograph. Bettmann/Corbis. Reproduced by permission.—Kopit, Arthur, photograph. AP/Wide World Photos. Reproduced by permission.—Lukas, Paul as Kurt Muller and Bette Davis as Sara Muller in the 1943 film version of Lillian Hellman's play *Watch on the Rhine*, photograph. Kobal Collection/Warner Brothers. Reproduced by permission.—McCoy, Sylvester (left) as Count and John Bowe as Figaro, in a scene from a 1991 production of *The Marriage of Figaro*, written by Pierre-Augustin Caron de Beaumarchais, photograph. © Donald Cooper/Photostage. Reproduced by permission.—McEnery, John as Weston conversing with Alex Kingston as Emma, in a scene from the 1991 Royal Shakespeare Company production of *Curse of the Starving Class*, written by Sam Shepard, photograph. © Donald Cooper/ Photostage. Reproduced by permission.—Nelson, Kenneth as Michael, Frederick Combs as Donald, Reuben Greene as Bernard, Cliff Gorman as Emory, and Keith Prentice as Larry in the 1970 film version of the 1968 play *The Boys in the Band*, written by Mart Crowley, directed by William Friedkin, photograph. Kobal Collection/Cinema Center/Leo. Reproduced by permission.—Pinter, Harold, 1961, photograph. The Library of Congress.—Ringwald, Molly, and Brian Kerwin in a scene from the Pulitzer Prize winning play *How I Learned to Drive*, written by Paula Vogel, at the Mark Taper Forum, Los Angeles, February 13, 1999, photograph by Jill Connelly. AP/Wide World Photos. Reproduced by permission.—Shepard, Sam, photograph. The Library of Congress.—Sheridan, Richard Brinsley, photograph. The Library of Congress.—Smith, Maggie as Claire (left to right), Eileen Atkins as Agnes, and John Standing as Tobias, in a scene from a 1997 production of *A Delicate Balance*, photograph. © Donald Cooper/Photostage. Reproduced by permission.— St. Peter's Basilica and surrounding square in Vatican City, photograph by George Freston. Hulton/ Archive. Reproduced by permission.—Thomas, Henry (left) as Wesley Tate and James Woods as Weston Tate in the 1998 film version of the 1998 play *Curse of the Starving Class*, written by Sam Shepard, directed by Michael J. McClary, photograph. Kobal Collection/Phillips, Ron/Media Entertainment. Reproduced by permission.—Vogel, Paula, photograph. AP/Wide World Photos. Reproduced by permission.—Wrestling scene at Drury Lane Theatre, from William Shakespeare's play *As You Like It*, engraving by Ellis, after painting by Shepherd. Hulton/Archive. Reproduced by permission.

Contributors

Greg Barnhisel: Barnhisel teaches writing and directs the Writing Center at the University of Southern California. Entries on *Curse of the Starving Class* and *Love for Love*. Original essays on *Curse of the Starving Class* and *Love for Love*.

Liz Brent: Brent has a Ph.D. in American culture, specializing in film studies, from the University of Michigan. She is a freelance writer and teaches courses on the history of American cinema. Entries on *The Advertisement*, *Blues for an Alabama Sky*, and *Wine in the Wilderness*. Original essays on *The Advertisement*, *Blues for an Alabama Sky*, and *Wine in the Wilderness*.

Lois Carson: Carson is an instructor of English literature and composition. Original essay on *How I Learned to Drive*.

Erik France: France is a librarian and teaches history and interdisciplinary studies at University Liggett School and basic writing at Macomb Community College near Detroit, Michigan. Original essays on *The Advertisement* and *The Man Who Turned into a Stick*.

Curt Guyette: Guyette has a bachelor of arts degree in English writing from the University of Pittsburgh. Original essay on *The Advertisement*.

Joyce Hart: Hart has degrees in English literature and creative writing and focuses her published writing on literary themes. Entries on *A Delicate Balance* and *The Man Who Turned into a Stick*. Original essays on *Blues for an Alabama Sky*, *A Delicate Balance*, and *The Man Who Turned into a Stick*.

David Kelly: Kelly teaches creative writing and drama as literature at Oakton Community College. Entries on *The Boys in the Band* and *How I Learned to Drive*. Original essays on *The Boys in the Band* and *How I Learned to Drive*.

Rena Korb: Korb has a master's degree in English literature and creative writing and has written for a wide variety of educational publishers. Entries on *The Marriage of Figaro* and *Men in White*. Original essays on *The Marriage of Figaro* and *Men in White*.

Laura Kryhoski: Kryhoski is currently working as a freelance writer. Original essays on *Blues for an Alabama Sky* and *Men in White*.

Daniel Moran: Moran is a secondary school teacher of English and American literature. Entry on *The Critic*. Original essay on *The Critic*.

Wendy Perkins: Perkins is an associate professor of English at Prince George's Community College in Maryland. Entries on *Mountain*

Language and *Watch on the Rhine*. Original essays on *Mountain Language* and *Watch on the Rhine*.

Ryan D. Poquette: Poquette has a bachelor of arts degree in English and specializes in writing drama and film. Original essay on *Y2K*.

April Schulthies: Schulthies is an editor who holds a master's degree in English literature and teaches English at the community college level. Entry on *Y2K*. Original essay on *Y2K*.

Chris Semansky: Semansky is an instructor of English literature and composition and writes regularly for literary magazines and journals. Original essay on *Y2K*.

Ray Warren: Warren is a freelance writer with a master of fine arts degree in writing from Vermont College. Original essay on *Men in White*.

The Advertisement

NATALIA GINZBURG

1968

Natalia Ginzburg, one of Italy's most admired playwrights of the post-World War II era, was granted the Marzotto Prize for European Drama for *The Advertisement* (1968). Originally written in Italian, its first translated performance was on the English stage.

The Advertisement centers around Teresa, a lonely woman separated from her husband, who rents out her spare room to Elena, a young woman attending university in Rome. From the moment Elena walks in the door, Teresa talks almost incessantly of her horrible childhood and her tumultuous marriage to Lorenzo, her estranged husband. After five years of marriage, Lorenzo left Teresa upon discovering her affair with his best friend. The play opens after she and Lorenzo have been separated a year. Teresa, however, is still obsessed with their relationship and is still in love with Lorenzo, although she broods resentfully over his treatment of her.

Elena moves into Teresa's spare room, and the two become friends. Elena enjoys Teresa's company, listening sympathetically to her long, sad monologues, although Teresa's demands on her attention prevent her from studying. When Elena meets Lorenzo, they are immediately attracted to one another and begin spending time together. After Elena admits to Teresa that she and Lorenzo are in love, Teresa at first seems to accept her pronounce-

ment calmly and rationally. However, as soon as Elena turns her back, Teresa shoots and kills her and then calls Lorenzo to confess her crime.

As in many of her plays, Ginzburg is concerned with the experiences of women in modern marriage and modern relationships. In the character of Teresa, she also explores the theme of obsessive love.

AUTHOR BIOGRAPHY

Natalia Ginzburg was born Natalie Levi on July 14, 1916, in Palermo, Italy. Her father was Jewish and her mother was Catholic, but Ginzburg was raised in a non-religious environment. She grew up in Turin, where her father was an anatomy professor at the university.

World War II and the fascist Italian government that instituted severe restrictions on the rights of Jews had a profound effect on Ginzburg's life. In 1938, the year in which anti-Semitic laws were passed in Italy, she married Leone Ginzburg, a Jewish publisher and antifascist political activist. In 1940 Leone was sentenced to live in the countryside as a means of political isolation. Natalia and their three children lived in the rural town of Pissoli until Armistice Day in 1943. During this time, Natalia's first novel, *The Road to the City* (1942), was published under the pseudonym Alessandra Tornimparte to avoid legal restrictions that banned Jews from publishing. In 1943 she moved with her family to Rome, where her husband was arrested for editing an antifascist newspaper. He died in prison in 1944 as a result of excessive torture at the hands of the Gestapo. Her father and two brothers were also arrested by the fascists, although one brother escaped. During this time, Natalia and her children lived in hiding from the Nazis in various locations throughout Rome.

After the war, Ginzburg moved to Turin, where she worked as an editor and translator, coming into contact with many prominent Italian writers. In 1950, she married Gabriele Baldini, a professor of English literature. They moved to Rome in 1952, where she remained throughout the rest of her life. Ginzburg continued to publish novels, many of them translated into English, from the 1950s to the 1970s. Her second husband died in 1969. In 1983 Ginzburg was elected to the Italian Parliament as an independent Left politician.

Between 1964 and 1989, Ginzburg wrote ten plays. Her first volume of plays, *I Married You for Fun and Other Plays* (1966), is comprised of four plays. Included in this collection is the prize-winning *The Advertisement*. Her second volume of plays, *A Town by the Sea and Other Plays* (1973), also contains four plays. Her final two plays were *The Armchair* (1985) and *The Interview* (1989). Ginzburg's last publication, *Serena Cruz or True Justice* (1990), is a novel based on the true story of an Italian family's efforts to adopt a four-year-old Filipino girl. Ginzburg died of cancer in 1991.

PLOT SUMMARY

Act 1

Teresa, a woman who is separated from her husband and living alone, has put an advertisement in the newspaper to rent a room in her house. Elena, a college student, comes to look at the room. Elena has been living in her aunt and uncle's house while going to college, but their children are too noisy and she can't study, which is why she wants to move. Elena is from the country and doesn't have much money, so she is willing to do light housework in exchange for the room.

Teresa soon begins talking incessantly about herself, explaining every detail of her marriage, while Elena listens politely, insisting that she is interested. Teresa explains that she had in fact put three different advertisements in the paper: one to rent out the room, one to sell an antique rosewood sideboard, and one to sell her house in the country. She says that she is married but that she and her husband are legally separated. She mentions that she had a terrible childhood because her father claimed that she was actually the child of his brother and so did not consider her to be his child. She was raised in her grandparents' house, where she lived with her parents and her brother, but her father and brother eventually moved to America. She couldn't stand living with her mother any more and ran away from home at the age of twenty to live in Rome. She soon found work as an extra in the movies at Cinecittà, the location of the Italian film industry. There she met Lorenzo, who happened to be on the set one day with a friend. Teresa and Lorenzo spent their first three days together in Teresa's apartment, doing nothing but sleeping and making love. But on the third day, Lorenzo went down to the store to buy cigarettes and didn't come back.

After Lorenzo disappeared, Teresa quit working for the film industry and got a job at a hair salon. One day, six months later, Lorenzo happened to walk into the salon. Teresa asked why he had never returned from going to the store for cigarettes, and he explained that he had run into a friend and forgotten all about her; then, by the time he remembered her, it was too late at night. The next day, his mother wanted him to visit her in the country; on the way back to Rome, he was in a car accident and injured his shoulder. Teresa assumed he was telling her "a pack of lies" but cried and begged him to stay with her anyway.

Teresa and Lorenzo soon moved in together. Before long, they got married because she thought she was pregnant, but it turned out that she wasn't. Teresa then learned that Lorenzo was actually very rich, although he lived like a poor university student. They began to spend his money thoughtlessly and recklessly, and he began collecting paintings, motorcycles, and cars.

Teresa goes on to describe a marriage in which Lorenzo continually criticized her, left her for days at a time, and forgot to come home any time he ran into a friend. Teresa also describes physical fights between them, in which he would hit her and she would bite him. But she also insists that their marriage was the happiest time of her life. Finally, Teresa cheated on Lorenzo, sleeping with his friend Mario. Lorenzo left her after coming home to find her in bed with Mario.

Act 2

Elena is now living with Teresa. Lorenzo stops by while Teresa is out shopping, and Elena meets him for the first time. She tells him she is very happy living there and that she and Teresa have become best friends. Elena mentions that Teresa is always talking about him and stays home all of the time in hopes that he might stop by.

Teresa comes home, and she and Lorenzo immediately begin bickering while Elena goes in and out of the room, preparing lunch. Teresa and Lorenzo

Natalia Ginzburg

rehash various conflicts and resentments. Lorenzo insists that he left Teresa because he no longer loved her, not because he discovered that she was cheating on him with his best friend. He says that he had to leave her because they were destroying one another. He claims that he is perfectly happy without a woman in his life, although Teresa accuses him of going to prostitutes.

Lorenzo agrees to stay for lunch, and Teresa points out that he has never been there for longer than fifteen minutes at a time. Teresa and Lorenzo continue to bicker about their marriage and about Lorenzo's family. Teresa complains that he doesn't give her enough money to live on and that she has to sell a piece of furniture to support herself. Lorenzo and Elena discuss their love of the countryside, which Teresa hates. Lorenzo invites Elena to see their house in the country, and Elena invites him to see her parents' house in the country.

Act 3

Teresa and Elena sit together, drinking their morning coffee. Elena explains to Teresa that she is moving back to her uncle's home because she can't get any studying done at Teresa's house, as she and Teresa are always talking. She insists that she is very fond of Teresa but simply must live somewhere that allows her to study. Elena explains that she was late coming home the night before because she went out to the movies with Lorenzo and two of his friends, after which she and Lorenzo walked around the city together. Elena then admits that she and Lorenzo have fallen in love, which is the real reason she is moving out.

Upon hearing this news, Teresa remains calm, cool, and rational. She says that she could tell they were in love and that she knows Lorenzo will never want her back, so it doesn't bother her. She insists that she and Elena will still be good friends and even offers to have her marriage annulled so that Elena and Lorenzo can get married. Yet, Teresa admits that she will always love Lorenzo and that she would be willing to take him back under any conditions. Then Teresa says that she's going to shoot herself one day so that Lorenzo will be a widower and will be able to marry Elena. She tells Elena she bought a pistol, back when she and Lorenzo lived together, so that she could shoot him. Elena begs Teresa to get rid of the pistol, and Teresa says she will.

When Elena goes into her room to pack, Teresa gets the pistol from her own room, walks into Elena's room, and shoots her. Teresa hurriedly calls Lorenzo to say she has shot and killed Elena. Just then, the doorbell rings. It is Giovanna, a young woman who is answering Teresa's new advertisement to rent the spare room.

CHARACTERS

Boy

At the end of act 1, a boy, the son of the grocer, comes to Teresa's door to let her know that they are willing to sell her the stray Siamese cat who wandered into their shop.

Lorenzo Del Monte

Lorenzo Del Monte is Teresa's husband. They were married and lived together for five years and have been legally separated for one year. When he

and Teresa first met, he was thirty years old. Lorenzo has a degree in engineering, but he does not have a job because he comes from a very wealthy family and does not need to work. However, when Teresa first met him, he was living like a poor university student, wearing the same old clothes every day. Their first three days together were spent in Teresa's apartment doing nothing but making love and sleeping. On the third day, Lorenzo told her he was going out to buy cigarettes but never returned.

Six months later, Lorenzo happened to walk into the hair salon where Teresa was working. He acted as if nothing had happened between them, and when Teresa asked why he never returned from the store, he told her a series of lies. Teresa nevertheless begged him to stay with her, and they eventually moved in together. Soon, they got married. At first they lived as if in poverty, but then they began a lifestyle of recklessly spending his money. He took to buying paintings, motorcycles, and cars. He also left Teresa alone for days at a time, claiming that he had gone to visit his mother, although it is not clear if he was telling the truth. He was very critical of Teresa and very controlling. They quarreled often, and he hit and punched her, although she also bit him and attacked him with a pair of scissors. When he found Teresa in bed with his best friend, he immediately left her. However, he insists that he did not leave because of the affair but simply because he did not love her anymore. In act 2, Lorenzo shows up at Teresa's house and meets Elena for the first time. He and Elena are immediately attracted to one another and share an interest in spending time in the country. In act 3, Elena tells Teresa that she and Lorenzo are in love. After Teresa shoots and kills Elena, she immediately calls Lorenzo to tell him what she has done.

Teresa Del Monte

Teresa Del Monte is a very lonely woman who talks incessantly to Elena, her young border, about her unhappy childhood and tumultuous marriage. Teresa has been separated from her husband, Lorenzo, for a year, but her life still revolves around him even though he only comes to visit her for fifteen minutes at a time. She is still in love with him and continually broods over both the good and bad elements of their relationship. She insists that, despite their violent quarrels and his cold treatment of her, she would take him back under any conditions.

Teresa continues to be supported by Lorenzo but is always putting ads in the newspaper in order to make more money. In act 1, she has placed three ads: one to rent out a spare room in her house, one to sell a piece of antique furniture, and one to sell their house in the country. When Lorenzo comes by to visit after a month's absence without explanation, he and Teresa immediately begin bickering about their marriage. Teresa expresses extreme resentment toward him about their relationship and about his family's treatment of her. Later, when Elena confesses to Teresa that she and Lorenzo are in love, Teresa appears to accept the situation in a calm, cool, and rational manner. She says she knows that Lorenzo will never want her back, so it shouldn't matter that he is now in love with Elena. She even offers to have her marriage annulled so that Elena and Lorenzo can get married. However, she also tells Elena that she may one day shoot herself, in which case Lorenzo would be a widower and could then marry Elena. Teresa explains that she bought herself a pistol when she was still with Lorenzo, thinking that one day she would shoot him. After Elena goes into her room, Teresa calmly gets her pistol and walks in after her. Teresa shoots and kills Elena, then immediately calls Lorenzo on the phone to tell him what she has done. She claims she did not intend to kill Elena, but it is unclear if this is true or not.

Giovanna Ricciardi

At the very end of act 3, just after Teresa has shot Elena, Giovanna Ricciardi rings her doorbell. When Teresa opens the door, Giovanna says she is answering the advertisement for the room and has come to look at it.

Elena Tesei

Elena Tesei is a twenty-year-old university student majoring in philosophy. She grew up in the country, where her parents run a small inn. Elena has little money and has been staying at her aunt and uncle's place in Rome while she attends college, but their children are too noisy, and she has trouble getting her work done. When the play opens, Elena has answered Teresa's add to rent out a room in exchange for light housework. Almost as soon as Elena comes in, Teresa begins talking incessantly about her unhappy childhood and her marriage. Elena listens politely and seems to be genuinely interested in what Teresa is saying.

MEDIA ADAPTATIONS

- *The Advertisement* was performed via radio broadcast in 1968 by the British Broadcasting Company.

In act 2, Elena has been living with Teresa for a while when she meets Lorenzo for the first time. Elena tells Lorenzo that she and Teresa have become best friends, that they have dinner together every night, and enjoy talking to each other. In act 3, Elena is about to move out of Teresa's house because, she claims, she cannot get any work done. She then admits to Teresa that she and Lorenzo are in love, which is the real reason she's moving out. She begs Teresa to remain her friend and is grateful when Teresa offers to have her marriage to Lorenzo annulled. Teresa tells Elena that she has a pistol and may shoot herself, but Elena begs her to get rid of it. When Elena goes into her room to pack, Teresa gets her pistol and shoots Elena, killing her.

THEMES

Modern Relationships

In many of her plays, Ginzburg explores the experiences of women in modern relationships and modern marriage. In *The Advertisement*, Teresa describes the course of her relationship with Lorenzo, which develops in a very nontraditional way that is characteristic of the 1960s when Italian culture was becoming increasingly modernized and secularized. Soon after they meet, Teresa and Lorenzo go to bed together, and they stay in bed for three days straight. When they meet again six months later, they move in together, although they are not married.

Teresa and Lorenzo eventually marry but only because they think Teresa is pregnant. After they are

TOPICS FOR FURTHER STUDY

- Ginzburg grew up during the years of Mussolini's rise to power in Italy. Learn more about Mussolini and the fascist era in Italy. What was the course of Mussolini's political career leading up to his position as a fascist dictator? What was the response of the Italian people to fascism? What changes did Mussolini effect in Italian politics, society, and economy during the 1920s and 1930s? Are any of these changes evident today?

- Learn more about the role of Italy in World War II. How did Italy come to be allied with Nazi Germany? What was the relationship between Hitler and Mussolini? How did the Italian-German alliance change and develop over the course of the war? What part did Italy play in the events of World War II? How was Italy affected by the Allied invasion of Sicily and the final years of the war?

- Important Italian playwrights of the twentieth century include Luigi Pirandello and Dario Fo, both of whom were awarded Nobel Prizes in literature. Pick one of these authors and learn more about his life, career, and major plays. What central themes does he explore in his plays? What social or political issues does he address? How were his plays innovative and experimental in form? How did the Italian public, Italian government, and international audiences receive his plays?

- In *The Advertisement*, Teresa works briefly as an extra in the Italian film industry, which was concentrated in the Cinecittà during the period in which this play was written. Learn more about the Italian film industry in the post-World War II era. What developments took place in Italian cinema during this period? Who were some of the major directors and actors? What were some of the important films of the postwar era?

married, however, it turns out that she is not pregnant. Although it is not mentioned directly, there is some implication that Teresa may have lied to Lorenzo about being pregnant to get him to marry her. However, *The Advertisement* was written three years before birth control became readily available in Italy, so it is believable that Teresa may genuinely have thought she was pregnant.

Though their lifestyle and their relationship are very nontraditional, Teresa and Lorenzo continue to harbor traditional expectations of marriage. They both accuse one another of not fulfilling their traditional marital roles. Teresa says that Lorenzo "was always telling me what I ought to have been like, how happy he'd have been if I'd been a *wife,*" while she herself "did nothing but tell him how I'd have liked him to be a *husband.*"

After five years of marriage, they separate. Although Lorenzo has no intention of reconciling with Teresa, they are unable to get divorced because divorce was not legal in Italy until 1970. Their options are either to obtain a "legal separation" or to have the marriage annulled. Lorenzo's mother wants him to get a legal separation "with guilt" so that he will not have to pay her alimony. But Lorenzo opts for a separation "by mutual consent." He helps Teresa find a place to live and continues to provide her with financial support, although she claims he does not give her enough money.

When Elena tells Teresa that she is in love with Lorenzo, Teresa offers to have her marriage to Lorenzo annulled so that he and Elena can marry one another. Although there was no legal divorce in Italy at this time, the Roman Catholic Church had a provision for marital annulment, but the criteria for annulment was relatively strict. *The Advertisement* was written just a few years before many of the traditional marriage laws in Italy dictated by the Catholic Church were either liberalized or abolished in favor of laws more in keeping with modern secular lifestyles.

In *The Advertisement*, Ginzburg explores the themes of modern relationships and modern marriage at a pivotal moment in Italian history when women and men were caught between modern lifestyles and traditional expectations as well as traditional laws about marital relationships.

Obsessive Love

The character of Teresa in *The Advertisement* is a case study in obsessive love. Teresa knows early on that her love for Lorenzo is irrational, and yet she feels she cannot help loving him. After they first meet, they go to bed together almost immediately. Although she has been with many men before and is quite popular, Teresa is in love for the first time in her life. Lorenzo then completely disappears without explanation. When he runs into her again by chance, six months later, he acts as if nothing unusual had happened between them. Although she knows that Lorenzo is lying to her about why he disappeared, Teresa begs him to become involved with her once again.

Throughout five years of unstable and tempestuous marriage, Teresa is so completely consumed by her love for Lorenzo that she believes herself to be happy in a relationship that sounds intolerable. Lorenzo is extremely critical and controlling of Teresa. Yet she always does what he wants her to do because, as she tells Elena, ''he was able to bully me because I loved him.'' Teresa adds that she lost her sense of self in submitting to his will, explaining that she obeyed him because ''I no longer had a will of my own left.'' In addition, Lorenzo was often cold and indifferent toward her, forgetting to come home any time he ran into a friend and often leaving her alone for days at a time, supposedly to go visit his mother. Eventually, they engage in violent quarrels. It is unclear from Teresa's description if Lorenzo was the primary aggressor in these fights, although it seems as if he may have been. Teresa describes fights in which he would slap and punch her and she would bite and scratch him, even injuring him with a pair of scissors on one occasion.

After five years of marriage, Teresa has an affair with Lorenzo's dearest childhood friend, Mario. Upon discovering them in bed together, Lorenzo immediately leaves Teresa. He later claims that he left her, not because of the affair, but because he no longer loved her. In fact, he says that he had stopped loving her long before this. After this incident, Teresa begs Lorenzo to come back to her, but he refuses. Even after Elena informs her that she and Lorenzo are in love, Teresa admits that she will always love him and that she would be willing to take him back under any conditions whatsoever.

Teresa's obsessive love for Lorenzo is so extreme and irrational that she even bought herself a pistol before they were separated, thinking that she would kill him one day. Her obsessive love culminates in the irrational decision to shoot and kill Elena out of jealousy. Teresa even states beforehand that she knows Lorenzo will never want her back, and yet Lorenzo is the first person she calls after killing Elena, as if she believes that somehow this act of violence will bring him back to her.

STYLE

Simile

Throughout *The Advertisement*, Ginzburg makes use of recurring similes in order to describe and characterize the relationship between Teresa and Lorenzo. A simile is a figure of speech in which one thing is described as being like something else in order to illustrate a particular quality or set of qualities.

Teresa and Lorenzo both describe their marriage in disparaging terms, using several recurring similes to portray the negative qualities of their relationship. At one point, their marriage is described as a monster. Teresa says that they would sometimes quarrel over a single word she might have used unthinkingly, upon which, she says, ''he'd drag out all the possible hidden meanings, so that word would grow and grow till it was like a monster.'' Likewise the negative elements of their marriage grow and grow to the point that the relationship becomes like a monster—an evil, violent, destructive thing that is out of their control.

Imagery

Lorenzo and Teresa both discuss their marriage using imagery of dirt and cleanliness in combination with similes comparing their relationship to the experience of drowning or suffocating.

Lorenzo compares his marriage to Teresa to the experience of drowning in order to express the feeling that the relationship is threatening to stifle his sense of individuality. According to Teresa, Lorenzo says that, with her, he ''always felt he was sinking into a well full of black, muddy, stinking water; he was gradually losing himself, bit by bit.''

Lorenzo's image of sinking into a well is repeated when he meets Elena and tells her that his marriage to Teresa made him feel like he was ''sinking into a black, muddy well.'' The comparison of their relationship to the experience of drowning is echoed in Lorenzo's repeated assertion that being married to Teresa was a stifling, smothering experience. He tells her, ''I can't breathe in your world!''

The image of dirty well water is contrasted with Lorenzo's description of his friendship with Mario as ''extremely delicate and pure and deep.'' The ''pure'' deep well of his feelings for Mario is thus contrasted favorably to his ''muddy'' feelings for Teresa. He claims that he refuses to let the fact that Mario slept with his wife ''poison'' their friendship, an image that continues the idea of well water as something pure that could potentially be poisoned.

Teresa picks up on Lorenzo's use of the terms ''pure'' and ''muddy'' to complain that he views his relationship with her as dirty, whereas his friendship with Mario is considered clean. She asks him:

> What about me? I betrayed you, too. Your friendship with Mario has been washed and cleaned and rinsed, and now it's just as good as new. That's what you said. Your feelings about me can't be washed and cleaned, and rinsed, I suppose? Those feelings were dirtied forever, I suppose, and you've chucked them away? . . . I suppose your feelings for me weren't delicate and deep.

Symbolism

In addition to the figurative language of simile, Ginzburg makes use of symbolic imagery to characterize the relationship between Teresa and Lorenzo.

They first meet on a movie set, where Teresa worked as an extra. She comments that, working at the film studio, she was ''never more than an extra.'' Her status as an extra in the movies is symbolic of her status in Lorenzo's life: she remains on the periphery of his world, an insignificant ''extra,'' who never captures his full attention.

When they first met, a strong gust of wind blew up the sand from the set, a desert, into an artificial sandstorm. The tumult and violence of a sandstorm becomes a symbol of their marriage; Teresa comments, ''Lorenzo says with me it was always like living in a sandstorm.''

Further, the movie set on which they met depicted the ruins of the ancient city of Troy. This symbolizes what is to become of their relationship and Teresa's place in it. Just as Teresa sits among the ruins of an ancient city on the movie set, so she also dwells in the past throughout the play, ruminating endlessly over the remains of a relationship long since fallen into ruin. At one point, when she argues with him over an incident that occurred earlier in their marriage, Lorenzo tells her to ''stop digging up ancient history.''

HISTORICAL CONTEXT

Mussolini and Fascism in Italy

Ginzburg's life and works were profoundly affected by Italian history, particularly the era of fascism. Italy's fascist era began with the rise to power of Benito Mussolini. Mussolini, who had been an ardent socialist journalist, broke away from socialism and formed the Fighting Leagues brigade in 1919. His squads of militant Blackshirts, as his followers were called, soon began taking over cities and provinces in Italy. In 1921 Mussolini organized his followers to form a political party known as the National Fascist Party. In 1922 he held a fascist convention in Naples in order to concentrate his Blackshirt brigades for an armed march into Rome, known historically as the famous March on Rome. King Victor Emmanuel III was asked to declare a state of siege and call in military troops to put down the threat of armed insurrection. The King, however, refused to order any resistance to the advance of Mussolini's troops. Instead, the King invited Mussolini to become Prime Minister of Italy. Thus, before the fascist brigades even reached Rome, Mussolini had triumphantly taken over the Italian government, without violence and without resistance.

For the next five years, Mussolini worked at consolidating his power as the head of state and leader of the fascist party. He took on the title of the *duce,* which means leader. In 1932 he publicly declared his intention to make Italy a world power through imperialist expansion. He began to see Nazi Germany under Hitler as a useful ally and made an official visit to Berlin in 1936 to meet with Hitler. In 1938 Hitler visited Mussolini in Italy, thus securing their alliance. Influenced by the policies of Nazi Germany, Mussolini instituted severe restrictions on the Jews of Italy in 1938. These anti-Semitic laws declared Jews to be ''unpatriotic'' and banned them from holding government jobs, teaching, and

COMPARE
&
CONTRAST

- **1960s and 1970s:** During the early 1960s, Italy continues to enjoy the postwar era "economic miracle" of unprecedented growth and prosperity. By the mid-1960s, however, the Italian economy suffers a downturn. With the economy in decline, Italy, during the 1970s, is in the throes of political instability. The years 1969–1982 are characterized by acts of domestic terrorism.

  1980s and 1990s: By the mid-1980s, economic conditions in the north of Italy have greatly improved, whereas in the south the economy is still weak. Mafia business practices and clandestine dealings with government officials dominate Italian politics and economy. Italian politics during the 1990s is characterized by scandal and turmoil. Widespread government corruption, particularly regarding the use of bribery, is brought to light in 1992. "Operation Clean Hands" results in the arrest and conviction of thousands of politicians, businessmen, and public officials for corruption and bribery, some in association with the Mafia. Many political parties are dissolved amidst the scandal, and new parties include a strong showing of neofascists in positions of power.

- **1960s and 1970s:** In the 1960s, the second Vatican Council meeting of 1962–1965 inaugurates the era of the Roman Catholic Church known as Vatican II, characterized by the liberalizing of many Church policies. In the 1970s, Italian society becomes increasingly secularized. In opposition to the dictates of the Catholic Church, divorce is made legal in 1970, and abortion is made legal in 1978. Civil marriage, unsanctioned by the Catholic Church, becomes increasingly common. In 1976, television and radio broadcasting is no longer a state monopoly regulated according to the values of the Catholic Church, and the new, privatized broadcasting companies air programs critical of traditional values.

  1980s and 1990s: By the mid-1980s, only 30 percent of Italian citizens regularly attend church (as compared to 70 percent in the 1950s). Pope John Paul II describes Italian society as "de-Christianized." The Concordat of 1985, agreed upon between the Vatican and the Italian government, rules that Roman Catholicism is no longer the state religion of Italy. Religious education is no longer compulsory in Italian schools. In the 1990s, the secularization of Italian culture and society as a result of the 1985 concordat and the liberalization of laws regarding marriage and reproductive rights continue to characterize Italian culture.

---

publishing. This last ruling profoundly affected Ginzburg's life, as her husband was a publisher and she a writer. In 1939 the Italian-German military alliance was formalized by the signing of the Pact of Steel between Hitler and Mussolini.

Italy in World War II

Germany began World War II in 1939 and was joined by Italy in 1940. But Italy did not fare well in the war due to inferior military resources, and Mussolini soon became subordinate to Hitler's military command. In 1942 the Allied troops invaded Sicily, signaling the beginning of the end of Italy's partnership with Germany and Mussolini's stranglehold over Italian politics. In 1943 his own fascist followers held a meeting of the Fascist Grand Council, at which they voted to ask the king to remove Mussolini from office. The king obliged, and Mussolini was arrested the following day when he showed up at his office in defiance of this decision. Mussolini was in prison less than two months before a German military operation successfully carried out his escape. The Germans allowed him to set up a puppet government, although he remained completely under their command. Meanwhile, the Allies were advancing through Italy defeating German forces. Mussolini was caught by Italian Communist supporters while trying to escape to Switzerland, and was shot and killed.

Italy in the Postwar Years

In 1944 Allied troops successfully liberated Rome from German control. World War II ended in 1945. By 1946 public sentiment in Italy leaned toward the dissolution of the monarchy in favor of a republic. King Emmanuel III had remained in power since the ousting of Mussolini but now abdicated the throne, naming his son, Umberto II, the new monarch. However, the monarchy was voted down, and both father and son were sent into exile. For the first time in Italian history, universal suffrage was instituted, allowing for women, as well as men, to vote on a Constituent Assembly. The result was the formation of a Constitution of the Republic of Italy, with a parliamentary system of government. The Italian constitution was set up in response to fascism, allowing for a weak central government and extensive civil liberties. The first parliamentary elections were held in 1948.

Italy enjoyed outstanding economic growth in the postwar years, adopting the phrase ''economic miracle'' to describe this postwar boom. By the mid-1960s, however, the economy began to slow down, resulting in the so-called ''hot autumn'' of 1969, during which labor unrest and general strikes were widespread.

Reproductive Rights and Marriage Laws in Italy

Ginzburg's play addresses concerns over the status of women in marital relationships during the 1960s. Although some changes in the status of women in Italy took place during the postwar years, significant changes did not occur until the period soon after *The Advertisement* was first produced. Women in Italy were granted the right to vote with the first elections of the new Italian Republic in 1948. However, most girls in Italy did not have the opportunity to receive a secondary (high school) education until the 1960s. Major changes in reproductive rights and divorce laws were instituted during the 1970s. Divorce became legal in Italy for the first time in 1970. Contraception became readily available after 1971. Many other traditional laws regarding marriage and family were abolished or liberalized in 1975. A referendum in 1978 legalized abortion by almost 68 percent of the Italian vote.

The practices of both civil (non-religious) marriage and couples living together without being married became more common throughout the 1970s.

CRITICAL OVERVIEW

Ginzburg's achievement in writing *The Advertisement* was honored with the international Marzotto Prize, which she was awarded in 1968. However, Ginzburg has been more widely recognized for her fiction, autobiographical novel, and nonfiction essays than for her dramatic writings. Only one of her ten plays has been translated into English.

Critics of *The Advertisement* focus on its feminist perspective, exploring the experiences of women in marriage and family in the historical context of a rapidly changing modern society. In the introduction to *Plays by and about Women,* in which *The Advertisement* is published in English translation, Victoria Sullivan and James Hatch focus on the character of Teresa as an example of the plight of women in modern society. They describe *The Advertisement* as a ''frightening portrait of female limitation,'' for ''her long-winded, egocentric monologues say something about the female state.'' Sullivan and Hatch comment that, ''Having been brought up with no particular goal except to catch a man, she cannot support herself economically or emotionally.'' Teresa's compulsive speech is interpreted as a function of her feelings of powerlessness as a woman; as Sullivan and Hatch observe, ''Teresa is a woman who has been reduced to talk as her only form of action.''

Giuseppe Faustini, in the *Dictionary of Literary Biography,* has characterized the central theme of Ginzburg's plays as the dissolution of traditional family roles in modern Italian culture. Faustini observes:

> Ginzburg's plays offer a microcosm of Italian society in transition. Her characters reflect the grief and anxiety that result from the disintegration of traditional social structures such as the institutions of marriage and family. She uses drama to examine the changing roles of marital and familial relationships and the effects of the political and social reforms that took place primarily in the 1960s and 1970s.

Faustini further points out Ginzburg's concern with the experiences of women in a changing society. In her plays, in particular, ''she attempts to liberate female characters who are often controlled by their male partners.'' The characters of Elena and

St. Peter's Basilica in Vatican City represents the influential role of the Roman Catholic Church portrayed in The Advertisement

Teresa in *The Advertisement* "struggle within a male-dominated world as they seek to assert themselves within the changing roles of wife and mother." Faustini notes that the struggle of women to effectively communicate their experiences is highlighted in *The Advertisement*, as Teresa and Elena "try to adjust to marriage and divorce as they attempt to make sense of their chaotic emotions resulting from their inability to communicate." In her plays more so than her novels, Faustini asserts, "Ginzburg is able to express her preoccupation with women's dependence on men as fathers, husbands, or lovers. She shows deep concerns about the disintegration of family life and about what she regards as parasitic male behavior."

CRITICISM

Liz Brent

Brent has a Ph.D. in American culture, specializing in film studies, from the University of Michigan. She is a freelance writer and teaches courses in the history of American cinema. In the following essay, Brent discusses the psychology of Teresa in Ginzburg's play.

Through her development of the character of Teresa, Ginzburg demonstrates the ways in which childhood experiences affect adult psychology. Teresa's character is clearly rooted in her childhood circumstances, which she describes as horrible. In her relationship with Lorenzo, in particular, Teresa reproduces the traumatic, unhappy experiences of her relationship with her father and her uncle Giacomo (who may or may not have been her real father). Lorenzo's treatment of Teresa in many ways mirrors the way men treated her when she was a child. Teresa is thus drawn to Lorenzo, even though he makes her miserable, because he represents to her the father(s) who ignored her throughout her childhood.

Teresa explains to Elena that her father always claimed that she was the child of his brother, Giacomo. In other words, Teresa's mother was suspected of having had an affair with her husband's brother. Teresa doesn't know for sure if Giacomo was her real father, but it was understood by everyone that he might have been. Since her father did not consider her to be his, he ignored her

WHAT DO I READ NEXT?

- Ginzburg's plays have often been compared to the plays of the nineteenth-century Russian realist writer Anton Chekhov. *Chekhov: Four Plays* (1996) includes translations of his most celebrated plays: *The Seagull, Uncle Vanya, The Three Sisters,* and *The Cherry Orchard.*

- Luigi Pirandello, the most celebrated Italian playwright of the twentieth century, received the Nobel Prize for literature in 1934. *Six Characters in Search of an Author* (1921), his most widely acclaimed work, is an experimental play in which characters who have been rejected by the author appear on stage to interrupt the dialogue of the legitimate characters.

- The Italian writer Giorgio Bassani, born in the same year as Ginzburg, is notable for his works depicting the lives of Jews in fascist Italy. His *Five Stories of Ferrara* (1956) includes five novellas tracing the growth of fascism and anti-Semitism in Italy from the 1920s through the 1940s. His celebrated autobiographical novel *The Garden of the Finzi-Continis* (1962) describes the once-aristocratic lifestyle of a privileged Jewish family decimated by the Holocaust.

- *The Little Virtues* (1962) is Ginzburg's collection of essays, based on her experiences in fascist Italy.

- *Family Sayings* (1963), also translated as *The Things We Used to Say,* is Ginzburg's autobiographical novel about her childhood and writing career.

- Dario Fo, one of the most celebrated Italian playwrights of the late twentieth century, was awarded the Nobel Prize for literature in 1997. His many plays became both popular and controversial as avant-garde political comedies. Fo's major plays are collected in two volumes: *Plays, 1* (1992) and *Plays, 2* (1994). *Plays, 1* includes *Accidental Death of an Anarchist* (1974), perhaps his best-known play, which is based on true events surrounding the arrest and imprisonment of an Italian anarchist who, in Fo's account, is thrown from a fifth-story window during a police interrogation.

---

and was cruel to her. When she was playing in the house, he would pick her up by one arm and throw her outside, claiming that she was not his child. He always said that he couldn't stand the sight of her and that he was going to move to America so he would never have to see her again.

Teresa always wondered why her uncle Giacomo did not come and claim her if she was really his child. Her only contact with him was when he would pass her on the street, and he would guiltily stop to give her some candies and then move on without a word. But Teresa always wondered, "Why doesn't he come and fetch me if I'm his?"

Eventually, Teresa was completely abandoned both by the man she knew as her father and by her uncle Giacomo. Her father moved to America and then sent for her brother to join him but left Teresa and her mother behind. After this, her uncle Giacomo no longer even stopped when he saw her on the street, but simply looked at her and moved on. Teresa thus grew up feeling cast aside by both her legal father and the man who may have been her biological father. This childhood experience has everything to do with her relationship with her husband, a man who ignores her and casts her aside throughout their marriage. Lorenzo regularly disappears without explanation and claims to have completely forgotten about her. Throughout their relationship, Teresa fears that he will never return from his frequent absences. This fear resonates with her childhood experience of having been ignored, forgotten, and abandoned by her father and uncle. The occasional moments of warmth Lorenzo offers Teresa resonate with her experience of being given scraps of attention by her uncle, in the form of a few sweets

---

from his pocket when he passed her in the street. Likewise, Lorenzo symbolically hands her a few morsels of affection during the course of their relationship but never really gives her his full attention or genuine love.

Teresa's fixation on Lorenzo as her object of affection develops in a manner that indicates that it is his careless treatment of her that resonates with her childhood experience of rejection by men. Lorenzo has physical features in common with Teresa's uncle: like Giacomo, Lorenzo is a small, short man. Although Teresa claims her first impression of Lorenzo was that "he was too small" and she remarks that she "never liked small men," she is unconsciously drawn to him, perhaps because his small frame reminds her of her uncle Giacomo. Throughout their marriage, Teresa continues to hope for that which is hopeless: that Lorenzo will truly love her and pay attention to her. Just as she experienced with her father and her uncle, Teresa wants more than anything to be loved by a man who will never love her. She tells Elena she would have liked "a bit of attention" from Lorenzo but "got no attention." In fact, she says, when he was out with his friends, he "never thought of me."

She first met Lorenzo by chance, and they spent two days and nights of passion together in her apartment. But on the third day he claimed he was going out to the store to buy cigarettes and never came back. When they run into each other six months later, he claims that he had met a friend at the store and had forgotten all about Teresa. He then tells her a "pack of lies," making up excuses for why he ran out on her. Even though she knows he is lying, Teresa feels she still wants him. When they run into one another by chance the second time, Lorenzo callously states that she shouldn't be upset about his walking out on her because she was never really a "person" to him anyway, as he doesn't really know her. Teresa's plea in response to this comment expresses the hope she harbored as a child, about how she wanted the men in her life to treat her: "I want you to realize that I'm a person. I want you to be considerate to me, and treat me with respect." Lorenzo's response to this plea is to walk out of the restaurant where they are talking and get into his car, prepared to leave her for good. But Teresa runs out after him, gets into his car, and begs him not to leave her. Lorenzo suggests she find a man who wants her and can give her what she wants and make her happy, but Teresa begs him to stay with her.

> TERESA'S CHILDHOOD WAS CHARACTERIZED BY THE VAIN HOPE OF REACHING, OF HAVING POSITIVE CONTACT WITH SOMEONE VERY DEAR TO HER: HER FATHER . . . ."

Teresa's pathetic display of sentiment for Lorenzo, a man who has abandoned her, lied to her, and essentially told her to get lost, resonates with her childhood feelings of wishing more than anything that the men who cast her aside (her father and uncle) would love her and welcome her into their homes, rather than throwing her outside as her father did, or disowning her as her uncle did. After Lorenzo leaves her, Teresa repeatedly writes and phones him to beg him to come back, but she gets no response. When Lorenzo stops by to visit Teresa, after they have been separated a year, she accuses him of not remembering anything she says to him or anything about her. She then brings up the time he went out to buy cigarettes and never came back, saying, "you'd forgotten I existed." Teresa's perpetual brooding over Lorenzo's disregard for her indicates the extent to which their relationship reproduces the trauma of her childhood, the trauma of being cast out by her father and her uncle, both of whom seemed to forget she existed.

Lorenzo's violent behavior toward Teresa also mirrors her father's rough treatment of her and his violent treatment of her mother. She says that she was frightened of her father, who "used to wake up in the middle of the night, and hit my mother, and make her nose and mouth bleed." When they're married, Lorenzo begins to hit and punch her during their arguments, which are often at night. Although Teresa doesn't mention if her mother ever fought back against her father, Teresa fights back against Lorenzo by biting him, and she even attacks him with a pair of scissors one time. Lorenzo claims that he left Teresa in part because he was afraid either he was going to kill her or she was going to kill him. And Teresa even bought herself a pistol, thinking that one day she might kill Lorenzo.

Teresa's traumatic childhood experiences have a significant effect on her adult experiences of the world. She tells Elena that, living alone after her separation from Lorenzo, she feels frightened at night and has a recurring nightmare. Her nightmare is clearly symbolic of her relationships with her father and her uncle, both of whom she wanted more than anything to pay attention to her and to love her. She describes her nightmare as:

> A wall, a courtyard, old furniture . . . rags and broken glass. I'm wandering about the place, rummaging among the rags. Then I beat on the wall, and try to call out. I try to shout out, but I haven't any voice. I know that on the other side of the wall, there's something dreadful. . . . Someone. A person very dear to me. And I can't reach whoever it is, because of the wall.

Teresa's childhood was characterized by the vain hope of reaching, of having positive contact with someone very dear to her: her father (whether he be Uncle Giacomo or the man she knew as her father). But the men in her life, including Lorenzo, have always put a wall between their feelings and Teresa, never allowing her into their hearts. No matter how hard she begs or pleads, they are deaf to her cry for love and attention, as if she hadn't a voice to call out with. Her irritating habit, as an adult, of talking incessantly is an outward expression of her feeling from childhood that she was being ignored by the man who should have been a father to her, as if he were deaf to her needs. As a result, she is left alone, cut off from all love by an impenetrable wall; she is left with nothing but the ruins of old relationships, the rags and broken glass that symbolize the meager scraps of attention or affection she received from her father, her uncle, and from Lorenzo.

Teresa reproduces the symbolic experience of the nightmare even in her efforts to obtain work as an extra in the film industry. She says, "I was always at Cinecittà, waiting at the gates in case they wanted me." This symbolizes her experience of her relationships with her uncle Giacomo and with Lorenzo, waiting and waiting for them to want her but always locked outside the gates of their affections. Despite being discouraged, Teresa remains full of hope that she will be "wanted." She says that, at the Cinecittà, she "hardly earned a penny" but was "always full of hope" that she would be hired as an extra or even become a star. Likewise as a child, she always wondered why her uncle Giacomo didn't claim her and take her home with him. Though he never even came close to treating her like she was his, Teresa remained full of hope throughout her childhood that he would one day want her.

Teresa's unconditional love for Lorenzo, despite his neglect, ill treatment, and downright rejection of her, indicates that, unconsciously, she regards him as a child regards a parent—in the sense that children generally want nothing but love and attention from their parents, no matter how badly they are treated by them. Toward the end of the play, she tells Elena:

> I do still love him. I shall always love him. That's the trouble. If he were halfway across the world, and just lifted a finger, I'd run to him. I'd run to him on all fours. I'd always take him back, even if he was old, and lost, and starving; even if he was flea-ridden, and syphilitic, with holes in his trousers. That's the truth. Living with him was hell, but I'd give my life, my whole life, to have the time back when we were together.

Source: Liz Brent, Critical Essay on *The Advertisement,* in *Drama for Students,* The Gale Group, 2002.

Erik France

France is a librarian and teaches history and interdisciplinary studies at University Liggett School and basic writing at Macomb Community College near Detroit, Michigan. In the following essay, he discusses the theme of dysfunctional families and how they shape adult relationships in Ginzburg's play.

The Advertisement tells a tragic story about the destructive effects of dysfunctional families. The inability of Teresa and Lorenzo to find a clear way of breaking family patterns keeps them from becoming healthy and complete adults. Their lingering co-dependent behavior, combined with Teresa's obsessive and desperately jealous clinging to something clearly unrealistic and unattainable (a happy and mutually respectful marriage with Lorenzo) leads, in fact, to Elena's death. Though Elena plays an active role in the situation that leads to her death, it is the failure of both Teresa and Lorenzo to fully let go of their disastrous relationship that sets the trap for Elena. If Lorenzo did not continue to drop by Teresa's flat from time to time, Elena would not have fallen in love with him, or vice versa—at least not in front of Teresa. The jealous and frustrated Teresa detects their mutual chemistry immediately, and when Elena later confesses that she and Lorenzo intend to be together, Teresa shoots and kills her. The play is filled with a litany of clues about how and why this happened. Even though Teresa and Lorenzo recognize most of the sources and symptoms of their psychological and emotional problems, tragically they never completely address them or recover from them. Elena quickly finds herself enmeshed in their unresolved problems, places herself in mortal danger, and is murdered in act 3.

The audience learns about Teresa's past because she tells her life story to Elena in act 1. Only minutes after first meeting her, Teresa tells Elena: ''I had a horrible childhood.'' Based on what she says about her family background, she is certainly telling the truth. This background is the primary key to understanding her personality and adult actions. As Robert J. Ackerman and Susan E. Pickering write in *Abused No More: Recovery from Abusive or Co-Dependent Relationships,* ''A woman builds her repertoire of behaviors around the structural models her parents provide. It is through these models that she first learns how men and women act towards each other.'' In Teresa's case, the odds were stacked against her from earliest childhood. Her father physically beat her mother and claimed that his brother, Giacomo, fathered Teresa. As a child, Teresa was frightened of her father and confused because no one would confirm or disprove the accusation. Her father was cold to her and favored her brother. ''He said my brother was his, but I wasn't,'' Teresa says. He cruelly said he couldn't stand looking at her and that he would abandon the family just so he wouldn't have to see her ever again. Eventually he did, moving to the United States.

By any standards, Teresa's father was clearly abusive and sadistic to her and her mother. To make matters worse, he would send Teresa's brother fine clothes, and eventually he sent money to her brother to join him overseas. By itself, the abusive pattern set by her father would have damaged Teresa's ability to have healthy adult relationships. But she had to endure even more abusive treatment at the hands of her paternal grandparents, with whom she and her mother were forced to live because they were apparently too destitute to live on their own.

Teresa's terrible childhood lumbered on, damaging her (and her mother) further. Her possible biological father, Uncle Giacomo, might have helped them, but he had made a permanent break with his parents, the very people with whom she was living, over disputed land. When Teresa was small, he occasionally gave her sweets, but ultimately even this small contact ceased and he abandoned her, too. Moving in with Teresa's grandparents presented more grief. They both scolded her, even though she did most of the housework and fieldwork, like a combination peasant and servant; they blamed her for their son's departure for America. After they

> "THERE WERE MANY PROBLEMS RIGHT FROM THE BEGINNING, AND NEITHER SEEMED ABLE TO STOP THEM. EVEN ON THEIR HONEYMOON, WHICH TERESA INSISTED ON HAVING IN HER OLD HOMETOWN, SHE IS BEDEVILED BY OLD FAMILY FORMS OF ABUSE."

died, Teresa and her mother moved to another relative's house, Aunt Amata's, and there her mother became a full-time servant. Her mother had worked herself so hard that one of her legs became lame. Determined to escape her mother's fate, Teresa fled for Rome when she turned twenty. Assuming that Ackerman and Pickering's theories are correct, Teresa—who had horrible role models to follow, little love, and much abuse and neglect of all kinds— would not have been equipped to create a healthy relationship. Denied physical affection, she craved it; denied financial security, she sought it; denied a loving father or loving male of any sort, she was ever on the lookout for one. All of these needs set her on a collision course toward Lorenzo, who came from a dysfunctional family of a different sort. Though they met by chance, it was not by chance that they became enmeshed with each other in a very unhealthy, mutually destructive adult relationship.

Lorenzo's childhood was vastly different from Teresa's. His father was dead, but his mother owned substantial property and agricultural resources, some of which were earmarked for Lorenzo upon her death. He lived in wealth and never wanted for material comforts, but these came at a price: his mother tried to control him through her purse strings, and, to an extent, she succeeded. Furthermore, he idealized his sister, who married, had nine children, and lived in comfort. But as an adult, Lorenzo acts out against the confines set by his mother. He hates being controlled and rebels constantly. Still, his mother never cuts him off financially, so his behavior is reinforced by her indulgence. By the time he and Teresa meet, he has finished an engineering degree but does not work. He is rich, spoiled, aimless, dilettantish, self-indulgent, and easily distracted. He has a pattern of staying with Teresa for a short time, running away, and then eventually returning, much like the pattern he has with his mother. However, Teresa's poverty makes her financially dependent on him and, indirectly, on his mother's financial dispensations. He never loves Teresa in a traditional way; rather, he feels sorry for her, and she provides a way to act out against his mother. Lorenzo tells Elena in act 2, ''I came to live with her because I wanted to annoy my mother . . . I *wanted* to live with a girl who was crazy and disorganized and confused.'' Given their dysfunctional family patterns and their inability to overcome them, the relationship between Lorenzo and Teresa was doomed from the start.

Dysfunctional family patterns spill over into Lorenzo and Teresa's marriage. They become co-dependent, a condition that reinforces negative attitudes and actions between them yet prevents them from coming to a healthy solution. There were many problems right from the beginning, and neither seemed able to stop them. Even on their honeymoon, which Teresa insisted on having in her old hometown, she is bedeviled by old family forms of abuse. Her Aunt Amata told her, ''You never deserved such a husband! Mind you hold on to him, you might easily go and lose him, a stupid crazy girl like you.'' And later, whenever they visited his mother, Lorenzo and his mother fought constantly. When Lorenzo and Teresa lived in Rome, they acted like crazy, spoiled children, wildly spending his money. He collected pictures, motorcycles, cars, and speeding tickets. He left her for days at a time, sometimes going back to see his mother, leaving Teresa anxious. They built a house in the country and then left it unoccupied, moving back to a Roman flat after only one night. ''He was disorganized,'' Teresa tells Elena, ''and *I* was disorganized, and the disorganization we managed to get into between us was unbelievable.'' Eventually, they began to fight whenever they were together. ''We used to have frightful scenes,'' Teresa says; ''he'd slap me, and I'd bite him and scratch him . . . and at five in the morning he'd go off on his motor-cycle, and I'd stay in bed crying.'' Hoping for Lorenzo to give her the unconditional love denied her in childhood, Teresa instead finds the same physical and emotional abuse committed by her father. Unlike her mother, though, Teresa fights back. And Lorenzo does not entirely abandon her, for he continues to give her money after they separate. But when they are together, they bicker constantly, even long after formally separating.

When the play begins, Teresa and Lorenzo have been separated for a year. Teresa has resorted to placing advertisements to try and control her life. But her life is actually out of control. She suffers from depression, insomnia, nightmares, and anxieties. She has aversions to old people and the countryside because they remind her of her childhood. She has no friends and hopes only for Lorenzo's permanent return, even though on a rational level she knows he will not live with her ever again. But he tortures her by returning occasionally, and he alleviates his guilt by giving her money. She lacks perspective and role models, people who could give her useful advice, and has no impulse control, she remains virtually paralyzed in an emotional sense. Her boarder, Elena, becomes her friend for a while, but upon meeting Lorenzo, Elena does the worst thing possible for their friendship by opting to leave with Lorenzo after she falls in love with him. Teresa, with her lack of impulse control and through murderous jealousy, shoots her. Interestingly, Elena is attracted to Lorenzo because he is like her own father, whom she dislikes on a conscious level because he lets her mother do most of the work at their country *pension* while he speaks English and plays games with guests. She seems to be acting out against her own somewhat dysfunctional family, for with Lorenzo she probably feels that she can correct the sins of her father and do a better job as his wife than Teresa has done. In any case, she will never have the chance to try.

By the end of the play, there is little hope for recovery because unattended dysfunctional family patterns have led to Elena's death and have permanently damaged the lives of the survivors. Though Lorenzo has attained a greater degree of self-knowledge, he remains enmeshed with his mother and Teresa. To get on with his life in a healthier manner, he needs to recover from family abuse as much as Teresa does.

Source: Erik France, Critical Essay on *The Advertisement*, in *Drama for Students*, The Gale Group, 2002.

Curt Guyette

Guyette has a bachelor of arts degree in English writing from the University of Pittsburgh. In the following essay, he examines the roles of fate and free will in the lives of the characters portrayed in Ginzburg's play.

In the play *The Advertisement*, by Italian author Natalia Ginzburg, a lonely woman separated from her husband places a newspaper advertisement seeking a student to share her apartment. From that simple beginning unfolds a story that ultimately ends in tragedy. Although there are three main characters, one—the woman named Teresa—holds center stage throughout. As in life, the vagaries of chance and irony play a key role in this drama. Fate plays a role in every existence, but everyone must make life choices, and with those choices come consequences.

The story of Teresa's troubled life is unveiled when a twenty-year-old philosophy student named Elena answers Teresa's ad seeking a roommate. The woman Elena meets is a compulsive talker still obsessed with the man she separated from a year ago, even though their five-year marriage was chaotic and mutually self-destructive. In the first act, Teresa reels off her life's story in a series of lengthy monologues. The speeches, however, aren't just a way for Ginzburg to move the story along quickly. The playwright's technique is used as a way to shed light on the psychological underpinnings of the drama's central character, who considers herself a victim of unfortunate circumstance. "Teresa is a woman who has been reduced to talk as her only form of action," editors Victoria Sullivan and James Hatch observe in the introduction to their 1973 collection *Plays by and about Women*. The portrait that emerges is a disturbing one. Teresa "reveals herself as the self-indulgent victim of her own desperately chaotic personality," note Sullivan and Hatch. The editors continue the description, writing:

> Her long-winded, egocentric monologues say something about the female state. Having been brought up with no particular goal except to catch a man, she cannot support herself economically or emotionally. Yet because of her demanding dependence and compulsive need to talk, no man can stand to live with her.

As a girl, Teresa's father accused her mother of cheating on him. He suspects that Teresa is not really his child, at first ignoring her and eventually abandoning both of them. The mother and daughter, left in dire financial straits, are forced to live with relatives. For a while, they reside with Teresa's aunt, who owns a small drapery shop. But as soon as she turns twenty, Teresa, determined not to spend her life "selling buttons," runs off to the adventure and uncertainty of life in Rome.

The Advertisement made its world premiere in 1968, a time when the women's movement was fast gaining momentum. It is not surprising that Teresa

> " . . . WHAT DEFINES THE INDIVIDUAL IS HOW HE OR SHE REACTS TO THE UNEXPECTED HAND THAT EACH IS DEALT."

is sexually liberated. Young and beautiful, she finds occasional bit parts in films that require her to strip down to bra and slip. In one, she eats grapes while the director encourages her to "waggle" her hips erotically. It is while filming one of these movies that she has a chance encounter with Lorenzo, a young engineer. They go out to dinner and then return to her apartment where they spend the next three days eating, sleeping, and making love.

Then Lorenzo leaves, saying he is going out briefly to get some cigarettes and doesn't come back. The abandonment is traumatic for Teresa, who gives up her attempts to become a movie star and finds work in a beauty shop. Six months later, again quite by chance, Lorenzo walks in to the beauty shop with a beautiful woman wearing a fur coat. Even though Lorenzo tells Teresa that he viewed her not as a person but as an object (with the revelation reducing her to tears), she pursues him and takes him to her bed once more.

Although Teresa didn't realize it when she first chased after Lorenzo, she soon discovers that he is quite wealthy. Instead of being a blessing, however, his riches are a kind of curse. After marrying, they become spendthrifts and live without purpose. Both are irresponsible. He buys and discards motorcycles and cars and piles up countless speeding tickets. Then they build a country villa, fill it with expensive paintings and antiques, but never move in.

Like the idle rich in F. Scott Fitzgerald's *The Great Gatsby*, the lack of struggle that defines daily life for the poor and working class leaves Lorenzo and Teresa free to pursue any sort of life they choose. But instead of putting that freedom to positive effect, they waste it on empty frivolity and spend far too much time focusing on their relationship of self-indulgence, which quickly becomes destructive.

Unlike the thoughtful and studious Elena, Teresa is no intellectual. Her husband goes so far as to describe her as "ignorant as a cook." Lorenzo is an intellectual, with a variety of interests from architecture to art but with a special passion for "pure physics." At his urging, Teresa tries to read books but can retain nothing. All of her attention is focused on her husband, and he finds that stifling. At first Lorenzo, a flawed character himself, attempts to help Teresa with what he describes as her "troubles and anxieties." What initially seemed to be love turns out to have been only pity. But her neuroses are so overpowering that they quickly begin to consume him. As he tells Elena, after making his entrance in the second act: "Instead of curing her anxiety I felt myself involved in it; I felt I was gradually sinking into a black, muddy well. I was losing my breath, my reason . . . a horrible sensation."

As a result, their marriage quickly dissolves into one of extreme dysfunction, marked by violent outbreaks. She'd bite and scratch him, and he would slap and punch her. "It was hell," Teresa tells Elena. Even so, she could not move beyond their relationship even after a year of separation. She'd sit alone in her flat, pining away for Lorenzo and yearning for a reconciliation that will never occur.

Through it all, she remains deeply disturbed. Hinting that more trouble is in the offing, Ginzburg ends the first act with a literary technique known as foreshadowing. By having Teresa allude to the terrible nightmares she experiences, the reader senses that something ominous awaits.

At the beginning of the second act, when Elena meets Lorenzo, she tells him how happy she is and what good friends she and Teresa have become. The fact that it all came about because of a stroke of good fortune is emphasized. "And to think," she says, "I came here just by chance, because of an advertisement!"

Lorenzo seems kinder than the man depicted by Teresa. He expresses concern for her well-being, is pleased that she has found a companion to ease her loneliness, and is continuing to support her financially even though Lorenzo knew she cheated on him by sleeping with his best friend. Despite his kindness, Teresa continues to berate Lorenzo and dredges up pieces of the past that he would rather forget. Having escaped the depressing whirlwind that was life with Teresa, he is trying to move on and find happiness. And, the author hints, a brighter future just might include Elena.

The brief third act opens with Elena describing her date the previous night with Lorenzo. Their relationship has progressed quickly. She's decided to move out of Teresa's apartment, telling her at first that the two spend so much time talking that she is having difficulty keeping up with her studies. But Teresa has already divined the real reason Elena is leaving. When Elena confesses that she and Lorenzo are in love, Teresa responds calmly that she knows. In fact, Teresa has already placed a new advertisement seeking another student to move into the room. Elena is taken aback by the display of equanimity. She expected Teresa to be upset, perhaps even irrational. After all, Teresa freely admits to being still in love with Lorenzo. But instead of anger, she summons up generosity, offering to obtain an annulment so that Elena and Lorenzo can marry.

As events reach their climax, both women philosophize about the unexpected twists of fate that have brought them to this junction. Elena says:

> What a strange thing fate is! To think I came here by chance, by the merest chance, answering an advertisement! I might easily never have looked in the paper that day, and never have come here at all! And I'd never have known either of you.

Teresa, understandably, is less enthralled by the same train of events:

> When people are happy, they never stop marvelling at the great intelligence of chance; because it's made them happy. And when they're unhappy, they're not at all surprised to discover how stupid chance is. Stupid and blind.

Listening to her friend speak, Elena is struck by how out of character she seems, sensing how odd it is that she seems so calm, cold, and rational. Teresa continues on, ruminating further about the role fate has played in what has turned out to be a terribly unhappy life:

> I could have married someone else, if I hadn't met him that day. I was so young and pretty. There were lots of men after me. I could have picked a nice, quiet, simple man, and had a settled, orderly life. Instead, I fall in love with him. That's my luck! He ruins me. Destroys me.

Life, however, isn't simply dictated by strokes of luck or misfortune. Fate plays a role in every existence, to be sure, but what defines the individual is how he or she reacts to the unexpected hand that each is dealt. Teresa's great flaw is her failure to realize that she is something much more than the victim of bad luck. In her mind, it is as if she bears no responsibility for the disaster that her relationship with Lorenzo became. After all, he seemed to thrive once they'd separated. Pursuing his passion for physics, he became productive and wrote a book about atoms. Had Teresa acted differently toward him, things might well have worked out for the better.

Even with their marriage in a shambles, she still has the opportunity to direct her life in a happier direction if she so chooses. She can do as Lorenzo did, sweeping away the pieces of a broken relationship to move on in search of contentment. Instead, she chooses to dwell on the past, sinking ever further into a pit of despair. It is a decision that leads to tragedy.

As the play builds to its climax, Teresa announces that she has a pistol in her purse and that she intends to use it, first on Lorenzo and then on herself. Elena begs her to throw the weapon away, and Teresa agrees. Relieved, Elena promises her distraught friend that she and Lorenzo will always be there for her. A few moments later—while both women are offstage—there is a gunshot. Teresa has killed Elena. The audience can't know for certain whether it was murder or an accident, but in either event, that newspaper ad that Elena read by pure chance has led her to an early grave.

Then the doorbell rings. It is another young woman who's come to see about the room she read about in a newspaper advertisement. 'And there you have it,' Ginzburg seems to be saying as the curtain falls. Life, with all its strange twists is, in the end, ironic.

Source: Curt Guyette, Critical Essay on *The Advertisement,* in *Drama for Students,* The Gale Group, 2002.

SOURCES

Ackerman, Robert J., and Susan E. Pickering, *Abused No More: Recovery for Women from Abusive or Co-Dependent Relationships,* TAB Books, 1989.

Faustini, Giuseppe, ''Natalia Ginzburg,'' in *Dictionary of Literary Biography,* Volume 177: *Italian Novelists Since World War II,* edited by Augustus Pallotta, Gale Research, 1997, pp. 141–49.

Ginzburg, Natalia, *The Advertisement,* translated by Henry Reed, in *Plays By and About Women: An Anthology,* edited by Victoria Sullivan and James Hatch, Random House, 1973, pp. 295–344.

Sullivan, Victoria, and James Hatch, ''Introduction,'' in *Plays By and About Women: An Anthology,* edited by Victoria Sullivan and James Hatch, Vintage Books, 1973, p. xii.

FURTHER READING

Bullock, Alan, *Natalia Ginzburg: Human Relationships in a Changing World,* St. Martin's Press, 1991.
    Bullock provides critical discussion of the works of Ginzburg in terms of her thematic focus on the experiences of women in modern relationships and the modern family.

Burke, Frank, *Fellini's Films: From Postwar to Postmodern,* Prentice Hall International, 1996.
    Burke offers an historical account and critical analysis of the films of the celebrated Italian director Frederico Fellini, whose works were popular during the period in which Ginzburg's play was written.

Jeannet, Angela M., and Giuliana Sanguinetti Katz, eds., *Natalia Ginzburg: A Voice of the Twentieth Century,* University of Toronto Press, 2000.
    Jeannet and Katz introduce a collection of critical essays on the works of Ginzburg in terms of her representations of modern life.

Ridley, Jasper Godwin, *Mussolini,* St. Martin's Press, 1998.
    Ridley provides a biographical account of the life and career of Benito Mussolini in the context of twentieth-century Italian history.

Stille, Alexander, *Benevolence and Betrayal: Five Italian Jewish Families Under Fascism,* Summit Books, 1991.
    Stille provides accounts of the experiences of five Jewish families in fascist Italy.

Zuccotti, Susan, *Under His Very Windows: The Vatican and the Holocaust in Italy,* Yale University Press, 2000.
    Zuccotti offers a critical historical account of the role of the Roman Catholic Church in the persecution of Italian Jews during the Holocaust.

Blues for an Alabama Sky

PEARL CLEAGE

1995

In a preface to the published version of her play *Blues for an Alabama Sky*, Cleage comments, ''I still believe that theatre has a ritual power to call forth the spirits, illuminate the darkness and *speak the truth to the people.*''

Blues for an Alabama Sky was first produced in 1995. In 1996, it was performed during the Atlanta Summer Olympic Games as part of the Cultural Olympiad. The play is set in Harlem, New York City, in 1930, at a time when, as Cleage states, ''The creative euphoria of the Harlem Renaissance has given way to the harsher realities of the Great Depression.'' Angel is a struggling blues singer and nightclub performer who cannot find a job. Her friend Guy, a costume designer, is also out of work but dreams of being hired to design dresses for the famous African-American singer and dancer Josephine Baker, who is living in Paris. Their neighbor Delia, a social worker, is trying to organize a family planning clinic in Harlem. Their friend Sam, a doctor, works long hours delivering babies at the Harlem Hospital.

Angel, who has no other source of income, allows herself to be courted by Leland, a very conservative, religious young man from Alabama, who claims he wants to marry her. Meanwhile, Delia, with the help of Sam, is successful in convincing a local church to support her proposal for a family planning clinic. Guy finally receives the long-awaited notice from Josephine Baker inviting

him to Paris to work for her. Angel, however, has gotten pregnant by Leland and obtains an illegal abortion performed by Sam. Furious about the abortion, Leland shoots and kills Sam.

In writing this play, Cleage was interested in portraying the lives of struggling African-American musicians, artists, and social activists in Harlem during the era of the Harlem Renaissance and the depression. Central themes of the story include economic hardship, reproductive rights, and homosexuality.

AUTHOR BIOGRAPHY

Pearl Michelle Cleage (pronounced ''cleg'') was born December 7, 1948, in Springfield, Massachusetts. She grew up in Detroit, where her father, a minister, founded his own denomination and became widely known for the fifteen-foot-high painting of the Black Madonna and Child, called the ''Shrine of the Black Madonna,'' which adorned his church. Cleage's mother was a schoolteacher who, along with Cleage's father, instilled in her a sense of responsibility to the African-American community. Cleage now describes her political orientation as that of an African-American Urban Nationalist Feminist Warrior.

Cleage studied drama and playwriting at a number of colleges and universities. She attended Howard University from 1966 until 1969, when she married Michael Lucius Lomax, an elected county official in Georgia (they were divorced ten years later). She attended Yale University in 1969 and the University of the West Indies in 1971. In 1971, she received a bachelor's degree from Spelman College and enrolled in graduate courses at Atlanta University. During the 1970s, Cleage worked as a writer, producer, and talk show host for a number of radio and television stations in Atlanta, Georgia. She served as the director of communications for the city of Atlanta and as press secretary to Mayor Maynard Jackson, the city's first African-American mayor.

From 1983 to 1987, Cleage was playwright-in-residence at the Just Us Theater Company in Atlanta, serving as artistic director from 1987 to 1994. In 1986, she founded the magazine *Catalyst,* of which she remained the editor for ten years. From 1986 to

Pearl Cleage

1991, Cleage taught as an instructor in creative writing at Spelman College, where in 1991 she was made playwright-in-residence. During the 1990s, she also served as playwright-in-residence at Smith College and Agnes Scott College. In 1994, Cleage married her longtime companion, Zaron Burnett Jr.

Cleage saw several of her one-act plays produced on the stage at Howard University in the late 1960s and at Spelman College in the early 1970s. During the 1980s, the Just Us Theater Company produced her plays *puppetplay* (1983), *Good News* (1984), and *Essentials* (1985). The year 1992 saw the production of two of her plays, *Chain* and *Late Bus to Mecca,* by the Women's Project and Productions and the New Federal Theater, and *Flyin' West* by the Alliance Theater Company in Atlanta. *Blues for an Alabama Sky* was first produced in 1995. In 1996, it was performed by the Alliance Theatre Company at the Summer Olympic Games in Atlanta as part of the Cultural Olympiad.

Cleage's nonfiction writings include *Mad at Miles: A Blackwoman's Guide to the Truth* (1990), which criticizes the celebrated jazz musician Miles Davis for his treatment of women, and *Deals with the Devil and Other Reasons to Riot* (1993), a collection of essays on American popular culture and mass media. *What Looks Like Crazy on an*

Ordinary Day— (1997), her first novel, was selected for the Oprah Winfrey Book Club. *I Wish I Had a Red Dress* was published in 2001.

PLOT SUMMARY

Act 1

Scene 1 takes place at 3:00 a.m. Angel, who is drunk, is being helped home to Guy's apartment by Guy and Leland, a young man who happened to be passing them on the street. Angel's boyfriend, Nick, an Italian gangster, has just gotten married and has broken off his relationship with her. During her nightclub performance at the Cotton Club, which Nick was attending, Angel interrupted her dance routine to yell and throw things at him from the stage. As a result, she has been fired, as has her friend Guy, who worked as a costume designer for the club. Guy's neighbor, Delia, awakened by the commotion, comes into his apartment to see what has happened. Delia, a social worker, is trying to organize the opening of a family planning clinic in Harlem. Guy explains that his dream is to get a job as costume designer for the celebrated African-American singer and dancer Josephine Baker, who is living in Paris.

Scene 2 takes place that Sunday afternoon. Since Angel had been living in an apartment paid for by Nick, Guy offers to let her live with him for a while. He doesn't tell her that he, too, has been fired, for fear of worrying her. Delia comes in to see how Angel is doing. Their friend Sam, a well-respected doctor at the Harlem Hospital, also stops by. He has just delivered twins and offers them all a drink in celebration. Sam, Delia, and Guy leave to go out for dinner, while Angel, still too hung over to eat, stays behind. Looking out the window, she sees Leland, whom she does not remember from the night before. After he explains that he helped Guy take her home, she suggests they go for a walk together the following Sunday.

Scene 3 takes place the following Wednesday afternoon. Angel comes home to Guy's apartment, having spent the whole day walking around Harlem, trying without luck to get a new job as a nightclub singer. Guy returns home and tells her that Nick has set up an audition for her at a club owned by his friend Tony T. Angel and Guy get ready to attend a

party in honor of the poet Langston Hughes, who has been out of town. Meanwhile, in Delia's apartment, Delia and Sam work together on preparing her speech to convince a local church to support the opening of a family planning clinic.

Scene 4 takes place the following Sunday evening. After Leland arrives for his date with Angel, Guy, Delia, and Sam leave to go out to the theater. Angel and Leland stay in the apartment and get to know one another. Angel learns that Leland is from Alabama and has recently come to Harlem to stay with a cousin. He tells her that his wife, Anna, died eight months earlier in childbirth, which the baby also did not survive. Leland explains that Angel reminds him of his wife, which is why she caught his attention. Angel also learns that Leland is very religious; she admits that she herself does not go to church. Angel kisses him and the lights go down.

Scene 5 takes place the following Friday evening. Guy tells Delia that he has finally received a telegram from Josephine Baker in Paris, stating that she likes his gown designs and requesting that she send her several sample gowns. After Delia leaves, Leland arrives for a date with Angel, who is not home yet. Guy invites him in but goes out before Angel arrives. Angel comes in, back from her "audition" with Tony T. She explains that Tony T. wanted to take her on as his mistress, supporting her in exchange for romantic companionship. Leland assumes that Angel has turned down Tony T.'s offer, although Angel hints that she has, in fact, accepted it since she has no other source of income. Leland tells Angel that he wants to be her man, although she warns him against the idea. He gives her a dress as a gift. After Leland leaves, Angel looks at the dress, which is entirely too conservative for her taste and looks awful.

Act 2

Scene 1 of act 2 takes place two weeks later on a Sunday afternoon. Guy is preparing a tea party to celebrate sending his five costumes off to Josephine Baker in Paris. Sam, Delia, Leland, and Angel are all there to celebrate. But when Leland finds out that Guy is homosexual, he calls it "an abomination." Guy angrily kicks Leland out of the apartment and then interrogates Angel as to why she intends to marry Leland even though she doesn't love him. Angel explains that she wants to marry Leland because he will provide her with financial stability. Meanwhile, in Delia's apartment, Delia and Sam kiss for the first time.

Scene 2 takes place two weeks later. Sam tells Angel that her test shows she is two months pregnant. Angel still hasn't found a job, and there is an eviction notice on the door of Guy's apartment. Guy, however, is unworried about their financial situation because he is counting on receiving money from Josephine Baker for his costumes. After Guy leaves, Leland, who hasn't come around to see Angel in two weeks, arrives and asks her to marry him. She accepts.

Scene 3 takes place the following day. The building in which Delia had hoped to open a family planning clinic has been set on fire in protest against the clinic. Sam, however, offers an alternative space in which to set up the clinic. Guy arrives home with a cable message from Josephine Baker, saying she loves all five of the costumes he made and inviting him to come to Paris and work for her. She has included a ticket on the boat to Paris, along with plenty of money to prepare for the trip. Angel arrives, and Guy tells her the good news and that he has also purchased a ticket for her to accompany him to France. After Guy and Delia go out to celebrate, Sam arrives. Angel tells him that she said would marry Leland but that she has now decided she wants to go to Paris with Guy and does not want to have the baby. Sam agrees to perform an abortion.

Scene 4 takes place the following morning. Angel returns home from getting the abortion and informs Guy about what she has done. After Guy leaves, Leland arrives with a rocking chair he has made for Angel. He tells her he wants her to rock all of their children in the chair and then gives her a diamond engagement ring. Angel lies to Leland about the abortion, telling him that she lost the baby due to a miscarriage. After he begins to question her, however, she tells him the truth, and Leland guesses that it was Sam who performed the abortion. He tells Angel she's lucky he isn't going to kill her for aborting his child. As Leland is leaving the building, Sam walks up, and Leland shoots him in the back with a pistol, killing him.

Scene 5 takes place two weeks later. Guy and Delia have not seen Angel since the morning Sam was shot. Guy invites Delia to go with him to Paris, and she agrees. Guy goes out, and Angel quietly slips into the apartment. Delia sees her, but the two women "both understand that things have changed between them forever," and they say nothing to one another. After Delia leaves, Angel sits at the window, calmly drinking a glass of champagne, contemplating her next move.

CHARACTERS

Angel Allen

Angel Allen is a thirty-four-year-old woman who, as the play opens, has been fired from her job as a backup singer at the Cotton Club. Angel has just broken up with Nick, an Italian gangster who recently married another woman. Angel, hurt by the breakup, saw Nick in the audience of the nightclub and interrupted one of her dance routines to berate him and throw things at him. As a result of the breakup, Angel has also lost her apartment, paid for by Nick, as well as all of her clothes and other belongings, since he will not allow her into the apartment to collect her things. Guy, her best friend, allows her to live in his apartment while she searches for another job. However, due to the depression, there are no singing jobs available for Angel, and she continues to be out of work while Guy supports her. Her only prospect is not a singing job but an opportunity to become the mistress of Tony T., a friend of Nick's. Angel is a practical woman who, although she would prefer a job as a singer, is not above selling herself to a man in exchange for financial security. In Leland, Angel sees an opportunity for financial stability as his wife, despite the fact that she does not love him. But, after she gets pregnant by Leland, she decides that she does not want the baby and chooses to abort it. She has had at least one abortion in the past, after she became pregnant by Nick. When Guy offers her a ticket to go to Paris with him, Angel decides that this is a better opportunity than marrying Leland. She first tells Leland that she has had a miscarriage and then admits to having had an abortion. After Leland shoots Sam, the doctor who performed the abortion, Angel disappears for two weeks. She returns to Guy's apartment just as Guy and Delia are leaving for Paris. But Angel seems to have cut all ties with her two friends, and the play ends as she sits in the window of Guy's apartment, figuring out what to do next. Angel is a woman who has always been able to do whatever it takes to survive, despite unfortunate personal and financial circumstances.

Leland Cunningham

Leland Cunningham is a twenty-eight-year-old man from Alabama who has been in Harlem only six weeks. Eight months earlier, his wife, Anna, died giving birth to a baby boy, who also did not survive. Leland encounters Guy and Angel on the street in the middle of the night and helps Guy to accompany Angel, who is drunk, back to the apartment. He later tells Angel that he was drawn to her because she looks like his deceased wife. Leland's manner is that of a Southern gentleman, and his dress is neat and conservative. He is very religious, with traditional, conservative values that are very different from those of Angel and her friends. Leland considers homosexuality "an abomination" and is even acquainted with the young men in the neighborhood who have been beating up on gay men. Because of this, Angel lies to Leland about Guy, saying that he is her cousin, rather than explaining that he is a friend who is gay. Leland continues to court Angel, even though her values and lifestyle are clearly very different from his. He tries to influence her to attend church, but she is not interested. He even buys her a very conservative dress, which is not at all her style. Before long, Leland asks Angel to marry him, and she accepts. After she tells him that she is pregnant with his child, he brings her a rocking chair he has made by hand, in which he says he wants her to rock all of their children. However, when Angel tells him she has miscarried the baby and then admits that she opted to abort it, Leland immediately figures out that her friend Sam was the doctor who performed the abortion. Leaving Angel, he encounters Sam outside of the apartment building and shoots him in the back with a pistol, killing him.

Deal

See Delia Patterson

Guy Jacobs

Guy Jacobs is a thirty-something homosexual man who has just been fired from his job as a costume designer for the Cotton Club. Guy's dream is to be hired by the famous African-American singer and dancer Josephine Baker, who lives in Paris, to design her costumes. He keeps a large picture of her in his apartment and constantly talks about how his life is going to change once she hires him. Guy is acquainted with the social circle of famous Harlem Renaissance poets and writers, particularly Langston Hughes. Guy is Angel's best friend. He defends her unruly behavior at the Cotton Club, even though he is fired as a result. He doesn't hesitate to let Angel live in his apartment with him

and even risks some danger at the hands of her former gangster boyfriend in order to sneak into her old apartment and grab some of her things. Guy doesn't tell Angel that he has been fired because he doesn't want to upset her, although this means taking lower-paying, less-glamorous jobs in order to support her. Guy explains to Delia that he met Angel in Alabama and was inspired to seek his fortune in Harlem because of her. He is very supportive and caring toward Angel, even though she can be a difficult person, because, as he tells her, "You let me see how beautiful I was." Guy finally receives a cable from Josephine Baker saying she loves his costumes and inviting him to come to Paris and work for her. She sends him a boat ticket to Paris and plenty of money to buy whatever he needs for his trip. He immediately invites Angel to go to Paris with him, as he now has enough money to buy her a ticket, as well. Angel accepts the offer, but after Leland shoots Sam, she disappears without saying anything to Guy. The day he is to leave for Paris, Guy invites Delia to accompany him in Angel's place, and she accepts. By the time Angel returns to his apartment in Harlem, Guy has already left to board the ship. However, Guy, always thinking of Angel's best interests, has paid the rent on his apartment a couple of months ahead of time, thinking that, if Angel returns, she will at least have a place to stay.

Delia Patterson

Delia Patterson, whose friends call her Deal, is a twenty-five-year-old social worker who is engaged in a project, spearheaded by Margaret Sanger, to open a family planning clinic in Harlem. Delia's apartment is across the hallway from Angel and Guy's. She is very shy with men but begins to date Sam after they work together on the family planning clinic. Two weeks after Sam is shot, Delia agrees to accompany Guy to Paris. Just as she is leaving, Angel returns to the apartment, but, as the stage directions state, "In that moment, both understand that things have changed forever between them." Delia leaves without saying a word to Angel.

Sam Thomas

Sam Thomas is a forty-year-old doctor at the Harlem Hospital. He works long hours delivering babies but also stays up late drinking with his friends on many nights. Sam is proud of his work delivering babies but is also aware of the problems many African Americans face raising children, due to the financial hardships caused by the depression. Sam is attracted to Delia, but he is aware of her shyness and is careful not to overwhelm her. He helps her to prepare her speech to the church about opening a family planning clinic. In addition to delivering babies, Sam also performs illegal abortions. He has previously performed an abortion for Angel, when she was pregnant by Nick. However, when she asks for another abortion, he is reluctant to go through with it, because this time the father is an African-American man, rather than a white man. However, Angel tells him that she does not want the baby, so he gives her the abortion. When Leland finds out, he shoots Sam in the back, killing him.

THEMES

Economic Hardship

A central theme of *Blues for an Alabama Sky* is economic hardship. Cleage set her play in 1930, early in the depression. The writers and artists of the Harlem Renaissance, which flourished during the 1920s, were hard hit by the depression because the struggle for economic stability detracted from the time and resources necessary to pursue artistic endeavors. Cleage thus focuses on the unknowns of the Harlem Renaissance, those struggling singers, dancers, and other artists who were so financially devastated by the depression that they were unable to successfully pursue their dreams. The character of Angel, in particular, is sidetracked from her goal of being a blues singer by the meager job opportunities available to her after she is fired from the Cotton Club. Angel's approach to addressing economic hardship is to rely on a man to support her. After she is fired, Guy takes her in and supports her, even though he, too, has been fired. Angel had been supported by Nick, a gangster who paid for her apartment and nice clothes in exchange for her favors as his mistress. After Nick gets married and breaks up with Angel, he passes her name on to another friend, Tony T., who offers to support her as his mistress. Angel is vague about her response to

this offer, but it seems that she accepts it, for lack of any better financial opportunity. However, when Leland asks her to marry him, she agrees, not because she loves him, but because she sees in him an opportunity for financial stability. Angel is a survivor and is not above doing whatever it takes to make her way in the world, even if that means selling her body to the highest bidder. Cleage thus portrays the ways in which a creative or artistic person, such as Angel, who is a singer and dancer, can be diverted from pursuing her dreams by the need to overcome economic hardship.

Family Planning

Family planning and reproductive rights are also important themes of this play. Delia's goal is to open the first family planning clinic in Harlem. As a social worker, Delia is working with Margaret Sanger, a pioneer in women's reproductive rights, to gain community support for the project. Delia's primary concern is to convince the popular Reverend Adam Powell of the Abyssinian Church in Harlem to support the opening of a clinic. Delia explains that she is ''trying to give women in Harlem the chance to plan their families'' through access to birth control. She comments that, because of the inaccessibility of family planning services, ''women are dying.'' Sam agrees to help Delia prepare her speech to Reverend Powell and the deacon board of the church, but his perspective on the issue is somewhat different from Delia's. He tells her that the issue of birth control in the African-American community is more complicated than she thinks. He explains that some African-American organizations interpret the efforts of Margaret Sanger, a white woman, as an act of ''genocide'' against the African-American community. He comments, ''What does family planning mean to the average colored man? White women teaching colored women how to stop having children.'' Sam helps Delia approach the issue as a matter of strengthening the black family through family planning. She changes her speech to focus on asking the church authorities ''for their help in building strong families with healthy mothers, happy children and loving fathers all over Harlem.'' With Sam's help, Delia successfully convinces the church to support the opening of a family planning clinic. Later, Margaret Sanger addresses the church congregation about her plans for the clinic, successfully gaining their support. However, after Sam performs an illegal abortion on

TOPICS FOR FURTHER STUDY

- Cleage has set her play in the context of the Harlem Renaissance movement in African-American literature. Learn more about one of the important writers of the Harlem Renaissance, such as James Weldon Johnson, Claude McKay, Countee Cullen, Wallace Thurman, Langston Hughes, Zora Neale Hurston, or Richard Wright. What are the major works of this author? What obstacles—financial, social, or personal—did this author overcome to become a successful writer? What central themes does this author address in her or his major works? In what ways did the Harlem Renaissance influence this author? In what ways did this author's work influence African-American literature?

- This play takes place during the era of the depression. Learn more about the depression. What events and circumstances led to the stock market crash of 1929? What effect did it have on the United States as a whole? How were the effects of the depression different in the South and in the North? Did it affect African Americans differently from white Americans? What effect did it have on the world economy? When and how did the depression end?

- Characters within the play mention two important African-American political leaders from the early twentieth century: Booker T. Washington and Marcus Garvey. Learn more about one of these men. What was his political philosophy? What influence did he have on the African-American community? What attitudes do the characters in this play have toward this leader and his politics?

- In Cleage's play, Angel is a struggling blues singer and nightclub performer. Learn more about the history of blues music. How and in what regions of the United States did the blues develop? Who were some of the important figures in blues music during the 1920s and 1930s? Learn more about one of these figures and her or his career.

- This play takes place in the era of Prohibition, during which the sale and consumption of alcohol was illegal. Throughout the play, the characters are seen drinking various kinds of alcohol without regard to such legal restrictions. Only Leland points out that Prohibition is still in effect. Learn more about the Prohibition era in the United States. What year was Prohibition instituted? What effect did it have on American culture? To what extent was the illegal sale and consumption of alcohol carried on? When was Prohibition repealed, and how did this come about?

Angel and is shot by Leland, press coverage of the incident creates a scandal which causes the community to withdraw support for the clinic.

Homosexuality and Homophobia

Homosexuality and homophobia are also central themes of this play. Throughout the play, Cleage explores the issue of homosexuality and homophobia (prejudice against homosexuals) in the African-American community. She portrays both the vital gay community in Harlem of the 1920s and 1930s and the virulent homophobia, which results in acts of brutality and violence against gays. Guy, who is homosexual, is clearly established in the gay community of Harlem, attending many parties and hobnobbing with famous gay writers. On first moving to Harlem, Guy had earned his living designing costumes for drag queens. One night, friends of his and Angel's, a gay couple, are beaten up by a group of men around the corner from their apartment building. Later in the play, a group of young men attack Guy as he is walking home from the store, but he successfully fights them off. It turns out that

Leland knows these men from his prayer meeting. Angel has been lying to Leland in order to cover up the fact that Guy is homosexual. When Leland finds out, he states that he thinks homosexuality is ''an abomination.'' Guy angrily kicks Leland out of his apartment for the insult.

STYLE

Setting: Harlem, New York

Blues for an Alabama Sky is set in Harlem, New York City, during the era of the Harlem Renaissance. This setting is important to Cleage's fictional story, which takes place in a real historical and geographic context. In order to appreciate the significance of this setting, it is helpful to have an understanding of the significance of Harlem to African-American history. Beginning in the late nineteenth century and throughout the twentieth century, the Harlem district of New York City came to be identified by its high concentration of African-American residents. African Americans began to occupy apartments in Harlem beginning in the 1890s. Lenox Avenue, in particular, became known as the African-American residential area of Harlem, and 125th Street was known as the ''Main Stem'' of Harlem's commercial district. In *Blues for an Alabama Sky*, Cleage refers to specific streets in Harlem that are historically significant, a stylistic choice that works to firmly locate her play in a specific historical and cultural context. Her description of the ''Time and Place'' in which the play is set mentions that Margaret Sanger was in the process of opening a family planning clinic on 126th Street. Guy mentions that the apartment Angel had been living in, paid for by her former gangster boyfriend, was on Lenox Avenue. As the play opens, Guy and Leland are helping a drunken Angel stumble down 125th Street in the middle of the night. At one point, Guy tells Angel that, in order to be successful, she needs to look beyond her small, limited world of Harlem, asserting, ''For prospects, you gotta look past 125th Street.'' Angel later states that she does not want to end up ''a broke old woman, begging up and down 125th Street.'' Toward the end of the play, a remark by Guy captures the sense that Harlem had once promised to be a bastion of African-American culture but became a disappointment to many, as the community suffered from the economic hardships of the depression era. He com-

ments, ''Harlem was supposed to be a place where Negroes could come together and really walk about, and for a red-hot minute, we did.'' Cleage thus utilizes a specific historical setting in which to capture the mood of an era through fictional characters.

Historical Fiction

Cleage's play can be categorized as historical fiction because of the stylistic choice of integrating real historical figures into a narrative focused on fictional characters. Cleage successfully and convincingly integrates the historical with the fictional, creating characters who are acquainted with such important historical figures as Adam Clayton Powell, the activist and political leader; Margaret Sanger, the pioneer in family planning; Josephine Baker, the famous nightclub performer; and Langston Hughes, the celebrated poet of the Harlem Renaissance.

HISTORICAL CONTEXT

Langston Hughes and the Harlem Renaissance

The Harlem Renaissance, also referred to as the New Negro Movement, designates a period during the 1920s in which African-American literature flourished among a group of writers concentrated in Harlem, New York City. Harlem Renaissance writers launched African-American literature into a new era, focusing on the experiences of black life and culture with an attitude of racial pride and self-determination for the African-American community. Two important magazines, the *Crisis* and *Opportunity,* were important promoters of the Harlem Renaissance, publishing the works of many young writers who pioneered the movement. The Harlem Renaissance also influenced artists and musicians exploring similar styles and themes. Langston Hughes (1902–1967) was one of the most important poets of the Harlem Renaissance. His first collection of poetry, *The Weary Blues,* was published in 1926. His influential novel, *Not Without Laughter* (1930), also garnered critical attention. Hughes is referred to many times in *Blues for an Alabama Sky.* The fictional characters of Cleage's play are members of Hughes's social circle, attending parties in his honor and associating with other significant figures of the Harlem Renaissance.

The Depression Era

Blues for an Alabama Sky is set in 1930, a year after the 1929 stock market crash that brought on the depression. The Harlem Renaissance petered out when the depression of the 1930s affected the financial status of many African-American writers and artists. Throughout the play, Angel makes a number of comments describing the economic conditions of the depression in Harlem. She has trouble finding a new job because, as she says, "the Depression has killed all the nightlife in Harlem." She goes on to explain, "There aren't any jobs doing anything, especially singing for your supper. Whole families sitting on the sidewalk with their stuff set out beside them. No place to sleep. No place to wash." Angel later adds, "I've never seen things this bad all over. Nobody's working and nobody's got prospects." Cleage thus demonstrates the effects of the depression on the African-American community in Harlem, particularly on the struggling writers, performers, and artists whose ambitions were thwarted by the economic difficulties brought on by the depression.

The Reverend Powell and the Abyssinian Church

Throughout the play, Cleage makes reference to several important political leaders in the African-American community, such as Reverend Adam Clayton Powell Jr., Booker T. Washington, and Marcus Garvey. The fictional characters in this play are acquainted with the historically real Reverend Powell, a popular pastor of the Abyssinian Church in Harlem. In the play, Delia successfully convinces Reverend Powell to support the opening of a family planning clinic. Historically, Powell worked as an elected public official, holding offices from the 1940s through the 1960s. In 1941, he was the first African American to be elected to the New York City Council. In 1945, he was elected to the U.S. House of Representatives, to which he was reelected for eleven terms. Powell was active in working for the passage of some fifty separate liberal legislative acts and bills to support civil rights, end segregation, and promote education and fair labor practices. He retired from politics in 1971 and died a year later.

The Black Arts Movement

In her introduction to *Blues for an Alabama Sky*, Cleage refers to herself as "a child of the Black Arts Movement." During the 1960s and 1970s, the Black Arts Movement, also referred to as the Black

Aesthetic Movement, emerged, embodying values derived from black nationalism and promoting politically and socially significant works of literature, often written in Black English vernacular. Important writers of the Black Arts Movement include Amiri Baraka (also known as LeRoi Jones), Eldridge Cleaver, and Ntozake Shange. Cleage began writing in the 1960s and 1970s, during the era of the Black Arts Movement, but her work did not emerge to gain national success until the 1980s and 1990s. *Blues for an Alabama Sky* thus shows the strong influence of the Black Arts Movement, with its focus on issues facing the African-American community, both in response to racist oppression imposed from outside the community and in response to internal divisions within the community.

CRITICAL OVERVIEW

Reviewers of *Blues for an Alabama Sky* frequently focus on the play's treatment of issues of race and gender in historical context. Freda Scott Giles, in the *African American Review*, compared *Blues for an Alabama Sky* to Cleage's plays *Flyin' West* (1992) and *Bourbon at the Border* (1997), commenting that, in all three, "Cleage seeks to bring us to grips with our American past and help us understand and acknowledge its impact on present conditions, especially with regard to issues of race and gender."

As critics have also observed, in *Blues for an Alabama Sky*, Cleage focuses on the unknown figures in a specific historical era, the ordinary people who make, and are made by, history, yet remain nameless in official historical accounts. Marta J. Effinger, in the *Dictionary of Literary Biography*, points out that *Blues for an Alabama Sky* is an example of Cleage's "obsession with history." She notes that while Cleage makes reference to a number of notable figures from the Harlem Renaissance era, "it is clear that the play examines what happened to ordinary people when the Harlem Renaissance ended." Giles concurs that in *Blues for an Alabama Sky*, as well as in several of Cleage's other plays, "Great events are seen not through the eyes of leaders and celebrities, but through the experiences of the ordinary people who lived them." As Effinger states, "the lives of black men and women" in this play "are dramatized as a struggle to gain access to the sparse opportunities in the early years of the Great Depression."

The Cotton Club, a popular jazz nightclub in Harlem, provides the setting for Angel's performance in Blues for an Alabama Sky

Critics also focus on the character of Angel as someone who ultimately does not take responsibility for the consequences of her actions, for her own life as well as for those around her. Giles comments that Angel, "accustomed to living in search of someone to take care of her, changes the lives of friends and lovers by failing to accept her responsibility for the shaping of her own destiny." Giles notes that Angel, "the pivotal character" in the play, "is called to account for her refusal to take responsibility for her actions." Giles goes on to assert:

> Angel . . . can only see her destiny in terms of the economic and emotional support of a man, and uses her body as the commodity through which she will achieve this support. Her myopic pursuit of self-interest strains her relationship with Guy to the breaking point and leads her to ignore the dangerous ground she treads in her relationship with Leland.

Effinger comments that the character of Angel "does not triumph" by the end of the play. Effinger states that Cleage once said that *Blues for an Alabama Sky* is her first play in which "one of her black female characters did not overcome obstacles." Effinger remarks that Angel "makes choices that destroy any possible opportunities," adding, "At the end of the play Angel is sitting alone in her apartment with the blues."

CRITICISM

Liz Brent

Brent has a Ph.D. in American Culture, specializing in film studies, from the University of Michigan. She is a freelance writer and teaches courses in the history of American cinema. In the following essay, Brent discusses the theme of dreams in Cleage's play.

An important theme of *Blues for an Alabama Sky* is the pursuit of dreams. While Angel is easily diverted from her dream of being a blues performer by the immediate concerns of economic hardship, Guy steadfastly pursues his dream without faltering for even a moment.

Guy's dream is to be hired as a costume designer for the famous African-American blues singer Josephine Baker, who is living in Paris at the time in which the play takes place. Josephine Baker (1906–1975) was an African-American dancer and singer who met with tremendous popular success performing in Paris music halls during the late 1920s. As Cleage states in the stage notes, in 1930, the citizens of Harlem were suffering the ill effects of the Depression, while "far from Harlem, Afri-

WHAT DO I READ NEXT?

- The much-celebrated experimental play *for colored girls who have considered suicide, when the rainbow is enuf: a choreopoem* (1977), by Ntozake Shange, addresses issues of race, class, and gender in the lives of African-American women.

- *Ma Rainey's Black Bottom* (1985), by August Wilson, is the most celebrated play by an African-American writer of the 1980s. It takes place in Chicago during the 1920s and centers on the blues singer Ma Rainey and her band.

- *Flyin' West* (1995), by Pearl Cleage, takes place on the frontier of the American West and concerns a family of African-American homesteaders.

- *Bourbon at the Border* (1997), published in *Flyin' West and Other Plays* (1999), by Pearl Cleage, is a play about a middle-aged couple in an apartment building in Detroit, reflecting back on their years of political activism during the 1960s.

- *The Collected Poems of Langston Hughes* (1994), edited by Arnold Rampersad, is an anthology of the best poems of Langston Hughes, one of the leading poets of the Harlem Renaissance.

- *The Power of Pride: Stylemakers and Rulebreakers of the Harlem Renaissance* (1999), by Carole Marks and Diana Edkins, provides an historical account of major figures in the Harlem Renaissance, including artists, writers, and intellectuals.

- *Classic Fiction of the Harlem Renaissance* (1994), edited by William L. Andrews, is an anthology of short stories by Harlem Renaissance writers such as Jean Toomer, Zora Neale Hurston, Claude McKay, Nella Larson, and Wallace Thurman.

- *Blues People* (1963), by LeRoi Jones (also known as Amiri Baraka), is a classic history of the development of blues music in the African-American community, written by one of the leading figures in the Black Arts Movement.

- *Jazz Cleopatra: Josephine Baker in Her Times* (1989), by Phyllis Rose, is a biography of Josephine Baker in historical context.

---

can-American expatriate extraordinaire, Josephine Baker sips champagne in her dressing room at the Folies Bergère and laughs like a free woman.'' For Cleage, as for the character of Guy, Josephine Baker is a symbol of freedom. Guy keeps his dream in sight at all times by placing a large photo of Josephine, as he calls her, in his workspace, a reminder of what he is striving for. Guy is intent on going to Paris to work for Josephine and sprinkles his conversation with French phrases, both real and made up, as if, in his mind, he were already there. He also sips champagne every chance he gets, as if by drinking an alcoholic beverage made in France, he is that much closer to realizing his dream come true.

But Guy doesn't simply indulge in idle dreams. He diligently pursues his dreams. He tells Delia, ''I'm going to drive Josephine crazy until she sends for me.'' Although it seems to others like an unrealistic goal, Guy never once doubts himself. He pursues his dream by first sending sketches of his costume designs to Josephine. In response, he receives a cable asking him to send several costumes for her to try on. At this point, he tells Delia, ''As far as I can see, all's right with the world. My dreams are about to come true.'' Finally, he receives the long-awaited cable inviting him to Paris to work for Josephine, with a first-class ticket and plenty of money enclosed.

Guy associates his dreams of creative and professional success with the idea of romance. He frequently describes everyday situations in the language of the romance novel, which indicates his view of the world as a place of infinite possibility, where one's wildest dreams may come true. He describes Leland, a stranger who helped him to drag a drunken Angel home at 3 a.m., as "A mysterious gentleman who came to our aid and then melted back into the Harlem night." Delia comments, "That's very romantic." To which Guy responds, "That's one of the secrets of life. . . . Learn to spot the romance." For Guy, spotting the romance means taking his dreams seriously and pursuing them diligently. As an example of what he means, Guy shows Delia a new costume design he has sketched for Josephine Baker. He tells her, "I dreamed it. I saw Josephine walking down the center staircase of one of those fabulous Folies-Bergère sets in this very dress." (The Folies Bergère was a popular Paris music hall where many of Josephine Baker's performances were staged.) Guy again adopts the language of a romance novel when he explains to Angel, who was too drunk to remember being helped by Leland, that the young man "saw a damsel in distress" and came to her rescue.

Angel, by contrast, has lost sight of her dream of becoming a blues singer and is instead pursuing immediate financial gain. As the play opens, she has just ended a relationship as the mistress of a gangster. Guy brings her home drunk and suggests she go to bed to sleep it off. But Angel replies, "I don't want to go to bed. What kind of dreams am I gonna have, hunh? No man. No job." From Angel's perspective, the only dream possible is the dream of a man or a job to meet her financial needs. Guy suggests she come to Paris with him, pursue the dream of a singing career, and "Give Josephine some competition." But Angel has no sense of romance and no sense of imagination with which to envision the ambitious dreams Guy pursues.

Angel is, in fact, disdainful of Guy's attempts to pursue his dreams, referring to him sarcastically as "some kind of genius with a dream." Guy then asks Angel, who has just accepted an offer to be a mistress of yet another gangster, "Is that your dream? Singing for gangsters?" When Leland passes on to Angel the message that Guy has finally received a cable from Josephine, he tells her that Guy said "it was a dream come true." Angel's response, however, is disdainful and pessimistic; she tells Leland, "I'm tired of Negro dreams. All they ever do is break your heart." Angel later comments, "Guy's a dreamer. He always was and he always will be, but I'm gonna hitch my star to somebody a little closer to home." Angel considers herself a practical woman who knows how to survive in a harsh world and will not waste her time on big dreams; she tells Leland, "I know how to take

> " ANGEL CONSIDERS HERSELF A PRACTICAL WOMAN WHO KNOWS HOW TO SURVIVE IN A HARSH WORLD AND WILL NOT WASTE HER TIME ON BIG DREAMS."

care of myself! I'm not going to be a broke old woman, begging up and down 125th Street, dreaming about fine clothes and French champagne."

Angel's goals, rather, are focused on the material comforts she hopes to gain through being supported by a man. She explains to Guy that, the whole time she was involved with Nick, "I kept thinking something wonderful was going to happen, but it never did. In my mind, I could see myself doing all these things with Nick—riding around in fancy cars, wearing furs, him giving me diamonds." When Guy asks Angel what she sees in Leland, she responds, "A rent check that won't bounce." From Angel's perspective, a rent check that won't bounce is a dream come true. As Guy later comments, Angel sees in Leland "her ticket to Paradise." Angel's idea of paradise is severely limited to practical matters such as paying the rent, whereas Guy's idea of paradise is a romantic dream of life in Paris where he will be acknowledged and rewarded for his creative genius and hard work as a costume designer.

Throughout the play, Guy's unfailing focus on his dream is contrasted with Angel's short-sighted focus on immediate financial concerns. When they receive an eviction notice, Angel is distressed, but Guy tells her not to worry because "I've been feeling Josephine in the air all day!" Angel, however, can think only of the immediate crisis, insisting, "Don't you understand? They're going to put us out on the street in seven days! One week!" She has no tolerance for the big dreams that prevent Guy from succumbing to such short-term setbacks. Angel insists on seeing only the concrete reality of the here-and-now and refuses to acknowledge any ambitious fantasies about the future. She tells Guy, "Whatever presence you're feeling hasn't got anything to do with Josephine. We're not in Paris. We're in Harlem. We're not strolling the boulevard. We're about to be evicted!"

Rather than banking on dreams, Angel acts according to the principles of luck. She tells Guy that she wishes she could bring herself some luck, and for Angel good luck means finding the right man to provide her with financial support and economic stability. She explains that she is interested in Leland because he "feels like luck to me." Leland later tells Angel that she "had a run of bad luck," but that he will change her luck by taking care of her. Angel flirtatiously asks, "You gonna be my lucky charm?" to which Leland responds, "I'm gonna be your man." From Angel's perspective, a man with money *is* a lucky charm. Guy, in contrast to Angel, is farsighted in his goals and dreams big, but is also willing to do the work of taking all the babysteps necessary to realize his dreams. Angel, however, thinks in terms of luck—the idea that events beyond her control will determine her future—and so is not motivated to work toward her goals.

In contrast to Guy, who dreams big and plans far in advance in order to realize these dreams, Angel is shortsighted, seeing only her immediate needs at hand and taking whatever solution will satisfy her concerns for the immediate future. She essentially prostitutes herself to wealthy men in exchange for clothes, lodging, and other material comforts, at the expense of her dreams, her personal feelings, and her long-term circumstances. Guy points out to Angel that she is too shortsighted, unable to imagine any possibilities beyond her immediate surroundings. He tells her, "For prospects, you gotta look past 125th Street. No law says we gotta live and die in Harlem, USA, just 'cause we happened to wind up here when we finally blew out of Savannah. The world is a big place!" Angel, however, responds with her own small-minded vision, retorting that the world is "getting smaller every day." Guy argues otherwise, telling her, "No it isn't. I can look out of this very window and see us walking arm in arm down the Champs Elysées" (in Paris).

Unlike Angel, Guy is able to see beyond his immediate circumstances to imagine a bigger and better future for himself. Angel comments, "Remember how you used to take those old broke-up binoculars whenever we'd go to the beach at home? The only Negro in the world ever tried to see Paris from the coast of Georgia." The image of the broken binoculars, through which Guy nevertheless looks out across the ocean to Paris, symbolizes his long-sighted vision of his dreams, despite the inadequate resources of his immediate situation. Angel, however, always focuses on her immediate finan-

cial needs—such as paying the rent—and is unable to use her imagination to envision her dreams, or anyone else's dreams, for that matter. She disdainfully says to Guy, "The myth of the magical Josephine. She practically lives with us but so far I haven't seen her share of the rent money!"

Throughout *Blues for an Alabama Sky*, Cleage emphasizes the importance of dreams to creating a meaningful life. She further demonstrates the difference between idle dreams of material luxury, and realistic, yet ambitious, dreams toward which the individual is willing to work with diligence and persistence. However, Cleage also explores the effects of poverty and financial hardship on creative individuals, often thwarting their ambitions and consuming them with the need to "pay the rent."

Source: Liz Brent, Critical Essay on *Blues for an Alabama Sky,* in *Drama for Students,* The Gale Group, 2002.

Joyce Hart

Hart has degrees in English literature and creative writing, and her published writing focuses on literary themes. In this essay, she examines the two female characters in Cleage's play, exposing how they are both sympathetic, as well as contradictory, images of one another.

Pearl Cleage, in her drama *Blues for an Alabama Sky*, has created two strong female characters who develop a relationship that exposes both their similarities and their incongruities. Throughout the passing sequences of the play, the women's stories weave in and out of one another's lives. In the beginning, the women bond with one another and experience mutual benefit, but, in the end, the characters are left connected to one another only through an irreconcilable grief. Cleage presents these women honestly, unafraid of exposing both their strengths and their weaknesses, as she strives, as stated in an interview in *American Theatre,* to be free of creating characters whose main roles are to portray only "the idea of positive images and role models." Rather, Cleage merely offers this relationship of two divergent women; then she leaves it to the audience to pick through the women's various personality traits to create their own role models.

Angel Allen, one of the two female characters in Cleage's play, is a thirty-four-year-old blues singer who is out of a job and has few prospects for her future. Angel is also a woman of the world who has been with many men and who, despite her talents, tends to rely on men to support her. She likes to wear flashy clothes, and she can be very manipulative. Her counterpart, Delia Patterson, is twenty-five years old and a social worker. Delia wears drab, old-womanish outfits to create a professional image that will foster confidence in her clients. Delia is a virgin. She is also a pioneering feminist. In the description of the female characters, Cleage states in the stage directions that Angel looks five years younger than she really is. Delia, on the other hand, because she wears frumpy clothes, looks older than her age. In other words, despite the fact that a nine-year age difference exists between the women, the time is bridged by the differences in the women's personalities. Throughout the play, Cleage repeats this same pattern, showing how the women's differences both bring them together and pull them apart.

The play begins with Angel having to be assisted into her apartment because she is drunk. She has lost both her job and her boyfriend. The audience is introduced to Delia when she runs over to Angel's apartment to see if she can help the intoxicated Angel. In this introductory scene, Cleage sets up the divergent qualities of the personalities of the two women. She juxtaposes the immaturity and carelessness of Angel with the sensibility and level-headedness of Delia. Delia worries about and is very supportive of Angel. She suggests that she can help Angel find a new job by teaching her how to type. Angel, once she is sober, tolerates Delia but eventually turns her nose up at the idea of typing. Angel is an artist and to take a job that requires typing, although it might buy her food, is beneath her. Angel would rather go hungry or rely on someone else to feed her.

Men support Angel both financially and psychologically. Men come first in her life, with her career maintaining only a secondary status. Delia, on the other hand, is independent of men, as much as a woman in the early 1930s could be. She is attracted to and respectful of them, but she does not rely on them for support. She recognizes their power, but she does not see herself as subservient to them. Delia accepts life's challenges in a way that inspires her, while Angel, when faced with difficulties, either turns to men or alcohol.

The women both share an affection for the character Sam, a Harlem doctor. It is through Sam's eyes that the audience is given a masculine point of view of the two women. Angel, upon interacting with Sam in one scene, tells him, ''I'm looking for a job. Let's get married.'' Although her sentiment is

> THE ELEMENTS THAT DELIA AND ANGEL FIND FASCINATING IN EACH OTHER, THEY TRY ON. IF THEY STUMBLE ON SOMETHING IN THEMSELVES THAT THEY DON'T LIKE, HOPEFULLY THEY WILL DISCARD IT. HOWEVER, CLEAGE IS A REALIST, AND JUST AS IN LIFE, SOMETIMES THIS DOESN'T HAPPEN.''

not totally sincere, Angel makes this statement as a test, trying to pull out Sam's feelings for her. Sam, who obviously cares for Angel, puts her down gently, telling her that she deserves a better man. The truth of Sam's affections is confirmed shortly afterward, when he reveals that he is interested in Delia. He is attracted to Delia's innocence, her zeal, and her independence. He appreciates Angel's beauty and artistic talent, but he is aware of the shallowness of Angel's motives.

While both women share the desire for a man, Delia develops a relationship with Sam that is built on mutual admiration and honesty. Angel, in the meantime, flirts with Leland, a complete stranger. Leland has been recently widowed, and Angel reminds him of his deceased wife. Whereas Delia opens herself up to Sam, exposing to him exactly who she is, Angel is aware that Leland is looking for a replacement for his wife, and she accommodates herself to his fantasy. Leland wants a ''god-fearing'' woman, so Angel plays the part.

Delia and Angel, although they have different ways of expressing it, share a passion for life. This is demonstrated, in particular, during a scene in which Delia receives a gift from her aunt. It is a fancy red dress, one that might be worn to a nightclub. Although the red dress clashes with the clothes that Delia typically wears, the stage directions state that she ''holds it up against herself and smiles.'' She looks at herself in the mirror and twirls around before placing the dress back on her bed and returning to her work. Later, when she looks over at the dress, she smiles, again. The color red and the flimsy material, which, if worn, would outline her figure rather than hide it, reflect her femininity and her latent sexual passions. Although she acknowledges these feelings, her work takes precedence over them.

As is seen later, it is through the scene of the red dress that the audience witnesses a connection between the two women. They are both women of passion. They both direct their feelings into their work: Delia focuses her feelings on issues of women's rights, whereas Angel uses her emotions to deepen the effect of her singing the blues. Although the women both can relate to the dress (and its implications), the way they direct and use their passions is quite different. Delia controls her feelings. She is more empathetic about other people because she understands her own psychology. She recognizes her passion, but she is willing to put it to the side when a more rational focus is demanded. In contrast, Angel's emotions are constantly bursting out of her, exposing themselves to, and affecting, everyone around her.

The red dress sets up another interesting aspect of the women's relationship, as shown when Angel comes over to Delia's apartment to announce that she has an audition for a new singing job. As she is talking to Delia, Angel eyes the red dress lying on the bed. When she finishes telling Delia her news, Angel asks Delia if she could borrow something to wear to the audition. Delia confirms what Angel already knows about Delia's normal wardrobe. ''Most of my stuff is . . . plain.'' At that moment, Angel pretends as if she has just noticed the red dress: ''Deal! What about this? Is it new?''

With this exchange, the audience sees the transparency of Angel. They also see how manipulative she can be. The difference in the women's wardrobe also portrays their dissimilar roles in society. Whereas Delia's goal is to blend in so that she can get her message across, Angel needs to stand out to capture people's attention. This scene also points out the giving nature of Delia as compared to the taking mode of Angel. However, the relationship works because the women mutually benefit from one another. Delia needs to give. It is through giving that she defines herself. In turn, Angel reminds Delia of her own feminine passion, and it is because of Angel's prompting that Delia decides to open up to Sam.

In the final scenes of the play, both the similarities and the differences between these women are even more emphasized. In regard to Angel, the audience gets to witness the length to which she will go to grab at any opportunity that comes her way in spite of the consequences that might befall the people around her. She first seduces Leland and becomes pregnant in an attempt to secure a marriage. In a twist of fate, she then discovers that Guy (her roommate) has received a large sum of money and has bought Angel and himself tickets to Paris. This is a dream come true for Guy, and his first reaction is to want to share it with Angel. Guy, who is homosexual, is not physically attracted to Angel, but this does not stop him from loving her. He is disappointed and hurt by Angel's desires to marry Leland, but he is even more disappointed when she tells him that she is willing to frivolously abort her pregnancy so she can go to Paris with him.

After the abortion, Angel faces Leland, first attempting to lie to him, then revealing her true feelings by telling him that she has been pretending to love him and now she's tired of him. Then she announces that she has aborted their baby. In this scene, all that Angel thinks about is herself. She has decided that since Guy is offering to support her, thus giving her a way out of Harlem and, supposedly, out of her misery, she can discard all the other people around her. She has no regard for Leland's feelings. The consequence of her insensitivity toward Leland leads to the death of Sam, whom Leland kills for performing the abortion. The death of Sam leaves Delia in mourning.

When Leland is imprisoned for murder, Angel, unable to face all the trauma she has created, runs away. The only two characters left, at this point of the play, are Delia and Guy. Their relationship is based on Angel: Guy is left with two tickets to Paris, and Delia needs to take a break to heal her wounds. Angel's affect is apparent on both of them. Guy has grown used to taking care of Angel, of having her tag along with him as a sister. He offers the Paris ticket to Delia, as he needs someone to share his joy. Delia, under Angel's influence, decides to be somewhat irresponsible for once in her life. When Guy asks Delia to go to Paris with him, she decides in his favor. So, in contrast to the earlier scene where Angel takes the red dress from Delia, Delia now takes the ticket to Paris from Angel. Delia has claimed a new outlet for her passions.

The play ends with a confrontation between Delia and Angel. Angel reappears just as Delia and Guy are leaving for Paris. Stage directions take over the final moments of the play, as the only dialogue spoken is Delia and Angel saying short good-byes to one another. The directions state that both women know that things have changed forever between them. Delia leaves "without looking back," while Angel goes to the window to think. This suggests that both women have come to a kind of crossroads in their lives, a time to take stock and revise. They have seen the best and the worst in one another, as well as in themselves. Right before this scene, Delia had remarked to Guy that the newspaper article on Sam's death sounded "so tawdry." Guy's response is: "It is tawdry. And so what? So are we all. Tawdry and tainted and running for our natural lives!" This is Cleage's main point. All people have their own crude sides. No one is different from another, because everyone is just trying her or his own best way to live. Cleage does not offer her definitions of which way is the best. She does not judge either Delia or Angel. What she does is allow them to expose themselves to the audience as honestly as she can. The two women do this best by demonstrating their differences in relation to one another. In their relationship, they learn about one another as well as discover themselves. The attractive elements they unearth in themselves, they keep. The elements that Delia and Angel find fascinating in each other, they try on. If they stumble onto something in themselves that they don't like, hopefully they will discard it. However, Cleage is a realist, and, just as in life, sometimes this doesn't happen.

Source: Joyce Hart, Critical Essay on *Blues for an Alabama Sky,* in *Drama for Students,* The Gale Group, 2002.

Laura Kryhoski

Kryhoski is currently working as a freelance writer. In this essay, she considers the exploitation of the African-American woman as a function of the play.

The African-American woman—arguably the most disenfranchised individual in American history—takes center stage in Pearl Cleage's *Blues for an Alabama Sky.* Angel, the main character of the play, provides a portrait of the subjugated or enslaved. However tempted one is to characterize Angel's problems as being a byproduct of her own self-destructive behavior, Angel is a victim. During a time of great poverty, in the face of an economy spiraling out of control, Angel turns away from the camaraderie or goodwill and comfort of her peers to find a way out of the oppression she experiences from day to day.

Angel's life is presented to the audience in bits and pieces throughout the course of the play. From the outset, Cleage throws her audience right into the

> **"** FOR ANGEL, THE ONLY MEANS OF SELF-EXPRESSION, OF ASSERTING HER OWN AUTHORITY AND POWER, IS FOUND THROUGH RAGE."

action, as a drunken Angel weaves her way home after hearing that her Italian gangster lover has "left" her to get married. And, it is through Angel's eyes that Delia learns about Angel's days working at Miss Lillie's as a prostitute. Delia's reaction is one of disgust, responding, "I don't know how you can talk about it like that . . . about what happened to you." Angel accepts her circumstance as a part of life, in her comment, "It was better than living on the street." Angel's friend Guy, too, is often enlightening in his interaction with Angel. He speaks to her, reminding Angel he is, as always, willing to be her support system and protector as Angel moves out of one bad relationship or situation into another. His aim is to comfort her, to smooth over the rough spots in Angel's life. After losing his job defending Angel's honor, he assures Delia, "Don't tell Angel. I don't want her to panic. I can take care of both of us if I have to. It won't be the first time."

Guy's comments reflect the strong sense of community among himself, Angel, Delia, and Sam. All of the characters not only enjoy strong friendships but also the benefits of a mutual support system. They seem to share a relationship based on emotional affinity and mutual trust. Delia, if somewhat naïvely, good-naturedly responds to Angel's job loss by offering her the opportunity to learn to type. And when Angel sees Delia's new dress, the first bright spot in an otherwise drab wardrobe for the social worker, Delia does not hesitate to lend the dress to Angel for her upcoming audition, meeting her attempt to protest the gesture with, "An audition is something special, isn't it?" A spirit of cooperation, one similar to that of a family unit, quickly takes shape amongst the characters. When Sam cures Angel's hangover with some aspirin and bootleg liquor, Guy does not hesitate to tell Sam, "your reward is that you get to take us all out for Sunday dinner." Sam graciously agrees, and the audience learns that Sam's volunteer efforts to provide dinner for the group are called upon by "Big Daddy" Guy on more than one occasion. But Guy also has a reward for Sam at the play's conclusion, sharing his new found success with Sam by inviting him to travel to Paris, "I will expect you [sic] to accompany me if I'm going to have any chance of returning home alive."

Sam also forgoes a party invitation celebrating Langston Hughes's return to Harlem and instead volunteers his time to assist Delia in writing a speech for Reverend Powell. The speech is of great import. Facing strong opposition from the Abyssinian Baptist Church in Harlem, Delia calls on Sam to help her convince the congregation of the need for a family planning clinic in their community. Her attempts at mobilizing a hostile community are brave if not revolutionary. According to Sam, in act 1, scene 3, "the Garveyites are already charging genocide and the clinic isn't even open yet." He goes on to say, "What does family planning mean to the average colored man? White women teaching colored women how to stop having children." Sam is cautioning Delia against a community that sees birth control as both a form of murder and a guarantor of white supremacy in number.

In an interview with Annette Gilliam in the *Washington Informer,* Cleage comments, "I will always write about Black people and our efforts to build a community where we can live safely. . . . These will always be my themes, regardless of the forum." The play offers the audience a chance to participate, and through Delia's brave struggles, to experience some of the excitement and enthusiasm fueling what Sam describes as "working tirelessly to save the [Black] race!" Sam shares Delia's vision of "strong families with healthy mothers, happy children and loving fathers all over Harlem." Exercising birth control and participating in family planning is not a means to diminish the Black population but instead a method by which "exhausted women and stone-broke men" can plan for future Black generations. Sam supports Delia but not without personal risk. He doesn't hesitate to offer to Delia the ground floor of his parents' brownstone to house the clinic, despite dangerous threats and a fire "set to run them out" of the original clinic site. Via Cleage, the audience is not only given a more intimate view of the community in Harlem, but insight into the personal motivations and brave efforts of some of its heroes and heroines alike.

Angel does not share the enthusiasm of her friends nor their political convictions. Nursing a hangover, Angel responds to Delia's enthusiasm for her mission by making a groan followed by an appeal to Sam and Guy, "Please don't get her all worked up! I can't take the history of the downtrodden without some aspirin!" It is a humorous moment but also predictable in light of Angel's character. Although this juke-joint songstress has the support of her offbeat family—a gay tailor, a doctor, and his newfound love interest, a young "free-loving suffragette"—Angel is a fringe element, remaining somewhat aloof from the group, absorbed by self-interest. Nor does she seem to be concerned with the success of her friends, except as a function of her own personal gain. Although embraced by her make-shift family, one showering her with love and unconditional support, she is unable to find solace or comfort in their devotion. "Angel" is an ironic name in and of itself: Angel considers everyone her "little sister," including Guy, yet she is a help to no one. She historically relies on the beneficence of others, leaving Guy to pick up the pieces when she runs out of options.

Angel's failure is, according to some critics, attributable to the destructive choices she makes. These choices destroy any possible opportunities she may have to triumph over her life circumstances. This idea is particularly evident in her interactions with Guy, her longtime male companion who has promised to provide for her, to take care of her, come what may. In a conversation with Delia, Guy reveals that he was fired from his job defending Angel's honor, his reasoning being that he "couldn't hardly stand by and let Bobby toss her out bodily into the street." Guy also reveals, in act 1, scene 1, that "it won't be the first time" he's had to take care of Angel. Guy's actions are not enough to soothe Angel's spirit. Delia discovers Angel's true attitude toward Guy after hearing her rather condemning comments, "Guy's a dreamer. He always was and he always will be, but I'm gonna hitch my star a little closer to home." Consequently, when Guy's dreams become a reality, Angel has already announced her pregnancy to Leland and has agreed to a loveless marriage. To further complicate the situation, Angel once again reacts to Guy's news by having an abortion and announcing to her fiancé that she intends to go to Paris to recuperate from her ordeal. Her actions, in turn, set off a horrible chain of events, events that ultimately cost Sam his life and leave Angel to fend for herself at the play's conclusion.

Angel has been shaped by her society. For Angel, experience has taught her the saddest of lessons: she only has faith in her own sexuality. Her sexual prowess is the only thing that gives her a sense of power and control over her world. The audience learns early on that Angel has worked as a prostitute. Sex was the key component of Angel's relationship with Nick, a relationship in which she was provided for until Nick's marriage. As further reinforcement, Angel is sent on a bogus audition, returning in disgust to report that she had been handed-off to her lover's gangster friend, Tony T. Says Angel of the alleged meeting, ''he [Tony] didn't want a singer . . . he wanted to keep a colored woman stashed up in Harlem so he could come by every now and then and rub her head for luck.'' Consequently, it is not surprising when Angel also resorts to using sex as a way to set her relationship with Leland in motion. In act 2, scene 1, Guy clearly recognizes this quality in Angel and confronts her with it. When Angel criticizes his ability to provide for her, he responds, telling her that she ''wouldn't dismiss it all so fast'' if he was a ''straight man'' offering to take her to Paris. And later on in the very same scene, Cleage drives this point home again, in Angel's own words. Angel tells Guy that she can't go to Paris because although she knows he loves her, he doesn't want to take her home. Guy responds by reminding her that she has and can lean on him, and Angel then betrays her own beliefs by making a distinction along sexual lines, pointing out to Guy that he ''can't get lost inside'' her.

Angel is a victim of her own harsh surroundings. She unwittingly destroys any chance she may have to be successful, in an effort to feel a sense of power and control. To anticipate disappointment, to predict and even prepare for failure is ultimately a way to avoid the pain Angel feels concerning her own life. It is safer for Angel to engage in cynicism and distrust than to risk having faith in Guy or Leland. This fear is evident in Angel's own remarks: ''All I'm afraid of is trying to lean on one more weak Negro who can't finish what he started!'' Angel is part of a world in which her voice doesn't matter, in which her success is limited by the kindness of a man. However seemingly cruel Angel's behavior is toward both Guy and Leland, it is understandable. Angel is raging against the confines of the society that defines her, she is one voice struggling to be heard. For Angel, the only means of self-expression, of asserting her own authority and power, is found through rage. In her interaction with Leland, for example, for every action, there is a reaction. Leland has pursued Angel because she reminded him so much of his dead wife, rather than

for any personal qualities she may have had. And when Leland hears that Angel has lost the baby, all he can think about is his pregnant wife and the disappointment he felt when she died, along with his unborn son. Leland does not acknowledge that Angel may have personal boundaries; instead, he crosses them and asserts what he needs, without regard for who she is. Angel recognizes what Leland is doing and lashes out at him in rage in act 2, scene 4, exclaiming, ''you want me to lie! That's all you ever wanted. Pretend I'm Anna. Pretend I love you. I'm through with it!'' Through the act of abortion, Angel has taken her power back, remaining true to herself.

Says Cleage, in her interview with the *Chicago Sun-Times*'s Hedy Weiss, ''When I got to the end of this play, I realized I was trying to make Angel do something that had not been justified by the characters and by their story. . . . I had to come to terms with what it meant for me to create a character that doesn't triumph.'' Despite the destructive, seemingly cruel behavior Angel engages in during the course of the play, Angel is a victim of circumstance. She is merely pushing against the invisible boundaries imposed on her by society to achieve a sense of autonomy and of freedom. It is in Angel's defiance of authority and the rage she feels against her own society that one can realize the tragic quality that defines her struggles as a Black woman. It is not hard, then, to hear ''all those crying colored ghosts'' that so plague Angel.

Source: Laura Kryhoski, Critical Essay on *Blues for an Alabama Sky,* in *Drama for Students,* The Gale Group, 2002.

SOURCES

American Theatre, Interview, Vol. 13, No. 6, July–August 1996.

Cleage, Pearl, *Blues for an Alabama Sky,* in *Flyin' West and Other Plays,* Theatre Communications Group, 1999, pp. 87–186.

Effinger, Marta J., ''Pearl Cleage,'' in *Dictionary of Literary Biography,* Volume 228: *Twentieth-Century American Dramatists, Second Series,* edited by Christopher J. Wheatley, The Gale Group, 2000, pp. 53–58.

Giles, Freda Scott, ''The Motion of Herstory: Three Plays by Pearl Cleage,'' in *African American Review,* Vol. 31, No. 4, Winter 1997, p. 709.

———, Review of *Bourbon at the Border,* in *African American Review,* Vol. 31, No. 4, Winter 1997, p. 725.

Gilliam, Annette, ''Romance, AIDS Explored in Pearl Cleage's New Novel,'' in *Washington Informer,* Vol. 34, February 4, 1998, p. 16.

Weiss, Hedy, ''*Blues for an Alabama Sky,*'' in *Chicago Sun Times,* March 17, 1998, p. 30.

FURTHER READING

Cleage, Pearl, *Deals with the Devil and Other Reasons to Riot,* Ballantine, 1993.
    Deals with the Devil is a collection of forty essays by Cleage on issues facing African Americans, covering such figures as Malcolm X, Clarence Thomas, and Arsenio Hall, as well as the films *Driving Miss Daisy* and *Daughters of the Dust.*

———, *What Looks Like Crazy on an Ordinary Day—: A Novel,* Avon Books, 1997.
    Cleage's first novel concerns an African-American woman who is HIV-positive and who falls in love with the man of her dreams.

Fabre, Genevieve, and Michel Feith, eds., *Temples for Tomorrow: Looking Back at the Harlem Renaissance,* Indiana University Press, 2000.
    Fabre and Feith offer a collection of essays on the continuing influence of the Harlem Renaissance on American culture.

Floyd, Samuel A., Jr., ed., *Black Music in the Harlem Renaissance: A Collection of Essays,* Greenwood Press, 1990.
    Floyd provides a collection of essays on African-American music of the Harlem Renaissance.

Hughes, Langston, *The Big Sea: An Autobiography,* A. A. Knopf, 1940.
    The Big Sea is an autobiography by Langston Hughes, one of the most important poets of the Harlem Renaissance.

Rodgers, Marie E., *The Harlem Renaissance: An Annotated Reference Guide for Student Research,* Libraries United, 1998.
    This is a reference bibliography with brief synopses of publications about the Harlem Renaissance. It is designed as an aid for students wishing to learn more about the Harlem Renaissance.

Spencer, Jon Michael, *The New Negroes and Their Music: The Success of the Harlem Renaissance,* University of Tennessee Press, 1997.
    Spencer offers an historical account of the musical developments of the Harlem Renaissance.

Watson, Steven, *The Harlem Renaissance: Hub of African-American Culture, 1920–1930,* Pantheon Books, 1995.
    Watson provides a history of the Harlem Renaissance in terms of its influence on African-American culture.

The Boys in the Band

MART CROWLEY

1968

Mart Crowley's first play, *The Boys in the Band*, is considered to be a groundbreaking work in American theater, the first truly honest portrayal of the lives of contemporary homosexuals. It opened in New York on April 14, 1968, at the off-Broadway Theater Four and ran for 1002 performances before being adapted to a successful motion picture. At a time when gay characters were seldom seen in commercial media except as crude stereotypes, this play presented a well-rounded view of what critics of the day referred to as ''the homosexual milieu.'' Taking place in an apartment in New York's posh Upper East Side, the action concerns nine acquaintances who converge for the birthday of one of their friends. The group includes Michael, a lapsed Roman Catholic alcoholic who is undergoing psychoanalysis; Donald, a conflicted friend who has moved far from the city to spurn the homosexual lifestyle; Harold, who is turning thirty and is morose about losing his youthful looks; Bernard, an African American who still pines for the wealthy white boy of the house where his mother was a maid; Emory, who revels in his homosexuality by acting flamboyant and girlish; and Larry and Hank, a couple that lives together despite the fact that they do not agree on the issue of monogamy. Joining them are a male prostitute who has been hired as a ''present'' for Harold's birthday and Alan, an old college friend of Michael's, who claims to be straight but who becomes a little too emotional when his manhood is threatened and who is strangely reluctant to leave each time he says

he is going. Modern audiences may find these character types overly familiar, in part due to the success of *The Boys in the Band*, which has bred countless imitations. Some of the plotting and staging devices used by Crowley show his inexperience as a writer, but his characters are presented with an honesty that is still effective today.

AUTHOR BIOGRAPHY

Mart Crowley was born in Vicksburg, Mississippi, in 1935. His early life was deeply rooted in the Catholic Church: he attended a Catholic high school and then went to the Catholic University of America in Washington, D.C., graduating in 1957. His family life was turbulent, with his father drinking heavily and his mother a hypochondriac who used drugs. Still, as Crowley told Ieva Augstums of *The Daily Nebraskan* in 1998, in one of his rare interviews, ''As for my parents, well, they were supportive knowing that they had a weird kid.'' In the early 1960s, he moved to Hollywood to work as a set designer and worked at several production companies. Eventually, from 1964 to 1966, he was a secretary for the actress Natalie Wood. It was during this time that he began writing *The Boys in the Band*.

The play was produced in New York in 1968 and proved to be a hit, running for over a thousand performances. Crowley himself wrote the screenplay for the 1970 film adaptation, which retained the original New York cast. He chose William Friedkin to direct, having been impressed with his work in adapting Harold Pinter's play *The Birthday Party* to film. The film was not as commercially successful as expected. Crowley's next play, *Remote Asylum*, was produced in Los Angeles in 1970, but it closed quickly. His greatest playwrighting success, after *The Boys in the Band*, was 1973's *A Breeze from the Gulf*, about his childhood in Mississippi. It won him second place in the New York Drama Critics' Circle award for that year. In 1979–1980, he served as an executive script editor and producer for the television series *Hart to Hart,* starring Natalie Wood's husband, Robert Wagner. Crowley wrote another small, seldom-produced drama, *Avec Schmaltz*, which was performed at the Massachusetts Theater Festival in 1984. One more significant play was his 1993 piece entitled *For Reasons That Remain Unclear,*

about a scriptwriter and priest who meet in Rome and recall their past history together. It has been performed several times and is bound, along with *The Boys in The Band* and *A Breeze from the Gulf*, in *Three Plays by Mart Crowley*, published in 1994 by Alyson Publishers.

PLOT SUMMARY

Act 1

The Boys in the Band opens in Michael's apartment in New York. Michael is preparing for the party: he has music on and drinks set out, and he is attempting to wrap a gift. The action begins with the arrival of Donald. Although Donald is not even familiar with the guest of honor, he has been invited to the party. It is revealed that he comes regularly to Michael's apartment on Saturday nights after seeing his therapist and then stays overnight before taking the long drive back to the Hamptons the following day. On this particular evening, however, Donald's therapist has cancelled, and he has arrived earlier than expected. Michael gives him some things that he bought for him to use during his weekly visits: scented soap, his own toothbrush, and hair spray. Before the guests arrive, they have a long discussion about their lives.

Donald talks about the work he has been doing with his therapist. He has recently realized that he was ''raised to be a failure'' by his parents, Evelyn and Walt. His father wanted him to be perfect, and his mother smothered him with love when he failed, and, as a result, Donald retreated from society, dropping out of college and leaving the city. He is currently working as a janitor and living in a small, rented room in a distant suburb. Michael explains that his own parents affected him adversely by spoiling him so that now he is used to not working, living on unemployment, and relying on others to pay his bills as he indulges himself in expensive travel and clothing. Donald notices that Michael is not drinking, and he responds that he is tired of following a drunken cycle of doing things under the influence of liquor that he should not have done and then drinking even more the next day to forget what he has done.

Michael answers a phone call from Alan, an old college friend. Alan is in the city visiting from his home in Washington, D.C., and he needs to talk with Michael. He is crying. Michael tells him to come over for a drink.

Larry and Hank, who are a couple, arrive with Emory, who is girlish and flamboyant. An awkward glance passes between Larry and Donald; later in the play, it is revealed that they once had casual sex, one night at a steam bath, and did not even learn each other's names. Bernard enters next. Michael explains that he was not openly gay when he was in college and asks them not to do anything that would let Alan know that they are gay. Alan calls back and says that he is not coming, so when the doorbell rings, they assume that it the birthday cake being delivered. The men are all dancing together in a line when Alan steps through the door.

Alan is uncomfortable with this roomful of obviously gay men. He attaches himself to Hank, who is wearing a wedding ring, and, in the discussion that ensues, they find that they each have two children, and Hank describes Larry as his "roommate." Emory interrupts several times with sarcastic, wry innuendoes about being gay. Later, when Alan is talking with Michael alone, he says that his friends all seem nice, specifically pointing out, "That Hank is really a very attractive fellow." The only one he does not like, he says, is Emory: "He just seems like such a goddamn little pansy."

Downstairs, the Cowboy enters: he is a handsome male prostitute that Emory has hired to sing "Happy Birthday" to Harold. When Alan returns from the bathroom, Emory makes sarcastic remarks about Alan's prudish attitude until, abruptly, Alan snaps, lunging at Emory, swearing at him, and punching him in the mouth. In the pandemonium that ensues, the guest of honor, Harold, arrives, and the Cowboy sings "Happy Birthday" to him and gives him a big kiss.

Act 2

Emory has ice on his swelling lip, and Alan sits on the couch with his hands over his ears. Harold discusses his depression over getting older and the pleasure he takes from drug use. In the meantime, Michael has started drinking and smoking, despite what he said to Donald earlier about quitting. Alan rushes out of the room to vomit, either from drinking too much or from self-revulsion, and Hank goes with him to watch over him. Michael and Harold discuss Michael's religious beliefs, and

Mart Crowley

Michael explains that Harold is keeping a secret cache of pills—"Hundreds of Nembutals, hundreds of seconals"—to kill himself with when he becomes too old and loses his good looks. After a brief time for eating and much more drinking, the lights are put out, and the Cowboy brings the birthday cake in for Harold, who opens his gifts. After the presents are open, they put music on, and once again the men are dancing with each other when Alan enters the room.

They decide to play a game. After several suggestions, Michael, who has gotten quite drunk, insists on playing a game that he just made up, called Affairs of the Heart. Each person must telephone the one person that he believes he has truly loved in his lifetime, and, if he makes contact, he must profess his love for that person. When several people do not want to play, Michael becomes aggressive with them. Alan asks Hank to leave with him, and Michael forcefully explains to him that Hank is not just Larry's roommate but his lover.

Bernard is the first to call. He calls Peter Dahlbeck, the son of the white family that his mother worked for as a domestic. When they were teenagers, Bernard and Peter had a brief romance one night, but they never talked about it again. Peter's mother answers the phone and says that he is out on a date, and Bernard spends the rest of the evening in a stupor, muttering that he should never have phoned. Emory calls Delbert Botts, whom he had a crush on in high school. At the senior prom, Emory found out that Delbert had told everyone that he was gay. When Delbert answers the phone, Emory refuses to tell him who is calling, and so he hangs up on him. Larry, who refuses to be monogamous with Hank, says that he is going to call ''Charlie,'' the name he has for all of the other people whom he sleeps with. Instead, Hank calls the answering service that they both share and leaves a message for Larry that he loves him. Larry still refuses to stay faithful, so Hank suggests a *ménage à trois*. Larry explains that he loves Hank, but it is pointed out that it does not count for the game if he did not say it over the phone, so he goes to the kitchen and calls from one of Michael's phones to the other.

Michael insists that Alan make a call, explaining to the others that a boy they both knew in college, Justin Stuart, said he had had several homosexual encounters with Alan. After being pressured, Alan takes the phone, dials it, and, stammering, finally gets around to saying ''I love you''; Michael takes the phone from him and finds out that it is Alan's wife at the other end. The party breaks up after that.

In the end, Donald and Michael are the only ones left. Donald starts to leave, but Michael, who has been brutal throughout the evening, breaks down and begs him to stay. Donald says that he is going to finish drinking the brandy in the bottle and then leave but that he will be back the next week. Michael heads out into the night to attend midnight mass at the Catholic church.

CHARACTERS

Bernard

Bernard is the one African American in the group. He has a small part in the play until the end when Michael initiates the Affairs of the Heart game. Encouraged to phone someone he loves and tell him that he loves him, Bernard chooses to phone Peter Dahlbeck, the son in the household where his mother worked as a domestic. Once, when they were drunk, Peter and Bernard were intimate with each other in the pool house, but they never spoke of it again. When Peter's mother answers and says that he is off on a date, Bernard spends the rest of the play angry at himself for having been so stupid as to have phoned.

Cowboy

The Cowboy is a handsome young man dressed in a cowboy outfit, hired for twenty dollars to sing ''Happy Birthday'' to Harold and spend the night with him. Unfortunately, he shows up early, before Harold arrives. He wants to get home early and get to bed because he hurt his heel while doing chin-ups. Throughout the play, he asks naïve questions, unable to keep up with the witty banter of the rest of the group. He leaves with Harold in the end.

Donald

Donald does not really know the other party guests well. He is a friend of Michael's. He lives outsude of New York, in a rented room in the Hamptons, where he has worked scrubbing floors since he dropped out of college. Donald comes to town on Saturday nights to see his psychiatrist, and then he stays at Michael's apartment.

Emory

Emory is the joker of the group and the most flamboyantly gay. He is always referring to himself and to the others as ''girls'' or ''Mary.'' He is the one who made most of the food for the party. It is his light, whimsical, girlish attitude that infuriates Alan, leading him to punch Emory at the end of the first act. During the game at the end of the play, Emory chooses to phone Delbert Botts, an older boy whom he had a crush on in junior high school and high school. Emory once embarrassed himself, begging Delbert to be his friend and buying him an expensive present, only to find out at the senior prom that Delbert had been laughing about him to others and was engaged to be married.

Hallie

See Harold

Hank

Hank left his wife and two children to live with Larry. He is a schoolteacher. Alan, noticing the wedding ring on Hank's hand, feels close to him, raising the possibility that Alan's attraction is not erotic but is because he identifies with Hank as the only other heterosexual in the room. In act 2, when Alan is feeling sick, Hank stays with him offstage. At the end of the play, when it is his time to phone the person that he loves most, Hank phones Larry, even though he knows that Larry has a difficult time committing himself to just one man.

Harold

It is Harold's birthday, and he is the last character to arrive, at the very end of the first act. He is a former ice skater. Harold copes with the depression and self-loathing that he feels by taking drugs: when he arrives, Michael mentions his being late and high on marijuana, and he explains, bitterly, "What I *am*, Michael, is a thirty-two year old, ugly, pock-marked Jew fairy." Later, commenting on the issue of beauty, he mentions his soul and notes, "if I could, I'd sell it in a flash for some skin-deep, transitory, meaningless beauty." Michael announces to the group that Harold is hoarding depressant drugs so that he can commit suicide before becoming old, a claim Harold does not deny. The Cowboy, who is beautiful and almost completely devoid of any intellect whatsoever, is attractive to Harold.

Larry

Larry is a commercial artist. He has had an affair with Donald in the past, although it was impersonal: they had sex but never even learned each other's names. As Larry explains it, "We haven't exactly met, but we've . . . Seen . . . each other before." Although he lives with Hank, Larry is reluctant to commit to a monogamous relationship, feeling that such a thing is unrealistic.

Alan McCarthy

Alan is an old college roommate of Michael's. Alan did not know that Michael was gay when they were in college, so Michael tries to keep it from him. Throughout the play there are several strong hints that Alan has homosexual feelings that he is trying to suppress. Alan is crying when he phones, asking to come over. Michael is afraid that Alan will find out that he is gay, a secret that is lost when Alan enters the apartment to find all of the men dancing together. Alan bonds with Hank after noticing the wedding ring on his finger and stays around him during much of the play, telling Michael when they are alone, "That Hank is really a very attractive

MEDIA ADAPTATIONS

- Mart Crowley wrote the screenplay for the 1970 film version of *The Boys in the Band,* which starred the entire Broadway cast (Frederick Combs, Leonard Frey, Cliff Gorman, etc.). It was directed by William Friedkin and is available on CBS/Fox Home Video.

fellow." After a few drinks, Alan becomes enraged at Emory and lunges at him, shouting, "I'll kill you, you . . . little mincing swish. You . . . freak. FREAK! FREAK!" Late in the second act, Michael insists that Alan call Justin Stuart, a man who had a gay affair with Alan in college. It seems that he is acknowledging his homosexuality when he phones and says "I love you," but when Michael takes the phone, he finds out that Alan has called his wife and committed himself to his heterosexual relationship.

Michael

The play takes place at Michael's apartment. Michael is a writer who has sold a screenplay that was never produced. For the most part, he travels the world, running up bills and getting other people to pay them. He is aging, losing his hair (a fact that is commented on several times throughout the play), and seeing a therapist to help him deal with the self-hatred that he feels about his lifestyle. He is well versed in cinema history and has a movie reference for just about every occasion. Early on, he explains to Donald that he has quit drinking and smoking because he is unable to "get through that morning-after ick attack" when he realizes the things that he has said and done the night before while drinking. Later, after the hostility between Emory and Alan subsides, Michael starts drinking again. His behavior becomes increasingly bizarre and offensive. He eventually makes up a "party game" that is meant to humiliate all of the guests. In the end, in a reversal of the first scene, Michael leaves his own apartment, intending to go over to midnight mass at the Catholic church.

TOPICS FOR FURTHER STUDY

- *The Boys in the Band* was one of the first plays to show gay life realistically. Research ways that plays and movies presented gay people before 1968 and explain what these depictions say about society's attitudes toward gays.

- Why do you think Crowley decided to set this play at a birthday party? Discuss how Harold's birthday affects each of the characters on the stage. Explain how you think the play would have been different if it had been set elsewhere.

- Use the Internet to find out about the many references to movies and literature that are made in this play, from Barbara Stanwyck to Lady Chatterly, ''Down to Earth,'' and so forth. Identify aspects from each that might appeal to the

characters in the play and then propose modern movies, books, and actors that they might like if this play took place today.

- If you were going to cast a revival of this play, which actors would you want to play each of the parts? Why?

- Do some research and come up with photos of the kinds of clothes and hairstyles you think these contemporary, urbane young men would have been wearing in the 1960s.

- How much do you think alcohol and drug use affects what goes on in this play? Research the chemical effects of alcohol and marijuana and use those findings to explain the behavior of Michael, Emory, Bernard, and the rest.

THEMES

Self-Image

Much of *The Boys in the Band* is concerned with the various ways that gay men thought of themselves in the late 1960s. Each of the different characters represents a lifestyle or perspective that has one meaning in mainstream society but that operates on an entirely different level within this small social setting of New York homosexuals. Michael, for instance, cannot come to any clear understanding of his own religious feelings because the Catholic Church, which he was raised believing in, rejects homosexuals like him. Bernard is comfortable with being the only African American in his group of friends and can joke about it and accept their jokes, but he is humiliated when he has to contact the world that he grew up in, where his family was considered socially inferior: the combination of the social expectations about race with the need to keep his sexuality a secret leaves him shattered in the end, barely able to function. Hank and Larry are hampered as a couple by Larry's reluctance to promise that he will be faithful: the

same problem, which affects many heterosexual couples, is made worse by the inability of homosexuals in 1968 to enter into any legally binding agreement like marriage. Harold's self-image is tied up in his youthful good looks, which diminish every day, causing his self-image to deteriorate before the audience's eyes. Emory seems to have a secure image of himself as a result of exaggerating the feminine aspects associated with homosexuality. His effeminate attitude makes him stand out, even among other homosexuals, but he is the member of the group who least wants to change who he is.

Alan is the play's most obvious example of someone whose image of himself does not match his behavior. When he calls Michael on the phone, he cries, and when he arrives in a roomful of obviously gay men, he develops a close bond with Hank, whom Alan describes as ''an attractive fellow.'' But after a short while and a few drinks, he lashes out at Emory, the most feminine of the group, shouting insults that were commonly used against homosexuals. Alan's behavior seems to be overcompensation or panic because this evening has made him aware of homosexual yearnings within himself, especially when Michael reveals his past relationship with Justin Stuart. In the end, though, Alan returns to his wife, raising the possibilities that he has either narrowly avoided an identity crisis or that the signs of his unwilling homosexuality were not true.

Humiliation and Degradation

As he becomes more and more drunk, Michael becomes more offensive to his friends, making racial slurs at Bernard and anti-Semitic statements to Harold and even calling Emory a ''nellie coward.'' His insults are bitter and crude, and the other men do not take them very seriously. This might be because they know that Michael is drunk and they forgive him, but it is also, in part, because they are used to living in a society that tries to heap degradation on homosexuals every day. To some degree, the anger that comes from Michael is a reflection of the anger that Alan lets out when he attacks Emory, even though Michael is openly gay and Alan is not. They both lash out in ways that reflect more on themselves than on the people they are attacking.

The game that Michael devises in the second act is indicative of the sort of humiliation that homosexuals felt at the time that this play was produced. In order to get the men to participate, Michael shouts at them, swears at them, and does what he can to be offensive. His behavior is terrible, but the results of the game can be seen as being good for the participants, forcing them to come to grips with the reality of their lives. In most cases—as with Bernard, who plays first—the game actually has harmful psychological effects, leaving them dispirited and without hope. One of the central messages of *The Boys in the Band* is that the reality of being gay in a predominantly heterosexual—and often homophobic—society, which these characters are forced to face, is often humiliating and degrading. Hank and Larry come the closest to finishing the game with some dignity, but they still have to deal with a fundamental difference about whether their relationship should be monogamous or not. The other character who leaves his humiliation behind is Alan, who leaves the gay world and goes back to the married life that society accepts as ''normal.''

Secrecy

The lives of the characters in this play are based upon keeping their sexual orientation a secret from the general public. They frequent places like bathhouses and gay bars where they can be open about their sexuality, but for the most part their lives are spent pretending that they are not gay, as Michael asks his friends to do when he thinks Alan is coming over. Keeping the fact that one is gay a secret is compared to living life in a closet, and so openly admitting that one is gay is called ''coming out of the closet,'' often shortened to ''coming out,'' as when Michael explains that ''long before Justin and I *came out,* we used to get drunk and 'horse around' a bit.''

Because this play takes place in a limited, pro-gay environment, it can be difficult for contemporary audiences to understand the threats faced by these characters if they did not keep their sexual identities private. Most homosexuals kept their sexual preferences a secret in the 1960s because they suffered innumerable prejudices from society at large, from offensive slurs to random acts of violence to employment and housing discrimination. Many states in the country had laws against sodomy, meaning that homosexuals could be arrested for their sexual practices alone. The numerous activities that are meant to raise public awareness of homosexuality have served to remove some of the shame and threat from being gay, allowing homosexuals to live more openly.

Gender Roles

Although all of the characters in this play are men, their homosexuality leads them away from stereotypical masculine behavior. The clearest example of this is Emory, who acts almost thoroughly girlish, from pretending to be a topless cocktail waitress when serving drinks to noting, when complimented on the food he has prepared, ''I'd make somebody a good wife.'' Emory has a complete list of feminine names that he calls the other men, like calling Bernard ''Bernardette'' or Harold ''Hallie.'' Like most of the others, he refers to other homosexual men as ''she'' or ''her'': in fact, his fight with Alan is a direct result of his saying, regarding Alan's wife, ''they'd love to meet him-*her.* I have such a problem with pronouns.''

Other than Emory, though, none of the characters in *The Boys in the Band* acts in a particularly feminine way. They may mock themselves for not conforming to traditional masculine values (as when Emory does his parody of a straight man by asking, with a deep voice, ''Think the Giants are gonna win the pennant this year?''), but most of the conversation goes beyond gender roles, creating a middle ground for men who are not masculine but still are men.

STYLE

Setting

The Boys in the Band is a play that takes place in New York City in the late 1960s. It reflects a social situation in which gay men were free enough to gather together privately but were still oppressed enough to feel the degree of self-contempt exhibited by most of the characters here. The characters engage in urbane, witty dialog that *New York Times* critic Clive Barnes characterized as "camp or homosexual humor." Noting the effect of gay culture on New York, Barnes went on to note, "Indeed, the New York Wit, famous the world over, is little more than a mixture of Jewish humor and homosexual humor seen through the bottom of a dry martini glass." From the characters' awareness of fashion and good places to shop to the fact that Michael is characterized as a world traveler, there is every indication that these people could not exist as they do in anything smaller than the western hemisphere's center of culture and commerce.

Even though the mood of the time and place is important to understanding the social dynamics of the characters, still, the play takes place in one enclosed place, Michael's apartment. The world outside is experienced only through the things that the characters say about how they live their lives. The telephone is important because it connects them to society beyond that one apartment: in almost every case when they telephone out, they suffer from rejection, giving audiences of all time periods the sense of how closed and insulated homosexual society could be, even in a major city like New York.

Structure

Although *The Boys in the Band* does not have a strong plot line in the traditional sense, it does center around one particular idea, keeping readers in suspense over the outcome. At the center of all of the revelations that come out on the night of Harold's birthday party is the question of whether Alan McCarthy is ready to admit to himself and to others that he is gay. There seems to be little doubt about his sexual orientation from the start, when he is described as crying, "Great heaves and sobs. Really boo-hoo-hoo time—and that's not his style at all." Later, when Alan shows up, it is clear that he can tell (or at least has a pretty good idea) that everyone at the party is gay, but he does not leave. He becomes irrationally upset about Emory's effeminate behavior, as if he is threatened by the sight of a man who is comfortable with acting unmanly. All of the signs indicate that Alan will eventually admit to being a homosexual, leading right up to Michael's revelation that Alan has engaged in homosexual behavior before, with Justin Stuart.

The portion of the play that takes place before Alan arrives serves to establish Michael's normal character and behavior. After Alan reconciles with his wife and leaves, Michael stays on stage trying to cope with the changes that Alan's presence have effected on his life. The whole drama is centered on Michael's relationship to what Alan knows and doesn't know and how Alan feels about himself. Michael is the central character, who is on stage throughout the play's running time, but his character is defined by what Alan does.

Style

The language used in *The Boys in the Band* is distinctive in its wit and cleverness, with frequent puns, sly put-downs, and allusions to movies, plays, and literature abounding. Just one instance would be the banter that ensues when a group of party guests arrives together:

> Emory: (Loud aside to Michael.) I think they're going to have their first fight.
> Larry: (Leans on landing) The first one since we got out of the taxi.
> Michael: (*RE:* EMORY) Where'd you find this trash?
> Larry: Downstairs leaning against a lamppost.
> Emory: With an orchid behind my ear and big wet lips painted over the lipline.
> Michael: Just like Maria Montez.
> Donald: Oh, *please.*
> Emory: (crossing to Donald) What have you got against Maria? She was a good woman.

To a great extent, this kind of language is a reflection of Mart Crowley's writing style, his way of keeping audiences entertained each moment they watch his play. Often, authors will write dialog that has all of the characters speaking with the same verbal style, and this is usually seen as a weakness, as a sign that the writer lacks the imagination to create different styles for each character. In this play, however, the consistency of speaking style helps to give readers a sense of the close-knit, unified worldview of this particular gay community. This is highlighted by the fact that the Cowboy does not "get" many of the sophisticated references: although he is gay, he is an outsider to this particular social circle, and so he is left out of the situation. The characters make fun of the Cowboy's simplicity, at his inability to keep up with their verbal banter, even though they accept him on a different, physical level.

COMPARE
&
CONTRAST

- **1968:** Homosexuality is considered a criminal act in many states.

  Today: Although a few states retain anti-sodomy laws (most notably Georgia, which went to the Supreme Court in 1986 to defend theirs), they are seldom enforced.

- **1968:** Homosexuality is listed as a disease by the American Psychiatric Association. Homosexuals go to psychiatrists to be "cured."

  Today: The APA dropped its disease designation in 1974. There is still conflicting research regarding whether homosexuality is genetic or learned.

- **1968:** When homosexual characters show up in movies or plays, they are often flamboyant comic characters or pathetically confused individuals who end up killing themselves. Homosexuals rarely appear on television.

  Today: Well-rounded gay characters are in-creasingly common on television, in plays, and in films.

- **1968:** Gays are considered promiscuous and incapable of forming lasting personal relationships.

  Today: Several states allow commitment ceremonies that accord gay couples legal rights similar to those given to heterosexual marriages. Gays still cannot marry, in part due to a "Defense of Marriage" act signed by President Clinton in 1996.

- **1968:** Homosexuals live in fear of physical attacks by those who are violently opposed to homosexuality.

  Today: Such attacks still occur, but most states and municipalities have hate crime legislation that threatens severe punishment to anyone who attacks someone because of his or her sexual preference.

HISTORICAL CONTEXT

Secret Meeting Places

At the time that this play was written, homosexuality was primarily an underground activity. Most large cities had homosexual communities, but these tended to stay to themselves, shut off from society at large. Most cities had clandestine gathering spots that were known as meeting places for homosexuals, but their existence was never officially recognized. For instance, certain areas of public parks, public rest rooms, train depots, balconies of movie theaters, and YMCAs were known among homosexuals as places to meet other gay men. Because of laws against homosexual activities and hostility toward homosexuals throughout the general public, the people who frequented these places tended to keep a low profile; still, their existence was fairly well known to the police, who would generally leave them alone, unless they were pressured for more arrests, such as when incumbent politicians were up for reelection.

Among the best-known places for gay men to gather in New York were the bathhouses. In *The Boys in the Band*, this is where Larry says that he and Donald had their brief, anonymous sexual encounter. Many major cities had public bathhouses dating back to the 1800s, when apartments with warm running water were scarce. By the start of the twentieth century, gay men had come to find the bathhouses, where men showered, steamed, and swam nude, to be convenient places to make acquaintances with each other. By the 1950s, there were bathhouses that catered exclusively to gay customers. Police could usually be bribed to leave these establishments alone, although they were always subject to raids. One of the most famous of the New York bathhouses was the Everard Turkish Bath, which opened in 1888 and was recognized as a meeting place for homosexuals by the 1920s. The one-dollar entrance fee included access to the pool, steam room, and a small cubicle with a cot in it. Other New York establishments included the New St. Mark's, Man's Country, and the New Barricks. In the 1970s and 1980s, with the rise of the Gay Pride Movement, the bathhouses became more open about being places for casual sexual encounters. By the mid-1980s, though, most closed down, as fear of the AIDS epidemic frightened away customers and public health officials moved to revoke the licenses of establishments that encouraged behaviors that would promote the spread of the disease.

The Stonewall Rebellion

The Boys in the Band premiered off-Broadway just a little more than a year before the single most significant event in the history of the Gay Rights Movement: the Stonewall Rebellion in New York. This event changed the way that the world looked at homosexuals and, more significantly, at the way that gays viewed themselves.

Throughout history, most societies have had a specific homosexual minority. In America, this group traditionally avoided confrontation, realizing that public exposure was usually followed by persecution. During the 1950s, for example, when some politicians gained fame for themselves by stirring up fear of Communism infiltrating our culture, there was a rise of virulent homophobia. Gays and suspected gays were fired from their jobs regularly by people who believed that Communists could get sensitive secrets from them with blackmail, by threatening to expose their sexual orientation. In the 1960s, on the other hand, many minority groups followed the methods and reasoning of the Civil Rights Movement to gain recognition and respect. It was the start of the Black Power Movement, the Woman's Liberation Movement, and the American Indian Movement, to name just a few. The very fact that a play like *The Boys in the Band* was reviewed in national publications indicates that the country was aware that there was a homosexual culture that was distinct but really not that different than the mainstream.

On the night of June 27, 1969, police raided the Stonewall Inn, a gay bar in Greenwich Village. The Village, as it is referred to in Crowley's play, was home to quite a few bars catering to gay clientele: the Checkerboard, the Sewer, and the Snake Pit were just a few. In spite of laws that made homosexual activities illegal, police generally left the gay bars alone, but in the preceding few weeks they had made a sweep through the Village and shut several establishments down. Several factors came together: the growing recognition of gays and their resistance to being treated like criminals for their private sexual lives, the fact that many patrons at the Stonewall Inn were there because their favorite bars had already been closed, and the heat of the summer night. As police began to lead the bar's customers out to paddy wagons, a crowd gathered and began to chant. The situation erupted into violence when the last patron put up a struggle; as police tried to subdue her, the crowd threw coins, bricks, and bottles. The police on the scene had to retreat into the empty bar, which protestors set on fire. When the riot squad arrived, they managed to disburse the crowd, but the following night, violence flared up again in the Village. Over the next few days, gay men and women from the outlying areas, who had heard about the fledgling rebellion, came to participate. Riots were averted, but the message was clear that homosexuals would no longer quietly accept laws or practices that relegated them to the status of second-class citizens.

As a direct result of the Stonewall Rebellion, gay rights groups proliferated. Ten days after the initial action at Stonewall, the first ''Gay Power'' meeting was held in Greenwich Village. The movement grew, working to raise society's consciousness of the homosexuals among them and, more importantly, teaching gays to be proud of who they are. In just a few years, the self-loathing displayed by the characters in *The Boys in the Band* already looked dated, a relic of a time when gays had to live in seclusion and to regret being the way they were—as gay poet Allen Ginsburg, quoted in Rutledge (put it in a speech soon after Stonewall), ''They've lost that wounded look fags all had ten years ago.''

CRITICAL OVERVIEW

The Boys in the Band was certainly not the first popular drama to have gay characters. For the most part, however, homosexuality was disguised in plays and film. One of the most powerful examples of this, which critics often point to as an immediate predecessor of Crowley's play, is Robert Anderson's 1953 drama *Tea and Sympathy,* about an effeminate boy who is mocked and threatened at a preparatory school. (He is given the nickname ''Sister-Boy,'' and the headmaster's wife makes it her mission to "cure" him sexually.) What makes *The Boys in the Band* such a groundbreaking work is that it was the first mainstream piece to show gay men in their own environment, interacting with each other, acknowledging camp posturing, in-jokes, and psychological torment without mocking or overemphasizing. Critics took note of the fact that the characters are gay, and they pointed out the ways in which that situation, though central to their personalities, was overshadowed by their basic humanity. As Clive Barnes put it in the *New York Times,* "The power of the play, which I saw at one of its press previews, is the way in which it remorselessly peels away the pretensions of its characters and reveals a pessimism so uncompromising in honesty that it becomes in itself an affirmation of life." In general, reviews were as positive as Barnes's, crediting Crowley with getting beyond the stereotypical aspects of each character to a deeper understanding.

Though it opened off-Broadway, the play gained the attention of national publications, bringing awareness of *The Boys in the Band* into households across the country that were in small communities where the subject was still much more hidden than it was in New York. It received favorable reviews in *Time, Newsweek,* and the *Nation;* Harold Clurman, the reviewer for the *Nation,* noted that, while not being "profound, moving or 'psychological,'" it is a polished piece of entertainment, with "a smooth veneer applied in a vein now becoming fashionable." The unsigned review in *Time* praised the cast, which it called "expert," noting that they "interact with such flawless skill, timing and grace that they could declare themselves an ensemble company right now and be ranked with the best." Like most mainstream publications, *Time*'s favorable review comes with a warning for the squeamish: "Uncompromising in its vision, totally unfettered in its four-letter speech, *The Boys in the Band* is a play that may be repellent for some viewers."

Two years after its theatrical debut, the play was revisited by critics and audiences when the screen adaptation of it opened. Because the screenplay was written and produced by Crowley and the same actors appeared in it, the reviews for the film often referred back to the play. Vincent Canby, a respected and influential critic, noted that "My reservations about [the film] all have to do with the source material, which sounds too often as if it had been written by someone at a party." After noting Crowley's talent for "comedy-of-insult," Canby notes that "there is something basically unpleasant, however, about a play that seems to have been

created in an inspiration of love-hate and that finally does nothing more than exploit its (I assume) sincerely conceived stereotypes."

Whether by coincidence of timing or a sign of the spirit of the times, *The Boys in the Band* was a groundbreaking work in a movement that gained power and popularity quickly. Soon after the play appeared, taking a bold and unflinching look at the gay world that many heterosexuals knew existed but knew little about, the Stonewall Rebellion pushed the Gay Power Movement into high gear. The play's greatest innovation was to show people that homosexuals are people too; within the next few years, dozens of advocacy groups sprung up across the country, taking over that function. As the GayGate web page explains it, the play became obsolete as soon as the Stonewall riots took place. To modern gays, the play that once seemed liberating is now a threat, reaffirming old stereotypes about self-hating, psychologically tormented homosexuals to straight audiences who take its overly dramatic elements as a lesson in gay life. Modern critics also find it difficult to accept this play as a look at gay life because it was written with no awareness of the most critical, sweeping social change to affect the gay community during the 1980s and 1990s, the AIDS epidemic. Reviewing a 1997 revival of the play for *Tucson Weekly,* Margaret Regan notes the undeniable effect of AIDS: "The specter of early death has unequivocally transformed the gay community, as plays like *Jeffrey* . . . so readily attest." But it is not only the absence of any knowledge of the disease that softens the impact of *The Boys in the Band* for Regan: "Some of the play's psychology is dated, too. Crowley trots out the old myth of the overbearing mother creating the gay son, a tiresome staple of antediluvian psychotherapy now mercifully laid to rest by more persuasive genetic research. And let's hope that the stereotype of the self-loathing gay man, alive and well in the play, is on the way to the same archetypal graveyard." Like most material that was considered cutting edge in its time, *The Boys in the Band* is considered a quaint and naïve museum piece, interesting for its historical value but not really relevant today.

CRITICISM

David Kelly

Kelly teaches creative writing and drama as literature at Oakton Community College. In this

A scene from the 1970 film adaptation of The Boys in the Band, *directed by William Friedkin*

essay, he discusses the historical significance of the play and looks at the reasons why its setting is so appropriate.

It was not too long after it changed the image that Americans had of homosexual men when it opened in 1967 that Mart Crowley's *The Boys in the Band* came to seem dated and irrelevant. Such things can happen. Everyone has had the experience of meeting someone who makes a startling first impression and then becomes tiresome as hours drag by; certainly an innovative artistic piece is just as likely to

lose its sheen once the novelty wears off. In the case of Crowley's play, the novelty was based on its respectful handling of the many facets of gay life. Coming at a time when the only homosexuals that showed up in popular entertainment were hysterical ''fruits'' or deviants bearing the burden of their ''unnatural crimes,'' *The Boys in the Band* brought the spectrum of personality types among gays to the American stage.

Not coincidentally, the same wind of change that brought the play popularity brought the Stonewall Rebellion fourteen months after it. It was

WHAT DO I READ NEXT?

- *The Boys in the Band* is compiled with Crowley's other most important works, *A Breeze from the Gulf* and *For Reasons That Remain Unclear,* in *Three Plays by Mart Crowley,* with a forward by Gavin Lambert. It was published by Alyson Publishers in 1996.

- Several lesser-known gay dramas from recent times are collected in the 1996 anthology *Staging Gay Lives: An Anthology of Contemporary Gay Theater,* edited by John M. Clum and published by Westview Press.

- John-Manuel Andriote's 1999 book *Victory Deferred: How AIDS Changed Gay Life in America* gives some perspective for how differently gay men and women see the world today from the way they saw the world when Crowley wrote this play.

- Tony Kushner won the Tony Award and the Pulitzer Prize in 1993 for his 1991 work *Millennium Approaches* and another Tony in 1994 for *Peristroika;* together, these plays comprise a sprawling work called *Angels in America.* The plays concern the interwoven lives of eight men in the post-AIDS world.

- Terrence McNally's play *Love! Valor! Compassion!* is somewhat like an updated version of *The Boys in the Band,* with a group of gay men gathering at a country house and peppering each other with witty dialog. The Tony-winning script was published in 1994 by Plume.

- *Stonewall,* by Martin Duberman, takes a narrative approach to history, following the lives of six gay men and women before and after the 1969 riot that changed gay history. It was published in 1993 by the Penguin Group.

- Some of the best gay fiction and memoirs of the vibrant period after the Stonewall riots were written by members of the Violet Quill Club. Many of these pieces, from authors such as Edmund White, Robert Ferro, and Felice Picano, have been collected in *The Violet Quill Reader,* published by St. Martin's Press in 1994.

---

bound to happen; the gay subculture in the late 1960s was too vibrant to be constrained, repressed by laws governing sexual commerce in a country that bragged about being the land of the free. It was so ready for mainstream attention that a play about eight gay men gathering in a room and talking openly became a runaway success with heterosexual audiences. It was so ready that a few drag queens resisting arrest at the Stonewall Inn one summer night could generate a melee of bricks and bottles, turning the tables on the police and making them hide in fear from the power of homosexuals, building over the next few days to one of late-twentieth-century America's most significant political moments.

After the riots in Greenwich Village that started at Stonewall brought the struggle for recognition to the streets, there was suddenly less need for a stage play to tell the world about gay diversity. Lacking its social impact, *The Boys in the Band* was vulnerable to the criticism that almost always comes up when a work is conspicuously popular. Detractors said it was facile; that it dealt in stereotypes; that, truthful as it was, it failed to present the *whole* truth; and that it should set a more positive example for young homosexuals, one not so despairing. As quickly as the play ascended, so too did it burn out in a flash. The world was different for gays at the start of the 1970s, and *The Boys in the Band* was already a relic.

In his introduction to the collection of his most significant works, *3 Plays by Mart Crowley,* the author mentions, while discussing the autobiographical element of his writing, that *The Boys in the Band* was originally going to be set in a gay bar but that he changed the setting to a birthday party after attend-

> LACKING ITS SOCIAL IMPACT, *THE BOYS IN THE BAND* WAS VULNERABLE TO THE CRITICISM THAT ALMOST ALWAYS COMES UP WHEN A WORK IS CONSPICUOUSLY POPULAR."

ing a birthday party for one of his friends. It is in such seemingly random decisions that art is born. What it might have gained in authenticity from being in a bar setting, the play would have lost in sympathy for its characters. The bar scene has always been a part of the urban gay scene. Much of the cause of this is the social pressures that kept homosexuality underground for most of the country's history. There were always secret meeting places known to insiders—certain park paths, movie balconies, subway platforms, and so forth—but these were out in the public, functional only for quick meetings, not for social bonding. It is only natural that gay bars would provide privacy in a social atmosphere. Still, a bar setting would have driven home the negative stereotyping that the play has been criticized for over the years. Any culture's bar scene is likely to highlight elements that the gay culture, in particular, has spent decades living down. A reputation for promiscuity, drug abuse, and for outrageous, decadent, open sexuality would only have been reinforced by a play set in a gay bar, with the extremes of the lifestyle shown at their most exuberant.

Besides, what could be more appropriate for a groundbreaking work than a birthday party carried out every time it is staged? Purists might insist that Stonewall represented the birth of the Gay Pride movement, but even they could not deny the significance of *The Boys in the Band* in bringing the culture to a point where Stonewall could occur. Like a birthday party itself, the play was a celebration when it first ran, a gathering for closeted gays who suddenly had a place to go to see other people like themselves. And, like a birthday party, there is always the specter of age, which leads inevitably to death, lurking somewhere about. In the play, Harold, the guest of honor, frets over the ravages of age and associates it with death, which he would wel-

come over the loss of his beauty. Ironically, in the real world, homosexuals had only a little more than a decade to celebrate their lifestyle out in the open before the advent of AIDS (which was originally called "gay flu" because it appeared to be some sort of virus that traveled among gays) cast the shadow of death over their lives. Since the early 1980s, it has been impossible to seriously discuss homosexual life without the impact of AIDS coming up. Those heady first days of liberation certainly seem like a party from today's perspective.

The play, though, does not seem like much of a celebration to audiences who experience it. Full of fighting, with egos broken, self-images rewritten, and the constant driving of the main character, Michael, to make his friends see the flaws in their lives, the action on stage shows no awareness of a new era dawning. Instead, it seems bent on trotting out the rottenness of every aspect of its times.

Critics who have dismissed the play for its self-loathing characters have a point but not as strong a point as they might think. The self-loathing aspect—such as Michael's cruelty to his friends or Harold's often-quoted introductory line about being an "ugly, pock-marked Jew Fairy"—are accurate reflections of their time. These men have a bunker mentality: like military men holed up in a bunker, they feel that they are under attack. They can realistically expect the violent, hostile world to come crashing into their lives at any time, and so they are ready for unmasking and humiliation at any moment. Under the circumstances, it is not surprising that they would take the preemptive step of bringing up their own faults. If society sees them as sick, and if, lacking adequate support, they believe that they are, then there would of course be a taint of dissatisfaction with themselves in everything they do.

Modern audiences are, on the whole, astute enough to account for the fact that this play happened at a different time. They know that the homophobia that was common in the 1960s has much to do with why Crowley's characters are so harsh toward themselves. From a modern perspective, it is almost embarrassing to see how much these men treat their sexual orientation as a curse. But it would be too simplistic to say that this sends a message that being gay is bad. People who take this message from the play either lack historical sense or they don't trust others to have understanding and so they take on the role of censorship to keep other people from getting the wrong impression. Nobody really looks to Michael, Donald, Emory, and all the rest as ''role models,'' and, with all that has happened during the past three decades, nobody expects them to provide a glimpse into the New York gay lifestyle anymore. Their only function now is to be interesting characters.

And they are interesting, in ways that are different from how they were interesting when the play first opened. Then, Michael, the angry, self-loathing party host, might have been taken seriously for his tortured Catholicism and his psychoanalytical interpretation of how his mother ''made'' him into a homosexual with her pampering ways. Now, it is merely interesting to know that people once thought that way. The religious positions declared by Michael and Harold show less interest in theology than showing themselves to be outside the mainstream Protestantism. It is ironic that Michael would try using psychoanalysis to ''cure'' his homosexuality: over time, homosexuality has become less stigmatized and has outlasted psychoanalysis, which has lost credibility. In fact, Michael's angst fits more closely with the recognized patterns of alcoholism than with anything his mother may have done.

The other most memorable characters are Emory and Alan. At the time, Emory might have come off as a crowdpleaser, a gay equivalent of the black-faced minstrel characters who embarrassed African Americans by talking in exaggerated dialects, acting out gross stereotypes of laziness and weak-mindedness. Today, though, Emory's giddy hysteria makes him the play's most vivid character, and his kindness toward Alan in the second act shows a depth of humanity that a stereotype could not have. Alan's fit of machismo, lunging at Emory while muttering slurs about gays, might seem dated, but the character is drawn with enough complexity to make him believable in any age. The other characters, though based in stereotypes, are the sorts that can be found in any gathering, and therefore they cannot be considered to be insults to their kind. Larry can't commit, but his partner Hank is the nesting type; Bernard is a minority within a minority; the Cowboy is kept around for his good looks and is dumb enough not to mind. Donald is the voice of reason that any good story will include.

Of course, *The Boys in the Band* is not as socially significant as it once was, but it is far from irrelevant. Times have changed, but there is enough insight in this play to give some insight to new audiences. The people who have written it off through the years seem to have mistaken it for a lecture on the social situation of gays, acting disappointed that they've come away from the lecture without taking any notes. It isn't a lecture; it's a party. Like any party, there are going to be unpleasant moments and moments when the meaning behind the rituals is lost in time, but the mood of celebration is still there every time this play is performed.

Source: David Kelly, Critical Essay on *The Boys in the Band,* in *Drama for Students,* The Gale Group, 2002.

Timothy Scheie

In the following essay, Scheie discusses the controversy over the representation of gay identity in the play The Boys in the Band, *calling into question what it means to be a ''gay spectator in the 1990s'' while assessing various audience reactions to the play over time.*

''Bellwether,'' ''watershed,'' ''crossroads,'' ''turning point'': with these and other ponderous terms, critics have hailed Mart Crowley's 1968 *The Boys in the Band* as the breakthrough production that brought frank and direct representations of homosexuality to American theatre. Where earlier plays had disposed of their ''deviant'' characters in a denouement that was often tantamount to a cleansing of the homosexual taint, spectators of *The Boys in the Band* witnessed for the first time a group of men discussing their sex lives, dancing together, kissing, and even having sex on a mainstream stage. The play takes the spectator to an exclusively gay birthday party at the apartment of Michael, a troubled man who coerces his guests into playing a truth game that elicits a series of witty barbs, confessions, and emotional outbursts as each tells the story of his life and loves. In a marked reversal of theatre tradition, the sole straight character, Michael's former college roommate Alan, is the outsider; it is his unexpected arrival that triggers an explosive scene in Crowley's play, and the restoration of order requires the purging of the straight man from the stage. *The Boys in the Band* was a hit (1002 performances). Thereafter, gay characters have frequently occupied center stage instead of the more pathologized regions of the margins, and ''gay plays'' have flourished in the years since *The Boys'* success.

Despite the play's groundbreaking status, the unflattering portrait of gay identity *The Boys in the Band* puts forth—a group of unhappy, self-destructive men who attend a boozy party that ends in an emotional bloodbath—did not leave all spectators with a feeling of exhilarating freedom. Infamous

> **"** UNLIKE BARNES, WHO
> SOUGHT THE UNIVERSAL BUT
> ULTIMATELY COULD NOT SEE PAST
> THE CHARACTERS'
> HOMOSEXUALITY, THE 1990S
> SPECTATOR, GAY OR STRAIGHT, CAN
> 'GET OVER' IT AND ACCEPT THESE
> CHARACTERS NOT AS THE
> DEFINITIVE REPRESENTATION OF
> GAYNESS, BUT AS ONE INFLECTION
> OF THE HUMAN EXPERIENCE
> AMONG MANY . . ."

lines such as "You show me a happy homosexual and I'll show you a gay corpse" fueled growing suspicions that the play, far from empowering, suggests instead the impossibility of a viable gay identity. One spectator writes, "I felt like I had been discovered . . . I wanted to fall into the earth. I was horrified by the depiction of the life that might befall me. I have very strong feelings about that play. It's done a lot of harm to gay people." *The Boys in the Band* starkly illustrates the dangers of entering representation, and the unease it has generated over the years refutes the commonsensical notion that increased visibility constitutes an unequivocal gesture of empowerment for a historically invisible and oppressed minority.

Consequently, when a new production of *The Boys in the Band* opened in New York City in the summer of 1996, nearly thirty years after the first run had ended, one might have anticipated that its tarnished reputation would have quelled the enthusiasm of potential spectators. This was not the case. Although it raised a few eyebrows, audiences generally received the revival well; after a successful run at the WPA theatre, it moved to the larger Lucille Lortel theatre for several more weeks. I saw the revival at both theatres and on each occasion witnessed what appeared to be a predominantly gay audience thoroughly relishing the show. I too enjoyed it, yet was not entirely comfortable with my reaction, nor with that of the audiences. After all,

aren't we supposed to have a problem with *The Boys in the Band*? I wondered at the audience's—and my own—willingness not only to tolerate but to derive pleasure from watching the taxonomy of pathetic and self-loathing characters that inhabit this play. After decades of discomfort or even disavowal, what had changed to make this play acceptable, meaningful, or at the very least entertaining for a gay spectator in 1996?

This begs the question of what it means to be a "gay" spectator in the 1990s in the first place. The idea of "gay" as a self-evident category of identity and an easily definable community has lost considerable currency in the age of the queer. In contrast with the struggle to make visible and to affirm proudly a viable gay and lesbian identity that characterized many theatre productions of the 1970s and 1980s, a queer commentary, informed by a poststructuralist and postmodern interrogation of fixed subject positions, reveals the margins, the internal contradictions, and the instability of identities, with no exemption for the categories of "gay" and "lesbian." From a queer perspective, the articulation of sexuality that presupposes a stable "gayness" assumes a naive, uncritical, and even dangerous position, one that, be it closeted, oppositional, or assimilationist, risks re-inscribing the categories of a heteronormative epistemological regime.

Although *The Boys in the Band*'s rehabilitation coincides more or less with the rise of the queer, it seems unlikely that this new critical sensibility could account for the play's new-found appeal. Theatrical performance has occupied a marginal and frequently discredited position in theorizations of queer, which more often examine television, film, and "everyday life" performances. A salient example of this trend would be Judith Butler's influential articulation of performativity, one of the most widely revoked theories in queer critiques, which borrows a theatrical vocabulary that suggests an affinity to the stage but rarely includes live performance in its discussion. When Butler does address the stage specifically, it is to define a "critically queer" performativity against the conventions of theatrical performance. Furthermore, conventional mimetic theatre—and there is no mimesis more conventional than the fourth-wall realism of *The Boys in the Band*—purports precisely to make visible the "reality" of its gay characters, and would more likely draw the reprimand of a queer commentary. Dramatic realism remains fraught for the representation of homosexuality, and critics have been quick to note that in even the most well-intentioned gay plays homosexuality is more often than not the problem in need of solving that motivates the plot. A more radical theatre, one that refuses recourse to a fixed identity that exists outside of its representation, would seem to demand a new mode of performance. In the 1980s, many artists eschewed the conventions of realism for a performance art that explicitly targets categories of identity, very often gendered and sexual identity, for deconstruction. In articulating the necessity of performance art, David Román writes that "realist drama is so embedded in the prevailing ideology of naturalized heterosexuality in dominant culture that it offers no representational position for gay men or lesbians that is not marginal or a site of defeat." While a materialist analysis of the history of realism and its reception—Elin Diamond's theorization of a realism without truth or "unmade" mimesis, for example—might refine such a sweeping critique, *The Boys in the Band* nonetheless exemplifies this tendency when in its denouement Michael has a near nervous breakdown and Donald embarks on an alcoholic binge. The revival, it should be noted, deployed no subversive performance strategies that issued an ironic or critical comment on the play; it played it "straight" (as it were).

Eve Kosofsky Sedgwick's analysis of the unstable distinction between minoritizing and universalizing discourses on homosexuality proves illuminating for an assessment of reactions to *The Boys in the Band*. Minoritizing discourses cast the homosexual as a segregated, distinct identity, while universalizing ones integrate gay men into society at large. Regarding AIDS and AIDS prevention, to use Sedgwick's example, a minoritizing discourse would speak of the male homosexual as part of a distinct "risk group," while the universalizing discourse would refer to "safe sex practices" that do not specify the sexual identity of the subjects involved. Neither, it should be noted, is inherently oppressive or unquestionably "correct." Universality or equal treatment under the law usually underlies civil rights initiatives, and is in word if not in deed an ideological underpinning of the American ideals of freedom and equality. However, exclusive recourse to the universal is not always a desirable trajectory for gay activism. As Sedgwick writes: "substantial groups of women and men . . . have found that the nominative category of 'the homosexual,' or its more recent near-synonyms, does have a real power to organize their experience of their own sexuality and identity." Universality can be synonymous with invisi-

bility, and staking a claim to a minority identity is crucial for many gay activist strategies. Making visible differences, however, is a double-edged sword: one person's Gay Pride march is someone else's idea of a freak show, or yet another's sell-out to the myth of a tolerant inclusive pluralism. What proves most interesting and productive for Sedgwick, and for the discussion that follows, is not which of the universalizing or minoritizing discourses is better or more true, but how these discourses align themselves in unpredictable and contradictory ways. They often uncomfortably intersect a single utterance to betray the "radical and irreducible incoherence" that inheres in discourse on sexual identity. The deceptively simple bumper sticker slogan "Gay rights are human rights" betrays this internal contradiction, at once defining a distinct community (gays) and erasing this difference under the rubric of the "human." This double movement radically disturbs the invocation of both gay and human identity; both stand on the shifting ground of a constitutive instability. The destabilized identity that emerges from Sedgwick's analysis makes hers a distinctly queer critical approach, one that proves particularly useful in that it does not simply refute the universalizing and the minoritizing discourses on gay identity but invites and even depends on an analysis of both to "queer" the identities they purport to describe.

The three reviews written by *New York Times* critic Clive Barnes during *The Boys in the Band*'s first run illustrate the contradictory interplay of these opposed discourses. In his 15 April 1968 review, *The Boys* draws his praise for its open representation of gay characters after decades of innuendo-laden closet-dramas: "The play, which opened last night at Theater Four, is by far the frankest treatment of homosexuality I have ever seen on the stage. We are a long way from 'Tea and Sympathy' here." However, Barnes ultimately grounds his enthusiasm for the play in distinctly universalizing terms:

> The point is that this is not a play about a homosexual, but a play that takes the homosexual milieu, and the homosexual way of life, totally for granted and uses this as *a valid basis of human experience* . . . The power of the play . . . is the way in which it remorselessly peels away the pretensions of its characters and reveals a pessimism so uncompromising in its honesty that it becomes in itself *an affirmation of life.*

Barnes hails the play for its daring "homosexual" content, but then draws the newly visible identity under the umbrella of a universal human identity. Thus validated as a card-carrying human,

Barnes's homosexual can serve as the hero who "affirms life" for all spectators, regardless of the particulars of their own lives. If *The Boys* is a play about "human experience," however, it is nonetheless about gay men, and homosexuality still constitutes the problem that drives the plot forward. The unsavory minoritizing tendencies of the play—evoked in Barnes's use of the word "homosexual," a juridico-medical term of pathological provenance—haunt Barnes's evaluation, and in his second review of 18 February 1969 he deploys a more ambivalent balance of the two discourses:

> The play is about a *homosexual birthday party*—or rather, to be precise, it is set at a homosexual birthday party. It is actually about *self-loathing and the malignant destructiveness* that develops from it. . . . But I do hope that Mart Crowley is wrong and that all homosexuals are not as wretchedly miserable as he paints them.

Barnes tries once again to dissociate the characters' sexuality from a more universal self-loathing, but concedes that this might not be possible and frowns on the troubled portrait of "homosexual" identity that emerges in Crowley's play. Barnes explicitly pathologizes the play's homosexual characters as "malignant," and tacitly opposes them to the relative "health" of the human (read: heterosexual) spectator. The stigmatized minority identity thwarts the desired elevation of its characters into the universal humanity, and Barnes tempers his praise for *The Boys in the Band* accordingly.

Barnes's assessment, no doubt a function of his mainstream readership, favors the liberal "we're-the-same-only-different" universal and vilifies the irrecuperably minoritizing aspects of the play, thereby failing to weigh the drawbacks of the former and the potential benefits of the latter, and *a fortiori* the instability of both positions. Barnes eventually could not see beyond the self-destructive stereotypes in Crowley's play. Adding to this concern, the dramatic events of the 1969 Stonewall riots upstaged *The Boys in the Band* and made visible in the streets a very different type of gay man, one who boldly took action in defense of his dignity. The powerless, self-blaming, washed-up characters of Crowley's play no longer announced the future, emblematizing instead a troubled past that contrasted starkly with the nascent gay liberation movement. Barnes's final review of 18 August 1970, written shortly before the play closed, betrays a marked change of heart:

> The "Boys in the Band" has just entered its third year at Theater Four on West 55th Street, and the damndest thing has happened to it. It has become a period piece.

Two years ago, when the theater was young and innocent, Mart Crowley's comic-tragedy seemed sensationally frank. To an extent it still is, but the liberating sense of breakthrough is missing. I am also more and more disturbed by the *antihomosexual* element in the play.

The breakthrough quality, the inclusion of gays in the great "human" family that validated the play, has dwindled to mere memory. Magnified to a "disturbing" level, the stigmatized minoritizing tendencies have eclipsed the universal value.

Gay history was moving very fast in the early 1970s. *The Boys in the Band*'s self-hating characters, who wished so desperately that they could be straight, not only alienated mainstream critics like Barnes but also quickly became anathema to the new mantra of Gay Pride. The new gay identity rallied those who proudly embrace their difference from the mainstream. Doric Wilson's 1982 play *Street Theater* crystallizes this sentiment in a scathing indictment of Crowley's characterizations. Wilson takes homosexuality out of a closeted apartment and, as the title indicates, brings it into the streets. *Street Theater* confronts the spectator with its own taxonomy of gay and lesbian types: leathermen, butch lesbians, hippie kids, "juicebums, hopheads, odd-balls, weirdos, queers . . . the usual gutter crowd you got to expect to contend with down here in the Village." Instead of wallowing in self-pity and mutual disdain, however, this diverse group defiantly bands together against the harassment of the police. *Street Theater* also includes in its cast the lead characters of Crowley's play, Michael and Donald, who, in preppie dress, refuse to participate in this counter-cultural community and berate the "uppity" gay and lesbian characters while loudly lamenting their own situation. As the characters angrily muster and prepare to join the incipient Stonewall riots at the end of the play, Donald exclaims, "You faggots are revolting!" "You bet you're sweet ass we are!" a closeted man retorts, before running off to the uprising in the first open expression of his new gay identity. Significantly, on the night of the incendiary raid on the Stonewall Inn, up on 55th Street *The Boys in the Band* was in the middle of its successful run. *Street Theater* would play thirteen years later in a small space in Tribeca and then in the Mineshaft leather bar. Its gay audience and use of a gay space stand in telling counterpoint to the mainstream appeal of *The Boys in the Band*. Wilson condemns Crowley's closeted and self-blaming characters for their complicity with the forces that repress them, a tacit alliance that perhaps contributed to the play's success in a mainstream venue. His critique of *The Boys in the Band* therefore operates through both universal and minoritizing discourses. The "universal" impulse that for Barnes validated *The Boys in the Band* is here branded a sell-out, as ill-regarded as the play's stigmatizing representation of a minority gay identity. In the place of the Michaels and Donalds who lament their exclusion from a heterosexual mainstream, Wilson draws an unambiguous battle line that ideologically but also very literally delineates the newly liberated and proud gay community, which coalesces into a unified "we," from the oppressive mainstream and those who fear to challenge it.

The proud gay identity had deposed the pathologized homosexual, and *The Boys in the Band* became a reference point, an important but provisional first step in the history of gay theatre. Often invoked but rarely studied or performed, in the 1970s and 1980s Crowley's play was virtually relegated to the toxic waste dump of cultural memory: a drum of tainted cultural sludge whose existence is readily acknowledged, but which would preferably remain buried—until now, that is. In recent years *The Boys in the Band* has resurfaced not only in New York, but also in Los Angeles, San Francisco, and even Fort Wayne, Indiana. A new edition of the play was also published in 1996. Who are these readers and spectators who find the play so appealing and have guaranteed its success in the 1990s? Are they good old-fashioned pragmatic liberals who see the universal struggle for "human" self-respect? Do they represent self-identified gays, for whom the characters' outdated angst serves as incontrovertible evidence that the fight for gay pride over the last thirty years has met with a great measure of success? Or are they critical queers, who find an exemplary illustration of the delusions of realism and the dangers that inhere in staking a claim to the "truth" of gay identity? Without surveys or interviews it is impossible, of course, to know who the audience members were and exactly how they received they play. However, Barnes and Wilson carve out two spectatorial positions, one striving for the universal and the other for a minority identity, from which they and others have historically condemned the representation of homosexuality in *The Boys in the Band*. To conclude, I would like to weigh how these positions might also serve as a justification for the play's renewed success, adding to them a third perspective, that of a queer commentary.

The universalizing liberal humanist account appeals, as is typical, to common sense and to a comforting belief in progress. From this perspective, one could maintain that times have changed for the better and that, although discrimination exists in many forms today, often brutally, gay men have achieved heretofore unknown visibility and acceptance. They have become a recognizable part of mainstream culture, and, without necessarily implying that the homosexual/heterosexual distinction is fading as a fundamental opposition for thinking about identity, it no longer represents the stigmatized and exclusionary opposition to the extent it once did. The more tolerant cultural climate generates revised readings of *The Boys in the Band*. John M. Clum writes that the 1968 audience was positioned to identify with the straight Alan, who looked upon the gay characters with disgust and pity and who, like the spectators, leaves the party-goers and their world behind for a "normal" life at the end of the play. In the 1990s, however, Alan comes off as an intolerant bigot, and the audience identifies with the gay characters as the play's heroes. It is the most outrageously effeminate character, the lisping interior decorator Emory, who emerges as the hero of the group when he defiantly stands up to the boorish insults of the drunk Alan and, at the risk of physical injury, dares to exhibit his sexuality while all the others attempt to pass as well as they can. Furthermore, the current range of gay personae on stage, film, and most recently television relieves *The Boys in the Band* of the heavy responsibility of being the first and only frank depiction of gay men a mainstream audience could see. Unlike Barnes, who sought the universal but ultimately could not see past the characters' homosexuality, the 1990s spectator, gay or straight, can "get over" it and accept these characters not as the definitive representation of gayness, but as one inflection of the human experience among many; even the nellyest queen can be elevated to the status of an Aristotelian hero. Criticism has come full circle, and a 1990s spectator might agree with what Barnes unsuccessfully attempted to establish in his reviews: that this is not ultimately a play about homosexuality, but the story of oppressed people who struggle against impossible odds and at great risk to maintain a sense of dignity in a hostile world.

It would be difficult to argue that the increased and hard-won acceptance of gays has in no way altered the reception of the play. The universalizing explanation of the revival's success nonetheless ignites the well-rehearsed critique of realism, which warns that even the most positive and ostensibly innocuous representations of gay characters betray a compromise with a heteronormative regime of power relations. In an eye-opening critique of Tony Kushner's *Angels in America,* for example, David Savran responds to those who greeted the complex and varied representations of gay men and persons with AIDS with enthusiastic approval. Savran identifies "ambivalence" as a dominant trope in *Angels in America,* and concludes that because Kushner's characters speak both from within and against the oppositional or alternative discourses (including Marxism, Mormonism, and liberal humanism), they ultimately neutralize dissent in an agreement to disagree. This consensus for inaction represents a fundamentally conservative ideal of a pluralistic state in which everyone has a place, or, more cynically, in which everyone *knows* her place. Savran questions the play's ability to challenge the order of white, heterosexual, and bourgeois America while also being an economically successful Broadway show. He ultimately reads this contradiction as a relationship of antagonistic complicity, and the "opposition between hegemonic and counter-hegemonic" that characterizes both the story within the play and that of its long and profitable run ultimately resolves in the myth of an inclusive pluralism. If even the sympathetic and empowered characters of Kushner's play are suspect, the troubled men in *The Boys in the Band* conform so completely to homophobic expectations that their appearance would seem to constitute not a liberating breakthrough for gay men but a naturalized justification of gay self-loathing. If gays are admitted to the table of "humanity," theirs is not a place of honor, no matter how valiant they show themselves.

A more militant and proud gay spectator might therefore feel anxiety instead of elation over inclusion—one might say absorption—into the mainstream and point out that the universalizing humanist account of the revival's success conspicuously fails to acknowledge the overwhelming *gayness* of it all: of the characters, of the audiences, and of the play's place in the history of the gay rights movement itself. It is, therefore, on very different grounds that the revival of *The Boys in the Band* might appeal to a minority gay identity, one that today finds itself somewhat a victim of its own success. Michel Foucault writes that repressive regimes unwittingly spawn new sites for sexuality. The proliferation of secret places where gay men congregate would confirm Foucault's hypothesis; without the constraints that create its necessity, that notorious corner of the public park would just be a shady grove of trees, not an outdoor cruising area in-

vested with intense sexual energy. However, these constraints have to varying degrees been eased, permitting a dispersal of gay sexuality from the confined but erotically charged crucible of those secret places out of society's sight—the unmarked bar, the bath house, the dark cruising area—which consequently lose some of their dire necessity. Men who would have met in a back alley gay bar thirty years ago might today openly express their sexuality without having to leave the circles of their institutionalized class, their neighborhood, their place of employment, or even their religious community. As feminists grapple with the question of exactly which women they are speaking of and for, gay activists and theorists similarly address a diverse community with a broad range of interests and characteristics, many of which would be incompatible in a single person. While many gay men choose to live in the gay "ghettos" of major cities and continue to frequent the "dark places," the difference between their much ballyhooed "homosexual lifestyle" and that of their straight neighbors is often riding on one increasingly less salient difference among a flood of possible similarities.

Anxiety over the increasingly ill defined gay identity lends urgency to a minoritizing counter-explanation of the revival's appeal. Harold's birthday party represents another one of those places out of society's sight where gay men meet. The characters in *The Boys in the Band*, though similar in some respects, are also black and white, nelly and butch, conservative and free-thinking, Catholic and Jewish, city-dwellers and suburbanites . . . the list could go on. They are a heterogeneous bunch who appear to have very little in common. They often don't even seem to like each other. In the opening scene, when Donald asks who is coming to the party, Michael replies, "the same old tired fairies you've seen around since the day one." A few lines earlier, he had stated only half-jokingly, "if there's one thing I'm not ready for, it's five screaming queens singing 'happy birthday.'" The party itself, with the exception of a nostalgic and riotous line dance sequence, serves up a steady flow of vicious insults that crescendo to an unbearable breaking point. One common interest above all others explains why these diverse characters come together in Michael's apartment: they are gay. Furthermore, it is not only in the action on stage that the WPA and the Lucille Lortel theatres joined the cruising spot and the bar as one of those dark places where gay men congregate; the revival brought gay men together in the audience as well. The dimmed house lights muted the differences among the spectators, who could collectively identify not with the characters' life in the closet, but with the distinctness of their minority gay identity and the strength of the bonds it forged between men, even if they were forged under constraint. *The Boys in the Band* created a certain *communitas,* the ritual reduction of difference, and fostered a clear-cut and unambiguous, if unproblematized, sense of gay identity.

Both universalizing and minoritizing tendencies, therefore, potentially explain the success of the revival. Wilson's double-bind becomes a win-lose or even a win-win situation in the 1990s. However, the chiasm of positive and negative assessments, articulated through both universalizing and minoritizing discourses on identity, generates a complex range of intersecting possibilities that coexist in contradictory tension. The revival therefore appeals to the third fictive spectator as well, the critical queer who, versed in poststructuralist theory, would make short shrift of the purportedly "true" and stable identities, be they human or gay. A queer commentary would reveal that the category of the human subsumes homosexuality into a universal ideal that in fact represents the norms and interests of a heterosexual society which itself only makes sense in opposition to the homosexual, and that, furthermore, the emergence of an ostensibly oppositional gay identity is just another effect of this same regime of power relations. "Human" and "Gay" are two sides of a single coin that conceal, while they gird, their opposite face. A contradictory internal logic undermines both the liberal humanist and the militant gay faith in mimesis and betrays the constitutive instability of the imaginary identities that these discourses erect.

The queer commentary appears to be the most theoretically evolved of the three hypothetical positions, and it offers a compelling critique of the other two. However, in this scissors-paper-rock scenario, queer in its turn is not immune to critique. The queer interrogation of identity has provoked unease in critics who note that it reproduces the occlusion of difference that has historically worked to the favor of some and the detriment of others, and that it absorbs gay identity once again into a universal, even if it is a universal refusal of identity. Sue-Ellen Case worries over the radical evacuation of the category "lesbian" in queer commentaries and wonders if they are not just one more mechanism to keep the lesbian in her historically invisible place. Leo Bersani sees queering as a fundamentally "de-

gaying" gesture, one that "repeats, with pride, a pejorative straight word for homosexual even as it unloads the homosexual referent." He takes Sedgwick to task specifically, protesting her claim that homosexuality inheres in the oppositions that support Western thought:

> It [Sedgwick's claim] rips us [gays] right out of our marginal status and relocates us, distinguished and incarnate, at the very heart of the epistemological endeavor, at the root of the western pursuit of knowledge.

By these accounts, "queer" represents the latest inflection of an old and all too familiar disappearing act. Case and Bersani refuse to relinquish the meaning of "gay" and "lesbian" as oppositional categories of identity, and resist their subsumption into both the universal Western humanity and the disturbingly similar "gayless" world of the queer.

There is no doubt that some queer theorizations have demonstrated a tendency to evoke an ideal, post-identity utopia as their implicit goal. Almost all, however, also warn that the present constraints are not easily dislodged and problematize the possibility of an autonomous, unilateral refusal of identity. Hitting on a crucial distinction, Jill Dolan writes that "to be queer is not who you *are,* it's what you *do.* To this one might add that even when "doing" queer you cannot simply cease to "be." Living on the near side of a perhaps not so imminent epistemological break, the fact that I "do" queer does not imply that I may wilfully shed the requisite identities, however imaginary, that I am constrained and/or privileged to "be"—gay, male, white, middle-class, and so on. Gay and queer are not mutually exclusive terms. In fact, the opposition between them is somewhat specious, for they are not fully commensurate: gay is a discursive position, but, until the advent of a post-symbolic utopia, queer will retain a measure of meta-discourse. Sedgwick fosters an uneasy co-existence of the two, and Bersani perhaps overstates the "degaying" gesture of her study. The analysis in *The Epistemology of the Closet* operates through the homosexual/heterosexual binary, not against it, and nowhere in it does Sedgwick contend that it is desirable, let alone possible, to eliminate "gay" as a defining category of identity. Sedgwick's stated aim to "render less destructively presumable 'homosexuality' as we know it today" could be read as a diminution of the category, but it also announces an attempt to enrich it, to rescue it from the poverty of unidimensional stereotypes and unquestioned normative assumptions.

The queer spectator therefore joins the humanist and the gay as fictive positions of hypothetical purity; none, in practice, enjoys autonomy from the others and freedom from contradiction. These three untenable extremes prove useful, nevertheless, by staking out a field of possibilities within which a spectator might locate a more viable, though inevitably ambivalent, position. Dolan plots one of these when she maintains that "'queer' opens spaces for people who embrace all manner of sexual practices and identities, which gives old-fashioned gays and lesbians a lot more company on the front lines," while also hoping that "we'll celebrate the achievements of gay and lesbian theatre and performance, along with the queer version, so that we can remember our history." Through the uneasy but necessary tension that arises between the universalizing queer and minoritizing gay tendencies housed in these two statements emerges a fourth possible spectator of *The Boys in the Band*. This spectator both "is" gay, because he cannot live outside of this category into which a society has interpellated him, and "does" queer by recognizing and interrogating the contradictory pressures that both shape and subvert this identity. The gay spectator "doing" queer might realize Dolan's hope, queerly keeping the category of gay open while recognizing *The Boys in the Band*'s uniquely significant situation as a play whose history, in 1996 as in 1968, participates in and is marked by that of gays themselves. Furthermore, although this position hovers somewhere near the gay/queer vector in this triangulated field, it nonetheless retains a certain measure of universal humanism as well, despite or, as Bersani might argue, because of its queerness. In the dark of the theatre, this spectator identifies with the community of spectators—not necessarily all gay—who come together and watch this play in a shared recognition of history, desire, and constraint, while never forgetting that the lights will come up to reveal this imaginary "we" as a heterogeneous crowd, transitory and provisional, whose few hundred individuals will quickly disperse into the city streets.

Source: Timothy Scheie, "Acting Gay in the Age of Queer: Pondering the Revival of *The Boys in the Band*," in *Modern Drama*, Vol. 42, No. 11, Spring 1999, pp. 1–12.

Joe Carrithers

In the following essay, Carrithers, focusing primarily on the movie version of The Boys in the Band, *discusses the concept of the "gaze" in terms of a heterosexual audience and homosexual subjects and argues that the film's gay stereotypes work to the advantage of the heterosexual norm.*

Few critics discussing spectatorship or the "gaze" of the spectator address the ways a heterosexual audience might view a film whose primary characters are homosexual. Even fewer of these critics address the ways such films attempt to accommodate these viewers. For a film to be successful, at least financially, it must attract the often larger heterosexual (straight) audience. A work such as *The Boys in the Band* (dir. William Friedkin), a 1970 Cinema Center Films release, modifies its images of gay sexuality in order to provide a "comfortable" experience for straight viewers. In films such as this one, which feature homosexual sexuality, there is a privileging of heterosexually inspired images (the most predominant being monogamous gay "marriage")—images that are antithetical to the redefinitions of sexuality and relationships supported by many gay men of the post-Stonewall generation. Such mediated depictions comfort the straight audience—primarily its men—by not forcing them to encounter (and, by extension, perhaps to accept) the possibility of other forms of sexuality, particularly nonmonogamous gay forms.

Simultaneously such a film negatively depicts those gay lives that do not follow heterosexual paradigms, reinforcing long-held stereotypes of gays as sad, troubled, and unhappy people. Gay viewers, hoping to see themselves and their lives reflected on the screen, find instead two equally distasteful options: either they must behave like straight men if they want to succeed, or they must accept a definition of their identity imposed by straight men. Richard Dyer says that by stereotyping, "the dominant groups apply their norms to subordinate groups, find the latter wanting, hence inadequate, inferior, sick or grotesque and hence reinforcing the dominant groups' sense of legitimacy of their domination." They can, in other words, take comfort in knowing they were right all along if no images on the screen call those stereotypes into question. In *The Boys in the Band*, this message emerges from the film's climactic scene, involving an emotionally brutal party game and its winners, which serves to reinforce the dominance of heterosexuality, not only by privileging monogamy and marriage, but also by "distorting, maligning or just plain ignoring" what the political action group Queer Nation, Los Angeles chapter, called in Frontiers "our true queer lives."

Writer/producer Mart Crowley's *The Boys in the Band* was performed first as a play in 1968 and then released as a film two years later, giving it a unique place in gay history. Its two versions appear on either side of the 1969 Stonewall uprising, a series of riots and demonstrations in New York City over incidents of police brutality and raids of gay bars. It remains perhaps "the most famous Hollywood film on the subject of male homosexuality." Yet its narrative becomes problematic for gay viewers because forms of sexuality that are alternatives to heterosexual paradigms—forms supported by activists since the beginning of the modern gay civil rights movement—are presented as failures. The only successful or happy men in the film are Hank and Larry, whose relationship most closely resembles (at the film's conclusion) a heterosexual marriage, and the token straight character, Alan, whom the other characters suppose to be gay (a "closet queen") but who exits the action with an intact heterosexual identity—wife and children included.

None of the other characters in the play or film elicits sympathy from the audience for gay men and their lives, a criticism that has been made for more than 20 years now. Michael is the main character, who is giving a birthday party for Harold. He suffers a brief nervous breakdown, and he and Donald, his ex-lover, are both in psychoanalysis to help them accept their identities as gay men—identities that persistently trouble them, causing them guilt. Harold is a guilt-ridden, unattractive Jew who must get stoned before appearing at his own birthday party. Cowboy is Harold's birthday present from Emory; he sells his body for money. Emory, the interior designer with an immaculately coiffed poodle, is too "nellie" (or effeminate) and therefore unable to assimilate fully into the mainstream of either gay or straight communities. Bernard, listed in the character outlines of the play simply as "twenty-eight, Negro, nice-looking," must face the prejudices of racism and homophobia; his role is remarkably peripheral. None of these men represents what might be considered an acceptable image of gayness because they are too stereotypical, as the character descriptions by Crowley indicate.

Indeed, *The Boys in the Band*, in its presentation of a social conflict between gay and straight identities, ultimately "functions" to the advantage of a straight spectator. That spectator's double is Alan, the token straight man who watches the proceedings. Peter Stallybrass and Allon White describe such conflicts: "In class society where

"GAY VIEWERS, HOPING TO SEE THEMSELVES AND THEIR LIVES REFLECTED ON THE SCREEN, FIND INSTEAD TWO EQUALLY DISTASTEFUL OPTIONS: EITHER THEY MUST BEHAVE LIKE STRAIGHT MEN IF THEY WANT TO SUCCEED, OR THEY MUST ACCEPT A DEFINITION OF THEIR IDENTITY IMPOSED BY STRAIGHT MEN."

social conflict is always present these sites [of symbolic and metaphoric intensity] do not necessarily coincide with the 'objective' conflict boundaries of an antagonistic class but will nevertheless function to the advantage of one social group rather than another." In this text, the advantage belongs to the straight audience. Laura Mulvey states, "mainstream film coded the erotic [or the sexual] into the language of the dominant patriarchal order," which, in this case, is heterosexual. Heterosexual audience members can reassure themselves of the stereotypes of gays, especially the negativity believed to be inherent in homosexuality.

The discussion that follows focuses primarily on the film version of *The Boys in the Band*, not the play or the 1968 printed version of the play as it was originally performed off Broadway. However, Hollywood's fidelity to the original script in preparing it for filming—using the playwright as the screenwriter—remains a remarkable achievement. The entire off-Broadway cast reprise their roles in the film, and the only major change in the scenes, aside from the opening credits montage, is the addition of a rainstorm that forces the party guests into Michael's apartment where they play the telephone "truth" game devised by Michael. Even though the film came out just one year after the Stonewall uprising, the impact of the uprising and the subsequent emergence of a new sense of identity for gay men (now known as "gay pride") do not appear. Although it is not too surprising that the film does not acknowledge these events—the uprising was barely mentioned in the mainstream media—what is surprising is the degree to which *The Boys in the Band* has kept rigid, pre-Stonewall stereotypes of gay men in public view for the past 25 years.

Typical—almost stereotypical—of the reactions to the play (and its later incarnation as a film) is John Simon's 1968 review: ''The homosexual part of the audience is to feel purged and to some extent vindicated by this play and production, whereas heterosexual spectators are to be made more aware of homosexual life styles and, if possible, sympathetic to them.'' He adds later that the play ''may prove a lesson in majority and minority coexistence—though at *The Boys in the Band* (as often, elsewhere) it is hard to tell which is which.'' Simon's suggestion becomes difficult to support because of the play and film's devalorization of homosexuality. Even Crowley admitted that Michael's self-hatred, echoed by most of the other gay characters, was the message ''that a very square American public wanted to receive''—a straight majority that the theater often needs for financial success. Gay viewers may search for a positive depiction of their lives, the diversity of their lives, but that search will be in vain. What is evident in *The Boys in the Band*, as in other gay films that become part of the so-called mainstream, is that ''cinematic identification not only functions to affirm heterosexual norms, but also finds its most basic condition of possibility in the heterosexual division of the universe.''

The division between homosexual and heterosexual is most apparent in the film's most predominant type of shot: the close-up. The screen often shows only one man, suggesting that he is not part of a community, but alone, separate, emotionally isolated. Each time the camera focuses on a group of the men (or the entire party), it soon changes back to close-ups. When Emory tells of his love for ''Delbert Botts, DDS,'' for example, the camera begins with Cowboy, Harold, and Michael also in the frame. It then zooms in on Emory, slowly removing the other men, isolating Emory. He cannot depend on the others; he must face the audience alone to be judged. And the straight audience, though unable to look at any other image on the screen, may find absurd or repugnant the tale of Emory's obsession for the straight married man who does not return his love. The straight viewer need not feel empathy, but he can instead feel more distance between himself and these gay men. Close-ups in other films may allow the audience to identify with the characters, connecting viewer and object. Here the close-ups

are of men describing the sadness of their lives. They speak of lost loves, the pain of coming out, the emptiness and self-hatred they often feel. Although gay viewers may empathize, straight men in the audience confront stereotypical depictions of homosexuality—they cannot make a similar emotional connection.

The scenes that most clearly illustrate the method by which *The Boys in the Band* affirms heterosexual norms involve the telephone truth game that ends the night of partying, confession, angst, and internalized homophobia. The rules of the game require participants to call ''the one person we truly believe we have loved.'' Players win points based upon how successful the call is. As Michael explains it:

> If you make the call, you get one point. If the person you are calling answers, you get two more points. If someone else answers, you only get one. If there's no answer at all, you're screwed . . . When you get the person whom you are calling on the line—if you tell them who you are, you get two points. And then if you tell them that you love them—you get a bonus of five more points! . . . Therefore you can get as many as ten points and as few as one.

Five of the party guests participate in the game—dubbed '''Affairs of the Heart,' a combination of the truth game and murder.'' Two of the characters ''win'' by accumulating as many points as possible—Alan, a married straight man, and Larry, whose emotional commitment soon emulates the model of monogamous heterosexual marriage. The others lose.

Bernard makes the first call but gains just two points. He then becomes depressed because he was unable to confess his love for a childhood friend. Emory accumulates only three when he calls the straight, married dentist he knew while they were still students in high school. He becomes too drunk to continue participating in the party activities. Hank, the school teacher who has left his wife and children for his gay lover, Larry, calls the answering service he and Larry use, asking the operator to leave a message for his lover. He gets seven points for his call. He then explains his need to ''come out'' to Alan and the other guests: ''Because I do love him. And I don't care who knows it.''

Exasperated at the constant bickering over his promiscuity, Hank's lover Larry calls Hank on another extension in Michael's apartment and gains 10 points (the maximum possible). He tells Hank, ''For what it's worth, I love you.'' Mimicking the remarks he said moments earlier about his inability to maintain a monogamous relationship, he says, ''In my own way, Hank, I love you, but you have to understand that even though I do want to go on living with you, sometimes there may be others.'' Philip Gambone writes about the years immediately after the Stonewall uprising: ''Monogamous gay mating, it was argued, was an unimaginative and even oppressive copy of heterosexual marriage; as gay and lesbian people, we were free to love, have sex with, and show affection for others outside the realm of 'marriage.''' When Larry joins Hank upstairs in the bedroom after this reconciliation over the telephone, it implies a possible curtailing of his extracurricular (or is it extramarital?) sexual activities. ''I'll try,'' says Hank on one extension; ''I will too,'' says Larry on the other. Hank will try to demand less of Larry's attention, to seek fewer signs of his commitment. In turn, Larry will try to be faithful, to be as monogamous as a spouse in a straight marriage should be.

The final, reluctant player—all others refuse to play the game—is Alan, who is forced to confront and question his sexuality (which he reaffirms as heterosexual). Michael demands that Alan play the game, mistakenly believing he will call Justin Stuart, a gay friend from his past. (Justin had claimed Alan was his lover.) Instead Alan calls his wife, Fran. He apologizes to her, reconciling with her after a disagreement, making this scene virtually an exact re-enactment of the reconciliation between Hank and Larry. Thus he also acquires 10 points, becoming co-winner with Larry. The remainder of the film depicts Harold's scathing indictment of Michael as ''a sad and pathetic man''; Harold leaving with his present, Cowboy; the departures of the game's two losers, Bernard and Emory; and a distressed Michael collapsing into Donald's arms. The conclusion leaves the viewer with three emotionally stable party guests: Alan, Hank, and Larry. Their status provides more comfort to the straight viewers than to the gay ones because their relationships perpetuate heterosexual norms.

The Boys in the Band unsettles some audience expectations about Alan, however, before the stabilizing ending. The questioning of Alan's sexuality begins early, when he telephones Michael just before the guests arrive for Harold's party. Michael, who has not told Alan he is gay, tries to persuade him not to come to the party; he does not admit that all of his guests are gay. Alan begins to cry over the telephone, saying he needs to talk to Michael, his old college roommate. After Alan's arrival at the party, his sexuality becomes more ambiguous (or questionable) with the attention he pays to Hank. He tells Michael, ''That Hank is really a very attractive fellow''; a statement he makes repeatedly and that begins to suggest that he desires more with Hank than just a conversation about sports, the topic that begins what amounts to a flirtation between the two men, who are or have been married to women. (That they are paired in the narrative remains a point overlooked by most critics, but it is one that calls into question the stability of heterosexual marriage.)

Michael confronts Alan: ''What you can't do is leave [the party before playing the truth game]. It's like watching an accident on the highway—you can't look at it and you can't look away.'' Neither can the audience. In one tight close-up after another, viewers watch the characters. They are forced to see and hear these men talk about their lives. The ensuing ''homosexual panic'' (the straight man's fear that he might be gay) reaches its apex with Michael's tirade against Alan: ''He knows very, very well what a closet queen is. Don't you, Alan?'' As evidence of that he cites Alan's earlier remarks about Hank: ''What an attractive fellow he is and all that transparent crap.'' That ''transparent crap'' gets reinterpreted with Alan's later, more confident heterosexual comments to his wife over the telephone and afterwards to the others. The fear of being gay (for either Alan or the heterosexual male spectator) must be removed so that, in Eve Kosofsky Sedgwick's terms, no longer is ''a man's man . . . separated only by an invisible, carefully blurred, always-already-crossed line from being 'interested in men.''' The straight men in the audience confront this fear and become more confidently heterosexual; they are not like those gay men on the screen.

Alan's reaffirmed identity (and perhaps the straight audience member's as well) as a heterosexual comes, though, after much attack from the others regarding his sexuality. Although Michael is the most adamant in directing his anger at Alan, the others—particularly Emory and Larry—take their turns as well. Larry notices Alan's attraction to Hank, for instance, and uses it as an opportunity to criticize Hank for behavior for which Hank has criticized Larry. At one point, when Alan and Michael start to go upstairs for a private discussion, Larry says to Alan, ''He'll [Hank] still be here.'' Although the party guests ''try to force Alan, the unexpected, 'straight' guest, into the stereotypical role of 'closet queen' . . . Alan returns the one quality they cannot accept: 'ambiguity.''' The audience, whether gay or straight, cannot maintain this sense of ambiguity about him. Alan enters Michael's apartment as a straight married man and leaves the same way; no questioning can negate that.

After Alan has been attacked for being a "closet queen" and has attacked Emory to defend himself, he pleads, "Hank, leave with me." The implication that he wants Hank as a sexual or romantic partner resurfaces, but also surfacing is the possibility that Alan feels homosexuality is something that can be escaped. He and the once-married Hank will remain straight (or become straight again) if they leave the "gay ghetto," the exclusive gay environment of Michael's apartment. As already noted, when Alan leaves the apartment, he does reaffirm his status as a heterosexual—a move that must serve as a comfort for straight audience members who earlier identified with Alan but who may be feeling as insecure as he about their sexuality. They can leave the theater; they can re-enter the heterosexually dominated world outside. They can "look away."

Even the physical placement of the actors reinforces the privileging of heterosexuality. During a private conversation with Michael in the bedroom, Alan stands most of the time that Michael sits. He can always look down on Michael. He is more brightly lit during the scene, even when he is sitting across from Michael. He is always in focus in the frame; Michael is not. And, in camera shots that include most or all of the people in the apartment, Alan is always placed differently. If the others face the camera, he faces away from it. If they sit, he stands. He is not part of the group; he is separate from it. The straight male spectator, watching his double on the screen, feels this same separation. He is not part of that community either. He too is just a viewer like Alan.

The heterosexual male spectator's fear of "contamination" from just watching a gay-oriented film also dissipates with the depiction of Hank and Larry's relationship, although their relationship at first confuses Alan and the straight audience members he represents. Alan "can't believe" Hank and Larry love each other. Their more stereotypically "masculine" appearances do not present a sexuality that is, in Foucauldian terms, "a secret that always [gives] itself away"—as Emory's more effeminate sexuality, for example, inevitably does. Film historian Russo argues that the "big lie about lesbians and gay men is that we do not exist . . . When the fact of our existence became unavoidable, we were reflected, on screen and off, as dirty secrets." Hank and Larry cannot be such "dirty secrets"; they act too much like heterosexual men, like Alan, like many of the straight men in the audience. Hank and Larry fit no commonly held stereotypes of gay men, as the others do. The equation of masculinity with the heterosexuality that they contradict illustrates a condition that "reflects the shame about our own homosexuality." That shame disturbs gay viewers who are unable to recognize themselves within the confines of a "happiness" represented only by Hank and Larry's model.

This should not suggest that Hank and Larry's relationship falls to support a positive image of a committed homosexual couple. Their characterization does avoid stereotyping. However, gay viewers must question whether this is truly a positive image. Most of the film depicts them constantly bickering, suspicious of each other's motives—hardly suitable role models for gay men wanting a monogamous relationship. Straight audiences may begin to assume that such relationships cannot last: gay men cannot be monogamous or committed to each other. They may suspect the game's resolution will not change Hank and Larry, and gay spectators may have the same suspicion. Larry, for example, voices the emotions gay men in unhappy or confining monogamous relationships might feel: "I love 'em all. And what he [Hank] refuses to understand—is that I've got to have 'em all. I am not the marrying kind, and I never will be." At that point, he adds, "Why am I always the g—damn villain in the piece? If I'm not thought of as a happy-home wrecker, I'm an impossible son of a bitch to live with." In this one sentence his identity moves from an image analogous to the "other woman" who breaks up a heterosexual marriage to the philanderer who demands the absolute freedom to cheat, like an unfaithful husband. Either scenario is unacceptable to Hank, whose requests for monogamy or proposed compromises (such as a ménage á trois) go unheeded. Indeed they often result in loud and frequent arguments. Larry's revelation of a prior sexual encounter with Donald prompts a fight—the "first one since the last one," Larry calls it. They even dispute their separate interpretations of previous arguments:

LARRY: We have no agreement.

HANK: We did.

LARRY: You did. I never agreed to anything!

Simply put, until the destructive truth game, they cannot agree. Then the agreement follows heterosexually constructed possibilities of monogamy and marriage. By the end of the film they have changed from having a relationship that permits one of the partners to be promiscuous with other men to a newly defined relationship with its basis in mutual consent to monogamy.

This presents, from one viewpoint, at least, a disturbing form of transgression. As Russo points out:

> What scares Alan and the audience, what they could not come to terms with or understand, is the homosexuality of Hank and Larry (Laurence Luckinbill and Keith Prentice), who are both just as queer as Emory yet ''look'' as straight as Alan. The possibility that there could be nonstereotypical homosexuals who are also staunch advocates of a working gay relationship is presented by the two lovers throughout the film.

And it is ''when Larry and Hank express affection for each other physically and verbally that the audience and the lone straight guest are most uncomfortable.'' Yet the film's concessions to the straight audience again make that discomfort disappear. The most obvious example is a scene that depicts Hank and Larry comforting each other in Michael's bedroom that was shot for the film but not used. Such changes still are being made in film and television; a similar shot of two gay men talking in bed, apparently after sex, for the television program *thirtysomething* in 1990 resulted in a reported loss of $1 million in advertising revenues for ABC. The episode with this scene never aired a second time, not even in syndication.

If the heterosexual audience cannot accept the two men together, neither can the characters in the film nor, it seems, the camera itself. Someone is always coming between Hank and Larry, trying to separate them just as Larry's numerous sexual encounters threaten to divide them. In a cab on the way to the party, Emory sits between Hank and Larry. Michael stands between them when they enter his apartment. Even Alan separates the couple visually; he sits between them after he arrives. The two men are seldom even in the same frame. The most notable exception occurs when Larry telephones Hank for the truth game after an argument about what constitutes a gay marriage. Their conversation is a two-shot scene that ends with both men facing the same direction—toward the stairs that lead to the bedroom. They behave in unison at last.

Neither they nor the other men, however, can be erotically associated in the bedroom, at least on camera. Three groups of men appear in the bedroom during the film. Michael and Donald are no longer involved in a relationship, so what might be erotic images of them together (Michael taking off his sweater, Donald's naked buttocks as he gets into the shower) are ultimately de-eroticized. The two do not desire each other; they are just friends. Michael and Alan confront each other in the bedroom, where Michael tries to justify his friendships with the other men. They remain separate, though, both physically and ideologically. Hank takes Alan through the bedroom after the fight with Emory, however they encounter Bernard and Emory, and another fight almost ensues. No sexuality is associated with the bedroom until Hank and Larry enter. Then the door is closed. We are not allowed to see two men making love. Heterosexual male viewers might have to recognize that Hank and Larry are lovers, but they do not have to see the two men sexually involved. They are not made too uncomfortable.

Larry and Hank ultimately settle for the possibility of a monogamous relationship, removing the sexual freedom celebrated by gay rights activists. Rather than upset straight viewers—a possibility likely with the representation of gay men whose sexuality is not readily apparent or whose relationships do not mirror heterosexual ideals at the end of the film—*The Boys in the Band* reminds its gay viewers of a more repressive era, a time when their sexuality was unacceptable and unaccepted.

The difference made by the events following the Stonewall uprising, articulated perhaps most clearly by Claude Summers, was ''the change from conceiving homosexuality as a personal failing or social problem to a question of identity.'' The film's appearance a year after Stonewall, in a form virtually unchanged from the version performed the year before Stonewall, suggests that it ''immediately became both a period piece and a reconfirmation of the stereotypes'' popularized before the uprising—''one Jew, one black, one Wasp, one midnight cowboy, one nellie queen and a married man and his lover.'' What dominates the literature about gays before Stonewall (like the play) is the belief that ''[i]dentification as a homosexual is frequently accompanied or preceded by feelings of guilt and shame and by a sense of (often quite justified) paranoia, for to be homosexual in most modern societies is to be set apart and stigmatized.'' The film version of this play reinforces those feelings of guilt and shame by its failure to acknowledge changes set into motion by the events at Stonewall.

Pivotal events in gay history—whether for the individual or the community often are overlooked. Edmund White, for example, writing about the morning after the initial uprising in June 1969, has his characters in *The Beautiful Room Is Empty* note the lack of attention garnered by the beginning of the modern gay civil rights movement: ''we couldn't find a single mention in the press of the turning point of our lives.'' Almost a year later than the events that end White's novel, *The Boys in the Band* commits the same offense as the press. A gay male after Stonewall may turn his attention toward finding positive representations that mirror his own. As Wayne Koestenbaum describes it, "Reading becomes a hunt for histories that deliberately foreknow or unwittingly trace a desire felt not by author but by reader, who is most acute when looking for signs of himself." Frequently the reader or viewer (in the case of a film like *The Boys in the Band*) is disappointed.

This gay male viewer confronts a film ostensibly about his community, his experience, his life, and his sexuality. However, the dominance of a heterosexual audience in this country means he also must accept that "I am neither there to be looked at, nor am I the agent of the look." What becomes obvious is that in films like *The Boys in the Band*, with its predominantly gay cast of characters, "heterosexual role playing was the role." For some gay men, the experience of watching the film "was like watching people from Venus." As one gay man points out, "I remember going to it with my wife and saying to her afterward, 'Look what you saved me from.' That was how I took the film at the time, which was how I think most people took it, a film about how inherently miserable most homosexual lives are." The film offers few alternatives to that reaction.

Today *The Boys in the Band* still places many homosexual men on opposite sides of a debate about its significance. Al LaValley remembers a panel discussion about this first "gay film" by Hollywood: "when Gay Lib used it as this icon of stereotypical pre-Stonewall homosexuality, I was just totally baffled . . . If homosexuals weren't like that, what was the need for Gay Liberation." This suggests at least one reason why the film, coming after Stonewall, became such a disappointment for gay men. As New York Times film critic Vincent Canby remarked after its opening, "There is something basically unpleasant . . . about a play [adapted into a film] that seems to have been created in an inspiration of love-hate and that finally does nothing more than exploit its (I assume) sincerely conceived stereotypes." The unpleasantness becomes even greater when the homosexual spectator is forced to acknowledge that, whether or not the stereotypes are "sincerely conceived," the love (at least happiness and comfort) goes mostly to straight men, like Alan, and the hate (self-loathing or psychological scars) to a majority of the gays.

Source: Joe Carrithers, "The Audiences of *The Boys in the Band*," in *Journal of Popular Film & Television*, Vol. 23, No. 2, Summer 1995, pp. 64–71.

SOURCES

Augstums, Ieva, "Pioneering Playwright Shares Experiences with UNL Students," in the *Daily Nebraskan*, March 13, 1998.

Barnes, Clive, "*Boys in the Band* Opens Off Broadway," in the *New York Times*, April 15, 1968, p. 48.

Canby, Vincent, Review of the movie *The Boys in the Band*, in the *New York Times*, March 18, 1970, p. 36.

Clurman, Harold, Review of *The Boys in the Band*, in the *Nation*, April 29, 1968, p. 60.

Regan, Margaret, "Birthday Bash: Millennium Theatre's *Boys in the Band* Is Older but Not Wiser," in *Tucson Weekly*, July 3–9, 1997.

Rutledge, Leigh W., *The Gay Decade: From Stonewall to the Present*, The Penguin Group, 1992, p. 3.

"The Theater: New Plays," Review in *Time*, April 26, 1968, p. 97.

FURTHER READING

Adam, Barry D., *The Rise of a Gay and Lesbian Movement*, rev. ed., Twayne, 1995.
    Called "the classic of its field," this academic text traces the movement for gay rights back to its origins in Germany in the 1890s. More concerned with gay politics than any of the characters in the play, it is still useful for background to the world that Crowley changed.

Kaiser, Charles, "The Sixties," in *Gay Metropolis: 1940–1996*, Houghton Mifflin, 1997.
    This much-lauded history of New York contains a long section explaining the ground-breaking impact of *The Boys in the Band* when it first appeared.

Marcus, Eric, *Making History: The Struggle for Gay and Lesbian Rights, 1945–1990*, HarperCollins, 1992.
    The Boys in the Band falls right in the middle of the area covered by this oral history, which includes interviews with people from all walks of life who talk about what it was like for homosexuals while the world was beginning to acknowledge gay rights.

Rutledge, Leigh W., *The Gay Decades: From Stonewall to the Present*, Plume, 1992.
    This book gives a detailed, month-by-month account of gay history right after the opening of *The Boys in the Band*, starting with Judy Garland's death on June 22, 1969, and continuing up into the 1990s.

van Leer, David, *The Queening of America: Gay Culture in Straight Society,* Routledge Press, 1995.

van Leer examines the ways in which homosexual sub-culture has been incorporated into mainstream America, a feat that *The Boys in the Band* is famous for.

The Critic

RICHARD BRINSLEY
SHERIDAN
1779

The Critic first premiered at London's Drury Lane Theatre on October 30, 1779. As its title suggests, the play follows a day in the life of a critic, Mr. Dangle, as he is entreated by members of the theatrical world for his patronage and support; the play's second and third acts feature Dangle (and another critic, Mr. Sneer) watching the rehearsal of *The Spanish Armada,* an historical tragedy written by their acquaintance, Mr. Puff. Although Puff's play is meant to arouse pity and fear—the two required tragic emotions according to classical standards—his play is a laughable hodgepodge of bombastic language and ludicrous events.

By the time of *The Critic*'s premiere, Richard Brinsley Sheridan had already enjoyed great success as a playwright: his first comedy, *The Rivals,* had opened at Drury Lane four years earlier and was followed by *The School for Scandal* (1777), widely regarded as his masterpiece. Sheridan had by this time also purchased an interest in Drury Lane and eventually became its manager; his experiences with actors, playwrights, directors, scenic designers and, of course, critics, all found their way into his play about Dangle, Sneer, and Puff. (Sheridan modeled some of the play's characters on people with whom he had worked.) The play is notable for its depiction of a playwright unable to withstand any criticism, an unscrupulous writer of advertisements, and its thorough parody of theatrical conventions. Though some may feel that mocking a bad play is

easier than composing a good one, many readers and viewers find *The Critic* an hilarious examination of an aesthetically terrible tragedy.

AUTHOR BIOGRAPHY

Richard Brinsley Sheridan was born on October 30, 1751, in Dublin to a family known for its artistic members. His grandfather, the Reverend Dr. Thomas Sheridan (1687–1738), was an author, schoolmaster, and friend of Jonathan Swift. His father, Thomas Sheridan (1719–1788), was a renowned actor, theatrical manager, and elocutionist. His mother, Frances Sheridan (1724–1766), was a novelist and playwright. Sheridan began grammar school in 1758 in Dublin while his parents pursued their careers in London; in 1759, his father relocated the family to Windsor. In 1762, Sheridan entered Harrow School, where he was often teased by other boys for being the son of an actor and for his less-than-fashionable wardrobe.

After leaving Harrow in 1768, Sheridan lived with his widowed father in Chelsea before moving with him to Bath. While at Bath, Sheridan and a former schoolmate from Harrow wrote *Ixion*, a farce, and submitted it to David Garrick, one of the most popular actors and directors of the day. Garrick was unimpressed. During this period, Sheridan also experimented with verse, composing ''The Ridotto of Bath'' and ''Clio's Protest; or, The Picture Varnished.'' The most important event in Bath, however, was Sheridan's meeting Elizabeth Linley, by all accounts a beautiful and talented young singer. Sheridan whisked her away to Calais, ostensibly to remove her from the pursuit of Captain Thomas Matthews, a suitor. In 1772, Sheridan and Linley were married by a village priest in Calais; upon their return, Sheridan fought two duels with Matthews in defense of his bride's honor. (Matthews was not killed during these duels.) In 1773, after a brief period of separation ordered by Sheridan's father, the two were officially married, this time in London.

London is where Sheridan's short career as a dramatist began and ended. His first play, *The Rivals* (1775), was an initial flop (partly due to bad acting) but a great success later that year after Sheridan revised it. (The play features Mrs. Malaprop, a woman whose linguistic faults have inspired the term ''malapropism.'') Other successes followed: his comic opera *The Duenna*, also in 1775, *The School for Scandal* in 1777, and *The Critic* in 1779.

Richard Brinsley Sheridan

While composing these works, Sheridan became manager of the Drury Lane Theater when, ironically, David Garrick retired and sold Sheridan his interest.

Sheridan was now a celebrity, but he would soon become as famous for his political rhetoric as he was for his plays. In 1780, he was elected to Parliament as a Whig; he continued his political career until only a few years before his death. He served as an under-secretary of state for foreign affairs, secretary to the treasury, an advisor to the Prince of Wales during the Regency crisis of 1788, and treasurer of the navy. In 1812, he lost his seat in Parliament after a number of stunning performances in House of Commons debates. His famous oration against Warren Hastings, the former governor general of India, was praised as a masterpiece of political speech. While enjoying his political success, however, Sheridan was beset by sorrow: in 1777, his wife delivered a stillborn child and in 1792 delivered a daughter, Mary, thought by many to be the daughter of another man. Sheridan's wife died later that year and Sheridan married Esther Ogle (daughter of the dean of Winchester) in 1795.

The Drury Lane Theatre burnt down in 1809 and was reopened in 1812—but without Sheridan as manager. He was arrested for debt in 1813 and never regained his seat in Parliament. Although he died a man hounded by financial worries, his death (on July 7, 1816) was mourned by many admirers, and he was given an elaborate funeral. Sheridan was buried in Poet's Corner of Westminster Abbey, near the grave of his friend, Dr. Samuel Johnson.

PLOT SUMMARY

Act I, Scene i

The play begins with Mr. Dangle, the critic, at breakfast with his wife. Dangle finds the morning newspapers too full of irritating news about politics; he therefore turns to the *Morning Chronicle* to find news of the theatrical world that interests him as a man with great passions for the stage. After Dangle remarks that his friend Puff's tragedy, *The Spanish Armada,* is being rehearsed at Drury Lane, Dangle's wife scolds him for taking no interest in affairs of state; Dangle counters her argument by pointing out that his various powers as "the head of a band of critics" make him an important man. Mrs. Dangle remains unimpressed.

Sneer, a fellow critic and friend of Dangle, arrives with two plays and asks Dangle to persuade one of the theatre managers to accept them for performance. The three discuss the faults of the modern theatre, specifically that it has lost its capacity to morally instruct the public and that the comedies have become too sanitized.

A servant enters and announces the arrival of Sir Fretful Plagiary, a talentless playwright who, as described by Dangle and Sneer, asks for honest criticism yet rejects any unflattering observations. As the two men discuss Sir Fretful's most recent "execrable" work, the playwright enters. Sir Fretful explains that he has sent his recent play to the manager of the Covent Garden Theatre, rather than Drury Lane, since Richard Brinsley Sheridan has *his* works performed there and might steal some of Sir Fretful's work out of envy. Sneer, true to his name, mocks Sir Fretful's worries and talents. Sir Fretful, slightly nonplussed, asks the men if there is anything they find that can be "mended" in his latest play—but, of course, he rejects all of their criticisms. Dangle and Sneer then invent a number of scathing complaints about Sir Fretful's work that they pretend to have read in the newspapers; despite

Sir Fretful's claim that he disregards the opinions found there, he suffers "great agitation" from their words as he pretends to laugh at the imaginary critics' complaints. Sneer asks Dangle if he can accompany him to the rehearsal of Puff's tragedy; Dangle agrees but asks Sneer to help him judge the merits of a family of Italian singers who are seeking his patronage and who have just arrived in Dangle's drawing room.

Act I, Scene ii

In the Dangles' drawing room, Mrs. Dangle attempts to converse with Signor Pasticcio Ritornello, an opera singer, and his two daughters. The French interpreter who has accompanied Pasticcio explains, in a very awkward fashion, that Lady Rondeau and Mrs. Fuge, two patrons of the opera, have sent the singers. Dangle and Sneer arrive, and Dangle is beseeched—in French and Italian—to put in a good word for the singers with the theatre managers about town. When a servant announces that Puff has arrived, however, Dangle asks his wife to escort the Italians and their interpreter into the next room.

Puff arrives and becomes the focus of the scene. Puff explains to Sneer that he is "a Professor of the Art of Puffing": an author who has taught newspapermen and advertisers how to inflate their diction so they may "enlay their phraseology with variegated chips of exotic metaphor" and "crowd their advertisements with panegyrical superlatives." Sneer asks if he can accompany Dangle to the rehearsal of Puff's play; Puff tells the two men that they may meet him in the green room later that day, since Puff first has to "scribble" a few paragraphs for the newspapers on a number of topics.

Act II, Scene i

Later that day, Dangle and Sneer meet Puff at the theatre, where the remainder of *The Critic* takes place. Puff explains that the threat of a Spanish invasion gave him the idea of writing an historical verse tragedy about the threat of the Spanish Armada faced by Queen Elizabeth in 1588. His play is set at Tilbury Fort, a stronghold at the mouth of the Thames where Elizabeth mustered her troops; the plot involves Tilburnia, the Governor of the fort's daughter, falling in love with Don Ferolo Whiskerandos, the son of the Spanish admiral. The theatre's under prompter enters and tells Puff that the actors are ready to rehearse; he also mentions that Puff will find the play "very short," since the actors have cut out the parts they found "heavy or unnecessary to the plot." For the remainder of *The*

Critic, Dangle, Sneer, and Puff watch the rehearsal and comment on the action unfolding before them, the two critics often calling attention to Puff's deficiencies as a playwright.

Act II, Scene ii

The rehearsal begins with two of Tilbury Fort's sentinels asleep at their posts; when Dangle asks Puff how the sentinels could be asleep "at such an alarming crisis," Puff explains that they must be so in order to allow the two approaching commanders to speak freely, which they would not do if the sentinels were awake. (As the play progresses, Puff responds to Dangle and Sneer's criticisms in a similarly defensive vein.) The characters Sir Walter Raleigh and Sir Christopher Hatton (the two approaching commanders) enter. Sir Walter explains that Philip, the king of Spain, has "struck at England's trade" with his armada. The two men also discuss the capture of Don Ferolo Whiskerandos, who has been taken prisoner and is being held at the fort. The Earl of Leicester, Commander in Chief, enters with his train and leads the other men in a prayer to the god of war, Mars. After they exit, the two sentinels rise and reveal that they were not, in fact, sleeping—they are spies of Lord Burleigh (Queen Elizabeth's chief minister) and will report to him what they have heard.

The morning cannons sound, the spies exit, and Tilburnia (the Governor's daughter) enters with Nora, her confidant. Tilburnia recites a ludicrous speech about the beauty of the morning and the sorrow of her heart. The Governor enters and tells Tilburnia that she cannot be wasting her time with "Cupid's baby woes," for the Spanish Armada is arriving. Tilburnia then employs (as Sneer calls it) "a kind of poetical second-sight": she looks offstage and begins describing (in great detail) the sights and sounds of the approaching fleet. Tilburnia begs her father to accept Don Whiskerandos's "noble price" for liberty, and the two engage in quick repartee, intended (by Puff) to sound like "a fencing match." Despite his daughter's pleas, the Governor remains unmoved and exits.

Don Whiskerandos enters in chains, accusing Tilburnia of not trying to win his freedom from her father. However, Tilburnia persuades him of her devotion with a melodramatic speech. After Puff's interruptions concerning their acting, the two exit. When Nora asks how *she* is to exit, however, Puff pushes her aside, yelling, "Pshaw! What the devil signifies how *you* get off!" Dangle and Sneer ask if Queen Elizabeth will enter, but Puff explains that she is only "to be talked of for ever" to raise the audience's expectations. Puff then instructs the actors involved in the second (or "under") plot to prepare, only to be told by the under prompter that the actors have cut the next scene entirely from the script. Allowing the cut to stand but vowing to "print it every word," Puff exits to prepare the actors for the final phase of the rehearsal.

Act III, Scene i

Puff's play proceeds with its "discovery scene." A justice (i.e., a judge) and constable enter and discuss the recent impression of military "volunteers"—some drunks and some prisoners—including one young man whose "clear convicted crimes have stampt him soldier." The justice sends the constable to fetch this particular youth. Before the constable returns, the justice's lady enters and remarks to her husband that one "prisoner youth" she has seen reminds her of their deceased son. When the young prisoner enters, he reveals (through a series of questions put to him by the justice) that he is, in fact, the justice's supposedly dead son. After a number of ridiculous plot clarifications, the prisoner, justice, lady, constable, and a number of other "near relations" all "faint alternately in each other's arms." The characters all revive and then exit. Dangle calls the scene "one of the finest" he has ever seen and says that it "would have made a tragedy itself." ("Aye, or a comedy either," cracks Sneer.)

A lone beefeater (i.e., a yeoman of the guard) enters; after his laughably short, four-line soliloquy, he exits. Puff explains that the soliloquy would have been longer had the beefeater not been observed. Lord Burleigh enters (who presumably by now has heard the report of his spies), sits in a chair, and "thinks" without ever saying a word. He shakes his head and exits. Puff explains the significance of his shake of the head in such detail that Sneer and Dangle are astounded. Sir Christopher and Sir Walter return, lamenting the fact that both of their nieces are in love with Don Whiskerandos; when the two nieces enter, their uncles withdraw to eavesdrop. The nieces (instructed by Puff) reveal their thoughts in a series of asides before Don Whiskerandos himself enters, searching for Tilburnia. Both nieces level swords against Don Whiskerandos as vengeance for rebuffing them, but then their two uncles leap from their hiding place and state that *they* will avenge their nieces' unrequited love; Don Whiskerandos, however, draws two daggers and holds them to the nieces' bosoms, creating a dramatic stalemate. Suddenly, the beefeater returns and orders the others to drop their weapons—which they inexplicably do. The nieces exit with their uncles, leaving Don Whiskerandos with the beefeater, who removes his costume and reveals himself as the Captain of the ship that had taken the Spaniard prisoner. Naturally, the beefeater "was himself an old lover of Tilburnia," and the two use the swords dropped by the uncles for a duel. The Captain kills Don Whiskerandos, whose dying word, cut off in mid-syllable, is completed by his killer.

The Governor enters in a panic, exclaiming that his daughter has grown "Distract" (i.e., mad) from the death of her lover. He exits, and Tilburnia and Nora enter, both mad and dressed in white satin. Tilburnia babbles in her "madness" for a moment before exiting to throw herself into the sea. Puff explains that her suicide will lead the play to its climax: the sea fight between the Spanish and English. An actor playing the Thames enters, accompanied by two actors in green, representing his banks. The battle includes a number of effects: cannon-fire, a procession of "all the English rivers and their tributaries," and the music of Handel. After its conclusion, Puff applauds his cast before remarking, "Well, pretty well—but not quite perfect—so ladies and gentlemen, if you please, we'll rehearse this piece again to-morrow."

CHARACTERS

Lord Burleigh

Lord Burleigh, the Lord Treasurer and chief minister under Queen Elizabeth I, appears in Puff's *The Spanish Armada* as a completely silent man. His simple shaking of the head communicates the need for the English to show a greater spirit if they are to defeat their Spanish enemies.

Mr. Dangle

Mr. Dangle is the critic of the play's title. Dangle's great love is the stage; the opening scene of the play shows him disregarding newspaper articles about important current events in favor of one that tells him about the theatre. "I hate all politics but theatrical politics," he explains to his wife as he hurriedly reads of a new play in production. Dangle finds great satisfaction in his position

as "the head of a band of cricticks," as his judgment of a play is so widely sought and revered. All members of the theatrical world seek his patronage because his word is enough to spark their careers; as he explains, there are "applications from all quarters" for his "interest." In act 1, scene ii, for example, Dangle receives some Italian singers in his drawing room and behaves like a king at court, despite the fact that he can barely understand them (or their translator). As his name suggests, there is something silly about a man who "dangles" around theaters and greenrooms, mingling with those who often hold a less-than-respectable position in London society. His self-importance makes him, therefore, an object of gentle ridicule: a man completely caught up in the work of others and determined to tell the public what it should think about its own tastes. Even his wife finds his devotion to theatrical matters laughable and unworthy of the effort with which he peruses them.

Nothing in the play suggests that Dangle is a harsh or brutal judge, as the term "critic" sometimes connotes. Indeed, each complaint he voices against Sir Fretful is followed by "tho' he's my friend" to suggest that Dangle takes no joy in trouncing someone's creative labors. When Sir Fretful arrives at Dangle's home, Dangle takes pains to spare his feelings when pointing out what he thinks of his latest tragedy: he prefaces his criticism by telling Sir Fretful that his first four acts are the best he "ever read or saw" before stating, "If I might venture to suggest any thing, it is that the interest rather falls off in the fifth." He furthermore calls the newspapers' attacks on Sir Fretful's work "ill-natured to be sure," despite the fact that Sir Fretful's work seems to warrant such censure.

Dangle's desire to criticize without offending is even more apparent when he watches the rehearsal of Puff's *The Spanish Armada* and asks polite questions about its flaws instead of jeering at them outright (as both Sneer and the audience do). Unlike many critics who make names for themselves by tearing down those of their contemporaries', Dangle enjoys his happy life as a man who reads plays in advance of their production and obtains the finest seats at the theatre.

Mrs. Dangle

Unlike her husband, Mrs. Dangle finds his devotion to the theatre childish and confounding. One of her first lines is, "Now that the plays are begun I shall have no peace"; it is this "lack of peace" caused by the constant influx of actors, managers, and playwrights into her home that Mrs. Dangle finds irritating. She scolds Dangle for taking no interest in contemporary politics and bemoans the fact that Dangle could, if he showed "the least spirit," have "been at the head of one of the Westminster associations." While amusing to the audience, Dangle's complete lack of interest in anything but the theater irritates his wife: "I believe," she tells him, "if the French were landed tomorrow, your first inquiry would be, whether they had brought a theatrical troop with them." Although Dangle tries to involve his wife in his theatrical pursuits, her attitude toward him is unchanging.

Early in the play, Mrs. Dangle complains that her house has become "the motley rendezvous of all the lackeys of literature" and "an absolute register-office for candidate actors, and poets without character." While Dangle enjoys having his patronage solicited by these "lackeys," Mrs. Dangle finds their presence unnerving. In act 1, scene ii, Sheridan offers the viewer an example of how Mrs. Dangle deals with these intrusions: after trying to understand both the Italian singer and his interpreter, she tells Dangle, "Here are two very civil gentlemen trying to make themselves understood, and I don't know which is the interpreter." Her frustration, however, does not deter Dangle from mingling with performers or abandoning his critical duties.

The Earl of Leicester

A favorite of Queen Elizabeth I, he appears in Puff's *The Spanish Armada* as the Commander-in-Chief of the military. In one of the tragedy's many unintentionally comic scenes, he leads the other characters in a prayer to Mars.

The Governor of Tilbury Fort

In Puff's *The Spanish Armada*, the Governor is the officer in command of Tilbury Fort, where the British troops are being mustered. His daughter, Tilburnia, falls in love with Don Ferolo Whiskerandos, who is being held prisoner at Tilbury Fort. When asked by his daughter to accept a "noble price" to free her lover, the Governor refuses.

Sir Christopher Hatton

Lord Chancellor at the time of the actual Spanish Armada crisis, he appears in Puff's tragedy based on the same. His niece eventually falls in love with Don Ferolo Whiskerandos.

Sir Fretful Plagiary

Sir Fretful is Dangle's friend and a playwright whose work is universally dismissed by all who read it as uninspired and whose personality is marked by tremendous insecurity. Many of the names in *The Critic* are comically indicative of the characters, and Sir Fretful Plagiary's fits him on two counts: he is immensely "fretful" when faced with criticism and often plagiarizes others' works (making his work a collection of "stray jokes" and "pilfered witticisms"). Before he arrives at Dangle's home, Dangle and Sneer discuss Sir Fretful's faults: he "allows no merit to any author but himself," he is "as envious as an old maid verging on the desperation of six-and-thirty," and he "is so covetous of popularity" that he would "rather be abused" in the press "than not mentioned at all." Of course, Sir Fretful finds none of these faults in himself, convinced as he is of his own genius. (He is so convinced, in fact, that he does not send his latest work to the Drury Lane Theatre for fear that Sheridan himself will steal his work!)

Sir Fretful's greatest fault, however, is his tendency to solicit others to give "free" and honest opinions of his work, only to reject any negative criticism with "petulant arrogance." Sir Fretful's conversation with Dangle and Sneer demonstrates this habit. When Sneer, for example, tells him that his play "wants incident," Sir Fretful remarks that "the incidents are too crowded"; when Dangle says that the "interest rather falls off" in the fifth act, Sir Fretful counters with, "Rises; I believe you mean, Sir." Sir Fretful further shows his inability to take any criticism when he asks Dangle and Sneer to recall what a newspaper said of him; despite Sir Fretful's laughter, he is obviously upset at having his work compared to "a bad tavern's worst wine."

Mr. Puff

A playwright and composer of advertisements, Puff is a friend of Dangle. His historical tragedy, *The Spanish Armada*, is rehearsed in acts 2 and 3. Puff calls himself a "Practitioner in Pangeyric" or "a Professor of the Art of Puffing": a man whose ability to "puff up" ordinary language earns him a living. Puff composes false reviews for plays in order to boost ticket sales, teaches auctioneers how to use inflated language to make their wares more alluring to bidders, and even pretends to be a widow (or other charity case) in the newspaper to solicit assistance from kind (yet gullible) readers. ("I supported myself two years entirely by my misfortunes,'' he explains.) Puff has various methods of ''puffing,'' such as ''The Puff Direct'' (in which he invents a positive review for a play the day before its premiere) or ''The Puff Collusive'' (in which he writes a piece denouncing a book or poem as too licentious or scandal mongering, thereby inciting the public to buy it immediately). At present, Puff has turned to the theatre, where he can indulge his ''talent for fiction and embellishment.''

During the rehearsal of his play, Puff exhibits all the nervous intensity one would expect from a director. Part of the humor of the rehearsal scenes lies in the way that Puff (like Sir Fretful in act 1, scene i) defends himself against every possible negative criticism of his play made by Dangle and Sneer. For example, after Sneer recognizes a line of Shakespeare's *Othello* in Puff's play, Puff explains, ''That's of no consequnce—all that can be said is, that two people happened to hit on the same thought. His shameless brand of self-defense is demonstrated throughout the play.

Sir Walter Raleigh

A soldier, explorer, poet and sometime favorite of Queen Elizabeth I, he appears in Puff's tragedy as a companion of Sir Christopher Hatton. Like Hatton's niece, Raleigh's niece also falls in love with Don Ferolo Whiskerandos.

Signor Pasticcio Ritornello

Signor Ritornello possesses one of the many ''outlandish throats'' found in the opera. He visits Dangle's home with his two nieces in order to secure Dangle's patronage. Unfortunately, he only speaks Italian and brings a French translator with him; when he tries to converse with Mr. and Mrs. Dangle, the result is comic cross-communication.

Mr. Sneer

One of Dangle's friends and fellow-critics, Sneer (as his name blatantly suggests) is a man always finding fault in those around him. His first conversation with Dangle reveals Sneer's assumptions about the theatre: feeling that the stage could be a ''school of morality,'' Sneer complains that ''people seem to go there principally for their entertainment!'' When Dangle complains of how comedies have been purged of all ''double entendre'' and ''smart innuendo,'' Sneer responds with a metaphor that reflects his judgmental mind and style of speech:

Our prudery in this respect is just on a par with the artificial bashfulness of a courtezan, who encreases

the blush upon her cheek in an exact proportion to the diminution of her modesty.

Throughout the play, Sneer makes a number of similar remarks, taking swipes at authors, actors, and newspapers. While Dangle is genial and indulgent, Sneer is bitter and unforgiving.

Sneer's chief role in *The Critic* is to offer a running commentary on Puff's *The Spanish Armada* when it is rehearsed in acts 2 and 3. His sarcastic heckling adds to the humor of Puff's unintentionally hilarious play and invites the audience to laugh at Puff's awful tragedy. For example, after Dangle praises Tilburnia's awful-sounding verse with, ''O!—'tis too much,'' Sneer remarks, ''Oh!—it is indeed''; similarly, when Puff explains that his characters must be allowed ''to hear and see a number of things'' not presented on stage, Sneer mockingly pretends to agree with him and states, ''Yes—a kind of poetical second-sight!'' Sneer makes comments like these throughout Puff's rehearsal; as Puff is wholly ''inflated'' with the false ideas of his own talents, Sneer serves as a means by which Sheridan mocks all writers of Puff's ilk, who find their own work beyond reproach.

Tilburnia

In Puff's *The Spanish Armada,* the daughter of the Governor of Tilbury Fort, who falls in love with Don Ferolo Whiskerandos. Never without Nora, her confidant, Tilburnia is a parody of the tragic heroine, torn between love and duty. She eventually goes mad after Don Whiskerandos's death and throws herself into the sea.

Don Ferolo Whiskerandos

In Puff's *The Spanish Armada,* the son of the Spanish admiral who is being held prisoner at Tilbury Fort. He is killed in a duel over Tilburnia. He is meant by Sheridan to be viewed as a parody of the exotic, alluring, and dashing foreign lover.

THEMES

Criticism

Naturally, *The Critic* explores the issue of criticism, specifically the different ways that

TOPICS FOR FURTHER STUDY

- Review the ideas set forth in Aristotle's *Poetics* about the necessary components of a tragedy and apply these ideas to a tragic work, such as *Oedipus the King* or Puff's *The Spanish Armada*.

- In 1776, Sheridan purchased an interest in the Drury Lane Theatre from David Garrick, one of the most highly praised actors of his day. Research the history of the Drury Lane Theatre and how it contributed to eighteenth-century drama as a whole.

- Puff's *The Spanish Armada* is set during the reign of Queen Elizabeth I but had echoes for Sheridan's audience of a possible contemporary crisis. To what degree did Sheridan's audiences feel the threat of a foreign invasion?

- At the end of Puff's play, Sheridan offers a number of stage directions that broadly outline what the audience sees during the climactic battle scene. How would you stage this battle and the "procession of rivers?" How would you make the scene as silly as the rest of *The Spanish Armada*?

- Compose a short script in which you parody the conventions of a cinematic form, like Sheridan does with tragedy. Consider science fiction, western, or detective films as possible subjects.

- Compose three different reviews of *The Spanish Armada*: one by Dangle, one by Sneer, and one by Puff himself. Be sure that each review accounts for its author's personality and aesthetics.

---

playwrights respond to critiques of their work. Sir Fretful Plagiary is the epitome of one who attempts to seem gracious and able to withstand any critical judgment of his plays; when faced with even the smallest quibble, however, his "fretful" nature becomes apparent. For example, Sir Fretful tells Dangle and Sneer that he is "never so well pleased as when a judicious critic points out any defect" in his work to him and that Sneer "can't oblige [him] more" than he would by offering his opinions. However, when Sneer tells him that the "events" in his latest play are "too few," Sir Fretful responds that the events are "too crowded"; when told by Dangle that the play's "interest rather falls off" at the end, Sir Fretful counters with, "Rises; I believe you mean, Sir." When Dangle's wife (who only defends Sir Fretful because "everybody else abuses him") states that she "did not see a fault in any part of the play from beginning to end," Sir Fretful exclaims, "Upon my soul the women are the best judges after all!" Of course, "best" in this context means "most flattering."

Unlike Sir Fretful, Puff does not become upset when faced with complaints about his play, *The Spanish Armada*. Instead, he offers what he finds to be logical explanations for every incident and line, however contrived or ridiculous. For example, when Sneer asks Puff how Hatton could never before have asked Raleigh about their preparations for war, Puff responds, "What, before the Play began? how the plague could he?" Similarly, when Dangle observes that the Beefeater's soliloquy of four lines is "very short," Puff explains, "Yes—but it would have been a great deal longer if he had not been observed."

Convinced of his own skill as a playwright, Puff becomes irritated when he learns of the cuts in the script made by the actors: although he initially calls them "very good judges" of what should be deleted, he later complains that they have cut "one of the finest and most laboured" scenes of his play. Although he lets the cuts remain, he vows to "print it every word," assured that his readers (if not his audience) will appreciate his talents.

Publicity and Advertising

While Puff is the play's primary playwright, Sheridan also uses him to satirize the means by which the skills of a playwright are found in the world outside of the theater, specifically in the world of advertising. Puff explains that he ''does as much business in that way as any six of the fraternity in town'' and that it is his talent for ''puffing'' up language to extraordinary heights that helps Puff make a living from the press. For example, Puff has taught advertisers to employ ''panegyrical superlatives'' to create appealing images of their products and capture consumers' interest; he has also used his talent for ''puffing'' to create false newspaper advertisements in which he pretended to be bankrupt, an invalid, and a widower in ordere to live upon the charity of credulous readers.

Puff's swindles are strikingly in tune with some modern advertising practices. For example, Puff uses the press to create false (and, of course, glowing) reviews of the work of his friends. A similar device was seen in 2001 when Sony Pictures came under fire for inventing positive critical reviews for its film *The Animal;* that same year, the company was criticized again for having employees pose, in television commercials, as theatergoers offering great reviews of *The Patriot.* Puff also composes stories wherein he sneaks in advertisements that seem glaringly out of place: for example, he recites a story he wrote about George Bon-Mot ''sauntering down St. James's-street,'' where he met Lady Mary Myrtle and said:

> I just saw a picture of you, in a new publication called THE CAMP MAGAZINE, which, bye the bye, is a devilish clever thing,—and is sold at No. 3, on the right-hand of the way, two doors from the printing-office, the corner of Ivy-lane, Paternoster-row, price only one shilling!

This is remarkably reminiscent of the advertising practice known as ''product placement,'' in which corporations pay to have characters in films use their clearly marked products. Many corporations selling things such as cars, food, and clothing use product placement as a means of exposing their products to a captive audience.

Finally, Puff also reflects a twentieth-century trend among advertisers when he describes his technique ''The Puff Collusive,'' in which he acts ''in the guise of determined hostility'' to presumably warn the public about the moral dangers of a new work of art (in the case of his example, a poem): ''Here you see the two strongest inducements are held forth;—First, that nobody ought to read it;—and secondly, that everybody buys it.'' When one considers the furor over certain books (such as *The*

Catcher in the Rye or *The Satanic Verses*), television shows (such as *N. Y. P. D. Blue* or *South Park*), or albums by artists as different as Elvis Presley and Eminem, one sees just how prescient Sheridan was in his creation of Puff and all his ''various sorts'' of ''Puffing.''

STYLE

Setting

The Critic takes place in two locations: Dangle's house and the theater where Puff's play is rehearsed; each setting reflects the values and assumptions of its principal character.

Dangle's house is a place where actors, singers, writers, and other ''lackeys of literature'' gather to solicit his approval and patronage. Dangle is a self-professed lover of the theater and his home reflects this; for while there, he does not engage in any conversation that is not about the theater. When reading the newspapers, for example, he dismisses the threat of a possible war in order to read about ''theatrical politics.'' In fact, Dangle's love of theater is so great and so ingrained in him that he often ''performs'' in his drawing room as if he were on stage. He finds Sir Fretful's latest play atrocious yet calls it ''finished and most admirable'' once he hears Fretful entering the room. Similarly, when Mrs. Dangle attempts to tell Sir Fretful that her husband and Sneer were just laughing at Sir Fretful's play, Dangle hides the truth from Fretful with the excuse, ''My friend Sneer was rallying just now . . . Sneer will jest.'' Dangle and Sneer's greatest performance occurs when they invent a series of negative reviews for Sir Fretful's work and pretend that they have read them in the newspapers. Because Sir Fretful is Dangle's friend, Dangle tries not to offend him; it is only through Dangle's elaborate and comic performance with Sneer that he can reveal what he really thinks about the author. As a man devoted to the theater, Dangle knows a great deal about acting on and off the stage.

Puff is, as he boldly asserts, a ''Professor of the Art of Puffing,'' and the theater where he rehearses his tragedy contains a multitude of ''puffed up'' actors and effects that revolve around Puff's preposterous script. At the theatre, Puff is invincible: he dismisses any remark about his play, however sugarcoated, and is always confident of his authorial and directorial powers. Puff's theatrical triumph occurs at the end of the play when his cast reenacts the defeat of the Spanish Armada: this hodgepodge of special effects, music, and actors portraying "The procession of all the English rivers and their tributaries" is laughable, rather than spellbinding, due to its highly "puffed" staging. Sheridan's point is that these "puffy" plays are a staple of British theater; by setting most of *The Critic* in a theater, Sheridan calls attention to his audience's taste—or the lack of it.

The Prologue

Almost all eighteenth-century plays featured prologues, recited on their opening nights by notable celebrities or writers and later reprinted in newspapers. As Mary E. Knapp points out in her 1961 study, *Prologues and Epilogues of the Eighteenth Century,* one purpose of the prologue was to "cajole the audience into a pleasant frame of mind so that they would be in a friendly mood before the curtain was drawn up." Another important function a prologue served was to point out the upcoming play's themes so that the audience could more readily identify them as the drama unfolded. The prologue to *The Critic* (written by Richard Fitzpatrick, a member of Parliament and lover of the theatre) is a history in miniature of the contemporary London stage and the degree to which it has decayed. Fitzpatrick begins by noting that "The Sister Muses"—tragedy and comedy—have, like earthly rulers, been misled by "evil counselors." Tragedy has fallen, since the time of John Dryden (1631–1700), into a series of plays featuring only ranting and raving characters who "bellow" so loudly that they no longer resemble real people. Comedy likewise has suffered by a preponderance of salacious jokes that cause "female modesty" to become "abash'd."

Fitzgerald, however, surprises the audience by explaining that the cures of these theatrical illnesses are sometimes worse than the diseases. Tragedy is no longer so histrionic, but "Now insipidy succeeds bombast." Comedy has been cleansed of inappropriate jokes, but now "the purest morals" are "undefil'd by wit." Fitzgerald's goal here is to communicate to his audience what he sees as the faults of his own era's theater—faults that will be exposed and exaggerated throughout *The Critic.* Fitzgerald also assists Sheridan's cause by enlisting the audience as the playwright's partners in satire,

telling them that *The Critic* will "brave the critick's rage," enrage "brother bards," and even "Newspapers themselves defy." If *The Critic* is to succeed as a comedy, its "chief dependence" must be the "alliance" of the audience, whose support will help Sheridan deflect the outcry he is sure will come his way as a result of his satire.

HISTORICAL CONTEXT

The Enlightenment

The Enlightenment and The Age of Reason are alternate names used by historians and critics to identify the eighteenth century. While the eighteenth century technically, of course, began in 1700, the term "eighteenth century" when used by literary critics has come to mean the years falling between the Restoration of Charles II in 1660 and the publication of Wordsworth and Coleridge's *Lyrical Ballads* (the book that sparked English romanticism) in 1798. In short, the eighteenth century was a period marked by incredible enthusiasm for science, history, and literature that the English had not enjoyed since the end of the Renaissance a century earlier.

The reasons for this sudden renewal of interest in the arts and sciences are complex but can be roughly understood by considering the terrible chaos that the nation had just endured and barely survived. The seventeenth century was marked by a civil war in which King Charles I and his army of loyalist "Cavaliers" fought with an army raised by the Puritan members of Parliament, who felt that Charles had grown too corrupt, too powerful, and too belligerent. Eventually, the Puritans defeated their Royalist opponents; after a trial by his enemies in which he could never have prevailed, Charles I was beheaded in 1649. The monarchy was—so the Puritans believed—abolished, and Oliver Cromwell, the military genius and commander of the Puritan forces, became the nation's ruler. (He was called "Lord Protector.") After Cromwell's death in 1658, his son, Richard, assumed the Lord Protectorship, continuing this historical period, known as the Interregnum, without a king. The citizens of England, however, found their new rulers worse than the monarch they had replaced; after a number of secret missions, negotiations, and meetings, the son of

COMPARE
&
CONTRAST

- **1700s:** Adam Smith's groundbreaking treatise on economics, *An Inquiry into the Nature and Causes of the Wealth of Nations,* is published in 1776. The book outlines the *laissez-faire* notion of economics that holds that the government should not interfere in business or trade.

  Today: Great Britain and the United States have, to some extent, adopted Smith's ideas, although attempts by the U.S. government to break up the Microsoft corporation sparked many debates about the role of the government in commercial affairs.

- **1700s:** Alexander Pope and Samuel Johnson's lengthy poems and essays (such as Pope's 1711 work *An Essay on Criticism* and Johnson's 1765 *Preface to Shakespeare*) are widely read; in their work, each writer offers his notions of what constitutes quality drama and poetry.

  Today: Literary criticism has somewhat given way to literary theory, a discipline that examines not only the workings of literary pieces but the ways in which these pieces are the products of economic struggles and gender identity.

- **1700s:** Satire dominates literary taste: by the time of *The Critic*'s premiere in 1779, works such as John Wilmot Rochester's ''A Satyr against Mankind'' (1679), Jonathan Swift's *Gulliver's Travels* (1726), John Gay's *The Beggar's Opera* (1728), Alexander Pope's *The Dunciad* (1729), and Laurence Sterne's *Tristam Shandy* (1767) prove themselves popular with the reading public.

  Today: Satire still flourishes in all genres: works such as Evelyn Waugh's *A Handful of Dust* (1937), Joseph Heller's *Catch-22* (1961), Kurt Vonnegut's *Slaughterhouse Five* (1969), and David Rabe's *Hurlyburly* (1984) are known for their satire and dark humor, much like that found in the work of Swift and Gay.

Charles I was brought out of hiding (from Scotland) to a tremendously warm welcome in London. Charles II was crowned in 1660, when the monarchy was restored.

This terrible war, coupled with a visitation of bubonic plague in 1665 and the Great Fire of London in 1666, stood in the English mind as horrible examples of the fury wrought both by man and nature. Enlightenment thinkers, therefore, sought to better understand both politics and science in an effort to ensure that similar events would never again occur. In 1662, the Royal Society (a government-funded organization of scientists working together and sharing information) was created; important books from this period include the first edition of the *Encyclopedia Britannica* (1768), Goldsmith's *History of the Earth and Animated Nature* (1774), Burke's *Reflections of the Revolution in France* (1760), Johnson's *Dictionary of the English Language* (1775), and Gibbon's *The Decline and Fall of the Roman Empire* (1776).

The first great dramatist of the age was John Dryden (1631–1700), whose comedy *Marriage á la Mode* (1673) and tragedy *All for Love* (1677) were immensely popular and reveal what would become the public's taste in both modes. Many eighteenth-century plays are ''comedies of manners'': plays that feature domestic plots, quick dialogue, and an ironic examination of the behaviors (or ''manners'') of the upper class. Examples of this genre include Sir George Etherege's *She Wou'd if She Cou'd* (1688), William Wycherley's *The Country Wife* (1675), William Congreve's *The Way of the World* (1700), and Sheridan's own *The School for Scandal* (1777), which cemented his fame as a comic playwright. Another popular comic form was the dramatic burlesque, in which theatrical conventions and means of productions became the subjects of satire: the Duke of Buckingham's *The Rehearsal* (1671), John Gay's *The Beggar's Opera* (1728), Fielding's *The Tragedy of Tragedies* (1731), and the famed actor David Garrick's *A Peep Behind the Curtain* (1767) are examples of this form. *The*

Critic is another example of dramatic burlesque, in which the audience laughs at actors playing the roles of actors struggling with their work. By the end of the century, however, drama fell into disfavor while the novel simultaneously exploded on the literary scene.

CRITICAL OVERVIEW

While modern critics generally applaud Sheridan's work and a modern reader may find *The Critic* a very amusing yet tame burlesque, its first production in 1779 caused a minor controversy in the London press. The play's unnamed first reviewer (in a review collected in *Sheridan: Comedies* (1986) edited by Peter Davison) admired the first act's wit and satire but complained that the second and third were "heavy and tiresome." He also scolded Sheridan for not attempting the "least originality" and called the play "an act of angry retaliation" rather than "a dramatic satire, founded on general principles." This same reviewer even wrote that Sheridan's satire on false advertisements for charity "may deprive some worthy objects of that relief which their distresses might otherwise receive from the benevolent." (He further complained that Puff and Sneer both mention the word "God" onstage "without censure.") Other eighteenth-century reviews were equally dismissive: in 1783, another unnamed reviewer (also collected in *Sheridan: Comedies*) called *The Critic* "the offspring of a pen that had in vain attempted to write a tragedy" and said that Sheridan "felt a malicious pleasure in decrying a species of composition which has been deemed superior" to Sheridan's own. Finally, the playwright Charles Dibdin, writing in his 1788 collection, *The Musical Tour of Mr. Dibdin,* challenged Sheridan to "write a tragedy so as to steer clear of his own lash"—something he felt Sheridan would find an impossible task.

Audiences, however, loved the play, which has become a favorite of actors, producers, and even critics since its premiere. Many twentieth-century readers echo the sentiments of Lord Byron as quoted in James Morwood's *The Life and Works of Richard Brinsley Sheridan,* who called it the "best farce" he had ever seen. In his 1970 study "Sheridan: The Last of the Great Theatrical Satirists," Samuel L. Macey discusses the twilight of dramatic burlesque in the eighteenth century: while the "restrictions imposed by the temper of the times" stifled some writers' will to satire, Macey praises Sheridan for allowing theatrical satire to exit the Enlightenment stage "with a bang rather than a whimper." In Philip K. Jason's 1974 essay, "A Twentieth Century Response to *The Critic*," he compares Sheridan's play to what he sees as its modern counterpart: Pirandello's *Six Characters in Search of an Author.* Like Macey, he praises how Sheridan balances the "multiple perspectives" that accompany any play while consciously calling attention to the actors within it performing their roles.

Some modern critics, however, praise Sheridan's craft while discounting his talents as a true artist. In his introductory essay to the Modern Library's *Eighteenth Century Plays* (1952), Ricardo Quintana argues that the work of Sheridan and his three chief contemporaries (Goldsmith, Fielding, and Gay) have "a depth generally lacking elsewhere" in Restoration drama. However, Quintana further remarks that Sheridan's "spectacular career" can "blind us to the fact that his wit and his remarkable sense of theater are not balanced by the insight and intuition of drama at its greatest." Similarly, in his book *Sheridan's Comedies: Their Contexts and Achievements* (1977), Mark S. Auburn calls *The Critic* "the most complete satiric play about the theater yet created" yet not up to the artistic level of Sheridan's previous (and more widely known) play, *The School for Scandal*:

> Beside the greater comedy, *The Critic* seems a remnant of his youth, a brilliant utilization of his experiences as a practical dramatist perhaps, but more nearly the product of an exuberance and an adolescent cynicism which the perfection of *The School for Scandal* seems to deny.

Of course, critical evaluations are often as varied as the opinions of Puff and Sneer. In his 1997 work *A Traitor's Kiss: The Life of Richard Brinsley Sheridan,* Sheridan's most recent biographer and critic, Fintan O'Toole, writes that *The Critic* allowed Sheridan to vent all the anxieties and frustrations he had amassed during his time as the manager of the Drury Lane Theatre: "Into it he poured all the vexations of the previous season, alchemically transformed into pure hilarity." O'Toole notes that of the twelve most often staged plays in England between 1776 and 1800, four were by Shakespeare and two (*The Duenna* and *The School for Scandal*) were by Sheridan. "With *The Critic* holding its place as one of the most frequently performed afterpieces," O'Toole concludes, "Sheridan the playwright continued to occupy a central place in

The Drury Lane Theatre in London, England

British cultural life.'' The fact that *The Critic* is still performed across North America and Europe attests to the fact that Sheridan still occupies, if not a central, at least a prominent place in twentieth-century theater.

CRITICISM

Daniel Moran

Moran is a secondary school teacher of English and American literature. In this essay, he examines the ways in which Sheridan's play parodies a number of tragic conventions.

In 1763, sixteen years before the premiere of *The Critic*, James Boswell co-authored a pamphlet in which he jeered at David Mallet's *Elvira,* a tragedy acted at the Drury Lane Theatre. Confessing to his friend Samuel Johnson that he felt somewhat guilty about the pamphlet, since he himself could not write a tragedy ''near so good,'' Boswell received another impromptu lesson from his mentor that found its way into *The Life of Samuel Johnson.*

WHAT DO I READ NEXT?

- Shakespeare's *A Midsummer Night's Dream* (1600) features a band of actors who rehearse their tragedy, *The Most Lamentable Comedy and Most Cruel Death of Pyramus and Thisby,* with hilarious results. Act 5 of *A Midsummer Night's Dream* features the play's performance.

- Like *The Critic,* Michael Frayn's farce *Noises Off* (1982) consists of rehearsals for a play where nothing happens as it should. Like *A Midsummer Night's Dream, Noises Off* ends with the audience watching the play they just saw being rehearsed.

- *The Rivals* (1775), Sheridan's first play, is a comedy concerning the thwarted (but eventually reconciled) love between Captain Absolute and Lydia Languish. The play is famous for the character of Mrs. Malaprop, Lydia's aunt who makes a number of ''malapropisms,'' humorous linguistic errors (''As headstrong as an allegory on the banks of the Nile'').

- Sheridan's *The School for Scandal* (1777), considered by many to be his masterpiece, follows the drawing room adventures of Lady Sneerwell and her group of gossips. Critics routinely praise the play as the perfect ''comedy of manners.''

- The American playwright David Mamet's *A Life in the Theater* (1977) concerns two actors—one young, one old—who discuss, in a series of vignettes, their work as actors and their struggles with their craft.

- The Renaissance team of Francis Beaumont and John Fetcher's *The Night of the Burning Pestle* (1613), like Puff's *The Spanish Armada,* features a number of dramatic conventions exploited for their comic potential.

- Henry Fielding's *The Tragedy of Tragedies* (1731), like *The Critic,* offers a mock tragedy through which Fielding parodies and satirizes specific authors and writers of his age. The printed edition of the play contains extensive footnotes by Fielding that identify his allusions and satirical targets.

- John Gay's *The Beggar's Opera* (1728) broke a number of theatrical conventions, both in its subject matter and political overtones. It was one of the most popular plays of the eighteenth century and inspired Bertolt Brecht and Kurt Weill's *The Threepenny Opera* in 1928.

- Tom Stoppard's *Rosencrantz and Guildenstern Are Dead* (1967) offers its reader a glimpse of Shakespeare's *Hamlet* through the eyes of two of its minor characters. Like Sheridan, Stoppard delights in exploring the nature of theater and its conventions.

Why no, Sir; this is not just reasoning. You *may* abuse a tragedy, though you cannot write one. You may scold a carpenter who has made you a bad table, though you cannot make a table. It is not your trade to make tables.

Boswell's conscience may have been bothering him because of a trend of thought sometimes found among those faced with the critical evaluation of tragedy: the genre is so revered and taken so seriously that mocking it is sometimes regarded as aesthetically sacrilegious, like finding fault with Michelangelo's *Pieta.* Comedy never tries to elicit the ''pity or terror'' (in Aristotelian terms) of trag-edy, and its faults are therefore regarded as less damaging to the work as a whole. Along these same lines, the benchmark for a quality tragedy is often a higher one than comedy, since laughter is suppos-edly easier to elicit than catharsis. This is why the most improbable plot devices in comedies are ac-cepted as part of the game, whereas the same improbabilities in tragedies are either glossed over or dismissed as unimportant in terms of the work's total effect on a viewer. In Shakespeare's *Twelfth Night,* for example, Viola disguises herself as a man and in doing so becomes *completely indistinguish-*

“ THE SPANISH ARMADA CAN BE READ AS A CATALOGUE OF THEATRICAL CONVENTIONS, EACH OF WHICH IS HILARIOUSLY PRESENTED BUT EACH OF WHICH ALSO PROVOKES A READER INTO RECALLING WHERE SIMILAR DEVICES OCCUR IN OTHER, ‘REAL’ TRAGEDIES.”

able from her twin brother—so much so that she excites the mourning Olivia into thunderous passion and never once causes her new master, Orsino, to question her gender. No viewer of this play would rail against this seemingly impossible device, yet if the same kind of incident occurred in *King Lear,* for example, audiences would have a much more difficult time ‘‘believing’’ it (to the extent that they suspend their disbelief and accept the action of any play as ‘‘real’’). Yet even the greatest tragedies have a number of events in them that are wholly implausible yet infrequently questioned by awestruck viewers and readers. As Puff explains to Dangle and Sneer, ‘‘a play is not to show occurrences that happen every day, but things just so strange, that tho’ they never *did,* they *might* happen.’’ That ‘‘might’’ is where plots become farcical (in the case of comedy) or awkward (in the case of tragedy).

Sheridan, of course, knew all of this from his years spent reading, attending, writing, and managing plays, and it is this central idea—that tragedies belong to a genre so exulted that anyone criticizing their creators (like Boswell) can actually feel guilty— that fuels *The Critic.* Sheridan made Puff’s *The Spanish Armada* a tragedy instead of a comedy because he knew that the humor would arise in direct proportion to the earnestness and seriousness of its performance. Had he made Puff’s play a comedy, everyone in the audience would be laughing *with* the characters rather than *at* them, and making his audience laugh at writers like Puff is crucial to Sheridan’s vision. Once the members of Sheridan’s audience start laughing at the

portentousness of *Puff’s* tragedy, however, they can begin to consider just how silly (and worthy of any number of pamphlets) the plots and conventions of even the greatest tragedies can be. As a viewer watches *The Critic,* therefore, he or she is invited to share in Sheridan’s laughter at tragic conventions and, ultimately, better appreciate those playwrights who are able to deal with these conventions in a way less laughable than Puff. ‘‘I improve upon established modes,’’ Puff boasts, and a careful reading of *The Spanish Armada* reveals Sheridan’s joy in parodying the established mode of tragedy and its conventions. Unlike Boswell, Sheridan never feels the slightest compunctions about mocking the genre or its less-than-talented disciples.

The Spanish Armada can be read as a catalogue of theatrical conventions, each of which is hilariously presented but each of which also provokes a reader into recalling where similar devices occur in other, ‘‘real’’ tragedies. The differences are merely ones of degree. For example, the opening scene of Puff’s play features two sentinels asleep at their post. When Sneer remarks that this is odd, considering the ‘‘alarming crisis’’ of a possible Spanish attack, Puff explains that the guards *must* be asleep, for Raleigh and Hatton would not speak if they knew the guards were watching them. This is a joke for the audience, but consider the death of Juliet in Shakespeare’s *Romeo and Juliet:* after she awakens from her drugged sleep in the Capulet tomb and learns that Romeo is dead, Friar Lawrence advises her to ‘‘Come, come away’’ and live among ‘‘a sisterhood of holy nuns.’’ When Juliet refuses, Friar Lawrence leaves the tomb, ostensibly because ‘‘the watch is coming’’ but really because had he stayed, Juliet would have been denied her opportunity to commit suicide. Moments later, the conveniently absent Friar returns with the lovers’ parents and confesses his role in their attempted elopement. Like Puff’s sleeping sentinels, Shakespeare’s Friar had to engage in an inexplicable action for the sake of dramatic expediency. This is similar to Hamlet’s dragging the body of Polonius into ‘‘the neighbor room’’ after he kills him; Hamlet may be doing so to spare his mother the horrible sight, but Shakespeare also knew that the actor playing Polonius had to get off the stage and having the actor jump up and exit after such an intense scene might break the spell of the moment.

Another theatrical convention skewered by Sheridan is the manner in which many playwrights struggle with the problem of exposition. After Hatton asks Raleigh why there is a ‘‘general muster’’ and "throng of chiefs" at Tilbury (although he plainly knows the answer), Dangle rightly asks Puff why, if Hatton "*knows* all this," Raleigh continues telling it to him; Puff explains that Hatton and Raleigh speak for the audience's sake. Information necessary to the plot is therefore presented but in such a way that its very presentation is laughably awkward. Jane Austen recognized the same problem and similarly parodied it in a play she wrote as a young girl, collected in her book *Love and Friendship:*

> Pistoletta: Pray papa how far is it to London?
>
> Popgun: My Girl, my Darling, my favourite of all my children, who art the picture of thy poor mother who died two months ago, with whom I am going to town to marry to Strephon, and to whom I mean to bequeath my whole Estate, it wants seven miles.

All playwrights face this challenge and meet it with varying degrees of success: to return to Shakespeare, consider the opening of *King Lear,* in which Shakespeare masterfully opens the play with the meeting where Lear divides his kingdom while simultaneously revealing his attitudes toward his daughters. Conversely, consider the opening of *Hamlet,* where Marcellus asks Horatio, who has returned to Denmark only two months ago, why Denmark is preparing "implements of war" in "sweaty haste." Why Marcellus, a royal guard, would not know anything about this and need to ask a civilian student is not explained, or even considered by many viewers. Even Shakespeare nods.

Once the exposition is out of the way, a playwright still faces the problem of information: a character needs to learn some fact or secret but must learn it in such a way that seems dramatically plausible. Eavesdropping, therefore, is the dramatist's friend; consider the number of plays in which a character learns something he or she is not supposed to by virtue of a good hiding place. In *Othello,* for example, the title character conceals himself so well that he can overhear Iago speak to Cassio of Bianca yet remain wholly unnoticed by Cassio, who speaks as freely as if he and Iago were on a deserted island. Similarly, *Hamlet* abounds in overheard conversations: Polonius and Claudius listen to Hamlet's "Get thee to a nunnery" tirade against Ophelia, and Polonius is killed while hiding behind a tapestry in Gertrude's room. As Puff proclaims, "If people who want to listen, or overhear, were not always conniv'd at in a Tragedy, there would be no carrying on any plot in the world." Sheridan knew this to be true: his own *The School for Scandal* relies heavily on eavesdropping to propel its plot. Here, however,

he takes great delight in laying bare the clumsy machinations of those who attempt to (in Hamlet's words) "hold a mirror up to nature" but fail.

The list of conventions thus parodied continues. Tilburnia's first speech mocks overdone pseudo-poetic language: she takes twenty lines to say, "It is morning and I am unhappy." The tendency for playwrights to imbue their characters with (in Puff's words) the ability "to hear and see a number of things that are not" is mocked by Tilburnia's description of the approaching armada; again, this is a ludicrous moment in Puff's play, but anyone who rereads Gertrude's description of Ophelia's death in *Hamlet* is faced with the same problem: from where did Gertrude get this information, and why did the person telling it not attempt to *rescue* Ophelia as she drowned? The playwright's necessary manipulation of props is mocked when Don Whiskerandos and the Beefeater happen to discover two swords dropped by Hatton and Raleigh; while humorous here, the same kind of manipulation occurs at the end of *Hamlet* when Hamlet and Laertes unknowingly switch swords during their final duel, thus allowing Shakespeare to kill them both with the same poisoned tip. Another tragic convention—madness—is often used by playwrights to solicit the pathos of the audience; such "mad scenes," however, often feature a character speaking in a way that cleverly reveals significant aspects of their personalities in a way that seems unlike "real" madness. (Lady Macbeth, for example, manifests her madness in sleepwalking while attempting to symbolically wash her hands of the guilt that plagues her.) This convention is ridiculed by Sheridan when he makes the mad Tilburnia babble such nonsense as:

> Is this a grasshopper!—Ha! no, it is my Whiskerandos—you shall not keep him—I know you have him in your pocket—An oyster may be cross'd in love!—Who says A whale's a bird?—

The more tragedies one has seen, the funnier Puff's play becomes. It is important to remember, however, that Sheridan does not do all this in an effort to mock the genre of tragedy as a whole; rather, he expresses his amusement with those writers who struggle with these conventions when composing their work and can only meet these challenges in the most dramatically clumsy ways. As a playwright himself, Sheridan knew of these struggles firsthand, and it is by presenting *The Spanish Armada,* a play where all of these struggles prove too great for Puff, that Sheridan invites his audience both to laugh at those who cannot meet the challenges of composition and to applaud those (like himself) who do. Puff's play, therefore, is a guide to Sheridan's aesthetics, albeit a guide that shows its user what *not* to do rather than what he or she should do. Great skill is needed to depict the work of an unskillful playwright, and, by examining the tragic conventions parodied in *The Spanish Armada,* a viewer can better appreciate the skills of tragedians who handle these conventions more adroitly than Puff.

Source: Daniel Moran, Critical Essay on *The Critic,* in *Drama for Students,* The Gale Group, 2002.

Mark S. Auburn

In the following essay excerpt, the author discusses the history of Sheridan's The Critic *and evaluates its status as "perhaps the most complete play about the theatre ever written."*

The Critic, which was first presented on 30 October 1779, is perhaps the most complete play about the theater ever written. It was both occasional entertainment and burlesque, topically oriented and aimed at posterity, a local development and an echo of an eternal form. From Aristophanes's *The Acharnians* to Shakespeare's "Pyramus and Thisbe," to Fletcher's *Knight of the Burning Pestle,* to Buckingham's *Rehearsal,* to Fielding's *Tragedy of Tragedies* or *Pasquin,* the comic dramatic urge at self-reflection has surfaced brilliantly. But the examples from the 1770s which influenced Sheridan failed to achieve lasting fame largely because they are too local, too tied to contemporary situations and personalities; only Garrick's *A Peep behind the Curtain* approaches the proper balance between timeliness and timelessness, yet it lacks the wit, satire, and brilliance to endure. What is surprising about *The Critic,* a greater play which adopted a similar form, is that it too is very local.

Consider the raw materials of *The Critic*: an absurd, thin-skinned playwright, a silly romantic tragedy on the subject of the Spanish Armada, a theatrical entrepreneur entranced not with literary worth but dramatic stage effects, newspapers filled with gossip and concealed advertisements, critical debates about the uses and meaning of dramatic entertainment, a theatrical world populated by actors who are selfish and managers who themselves are playwrights. Stripped of contemporary associations, these subjects will be of interest as long as artistic impulses are channeled through the medium of the stage; but in Sheridan's play, each has purely local satiric applications which to a great extent determined the original success of *The Critic,* but

which, it seems, would also prevent lasting fame. Both playwrights were recognized as specific individuals; the subject of Puff's tragedy held immense contemporary concern; and the critical themes were the stuff of the day.

Parsons, who portrayed Sir Fretful Plagiary, openly imitated the dress and mannerisms of Richard Cumberland, author of *The West Indian* and more recently *The Battle of Hastings,* a historical tragedy produced by Sheridan at Drury Lane 24 January 1778. On 20 March 1779 Cumberland had given a prelude to his musical piece, *Calypso,* for its Covent Garden production: that prelude was commonly known as *The Critic.* No one failed to recognize Parson's impersonation, and the *Lady's Magazine* for October 1779 went so far as to say that Sir Fretful Plagiary "exhibits one of the most harsh and severe caricatures that have been attempted since the days of Aristophanes, of which a celebrated sentimental writer is evidently the object: a great part of what is said by his representative being literally taken from his usual conversation, but with pointed and keen additions." Cumberland so felt the imputation that in his *Memoirs* (1807) he avoids mentioning the character's name completely, but casts oblique aspersions on Sheridan by citing a conversation between himself and Garrick following the introduction of *The West Indian* in which Garrick supposedly counterfeited the reading of a bad review of the comedy, then revealed his joke. The implication is clear: in staging Sneer's attack on Sir Fretful, Sheridan was merely retelling a worn-out story, Cumberland would have us believe, plagiarizing it in fact from life.

The other playwright of *The Critic,* Puff, was also from real life. Consider his thoughts on the subjects of drama:

What Shakespeare says of Actors may be better applied to the purpose of Plays; *they* ought to be "the abstract and brief Chronicles of the times." Therefore when history, and particularly the history of our own country, furnishes any thing like a case in point, to the time in which an author writes, if he knows his own interest, he will take advantage of it; so, Sir, I call my tragedy The Spanish Armada; and have laid the scene before Tilbury Fort.

On 18 June 1779, Spain declared war on England; on 16 August 1779 the war came home to London in the form of reports that the French and Spanish fleets had evaded a British squadron and were in the Channel. Volunteer companies were formed, the militia mobilized, and not until mid-September did invasion fever die down. In the

Public Advertiser and the *Lady's Magazine,* Queen Elizabeth's speech to the army at Tilbury before the arrival of the Spanish Armada was reprinted; theatrical entertainments were given on the subject; poems were printed in the newspapers; correspondents employing Roman pseudonyms offered copious advice; and Covent Garden produced a topical musical farce on the war preparations titled *Plymouth in an Uproar.*

One of the theatrical entertainments on the subject is particularly interesting. During the summer of 1779 there was produced at the theater at Sadler's Wells a pantomime-pastiche, advertised as

> A new favourite Musical Piece consisting of Airs serious and comic, Recitatives, Choruses, &c., called *The Prophecy: or, Queen Elizabeth at Tilbury.* In the course of which will be introduced a variety of Machinery and Decorations, particularly an emblematical Frontispiece, at the top of which, in a small Transparency, will be represented the Destruction of the famous Spanish Armada, and the view through the said Frontispiece will be closed by a Moving Perspective, representing the present Grand Fleet. The Recitatives and Choruses by Mr. Olive, the Airs selected from the best Masters, and the Paintings by Mr. Greenwood. Rope-dancing by Signora Mariana and Mr. Ferzi.

Pastiches of this sort almost always were mainly the creations of theatrical managers (Sheridan, of course, was behind *The Camp*, a similar topical exploitation piece), so we may assume that the author-director of *The Prophecy* was the manager of Sadler's Wells, who happened to be Thomas King, the great Drury Lane actor. King, veteran of Bayes in *The Rehearsal* and *The Meeting of the Company,* creator of Glib in *A Peep behind the Curtain,* created Puff, author of *The Spanish Armada.*

These local references seem by themselves enough to doom *The Critic* to mere topicality. But there is more in the way of local and domestic jokes. The manager who writes was Sheridan himself, and Mrs. Dangle is bothered by foreign singers because that same manager had recently assumed ownership of the opera house, as Sheridan had done in real life. Dangle was recognized by many as Thomas Vaughan, author of a farce produced under Sheridan's direction called *The Hotel* (DL, 20 Nov. 1776) and a theatrical amateur and "dangler" about the Green Room. Miss Pope's portrayal of Tilburina was a take-off of Mrs. Crawford's tragic acting, while the younger Bannister's acting of Don Ferolo Whiskerandos mimicked William Smith's portrayal of Richard III. Sheridan was known for writing "puffs" for Drury Lane, and the "puff direct" of which Puff gives an example was most likely a

> THE VERY BRILLIANCE OF *THE CRITIC* ARISES BECAUSE ITS INFORMING DESIGN IS NOT TOPICAL, BECAUSE ITS RIDICULE IS NOT SPECIFIC SATIRE BUT GENERAL COMIC CRITICISM."

"puff preliminary" for Elizabeth Griffith's *The Times,* a comedy to be produced little more than a month after the introduction of Sheridan's afterpiece.

Such topicality might assure a successful, financially rewarding run. In the previous season, Sheridan's slight pastiche, *The Camp* (15 Oct. 1778), had run for fifty-seven performances as an afterpiece and brought in an average of £228 a night for its first ten performances, an amazing achievement in a season for which non-benefit performances averaged only £183. The literary features of *The Camp* are hardly significant: a little characteristic and a little witty dialogue, a pair of national characters (Irish and French), some avaricious countrymen and their self-interested exciseman, some fine ladies, a briefly presented fop, and two minor, subordinated lines of action (one of a clever wit duped, the other the familiar boy-gets-girl sort) coexist merely to provide a theatrical visit to the military camp at Coxheath, then actually populated with soldiers and the focus of a great deal of contemporary interest. There were a few songs, some marching and dancing, and most important, splendid perspective views executed by De Loutherbourgh "which exceeds every Thing in Scenery we have ever seen." It should not be surprising that when audiences would pay to see such drivel, Sheridan would give them more—and he did, in another pastiche, *The Wonders of Derbyshire,* later the same season. *The Critic,* in a similar fashion, has topical subjects, local and domestic jokes, songs which were popular enough to warrant separate publication, and De Loutherbourgh scenery which "seems to bring nature to our view, instead of painting views after nature."

And yet, *The Critic* is obviously a great deal more than just a topical burlesque. "Whoever, delighting in its gaiety and wit, remembers that *The*

Critic was written in one of the darkest hours of English history'' when invasion seemed imminent? We may no longer view Sir Fretful Plagiary as a caricature of Cumberland, or know that Puff is Thomas King, veteran actor and theater manager; but who fails to be delighted by timelessness encased in timeliness? The very brilliance of *The Critic* arises because its informing design is not topical, because its ridicule is not specific satire but general comic criticism. *The Critic* is clearly burlesque in its widest sense, rarely parody, the most topical form of burlesque.

Parody is a subspecies of satire, the direct mockery by imitation of a given, specific, external object. In one of the precursors of *The Critic* , *The Rehearsal,* numerous speeches, lines, and situations echo and ridicule speeches and situations from contemporary Restoration heroic plays. The viewer of that play today, or even the mid-eighteenth-century auditor, is unlikely to derive the pleasure contemporary audiences felt; even the reader of a good annotated edition will probably fail to enjoy all the literary satire Buckingham intended. *The Rehearsal* lasted on stage because its timeless frame permitted massive changes in its parodied content. Cibber and Garrick injected contemporary commentary, mimicked the behavior of contemporary actors, in essence made the play of their time in spite of its origins. They, and modern producers, must do so because true parody—specific satire of a specific object—is lost when the object it mocks is lost: *Shamela* without *Pamela* is not very amusing and even the early chapters of *Joseph Andrews* seem misleading to many who do not know Richardson's novel. Burlesque, however, is not parody—not specific satire—but general ridicule of classes of objects. Parody takes the characteristics of specific objects, redefines them to expose their absurdity, and moves toward damnation of the whole class through damnation of the objects; burlesque creates the characteristics of the whole class by granting characteristics to an absurd imaginary individual example which in and by itself has no direct resemblance to any individual member of the whole class. Parody is particular, burlesque is general; parody is almost always highly topical; burlesque may have some topical features, but as a whole, is barely topical in itself.

The burlesque of *The Critic* has lasted longer than that of *The Rehearsal* or *The Tragedy of Tragedies* because *The Critic* chose as its objects those of a larger, less definable, less topical class. Buckingham's play mocks a rather local group of objects, heroic plays; Fielding's play attacks nearly the same set of rather local phenomena. But Sheridan's play mocks a large, amorphous class: *The Spanish Armada* is absurd not just as heroic drama, historical drama, domestic tragedy, or romantic tragedy, but as poorly conducted serious drama of any time. Unprepared discoveries, clumsy exposition, wild coincidences, pretentious dialogue, excessive spectacle are faults not of any single genre but of any kind of wretched play. Obviously, both *The Rehearsal* and *The Tragedy of Tragedies* burlesque the general as well as parody the particular; but insofar as they ridicule the particular they remain local. *The Critic*, even encased in topical references, has more endurance precisely because it ridicules the general more consistently.

This is one reason why, for instance, searching for passages from other eighteenth-century plays parodied in *The Critic* is such a fruitless business: there are very few if any because Sheridan was not attacking specific plays. This is one reason why Puff, and not Sir Fretful Plagiary, is the author of *The Spanish Armada:* Sir Fretful's association with Cumberland was too strong, and to ridicule Cumberland's *Battle of Hastings* was to tie *The Critic* to a merely local event; the association of Puff as the author of the tragedy with King as the author of an entertainment on a similar topic is convenient, but not necessary to make the satire against bad drama effective.

Moreover, *The Critic* is not just an attack on bad drama, but a comic castigation of sloppy theatrical practices in general. Literature is not Sheridan's target, as it was largely for Buckingham and Fielding; instead, his aim is to ridicule the excesses of professional, practical theater, and not just theater in production but theater in all its aspects. Dangle is every theatrical hanger-on—the amateur of dubious influence, the critic of unsure tastes, the hypocrite of uncertain loyalties. Sneer is every dramatic critic—self-interested for the two plays he brings to Dangle, but cynical concerning anyone else's efforts. Sir Fretful is every thin-skinned author, and he became Cumberland not so much because Sheridan's text called for it as because Parsons chose to emphasize it: later actors have played the role successfully without reference to the sentimental playwright. Puff is beyond correction, a hackneyed playwright and a spectacle-monger. The Italian visitors come unprepared, ignorant of language, naïvely trusting in their own talents—a perfect reflection of many theatrical hopefuls. The self-interested managers, the upstaging actors and actresses, the practical designers and prompters are theatrical characters of all time. The aim of *The Critic* is clear, and the barb hits and sticks to the theatrical target.

Yet, as in *The Rivals* or *The School for Scandal* where sentimentality seems approved of as well as damned, many have doubted the aesthetic integrity of *The Critic*. The tacking together of the manners scenes of the first act with the more highly artificial burlesque rehearsal of the second and third acts seems a cynical attempt to utilize materials on hand, not to create a unified work capable of achieving the aesthetic integrity Sheridan sought (and failed) to give *The Relapse* or successfully lent to his other comic masterpieces. Early reviews remarked that Sheridan would have done better to play the first act as a prelude, or to integrate it with the second and third. It is, of course, a kind of prelude already. Yet its duration is such that it overshadows much of the rehearsal: it might have been integrated, but only at the possible expense of vitiating the effects of the rehearsal. Moreover, the attacks on newspaper puffery, on the selection of plays, on the influence of amateurs, and on the vanity and hypocrisy of authors and critics that constitute the satire of act one seem in many ways irrelevant to the attack on theater in production that constitutes the satire of acts two and three. Of course, Sheridan was attacking theater in all its aspects; his failure, if there was one, was to separate the various aspects of his target so completely that in acts two and three we lose sight of theater as a whole while we focus only on theater in production.

The serious use of spectacle might be considered a flaw; De Loutherbourgh's scenes and effects were lavishly praised for their verisimilitude, not their mockery of theatrical effect: *The Critic* was in part successful for many of the same reasons *The Camp* was—for its magnificence, battle, noise, and procession. Clearly, the representation of the defeat of the Spanish Armada by the English fleet, chorused with the popular and rousing song, ''Britons Strike Home,'' evoked surprise, delight, and patriotic sentiment; and the procession that followed of *''all the English rivers and their tributaries''* was a theatrical extravaganza matching Garrick's *Jubilee*. Puff's final ''Well, pretty well—but not quite perfect—so ladies and gentlemen, if you please, we'll rehearse this piece again to-morrow'' would be hard pressed to bring things into burlesque perspective. But I suspect Sheridan was laughing at his audience and their desires, that he was saying in effect ''Here you have it, and you have nobody to blame but yourselves if you fail to see the self-satisfied stupidity of your tastes.'' In his time the line was his joke; in our time the joke is ours, for no modern production of *The Critic* fails to burlesque the final flourish with scenery and props falling and colliding. Moreover, Sheridan's ridicule of the theater in all its aspects would be complete only if the audience, the most important constituent, received its corrective lash, too. They did, and that is yet another reason why *The Critic* is the most complete satiric play about the theater yet created.

The informing principle of *The Critic*, then, is broad burlesque of theater in all its aspects. Such a work should not be judged by standards of unity induced from works not designed according to the same principle. Students of the play would be wrongheaded to attack *The Critic* because some characters are drawn inconsistently or because some characters disappear from the representation or because the ''plot'' lacks unity of tone, just as readers would be wrong to criticize *The Dunciad* for ridiculing nonliterary targets like education or to fault *Tristram Shandy* for its failure to bring all aspects of its narrative to a probable conclusion. Pope's work, designed to ridicule intellectual dullness in all its aspects, had neither to fulfill the demands of an allegorical satire on learning like *The Battle of the Books* by focusing specifically on literary matters nor to satisfy the principles of narrative coherence and characterization of an allegorical and personal satire like *MacFlecknoe*. Sterne's work, designed as a uniquely personal expression employing a fictive ''I'' narrator burlesquing a wide variety of literary forms including the periodic essay, the novel, and the confession while telling a ''story,'' had neither to achieve a principle of narrative coherence similar to that of *Clarissa* or *Tom Jones* nor to create a sense of closure arising from the resolution of the instabilities in the relationships among characters similar to the sense of closure created in Richardson's or Fielding's novels. Just as we value *Tristam Shandy* though it is not a novel, or *The Dunciad* though it is not strictly a satire on literature, so we should value *The Critic* though it is not just a burlesque of theatrical literature, as are *The Rehearsal* or *The Tragedy of Tragedies*.

For what should we praise *The Critic*? How can we explain the unique pleasures derived from its reading or representation? The answers lie largely, I think, in the succession of comic ''moments,'' into which Sheridan packed all the comic techniques he had developed in his earlier works. In a manner characteristic of his indolent genius, he chose only the loosest of informing principles—that of burlesque of all aspects of theater—to bring them together.

As we have seen elsewhere in this study, Sheridan's greatest skills lay in the creation of comic moments. He could unify them around and through action and character as in *The Rivals, The Duenna, A Trip to Scarborough*, or *The School for Scandal*, but even in those works problems remain. The two most unified by plot—*The Duenna* and *A Trip to Scarborough*—fail to reach the heights of great comic literature; *The Rivals*, though a great work of comic art, nevertheless has aesthetic problems, largely of unity; *The School for Scandal* is great unified comic art, but fails as "morally serious comedy." The maker of moments could only barely bring his moments together. In a sense, Sheridan was always making parts—sketching scenes but not plots, writing dialogues to ideas, not to characters in conflict; and the sheer mass of short uncompleted fragments he left, if not the works into which he molded some of these moments, confirm that this was his method of creation. The moments of *The Critic* show particularly his great skill as a maker of comic dialogue. Sheridan's comic dialogue, indeed the dialogue of all great creators of dramatic comedy, is amusing for one of four principal approaches used either separately or in combination: character, situation, manifest absurdity, or wit.

In amusing dialogue based on character, the faults or foibles of the character are displayed in a comic way, so that we smile not at *what* the character says but at the fact that *he* says it. Verbal tics, dialect oddities, and comically repetitive or predictable assertions of belief all fall into this category. To utilize a stage Jew or Irishman, to display an irascible father, a disappointed old bachelor, or a ridiculous fop is to employ dialogue based on character.

Nearly as frequently encountered among comic kinds is dialogue based on situation. We laugh through our superior knowledge of the circumstances and enjoy the dramatic irony of the concealed facts which we, and perhaps some of the other characters, share. The reiteration of belief in an adulterer *manqué* while the partner in his sin is to our knowledge concealed on the scene, or the imposition by means of disguise of a clever person on a stupid one, are good situational techniques which may lead to the development of amusing, ironic dialogue.

Manifest verbal absurdity is the basis for a third kind of comic dialogue. Puns, intentional or otherwise, mistakes of grammar, excessive, inappropriate or badly designed comparisons are the most commonly encountered comic verbal absurdities. Here the character need not himself be amusing—though most frequently he is—for he can be so briefly displayed as not to develop any character, he can report the words of others, or he can make mistakes which are not truly an aspect of his character as we perceive it.

Historically the most valued of amusing comic dialogue is that based on wit. Wit, that intellectual excellence which we can admire apart from character (hence our admiration for the witty speech of even those characters by whom we are not amused), employs unusual or apt comparisons and irony in obvious or subtle manners. Like manifest absurdity, wit can be an aspect of characterization; and like amusing dialogue based on character, wit can be made an aspect of situation, as when a speaker who is witty ironically comments to a butt who fails to recognize the irony. (Note that manifest absurdity is not the same thing as false wit; false wit amuses largely as an aspect of character, for it is intentional, i.e., intended as wit.)

Of these four kinds of comic dialogue, those based on character and situation are the most commonly employed, that based on manifest absurdity the least attempted, and that founded on wit the least frequently achieved. As a general principle we can say that the great and memorable scenes of comic dramatic literature employ at least three and often all four kinds of comic dialogue in concert. Indeed, the failed attempts of a good many third-rate dramatists of Sheridan's day as well as the successes of many comic dramatists of genius in all times suggest a corollary, quantitative principle: the more aspects or different representatives of amusing character, the more ironic levels of comic situation, the more manifest absurdity, and the more striking and original wit all used in concert, the more probable the creation of memorable, amusing comic dialogue. Two scenes I have touched on frequently in this study—Jack's imposition on Mrs. Malaprop, and the screen scene of *The School for Scandal*—demonstrate both the concert and the quantitative principles admirably, for both scenes depend upon widely different and striking characters, several levels of situational irony, manifest absurdity (to a lesser extent), and wit all used together. Both principles underlie the success of the dialogue in the moments of *The Critic*.

Take the famous roasting scene of Sir Fretful Plagiary. The scene begins with an immediate situational irony, prepared for by witty characterization, so that we await with pleasure the arrival of ''the sorest man alive . . . [who] shrinks like scorch'd parchment from the fiery ordeal of true criticism.'' Dangle's attempt to second Sneer's remarks on Sir Fretful are stopped by the playwright's entrance.

> Dangle. Ah, my dear friend!—Egad, we were just speaking of your Tragedy—Admirable, Sir Fretful, admirable!
> Sneer. You never did anything beyond it, Sir Fretful—never in your life.
> Sir Fretful. You make me extremely happy;—for without a compliment, my dear Sneer, there isn't a man in the world whose judgment I value as I do yours.

Sneer's cynical double entendre is answered by Sir Fretful's so that we are led to expect a battle of wits. Mrs. Dangle's immediate complication of the scene's irony—''They are only laughing at you, Sir Fretful''—sparks the first of a series of amusing asides in which Sir Fretful reveals his character by revealing his irritation—''A damn'd double-faced fellow!''—and we quickly see that Sir Fretful is not capable of matching Sneer's wit by insinuation, innuendo, and double entendre. As the scene continues, Dangle's lack of wit contrasts with Sneer's witty remarks. Both men are willing to discomfit Sir Fretful, and increasingly situation becomes less important than character and wit. At first Sneer's wit is chiefly in subtle ironic one-liners or occasionally, in neatly prepared jokes. Despite the fact that the subject matter of the conversation is directed outside the immediate situation, Sneer is able to turn it back on Sir Fretful, as in this exchange: Sir Fretful fears that the manager (i.e., Sheridan) might steal something from his tragedy were he allowed to read it.

> Sir Fretful. And then, if such a person gives you the least hint or assistance, he is devilish apt to take the merit of the whole.—
> Dangle. If it succeeds.
> Sir Fretful. Aye,—but with regard to this piece, I think I can hit that gentleman, for I can safely swear he never read it.
> Sneer. I'll tell you how you may hurt him more—
> Sir Fretful. How?—
> Sneer. Swear he wrote it.

Situational irony is added to wit and character as the basis for the amusing dialogue which develops as Sneer quotes the imaginary review to an increasingly discomfited Sir Fretful:

> Sneer. Why, [the critic] roundly asserts that you have not the slightest invention, or original genius

whatever; tho' you are the greatest traducer of all other authors living.
> Sir Fretful. Ha! ha! ha!—very good!
> Sneer. That as to Comedy, you have not one idea of your own, he believes, even in your common place-book—where stray jokes, and pilfered witticisms are kept with as much method as the ledger of the Lost-and-Stolen-office.
> Sir Fretful.—Ha! ha! ha!—very pleasant!
> Sneer. Nay, that you are so unlucky as not to have the skill even to *steal* with taste.—But that you gleen from the refuse of obscure volumes, where more judicious plagiarists have been before you; so that the body of your work is a composition of dregs and sediments—like a bad tavern's worst wine.
> Sir Fretful. Ha! ha!
> Sneer. In your more serious efforts, he says, your bombast would be less intolerable, if the thoughts were ever suited to the expression; but the homeliness of the sentiment stares thro' the fantastic encumbrance of its fine language, like a clown in one of the new uniforms!
> Sir Fretful. Ha! ha!
> Sneer. That your occasional tropes and flowers suit the general coarseness of your stile, as tambour sprigs would a ground of linsey-wolsey; while your imitations of Shakespeare resemble the mimicry of Falstaff's Page, and are about as near the standard of the original.
> Sir Fretful. Ha!—
> Sneer.—In short, that even the finest passages you steal are of no service to you; for the poverty of your own language prevents their assimilating; so that they lie on the surface like lumps of marl on a barren moor, encumbering what it is not in their power to fertilize!—
> Sir Fretful. [*after great agitation.*]—Now another person would be vex'd at this.

Of course, we value this scene most for the wit; but the dialogue, amusing by virtue of situational irony and character as well as wit, explains why we find the scene more pleasureable than the subsequent witty exchange among Sneer, Dangle, and Puff on the art of puffery. Pleasant as this later scene is, witty and absurd as Puff's explanations of his art are, scathing as the continued indictment of newspapers and the theater becomes, the scene does not achieve the levels of comic enjoyment possible in the roasting of Sir Fretful. It is too much like those virtuoso recitations continually attempted by the characters of Samuel Foote. Sheridan could outdo Foote in this regard, but as the juxtaposition of these two scenes shows, he could also do more in blending character, situation, and wit.

The moments of the first act of *The Critic*—Mr. and Mrs. Dangle's daily jangle, Sir Fretful's roasting, the Italian singers, and Puff's art of puffery—are all bound together by their burlesque of the theater in all its aspects. Character largely informs the first scene between the Dangles; character, situation, and wit melds in the dialogue of the second; character to a very small extent, manifest absurdity, and situation make amusing the display of the Italian singers and their French-speaking interpreter; wit, and to a lesser extent, characterization make effective the satiric dialogue of the fourth scene. Any of these scenes could be removed from the burlesque; any could be exchanged with another and not disturb seriously the connections among them, for there is no significant development of character or action. Each is amusing basically for itself; each could have been, and I suspect was, written at a different time; and they were brought together here only by means of the loosest of informing devices.

The two rehearsal acts are moments in that the particular sections of the satirical target under attack at any given time could have been attacked earlier or later in the presentation; there is no principle of development underlying the satire. But the continuity of the unfolding play within the play provides a unity not to be found in the first act, and this, together with Sheridan's employment of amusing dialogue constantly based on a rich interaction of character, situation, absurdity, and wit gives to acts two and three of *The Critic* a sustained power not to be found in act one. Puff is oblivious to the quality of his play and speaks of its absurdities as if they were excellencies; his character is further revealed by his comically unjustifiable pique at the actors' cuts. We are amused too by the irony of the situation. Our own critical standards and the efforts of raisonneur Sneer reveal the concealed truth of the intellectual and creative aesthetic poverty of *The Spanish Armada* which Puff cannot recognize, Dangle only occasionally seems to notice, and Sneer sarcastically exposes. The manifest absurdities of the dialogue of the play within the play—metaphors piled upon one another with no regard to their aesthetic appropriateness, bathos where there should be pathos—are joined by the manifest absurdities of Puff's explanations. Sneer's ironic commentary adds a dimension of wit—wit of an obvious but nonetheless pleasurable sort.

Demonstration of this interaction in any of the various moments of acts two and three threatens to overwhelm even the heavy-handed irony of this section of *The Critic*. So rather than explicate a scene or two, let me point to Sheridan's use of three other comic devices of dialogue—repetition, diminution, and what I will call accidental wit. All reinforce the complex interplay of the dialogue. In

act one Sheridan had used repetition to good effect with Dangle's tag lines, ''tho' he's my friend!'' In act two it becomes the principle upon which we find the agreement of all those present on stage in *The Spanish Armada* to pray to Mars amusing: ''And me!'' ''And me!'' ''And me!'' ''And me!'' Diminution—a kind of repetition for the specific effect of reduction—adds to character in act one as Sir Fretful's responses to the imagined criticism gradually change from ''Ha! ha! ha!—very good!'' to a half-hearted ''Ha!—''; it serves both purposes of characterization and absurdity in this stichomythic exchange between two characters of *The Spanish Armada:*

> ''Tilburina.
> ''A retreat in Spain!
> ''Governor.
> ''Outlawry here!
> ''Tilburina.
> ''Your daughter's prayer!
> ''Governor.
> ''Your father's oath!
> ''Tilburina.
> ''My lover!
> ''Governor.
> ''My country!
> ''Tilburina.
> ''Tilburnia!
> ''Governor.
> ''England!
> ''Tilburina.
> ''A title!
> ''Governor.
> ''Honor!
> ''Tilburina.
> ''A pension!
> ''Governor.
> ''Conscience!

The crescendo of economic concerns completely deflates the repetition:

> ''Tilburina.
> ''A thousand pounds!
> ''Governor.
> ''Hah! thou hast touch'd me nearly!

But perhaps the funniest lines are built on accidental wit—a combination of character, situation, manifest absurdity, and the approximation of wit. Consider just two examples, both of them Puff's explanations for problems in his play. Sneer criticizes the decorum of the dialogue:

> Sneer. But, Mr. Puff, I think not only the Justice, but the clown seems to talk in as high a style as the first hero among them.
> Puff. Heaven forbid they should not in a free country!—Sir, I am not for making slavish distinctions, and giving all the fine language to the upper sort of people.

Or perhaps the funniest lines of the play:

Enter A Beefeater.
''Beefeater.
''Perdition catch my soul but *I* do love thee.
Sneer. Haven't I heard that line before?
Puff. No, I fancy not—Where pray?
Dangle. Yes, I think there is something like it in
    Othello.
Puff. Gad! now you put me in mind on't, I believe
    there is—but that's of no consequence—all
    that can be said is, that two people happened to
    hit on the same thought—And Shakespeare
    made use of it first, that's all.
Sneer. Very true.

Such effects make the moments of the rehearsal scenes particularly amusing. And even if the informing principle—to burlesque the theater in all its aspects—seems loose, we can be happy that Sheridan was able to cast upon it here and sorry that never again would he bring his ''moments'' together.

With *The Critic* we come to the end of Sheridan's achievement as comic dramatist. There would be another year or two of active work in the theater, but no more literary achievement. On 12 September 1780 Sheridan was elected Member of Parliament for Stafford, and though he remained associated with Drury Lane for more than thirty years, only one major theatrical effort was to come, the pompous and absurd *Pizzaro*. He kept his hand in, however, and not just in the till; he participated in correcting and revising other dramatists' work, in coaching and advising actors, and in organizing a few spectacular entertainments; he continually promised definitive editions of his own works and continually projected another play, especially when money was short. But never again would he produce a comedy. Perhaps Sheridan knew his powers were going or had gone; perhaps he felt he never would be able to focus the energy necessary to create another masterpiece.

Why have so many great English comic dramatists stopped writing for the stage at relatively young ages? Congreve had produced all his comedies by the time he was thirty; Etherege saw his last play on stage when he was barely forty, Wycherley when he was in his mid-thirties; Wilde's best play comes from his fortieth year, Synge's from his thirty-sixth, Jonson's four or five best from his late thirties and early forties, Coward's three or four from his early thirties, Vanbrugh's from his early thirties, Sheridan's and Farquhar's from their late twenties. Of course, one cannot give a single answer, unless one wants to invoke so vague a term as ''comic spirit'' or attribute to youth an exuberance many have

displayed in maturer years. Congreve was disgusted with developments in popular taste; Farquhar and Synge died young; Wilde was forbidden a public forum for his wit; and Sheridan entered Parliament to embark on a new and brilliant career. Beyond these few reasons, we can only speculate. In Sheridan's case, particularly when a new comedy would have meant so much to his always precarious financial position, why did he fail to employ his obvious talents as a comic dramatist? Michael Kelly, a talented musician and performer, relates an anecdote that reveals much:

One evening (probably in the late 1780's or early 1790's) that their late Majesties honoured Drury Lane Theatre with their presence, the play, by royal command, was the ''School for Scandal.'' When Mr. Sheridan was in attendance to light their Majesties to their carriage, the King said to him, ''I am much pleased with your comedy of the 'School for Scandal;' but I am still more so, with your play of the 'Rivals;'—that is my favourite, and I will never give it up.''

Her Majesty, at the same time said, ''When, Mr. Sheridan, shall we have another play from your masterly pen?'' He replied, that ''he was writing a comedy, which he expected very shortly to finish.''

I was told of this; and the next day, walking with him along Piccadilly, I asked him if he had told the Queen, that he was writing a play? He said he had, and that he actually was about one.

''Not you,'' said I to him; ''you will never write again; you are afraid to write.''

He fixed his penetrating eye on me, and said, ''Of whom am I afraid?''

I said, ''You are afraid of the author of the 'School for Scandal.'''

I believe, at the time I made the remark, he thought my conjecture right.

However contrived his anecdote sounds, Kelly was correct, of course: Sheridan did not finish another dramatic comedy, though he lived on for thirty-seven years after *The Critic*. And Kelly was correct in another way, for though today we may value all of Sheridan's dramatic works, he is still largely remembered as the author of *The School for Scandal*. Beside the greater comedy, *The Critic* seems a remnant of his youth, a brilliant utilization of his experiences as a practical dramatist perhaps, but more nearly the product of an exuberance and an adolescent cynicism which the perfection of *The School for Scandal* seems to deny. Still, *The Critic* is a more stageworthy work than either of its major competitors in its time and in ours, *The Rehearsal* and *The Tragedy of Tragedies;* for even Sheridan's burlesque achieves, however artificially, a fusion of wit which only Wilde and Coward have since reached. What a pity that the greatest Georgian playwright would henceforth produce only *Pizarro*.

Source: Mark S. Auburn, *"The Critic,"* in *Sheridan's Comedies,* University of Nebraska Press, 1977, pp. 157–75.

SOURCES

Auburn, Mark S., *Sheridan's Comedies,* University of Nebraska Press, 1977, pp. 165–75.

Austen, Jane, *Love and Friendship,* Frederick A. Stokes Company, 1922, p. 167.

Boswell, James, *The Life of Samuel Johnson,* Penguin Books, 1986, p. 101.

Dibdin, Charles, *The Musical Tour of Mr. Dibdin,* in *Sheridan: Comedies,* edited by Peter Davison, Macmillan Education, 1986, p. 193.

Jason, Philip K., *"A Twentieth Century Response to The Critic,"* in *Sheridan: Comedies,* edited by Peter Davison, Macmillan Education, 1986, p. 207.

Knapp, Mary E., *Prologues and Epilogues of the Eighteenth Century,* Yale University Press, 1961, p. 9.

Macey, Samuel L., *"Sheridan: The Last of the Great Theatrical Satirists,"* in *Sheridan: Comedies,* edited by Peter Davison, Macmillan Education, 1986, p. 198.

Morwood, James, *The Life and Works of Richard Brinsley Sheridan,* Scottish Academic Press, 1985, p. 106.

O'Toole, Fintan, *A Traitor's Kiss: The Life of Richard Brinsley Sheridan,* Farrar, Straus and Giroux, 1997, pp. 151–57.

Quintana, Ricardo, *"Introduction,"* in *Eighteenth Century Plays,* Modern Library, 1952, pp. xvi–xix.

Review of *The Critic,* in *Sheridan: Comedies,* edited by Peter Davison, Macmillan Education, 1986, pp. 191–92.

Review of *The Critic,* in *Sheridan: Comedies,* edited by Peter Davison, Macmillan Education, 1986, pp. 192–93.

FURTHER READING

Aristotle, Horace, and Longinus, *Classical Literary Criticism,* translated by T. S. Dorsch, Penguin Books, 1975.
   This collection features Aristotle's *Poetics,* his treatise on tragedy that stands as the supreme piece of criticism for tragedies of any age.

Eighteenth Century English Literature, edited by Geoffrey Tillotson, Paul Fussell, and Marshall Waingrow, Harcourt Brace Jovanovich, 1969.
   In addition to *The Critic,* this comprehensive anthology features selections from all the famous Enlightenment writers, such as Alexander Pope, Jonathan Swift, Samuel Johnson, James Boswell, John Gay, Henry Fielding, and Edward Gibbon. This is an indispensable book for any student of Enlightenment literature or thought.

Eighteenth Century Plays, edited by Ricardo Quintana, Modern Library, 1952.
   This collection of eight plays features Sheridan's first play, *The Rivals;* the volume also contains John Gay's *The Beggar's Opera* and Oliver Goldsmith's *She Stoops to Conquer,* two other popular Enlightenment comedies. Quintana's introduction surveys the eighteenth-century theater.

O'Toole, Fintan, *A Traitor's Kiss: The Life of Richard Brinsley Sheridan,* Farrar, Straus and Giroux, 1997.
   This recent (and critically praised) biography examines Sheridan's plays and political career in detail, often discussing the significance of Sheridan's Irish roots.

Curse of the Starving Class

SAM SHEPARD

1977

Sam Shepard's *Curse of the Starving Class* at first reading is a very strange play. The playwright seems not to have been able to decide whether he wanted to write a realistic social protest play or a symbolic drama, and the characters also are at times little more than stock types from gangster movies. But a closer look at this play reveals that it is a very sophisticated drama that seeks to link deep archetypal themes of human suffering and fate to very specific and contemporary political and social issues. The family whose plight is dramatized are indeed beset by a curse about which they can do nothing, but Shepard refuses to specify what that curse is. The play is clearly a symbolic drama, but it is no allegory; the symbols are used more for their resonance and imagistic power than for any one-to-one correspondence with the themes of the play. The play is fragmented, decentered, at times incoherent. Parts of it seem lifted from B-grade movies; other parts seem like Greek tragedy barely altered. In this pastiche lies the play's power.

AUTHOR BIOGRAPHY

One of the most famous playwrights in contemporary America, Sam Shepard's fame comes in part from what some critics have called a ''self-made myth.'' Shepard is tall, dark, and handsome; he is rough and rugged; he is a brilliant and successful writer and actor who has been romantically linked

Sam Shepard

with a glamorous movie star for years. After many years of struggle in the theatre, Shepard finally gained a great deal of note for his work in films in the 1980s, and the American public at large became familiar with this man who seems to have been born already on his way to being an American icon.

Shepard's family background and upbringing place him solidly in the narrative of the American artist of modest circumstances who completely remakes himself. Shepard was born Sam Shepard Rogers VII on November 5, 1943, at Fort Sheridan, a military base, in Illinois. Shepard's family lived on army bases until 1955, when they finally settled in Southern California. In Duarte, Shepard worked on the family's avocado farm and raised ranch animals (one year raising the grand champion yearling ram at the Los Angeles County Fair). In 1961, after graduating from high school, he enrolled in a junior college but dropped out after one year, joining the Bishop's Company theatre troupe.

When the Bishop's Company arrived in New York and left again, Shepard stayed, got a job as a waiter at the Village Gate jazz club, and officially changed his name. At this point, he also started writing plays, and in 1964, the bohemian center St. Mark's-in-the-Bowery was the venue for two of his plays: *Cowboys* and *Rock Garden*. These plays

received a favorable review from the *Village Voice,* which encouraged Shepard to continue writing. The following year, Shepard saw six of his plays produced in small theatres in New York, and in 1966, Shepard became the first playwright to receive three Obie Awards in one year (winning for *Chicago, Icarus' Mother,* and *Red Cross.*

The late 1960s saw Shepard's career accelerate dramatically. In 1967, he was finally able to quit his day job (he was still waiting tables) when he received fellowships from Yale and the University of Minnesota and a Rockefeller Grant. Four of his plays were produced that year, and he also began work in film, writing a screenplay and working with Italian director Michelangelo Antonioni on Antonioni's movie *Zabriskie Point* (released in 1969). As the decade closed, Shepard was awarded a Guggenheim Fellowship, joined a rock band (the Holy Modal Bounders), received two more Obie Awards, and married actress O-Lan Johnson.

In the 1970s, Shepard began to achieve fame to accompany the successes he enjoyed in the 1960s. He and his family (now including a son) moved to London in 1971, where he continued writing plays that are produced in London, New York, and even Edinburgh. After publishing a book of poems and prose, *Hawkmoon,* in 1973, Shepard and his family returned to California in 1974. Shepard began working with the Magic Theatre in San Francisco in 1975; this theatre became his primary venue. In 1977, Shepard wrote and won an Obie Award for *Curse of the Starving Class,* and even published a book about his tour with Allen Ginsberg and Bob Dylan. He won a Pulitzer for *Buried Child* in 1979. He was also acting more frequently in films in this period, appearing in Terence Malick's *Days of Heaven, Resurrection,* and *Raggedy Man* by 1981.

True fame came to Shepard by the early 1980s. Although he continued to write very successful plays, including *True West, Fool for Love,* and *A Lie of the Mind,* he also wrote successful screenplays— the most notable being *Paris, Texas,* which won the Palme d'Or at the 1984 Cannes Film Festival. At this time he also appeared in films such as *The Right Stuff, Baby Boom,* and *Country.* In 1982, Shepard fell in love with and began living with the actress Jessica Lange. Today, he is still with Jessica Lange; in 1984, he was officially divorced from O-Lan. Shepard continues to write and act in films, and his plays continue to be produced all over the United States.

PLOT SUMMARY

Act I

The play opens on Wesley, who is loading broken pieces of the family's front door into a wheelbarrow. His mother, Ella enters, and Wesley and she talk about the events of the night before. Wesley embarks upon a long monologue narrating the events of the previous night before leaving, at which point Ella begins talking to nobody in particular about the start of menstruation. As she speaks, her daughter, Emma enters and joins the conversation in progress. When Ella asks what Emma is carrying, Emma tells her that they are the materials for her 4-H demonstration on how to cut up a frying chicken, and then she immediately starts looking for her chicken in the refrigerator. Emma decides that Ella boiled her chicken and storms out.

Wesley re-enters and starts yelling to the off-stage Emma about her chicken. The three of them begin arguing about whether they are the starving class, while Wesley urinates on Emma's chart. Emma then yells down that she is going to take the horse and leave. Later, when Wesley and Ella talk, Ella tells him that she is going to sell the house and use the money to go to Europe. Wesley leaves and Emma returns, covered in mud from being dragged by the horse. Emma tells Ella of her dream of going to Mexico and becoming a mechanic.

Taylor enters and talks with Emma, who calls him creepy. Taylor explains that selling is in Ella's best financial interests. Wesley enters, sets up a small fenced enclosure in the kitchen, exits, and re-enters with a lamb. The three of them converse tensely until Ella enters. Emma leaves; then Taylor and Ella leave for a "business meeting." Wesley is left on stage, talking to the lamb, when Weston's voice is heard outside. He enters, drunk, and begins yelling at his son, Wesley. He has brought a bag of artichokes that he bought while visiting his worthless desert property. The curtain falls as Wesley and Weston discuss how to rid the lamb of the maggots that are infesting its digestive tract.

Act II

The curtain opens on Wesley again, who this time is building a new front door for the house. Emma is with him, and the two of them discuss the potential sale of the house and Ella's relationship with Taylor. Wesley describes the suburbanization going on around them as a "zombie invasion" and tells her he dreams of going to Alaska. Weston stumbles in, even drunker, and wants to know where Ella is. He tells the children that he has found a buyer for the house, and Emma leaves abruptly. Weston and Wesley discuss the "poison" that Weston feels has infected him all of his life. When Wesley tells him that Ella is thinking of selling the house, Weston explodes and threatens to kill her and Taylor. After this outburst he passes out.

When Weston comes to, he starts up again where he left off, rejecting Wesley's suggestions that they plant avocados on their land. Mumbling about his experience flying planes in the Second World War, he passes out again. Ella re-enters with groceries and throws the artichokes on the floor. She tells Wesley that she knows about Weston's foolish purchase of desert land sight unseen, and Wesley deduces that it was Taylor who sold him the land. As Wesley and Ella argue, Ella speaks of the curse she sees operating on the family.

Ellis enters, laughing at the passed-out Weston who is slumped on the kitchen table. He pulls out the $1500 that he owes Weston for the purchase of the house, and Ella tells Wesley to throw him out. As Ellis talks to them, they learn that Weston owes money to some "pretty hard fellas." Wesley offers to take the money to those men, but Ella forbids it. Taylor appears and tells Ella that he has the final draft of the deed of sale. Taylor is in disbelief, and Ellis threatens him. Taylor argues that Weston is legally incompetent to sell the house and boasts that he has "corporations" and "executive management" behind him.

While he is fulminating, Sgt. Malcolm enters and informs the family that Emma has been arrested for riding her horse through the Alibi Club and shooting up the bar. Taylor leaves, and Wesley yells at the policeman to arrest him for being a confidence man. Ellis grabs the money back from Wesley (feeling that now he is owed for the damage to his bar), and the act closes as Ella agrees to come to the police station to pick up Emma.

Act III

Weston in new clean clothes and the lamb in its enclosure are on stage, and Weston is telling the lamb his story about castrating lambs and throwing their testes onto a roof for an eagle to eat. Wesley appears, bloodied, and tells Weston that he has tried to get the money back. Weston tells Wesley that he got up early and took a walk around the house and decided he wanted to stay, so he cleaned up, bought food, made a huge breakfast, and did all of the laundry. Inviting Wesley to have some breakfast, he tells him (as Wesley walks off) that he is reconsidering the idea of planting avocados. Ella enters, asks why the lamb is back in the kitchen, and tells Weston that she has been at the jail, visiting Emma. Weston tries to be civil to Ella, but she starts screaming at him. He tells her to take a nap on the table because "it'll do wonders" for her. She climbs up and stretches out on it as Wesley, completely naked, enters. He picks up the lamb and carries it off.

Ella falls asleep on the table and Wesley, dressed in Weston's old clothes, enters. He tells Weston that he butchered the lamb for food, but Weston yells at him and shows him the newly stocked refrigerator. Wesley tells Weston that his creditors are going to kill him. Weston considers fleeing to Mexico, and Wesley muses about finding Taylor to get the money for the desert land back. Weston exits and Emma enters. Wesley tells her, when she asks if he is going to take over the role of "Daddy Bear," that he feels himself becoming his father, that as he put on Weston's clothes, he could feel something "growing on" him. Emma picks up Ella's pocketbook, steals from it, and then tells Wesley that she is going to begin a life of crime. As Ella calls her name out in a dream, Emma quickly leaves.

Ella wakes up, and a huge explosion offstage follows upon this. Emerson and Slater enter, laughing and holding the bloody carcass of the lamb. They say that they blew up Weston's car. They menace the family a little and leave. Wesley and Ella talk about Weston's eagle story as the play ends.

CHARACTERS

Ella

Ella is the mother of the family in *Curse of the Starving Class*. As the play opens, she and Wesley are both surveying the chunks of the door broken down by her husband Weston. Where Wesley seems angry with her for provoking Weston to anger, Ella holds that the incident was entirely Weston's fault. She quickly changes topics, though, and throughout the play she continues to switch her moods and attention immediately, as if she wants nothing to affect her very deeply. She tends to ignore the things

going on immediately around her. It is clear, though, by the way she will just as quickly return to a topic, that she is simply trying to keep things under the surface.

The play, as it proceeds, provides insight into Ella's true desires. She has very little affection or even respect for her husband. Without her husband's knowledge, she is seeking to sell her house (with the help of the lawyer Taylor) and dreams of using the money to go to Europe. Although she clearly does not love her husband in the time depicted in the play, in the third act we see her interact with Weston almost kindly and tenderly, and as the play closes, she recalls the story about the lambs that Weston tells—in fact, she tells Wesley that the story "just went right through me."

Ellis

Ellis is the owner of the Alibi Club, the bar where Weston spends his time. He is greedy and seeks to take advantage of the family. He comes to the house to claim it; Weston has signed the deed over to him for $1500, and even though Weston is an alcoholic and was drunk when he signed the agreement, Ellis is unwilling to nullify their agreement. Even though it is Weston's choice to drink the way he does, Wesley and Ella clearly resent Ellis for being the man who is immediately responsible for his drinking. Eventually, while Ellis is in the house, he is told that Emma has shot up his bar, and he reclaims the money from Wesley and leaves. In the symbolic structure of the play, Ellis represents the greed of the petty business owner and the tendency of people to take unfair advantage of each other. However, like most of the villains in this play, Ellis is a very two-dimensional character, seemingly taken directly from B-grade movies of the 1930s and 1940s.

Emerson

Emerson is a small man to whom Weston owes money. He appears, with Slater, at the end of the play, when he blows up Weston's car. He is menacing and laughs at the family's plight. Even more than Ellis, he (and his partner Slater) is a character of no depth, taken directly from gangster movies. Their entrance is unnecessary, their incessant giggling is both funny to the audience and entirely gratuitous, and the bloody slaughtered lamb they hold is so obviously and clumsily symbolic that Shepard almost appears to be making fun of the audience's desire for an ending that ties up the symbolism of the play.

Emma

Emma is Weston and Ella's daughter and Wesley's sister. Emma is probably about thirteen or fourteen years old, and as the play opens, she is just beginning to menstruate (which is another echo of the "curse" of the title). At first glimpse, she is the model of the good American farm girl, raising chickens for the 4-H and dressed in her uniform. However, her character is much darker and stranger, compelled by forces much deeper than her understanding. She wants out of the household and dreams of riding the family's horse, going to Mexico, and becoming a mechanic. In the middle of the play, offstage, she rides her horse through the Alibi Club and shoots the place up with a rifle. At the end of the play, in a bizarre speech that seems to have been taken directly from a bad gangster movie, she announces that she has decided on a life of crime and ostensibly leaves the house and steals the car, which immediately is blown up by Emerson and Slater. Whether or not she is killed in this incident is never revealed, but, as she is not meant to be a realistic character, whether she survives or not isn't particularly important.

The family turmoil of the play and the disjointedness of the family's life is reflected in her behavior—bizarre, violent, antisocial, seemingly motivated by images she has seen on television and in action films. In her desire to flee her doomed dreams and her propensity to violence, she embodies the family "curse," the "nitroglycerine of the blood" alluded to in the play.

Malcolm

Sergeant Malcolm comes to the house in the second act to inform the family that he has arrested Emma for shooting up the Alibi Club. He is entirely a plot device, without any depth of character.

Slater

Slater is Emerson's partner. He is the follower of the two and enters holding the skinned lamb. Like Emerson, he is a stock character from a gangster film with no depth.

Taylor

Taylor is a lawyer retained by Ella in her efforts to sell the house. He also seems to have seduced Ella as part of their business agreement. We learn that he has also sold worthless desert land to Weston, and as a result, Weston attempts to get his money back from the transaction. On one level of symbolism, Taylor represents the real-estate developers and

MEDIA ADAPTATIONS

- *Curse of the Starving Class* was adapted as a film in 1994 by Shepard and Bruce Beresford and produced by Breakheart Films. In addition, playwright Sam Shepard is himself an actor and can be seen in over a dozen wide-release films (many with his longtime partner Jessica Lange), including *Country, Places in the Heart,* and *The Right Stuff.*

speculators who caused the rapid suburbanization of southern California farmland in the 1940s and 1950s; more generally, he represents the incursions of predatory capitalism into the lives of the poor and working classes. However, on the deep symbolic level, on which this play also operates, Taylor is simply another manifestation of the "curse" under which this family labors. Like Ellis, Emerson, and Slater, Taylor is another entity that injects itself inside the family, causing it to hemorrhage and die.

Wesley

Wesley is the son of Weston and Ella. He is approximately seventeen years old (although his age is never specified) and angry about his situation in life. He dreams of leaving the family and going to Alaska. Whereas his mother, influenced by romantic notions, seeks to flee to the ancient countries of Europe and his sister, influenced by thriller films, wants to lose herself in Mexico or in the one-gas-station towns of southern California, Wesley wants to find another new frontier. His family, presumably, has sought out this frontier of southern California, a frontier that is disappearing rapidly. But because of the "curse" on the family, he must seek out the new and uninhabited.

Wesley is also the most physical character in the play. As the curtain opens, he is engaged in physical labor (putting the broken pieces of the door into a wheelbarrow) and in a shocking scene soon after, he drops his pants and urinates on his sister's

4-H project. Immediately after this, he complains about being hungry and is associated closely with the maggot-infested lamb that he brings into the kitchen. His physicality is strong and at times disturbing. Wesley also introduces one of the most important themes into the play: the theme of germs and infections. In the first act, when his mother tells him to take the lamb outside, he tells his sister that she is afraid of ''Germs. The idea of germs. Invisible germs mysteriously floating around in the air. Anything's a potential carrier.''

Weston

Weston is the father of Emma and Wesley. He is a violent alcoholic who resents the poverty of his family, and as a result, he spends his time drinking at the Alibi Club. He has become involved with gangsters and owes them a great deal of money. To solve his money problems, he sells his house to Ellis. Suffering from his family curse, he is violent and even threatens to kill Taylor and his wife when he learns that they are plotting to sell the house. He has had a previous dealing with Taylor in which he bought a piece of property from him. During the play, he discovers that the land he bought is worthless.

Like Wesley, Weston grew up on a farm, and he reminisces about this with Wesley. In fact, in the first two acts, Weston tends to live in the past, telling stories about his upbringing and about his experiences in the war. But when the third act opens, Weston has changed dramatically, it seems: he is dressed in new clean clothes and has sobered up; he is folding the laundry and talking to the lamb. He begins making, not destroying, a home and even tells Wesley that he has plans to turn their land into an avocado orchard. But there is a ring of strangeness to his story, for he is telling the lamb his story about castrating lambs and throwing their bloody testicles up on a roof. In the symbolic structure of the play, he represents the man cursed to his fate, whose efforts to secure his house or body from outside invaders will always be thwarted.

THEMES

The Disappearing Frontier

Shepard's work, from his first play *Cowboys* to his most recent scripts, is suffused with images of cowboys, frontiersmen, and pioneers. When he was asked by a *Theatre Quarterly* interviewer in 1974 why he wrote about cowboys, Shepard replied:

> Cowboys are really interesting to me—these guys, most of them really young, about sixteen or seventeen, who decided they didn't want to have anything to do with the East Coast, with that way of life, and took on this immense country, and didn't have any real rules.

Shepard's fascination with images from the Western frontier also derives from his sense that something great and important in the American character has disappeared.

In *Curse of the Starving Class*, the unnamed family on which the play centers are all affected by their unidentifiable sensation that a frontier has disappeared. They live in southern California, a place that was initially a true frontier and then in the depression became the land of dreams for poor migrants from the Dust Bowl and the South. But it, too, is changing, going from being some of the richest farmland in the United States to becoming the suburban sprawl of Los Angeles. Each of the characters responds to this differently. Ella wants none of it; she seeks to sell the house and use the money to go to Europe (the very opposite of a frontier). Weston is lost, beaten-down, and drunk, and he has sought to buy more land on an even more remote frontier—the desert. The children both romanticize the frontier. Emma sees herself as a character in a movie, pumping gas and fixing cars at a remote town far from civilization, while Wesley (like his father, perhaps?) still seeks for the real frontier: Alaska.

Although Shepard has denied that he is trying to write social protest plays, *Curse of the Starving Class* reads like one. In this play, the frontier disappears because of predatory capitalism (represented largely by Taylor, the lawyer who wants to buy the family's house in order to create a suburb and who sells Weston worthless land). But capitalism and greed also work on a much more personal level to ruin the family. Ellis knows that Weston is a drunk and is not responsible for his own actions; nonetheless, he is happy to keep making money off his drinking and to take advantage of Weston by buying his house. The frontier, a land where a man could take his fate in his own hands and be the master of his destiny, is entirely gone in this play, replaced by the ''curse'' that marks this family and the ''starving class'' to which they belong.

TOPICS FOR FURTHER STUDY

- Research the different ways in which plays go from being written to being produced in America. Who writes plays? What different kinds of plays are there? What is community theatre? Regional theatre? What does a "Broadway play" mean? What is the difference between Broadway, off-Broadway, and off-off-Broadway? Who pays for each kind of play to be produced?

- Divide into groups as a class, with each group directing a section of one of the acts of *Curse of the Starving Class*. Pay attention to the property list provided and find those items. Dress the characters as Shepard specifies. As you watch the play, think about other ways the groups could have directed the scenes and how that would have changed the understanding of the play.

- The history of southern California—the transformation of a hostile land into a farming paradise and then into suburbia—in many ways mirrors the history of the United States as a whole, and *Curse of the Starving Class* alludes to many of the currents in that history. Research the history of Los Angeles and its suburbs, focusing on how irrigation caused the desert to bloom and on how this farmland attracted migrants from the American South and Southwest and from Mexico.

- Sam Shepard is not only a playwright and screenwriter but he has also become a noted actor. See some of his movies (good candidates include *Days of Heaven, Country,* and *The Right Stuff*) and compare the themes of those movies to the themes of *Curse of the Starving Class.*

Family Curses

In a way, *Curse of the Starving Class* is an updating of one of the oldest extant play cycles, Aeschylus' *Oresteia.* That trilogy, written in the fifth century B.C.E., tells the story of the house of the Greek hero Agamemnon, who brought a curse upon his family by sacrificing his daughter Iphigenia in order to obtain favorable winds for his army's voyage to Troy. In the ten years he is gone at the Trojan War, his wife Clytemnestra takes up with another man, and upon Agamemnon's return, she and her lover murder her husband. Orestes, Agamemnon's son, must avenge his father's death. The cycle of violence cannot end—murder must answer murder—until the gods themselves intervene.

The family of *Curse of the Starving Class* seems similarly doomed. They suffer under a "curse" that is peculiar to them, not just to their class. Ella says in the second act that this curse is "invisible but it's there. It's always there. It comes onto us like nightmare." At other points, characters refer to the curse as a germ, as an infection, and as nitroglycerin in the blood. The curse dooms them to violence, poverty, and self-destruction, and the result is al-ways to explode the enclosing structure of the family. Weston's drunkenness breaks the family apart and, literally, damages the integrity of the house itself when he breaks down the door. Ella sleeps with the lawyer who is trying to take their house away. Emma, when she figuratively becomes a woman (has her first menstrual period), undertakes a life of crime and violence.

But it is Wesley who is the real emblem of the curse. At the start of the play, in a long monologue, he narrates his father's rage of the previous night. In this monologue, he switches between first and third person, as if he were watching things happen to him from the outside. Food, the symbol of a healthy family, is literally pissed on by him when he urinates on his sister's chart of how to cut up a frying chicken. And at the end of the play, after Weston has sobered up and decided to return to the family, Wesley changes into Weston's old filthy clothes and butchers the lamb that is, in part, the symbol of the fragility of the family. As he reaches manhood, the curse takes hold of him, and he is compelled to behave in a way that ensures the destruction of himself and of his family.

STYLE

Symbolism

Curse of the Starving Class uses symbolism a great deal, but Shepard uses it in a jarring way. His symbols—the lamb, the broken door, the refrigerator, the old car—jump out at the viewer and almost announce ''I am a symbol!'' But Shepard uses them less as true symbols than as evocative images. This play cannot be ''decoded'' as an allegory in which we can reduce the refrigerator to a representation of spiritual hunger, the lamb to a representation of sacrifice and innocence, and the door to a representation of the barrier between the family and the outside world. These objects are indeed symbolic, but they are meant to hit the audience with their power. It is shocking to see a live lamb on stage and even more shocking to see it bloody and dead; similarly, the centrality of the refrigerator to every scene and the constant opening and closing of its door reminds us of the theme of hunger and starving, but Shepard refuses to nail down its meaning for us.

The symbols work together to undermine the realism of the play. Realism, a style of drama that seeks to represent the world on the stage just as it is in real life, was out of favor in the 1960s, the decade in which Shepard began writing. Symbolic dramas were popular, and Shepard wrote those kinds of plays in his early career. With *Curse of the Starving Class*, Shepard moved more toward realism, to the social dramas of such classic realists as Ibsen. But Shepard retains the symbolic structure of his earlier plays. These people are not meant to be accurate representations of real people, nor are we meant to believe that this family had a lamb, brought it inside, and then butchered it. Like the stock gangsters whose entrance signals the end of the play, these symbols break down the illusion of reality. The drama is here to create an impact: whereas the realistic story of the family appeals to our minds and emotions, the symbols affect us on a subconscious level.

Motif

Closely connected to the symbolic structure of the play is its use of motif, or a recurring image. Two motifs, very near each other in meaning, recur throughout *Curse of the Starving Class*: images of inside/outside and images of disease and sickness. Obviously, these two motifs are related to each other, for disease is the intrusion of an entity that should be kept outside the body. Shepard, though, does not define the family's curse just as a disease, though; this ''curse'' is more historical and supernatural, like the curses that afflicted the great families of Greek tragedy.

The first motif almost overwhelms the play with its omnipresence. The play opens on an image of the breakdown of the barrier between outside and inside, the shattered front door that allows all sorts of undesirable elements to enter the house. As the play continues we constantly see this theme emphasized: conversations in the kitchen are conducted in a normal tone of voice, but conversations between one person in the kitchen and another person outside the room are almost always furious screaming matches; the refrigerator's constant opening and shutting reminds us that ''inside'' is an empty place; even the lamb, when brought onstage by Wesley, is placed into a small penned enclosure. Inside has become a hollow, void place to the family, and as a result, they want out—Ella to Europe, Emma to Mexico, Wesley to Alaska, Weston to an alcoholic stupor.

Disease and sickness, and images of a poison circulating through the blood, complement the motif of inside/outside. The curse on the family is described by both women as something that breeds internally in Weston and Wesley and is inevitable. Also inevitable, and also treated as a ''curse,'' is Emma's menstruation (which is another image of the inside escaping to the outside). Ella warns Emma that swimming during her period could kill her. Even the lamb suffers from an invasion of a harmful force in its body: maggots have infested its digestive tract. When the body's defenses fail and intruders are allowed to breed inside the body, the play tells us, the body will soon fall to those forces that threaten it.

HISTORICAL CONTEXT

Urban Sprawl

As a country whose greatest natural resource has always been its seemingly endless supply of land and space, the United States settlement and development has generally followed the same pattern. New land—Plymouth Rock, California, Alaska,

COMPARE
&
CONTRAST

- **1970s:** Oil and gas shortages precipitate an energy crisis in the United States. Cars line up for gasoline, and President Ford appoints an "energy czar" to head U.S. energy policy efforts. As the crisis ends, both politicians and the public realize that these "shortages" were created artificially by oil-producing countries and oil companies in order to boost profits.

  Today: The U.S. again faces an energy crisis, but this time the shortages and exorbitant prices affect electricity. California suffers from "rolling blackouts," and the major population centers of the East Coast are warned about similar blackouts or brownouts. President George W. Bush proposes an energy policy that stresses greater production, but many citizens mistrust this policy because of Bush's and Vice-President Dick Cheney's ties to oil companies and the energy industry.

- **1970s:** In Los Angeles, suburbanization continues unabated. The central city suffers while middle-class people flee to suburbs that sprawl ever farther into what was once farmland.

  Today: After riots, fires, a major earthquake, landslides, and flooding, Los Angeles continues to grow. However, many people move back into the central city to work in the burgeoning entertainment industry.

- **1970s:** With the "first wave" of feminism, women begin demanding equal treatment by the law and by their husbands. Laws against marital rape, for instance, gain ground in many states that had previously resisted them. Conservatives, however, decry feminism, blaming it for rising divorce rates and what they see as a "breakdown" of the nuclear family.

  Today: Feminism is in its "third wave." As many of the issues feminists initially fought for have become law, feminist groups turn their sights on other issues. However, many of the same issues (such as access to abortions and birth control, equal pay for equal work, and affirmative action) still remain to be resolved.

---

or anywhere in between—is settled and cleared for farming or industry by rugged individualist pioneers; more people move near that newly desirable land, and towns spring up; the towns grow so big and encroaching that the rugged individualists feel crowded by city life (or are unable, economically, to survive) and move on to find new frontiers.

California, especially southern California, is perhaps the best laboratory to examine this development. When the Spanish first explored the area of Los Angeles and the San Gabriel and San Fernando Valleys, the region was arid, almost desert. Large-scale irrigation beginning in the late nineteenth century "made the desert bloom," and soon the area (along with the Imperial and Central Valleys) was America's richest farmland, producing citrus fruits, melons, berries, even lettuce and other water hungry crops. The agriculture drew refugees from the Dust Bowl states during the Great Depression, and poor people thronged to southern California. At the same time, land speculators were buying the land of Los Angeles, Ventura, Orange, and Riverside counties and preparing it for residential development. Advertising in newspapers around the country, they encouraged people to come to "Sunny California!" to retire or simply to flee the frigid northern climates or unhealthy cities of the East. Los Angeles grew dramatically in the middle of the twentieth century, becoming one of America's largest cities.

But the people who came to Los Angeles did not want to live in the same kinds of overcrowded cities many of them had left back East. They wanted large houses, cars, two-car garages, front and back yards. But with the millions of people who now lived there, there simply was not enough room in the city. The speculators and developers then began building subdivisions in the areas immediately surrounding the city. Ever more land was needed, and the developers set their sights to the farmlands surrounding the city. City-dwellers seeking lower taxes, lower crime rates, and less congestion came to these suburbs. "Urban sprawl" came to Los Angeles.

Today, Los Angeles is one of the largest urban conglomerations in the world. Some population geographers see the U.S. cities of Los Angeles and San Diego and the Mexican city of Tijuana as one immense "megalopolis," a mega-city with tens of millions of inhabitants. The open spaces that once separated them have largely disappeared; similarly, the farmland that once was the area's largest economic resource has long since given way to other industries. Caught up in this are families such as the one in *Curse of the Starving Class*, whose land is coveted by subdivision developers like Taylor. In the play, as in the real world, these families were often taken advantage of, selling their land for well below market rates and finding themselves with nowhere to go and little money to sustain them.

CRITICAL OVERVIEW

Curse of the Starving Class is not only the first play of what is known as the "family trilogy" (the two other plays in that trilogy are *Buried Child* and *True West*), it also stands as the initial play of the second phase of Shepard's career. A very prolific playwright, Shepard saw numerous of his plays produced in most years from the time of his first play (1965) to 1978, the year of *Curse of the Starving Class*. This start of the second phase of his career is often interpreted as a move away from radical experimentation toward a greater inclusion of "realism," or the kind of theatre that attempts to portray on stage things as they actually are in the world, both in terms of the construction of the play and in its content. Charles R. Lyons, in his essay "Shepard's Family Trilogy and the Conventions of Modern Realism," writes that these plays "break with Shepard's earlier dramatic writing by implementing several of the conventions of dramatic realism." However, Lyons argues, Shepard never becomes a true "realist." Rather, he just "borrows" realism but does so in such a way that it "complicates the strategies of dramatic real-

ism" and "fragment[s] the possibility of narrative unity with significant disjunctions, interstices, and inconsistencies."

Critics of the play's initial productions noted its dark tone and, often, its similarity to the play *The Cherry Orchard* by the nineteenth-century Russian playwright Chekhov. Reviewing the 1978 production of the play at the Joseph Papp Public Theatre in New York (not the original production; it was first put on in 1977 in London), Douglas Watt of the *New York Daily News* called the play "a bitter farce, a desolate tragicomedy variation on a favorite theme of the author's, the stifling of the American spirit by unseen, unknown forces gobbling up the land and the soul of its people in the name of progress." Richard Eder, writing for the *New York Times* about the same production, compliments Shepard's "images of considerable power" and "style that oscillates between realism and savage fantasy" and feels that the play "reads well" but was not constructed to actually be staged. In the *New York Post,* Clive Barnes was impressed by the raw power of the play but thought that the play was "probably too muddled and too indirect to compensate for the fever-heat of its passion."

Other reviewers shared these same ambivalent sentiments. Howard Kissel of *Women's Wear Daily* was caught up in the weirdness of the play but felt the ending fell short: the "concluding images seem contrived, manipulative and self-indulgent." Stanley Kaufmann, writing for the *New Republic,* called Shepard "phenomenal" and "the best" playwright in America under forty but argued that in this play, Shepard showed more talent than careful craftsmanship: "it contains so much, yet ultimately it is not enough." John Beaufort of the *Christian Science Monitor* praised the power of the imagery but concluded that the play was "in the main unpleasant" and that "there is little nourishment in this case history of the spiritually starved." And, reviewing the earlier London production of the play, John Lahr wrote in the *Village Voice* that "there is not enough work in" Shepard's script because "the play leaves too much unexplored. The characters don't show; they tell."

Recent critical opinion on this play has elevated its reputation. The strange and jarring play is now understood as an oscillation between realism and symbolism, and both critics and audiences, by now familiar with Shepard's method, accept the play's violent language and mordant tone.

Henry Thomas, as Wesley, and James Wood, as Weston, in the 1994 film adaptation

CRITICISM

Greg Barnhisel

Barnhisel teaches writing and directs the Writing Center at the University of Southern California. In this essay, he examines themes of disease, invasion, and breaching in Curse of the Starving Class.

Although it is not a symbolic drama whose meaning lies only in the interaction of its symbols, neither is *Curse of the Starving Class* a truly realistic drama, in which the audience is meant to empathize with the characters as real people. Critic Stephen J. Bottoms identifies Shepard's style, or school, as ''grotesque realism'' and writes that ''the action of *Curse* veers wildly between a range of clashing generic styles, from kitchen sink banality to exaggerated melodrama, and from broad comedy to ritualized symbolism, thwarting any attempt to read into it a unified depiction of a stable or unified real world.'' With the style of the play ''veering wildly'' as it does, viewers latch onto the stable elements of the play—the symbols, the images, the motifs. Through these motifs, Shepard attempts to convey the power of the play.

The play is structured, in its images and symbols, on the difference between inside and outside

and on the dangers inherent in letting things from the outside begin to inhabit the inside. David J. DeRose writes about the play:

> [It] is about violation and invasion; about the all-too-sudden invasion of a once-rural farming community by sprawling suburban housing developments; about the poisonous violation of one's physical being by invisible biological 'curses' like genetic conditioning, microscopic germs, maggots, even menstruation; about the impersonal invasion of uncontrollable socio-economic forces into the family unit; and about the terrifying violation of a house at night by a drunken father who smashes down the front door, leaving home and family vulnerable to even further violation.

Weston explicitly states the theme in his first appearance, wanting to know ''Is this the inside or the outside?'' when he sees the lamb in the kitchen. Each main character, each event, each symbol carries with it this tension between a barrier and an invader attempting to breach it.

The play opens on an image of a breached defense. The family's front door lies in shards on the floor, and Wesley is picking up the pieces, hoping to rebuild the family's symbolic gate for keeping out the outsiders. But their conversation reveals to us that even before this happened, the difference between outside and inside was already perverted: the

WHAT DO I READ NEXT?

- *Buried Child* (1978) is the second of Shepard's "family trilogy." It examines many of the same themes as does *Curse of the Starving Class.* In 1978, the play won the Pulitzer Prize for the best American play of the year. The trilogy ends with *True West,* the story of two brothers.

- Many of the plays of the German playwright Bertolt Brecht use techniques of pastiche and the undermining of naturalism to achieve an effect on the viewer. Brecht's theories about drama and how drama can have a social impact were very influential among American playwrights (Shepard included) in the 1960s. Some of Brecht's best-known plays include *The Caucasian Chalk Circle, Mother Courage and Her Children, Galileo,*

The Threepenny Opera, and *The Good Woman of Szechwan.*

- Mike Davis's *City of Quartz* (1990) is an extremely detailed and provocative study of the history of Los Angeles. His argument is that every aspect of L.A.—from the organization of the police department to the zoning laws to the design of park benches—was designed with the intention of isolating the wealthy from the large masses of poor and minority people.

- The classic story of poor rural people moving to California is John Steinbeck's *The Grapes of Wrath* (1939). The Joad family, impoverished farmers from Oklahoma, pack up their truck and move to find work in California, only to discover that the earthly paradise is not what they imagined.

---

door was locked to keep one of the family members out. The body, the house, was itself already weakened before the play begins, being infested with termites.

Once the door is broken down, though, anything can come it, and does. Weston returns, drunk, and brings anger and spite to the house. Taylor, the true agent of disease, comes in and infects Ella, recruiting her to help him. Ellis enters and brings money in exchange for the house but then takes that back. Finally, the motiveless violence of Emerson and Slater walk in like an opportunistic infection that takes advantage of an already weakened body. Images of such infections run through the play, from Emma's description of the family's curse as being "in the blood" to the maggots that have taken up residence in the lamb's body.

Food, along with the theme of hunger and starving, also works with this theme of inside/outside. All of the family seem obsessed with food: Ella offers Wesley bacon and bread, Emma is giving a presentation on frying chickens, Wesley stares in the empty refrigerator, and (after his conversion)

Weston stocks the refrigerator full of food. The family denies they are of the "starving class," but the dearth of food in the house gives the lie to their claim. Just after finding an empty refrigerator, Emma yells, "Eat my socks!" Finally, in an act intended as a last stand against hunger, Wesley butchers the lamb that has represented both the family and Wesley himself. This butchering, which Wesley intended as a practical act, turns out to be useless and redundant, since Weston has already bought food. Killing the lamb becomes just another violent act committed as a result of the curse.

Ella and Weston, although cursed in different ways, both unwittingly facilitate the breakdown of the house. (The word "house" here needs to be understood both literally and figuratively, as in Greek tragedy or Poe's "Fall of the House of Usher.") Weston, of course, literally breaks the house, smashing the door. He also injects his drunken, violent self into the kitchen and lodges himself there. But in the third act, he seems to have shaken off the curse. He cleans himself up, purchases food for the family (the lack of food is another symptom of this "curse of the starving class"), and takes care of the lamb, which represents the family itself. But even though Weston seems to have left his curse behind, Wesley has now come into his birthright and will see the family destroyed. Ella breaks down the barriers of inside/outside the family in a different way, inviting an outside (Taylor) in and helping him take the family's house. Not coincidentally, she also has sex with him, bringing something from inside the marriage and giving it to an outsider.

Emma's disease is of a different sort, or sorts. When we first see her, her mother is lecturing her on the dangers of her first menstrual period (which she calls "the curse"). Her mother tells her that her menstruation is not just her insides escaping but that it also can contribute to an invasion from the outside. "You should never go swimming when that happens," she says. "The water draws it out of you." But Emma's more dangerous infection or curse is her infection by popular media images. She dreams of scenes from action films and wants to be a mechanic or ride off on her horse or flee to Mexico like "that guy" who wrote *The Treasure of the Sierra Madre* or live a life of crime. The men who arrive at the end of the play and (apparently) kill her, Slater and Emerson, seem to have emerged from her movie-spawned fantasies.

Of all of the characters, this outside/inside tension most profoundly affects Wesley. In the course of the play, he comes into his manhood; he grows into the curse and takes it on as his birthright, just as his father resolves to leave it behind. But throughout the play, Wesley is struggling to keep the inside inside and the outside outside. He tries to build a new door, he erects an enclosure on stage for the lamb, he does and says different kinds of things when in the kitchen (onstage) and out of the kitchen (offstage).

But he cannot withstand the pressure on him, and his strange syntactic choices in his first monologue exemplify this. In that speech, he begins by narrating the events of the previous night in the past tense: "I listened like an animal . . . I could feel the space around me." Then he switches abruptly to the present: "I picture him sitting. What's he doing?" Finally, the speech ends as Wesley seemingly loses his grip on grammar, using only the present participial forms of verbs: "Woman screaming . . . Dad crashing away . . . ignition grinding." Modes of narration (past, present, nongrammatical) mix as his ability to narrate "normally" breaks down. He is trying to fight off an irresistible force whose nature

> EACH MAIN CHARACTER, EACH EVENT, EACH SYMBOL CARRIES WITH IT THIS TENSION BETWEEN A BARRIER AND AN INVADER ATTEMPTING TO BREACH IT."

we do not yet know. But we soon see examples of his bizarre behavior, his breaching of the border between what should be inside and what should be outside, when he urinates on Emma's poster and, later, when he comes on stage utterly naked.

Wesley does this because of the "curse" that lies on the family. This family was doomed from the beginning, for an intruder older than any character in the play has already fixed their fate. This "curse," as Ella calls it, is carried inside the men like a disease and infects them from the inside until it destroys them. Emma describes Weston's curse:

". . . a short fuse they call it. Runs in the family. His father was just like him. And his father before him. Wesley is just like Pop, too. Like liquid dynamite. . . Nitroglycerine. In the blood." In the second act, Weston himself tells Wesley that he remembers the "poison" starting to act in him: "I saw myself infected with it. . . I saw me carrying it around. His poison in my body. You think that's fair?" Ella says that the curse infests the men's body even to the molecular level. "It goes back and back to tiny cells and genes," she says. "To atoms. To tiny little swimming things making up their minds without us." These quotes bear significant resemblance to one of Shepard's statements about his attraction to Greek tragedy: he said that the plays evoke "emotional states, these forces [that] go so far back that they go right to the birth of man. And we're still living in the shadow of these things."

The inside, then, betrays the body itself, and this betrayal is foreordained. There is nothing Weston, or Wesley, can do about it. The fatalism of Weston's story of the lambs and the eagle resonates here, for there are no winners in Weston's view: the lambs are castrated, and the eagle and cat kill each other. In the family's life, just as Weston changes himself and symbolically joins the family again, Wesley takes on his old role, acting as disrupter and killing the lamb that, because of Weston's care for it, has come to represent the family. The curse operates unimpeded.

The social commentary of the play, its inclusion of the theme of suburbanization and urban sprawl, is another manifestation of the theme of infection from inside. Taylor does not use brute force (as do Emerson and Slater) to relieve the family of their land; he insinuates himself inside the family in order to accomplish this. His goal is to buy their land so that he can develop a suburb, but in the process, he contributes to the destruction of the family by seducing Ella and earning Weston's rage (for selling him worthless land). The suburb comes into being and destroys the farmland, not because of governmental order, but because the farmers themselves allow it to happen by selling their land. They, the insiders, invite the outsiders in and allow them to destroy the body (here understood as the stretches of farmland that once characterized southern California). They invite in the ''zombie invasion,'' as Wesley calls it.

Curse of the Starving Class is a strange play. It isn't quite realistic, but it isn't quite purely symbolic either. Should we be emotionally affected by it? Is it a social protest play? Shepard denies that he is interested in writing social commentary; at other times, he has stated that his plays of this period were influenced by the classic Greek tragedies, which sought to elicit ''pity and fear,'' in Aristotle's words, from audiences. Is it for this that he includes stock characters, clearly taken from B-grade gangster movies? Is this why he makes the characters so erratic, moving, in a beat, from hollering rage to calm? Is this why, in a word, the play constantly makes the audience aware that it is watching a play but at the same time succeeds in genuinely emotionally reaching that audience?

Source: Greg Barnhisel, Critical Essay on *Curse of the Starving Class,* in *Drama for Students,* The Gale Group, 2002.

Charles R. Lyons

In the following essay excerpt, the author discusses Shepard's merging of archetypal familial relationship paradigms with the realism associated with his style.

Curse of the Starving Class displays its schematic organisation by dividing up most of its text among four principal family member/speakers in a artificially symmetrical scheme—Weston/Wesley; Ella/Emma. This contrived conflation of names suggests, early in the play, that the text relates the younger figures to the older; and, as the play progresses, we see certain ways in which the children replicate or substitute for their parents. In general, *Curse* voices and reiterates a process in which self-identification takes the form of assuming aspects of the identity of another. The text also voices resistance to that process. The language suggests that the assimilation of the physical traits or behaviour of the older by the younger is either an inevitable or natural process of inheritance, a logical transfer of some substance from one person to another: the physical image of the father reproduced in the body of the son, the poison of the father inherited by the son, the curse of menstrual blood inherited by the daughter.

Curse of the Starving Class brings the problematic father to the foreground even though, at one provocative moment, the mother works with the idea of her son as the replication of her father rather than her husband in a moment that relates to the son/grandfather connection of *Buried Child.* The text demands that the actor playing Wesley urinate on the charts that the character, Emma, has prepared for an oral presentation, revealing his penis to the audience, in an exhibitionistic gesture the stage directions place 'downstage'. While this act also clarifies the hostility of the relationships among the family structure, the incident functions primarily to display the son's circumcised penis that Ella will soon identify as identical to that of her father. Here she focuses upon her dream of Wesley as the replica of her father:

> Why aren't you sensitive like your Grandfather was? I always thought you were just like him, but you're not are you? . . . Why aren't you? You're circumcised just like him. It's almost identical in fact.

This statement implies that the father, Weston, is not circumcised, and this indirect suggestion works to undermine or complicate the several processes in which Wesley attempts to present himself as the replica of his father.

Weston narrates a significant action in which he removes his clothing, refreshes or purifies himself in a cleansing bath, and walks naked through his house in a deliberate celebration of his reconstituted identity. In Wesley's attempt to incorporate the identity of his father, he acts out what Weston only tells us about. That is, the text of this play presents the father's action in the less 'present' form of narration and demands that the son enact the sequence, in a scene that displays his body to the audience. Consequently, the imitation has more theatrical substance—both in its dramatised presence and exhibitionist quality than the original narration that exists only as speech.

The language of the play—and its visual display of the narrative field, the space in which the story plays itself out—works both to incorporate the presence of the father and to dislocate that image. The play opens with the son's narrative recitation of the destructive arrival and abrupt departure of the father as an event in the immediate past; the text clarifies that the father's presence is periodic rather than continuous; and the text removes his ownership of the land and distances him as the sexual partner of his wife, replacing him with a surrogate lover. Wesley's actions attempt to appropriate and displace the presence of the father and in this assimilation to lose his own identity.

Shepard's problematising of the father figure is conventional. In all of Chekhov's major works, the father's absence contributes to the deteriorating state of the immediate environment: for example, in *The Cherry Orchard,* the death of Ranesvskaya's husband, the man whom she married from outside her class, allows the transgressive behaviour that accelerates the decline of the estate and its purchase by the former peasant, Lopahin. Nora's independence is drained by her father's behaviour toward her in Ibsen's *A Doll's House*; and in *Rosmersholm,* Rebekka's recognition that Dr. West, the mentor with whom she had a sexual relationship, was actually her natural father, disallows her relationship with Rosmer. The problematic father becomes a staple of American realism as evidenced by *Long Day's Journey, All My Sons, Death of a Salesman,* and *The Glass Menagerie.* We even see this figure in *Who's Afraid of Virginia Woolf?* in the representation of the illusory father's weakness. The patriarchs of Shepard's trilogy continue to play out this convention.

In more obvious instances of self-consciousness, *Curse of the Starving Class* displays an overt symbolism that extends the kind of metaphoric use of scene and objects that characterises the texts of Ibsen and Chekhov. First of all, the centrality of the refrigerator to which the inhabitants of this house go again and again, seeking nourishment that will abate

> **" THE LANGUAGE OF THE PLAY—AND ITS VISUAL DISPLAY OF THE NARRATIVE FIELD, THE SPACE IN WHICH THE STORY PLAYS ITSELF OUT—WORKS BOTH TO INCORPORATE THE PRESENCE OF THE FATHER AND TO DISLOCATE THAT IMAGE."**

their appetite, gives this object, in repeated use, a kind of inconographic value. The refrigerator is both a failing source of nourishment and the repository for the inadequate nourishment the parents provide for themselves and their children. The function of this rather banal and obvious symbol is not as significant to this discussion as the blatancy of its use. The lamb provides a more typical symbolic use of a material object. Here the performed text presents a familiar symbol of Judeo-Christian theology: the Pascal lamb sacrificed in the Passover as a substitute for the firstborn son, as that figure is articulated by the Hebrew Bible and transformed in the New Testament into the image of the Christ himself, the lamb or son of God, sacrificed to atone for the sins of all mankind. The complex conflation of lamb, firstborn son, and the symbolic sacrifice of Isaac, which is reified in the Christian passion and the relationship between human father and son and Divine Father and Son—all these resonances amplify the living stage property of the maggot-infested lamb that Wesley nurtures and eventually sacrifices as he acts out his imitation of his father. These images also inform Weston's monologue in which he describes the fight between the tom cat and eagle that takes place while he castrates sheep. For our purposes, the mythic signficance isn't as important as the ways in which the text operates to incorporate this material, to formulate a self-conscious image of the self as a son who is the victim of the dominating presence or residual authority or constraining identity of the father. Ella assists Wesley in that project as she prompts him to re-tell his father's story of the self-destructive hostility of eagle and cat that in combat and death merge into each other to form 'one whole thing'. The unity here, of course, is the merging of mutually self-destructive acts, a unity that does not provide a figure that successfully integrates the various elements of *Curse* into cohesive narrative structure. That refusal to spell out a coherence extends the inconclusive resolution of modern realism—typified in *Ghosts'* refusal to reveal whether Fru Alving gives the fatal sedative to Oswald in the immediate future. The problematic nature of this story's assertion of wholeness, in combination with the theatrical shock of the explosion that denotes the destruction of the Packard and the apparent death of the young girl, aligns with the final shocking images that terminate many of the texts of modern realism: Treplev's suicide, Hedda's suicide, Julie's murder/suicide, the figure of the bound Captain in *The Father*.

Shepard's text merges images that are, clearly, highly resonant cultural artifacts, with the conventional representation of problematic sons who are caught within the coordinates of a role determined by their father's identity. Shifting among the conventional schemes of modern realism and the self-conscious invocation of mythical parallels, *Curse of the Starving Class* attempts to identify the father as both castrator and wastrel and tries to identify the son as both inadequate substitute for the father, and as the failed redeemer of familial guilt through his performance of a ritual sacrifice. In an ambiguous transfer of sexual roles, the menstruating young woman enacts her father's prodigality, and in being blown-up in his Packard, wired to murder him, becomes his surrogate.

True West removes the figure of the father completely except for the ways in which his character is embodied in the language and interaction of the antithetical sons. As a presence in the embedded narrative, however, the father of *True West* becomes a significant figure, a physically and mentally disabled man in deliberate self-exile, pursuing his self-sufficient but self-destructive course. Here *True West* exercises a structural convention that is a particularly American variant of dramatic realism: the opposition of two brothers caught in a triangular relationship with a father. Consider, for example, the competitive brothers in O'Neill's *Beyond the Horizon* who, like Austin and Lee, exchange roles; the sequence of paired brothers in the plays of Arthur Miller; the ambivalent affection and hostility that marks the relationship of Jamie and Edmund in *Long Day's Journey into Night*. In *True West* the convention provides a structure in which the playwright may display the negotiation that takes place between the brothers as they attempt to define themselves through their difference or likeness to the absent and problematic father.

Shepard conflates the paradigmatic relationship of brothers with the convention of the external figure who invades the scene and attempts to dispossess the inhabitant(s). Here that space gains resonance because its comforting, if banal, dimensions belong to the mother. However, the psychic territory over which these men do battle focuses more upon the father than the mother. Lee, apparently less connected to the 'real' world than his educated brother, acts out a role that, in itself, seems to enact his father's failed western mythology. Ironically, Austin himself trades upon a more self-conscious fictionalising; and, to compound the irony, Lee is able to market his mythologising more successfully than Austin in the negotiation with Saul Kimmer, the Hollywood producer—although he depends upon Austin's mediation of plot/myth into scenario/text. In *True West* the embedded narrative includes the ostensible biographies of its principals, the Ivy League university student opposed to the nomad—but the primary embedded narrative becomes the scenario of Lee's western drama, the compressed text-within-the-text.

In summary, I would describe this group of three related texts as a theatrical attempt to articulate the processes of exorcising the presence of the father, and assimilating his energy by appropriating self-consciously both the aesthetic conventions of realism, and the archetypal paradigms in which we perceive the relationships of father and son. One of the difficulties of reading dramatic texts with the perspectives of psychoanalytic theory is the difficulty in separating the archetypal from the conventional. Reading the Ibsen canon, with the insistent repetition of the sexual triad that remains constant throughout its variety of theatrical modes, it is possible to see the ways in which theatrical convention serves an idiosyncratic and obsessive central drama. The combination of Ibsen's idiosyncrasy and the materialist demand for contemporary detail forged many of the conventions that shape the realist project. Shepard both uses those conventions and ironically foregrounds their artifice in a curious explication of familial relationships that seem to me, at this point, more conventional than archetypal, more self-conscious than unconscious, more public than private, more aesthetic than psychological, more theatrical than autobiographical.

Source: Charles R. Lyons, ''Shepard's Family Trilogy and the Conventions of Modern Realism,'' in *Rereading Shepard,*

A scene from the 1991 theatrical production of Curse of the Starving Class, *featuring John McEnery and Alex Kingston*

edited by Leonard Wilcox, St. Martin's Press, 1993, pp. 125–29.

David J. DeRose

In the following essay, the author discusses Shepard's creation of an "intricate network" of elements to create a "mythic subtext" of forces infecting the lives of his characters.

In *Curse of the Starving Class*, it is not just the father's ghost who refuses to die but also a family curse, an inherited predisposition toward violence, a "nitroglycerine of the blood" that flows through the son's veins as it does through the father's. Like the unseen forces at work on Shepard's earlier characters, this blood curse, transmitted from generation to generation by "tiny cells and genes," is a powerful yet invisible force, imposing itself upon the characters in the play without their consent. And, without their consent, it turns them against each other, so that the curse of Shepard's "starving class" family is to be forever locked in battle: clinging to each other for life, yet fighting to the death.

Curse of the Starving Class starts in the wake of an act of domestic violence. The play opens to the family's teenage son, Wesley, cleaning up the pieces of a broken door. The previous night, his father, Weston, had arrived home drunk to find that the door to the house had been locked against him by his wife, Ella. In an intoxicated rage, Weston battered down the door with his body, then disappeared. The next morning, as Ella enters the kitchen setting of the play to make herself some breakfast (there is nothing in the house to eat but bacon and bread), Wesley describes the events of the previous night as he experienced them from his bed. Wesley's sensory-specific monologue, similar to those of Shepard's early plays, creates a heightened sense of the physical and emotional invasion of his being by his father's violence. He is an open receiver, sensing the "space around me like a big, black world," and aware that "any second something could invade me. Some foreigner. Something undescribable." What invades Wesley's being is the sound of his father smashing down the door to the house and the terror of knowing he is vulnerable to the same violence: "Man cursing. Man going insane. Feet and hands tearing. Head smashing. Man yelling. Shoulder smashing. Whole body crashing. Woman screaming. Mom screaming. Mom screaming for police". Weston's violent attack upon his own home and his terrorizing of his wife and family are

> BOTH THEMATICALLY AND THEATRICALLY, *CURSE OF THE STARVING CLASS* CONTAINS IMAGES OF VIOLATION AND INVASION BY HOSTILE, UNCOMBATABLE FORCES."

both literal and symbolic destruction of the protective circle of the family. He not only violates their safety, but by virtue of his absence as father and protector, he leaves them open to attack and invasion from others. Wesley is particularly sensitive to this sense of defenselessness, for he clearly wants to open himself to his father, but in so doing, he risks devastating emotional violation.

Both thematically and theatrically, *Curse of the Starving Class* contains images of violation and invasion by hostile, uncombatable forces. The play is about the all-too-sudden invasion of a small Southern California ranching community by the suburban sprawl of housing developments and superhighways; about the violation of one's physical being by poisonous "curses" such as genetic conditioning, microscopic germs, bloodlines, violence, even menstruation; about the impersonal invasion of uncontrollable socioeconomic forces into the family unit; and about the terrifying violation of a family home at night by a drunken father who smashes down the front door, leaving house and family vulnerable to even further violation.

The stage setting itself is an image of the violation of the home and family: kitchen furniture is set against a stark, open stage. There are no doors, no walls, only red-checked curtains suspended in midair to suggest the farmhouse windows. The first image one sees on this exposed kitchen set is Wesley filling a wheelbarrow (a piece of outdoor equipment) with the shattered remains of the door to the house, the only barrier between family and outside world. Any sense of interiority or of the domestic comfort of the home is immediately undermined. When the father, Weston, eventually returns midway through the play, he finds a live lamb in his kitchen. He ponders aloud this lack of differentiation between the interior and the exterior: "Is this the inside or the outside? This is

inside, right? This is the inside of the house. Even with the door out it's still the inside. (to lamb) Right? (to himself) Right." The home—including the comforting reality the word *home* conventionally suggests—has been left exposed by the dissolution of the family and the estrangement of the mother and the father. It cannot be repaired. Even when Wesley builds a new door in an act symbolic of his desire to keep the family intact, strangers walk straight onto the stage and into the family kitchen.

Those strangers appear as the result of Weston's and Ella's individual attempts to sell the house and the farm without the other's knowledge. Ella has been dealing with Taylor, a slick attorney who has made her sexual seduction part of their business transaction. Weston has cut a deal with a sleazy bar owner, Ellis, who intends to turn the home into a steak house. Weston, it turns out, needs the money to pay off some heavy debts he has run up with local thugs.

The peculiar characterization of these intrusive strangers, with their threatening appearance and cold, criminal attitudes, is completely foreign to the domestic setting of the play and realistic characterizations of the family members. In a review of the original London production, Charles Marowitz noted that "these outside characters . . . waft on in a style peculiar to themselves with no reference to the ongoing, naturalistically pitched main situation" (Marowitz). Wesley draws attention to this peculiarity when he describes the forces at work upon his family as a zombie invasion: "It's a zombie invasion. Taylor is the head zombie. He's the scout for the other zombies. He's only a sign that more zombies are on their way. They'll be filing through the door pretty soon". Taylor is the first "zombie" to stroll unannounced into the kitchen, but others follow, including two moronic hired thugs, Emerson and Slater. These unannounced entrances become increasingly bizarre and threatening, climaxing with the offstage explosion of Weston's car (with his daughter, Emma, in it) as Emerson and Slater enter, giggling hysterically "as though they'd pulled off a Halloween stunt," holding out the carcass of a slaughtered lamb.

Watching these otherworldly characters burst onto the stage of this domestic drama is like watching the intersection of one plane of reality with another. Their sudden appearance is as alien and disruptive as that of Cody's cowboy brothers at the end of *Geography of a Horse Dreamer* or the business-suited men at the end of *Cowboys #2*. But, in *Curse of the Starving Class*, these figures resound with both theatrical and thematic significance. On the one hand, these characters are like the intrusive figures of Shepard's earliest plays: theatrical manifestations of the self's exposure to a world so strange as to unfix permanently one's preconceptions of reality. But they are also grounded in Shepard's personal experience as a teenager in Duarte, California. The lawyers and thugs represent the developers and real-estate hustlers who exploited Los Angeles's postwar population boom by literally wiping out the tiny farming communities that lay east of the city in the Central Valley. As superfreeways and mass housing developments began to spread into the rich farmland, small communities like the one in which Shepard grew up were literally wiped out of existence as fast as buildings could be erected and roads constructed. Postmodern America, with its shopping malls and fast-food chains, rapidly made the rural life-style of Shepard's "starving class" family obsolete.

Shepard has repeatedly claimed that such socially significant interpretations of his plays are not within his field of concern as a dramatist: "I'm not interested in the American social scene at all," Shepard has said of his family plays. "It totally bores me". Turning to the family for inspiration, Shepard hoped to "start with something personal and see how it follows out and opens to something bigger". The "something bigger" Shepard pursued was not the social relevance he had courted with American pop culture plays like *Operation Sidewinder* but rather the archetypal "mythic emotions" that classic tales of the family had evoked in ancient Greek tragedy. According to Shepard, his family plays are intended to strike a more universal chord; by self-consciously using the term *curse*, for instance, and employing images of hereditary violence to suggest a link between his own "starving class" family and such infamous family lines as those dramatized in Aeschylus's *Oresteia*, Shepard attempted to raise his domestic melodrama to the level of modern myth and to tap the collective contents of our repressed mythic consciousness.

Shepard employs an intricate network of images in *Curse of the Starving Class* to establish a mythic subtext in the shape of unseen forces infecting the characters and determining their fates. As in earlier plays, those forces can take on physical manifestations. For instance, long before the broader, hereditary nature of the title's curse is hinted at, a more immediate "curse" arises: Emma is stricken with her first menstrual period, the "curse" of womanhood. Her mother, Ella, warns against sanitary napkins purchased in gas stations: "You don't know whose quarters go into those machines. Those quarters carry germs . . . spewing germs all over those napkins".

Ella's maternal warning is the first of many images related to microscopic forces at work in the lives of the characters. Later, when Wesley brings a maggot-infested lamb into the kitchen, concern is again expressed over the presence of "invisible germs mysteriously floating around in the air". It is Ella who ties the power of such microscopic presences to the ancient curse of fate and heredity that condemns the family to repeated acts of violence and self-destruction:

> Do you know what it is? It's a curse. I can feel it. It's invisible but it's there. It's always there. It comes onto us like nighttime. Every day I can feel it. Every day I can see it coming. And it always comes. Repeats itself. It comes even when you do everything to stop it from coming. Even when you try to change it. And it goes back. Deep. It goes back and back to tiny cells and genes. To atoms. To tiny little swimming things making up their minds without us. Plotting in the womb. Before that even. In the air. We're surrounded with it. It's bigger than government even. It goes forward too. We spread it. We pass it on. We inherit it and pass it down, and then pass it down again. It goes on and on like that without us.

Shepard once said that Greek tragedy evokes "emotional states, these forces . . . [that] go so far back that they go right to the birth of man. And we're still living in the shadow of these things". In *Curse*, Shepard injects mythic dimensions into the lives of his characters through the presence of a biological fatalism, determined by forces "making up their minds without us," continuing into the future "on and on like that without us." The characters find themselves helpless in the grasp of an inexplicable presence in their lives: "It comes even when you do everything to stop it from coming."

The new dramatic agenda Shepard sets for himself with *Curse of the Starving Class* is not one he easily assumes. In spite of the sophistication of imagery, the domestic setting and story, and the dominant surface realism of *Curse*, the play shows definite signs of a strain between the heightened theatrical reality of many of Shepard's earlier plays and his new intentions as a family dramatist. Putting aside Shepard's use of such disparately drawn characters as Emerson and Slater to reinforce the theme of invasion, one is still left with numerous disturbing and incongruous images and events that appear to have no connection to Shepard's thematic intentions but are instead the vestiges of an earlier stage aesthetic.

Within Shepard's family plays, the mixture of surface realism and a heightened sense of a theatrical presence lurking beyond that realism led one critic to comment ''one feels the need for a word such as 'Lnova-realism' to describe the style into which Shepard's plays have settled''. His stage actions and images are not just real, they are ''suprareal''—in the sense that, when set against the created fictional ''reality'' of the play, they become overwhelmingly vivid and material. *Curse of the Starving Class* opens, for instance, with a string of typically Shepardesque non sequiturs that transform the stage reality into a series of perpetual presents. Wesley and his mother, Ella, are discussing Weston's drunken appearance of the night before when Wesley suddenly launches into an extended monologue in which he recounts the previous night's events. Just as suddenly, he leaves the stage and Ella starts speaking to the empty space. She appears to be rehearsing the lecture she will give to some (unidentified) girl who is having her first menstrual period. Perhaps a minute into this lecture, Ella's daughter, Emma, enters. Ella ''talks to her as though she's just continuing the conversation''. Emma responds, in turn, as though she has been present for the entire speech.

While some productions of the play might attempt to smooth the jagged edges of these individual moments and create a realistic narrative line, this sequence of events is far too bizarre to overlook, especially at the beginning of the play. Some directors have blocked the mother-daughter scene as though Ella is aware of Emma's presence just offstage and well within earshot. But Shepard's stage directions indicate no such assumption, stressing that Ella ''speaks alone'' at the beginning of the speech and that Emma does not enter, nor is she heard offstage, until later. The causal and temporal reality of the scene are thus unfixed, and the sequence of events resembles a description of schizophrenic reality: ''an experience of isolated, disconnected, discontinuous material signifiers which fail to link into a coherent sequence''.

But to what end? Neither Wesley's transfixing monologue nor Emma's dreamlike materialization in the middle of her mother's discourse serves to reinforce any apparent dramatic or thematic intention on Shepard's part. Such irrational, discontinuous images are without context in this play, seeming to exist for their own sake as unqualified material images. The same is true of Shepard's startling use of the unqualified physical presence of the actor playing Wesley.

Early in the play, this actor must, without warning or explanation, unzip his pants and urinate on Emma's 4-H club charts. Later, he is required to walk naked onto the stage, again without warning, and scoop a live lamb into his arms, carrying it off. Linked to the unexpectedness and inexplicability of his actions, the purely physical reality of the actor—either exposing his genitals to urinate or entering naked—is so strong that the created illusion of his character and the fictional stage reality are shattered. Such physical nudity creates a heightened stage reality: there is no such thing as a naked ''character'' on stage. When the actor sheds his clothing, he sheds the illusion of character, of acting, and brings a new level of physical immediacy or ''suprapresence'' to the stage. This effect is intensified by the presence of the live lamb. The unqualified existence of the animal—that is, its immediate physical presence without the created pretense of character or performance—is far more ''real'' than the fictional reality of the play. The image of the naked actor scooping the live lamb into his arms and carrying it offstage transcends the realm of scripted reality in favor of the suprareal.

Had these events occurred in just about any Shepard play previous to this one, they would have been equally shocking perhaps, but they would also have been an integral, vital part of Shepard's phenomenological stage consciousness. However, in *Curse of the Starving Class*, Shepard is both telling a conventional story and introducing sustained characters and a narrative discourse into his writing. If he is ''dramatizing a condition,'' as Robert Corrigan might suggest, that condition is the thematically anchored state of invasion in which the characters find themselves. If these instances of heightened reality have any relation to that condition, it is only to intensify the physical and psychic discomfort suggested by the presence of a pervasive curse and of microscopic physical forces. They add, in John Glore's words, ''a tone of foreboding anxiety'' by virtue of their ''erratic disruption of a surface realism''. More likely, though, is that Shepard, trying to find his way through a full-length domestic drama for the first time in his career, turned without thinking to the techniques of a stage aesthetic that had been part of his highly intuitive modus operandi for more than 10 years.

The stories that open and close *Curse of the Starving Class* indicate the direction Shepard's drama is to take from this point on in his career. The play begins, as mentioned earlier, with Wesley's vivid account of the violent events from the previous night. The story is extremely sensory-specific, allowing the stillness and silence of the night to stretch the perceptual boundaries of the boy in his bed, and allowing the sense of sound to become acute, dominating all other experience. The telling of the story is a solo riff, in which Wesley steps out of the action of the play to create a moment, much like those in Shepard's early plays, in which the incantatory power of the language takes the audience beyond the confines of the stage.

By contrast, the final story of the play is far more literary, intended as far less of a visceral experience and more of a metaphorical comment on the events of the play. Weston begins the story at the top of the third act, and Ella finishes it as she stares at the gutted lamb that Emerson and Slater have dropped in the middle of her floor. Weston tells of a day he was castrating lambs and of an eagle that began swooping down out of the sky to grab the testes as Weston threw them over his shoulder onto the roof of a small shed. Each time the eagle would snatch the testes up in his talons, Weston would jump involuntarily to his feet, yelling, "with this icy feeling up my backbone". When Ella tells what she claims is the same story at the play's conclusion, she describes a substantially different course of events in which the eagle accidentally scoops up a cat and carries it off into the sky: "And they fight. They fight like crazy in the middle of the sky. That cat's tearing his chest out, and the eagle's trying to drop him, but the cat won't let go because he knows if he falls he'll die . . . And they come crashing down to the earth. Both of them come crashing down. Like one whole thing". This story, so clearly a metaphor for the self-destructive way in which the family members cling most desperately to those with whom they fight most savagely (namely themselves), ends the play on a powerful but dramatically conventional note. Wesley's incantatory monologue is the last of its kind in Shepard's family plays, and Ella's heavily laden metaphor is the first of many that Shepard will employ in the plays that follow. Yet, with each successive family play, Shepard's use of such traditional literary and dramatic conventions

increases as his talents as a realistic dramatist grow. With each new play he also makes a greater effort to forcibly subjugate his highly theatrical intuition—the trademark of the "old Shepard"—to his new dramatic strategies and thematic concerns as a family dramatist.

Source: David J. DeRose, "The Father, the Son, and *The Holy Ghostly*," in *Sam Shepard,* Twayne Publishers, 1992, pp. 90–99.

Landy F. Sparr, Susan S. Erstling, and James K. Boehnlein

In the following essay excerpt, the authors discuss a variety of common interfamilial themes in Shepard's Curse of the Starving Class.

Shepard captures the promise and failures of a family, the humor, beauty and bleakness that characterize a group of people trying to live together. His plays are not solely comments on family desolation, but on the family spirit that continues to assert itself to survive.

The Tate family is losing its cohesiveness. It is "starving" for emotional connectedness and a sense of identity and purpose. The family members barely operate as a group except for a place to sleep and eat—and even those most primary and elemental functions of the family can no longer be counted on. Sleeping occurs in a disorganized fashion (in the car, on the table), and eating occurs with no predictable pattern. Even the front door is broken down, leaving them open to invasions from the external world. Caring is expressed in an off-hand manner. When there is no food in the house, the father brings home a bag of artichokes; in an attempt to care for a sick animal the son brings a lamb with maggots into the kitchen.

The family seems unable to provide its members with meaning and context for rites of passage such as Emma's first menstruation. The father describes his own inability to grapple with the transitions in life, "the jumps." The only way to find personal purpose is through escape fantasies—sell the land, go to Europe, ride off on a horse. In one hopeful moment, the father exclaims that what he has been searching for is right "inside this house" but family members are unable to join him in his new-found optimism.

Shepard has said that in writing family plays he entered into "the earthquake zone." He said, "You got to or you end up writing diddlybop plays." He tried to be honest in his writing. His primary theme

> A FAMILY'S BELIEF SYSTEM INFLUENCES BOTH ITS CONDUCT AND THE RITUALS IT CREATES TO DEAL WITH NORMAL EVENTS AND EVENTS THAT REQUIRE CHANGE . . . THE VULNERABILITY THAT SHEPARD'S CHARACTERS FEEL IS A DRAMATIC PORTRAYAL OF THE LACK OF FAMILY COHESION."

is the inescapability of the mysterious family bond. Like other American family plays such as Tennessee Williams' *The Glass Menagerie* or Eugene O'Neill's *Long Day's Journey into Night,* there is considerable tension among family members but here the tension is more overt. The characterizations achieve a passionate and uniquely American rowdyism. Shepard's families have an amazing capacity to tolerate eccentric behavior. It has been said that Shepard sees the nuclear family as a war zone where blood (heredity) begets blood (homicide).

The Tate family is no match for a Shepard-depicted raging consumer society where material goods are valued above land and people. Malicious 20th-century encroachment is one of Shepard's social activist themes; the New West of suburbs, freeways, color T.V.'s, and modern shopping developments contributes to a breakdown of personal relationships, and worship of the new trivializes the past. With the past forgotten, the present takes on a transcendent immediacy because in a rapidly changing consumer-oriented society, goals become meaningless. Shepard suggests that the American underclass, uprooted and exploited, suffers the repercussions.

Even though Shepard glorifies the frontier (Old West) and its concomitant individualism, he also has an attachment to 1960s-style politics with its dread of the "system" and its pastoral ideals. In Shepard there has always been this tug-of-war between radical ideals and conservatism. This provides a source of dramatic tension in his writing that is never fully resolved.

Additionally, *Curse* illustrates common inter-familial issues that may be characterized as follows:

1. Differentiation

A basic concern of Shepard's characters is the struggle for individuation in the face of constraining family ties. This is a universal issue but in a family as bereft and isolated as the Tates, individuation is nearly impossible. Attempts to save the self are associated with fantasies of flight or escape that often end in destruction—alcoholism, selling the ranch, "zombie" cities, explosions. The family does not have a cohesive structure to assist its members in defining their identities. Even the names—Weston, Wesley, Emma, Ella—contribute to a lack of differentiation and an uncertainty as to who is who. Each person is struggling to make a mark and sometimes it is in competition with or at the expense of another.

In the Shepard play, *Action*, the main character describes the continuing struggle to be a separate self while yearning to be in a family.

> "Just because we're surrounded by four walls and a roof doesn't mean anything. It's still dangerous. The chances of something happening are just as great. Anything could happen. Any move is possible. I've seen it. You go outside. The world's quiet. White. Everything resounding. Not a sound of a motor. Not a light. You see into the house. You see the candles. You watch the people. You can see what it's like inside. The candles draw you. You get a cold feeling being outside. Separated. You have an idea that being inside it's cosier. Friendlier. Warmth. People. Conversation. Everyone using a language. Then you go inside. It's a shock. It's not like how you expected. You lose what you had outside. You forget that there even is an outside. The inside is all you know. You hunt for a way of being with everyone. A way of finding how to behave. You find out what's expected of you. You act yourself out."

2. Boundaries

The Tate family frequently violates traditional psychological boundaries—marital, parental, sibling, personal, or the family group as distinct from the outside world. The boundary theme starts at the play's opening with the mother admonishing the son for attempting to clean up debris from the front door that was broken down by the father. The gate between the family and the world outside has been destroyed and the son is not allowed to restore it. There is uncertainty about who is in and out of the family and who is performing what roles and tasks within the family system. Boundary diffusion is reflected in Wesley's comment, "like any second something could invade me. Some foreigner. Something undescribable". Generally, the greater the family boundary ambiguity, the greater the individual and family dysfunction.

3. Marital Disintegration and Parental Ineffectiveness

Shepard depicts two basic themes critical to family therapy—marital disintegration and parental ineffectiveness. The marital relationship portrayed in *Curse* is minimally existent, and at best is characterized by hostile undermining. There is no sense of marital sanctity—children and con men are invited by each marital partner to conspire against the other. The parents are almost never on stage together in a conscious state, and the only time siblings unite is in joint escape fantasies. The parents' lack of communication affects the whole family. It appears that characters are often unaware of what the other is saying because they rarely comment on what has been said. The breakdown of dialogue reflects in dramatic form the inability to sustain interpersonal relationships.

Yet, a closer look reveals Shepard's perception and instinct about marriage. The spouses do communicate with each other, only they send messages through their children. There is a symmetry between spouses as they separately engage in identical plans to sell the ranch. They are so close that Ella can "smell" Weston's skin through the front door. Shepard captures the tensions inherent in marriage. Weston and Ella have remained together because family bonds are not easily broken and emotional distancing is easier or more comfortable than severing the bonds.

Shepard's characterization of the parent-child relationship reflects similar tensions. The parenting function has been partially assimilated by the children. The parents seem unable to either provide for their children or exert authority over them. At times it appears to be outright neglect, yet there are glimpses of intended caring. We have an illustration of adolescent conflict—the daughter's need to break the family bond alongside her need to stay connected. She acts erratically after learning that her parents are separately trying to sell the ranch (all that holds them together). Is her behavior a desperate attempt to unite the parents in an act of authority or caretaking?

4. Uprootedness and Family Isolation

Shepard has a keen sense of a family that is unconnected to a community. His families seem adrift, disconnected from the moorings of religion, neighborhood, or extended family. Family members are not sure why they are where they are and constantly entertain fantasies of moving on. This may be Shepard's indictment of contemporary American society but there have always been families like this—disorganized families that seem unable to develop or support relationships that enhance their lives as a group or as individuals.

Shepard's characters do not relate to society; there is no world outside; they cannot see beyond their own mental states. They react rather than interact. Allegorically, the family that sees no way out of its situation turns on itself, and its members tear each other apart like the eagle and the cat. The only positive connection with the larger world is Emma's 4H involvement and this is thwarted by family members—her mother boils the chicken Emma has bred for demonstration and her brother urinates on her 4-H posters.

5. Family Identity, Goals, and Moral Purpose

Reiss and Oliveri have established the importance of understanding a family's belief system or operating paradigm as a way of interpreting its attitudes and behavior. Shepard's Tates seem to view themselves as failures, exploited and isolated, controlled by elements outside themselves, and destined to live out a "curse" passed on by former generations. There is no prevailing sense of unity or cohesion, and while much of the play takes place in the kitchen, people come and go randomly. The one attempt by Weston to insert hope and direction into the family is rejected, especially by Wesley, who has accepted the family belief that it is too late to start over. The father's new sense of purpose, based on his feeling of connectedness, does not fit with the family's operating paradigm.

Another reflection by Shepard of the difficulty of family transitions comes through Weston's voice: "The jumps. I couldn't figure out the jumps. From being born, to growing up, to dropping bombs, to having kids, to hittin' bars, to this". The father did not have for himself, nor is he able to pass on to his children, an ability to integrate the transitions between life events and stages. These transitions or "jumps" that mark a family's progression through the life cycle are usually facilitated through ritual and ceremony that mark change, place an event in context, and promote growth. Ella's weak attempt to address the onset of her daughter's menstrual cycle, clearly a rite of passage, is an example. More important than her mother's giving her incorrect and frightening information is that the subject is cut off and dropped.

A family's belief system influences both its conduct and the rituals it creates to deal with normal events and events that require change. Recognizing the significance of ritual, Imber-Black and her associates have developed an approach to families that creates new, alternative, and useful behavior patterns. The vulnerability that Shepard's characters feel is a dramatic portrayal of the lack of family cohesion.

6. Intergenerational Legacies

Shepard acknowledges the power of past generations on current family attitudes and behaviors. Weston Tate has been "poisoned" by his father, and Wesley the son feels himself becoming like his father. Family members feel biologically and psychologically determined. One established legacy is that Weston's father lived "apart" even though he was "right among them." Weston's alcoholism allows the same behavior in this generation of the Tate family. Each family member lives apart although they are right among each other— they need distance or they fear being engulfed.

Shepard deliberately appropriates mythical material to formulate his images of fathers and sons. The principal energy in the text actually works to articulate an image of the male characters as sons rather than fathers. Weston's authority role is highly undermined because his presence is periodic rather than continuous. The play works both to incorporate and dislocate the parents' presence, particularly the father's. Wesley appropriates aspects of Weston's identity, but in the end proves to be an inadequate substitute.

There is less exploration of the female past in this family. We know nothing of Ella's family origin and the psychological legacy she passes on to Emma. One might assume that Shepard is writing from personal experience which is why we see male generational patterns explicated more clearly in his plays.

Finally, there is a legacy of menace and an anger even during the play's punchy comic sections. The menace is palpable.

"Do you know what this is? It is a curse. I can feel it. It's invisible but it's there. It's always there. It comes onto us like nighttime. Every day I can feel it. Every day I can see it coming. It always comes. Repeats itself. It comes even when you do everything to stop it from coming. Even when you try to change it. . . . It goes forward too. We spread it. We pass it on. We inherit it and pass it down and then pass it down again. It goes on and on like that without us".

Source: Landy F. Sparr, Susan S. Erstling, and James K. Boehnlein, "Sam Shepard and the Dysfunctional American Family: Therapeutic Perspectives," in *American Journal of Psychotherapy,* Vol. XLIV, No. 4, 1990, pp. 568–72.

SOURCES

Barnes, Clive, "Shepard's *Starving Class* Offers Much Food for Thought," in *New York Post,* March 3, 1978.

Beaufort, John, "Off-Broadway: Tale of a Blighted Family," in *Christian Science Monitor,* March 3, 1978.

Bottoms, Stephen J., *The Theatre of Sam Shepard: States of Crisis,* Cambridge University Press, 1998.

DeRose, David J., *Sam Shepard,* Twayne, 1962.

Eder, Richard, "Theatre: *The Starving Class,*" in *New York Daily News,* March 3, 1978, p. C4.

Hart, Lynda, *Sam Shepard's Metaphorical Stages,* Greenwood Press, 1987.

Kaufmann, Stanley, "What Price Freedom?" in *New Republic,* April 8, 1978, pp. 24–25.

Kissel, Howard, Review of *Curse of the Starving Class,* in *Women's Wear Daily,* March 3, 1978.

Lahr, John, "A Ghost Town of the Imagination," in *Village Voice,* July 25, 1977, pp. 61–62.

Lyons, Charles R., "Shepard's Family Trilogy and the Conventions of Modern Realism," in *Rereading Shepard,* edited by Leonard Wilcox, St. Martin's Press, 1993.

Watt, Douglas, "In the End, Emptiness," in *New York Daily News,* March 3, 1978.

FURTHER READING

DeRose, David J., *Sam Shepard,* Twayne, 1992.
Part of the immensely useful Twayne's *U.S. Authors* Series, this book provides a concise introduction to Shepard's life, short descriptions of almost all of his works up to *States of Shock,* and discussions of the themes and techniques that characterize Shepard's work as a whole.

Randall, Phyllis R., "Adapting to Reality: Language in Shepard's *Curse of the Starving Class,*" in *Sam Shepard: A Casebook,* edited by Kimball King, Garland, 1988.

Randall argues here that, although *Curse of the Starving Class* is indeed a more realistic play than the works that preceded it, Shepard retains a use of language in this play that ''we do not ordinarily associate with realistic drama.''

A Delicate Balance

EDWARD ALBEE

1966

In 1994, after enduring a lull in his theatrical career, Edward Albee won his third Pulitzer Prize for drama. In 1996, Edward Albee's play, *A Delicate Balance*, celebrating its thirtieth birthday on Broadway, won a Tony Award for the best revival play of the year. Together, these awards mark the enduring qualities of both the playwright and his play.

A Delicate Balance was first produced at the Martin Beck Theatre on Broadway on September 12, 1966. It came four years after Albee's other huge Broadway hit *Who's Afraid of Virginia Woolf?* (1962). Both of these plays deal with a recurring theme of Albee's, which entails a sense of missed opportunity and loss. Both plays also deal with dysfunctional relationships. Both were commercial successes, more easily understood and appreciated by general audiences than Albee's previous and intermediate plays that leaned toward the absurd. One main difference between the two plays is that *Who's Afraid of Virginia Woolf?* is known as the play that almost won the Pulitzer (it was nominated, but one of the Pulitzer committee members deemed its language and subject matter too crude), whereas *A Delicate Balance* did win the coveted prize.

Albee's career took a slight downturn after the success of *Who's Afraid of Virginia Woolf?*, at least in reference to audience appeal and critical approval. It wasn't until the production of *A Delicate Balance* that Albee would again enjoy popular,

critical, and financial success. Although *A Delicate Balance* won Albee his first Pulitzer Prize, most critics at the time considered the play, as Steven Drukman writes in *American Theatre,* to be one of Albee's "last gasps." Although it would not be Albee's last gasp, Albee would have to wait almost ten years before he would win his second Pulitzer (for *Seascape* [1975]) and then again almost another twenty years before he would again claim the prize for his *Three Tall Women* (1994).

Despite his erratic successes, Albee has had an extremely significant impact on American theater. His play *A Delicate Balance* has often been credited with creating an archetype for American drama with its classic study of the American family, albeit a quite dysfunctional one. The play looks into the confusion that erupts in a modern family's attempt to avoid pain and discomfort, which, as Albee demonstrates, only creates more pain and discomfort. The play's major themes are denial of emotions (and often reality itself), loss of opportunities and potential, and regret over paths not taken as reflected in the lives of a very well-to-do suburban couple who have retired but find their long-sought freedom about to collapse. In the period of one weekend, their home comes under attack by emotionally wounded family members and friends, who, in the end, expose the couple's own emotional insecurities. The scenes are not easy for audiences to take, but, as Albee states in an interview with Richard Farr in *The Progressive:*

> If I wrote plays about everyone getting along terribly well, I don't think anyone would want to see them. . . . You have to show people things that aren't working well . . . in the hope that people will make them work better.

AUTHOR BIOGRAPHY

Edward Albee was adopted in Washington, D.C., two weeks after his birth on March 12, 1928, by Reed A. Albee (who, after retiring from his father's theatre business, raised horses) and Frances (Cotter) Albee (who once worked as a live mannequin for the upscale Bergdorf department stores). His adopted grandfather, Edward Franklin Albee, for whom he was named, was part owner of the Keith-Albee Theatre Circuit, a coast-to-coast chain of over two

Edward Albee

hundred vaudeville theaters. As stated in Richard E. Amacher's book *Edward Albee,* upon his adoption, Albee was immediately taken to a "sprawling Tudor stucco house in Westchester [New York]" where he lived out his early years in a "world of servants, tutors, riding lessons." As a child, Albee spent his time in New York during the summers and in Miami or Palm Beach during the winters. Albee's mother is quoted as saying (in Amacher's book) that "there was a Rolls to bring him . . . to matinees in the city" and that he had at his disposal "a St. Bernard to pull his sleigh in the wintertime." At the age of twelve, Albee wrote his first play, a three-act sex-farce.

Albee's education was marked by several dramatic departures from school. He was expelled from Lawrenceville Preparatory School (New Jersey) and Valley Forge Military Academy (Pennsylvania). Later he graduated from the private high school Choate Rosemary Hall (Connecticut) but then was dismissed from Trinity College "in his sophomore year, reportedly for failure to attend Chapel and certain classes," writes Amacher.

Due to family tensions, especially between Albee and his mother, Albee left home at the age of twenty. It was at this time, with the aid of a family trust from his grandmother, that Albee moved to

Greenwich Village and took on a series of odd jobs. It would not be until ten years later, right before Albee turned thirty, that he would write his first hugely successful play *The Zoo Story.* From there, according to Richard Farr writing in the *Progressive,* "Albee went on to write a series of chilling attacks on the American domestic verities." His first full-length play, *Who's Afraid of Virginia Woolf?* (1962) is one such play as is *A Delicate Balance* (1966), which was to become Albee's first experience in winning the Pulitzer Prize (1967). Albee would eventually capture two more Pulitzer Prizes with his plays *Seascape* (1975) and *Three Tall Women* (1994). It should be noted that both *Whose Afraid of Virginia Woolf?* and *A Delicate Balance* were made into successful movies, with *Whose Afraid of Virginia Woolf?* wining five Academy Awards.

In Albee's plays, he often wrestles "with the obsessive influence of his adoptive mother," relates Lawrence DeVine in his review of Mel Gussow's *Edward Albee: A Singular Journey: A Biography.* This theme is partly played out in *A Delicate Balance* but does not seem to have been put to rest until Albee "was nearly 65 years old," states De Vine. After a tailspin in his theatrical career, which lasted almost twenty-five years, Albee wrote and saw successfully produced his play *Three Tall Women* (which won him his third Pulitzer). Albee admits that this is a play that describes three different stages of his mother's life (she was, in fact, six feet two inches tall). With this play, writes De Vine, Albee psychologically "took off his hair shirt," and professionally achieved renewed success "after enduring a long period of critical neglect and abuse." He was also successful, at this time in his life, in overcoming a long bout with alcoholism.

In 1996, President Clinton presented Albee with a Kennedy Center Lifetime Achievement Award, honoring him for his lifetime's contribution to the nation's culture. In his article "A Question of Identity," Robert Brustein quotes Clinton as saying that Albee's first play, *Zoo Story,* was "a play that took the American theater by storm and changed it forever." Clinton then added, "In your rebellion, the American theater was reborn." Over his professional career, many critics have made similar statements and have hailed Albee as the successor to such acclaimed playwrights as Arthur Miller, Tennessee Williams, and Eugene O'Neill. Albee is also credited with inspiring a new generation of dramatists and remains one of America's most celebrated playwrights.

PLOT SUMMARY

Act 1, Friday Night

The play opens with Agnes, the female lead and a "handsome woman in her late 50's," discussing the possibility of suddenly and quite easily losing her mind. She speaks in a soft voice with a "hint of a smile on her face," suggesting a state of peace, despite the subject matter of her conversation. Her husband, Tobias, responds to her by reminding her that "there is no saner woman on earth" than herself. Tobias, as he speaks, seems to have nothing more important on his mind than deciding what kind of drink he wants to make for himself.

When Tobias reassures Agnes that "we will all go mad before you," Agnes admits that she could not really go mad because she needs to take care of him. But this does not stop her from discussing the topic. At one point, she refers to her musings of potential madness as "theoretically healthy fear," but she quickly catches herself and corrects her definition to "healthy speculation."

The couple is sitting together enjoying their drinks, when, somewhat disjointedly, Agnes brings up the topic of her sister Claire. Agnes exclaims that although she is astonished by her own thoughts of madness, it is her sister who astonishes her the most. But when asked by Tobias to explain her statement, Agnes declares that she doesn't want to "use an unkind word" at the moment because the couple is being "cozy." However, this does not stop her degrading remarks about Claire. When Agnes begins negatively criticizing her sister, Tobias stands up and moves to another chair, stating his reason as "It's getting uncomfortable." Agnes comes back with the remark, "Things get hot, move off, huh?"

Agnes continues to discredit her sister, and Tobias continually tries to discourage her, to the point of telling her that he thinks she should apologize to Claire. Agnes becomes a bit ruffled at the suggestion and then returns to her subject of possibly going mad but decides that she never could do such a thing because she is so stable. "There are no mountains in my life . . . nor chasms. It is a rolling, pleasant land," she says. To which Tobias asserts, "We do what we can." Agnes then declares their life's motto.

Claire appears in the room and apologizes to Agnes. This catches Agnes off guard, and she asks Claire what she is apologizing for. Claire responds, "that my nature is such to bring out in you the full force of your brutality." This brings out a long diatribe from Agnes concerning Claire's lifestyle. At this point, Agnes leaves to telephone her daughter, Julia, and Tobias and Claire share a conversation and another drink.

Claire senses that Tobias and Agnes's daughter Julia might be going through yet another divorce and predicts that Julia will be coming home shortly. Then Claire suggests that when Julia does arrive, Tobias should shoot Julia, Agnes, and then herself. Tobias says that the only way he could commit such an act would be if he were in a high state of passion, which Claire laughs at, unable to see him outraged by anything.

As Claire drinks, Tobias suggests that she rejoin Alcoholics Anonymous. Claire, in turn, asks Tobias what he has in common with his very best friend, except for "the coincidence of having cheated on your wives in the same summer with the same woman."

Agnes reenters the room, announcing that Julia is coming home. Tobias then tells the story of a cat that he once had. He and the cat pleasantly tolerated each other until one day Tobias realized that the cat had been totally ignoring him. After several attempts to make the cat pay attention to him, Tobias ends up slapping the cat in the head. He says that he found he hated the cat because he felt as if she were accusing him of something, and shortly after this incident, Tobias took the cat to the pound and had it put to sleep. Claire and Agnes both assure him that he did the best he could. "You probably did the right *thing*," Claire says. "Distasteful alternatives the less . . . ugly choice."

There is a knock on the door, and Harry and Edna (Agnes and Tobias's best friends) ask if they can stay there. They have been frightened by something intangible and do not want to return to their own home.

Act 2, Scene 1, Early Saturday Evening

Act 2 opens with Agnes and her daughter Julia discussing the fact that Harry and Edna are occupying Julia's old bedroom. Agnes insists that Julia accept the situation. She does not want to discuss anything. She does not know how long Harry and Edna are planning on staying and is not really clear why they are there. Harry and Edna have spent the entire day in their room, not coming out even for meals.

Tobias then enters, and Agnes departs, leaving Tobias and Julia throwing insults at one another. Julia whines about not having her room and the fact that no one seems to know why Harry and Edna are there or how long they are planning on staying. Tobias then discredits Julia for all the broken marriages that she has accumulated. There is mention of Julia's brother who died while still young. During this conversation, Tobias fixes himself a drink.

Claire enters and chides Julia about her new divorce and about constantly returning home. Julia teases Claire about her drinking. Agnes arrives to announce that dinner is ready. She makes the statement, "It's one of those days when everything's underneath." When asked if she knows what is going on with Harry and Edna, Agnes tells them that she knocked on the door but was too embarrassed, irritated, and apprehensive to pursue the matter. After asking Tobias for a drink, she announces that "there is no point in pressing" the issue of Harry and Edna. At the end of scene 1, Harry and Edna appear with their coats over their arms. They announce they are going home but will return with their suitcases.

Act 2, Scene 2, Later That Night

Scene 2 opens with Julia and Agnes in the room alone after dinner. Julia is disgusted with her mother's desire to control everyone's conversations and emotions. Agnes's response is, "When we are dealing with children . . ." She then tells Julia that she will do what she must to keep the family in shape. Agnes then adds, when Tobias enters the room, "There *is* a balance to be maintained . . . and I must be the fulcrum."

Julia returns to her insistence that she wants her room back. To this end, Agnes tells Julia to go up to the room, while Harry and Edna are gone, and barricade herself there. She also suggests that Julia "take Tobias' pistol while you're at it!"

Claire enters the room, and a heated discussion ensues, ending with the topic of what they should do about Harry and Edna. Claire says, "You've only got two choices, Sis. You take 'em in, or you throw 'em out." When Agnes and Tobias leave to help Harry and Edna (who have returned) unload their suitcases from their car, Julia asks Claire what she thinks Harry and Edna want. Claire responds, "Comfort." When Julia states that this is her home, Claire says, "We're not a communal nation, dear, giving, but not sharing, outgoing, but not friendly. We submerge our truths and have our sunsets on untroubled waters.''

When Edna enters, she and Julia argue. Edna, in essence, tells Julia that it is time for her to grow up. Julia reminds Edna that she is a guest in the house, to which Edna responds that she and Harry are Agnes and Tobias's best friends. When Harry enters the room, he goes to fix everyone a drink at the bar, but Julia stands in front of the bar and insists that he stay away from it. Julia becomes emotionally frustrated and starts yelling, ''THEY WANT.'' Then she changes her statement to, ''I *want*'' and then ''I WANT ... WHAT IS MINE!!'' Julia leaves the room, and Agnes reminisces about the death of her son, ''an unreal time.'' She says that she suspects that Tobias has been ''unfaithful,'' and she asks Harry and Claire to confirm it, but they both deny it.

After Tobias announces that Julia is in hysterics, Julia then appears in the room with a gun in her hand. She insists that Harry and Edna leave. She eventually gives the gun to Tobias, and Agnes says, ''How dare you come into this room like that! How dare you embarrass me and your father!'' Edna then begins to criticize Julia, to which Julia responds that Edna has no right to tell her what to do. Edna comes back with the statement, ''*We* have rights here. *We* belong.'' Edna then declares that she and Harry are staying there forever, ''if need be.''

Act 3, Early Sunday Morning

Act 3 begins with a conversation between Agnes and Tobias. Tobias has stayed up all night, having given up his room to his daughter and not feeling quite comfortable enough to sleep with his wife in her room. Agnes confesses that she saw Tobias standing in her room in the night and refers to him as a stranger. They ask one another if either has had a clear thought on what to do about Harry and Edna. Agnes defers to Tobias, telling him that it is his role to make all the decisions. Tobias tells her that she is copping out. There is also a brief discussion between Tobias and Agnes about their sexual relationship. Agnes reminds Tobias of the times when he ''spilled'' himself on her ''belly,'' preventing Agnes from getting pregnant after the death of their son.

Near the end of act 3, Claire, Julia, Tobias, and Agnes all discuss their versions of why Harry and Edna are there and what they should do about it.

Then Harry and Edna join them, and everyone in the room is drinking, despite the early hour of the morning. Edna announces that Harry wants to talk to Tobias alone, and the women leave the room. Harry tells Tobias that if the circumstances were reversed, he and Edna don't think they would allow Tobias and Agnes to live at their house, in spite of the fact that they are best friends. Then Harry asks Tobias, ''You don't *want* us, do you, Toby?''

Tobias then delivers what the author refers to in the script notes as Tobias's ''aria.'' It ends with Tobias answering that he does not really want Harry and Edna to stay there but that because they are friends, Harry and Edna have the right to be there. Agnes then talks with Edna as Tobias goes with Harry to get the suitcases and put them in the car. Agnes states, ''Everything becomes ... too late, finally.'' The play ends on Agnes's thought that people sleep at night because they are afraid of the darkness. ''They say we sleep to let the demons out—to let the mind go raving mad. . . . And when the daylight comes again . . . comes order with it.''

CHARACTERS

Agnes

Agnes is the main female character of the play. She is woman in her fifties, well off, and married to Tobias. She is also the mother of Julia and the sister of Claire. Agnes believes herself to be the fulcrum of the family, keeping everyone in balance. She often maintains this balance, or order, by not confronting issues, not taking a stand, and not processing emotions. She tries to keep the peace by not dealing with anything that might upset it.

On the surface, Agnes is completely supportive of her husband, Tobias. She looks to him to confirm her thoughts, and, likewise, she confirms his. It is not until near the end of the play that she brings up issues that show cracks in her relationship with her husband. When the memory of the death of her son is brought to the surface of her thoughts, she reminisces about how difficult a time that was for her, a time when she questioned everything, including her husband's love and faithfulness to her.

Although she feels as if she is the fulcrum, Agnes begins and ends the play on her musings of insanity. She wonders if she could just suddenly slip off into madness and what that would be like. She wonders what her husband would do if that happened. Would she be an embarrassment to him? Embarrassment is a very large issue with Agnes. She is easily embarrassed by her sister Claire, who Agnes believes has wasted her life and her potential. When Claire insists that she is not an alcoholic, Agnes states sarcastically, ''that's very nice.'' Then she lists all the times that Claire has vomited, fallen down, and called from the club to have someone come and get her. She concludes this commentary with the words: ''If we change for the worse with drink, we are an alcoholic.''

Agnes's relationship with her daughter, Julia, does not fare much better. Julia also embarrasses her mother. When Julia becomes hysterical, Tobias asks Agnes to go talk to their daughter. Agnes's response is, ''I haven't the time.'' Instead of empathizing with Julia, Agnes becomes more self-absorbed. She tells her husband that she has suffered far more than her daughter. This same self-absorption is apparent in all of Agnes's relationships. She easily becomes lost in self-pity and at the same time believes herself to be above everyone around her. If she is the fulcrum of the balance in the family, Albee portrays her as a very unstable one. Albee has admitted that the character of Agnes is based on his real-life adopted mother.

Claire

Claire is Agnes's younger sister. She claims that she is not an alcoholic but rather a willful drinker. Of all the characters in the play, whether it is due to the alcohol or not, Claire has the loosest tongue. She speaks her mind and is the least affected by social politeness.

Claire lives with Agnes and Tobias and appears to have no means of support except for them. Her main role in life seems to be to annoy and embarrass her sister. She is everything that Agnes dislikes. Claire makes the statement, after telling Tobias that he would be better off if he killed Claire, Julia, and herself, that she will never know whether she wants to live until Agnes is dead. With this statement, Albee makes it sound as if Claire holds Agnes up as a role model, a model that she has never been able to reach. And instead of trying to reach it, she has done everything to live her life in a diametrically opposed manner.

Claire's relationship with Julia is closer than her relationship with anyone else. She and Julia

MEDIA ADAPTATIONS

- A movie adaptation of Albee's *A Delicate Balance* was produced in 1973 and directed by Tony Richardson. It stars such actors as Katharine Hepburn, Paul Scofield, Lee Remick, and Joseph Cotton.

---

identify with one another in their roles as the ''other''—people on the periphery of Tobias's and Agnes's lives. Claire and Julia are the rebels, the failures, the embarrassments that must be tolerated. When Julia arrives home, Claire greets her more honestly, more warmly than do Julia's parents.

Despite Claire's open disdain for her sister, she has never told Agnes about Tobias's affair. It is not clear if she does this out of love or out of spite. She keeps the affair a secret, almost as if she has a hidden weapon that she protects in case she may have to use it one day. When Agnes comes right out and asks Claire to confirm her suspicions about Tobias, Claire's answer is, ''Ya got me, Sis.'' Shortly after this exchange, Agnes describes Claire in this way: ''Claire could tell us so much if she cared to . . . Claire, who watches from the sidelines, has seen so very much, has seen us all so clearly . . . You were not named for nothing.'' Claire is said to closely resemble Albee's aunt Jane, an alcoholic and frequent visitor to the Albee home.

Edna

Edna is Harry's wife. It is not clear if she is really Agnes's friend or if she and Agnes know one another only because their husbands are friends. Edna arrives one day at the door of Agnes and Tobias's home. She takes it for granted that they will let her and Harry stay there for however long it takes them to get over their unnamed fear.

Despite the fact that the relationship between Edna and Agnes is not clear (their names are very similar), Edna sometimes takes on the role of mother to Julia. Although Edna's manner is dissimilar, her sentiments are comparable to Agnes's. Edna is not afraid to voice her opinions. Edna tells Julia that she is no longer a child and should take more responsibility for her life. She also declares that Julia no longer has rights in her parents' house.

Edna also confronts Agnes and tells her to stop making fun of her and her husband, Harry. Although Edna may not be able to name the fear that has driven her out of her own house, she appears to be quite capable of naming the things that other people are doing wrong in their lives.

But then again, it is Edna, in the end, who realizes that there are boundaries, even between friends. She understands that there are some boundaries that should not be pushed, some things that "we may not do . . . not ask, for fear of looking in a mirror." And it is also through her reflection that the play resolves. Edna has looked into that mirror at the end of the play and has decided that if the tables were turned, if Agnes and Tobias had come to her, she would not have allowed them to stay at her house.

Harry

Harry is Edna's husband and Tobias's best friend. At one point in the past, Harry and Tobias, coincidentally, had an extra-marital affair with the same young woman. Besides both having been businessmen and meeting at the same club, it is unclear what else Harry and Tobias have in common except that they have known one another for a long time and neither sleeps with his wife. Harry is something of a reflection of Tobias, but he is even more reserved. Of all the characters in this play, Harry speaks the least. And when he does speak, he is a man of few words with lots of pauses around each one. He prefers to talk around things rather than going at them straight on. He also avoids questions, as when Agnes tries to find out why he and his wife have come to their home. Instead of giving Agnes an answer, he compliments the furnishings in Agnes's home. He also has the tendency to repeat himself; at one point he repeats the same line four times when he tries to explain how fear has driven his wife and him out of their home. It is Harry, in the end, who tells Tobias that he and Edna have decided to leave. Although Harry prompted the discussion with Edna about resolving the issue of staying at their friends' house, it is implied that Edna made the decision and that Harry just delivered the message.

Julia

Julia is the thirty-something daughter of Agnes and Tobias. She has just recently been divorced for the fourth time and has returned home. Her father calls her a whiner, and her mother has little time for her. Julia, based on a relative of Albee's, his cousin Barbara, has set a pattern in her life of marrying for the wrong reasons and then divorcing and returning home. Her parents welcome her, although they make it clear that they wish she would establish an independent life of her own.

Julia is the catalyst of the play. While the other characters either hide their emotions in alcohol or avoid confrontations by smothering their feelings in banal social sweet talk, Julia brings matters to the forefront. She has wants, and she demands that they be at least heard, if not satisfied. The most obvious thing that she wants in this play is her bedroom in her parent's home. However, upon her return, she discovers that her room is being occupied by Edna and Harry, her parents' so-called best friends. In her attempts to regain control of her bedroom, Julia makes everyone confront the issues of the play, namely, defining relationships, wants, needs, and rights. At one point, Julia forces the issue first by having an emotional tantrum, then by upsetting the furniture and all the clothes in her bedroom, and finally by threatening everyone with a gun.

Julia tends to put down her mother and commiserate with her mother's sister Claire. Julia acts as if she is Claire's friend, until Claire points her finger at Julia and lets her know that Julia is as much a visitor in her parents' home as Harry and Edna are.

Julia, Claire, Harry, and Edna are portrayed as invaders in the lives of Agnes and Tobias. They all have their own reasons for needing to be there: none of them is able to make it alone in the outside world. Julia falls back on her childhood to claim her spot, even though she is nearing middle age. She has little empathy for the others who are also seeking comfort in the same house.

Tobias

Tobias is Agnes's husband and the father of Julia. He is a well-to-do, retired businessman. Although he is tolerant of people around him, he, like his wife, tends to avoid emotional topics. His tolerance toward his sister-in-law Claire is shown in his nonjudgmental attitude toward her drinking. Although he encourages her to return to Alcoholics

Anonymous at one point in the play, he does not berate her for drinking. In some ways, he even encourages it or at least does not discourage it. There are a few subtle insinuations that Claire and Tobias might have at one time had an affair, but this is initially only alluded to by script directions that have Claire open her arms to Tobias in a "casual invitation." Later in the play, Agnes asks Tobias (when he cannot sleep) if he went to Claire.

Whether Tobias had an affair with Claire is not certain; however, his infidelity is. Claire knows about an affair that Tobias had with a young woman, but she has never told Agnes about it. Claire only uses the information to taunt Tobias. Some critics have suggested that the young anonymous woman with whom Tobias had the affair was actually Claire. Despite all this, Tobias appears secure in his marriage with Agnes, even though they have not shared the same bed for many years. Their marriage seems to have become something of a habit. Tobias shows very little affection to his wife except in the way that he reinforces her thoughts, giving her assurances, for instance, that she, of all people, should not worry about going mad.

Tobias appears to be closer to his daughter than Agnes is. However, the degree of intimacy is not considerably greater. Tobias is the more concerned parent when Julia becomes hysterical, although he does nothing but ask Agnes to console her. It is Tobias who takes the gun away from his daughter, and it is Tobias to whom Julia apologizes for her outburst.

If Agnes is the fulcrum, then Tobias is the energy behind the fulcrum that works at keeping a balance in this dysfunctional family. He is constantly asking people to talk more kindly about one another. Or, in the least, it is Tobias who keeps silent while fury flares around him. It is also Tobias who serves everyone drinks, as if trying to soften the edges of their grievances with alcohol.

It is Tobias's friend Harry (and his wife, Edna) who bring the play to its conclusion, forcing Tobias to define what friendship is all about. In the end, Tobias proclaims that friendship is not about wants but rather about rights. Tobias's friend Harry has the right to move into Tobias's house even if that is not what Tobias, or the rest of his family, wants. Contradicting this conclusion is the story concerning his cat that Tobias tells in the middle of the play. In this case, the cat wanted to be left alone. Tobias was

uncomfortable with the cat's noncompliance, and eventually he hits the cat and then has the cat put to sleep. But disregarding the cat, Tobias seems true to his definition of friendship. He has, after all, allowed his sister-in-law to live off him. He allows his thirty-something daughter to continually move in and out of his house, and he tolerates his wife. He also tolerates his friend Harry's moving into his house uninvited. At the end of the play, Tobias questions Harry's efforts at friendship and honesty. Then he apologizes. Albee admits that the character of Tobias is based on his adopted father.

THEMES

Loss

There are many different kinds and levels of loss in Albee's play *A Delicate Balance*. Most obvious is the loss of balance that has been precariously maintained by Agnes, the main character in the play and mistress of the house in which the play takes place. Agnes begins the play musing about sanity, a condition, at least in Agnes's mind, that can easily be lost. Agnes wonders what would happen if she were to lose her sense of the rational. Who would take care of things? The way in which Agnes maintains the delicate balance in her home, as well as the delicate balance of her sanity, is to lose contact with her own emotional reality. She also tries to convince everyone else to supress his or her emotions. Agnes believes that by saying that the emotions are gone, circumstances will return to some condition that resembles normalcy.

A loss of opportunity is another kind of loss that is represented in Albee's play. Agnes has lost the opportunities of youth, of having another child. Agnes's sister Claire has lost her opportunity at married life, having children, doing something with her life other than getting drunk. Julia, Agnes and Tobias's daughter, has lost several marriages and the opportunity to have children. She has also lost her room, symbolic of having lost her childhood. Julia has also lost a brother, who died in his youth. This loss Agnes mourns as a loss of love. After the death of the child, Tobias and Agnes no longer attempted to have more children. This eventually lead to the loss of their sexual life together.

There is also the overall loss of privacy and peace when Agnes and Tobias are invaded by

TOPICS FOR FURTHER STUDY

- Although Albee's *A Delicate Balance* has often been described in realist terms, several critics point out absurdist elements in the play (such as the abstract fear that drives Edna and Harry out of their house). Do research on both the theories of realism and absurdism; then examine the play and write a report on examples of both of these theories and how Albee uses them.

- One of the most disparaging societal elements for young people of the late 1950s was the concept of conformism. The 1950s gave birth to mass-produced, suburban housing in which one or two building designs were used to develop whole neighborhoods, eliminating a sense of uniqueness and individuality. Conformism has also been partially blamed for the spread of the anticommunist paranoia of McCarthyism. Write a research paper on the concept of conformism,

providing current examples of it in the United States. Compare the 1950s with your generation. What elements of conformism exist today? How might conformism be used in a positive way? What are some of its negative aspects?

- Albee has stated that Samuel Beckett more than any other playwright influenced Albee's writing. Read one of Beckett's plays (*Happy Days* or *Waiting for Godot* might be good choices), and then compare Beckett's style of writing, his choice of themes, and his characters to those found in Albee's *A Delicate Balance*.

- Alcohol is used quite liberally throughout this play. Research alcoholism in the United States, and write a paper on the effects of alcohol both on the person who abuses it and on their families. Then conclude your paper with an analysis of how alcohol affects each of the play's characters.

Claire, Julia, Harry, and Edna, who all want to live with them. The crowding of the house, the battles for space and understanding, the irritations and frustrations of trying to compromise, all eventually lead to the ultimate loss of balance. Where patience and social sensibility once were the rule, chaos and emotionalism reign. And the play ends with Agnes once again contemplating the loss of her sanity.

Escape from Reality

Reality in this Albee play is something that most of its characters try to escape. The most obvious escape route is through alcohol. Its presence is so entwined in the dialogue that it becomes almost a character itself. Every scene revolves around the bar and decanters of brandy, cognac, anisette, and gin. Claire is alcohol's most wounded victim, but she is also the one who, although she has the most trouble dealing with reality, sees reality the clearest. Tobias is not as ruled by alcohol but uses it to calm himself enough to maintain his patience and usual silence.

Agnes, on the other hand, has a preprogrammed script in her head that contains all the social rules of conduct. She is easily embarrassed and uses most of her energies attempting to keep others from saying or doing things that go against her rules. In other words, she escapes the nasty or difficult parts of life by defining them as taboo subjects. Agnes hides from reality behind the rules. If the rules do not offer shelter, she then escapes reality through pure avoidance. She does not want to talk about things that are unpleasant, unless, of course, she is discussing her sister's poor excuse for a life. She avoids her daughter's temper tantrum, assuming that her daughter will eventually work things out on her own. Agnes, in the meantime, does not have time to deal with all those emotions. Even though she suspects that her husband had an affair, she only asks the people whom she knows will not confirm her suspicions.

Julia escapes from reality by marrying men on a whim and then abandoning them when things do not work out. She then runs home and wants to crawl back into the womb. She has not evolved into a mature woman although she is in her mid-thirties, she would rather go home to her parents and reclaim the room in which she grew up. Her energies are used in fighting for her right to return home rather than in fighting for a life of her own.

Harry and Edna are the most obvious escapees as they run from their own home and set up camp in the home of Agnes and Tobias. They run from a general sense of fear or dread, not even knowing what they are afraid of. All they want to do is escape by hiding, all day if they must, in a bedroom in their friends' home.

Fear

Fear could easily be argued as another character in Albee's play. It is an unnamed fear that moves Harry and Edna out of their house and into the middle of the chaos in the home of Agnes and Tobias. As Harry and Edna explain it: ''WE GOT . . . FRIGHTENED.'' ''We got scared.'' We . . . were . . . terrified.'' The fear is described as darkness, as when Agnes says: ''I wonder if that's why we sleep at night, because the darkness still . . . frightens us?'' Agnes also labels fear as ''the terror. Or the plague,'' and she states that Harry and Edna have brought the plague with them. And she claims that the only solution is isolation.

There is also Agnes's fear of going insane and her fear of confrontation; Tobias's fear of having another child; Julia's fear of growing up and her fear of being displaced in her parents' lives; and Claire's fear of life and her fear of love, the one thing that she desperately wants.

STYLE

Setting

The entire play takes place in one room, ''the living room of a large and well-appointed suburban house.'' In that room is a bar, which is well stocked with bottles of liquor. Time changes from Friday night to Saturday evening, then later the same Saturday, and eventually to early Sunday morning, but the setting remains the same. This one room is the focal point of the house, where all the characters can meet to argue about the living arrangements in the other rooms of the house.

Dialogue

In this play, there are very few dialogue passages that are written without script directions (written in italics inside parentheses before the actual printed dialogue). Although it is common practice for playwrights to supply some interpretation of how the dialogue should be delivered, Albee supplies these directions quite liberally and quite specifically. For instance, in the opening scene, he directs Agnes's first lines with these directions: ''*(Speaks usually softly, with a tiny hint of a smile on her face: not sardonic, not sad . . . wistful, maybe).*'' In a later line for Tobias, Albee directs the actor to deliver it in this way: *(Very nice, but there is steel underneath).* For one of Claire's lines, Albee suggests that the actor speak, ''*(to Agnes' back, a rehearsed speech, gone through but hated).*''

Albee's directing almost every line of dialogue demonstrates that he has very specific psychological meanings behind his words. He is aware of the characters' thoughts and the emotions behind their words and wants to make sure that the actors understand them. He is not willing to allow the actors to interpret the play on their own. He uses terms like ''quiet despair,'' ''surprised delight,'' ''slight schoolteacher tone,'' and ''the way a nurse speaks to a disturbed patient.'' He often writes directions about how the actors should hold their hands, turn their heads, or change their facial expressions to include a narrowing of their eyes. The longest script notation that Albee writes occurs toward the end of act 3, before a monologue delivered by the character Tobias. Albee's directions read:

(This next is an aria. It must have in its performance all the horror and exuberance of a man who has kept his emotions under control too long. Tobias will be carried to the edge of hysteria, and he will find himself laughing, sometimes, while he cries from sheer release. All in all, it is genuine and bravura at the same time, one prolonging the other. I shall try to notate it somewhat).

It should be noted that he does.

Dilemma

The central concept around which this play is built is the dilemma of what to do with Harry and Edna. Their situation is the focal point for all the characters, including Harry and Edna themselves. Albee uses this dilemma to cause emotions to rise. As his characters try to figure out what to do about the Harry and Edna, they have a series of discussions or debates that slowly rise in emotional temperature. Each character has his or her definition of what the dilemma is, as well as a means for resolving it. The tension in the play rises with the rise of emotions as the characters move toward a climax or a moment of truth. This moment is played out most specifically by Tobias and Harry in the conversation that defines their friendship: one that is built on rights and responsibilities rather than love and affection. In the end, Harry and Edna decide to go back home, thus solving (or at least releasing some of the tension of) the dilemma.

HISTORICAL CONTEXT

The tone of Albee's play *A Delicate Balance* reflects the overall social setting of the late 1950s. The postwar era was a time, in American culture, of very mixed messages. The older generation was caught up in putting on a good, social face while the younger generation was practicing drills at school on how to protect themselves from the radioactive fallout of atomic bombs. It was a time when parents (mostly mothers) were still greatly influenced by Emily Post, a socialite writer whose very name was an icon for social grace. Her books, such as *101 Common Mistakes in Etiquette and How To Avoid Them, Etiquette in Society, in Business, in Politics, and at Home,* and *The Secret of Keeping Friends,* defined success in life in terms of charm, proper social graces, and elegant and considerate speech. Television, which was impacting American society for the first time, aired shows like *Ozzie and Harriet, Leave It to Beaver,* and *Father Knows Best,* all of which depicted idealized families that lived in properly kept homes, whose members neither raised their voices nor stepped outside of the perimeters of their prescribed roles. In other words, these television families lived according to Emily Post's standards. With these role models, parents, generally speaking, taught their children to hide their emotions, to control their tongues, and to avoid confrontation. The socially correct behavior was to acquiesce rather than to make a scene.

In the meantime, Americans had grown increasingly more aware of the realities of war, more leery of the conformist mentality that had allowed the spread of Nazism in Germany, and of the paranoia of Senator McCarthy's anti-Communism

crusade. And the younger generation began experimenting with drastic change. Even if the majority of teenagers could not put their fingers on what was bothering them, there was a growing number of writers and artists who could. One of them was British playwright John Osborne, whose first play *Look Back in Anger* impacted British theatre in a similar way that Albee's first play *Zoo Story* impacted American theatre. Osborne was referred to as one of the Angry Young Men, a term applied to English writers of the 1950s who expressed social alienation and rejected outmoded bourgeois values. In Osborne's plays there existed no rules and no social etiquette, and this shocked the older generation of theatergoers and influenced many American writers.

Around this same period, in the United States a group of writers were being referred to as the Beat Generation. Their works critiqued the conformism of the 1950s. One of the techniques used by Allen Ginsberg and Jack Kerouac, two of the more famous members of the Beat Generation, was to explore different forms of language and its expression, as they tried to put down in print an impression of spontaneity.

Another type of theatre that became popular during the 1940s and 1950s was referred to as Absurdist Theatre. French playwright Eugene Ionesco was famous for his absurdist plays and his style was transported to American theatre. Young actors and playwrights began off-Broadway productions in which they were able to perform new and experimental plays. By keeping production costs down and by using unknown casts instead of star performers, producers were able to offer interesting theatre at low prices. This fit in well with playwrights who wrote in the absurdist mode, either in all of its manifest forms or at least in part of them, sometimes even including incomprehensible language. In absurdist plays there is a loss of causal relationships, and everything becomes senseless. Albee's early plays, including his *Zoo Story,* are considered absurdist plays because of their illogical or irrational elements. Harold Pinter, a contemporary of Albee's, is also defined as an absurdist, as is Samuel Beckett, one of Albee's role models.

Somewhere in between a romantic or an idealized view and the irrational absurdist view is the realist. In the 1950s and early 1960s, plays that leaned more toward realism were more likely to meet with commercial success, which is exactly

COMPARE & CONTRAST

- **1930s:** Alcoholic Anonymous (AA) is founded in Cleveland, Ohio, and within four years its membership grows to 100.

  1950s: The Twelve Step program of AA offers those who are suffering from alcoholism a way to grapple with their dependence. It is estimated that there are now over 100,000 members in AA.

  Today: Membership in AA is now international and includes over 2 million members.

- **1930s:** Dogs and cats roam freely without restrictions and without protection from cruelty caused by humans.

  1950s: The American Humane Association is formed in an attempt to protect animals.

Today: It is estimated that over 40,000 dogs and cats are euthanized each day in various animal shelters and veterinarian offices throughout the United States.

- **1940s:** During World War II, women take on a more independent role in American society, and birth rates drop as divorce rates rise.

  1950s: It is calculated that there are over one million divorced people living in the United States.

  Today: It is calculated that there are over 2.5 million new names added to the divorce list each year, with an estimated figure of over 20 million divorced people living in the United States.

---

what happened with two of Albee's plays at that time, *Who's Afraid of Virginia Woolf?* and *A Delicate Balance.* By definition, a realist play is one that is concerned with the ordinary elements of life with a focus on present, specific action. A realist employs simple, direct prose with an emphasis on the characters' inner selves. It is through Albee's direct prose that the psychology of his characters is exposed, even as the characters try to hide it either from the other characters or from themselves. For Albee, this form offered a vehicle to deal with his unpleasant and sometimes debilitating relationship with his mother, who is a reoccurring character in Albee's plays, such as Agnes in *A Delicate Balance.*

CRITICAL OVERVIEW

A Delicate Balance is one of Albee's most long-lived plays, enjoying receptive audiences and reviews both in the 1960s, when it was first produced, and more recently in the 1990s and 2000s, when it experienced a revival. Although not every review has been positive toward Albee and his work, most

acknowledge his impact on American drama, with *A Delicate Balance* being credited as one of his more influential plays. As Harold Clurman in his 1966 *New York Times* article writes, ''Albee seems to excite everyone to a defiant admiration or to a determined denunciation.'' Clurman goes on to declare, ''Albee is a master of stage speech,'' which he says is ''extremely studied and remarkably euphonious.'' He also states that *A Delicate Balance*

> comes closest . . . to a synthesis of Albee's traits and talents. Though still somewhat withheld by the mask of comedy and vindictive humor, it voices his particular ache in the most genuinely compassionate tone of which he is now capable.

Another 1960s reviewer, this time Walter Kerr in the *New York Times,* believed that the main theme of *A Delicate Balance* was hollowness, and that Albee, Kerr states in a somewhat sarcastic tone, did a good job in presenting it as it is, ''offered to us on an elegantly lacquered empty platter the moment the curtain goes up.'' Kerr then goes on to question how a playwright might offer hollowness. He states that Harold Pinter, a British playwright in Albee's time, did it through suggestion. Pinter never used ''the word 'fright'; he simply frightens us. Mr.

A scene from the 1973 film adaptation of A Delicate Balance, *starring Katharine Hepburn and Paul Scofield*

Albee, on the other hand, plays out his hand all too readily, revealing that there is so little in it.'' Kerr felt that Albee, rather than making the audience feel frightened, only allowed the audience to listen to the details of other people's fright. He then goes on to liken the images that Albee presents to ''chocolate Easter bunnies that crack wide open at the very first bit [sic].''

In a book published in 1987, giving the critic a more distanced view on Albee's works, Gerry McCarthy in his book *Edward Albee* writes that *A Delicate Balance* ''is a remarkably clear and deft piece of work.'' McCarthy believes that at the time Albee wrote this play, he had eased into a more comfortable relationship with his writing and because of this *A Delicate Balance* reflects a new sense of ''coolness.'' McCarthy continues, ''His style allows the structure of the play to be more carefully arranged,'' and the way he defines the central concern of this play ''is meticulously controlled through a disciplined, highly articulate prose.''

On April 21, 1996, Albee's play was revived and presented at Lincoln Center in New York. Vincent Canby, writing a review of this revival production in the *New York Times,* tells his readers,

''This production has the impact of entirely new work.'' Canby's claim is backed up later when the play wins a Tony Award for best revival. Canby adds that audiences should expect ''an evening of theatrical fireworks that prompt astonished oohs and ahs, genuine laughter and a certain amount of delicious unease.''

Since the 1996 revival, Albee's play has enjoyed new productions around the globe. A press release from the Circle Theatre in Dallas, Texas, describes Albee's play as being ''filled with shades of meaning, subtleties, and whole paragraphs of brilliant dialogueue,'' which has made it ''classic theater.'' In a review in the *Seattle Post-Intelligencer* in January 2001, theatre critic Joe Adcock states that Albee has ''expanded'' Jean-Paul Sartre's (a French existentialist writer's) theory of hell. In Albee's play, ''hell is still other people. But now there are six of them. They spread themselves out over three acts. Their damnation lasts nearly three hours.'' Adcock continues by stating that Albee also ''expands the dimensions of hell,'' as hell not only exists on the stage but ''spills out into the auditorium . . . and his characters and his story torture the audience.'' Writing during the same week, only this time in the *Seattle Times,* critic Misha Berson describes the play and the playwright in more flattering terms. ''What Albee brings to the subject [of extinction] . . . is a scalding wit and . . . a gift for poetic reverie and a rare 'delicate balance' of social satire and compassionate absurdity.''

CRITICISM

Joyce Hart

Hart has degrees in English literature and creative writing and is a freelance editor and published writer. In this essay, she examines the character Tobias and the story of his cat and then uses the story as Albee's metaphor for Tobias's inability to love or make contact with his wife.

In the book *Conversations with Edward Albee* (edited by Phillip C. Kolin), Albee articulates one of the motivating forces behind the actions of the characters in his play *A Delicate Balance*. He states, ''The [delicate balance] is between what we should be doing and what we ultimately decide we need to do to protect ourselves.'' Throughout *A Delicate Balance*, Albee demonstrates various ways in which his characters create barriers between themselves and others in order to avoid facing one another and their fears. These fears run a whole gamut of emotions and are displayed in idiosyncratic ways depending on which character is involved, what a character's relationship is with the other characters, and, for some, what lessons they have learned from the past. In terms of lessons learned, Tobias's story of his cat illuminates some of his fears and can be used to help understand the decisions he makes as he, like all the other characters, desperately tries to maintain that delicate balance.

In the first act of *A Delicate Balance*, in the middle of an awkward battle of insults between his wife, Agnes, and his sister-in-law, Claire, Tobias falls back into a reflection of his relationship with a cat that once lived with him. The fact that he remembers this cat while sitting in his parlor with two women fighting cues the reader that there is more than memory going on here. Thoughts are recalled by association, so there should be a connection between what Tobias is witnessing in the present and what he suddenly finds himself remembering.

Tobias's relationship with his cat develops over several years. He'd had the cat since he was a child, so he was famialiar with the cat's manner-

isms. The cat didn't like people, in general, but seemed only to tolerate them. However, Tobias believed that the cat liked him, or, as he says, ''rather, when I was alone with her I could see she was content; she'd sit on my lap. I don't know if she was happy, but she was content.'' Relating this part of the cat story while listening to his wife argue might make the reader wonder if this is a comment about Tobias's feelings for his wife. Throughout the play, there is little observable evidence of Tobias's affections for his wife or, for that matter, of Agnes's love for Tobias. They are not sleeping together, nor do they even share a bedroom. Their conversations with one another are cordial but demonstrate only surface emotional content unless they touch on subjects that are almost too painful to bear. So there remains the question of whether Tobias really loves his wife or, like the cat, merely tolerates her. Or, turning this statement in another direction, does the cat represent Agnes? Is Tobias looking at Agnes as he looked at his cat? Does Tobias feel that Agnes doesn't really like people but that she feels, if not happy, at least content living with Tobias? It is interesting to note that at the end of this part of the cat story, Tobias pauses, allowing Agnes to reflect on the portion of the story that Tobias has related so far and to respond to his commentary, which she does. As soon as Tobias mouths the words ''she was content,'' Agnes replies: ''Yes.''

Tobias then continues with his cat story, stopping to correct himself when he states that he suddenly realized one day that the cat no longer loved him. Tobias says: ''No, that's not right; one day I realized she must have stopped liking me some time before.'' The fascinating point that is being made here is that Agnes and Tobias's relationship compares quite consistently with this observation. Whether Tobias is aware of this on a rational level or is bringing up the memory of the cat in reaction to a subconscious realization is not clear. However, it can be quite successfully argued that Albee is aware of the connection. Later in the play, Albee exposes two incidents that occurred much earlier in the marriage of Agnes and Tobias, either of which could have caused Agnes to have ''stopped liking'' Tobias ''some time before.''

It is unclear which incident happened first, but the one that is mentioned first in the play is Tobias's alleged infidelity. The woman who was involved in this extramarital affair is never named, but some critics have analyzed the play and concluded that the woman was none other than Agnes's sister Claire. There are a few clues provided by Albee that

WHAT DO I READ NEXT?

- Albee's writing is often compared to Eugene O'Neill's. In *Long Day's Journey into Night* (1956), O'Neill tells a story about an unhappy, dysfunctional family in which the youngest son is sent to a sanatorium to recover from tuberculosis, all the while despising his father for sending him there. The young man's mother is wrecked by narcotics, and his older brother is an alcoholic.

- When Albee's writing leans more toward the absurd, it is often compared to Harold Pinter's. One of Pinter's more famous plays is *The Homecoming* (1976), which is set in an old house in North London, where an aging father lives with his two sons and his younger brother. The action begins when Teddy, another one of the father's sons, who has been away from the family for six years, brings his wife home to visit the family she has never met. As the play progresses, the younger brothers make passes at their sister-in-law until they all but make love to her in front of her stunned husband.

- Albee has said that Eugene Ionesco is one of his role models. In *Rhinoceros* (1959), as in many of his early plays, Ionesco startles audiences with an absurd world that invariably erupts in both laughter and anxiety as the population of a town slowly transforms into a herd of rhinoceros with only one human, at the end, remaining. This is Ionesco's statement against conformity, especially in reference to the brutality of the Nazi movement of his time.

- If Albee were to choose the playwright who most impressed him, it probably would be Samuel Beckett. In *Happy Days* (1961), Beckett explores relationships that bind one person to another by showing the mutual dependency of a woman, Winnie, who is buried in a mound of dirt (first up to her waist and later up to her neck) by her frustratingly silent mate, Willie.

- Known as the Albee play that did not win the Pulitzer Prize, *Who's Afraid of Virginia Woolf?* (1962) has often been described as a thematic precursor to *A Delicate Balance. Who's Afraid of Virginia Woolf?* is a play in three acts with the action taking place in the living room of a house belonging to a middle-aged couple, George and Martha, who are drunk and quarrelsome. When another couple stops by for a nightcap, they are enlisted as fellow fighters, and the battle begins. A long night of malicious games, insults, humiliations, betrayals, painful confrontations, and savage witticisms ensues. The secrets of both couples are laid bare, and illusions are viciously exposed.

- In order to better understand the disease of alcoholism, James Robert Milam and Katherine Ketcham have written *Under the Influence: A Guide to the Myths and Realities of Alcoholism* (reissue edition 1984). Based on scientific research, this book examines the physical factors of alcoholism and suggests a stigma-free way of understanding and treating alcoholics. Some of the topics in this book include ways of defining an alcoholic, stages of alcoholism, how to choose a treatment program, why prescribed drugs can be dangerous and even fatal for alcoholics, and how to ensure a lasting recovery.

- Called one of the Angry Young Men (a group of writers in England who freely expressed their disdain for established British society), John Osborne is said to have changed the face of British theatre with his play *Look Back in Anger.* It was first performed in 1956, and although the form of the play was not new, its content was. The play centers on disenfranchised youth, an unusual topic at the time, with its hero, Jimmy Porter, frustrated with his position in society, which he can never overcome because the traditional possessors of wealth and privilege will forever hold him in his place.

support this claim, such as the fact that Claire is aware of the affair to the point of complete certainty. Albee also suggests in his script directions that Claire "*raises her two arms . . .* [in a] *casual invitation.*" The tone of the conversations between Tobias and Claire are also much more relaxed and more openly honest than Tobias's exchanges with Agnes. In addition, toward the end of the play when Tobias tells Agnes that he had trouble sleeping one night, she asks if he went to Claire.

The other event that marred the couple's affections for one another and could have been the cause of Agnes's no longer liking Tobias happened upon the death of their son, Teddy. Through guilt or fear of loss, Tobias, at that point, refused to have any more children. "I think it was a year, when you spilled yourself on my belly, sir?" Agnes says to Tobias in act 3. And then "you took to your own sweet room. . . . And *I* must *suffer* for it. . . . And I have made the best of it. Have lived with it." Either of these incidents, the alleged affair or the death of the child and subsequent loss of sexual contact, could be cause for Agnes to have stopped liking Tobias.

Tobias continues his story about the cat with the comment that he suddenly realized that his cat was no longer in the room with him, reflecting, perhaps, on the observation that even though Agnes's physical self is present, he senses that on the emotional level, she removed herself from him a long time ago. It is through the cat's absence that Tobias finally realizes a new pattern in the cat's life, a pattern that Tobias interprets as "she didn't like me any more. It was that simple."

When he comprehended his cat's new behavior, Tobias relates, "I tried to force myself on her." After hearing this comment, Agnes cannot contain herself and responds: "Whatever do you mean?" From this point of the story on, Tobias confesses that he became somewhat obsessed with trying to make his cat like him again. When the cat gives him no sign of returning his attempts at affection (she wouldn't purr when he petted her, for instance), Tobias became irritated, shook her, and when the cat responded by biting him, Tobias slapped her across the head. "I . . . I *hated* her!" he says. Eventually Tobias had the cat euthanized.

Fascinating correlations exist even in this part of the story. Although Agnes is still alive, therefore contradicting the end of Tobias's cat story, there is a sort of playful and ironic conversation between

> " THERE COULD ALSO BE THE CLAIM THAT ON A PSYCHOLOGICAL LEVEL TOBIAS HAS KILLED HIS WIFE SINCE HER EMOTIONS FOR HIM HAVE BEEN BURIED, AT LEAST THE MORE PASSIONATE, PLEASANT ONES."

Claire and Tobias in which Claire suggests that Tobias should kill Agnes (as well as his daughter and Claire herself). The only emotional response Tobias has to this suggestion happens when Claire also tells him that he should kill Agnes before he kills her. "But it would have to be an act of passion—out of my head, and all that," he says. He does not question whether or not he could kill his wife, only that he could not kill her unless he was in a state of "passion." As a matter of fact, the only question he posits in this exchange is to ask Claire: "Do you really want me to shoot you?" Since Tobias was in a state of "passion" when he had the cat killed, there still remains, at least on a speculative level, a connection between his cat and his wife. There could also be the claim that on a psychological level Tobias has killed his wife since her emotions for him have been buried, at least the more passionate, pleasant ones.

There are moments when Agnes's emotions do rise to the surface. However, these emotions usually are followed by accusation. She often insinuates to Tobias that she knows that he had an affair with her sister. She blames Tobias for not being strong in his relationship with their daughter, therefore encouraging Julia's many divorces. In the third act of the play when Agnes recalls Tobias's refusal to make sexual contact with her following the death of their son, she, on one hand, absolves Tobias by stating that he did not want to create any more children because he was "racked with guilt." On the other hand, she then adds the word "stupidly," referring to his guilt, and adds: "and *I* must *suffer* for it."

Agnes's accusation fits well into Tobias's story of his cat when he adds another interesting element to his tale while summarizing his emotional response to the cat story:

I had *lived* with her; I had done . . . *everything*. And
. . . and if there was a, any responsibility I'd failed in
. . . well . . . there was nothing I could *do*. And, and I
was being accused.

The key words in this statement are "responsibility" and "accused." The first of these words,
"responsibility," is a theme that is either overtly
expressed or subtly suggested throughout the play.
Agnes refers to Tobias, at one point, as a man who
provides a good home for her and her sister Claire.
In other words, he is responsible for the welfare of
two middle-aged women, giving them food and
shelter as any responsible man would do. Tobias, at
the end of the play, also mentions responsibility in
reference to his friend Harry, who has come to stay
in Tobias's house. Tobias feels more responsibility
than friendship toward Harry. In the same way,
Tobias feels responsible for Agnes, even though the
emotions between them have died. The other key
word, "accused," fits Agnes's overall tone, as
mentioned previously.

In concluding his story about his cat, Tobias
makes the statement, "I had her killed." Immediately following his words, Agnes tries to soften the
impact of these words by simplifying the act: "You
had her put to sleep. She was old. You had her put to
sleep." In reaction, Tobias restates that he had the
cat killed. He even raises his voice and repeats his
statement, taking full responsibility for the cat's
death. At this, Agnes again tries to ease Tobias's
guilt. "What else could you have done?" This time,
Tobias reflects on his actions. He wonders about
other things that he might have done to avoid
destroying the cat completely.

It is through these reflections that the audience
becomes aware of the workings of Tobias's mind.
Tobias's contemplations on what other actions he
could have taken with his cat also provide hints as to
how he has resolved his relationship with Agnes:

I might have tried longer. I might have gone on, as
long as cats live, the same way. I might have worn a
hair shirt, locked myself in the house with her, done
penance. For *something*. For *what*. God knows.

If Tobias has learned anything from his experience with his cat, it is that he must build up tolerance
and patience. He has learned to live with his wife.
He does not force her to love him and has found
ways to maintain his sense of responsibility toward
her and their marriage. His conclusions may not be
psychologically healthy (he stills seems to hold on
to guilt and a need for punishment), but it could be
noted that he has not killed Agnes. That, at least, is
some improvement.

Source: Joyce Hart, Critical Essay on *A Delicate Balance,* in
Drama for Students, The Gale Group, 2002.

Richard Farr

*In the following interview, Albee discusses the
social and political background and content of
his work.*

Despite wealthy adoptive parents who sent him to
exclusive schools like Choate, Valley Forge, and
Trinity College, playwright Edward Albee didn't
have an easy start. He was expelled from most of the
schools, or expelled himself. At eighteen he expelled himself from his parents' home and spent a
decade drifting in and out of casual jobs.

He was a messenger for Western Union when,
at twenty-nine, he wrote an angry, deeply disturbing
one-act play called *The Zoo Story*, in which a
businessman on a park bench is coerced into stab-
bing a vagrant.

The play was a sensation, the critics hailed it as
the first work of a hugely original talent, and Albee
went on to write a series of chilling attacks on the
American domestic verities, most notably *The American Dream* (1961), *Who's Afraid of Virginia Woolf?*
(1962), and *A Delicate Balance* (1966)—which
won Albee his first Pulitzer prize.

Albee said from the start that he hated the
commercial values of Broadway, and he was one of
the founders of the Off-Broadway movement. Perhaps the critics decided that the very successful
Angry Young Man needed a lesson in humility.
After 1966 his reputation went into a quarter-cen-
tury tailspin, as each new offering "failed" to live
up to the promise of the early work. Albee continued
to produce original drama at the rate of one play per
year. Critics responded by dismissing nearly all of it
as willfully experimental and obscure, and Albee
responded to their criticism by dismissing the most
powerful New York critics, by name, as know-
nothings.

Albee has always been an experimentalist, and
he seems not to have cared that some of his work has
not been well received. So there was some irony in
the relief critics expressed in 1992, when he won
another Pulitzer for *Three Tall Women*. "Albee has
done it again," was the cry, as if the entire theater
community had been waiting thirty years to see if
the old dog could jump through the hoop one more
time. Albee is a name to reckon with again. *A*

Delicate Balance has just celebrated its thirtieth birthday on Broadway by winning three Tony awards, including Best Revival.

Albee travels constantly, teaching and lecturing, but in New York he can be found in a cavernous TriBeCa loft, an abandoned cheese warehouse he bought eighteen years ago in the days before cavernous TriBeCa lofts were fashionable. Despite the gray hair, he doesn't look close to his sixty-eight years. We sit on black leather couches in the middle of his extraordinary art collection. A Dogon granary door is propped up just behind the author, a Picasso sketch stands in a frame on a desk, and a Japanese grain-threshing device sits on the floor nearby. An Australian aboriginal war axe lies dangerously on the table between us.

Q: Your plays don't express very overtly political sentiments. Is that because you don't want to seem to be getting up on a soapbox?

Albee: I do think that all of my plays are socially involved, but sometimes very subtly and very indirectly. Certainly *The American Dream* was socially involved. It's about the way we treat old people, the way we destroy our children, the way we don't communicate with each other. *The Death of Bessie Smith* was a highly political play. Sometimes it's subtle and sometimes it's fairly obvious.

Q: It has been suggested that *Who's Afraid of Virginia Woolf?* is "really" about two gay couples.

Albee: If I had wanted to write a play about two gay couples, I would have done it. I've had to close down a number of productions that tried to do that play with four men. It doesn't make any sense; it completely distorts the play. Changing a man into a woman is more than interpretation: It's f—ing around with what the playwright intended.

Q: Do you try to exercise strong control over how your plays are produced?

Albee: I always tell actors and directors—whether I'm working with them or not—do whatever you like so long as you end up with the play that I wrote. There's more than one way to skin a cat, lots of different interpretations. The only time I really complain is if, either through intention or inattention, the director distorts my play.

Q: Many of your plays are about families, especially about family dysfunction.

Albee: This has been going on ever since drama was invented. *Oedipus Rex* is about family and

> " IF I WROTE PLAYS ABOUT EVERYONE GETTING ALONG TERRIBLY WELL, I DON'T THINK ANYONE WOULD WANT TO SEE THEM."

family dysfunction; *King Lear* is about family and family dysfunction. Nothing new about it. If I wrote plays about everyone getting along terribly well, I don't think anyone would want to see them. All serious theater is corrective. You have to show people things that aren't working well, and why they're not working well, in the hope that people will make them work better.

Q: But some playwrights don't focus on the family so much.

Albee: Which ones? Brecht maybe. But the atomic family is such a central part of human society. You can't get away from it.

Q: What is your attitude to marriage and the traditional family?

Albee: As with all things: When it works, it's fine. When it doesn't, do away with it.

Q: Is the legalization of gay marriage an important issue?

Albee: Why do you ask? Look, one day I'll write a play about a dysfunctional gay marriage. OK?

Q: Are you working on a play now?

Albee: I have two plays, one that I'm writing now called *The Play About the Baby*—that's the title of it—which I'm halfway into, and there's another one floating around in my head called *The Goat*, which very much wants to be written down.

Q: Do you write every day?

Albee: If writing is thinking about writing then I'm writing all the time. There isn't a day that goes by when I'm not thinking about a new play. But the literal writing down of a play—I seldom do that more than three or four months out of the year. That happens only after the play is fully formed in my mind: I wait until I can't do anything else but write it down. I never make notes because I make the assumption that anything I can't remember doesn't belong there in the first place.

Q: Do you do much rewriting?

Albee: I may, in my head, before I write things down. A lot of the writing is in the unconscious. I do very little rewriting once I write a play down on paper, very little.

Q: What's the role of comedy in drama?

Albee: I've found that any play which isn't close to laughter in the dark is very tedious. And conversely, even the purest comedy, if it isn't just telling jokes, has got to be tied to reality in some way. I think a play should do one of two things, and ideally both: It should change our perceptions about ourselves and about consciousness, and it should also broaden the possibilities of drama. If it can do both, that's wonderful. But it's certainly got to do one of the two.

Q: Does the artist have a duty not to preach politics in his work?

Albee: Most serious drama is trying to change people, trying to change their perceptions of consciousness and themselves and their position as sentient animals. Sometimes it's very overtly political and sometimes very subtly so. The way we vote, the way we function as a society, is determined by our sense of ourselves and our consciousness, and to the extent that you can keep people on the edge, alive, alert, and reexamining their values, then they will deal more responsibly with the particular issues. But didacticism belongs in essays.

Q: Isn't there any good art that's didactic? Dickens? Goya?

Albee: In the second half of the twentieth century things get more complex and it's harder to think of examples. David Hare does write didactic plays: *Racing Demon,* for instance, which I have retitled, not unaffectionately, *Raging Didacticism.* When there's too much didacticism going on I start sighing. I say: I know this stuff—dramatize it for me!

Q: You have always opposed the commercial pressures and values associated with Broadway. Do you feel uncomfortable with the success that *A Delicate Balance* is enjoying there now?

Albee: I never feel bad about getting awards; if they're giving out awards, I'd like to have them. But I don't care. They don't matter. The plays that seemed to matter on Broadway this year were very

different from what usually wins. None of them originated on Broadway. So maybe something better is happening, though I think it's a little strange.

Q: You have taught at various institutions. Do you make any conscious effort to radicalize your students?

Albee: I do, yes. I probably shouldn't because I'll probably get thrown out—we're talking about Texas, where I teach now. I don't give them grades on how radical they've become, but I do talk a lot about their responsibilities. And I do often mention right at the beginning that there isn't a single creative artist whose work I respect who has been anything other than a liberal.

Q: Ezra Pound?

Albee: Well . . . there are exceptions.

Q: Have your students changed, politically?

Albee: Even back in the "activist" sixties and seventies I would talk to a lot of students and most of them couldn't argue dialectics for more than thirty seconds. They had an emotional involvement and they had a few slogans but they were not informed. Anyway, I teach aspiring writers, almost all of whom are liberal because they realize that anything that is not liberal is not going to respect their freedom of speech, freedom of activity. So quite selfishly, they are liberal, though how they will vote when they make it I have no idea. Some of them will get rich, go to Hollywood, and start voting Republican. Even in a democracy, things like that happen!

Q: In 1961, you said that we were ruled by "artificial values," and you spoke with contempt of the view "that everything in this slipping land of ours is peachy keen." Have we slipped further into "artificial values"?

Albee: I think we've slipped a lot further. We have to go back to the fundamental responsibilities of democracy. Democracy is fragile and it must be made to work, which demands an awful lot of effort on everybody's part. I find the real and planned incursions against our civil liberties frightening and dangerous. The so-called religious right of the Republican Party—the Christian right, they call themselves, although in my view they are neither Christian nor right—is after a totalitarian state. But none of these things would be allowed to happen if we had a population a) that bothered to vote; b) that informed itself of the issues; and c) that understood that democracy is a participatory governmental system. We don't live up to our responsibilities to democracy.

Q: Would you describe yourself as a capital-D Democrat?

Albee: The first time I ever voted was in a New York City mayoral election. There were three candidates: a Democrat who was perfectly OK but a hack; a Republican who was probably not as terrible as all Republicans are these days; and a candidate for the American Labor Party who everyone said was a Communist. He was actually a leftwing socialist, and he was the only person who a sensible person could have voted for. But the whole question of what is leftwing has shifted so. My God, Nelson Rockefeller would be considered leftwing now. I not only voted for the American Labor Party once, I also voted Republican once—no, twice—to get Javits reelected. But yes, I'm a Democrat, though I'm afraid I'm much more of an unreconstructed New Deal Democrat than most, perhaps because that was when I first had some political consciousness.

Q: People are criticizing Clinton for being too conservative.

Albee: Clinton needs a lot of criticism, but don't let's criticize him so much that Dole gets elected. Wait until he gets his second term, if he gets it. Then you'll find a much more liberal President because he won't be up for reelection.

Q: What's it like, in these conservative times, to work on NEA grant committees?

Albee: I don't get asked as much as I did. I'm a troublemaker. The pressures that were put on us occasionally to find as many worthwhile sculptors in North Dakota as there were in Brooklyn—well, I'm in favor of populism within rational limits, but . . . I also served for a while on the New York State Council for the Arts, but I was equally vocal there, and I'm not invited to do those things too much now.

Q: Did you enjoy them?

Albee: Yes, I considered it a civic responsibility. You know, in the thirties there was a huge arts program, for the visual arts especially, where a great generation of abstract painters was put to work decorating public buildings. And a lot of writers was put to work in schools. But nobody remembers that. They all think the National Endowment was the first time anyone had thought of using creative artists for the public good. We spend about thirty-eight cents per person per year on support of the arts in this country. In Germany it's five or six bucks. All the howling that's taking place in the fens of ignorant Republicanism attacking these supposedly huge grants is preposterous, it seems to me—sinister and cynical and totally fallacious. This is less money per year than you pay for one pack of cigarettes. If you don't want to educate yourself, you have a responsibility to educate other people, educate your children; this is part of the responsibilities of democratic life.

Q: However, there's a widespread sense that art is really just entertainment for highbrows.

Albee: Not only that! Art is dangerous. It's obscene. It's anti-god. And these arguments that the philistines come up with wouldn't work if people were educated to want art.

Q: You helped to create the Off-Broadway movement in the early 1960s, which seems to have been a period when anything was possible in the arts. Why have things gone from there to here?

Albee: A combination of fear and greed. I remember a time, I can't give you a date, but all of a sudden college students were informed—I don't know by whom—that what you did was graduate, get a cushy job, and vanish into society. I see it more and more. Mind you, my playwriting students haven't figured it all out yet. They still think that individuality has some virtue; they still think that their responsibility, if they possibly can, is to change the way people think.

Q: So, despite the slough of cultural-conservative despond, you see grounds for optimism?

Albee: How old are we, as a country? Two hundred years? I think we'll survive Gingrich and Dole.

Q: What's best in contemporary American theater?

Albee: I don't make lists. I always leave somebody good out. We have so many good playwrights in America now, a whole new generation.

Q: Is there any dominant theme or style emerging?

Albee: We have great diversity of style. I do find that the more naturalistic a play is, the more popular it tends to be.

Q: Is that a criticism?

Albee: Yes.

Q: Why is naturalism a problem artistically?

Albee: Theater audiences have been trained towards naturalism. The critics don't like experimental plays generally, and they steer audiences away from them. It's part of the fear of the intellectual in American culture. A big problem in this country.

Q: Do you have an aversion to musicals, in general?

Albee: I think it's a bastard art form. The music isn't usually very good. I used to like junk musicals when Rodgers and Hart wrote them, and Cole Porter, but then they didn't have any pretense. The stuff that's on now is supposed to be serious music writing and serious theater, but it's just pretentious, middle-brow junk. I dislike it a lot. The last musical I liked a lot was *Evita,* because it was politically interesting.

Q: I notice that one of the theater reference books lists your religion as Christian. For an Absurdist playwright that seems odd.

Albee: That may just be a weird oversimplification of something I said at one time. I'm a great admirer of the revolutionary leftist politics of Jesus Christ, and I am a Christian in the sense that I admire him a great deal. But I don't have any truck with the divinity or with God, or any of that stuff. I just think he's an interesting revolutionary social thinker—and that makes me a Christian, does it not?

Q: Many of your plays seem to be about the maintenance or collapse of illusions. As if the goal is to live life without illusions.

Albee: I don't think there's any problem with having false illusions. The problem is with kidding yourself that they're not false. O'Neill said, in that extraordinary play that nobody does, *The Iceman Cometh,* that we have to have pipe dreams. I think *Virginia Woolf* was in part a response to that; it's better to live without false illusions, but if you must have them, know that they are false. It's part of the responsibility of the playwright to help us see when they're false.

Q: There seem to be Chekhov-like and Beckett-like elements in your plays. Are you influenced by other playwrights?

Albee: I certainly hope so. You learn from people who've come before you and who have done wonderful things. The trick is to take the influences

and make them so completely you that nobody realizes that you're doing anything else but your own work.

Source: Richard Farr, Interview with Edward Albee, in *Progressive,* Vol. 60, No. 8, August 1996, pp. 39–41.

E. G. Bierhaus

In the following essay, the author analyzes Albee's A Delicate Balance *not in terms of personal relationships, as it is usually discussed, but in terms of its politics, which, he writes, makes the focus of the play ''a moral and intellectual one.''*

W. H. Auden in *The Dyer's Hand* lists six functions of a critic, the fourth being: ''Give a 'reading' of a work which increases my understanding of it.'' In giving a new reading of Edward Albee's *A Delicate Balance,* I hope to increase the reader's understanding of this play by making him more aware of its ambiguities and by pointing out to him new associations within it. Although no one reading of *A Delicate Balance,* however careful, can reveal or distil or explain its full meaning simply because no work of art can ever finally be fully understood, a new reading does provide a new focus which changes the play's perspective.

My reading of *A Delicate Balance* is new because I do not think its primary focus is on the responsibilities of friendship. This is present but secondary. The primary focus is rather political, making the focus both a more moral and intellectual one. In friendship the emphasis is on the rights of the friend, in politics on the rights of the individual or self, in this case Tobias. To substantiate this reading, I shall examine three aspects of *A Delicate Balance* which to my mind require further attention: the significance of the characters' names, the surprising permutations of the characters, and finally the parable of Tobias and the cat.

I

Names have many resonances for Albee: biblical (Jerry and Peter in *Zoo Story*), historical (George and Martha in *Who's Afraid of Virginia Woolf?*), sexual (*Tiny Alice*). ''The Players'' in *A Delicate Balance* are no exception. (Notice that we have players instead of a cast because this is to be a contest.) Agnes, lamb of God, is also a third century saint, a virgin martyr who was decapitated because her body refused to burn at the stake. Agnes, a transliteration of the Greek . . . (pronounced hagnós), means ''pure'' and ''chaste.'' Tobias means ''God is good.'' In *The Book of Tobit* Tobias cures his father's blindness with the help of the archangel Raphael, his guardian. Edna also appears in *The Book of Tobit* as Tobias' mother-in-law. Harry is the diminutive of Henry, a name which evolved from the Old German words for "house," or "home," and "ruler."

Julia is the feminine form of Julius. "The Romans supposed the name to be derived from Greek . . . 'downy,' but there is no good evidence for this." Downy means "feathery" or "fluffy," but it is also slang for "wide awake" or "knowing." Claire of course means "to make clear" as Agnes observes: "Claire, who watches from the sidelines, has seen so very much, has seen us all so clearly, have you not, Claire. You were not named for nothing." Lastly, there is Teddy. Teddy, the dead son of Agnes and Tobias, is the diminutive of Edward, an Old English compound meaning "rich," "happy," and "ward," "guardian," and of Theodore, Greek for "god's gift." Edward and Theodore are both saints; Edward is also a king and martyr.

The resonances are various and conflicting, though always pertinent and never deceptive. Agnes, more wolf than lamb (". . . I am grimly serious. Yes?"), far from saintly ("We do not attempt the impossible," and "I'm not a fool," both saintly imperatives), more sacrificing than sacrificed (to Claire: "If you are not an alcoholic, you are beyond forgiveness," and to Julia: "How dare you embarrass me and your father!" [notice the "me" first]), is neither pure nor chaste in either the physical or spiritual sense (Claire to Julia: "Your mommy got her pudenda scuffed a couple of times herself 'fore she met old Toby," and Agnes to Tobias: "We must always envy someone we should not, be jealous of those who have so much less. You and Claire make so much sense together, talk so well").

Although Agnes considers herself blessed in a qualified way (". . . it is simply that I am the one member of this . . . reasonably happy family blessed and burdened with the ability to view a situation objectively while I am in it," and "There are many things a woman does: she bears the children—if there *is* that blessing. . ."), she also jokingly calls herself a "harridan," *e.g.,* a hag (". . . rid yourself of the harridan. Then you can run your mission and take out sainthood papers"). Ironically this last is addressed to Tobias, the only member of her family who is foolish enough to attempt the impossible.

Instead of having a blind father as in the apocrypha, this Tobias has a blind wife. Agnes is *not* the one member of her family who can view a

Maggie Smith, Eileen Atkins and John Standing in a scene from the 1997 theatrical production of A Delicate Balance

situation objectively while in it. Claire does this much better: "Harry wants to tell you, Sis." If Agnes weren't so afraid of silence, Harry would have explained his presence sooner. Moreover Agnes' remark to Julia, ". . . nobody. . .*really* wants to talk about your latest . . . marital disorder. . .," is simply untrue. Claire does: "I have been trying, without very much success, to find out why Miss Julie here is come home." Agnes can't even see herself properly:

AGNES. There was a stranger in my room last night.
TOBIAS. Who?
AGNES. You.
TOBIAS. Ah.

It doesn't occur to Agnes, as Tobias' "Who?" suggests it does to him, that she herself is the stranger.

Even Harry and Edna are sufficiently self-aware to recognize that in a similar situation they would not grant sanctuary to Tobias and Agnes. Julia also questions her mother with new insight: "I must discover, sometime, who you think you are." Agnes' "icy" reply is significant: "You will learn . . . one day." We all learn by the end of the play: Agnes thinks of herself as guardian, but she is in fact

> MY READING OF *A DELICATE BALANCE* IS NEW BECAUSE I DO NOT THINK ITS PRIMARY FOCUS IS ON THE RESPONSIBILITIES OF FRIENDSHIP. . . . THE PRIMARY FOCUS IS RATHER POLITICAL, MAKING THE FOCUS BOTH A MORE MORAL AND INTELLECTUAL ONE."

mad. So she does "lose her head" because she refuses to be burned, one method of inoculation against the plague, the play's chief metaphor.

Although Tobias begins drinking anisette, he switches to brandy—Claire's drink. Brandy burns. It is brandy that Tobias later offers to Harry at the end of Act III, but he refuses: "No, oh, God no." Harry has been burned enough for one week-end. Like Tobias, he was foolish enough to attempt the impossible and failed. That's why he leaves. Tobias has no place else to go. Although his house is not a home as Agnes uncomfortably reminds him: "Well, my darling, . . . you do not live at home," it is *his:* "I have built this house!" He is therefore free to exclaim to Harry: "I want your plague! . . . Bring it in!" But Agnes does not want it, and because she is nanny and drill sergeant (her drink is cognac: "It is suppose to be healthy") and *not* saint and martyr, Harry and Edna leave. Tobias remains to join Claire and Julia, "the walking wounded" (a deft description of sanity—and sainthood?), in another drink, while Agnes, the "steady wife," plans for them another day.

Harry and Edna return to their house where Harry can again be the ruler. The terror is still there, but they don't seem so overwhelmed by it. Their support of one another which at their entrance comes across as awkward and impersonal has mellowed. A tenderness has entered their relationship— Edna: "I let him think I . . . wanted to make love"— which coupled with the quiet acceptance of their failure—Edna: "We *shouldn't* have come. . . For our own sake; our own . . . lack"—lends a grace to their endurance which is not available to Tobias and Agnes who are locked in their separate worlds.

Their lives may be the same, as Edna observes, but their responses are not. Harry and Edna at least have the vitality to feel, act, and see. Therefore the ramifications of their departure, which is final,

> EDNA. I'm going into town on Thursday, Agnes. Would you like to come?
> [*A longer pause than necessary,* CLAIRE *and* JULIA *look at* AGNES]
> AGNES. [*Just a trifle awkward*] Well . . . no, I don't think so, Edna; I've . . . I've so much to do. . .

is less severe for them than for Tobias because they have each other. Tobias is left with two resigned drinking companions and a house manager nattering away about millenniums.

Immunity to the plague is acquired through testing, which leaves one burned or isolated "unless we are saints" (Agnes' sarcastic alternative):

> CLAIRE. So one night . . . I'd had one martini—as a Test to see if I could—which, given my . . . stunning self-discipline, had become three;
> EDNA. We mustn't press our luck, must we: test.

The characters' immunity, Claire and Agnes excepted, exists in various stages: Tobias' is beginning; Harry and Edna's is advancing, though they resist it; Julia's is progressing nicely. Although she endured as a young girl a "two-year burn at suddenly having a brother" and subsequently has known four husbands (know in the biblical sense is sexual), Julia is still not sufficiently "wide awake" for the "great big world." She needs to return home to Tobias and Agnes.

Claire is the only character who believes her immunity to be complete: "I've had it. I'm still alive, I think." Without Claire who feels "a little bigger than life" and who is the real nexus of the household, we would have no way to identify the degree of Julia's immunity, or her ambivalence to it. Nor could we see by the end of the play that Agnes who is "neither less nor more than human" is also immune. For her inoculation is different from the others. They *resign* themselves to reality whereas Agnes *creates* her own—"I'm as young as the day I married you." They confront their demons in the daylight, but Agnes—"well, you know how little I vary"—quarantines hers in the unknown chambers of her heart. Thus the plague (and the play) becomes less mysterious when associations with the characters' names are permitted to illuminate it.

II

One of the consummate strengths of *A Delicate Balance* is its universality. It speaks not only to its time, but out of it. Every year is a plague year somewhere, and no one is immune. As Hamm remarks in *Endgame* (a play with which *A Delicate Balance* has close affinities): "... you're on earth, there's no cure for that!" A major technique Albee employs to create this universality is characterization. This is partially achieved by the resonances, associations, and echoes the names of the characters have with life external to the play which fixes it in an historical—and literary—continuum. It is also partially achieved by the permutations of the characters themselves.

Just as Albee clues us in to the significance of names through Claire, so he clues us in to the significance of permutations by describing Harry and Edna as "very much like Agnes and Tobias." These internal resonances are as numerous and complex as the external ones. Furthermore, they determine the play's action and generate its vision, foci which are not coterminous.

When Claire declares to Tobias that "'Love' is not the problem. You love Agnes and Agnes loves Julia and Julia loves me and I love you. We all love each other; yes we do," she acknowledges that the boundaries of love in their household are set though circuitous. Trouble arises when these boundaries are challenged, *e.g.,* by Harry and Edna:

> TOBIAS. I almost went in *my* room . . . by habit . . . but then I realized that your room is my room because my room is Julia's because Julia's room is. . .

But while the boundaries are openly agreed upon by Agnes, Tobias, Claire, and Julia, they are constantly being unconsciously crossed: Claire, "like sister like sister"; Tobias, "My name is Claire"; Tobias calls Claire Agnes; Agnes becomes Julia's father, Tobias her mother; Claire calls Julia "daughter"; Harry becomes Tobias; Edna becomes Agnes. What this means is, as Claire points out, that like Tobias' friends they are all "indistinguishable if not necessarily similar ..." They share a common environment. "When one does nothing, one is threatened by the question, is one nothing?" It is a question which threatens them all.

It is in fact the terror. Tobias' despairing "Doesn't friendship grow to [love]?" is rhetorical for everyone except himself. Claire had already answered it: "We're not a communal nation...; giving, but not sharing, outgoing, but not friendly." An earlier assessment by Claire had driven Tobias to examine his boundaries:

> TOBIAS. We'll do neither, I'd imagine. Take in; throw out.

CLAIRE. Oh?
TOBIAS. Well, yes, they're just . . . passing through.
CLAIRE. As they have been . . . all these years.

A later claim by Edna pushes his examination further: "We are not . . . transients . . . like some." But they *are* transients. All of them. They each try the other's roles in an effort to belong, and although they meld perfectly (Julia talks like Claire, Tobias repeats Agnes, Harry mixes drinks like Tobias) they find that the new skin is just like their old one: "dry . . . and not warm." As Tobias eventually, discovers, boundaries bind (blind?) more often than they enclose.

A Delicate Balance is neatly constructed. Agnes both opens and closes the play. Her opening speech is seemingly a descant on whether or not she will go mad, but upon closer examination we find that what really astonishes her most "is Claire." This of course italicizes Claire's enlightenment and establishes straight away the conflict between the two. It is the major conflict of the play with Tobias as the stake. Each wants to persuade him to embrace her vision of the world: Agnes, instinctively selfish, demands order; Claire, instinctively generous, accepts the absurd. Agnes wants "peace," Claire "merely relief." The appearance of Harry and Edna forces Tobias either to choose between these opposing visions or to adopt one of his own. He opts for the latter, and it becomes a last, desperate effort to inject meaning into his life ("God is good").

Harry and Edna are thus pivotal because they upset the delicate balance of this trio. (The play is full of delicate balances: one exists between each of the characters, between appearance and reality, between the play and its reader or spectator.) But Harry and Edna are like Tobias and Agnes, Tobias is like Claire and Julia is like Agnes. Thus all the characters are pivotal, although each is "moving through his own jungle." "All happy families are alike," Claire tells Tobias, Agnes and Julia, quoting the opening of Tolstoy's *Anna Karenina.* And so are unhappy strangers.

III

As with Jerry's parable of the dog in *Zoo Story,* Tobias' parable of the cat is an analogue of the whole play. The parable contains eleven salient points: (1) the cat existed before Tobias met Agnes; (2) the cat was feminine; (3) she didn't like people; (4) but she was contented with Tobias; (5) one day he noticed that she no longer liked him; (6) he shook her; (7) she bit him; (8) he slapped her; (9) she judged him, accused him of failing; (10) he felt *betrayed*; (11) he had her killed.

Agnes is the obvious analogue to the cat: she is feminine, she replaces the cat in Tobias' affection, she does not like people (''You would not have a woman left about you—only Claire and Julia . . . not even people''), and she is contented with Tobias (''. . . I have reached an age, Tobias, when I wish we were always alone, you and I, without . . . hangers-on . . . or anyone''). Tobias noticed that Agnes no longer liked him after the death of Teddy, ''god's gift,'' Tobias' ''ward'' *and* ''guardian'' (his archangel?), whose death that hot, wet summer permanently altered the balance of all their lives. (AGNES. ''Ah, the things I doubted then: that I was loved—that *I* loved, for that matter!'') Tobias then ''shook'' Agnes by being unfaithful; she ''bit'' him by ''trying to hold [him] in.'' He ''slapped'' her by sleeping alone. She then judged him, accused him of failing (''Did my husband . . . cheat on me?'' and ''*You* could have pushed her back . . . if you'd wanted to''). Since married to Agnes, Tobias has felt betrayed by Teddy's death, Agnes' failure as a mother, Claire's infidelity with Harry, Julia's failure as an adult, and finally by Harry's refusal to ''stay.''

The analogue seemingly breaks down with point eleven: Tobias does not kill Agnes. Nor does Agnes kill Tobias. She does, however, see to it (Agnes is never blind to her own needs) that he is ''put to sleep,'' her euphemism for killing, by injecting him with the plague, *e.g.,* by thwarting *his* vision which is to make Harry and Edna stay, by withholding her succor from him and them. And her injection, like the vet's, succeeds where his fails.

Albee carefully prepares us for this reversal in two ways. First he identifies Tobias with Claire (this identification began when Tobias switched to Claire's drink, brandy). Immediately before the parable, Agnes ''decides Claire is not in the room,'' which is the reaction of the cat in the parable. During the parable Agnes again identifies herself with the cat when she wants to know if Tobias hurt her when he slapped her, while Claire identifies herself again with Tobias by asking what did he do, e.g., with the cat. Thus we intuitively feel that Tobias, like Claire, will succumb to Agnes' authoritarianism.

Second, Albee places the following exchange immediately after Tobias' ''I had her *killed*!'' which terminates the parable:

AGNES. Well, what else could you have done? There was nothing to be done; there was no . . . meeting between you.
TOBIAS. I might have tried longer . . . I might have worn a hair shirt, locked myself in the house with her, done penance.
CLAIRE. You probably did the right *thing*. Distasteful alternative; the less . . . ugly choice.
TOBIAS. Was it?
[*A silence from them all*]
AGNES. [*Noticing the window*] Was that a car in the drive?
TOBIAS. ''If we do not love someone . . . never have loved someone. . .''

Each of these speeches foreshadows the end of Act III: Agnes' ''. . . what else could you have done?'' is precisely her response to the departure of Harry and Edna, as is Tobias' ''I might have tried longer.'' Claire's ''distasteful alternative'' is comforting and pragmatic, while Agnes' nervous remark about the ''car in the drive'' parallels her breaking the silence with her—and the play's—concluding speech. But it is Tobias' quiet ''Was it?'' that is the most revealing, for he is suggesting that ''the less ugly choice'' might have been his own death. This is reinforced by his quoting Anges' ''If we do not love someone . . . never have loved someone'' which was originally her reply to Claire's ''Or! Agnes; why don't you die?'' The implication is that if one does not love someone, the generous ''reflex'' is to sacrifice oneself. This is what Tobias should have done with the cat; this is what he tried to do with Harry and Edna: ''I DON'T WANT YOU HERE! I DON'T LOVE YOU! BUT BY GOD . . . YOU STAY!!'' The reversal is complete: Tobias is ultimately the cat as he is the saint. But because God is dead—''The bastard! He doesn't exist!,'' to quote Hamm once again—sainthood is dead as well. As Julia explains, she first thought of her father as a saint, then as a cipher, and finally as a ''Nasty, violent, absolutely human man.''

This is what we are left with at the end of *A Delicate Balance*: three absolutely human beings—Tobias, Claire, Julia—seeking alcoholic ''relief'' from the disorder and ''debris'' of their stultifying existence, while the fourth member of their household, Agnes, speaking ''To fill the silence,'' remarks upon ''the wonder of daylight'' before blithely welcoming the new day. The conflict is over. Agnes has won. The price? *Three* early morning drinkers and that ''living room of a large and well-appointed suburban house'' thoroughly infected with the plague.

Since 1966 when *A Delicate Balance* was first produced, the environment of America has become increasingly disordered and dirty. Mr. Nixon is a permutation of Mr. Johnson who was "very much like" Mr. Goldwater; Democrats become Republicans, Republicans Democrats: "everyone [is] moving through his own jungle." We are all "players," strangers in a room; our endings, like Agnes' (and like that unfinished sentence ending *Finnegans Wake* which continues on the first page of the book), are reminiscent of our beginnings, dependents seeking "relief." And this brings me back to W. H. Auden, whose sixth function of a critic is to "Throw light upon the relation of art to life. . ."

Source: E. G. Bierhaus, "Strangers in a Room: *A Delicate Balance* Revisited," in *Modern Drama,* Vol. 17, No. 2, June 1974, pp. 199–206.

Michael E. Rutenberg

In the following essay excerpt, the author explores the themes of death, friendship, family, and their resistance to change in Albee's A Delicate Balance.

Notwithstanding the fact that Edward Albee received the Pulitzer Prize for *A Delicate Balance*, it still remains, aside from *Tiny Alice*, his most underrated play. Premiered on September 12, 1966, at the Martin Beck Theatre, its generally mild reception generated immediate controversy over Albee's continuing talent as a first-rate playwright. Martin Gottfried, reviewing for *Women's Wear Daily,* called the play "two hours of self-indulgence by a self-conscious and self-overrating writer." Robert Brustein, now Dean of the revitalized Yale School of Drama, said the writing was "as far from modern speech as the whistles of a dolphin." Conversely, John Chapman called it "a beautiful play—easily Albee's best and most mature." And Harold Clurman considered it "superior to the more sensational *Virginia Woolf.*"

While the critics could not agree on the play's merits, they seemed to be in general agreement on its theme, which they stated in various ways as man's responsibility to man. Albee had hinted at the theme before the play's opening (he wasn't going to be misunderstood again) when he revealed that the new work was about "the nature of responsibility, that of family and friends—about responsibility as against selfishness, self-protectiveness, as against Christian responsibility." In their reviews the critics simply paraphrased what Albee had said about the responsibilities of friendship since a major plot episode concerns the protagonists' best friends.

Norman Nadel claimed that the "delicate balance" was between "the right of privacy and the

> EACH AND EVERY RELATIONSHIP HANGS IN THE BALANCE OF TIME, DOGGEDLY RESISTANT TO CHANGE."

obligations of friendship." *Vogue's* reviewer echoed the other critics when he remarked that it is "when our friends make demands on us that we fail them." Leonard Probst, reviewing for NBC-TV, said in his one minute critique that "the delicate balance is the balance between responsibility to friends (when they're in trouble) . . . and the conflict with our own reasonable desires." John Gassner, in analyzing the play's structure, concluded that it was most concerned with saying "if we do not want to betray a friendship, we do not really want to carry it very far." With this general agreement on its theme, the critics turned out an onslaught of reasons why the new play was not well written.

Norman Nadel, referring to the neighboring couple who decide out of a private fear to stay on indefinitely, commented that their personal problem split the play into two parts which "do not relate as they should." John Gassner, writing for the *Educational Theatre Journal,* concluded that Albee had brought too many other elements into the play to simply resolve the friendship theme. Perhaps the most outspoken criticism of the play's structure came from the *Village Voice.* Michael Smith wrote that the play's crisis had "not been resolved but uncreated . . . [because] . . . Harry and Edna, quite on their own, simply go away. . . . Balance has been restored not by the called for heroic leap, but by removal . . . this play is a cop-out."

Each critic's evaluation was based on the premise that Albee had not carefully thought out the play's events as it related to the problem of friendship and its ensuing responsibilities. Professor Gassner, concentrating on what he considered Albee's intention, went so far as to say that certain major characters should not have been included in the play—specifically, that the alcoholic sister's appearance seemed somewhat arbitrary and the daughter's sudden homecoming uncalled for. Walter Kerr complained that "there are no events—nothing follows necessarily from what has gone before, no two things fit, no present posture has a tangible past.'' The critic for *Newsweek* summed up all the adverse criticism when he said there was a division between theme and procedure.

But the play examines more levels of our existence than the need for truer friendship among men. Once properly understood, the play's events are perfectly sequential (though I am not categorically against a plotless play as we shall see in the chapter on *Box-Mao-Box*), revealing an analysis of the modern scene that goes deeper than the reviews imply. One of the elements not discussed in any of the reviews is a continuation, and I believe culmination, of a major Albee theme.

From the very first Albee drama, through this play, two characters continually make their appearance: that domineering, man-eating, she-ogre of the American family—Mom—and her playmate, that weak-willed, spineless, castrated, avoider of argument—Dad. Together these two have woven their way through every single play of Albee's with the exception of *Tiny Alice*—although some critics have made an incorrect case for the existence of this sado-masochistic pair there also. Mom and Pop first showed up obliquely in *The Zoo Story* when Jerry began explaining his orphaned status to Peter. They next appeared as characters in both *The Sandbox* and *The American Dream*, its extention, playing out their roles of emasculator and emasculated, with Mom doing her part with such zest and relish that it made her male audience cringe with empathic pain. Even *Bessie Smith*, Albee's supposed civil rights play, got out of hand when his obsession with the battle of the sexes allowed the play's original theme to get away from him. It did, however, plant the seed of Daddy's fight for survival which came to fruition in the highly successful *Virginia Woolf*. The play's huge success is directly attributable to both the rich verbal texture and the fact that for the first time Albee gave Mom a formidable antagonist. This time Daddy would fight to the death before acquiescing to Mom's husband-destroying intentions.

Many critics have been quick to insist that Albee was really writing about his own foster parents and not about a typically American condition. A look into the many sociological texts on American life would negate that analysis. One such treatise, examining Dad's position in the American home, bluntly asserts that ''in few societies is the role of the father more vestigial than in the United States.'' This same text vividly points out that the success of such comics as *Blondie* (now seen on

television) or its home-screen predecessors, *The Honeymooners* and *The Flintstones,* is that the American public is convinced that the American father is a blunderer and has given up authority, because with him at the head ''the family would constantly risk disintegration and disaster.'' One further example, this time analyzing Mom, should suffice as a preamble to the conflicts set forth in *A Delicate Balance.* The following condensed statement on Mom can be found in a standard sociology textbook sold in most college bookstores across the country:

> 'Mom' is the unquestioned authority in matters of mores and morals in her home. . . . She stands for the superior values of tradition, yet she herself does not want to become 'old.' In fact, she is mortally afraid of that status which in the past was the fruit of a rich life, namely, the status of the grandmother . . . Mom—is not happy: she does not like herself; she is ridden by the anxiety that her life was a waste.

A Delicate Balance is a continuation of the Mom and Pop relationship as they enter the age of retirement. Through a rather bizarre event, Albee has forced the famous couple to re-examine the sum total of their lives with conclusions startlingly similar to the ones reached by the above sociological analysis. Albee wrote this play on boat trips to Europe. The relaxed slow pace of the ship's journey fit the needs of the playwright as he began to write his most introspective play. This particular style, not common to the American stage since it isn't filled with obvious physical action, was alien to many of the critics. Walter Kerr, in particular, reacted traditionally when he claimed that the play was ''speculative rather than theatrical, an essay and an exercise when it might have been an experience.'' In spite of Kerr's criticism, Albee went on to develop the introspective technique further until he completely broke from theatrical narrative in *Box-Mao-Box.*

Mom and Pop begin *A Delicate Balance* in ''the living room of a large and well-appointed suburban house.'' The couple, it will be remembered, started their careers as typically middle-class, later moved on to the university as intellectuals, and have now become well-to-do as they prepare for retirement. Placing Mom and Pop in the privileged class at the end of their lives is quite correct, because it is the symbolic end—the fitting reward for the dedicated American life. The American dream has come true; Mom and Pop have enough money now to isolate themselves from people and avoid any commitment to society. At one point in the play, Mom (Agnes) remarks, ''I have reached an age, Tobias, when I wish we were always alone, you and I, without . . . hangers-on . . . or anyone.'' We find the two, self-isolated at the beginning of the play, as Agnes speaks to her husband, having quietly contemplated the possibility of going mad:

> AGNES: . . . that it is not beyond . . . happening; some gentle loosening of the moorings sending the balloon adrift.

There is a death wish in her thought of insanity. Not verbalized yet, it's subliminally in her very description of madness. A recent movie, *Charlie Bubbles,* commenting on our society today, used the same imagery to suggest the death or suicide of its hero. At the end of the film, Charlie, totally alienated from his society and unable to live alone, performs the ultimate retreat from life as he steps into a balloon and sails out of this world.

Death is not a new concern in Albee's writing. *The Zoo Story* states that only at the supreme moment of death is there any human contract. *The Sandbox* and *The American Dream* are noticeably concerned with the death and removal of grandma from the American home. The title of *The Death of Bessie Smith* speaks for itself. *Virginia Woolf* builds to the death of the imaginary child which symbolizes the demise of all illusions. Finally, *Tiny Alice* examines the death and subsequent martyrdom of a lay brother. This ever-present concern with death is continued in *A Delicate Balance* and is instrumental to the deepest meanings of the play.

Agnes is reassured by Tobias (Pop) that ''there is no saner woman on earth,'' but unwilling to reciprocate her husband's support, she replies in her typically emasculating way that she ''could never do it—go—adrift—for what would become of you?'' Once again, as in all the past plays, Pop is reminded of his ineffectualness and total reliance on Mom. Presumably his life would disintegrate should Mom suddenly expire. Agnes continues her preoccupation with insanity, admitting now that thoughts of old age motivate her:

> AGNES: Yes; Agnes Sit-by-the-fire, her mouth full of ribbons, her mind aloft, adrift, nothing to do with the poor old thing but put her in a bin somewhere, sell the house, move to Tucson, say, and pine in the good sun, and live to be a hundred and four.

Ironically, in an earlier version of Mom, notably *The Sandbox*, she put her mother in a bin to die—which grandma promptly did. Agnes now wonders when it will be her turn to inherit the fate of our senior citizens. Tobias, too, is aware of his coming old age for he says a moment later, ''I'm not

as young as either of us once was.'' Agnes, still unnerved over her future, asks Tobias to tell her what he'd do if she really did go insane:

> TOBIAS: (*Shrugs*) Put you in a bin somewhere, sell the house and move to Tucson. Pine in the hot sun and live forever.
> AGNES: (*Ponders it*) Hmmmm, I bet you would.
> TOBIAS: (*Friendly*) Hurry, though.

Tobias is presumably joking, but under the friendly kidding is the same hatred that made George pull out a phony rifle in *Virginia Woolf* and shoot Martha. Agnes, somewhat taken aback by Tobias's admission that her senility and eventual death would not disturb him in the least, retaliates by assuring him that the perpetual blandness of her emotions would never lead to the psychological disintegration of insanity. She says, ''I can't even raise my voice except in the most calamitous of events.'' Actually she makes the case for eventual psychosis even stronger by admitting that her personality doesn't allow her to respond normally to most events that circumscribe her life. She begins to consider various chemical ways to induce psychosis, and there is a hint that she would like to try LSD or its narcotic equivalent to induce the excitement needed to bring about a drastic change in her day-to-day boredom. She quickly gives up this idea of chemical madness when she realizes it isn't permanent:

> AGNES: Ah, but those are temporary; even addiction is a repeated temporary . . . stilling. I am concerned with peace . . . not mere relief.

Here, Agnes unconsciously wishes for death, the permanent peace, because it has begun now ''to mean freedom from the acquired load and burden of the irrational.'' Still unable to rid her mind of its chronological inheritance, she resumes describing the dreary picture of their remaining years:

> AGNES: You have hope, of growing even older than you are in the company of your steady wife, your alcoholic sister-in-law and occasional visits . . . from our melancholy Julia. (*A little sad*) That is what you have, my dear Tobias. Will it do?
> TOBIAS: (*A little sad, too, but warmth*) It will do.

Ted Hoffman, reviewing for New York radio station WINS, was completely correct when he realized that so much of *A Delicate Balance* ''deals with the loneliness and corrosion of growing old.'' This theme, introduced early in the play, propels the play's action and is directly related to its resolution.

This first section of the play ends as Claire, Agnes's alcoholic sister, enters and apologizes for her somewhat inebriated condition. She neverthe-less accuses her sister of mistreating her because she is a drunk. Agnes defends herself in a way that Albee's heroine has never done, foreshadowing the change that will take place in her by the time the play ends:

> AGNES: . . . If I scold, it is because I wish I needn't. If I am sharp, it is because I am neither less nor more than human . . .

Only in this play does Mom apologize for her unpleasantness. This gnawing self-awareness later becomes a factor in her surprising decision to step down, at the end of the play, and relinquish her long-held role as head of the family. She leaves Claire and Tobias together in order to call her daughter Julia who is far enough away from her mother to effect a time differential of three hours. No sooner has Agnes left the living room than Claire asks Tobias why he doesn't kill Agnes. Tobias replies ''Oh, no, I couldn't do that,'' intimating that he doesn't have the guts for an act of bloody passion.

Albee uses Claire periodically as a quasi-narra-tor, sardonically commenting on the action. I find this practice unnecessary and her peripheral posi-tion alienating and at odds with the otherwise tight entanglement of his characters. One illustration of this annoying practice should be sufficient. When, in the midst of family crises, father, mother, daugh-ter, and audience became deeply involved with the situation at hand, Albee breaks this involvement and, using Claire, gets cute:

> CLAIRE: (*To* TOBIAS, *laughing*) Crisis sure brings out the best in us, don't it, Tobe? The family circle? Julia standing there . . . *asserting;* perpetual brat, and maybe ready to pull a Claire. *And* poor Claire! Not much help there either, is there? And lookit Agnes, talky Agnes, ruler of the roost, and Maitre d', *and* licensed wife—silent. All cozy, coffee, thinking of the menu for the week, *planning.* Poor Tobe.

Ostensibly, Claire's monologue is supposed to alienate the audience, in the Brechtian sense, by describing the moment while it's happening. Claire, in giving us information that is not necessary to the plot, serves no purpose other than to hold up the action while the viewer is jolted out of his empathy. Albee has used the aside as far back as *The Sandbox*, where Grandma talked to the audience and com-mented on the action. He used it again to less advantage in *Everything in the Garden*, but in these examples the aside was presentational in that the characters talked directly to the audience. It is clear now that Albee's periodic experiments with presen-tational speeches was a long-time predisposition,

which eventually found its form in the later *Box-Mao-Box.* However, *A Delicate Balance* is struc-tured representationally and periodic comments on the action from the sidelines does not work well in a post-Ibsen play.

Claire does serve another purpose, and it is here that her presence is effective. Claire tells the truth. She sees (clairvoyant) and tells it like it is. Per-haps this is why she drinks. She cannot cope with what she perceives and rather than kill herself or go insane, she drinks. When she isn't com-menting sarcastically on the action, her propensity for the truth prods the characters on toward the play's resolution. The first truth emerges when Claire forces Tobias, now retired, to examine the genuineness and durability of his past business friendships.

> CLAIRE: . . . With your business friends, your indis-tinguishable if not necessarily similar friends . . . what did you have in common with them?
> TOBIAS: Well, uh . . . well, everything. (*Maybe slightly on the defensive, but more vague*) Our business; we all mixed well, were friends away from the office, too . . . clubs, our . . . an, an environment, I guess.
> CLAIRE: Unh-huh. But what did you have in com-mon with them?

Claire asks the question twice more, but all Tobias can answer is ''please, Claire.'' Claire's insistence serves two purposes: first, it reveals the relative superficiality of most friendships because Tobias cannot think of one thing he has had in common with his friends except proximity. An eminent sociologist came to the same conclusion when he noted that ''Americans change both resi-dence and job with the greatest of ease; and with each change of either, friends are changed, too.'' Second, this brief revelation foreshadows and pre-pares the audience for the final tragic event concern-ing Tobias's closest friends.

Claire has made her point and is soon on to a new subject. She asks Tobias why he's switching from anisette to brandy. Tobias replies that the effects of anisette don't last as long. We realize that quiet, well-mannered Tobias looks to escape his surroundings by dulling his mind and memory for as long as possible. It is interesting to note that while Claire is said to be the alcoholic, Tobias drinks as often and as much as she does. Tobias is not off the hook though, because Claire will not let him forget. Reminding him of the time he was unfaithful to Agnes, she builds more evidence to dispel the image of tranquil, thoughtful Tobias, happily spending the final years of his life as the devoted, loving husband.

Claire then lies on the floor, arms outstretched in what Albee calls ''a casual invitation.'' Tobias only moves away; he is not interested. Later we find out that he's not sexually interested in his wife either. Years of constant emasculation have debilitated his sex drive until he is now like George in *Virginia Woolf*: impotent.

Impotency in Dad is a recurring theme in Albee's plays. We first hear of it in *The American Dream* (though Mommy and Daddy have no children in *The Sandbox*) when Mommy refers to Daddy's impotency as a result of a recent operation. The theme again appears in *Virginia Woolf* if we consider the inability of George and Martha to have a child. Impotency suggests loss of manliness as well as depletion of physical strength—both characteristic of the American daddy, according to Albee. It also implies sterility or the inability to produce a new generation. We do not create anything new; we only perpetuate, the old. At one point in the play Agnes corroborates this indictment. Talking about her only daughter she admits: ''We see ourselves repeated by those we bring into it all. . . .'' At another moment Claire makes the same observation when she says: ''We can't have changes—throws the balance off.''

Claire's remark also clarifies the title of the play, which is meant to mean the delicate balance of the *status quo,* whether it be in reference to an existing relationship within the family, a friendship outside, or the general state of affairs within the country or, for that matter, the world. Each and every relationship hangs in the balance of time, doggedly resistant to change. This difficulty of change within our lives is dramatically depicted as the play progresses, developing into the major theme of its denouement.

Unwilling to recognize Claire's open invitation to have sex with her, Tobias changes the subject, confessing that he can't remember the last time he saw his wife cry, ''no matter what,'' indicating she is as dried up emotionally as he is sexually. Tobias asks Claire why Alcoholics Anonymous never helped her. She replies, in a rather descriptive monologue, that she could not accept a belief in God—the first tenet of the organization. Besides, she doesn't admit to being an alcoholic. Agnes re-enters and stuns Tobias with the news that their daughter, Julia, is coming home after the dissolution of her fourth marriage. Apparently everyone has been aware that the breakup was coming, except Tobias. He offers to talk to his son-in-law in an effort to save the marriage, which seems, from Agnes's reaction, to be a new role for her husband:

> AGNES: (*As if the opposite were expected from her*) I wish you would! If you had talked to Tom, or Charlie, yes! even Charlie, or . . . uh. . . .
> CLAIRE: Phil?
> AGNES: (*No recognition of* CLAIRE *helping her*) . . . Phil, it might have done some good. If you've decided to assert yourself, finally, too late, I imagine. . . .

This sudden turnabout for Tobias is structurally important because it represents the first manifestation of an inner crisis that will grow during the course of the play, finally forcing Tobias to act contrary to his nature, in a last-ditch attempt to hold together his fast disintegrating ego. Agnes's remark, ''too late, I imagine,'' foreshadows the tragic failure of his attempt.

Claire breaks in and alters the mood temporarily by singing a little ditty about Julia's ex-husbands, which is Albee's way of reintroducing the death theme. This time it is to inform us of the death of four marriages, the stigma of which, Julia carries with her:

> CLAIRE: (*A mocking sing-song*) Philip loved to gamble. Charlie loved the boys. Tom went after women, Douglas. . . .

It seems that Julia has a knack for picking marriage partners who must fail her. Unconsciously she doesn't want these marriages to work because she needs a reason to return home to the protection of her parents and to resume the old parent-child relationship. Whatever happened over the years, we can only know that Julia feels deprived of something in that relationship and keeps coming back to get it. Agnes reinforces Julia's neurosis by taking her back into the house and allowing her to resume the mother-daughter premarital kinship because it gives her the illusion she is still young enough to have an unmarried daughter.

Cued by Julia's homecoming, Tobias obliquely gives us the needed information about Julia's years at home. He does this by confessing to a rather pathetic and apparently unrelated incident in his past. It seems that for many years before his marriage to Agnes, he and a pet cat enjoyed a mutual affection. One day Tobias realized that his pet cat no longer liked him; it would not come to him when called, and retreated whenever he approached. The cat's unexplainable rejection made Tobias all the more anxious to win back his pet's love. Finally, after many overtures, in desperation and utter frustration, he shook the cat violently yelling, "Damn you, you like me; God damn it, you stop this! I haven't *done* anything to you." Frightened at the outburst, the cat bit him, and Tobias, in retaliation, viciously smacked it. Tobias describes the outcome:

> TOBIAS: . . . She and I had lived together and been, well, you know, friends, and . . . there was no *reason*. And I hated her, well, I suppose because I was being accused of something, of . . . failing. But I hadn't been cruel by design; if I'd been neglectful well, my life was . . . I resented it. I resented having a . . . being judged. Being betrayed.
>
> CLAIRE: What did you do?
>
> TOBIAS: I had *lived* with her; I had done . . . *everything*. And . . . and if there was a, any responsibility I'd failed in . . . well . . . there was nothing I could do. And, and I was being accused
>
> CLAIRE: Yes; what did you do?
>
> TOBIAS: (*Defiance and self-loathing*) I had her killed.

Almost every critic referred to the "cat story." It is obviously Albee at his best. The critics likened it to the dog monologue in *The Zoo Story*, maintaining that the telling of it meant more than the unfortunate experience of one man and an animal. Henry Hewes thought it meant that Albee was trying to puncture the myth that "people who are sufficiently happy together and are enough in love to get married will forever remain in love." Other reviewers thought the account was a lesson on friendship and tied the monologue to what they thought was the major point of the play. This is not at all the case. What Albee wanted, in having Tobias relate the tale, was to have the audience realize Tobias's sense of failure as a father. The thought is so unbearable that he is unable to confess it directly. The narrative implies that like the cat, Julia once loved and related to her father and that despite his attempt to provide a home for his daughter, she inexplicably withdrew from him until they now no longer communicate. The last thing Tobias says before he begins the cat story concerns his failure to relate to her. Filled with anxiety, he reneges on his earlier offer to talk to his daughter about reconsidering the dissolution of her marriage:

> TOBIAS: (*Not rising from his chair, talks more or less to himself*) If I saw some point to it, I might—if I saw some reason, chance. If I thought I might . . . break through to her, and say, "Julia . . . ," but then what would I say? "Julia . . . ," then nothing.

Tobias blames himself for his failing relationship with his daughter and her resulting inability to develop a satisfactory and durable relationship with a man. The results of his ineffectualness are all around him. Guilt ridden because of his failure as husband and father, he privately yearns for change.

In talking about *A Delicate Balance*, Albee has said that it "is about the fact that as time keeps happening options grow less. Freedom of choice vanishes. One is left with an illusion of choice." The experience has been as crushing for Tobias and Agnes. They too must live the remaining years without illusion. But their reality is somewhat different from learning that their closest friendship was at best superficial; what they learn is that there comes a time in every life when hope of change no longer exists. What they have made of their lives must now stand because it is too late for undoing. Tobias cannot change his skin. Even his impassioned plea to Harry is an indication not of strength but continued weakness because of its uncontrollable hysterics. Tobias a long time ago chose passivity; he must now accept its outcome.

It is interesting to read Harold Clurman's analysis of Tobias, based on his belief that the play had only to do with that "insuperable difficulty of loving one's neighbor." He feels that the character of Tobias should have been played not as a little man but rather as an "outwardly imposing figure, a very 'senator' of a man, a pillar of our business community in whom the springs of sensibility have begun to dry through disuse. The welling up of his being in the play's crisis would then become more stirring and, what is more important, exemplary." What Clurman has neglected to see, however, is that Tobias does not succeed in his attempt at rescuing his life from the quicksand of indifference. What is exemplary is not his sudden feelings of remorse for a life of aloofness, but his realization that despite his willingness to change, the patterns of his past are forever stamped in the anguished memories of a wasted life and in the knowledge that choice ceases to exist as we approach the termination of our lives. Tobias was, and must remain always, small. This theme is summed up rather movingly by Agnes at the end of the play:

> AGNES: Time. (*Pause. The look at her*) Time happens, I suppose. (*Pause. They still look*) To people. Everything becomes . . . too late, finally. You know it's going on . . . up on the hill; you can see the dust, and hear the cries, and the steel . . . but you wait; and time happens. When you *do* go, sword, shield . . . finally . . . there's nothing there . . . save rust; bones; and the wind.

Despite the mixed reception *A Delicate Balance* received from the critics, on May 1, 1967,

Albee was given the Pulitzer Prize. The next day he officially accepted the award, but remembering the controversy over the Pulitzer Advisory Board's decisions to overrule John Gassner and John Mason Brown when they proposed that Albee be given the prize for *Virginia Woolf*, he warned that it "is in danger of losing its position of honor and could foreseeably, cease to be an honor at all." The following day, speaking at a news conference, he reiterated his feelings, listing exactly why he accepted the award:

> I have decided to accept the award for three reasons: First, because if I were to refuse it out of hand, I wouldn't feel as free to criticize it as I do accepting it. Second, because I don't wish to embarrass the other recipients this year by seeming to suggest that they follow my lead. And finally, because while the Pulitzer Prize is an honor in decline, it is still an honor, a considerable one.

Originally underrated by the majority of New York critics, yet heralded by the Pulitzer Committee as the best play of the year, *A Delicate Balance* has shown Edward Albee at his most sympathetic, his most gentle. There is more delicateness and maturity in this play than any of his other works, and it will prevail "not only [as] a brilliant and searching play but [as] a strangely beautiful one."

Source: Michael E. Rutenberg, "*A Delicate Balance*," in *Edward Albee: Playwright in Protest*, DBS Publications, Inc., 1969, pp. 137–51, 163–64.

C. W. E. Bigsby

In the following essay, the author analyzes the strengths and weaknesses of Albee's A Delicate Balance.

In 1962 Edward Albee's *Who's Afraid of Virginia Woolf?* narrowly avoided winning the Pulitzer Price. Although the previous award had gone to an insipid musical, no prize was offered in 1962–63. When another of Albee's plays is awarded the self-same prize some five years later, then, the critic is posed with an obvious problem. Have the Committee, one of whose members reportedly called *Who's Afraid of Virginia Woolf?* "a filthy play," become more catholic in their taste or has Albee compromised the values and the manner which had formerly made his work unacceptable? The answer, I believe, is that Albee has achieved what is clearly a rare distinction. He has played a part, small though it is, in the long process of educating the Pulitzer Prize Committee. For while *A Delicate Balance* is without doubt a lesser play than *Virginia Woolf* there seems little doubt that it does demonstrate Albee's contin-

ued determination to bring to the American theater both the lucidity and passion it has so often lacked and that desire to experiment without which any theater is in danger of vegetating.

Where *Who's Afraid of Virginia Woolf?* had examined the impotence of contemporary society, *A Delicate Balance* attempts to penetrate to the fear of which this impotence is merely one expression. Rather like T. S. Eliot's *The Family Reunion* it tries to delve below the surface of a precarious urbanity to the spiritual terror which exists just below the surface. In Eliot's words it is concerned with "The backward look behind the assurance . . . the backward half-look / Over the shoulder, towards the primitive terror."

The play is set in the living room of a large and well-appointed suburban house and the action centers on six characters linked either by familial ties or by the familiarity of long association, falsely confused by them with "love." Against this setting they act out a ritual which, like those in Eliot's play and Albee's own earlier work, forces them to face the spectres of their own fears.

Agnes and Tobias are approaching sixty and it is clear that they have evolved a workable relationship which, while protecting them from obvious loneliness, equally clearly has left them fundamentally estranged from one another. They live with Agnes's sister, an alcoholic who had once been Tobias's mistress. Into this tense but apparently reassuring atmosphere there intrude both their daughter, Julia, returned from the latest of her marital failures, and their "best friends," Harry and Edna. These three arrivals come in search of comfort, hoping to find some refuge from sudden crises in their own lives. In this atmosphere, however, the delicate balance of middle-class temporizing is disturbed, and for a moment they are forced into the sort of introspection which can lead either to a deeper perception or back into the anesthesia of contemporary life. Seeking comfort they find themselves face to face with their secret fears. As Eliot's Harry says in *The Family Reunion*, "the last apparent refuge, the safe shelter / That is where one meets them. That is the way of spectres."

When Harry and Edna arrive they are terrified, having just undergone a frightening experience which they are unable or unwilling to specify beyond the fact that "it was all very quiet, and we were all alone . . . and then . . . nothing happened, but . . . WE GOT . . . FRIGHTENED . . . We . . . were . . . terrified . . . It was like being lost: very young again,

> *A DELICATE BALANCE* IS ALBEE'S ACKNOWLEDGMENT OF THE FACT THAT 'WE'RE NOT A COMMUNAL NATION' AND THAT THERE IS A DESPERATE NEED TO REESTABLISH HUMAN RELATIONSHIPS ON JUST SUCH A FIRM FOUNDATION OF TRUTH.''

with the dark, and lost.'' Faced with what William James has called ''an irremediable sense of precariousness'' and Tolstoy an awareness of the ''meaningless absurdity of life'' they try to win their way back to ''sanity'' through contact with the ''normal'' world of suburban living. But as Camus has pointed out, this awareness of absurdity can itself emerge from the apparently reassuring repetitions of daily life. As he says, ''It happens that the stage-sets collapse. Rising, tram, four hours in the office or the factory, meal, tram, four hours of work, meal, sleep . . . this path is easily followed most of the time. But one day the 'why' arises and everything begins in that weariness tinged with amazement.'' It is precisely with this moment of enlightenment, then, that Albee is concerned in *A Delicate Balance*. For he shares with Eliot something of the conviction voiced by Harry in *The Family Reunion*. His characters, like Eliot's, ''are all people / To whom nothing has happened, at most a continual impact / Of external events''; they ''have gone through life in sleep / Never woken to the nightmare.'' In this, his Pulitzer Prize-winning play, then, they are forced, for a while, to do precisely this: to wake to the nightmare.

The delicate balance which Agnes and Tobias have contrived in order to survive is not threatened by Claire, who, having been categorized as an alcoholic, can be safely ignored. The real threat is implicit in the very strategy by which they live. For accepting, as they do, that the ordered structure of daily routine in turn suggests a kind of ''cosmic purpose,'' any disruption of that routine must imply a disruption of the very foundation of their existence. Thus it is that when Edna arrives and detects some change in the room Agnes is immediately apprehensive until she realizes with ''relief'' that the change is merely a rearrangement of the room, itself a part of an established routine. As Claire points out, ''the drunks stay drunk; the Catholics go to Mass, the bounders bond. We can't have changes—throws the balance off . . . Just think, Tobias, what would happen if the patterns changed; you wouldn't know where you stood, and the world would be full of strangers.'' Perhaps it is no longer surprising to find that this is an insight shared by Eliot's characters, ''We only ask to be reassured / About the noises in the cellar / And the window that should not have been open . . . Hold tight, hold tight, we must insist that the world is what we have always taken it to be.''

When the precarious balance of this compromise is threatened, however, there remains only the retreat into illusion. In Claire's case this involves a simple resort to alcohol, but Albee is concerned here with a final and more dangerous subterfuge—complete alienation from a threatening reality. When the play opens Agnes is speculating on the possibility of going mad, becoming a schizophrenic, ''since I speculate I might, some day, or early evening I think more likely—some autumn dusk—go quite mad, then I very well might.'' Since the action of the play takes place on just such an autumn evening there can be little doubt that the ''insanity'' does occur and that far from offering a protection it precipitates a sudden and frightening awareness of absurdity. Moreover it seems likely that Edna and Harry, who are described by Albee as being ''very much like Agnes and Tobias,'' are to be taken as representing the other half of the schizophrenic personality. Indeed there is a real sense in which Harry and Edna act as substitutes for those whose home they have effectively taken over, Edna herself taking on the role and function of the mother while Harry is actually referred to as ''being Tobias.'' So that while the friends can be granted a separate identity they can also be seen as expressions of the suppressed fears of Agnes and Tobias.

R. D. Laing has pointed out that ''the behaviour that gets labelled schizophrenic is a special strategy that a person invents in order to live in an unlivable situation.'' To Agnes it is indeed just such a strategy to be employed ''if all else should fail; if sanity, such as it is, should become too much.'' But as Albee had insisted in *Who's Afraid of Virginia Woolf?* those who retreat into insanity remain ''undeveloped'' and incapable of establishing genuine relationships, so that the illusion is ultimately worse than reality. The danger in fact in real terms is that the protective schizophrenia may become a total substitute for reality—a danger which Agnes recognizes when she accept the chance that "I could not . . . come back." At the very least, Albee insists, such a response must leave the individual totally alone, a fact which is emphasized by Agnes's description of this madness as a process of "becoming a stranger in . . . the world, quite . . . uninvolved." If this has overtones of Camus' *The Stranger,* however, Albee shows no tendency to exult in the sheer indifference of this stance. For clearly what he is calling for here, as in his earlier plays, is a courageous determination to face the world as it is, for to him, as to Nietzsche, "we no longer believe that truth remains truth if the evil is withdrawn from it." Or as Camus expresses it in *The Myth of Sisyphus,* "There is no sun without shadow, and it is essential to know that night." Significantly, indeed, of the play's three acts, two take place during the night, a time when, as Agnes admits, "we . . . let the demons out" and discover "the dark side of our reason."

To Albee the individual poised between the "leap of faith" which had tempted Julian in *Tiny Alice* and the bourgeois contentment seized upon by Agnes and Tobias should turn towards the one source of possible renewal—man. As Camus had said, "There are gods of light and idols of mud. But it is essential to find the middle path lending to the faces of man!" It is precisely the failure of the play's characters to do this, to establish the importance of human contact, of love, which is the essence of their predicament. It is this which endows them with a sense of guilt which has to be expiated. Claire, for example, identifies the consequences of her own retreat from reality as consisting in a destruction of that very love which alone could redeem her. The alcoholic whom she describes is, indeed, an obvious archetypal figure in a society which, as Albee has insisted in many of his plays, reverts to the bottle as part of its refusal to face the real, adult world: "your eyes hurt and you're half dead and your brain keeps turning off . . . and you hate . . . yourself, and everybody. Hate, and, oh God!! you want love, l-o-v-e, so badly . . ." But in this society, as Albee had stressed in *The American Dream,* even the word "love" has become corrupted. It becomes an expression of self-pity and greed or simply a means of describing social relatedness, so that there is clearly a savage irony in Claire's declaration that "You love Agnes and Agnes loves Julia and Julia loves me and I love you. We all love each other." In fact she feels con-

strained to add, "We love each other . . . to the depths of our self-pity and our greed. What else but love? . . . love and error."

Like Claire, Tobias too has withdrawn from what he sees as the harsher realities of life. He has become "too . . . settled," too "dried up." He has given up trying to make contact and is reduced in an ineffectual cipher primarily because he is afraid that to love is to become vulnerable. Unable to adjust to the loss of his son Teddy, who had died at the age of two, he refuses to accept the implications of love, choosing to substitute a kind of painless coexistence which inevitably leads to a breakdown of human values. When Julia and Claire appeal to him to rescue them from their desperate situation he can only mumble, "It's too late . . . or something." Such a reaction leads directly to what Agnes identifies as "the demise of intensity, the private preoccupations, the substitutions." Life becomes nothing more than the pointless tedium which Samuel Beckett had identified. As Claire says, "We're waiting, aren't we? . . . Waiting. The room; the doctor's office; beautiful unconcern: intensive study of the dreadful curtains."

If Tobias's distrust of the commitment involved in love is the cause of his isolation, however, it is also the cause both of his guilt and his fear. In order to clarify his feelings he tells a long parable of his relationship with a cat which in some ways parallels the story of Jerry and the dog in *The Zoo Story.* Tobias's cat, which had lived with him contentedly for fifteen years, had suddenly withdrawn its affection, refusing to stay in the same room, refusing even to purr. Tobias describes how he had become progressively determined to restore their relationship. His failure in this, however, had turned his affection to hatred, for he had come to feel that the cat's attitude implied an accusation; he felt that he had been betrayed. Finally, when his approaches are repelled, he has the cat killed so that it will no longer reproach him. It is precisely this failure to persevere in love merely because it is not returned which is the source of Tobias's sense of guilt. For Albee's point here is essentially that which Arthur Miller makes in *After the Fall,* namely that there is a need to renew love even in the face of inevitable failure. In place of Albee's cat Miller uses the image of an idiot child who is virtually incapable of responding to love but who for that very reason demands the renewal of that love even in the knowledge of its eventual failure. So here Tobias admits that "I might have tried longer. I might have gone on, as long as cats live, the same way. I might have worn a hair shirt. locked myself in the house with her, done penance.'' This sort of commitment clearly becomes especially vital in a society in which, as Tobias finally admits, our main dialogue is ''with ourselves'' Where Miller's hero discovers that the origin of all cruelty and treachery is the self, Edna similarly acknowledges that ''the one body you've wrapped your arms around . . . the only skin you've ever known . . . is your own.''

Erich Fromm has pointed out that for many, marriage itself is an attempt to counter just such a feeling of isolation; ''the main emphasis'' in such marriages, he points out, is ''on finding a refuge from an otherwise unbearable sense of aloneness.'' When this fails, as it does time and again for Julia, ''they continue to remain children, to hope for father or mother to come to their help when help is needed.'' So it is that Julia returns to her home and demands access to her own room—a room which clearly functions as a refuge, a womb, ''Warmth. A special room with a night light, or the door ajar so that you can look down the hall from the bed and see Mommy's door is open . . . back from the world? To the sadness and reassurance of your parents? . . . You're laying claim to the cave.'' Julia's insanity— she becomes hysterical and eventually catatonic— is indeed an expression both of her failure to understand the real nature of love and of her inability to face a world in which the connection between individuals is continually threatened. As Fromm has pointed out, ''If the nature of sanity is to grow out of the womb into the world, the nature of severe mental disease is to be attracted by the womb, to be sucked back into it—and that is to be taken away from life.''

Albee is not content, however, merely to state the dilemma of the alienated individual brought face to face with the corruption of human values. Neither is he content to slip into the determinism of Samuel Beckett. For in the coarse of the play Tobias gradually stumbles towards a realization both of the fact of his own isolation and of the real nature of the relationship which exists between himself and those he had taken to be his ''best friends.'' He finally admits that he does not love them. He admits that they are a threat to his peace of mind. But by a supreme effort of will he tries to overcome the temptation of his own self-interest and in doing so goes some way towards expiating his sense of guilt. ''I DON'T WANT YOU HERE! I DON'T LOVE YOU! BUT BY GOD . . . YOU STAY!!''. In this moment he succeeds in transcending the egotism

which has undermined the other relationships in the play, and he faces the brutal truth from which he had previously averted his eyes.

To Agnes, Edna and Harry represent only the fear which can upset her compromise with existence. She refers to them as a plague, a ''mortal illness'' which has descended on them and which must be rejected. The only response is to ''isolate . . . quarantine . . . ostracize,'' unless we are saints. Tobias is potentially just such a saint. For to him Edna and Harry, and thus the terror, the sense of absurdity which they represent, must be embraced and not denied. Indeed it finally seems to him that if life is solely dedicated to preserving ourselves and the compromise which we have contrived, then love does not exist and there is no purpose. As he asks, ''When we talk to each other . . . what have we meant? Anything? When we touch. when we promise, and say . . . yes, or please . . . with *ourselves?* . . . then it's all been empty.'' In response to Tobias's growing concern with his fellow man and with the need to face the darker side of the human condition, Agnes counterposes the family unit, ''Blood holds us together when we've no more . . . deep affection for ourselves than others.'' By now, however, Tobias is on the verge of the realization which had been implicit in *Who's Afraid of Virginia Woolf?*, namely that genuine human contact becomes possible only when individuals are prepared to face the world as it really is without recourse to protective illusions, to the bottle or to the womb. As Erich Fromm has said, ''The ability to love depends on one's ability to emerge from narcissism, and from the incestuous fixation to . . . clan.'' Perhaps this provides a clue, indeed, to Albee's dedication of the play to John Steinbeck whose Joad family had been brought to a similar understanding in *The Grapes of Wrath* that ''Use' ta be the fambly was fust. It ain't so now. It's anybody.''

Edna and Harry, then, represent both those acquaintances who never really become anything more than strangers and those aspects of the human condition—the sense of absurdity, of precariousness—which we are afraid to acknowledge in our own lives. Insofar as Tobias succeeds in accepting them at the end of the play, therefore, he emerges as one of Albee's ''reality-heroes''; a saint who accepts the Old Testament directive to ''love the stranger'' and who fulfills William James's primary Christian injunction, ''a man must die to an unreal life before he can be born to a real life.'' Like George in *Who's Afraid of Virginia Woolf?* and Julian in *Tiny Alice*, he has tentatively accepted an unpalatable truth and moved to establish genuine relationships. In essence he has followed the advice offered by Lafeu in *All's Well that Ends Well,* ''we make trifles of terrors, ensconcing ourselves into seeming knowledge when we should submit ourselves to an unknown fear.'' Where Harry has to learn, in *The Family Reunion,* to face the Furies whom Aeschylus describes as ''Armed with arrows of the dark, with madness, false night-terrors / To harass, plague, torment,'' Tobias has to learn a similar lesson in Albee's play. Indeed in a sense Harry and Edna fulfill the same functions as do the Furies in Eliot's play. For they too bring ''death and terror, blight and poison'' but can similarly be transformed if they are accepted instead of being banished.

A Delicate Balance is Albee's acknowledgment of the fact that ''We're not a communal nation'' and that there is a desperate need to reestablish human relationships on just such a firm foundation of truth. For to him if we continue to ''submerge our truths'' on ''the grassy bottom'' and prefer to ''have our sunsets on untroubled waters,'' then the essential need for humanity is to ''develop gills.'' The urgency of this transformation is underlined by the warning that ''Everything becomes too late finally.'' Where the apocalyptic alternative to this necessary human response had been made abundantly clear in *Who's Afraid of Virginia Wolf?* he now once again stresses that the alternative is ''rust; bones, and wind.''

If the world which he is describing is indeed a sterile one, this state of affairs, as we have seen, is a result of man's failure of nerve. Tobias, for example, unwilling to face the loss which is an endemic part of life, withdraws his affections from his wife—a sexual withdrawal which guarantees sterility. By the end of the play, however, he has regained something of his courage and achieved an insight into his private fears which, logically enough, comes to him as it does to Eliot's protagonist:

Not in the day time And in the hither world
Where we know what we are doing
There is not its operation . . .
But in the night time
In the nether world.

It follows from this that the apparently trite ending should not be taken at face value, for Agnes's expansive welcome of the returning day is clearly Albee's ironical comment on the ease with which the individual rejects new perception. Indeed when Robert Brustein accuses Albee of closing his play ''with one of those vibrato rising sun lines familiar

from at least a dozen such evenings,'' he is demonstrating little less than a failure to understand the whole point of the play. To a mind which grasps desperately at the apparent order of daily routine as a welcome escape from the more painful realities of life, the return of day provides a welcome excuse to escape the perceptions of the night. Tobias, however, had regretted that ''when the daylight comes the pressures will be on, and all the insight won't be worth a damn.'' In this context the play's final lines have a searching irony as Agnes welcomes the return of day as the return of unconsciousness, for ''when the daylight comes again . . . comes order with it.'' As Erich Fromm has emphasized, ''the strict routine of bureaucratized, mechanical work'' serves merely to keep people ''unaware of their most fundamental human desires, of the longing for transcendence and unity.'' So Agnes closes her eyes to the perceptions of the night and consoles herself with a return to her former coma: ''Poor Edna and Harry. Well, they're safely gone . . . and we'll all forget . . . quite soon. Come, now; we can begin the day.'' To Albee, however, it is less Agnes's willing retreat from the brink than Tobias's stumbling perception which is significant. For, like Williams James, he believes that ''Truly the light is sweet, and a pleasant thing it is for the eyes to behold the sun: but if a man live many years and rejoice in them all yet let him remember the days of darkness . . .'' If Tobias's affirmation is only a tentative, even a slightly prevaricating one, perhaps it is an indication of the truth of his earlier perception—an understanding shared by George in *Who's Afraid of Virginia Woolf?* that ''once you drop you can come back up part way . . . but never really back again.''

The fact remains that man is free to act. If he chooses again and again to retreat into illusion and to elevate his own sense of guilt above the need for comparison, it remains clear that there is no inevitability in this choice. So it is that Claire insists that she is not an alcoholic, although it ''would be simpler if I were.'' Indeed the distinction which she makes between herself and the alcoholics is at base the same distinction which Albee has always been at pains to make between Beckett's passive victims and his own protagonists: ''they couldn't help it; I could, and wouldn't . . . they were sick, and I was merely wilful.'' Agnes, indeed, admits that man's absurdity is largely of his own making: ''We manufacture such a proportion of our own despair.'' The door is thus clearly open for amelioration, and the suffering, which perhaps significantly takes place between Friday and Sunday, can result in redemption. The possibility always exists, as Claire says, that ''a breeze might rise and stir the ashes.'' If Albee is getting more urgent, perhaps even more shrill, in his effort to force the need for love in a world seemingly intent on self-destruction, and content to find purpose in the sham order of bourgeois society, it is because he is strongly aware of the attractiveness of illusion. Albee is not a social reformer. He is concerned with moral and spiritual reform but he brings to this all the urgency of the committed. Indeed the very fact that he allows the last word to Agnes is a demonstration of his growing fear that his is a voice echoing in the wilderness. In fact it is possible to see *A Delicate Balance* as in part an expression of Albee's own sense of artistic frustration; the frustration of a dramatist able to command the attention of an audience in the theater but unable to wring from it an admission of the nexus which exists between the drama enacted on stage and their own lives. The audience, like Tobias, ''can sit and watch . . . can have . . . so clear a picture, see everybody moving through his own jungle . . . an insight into all the reasons, all the needs . . . the dark sadness.'' But the return to routine, to daylight, as we have seen, means that ''the insight won't be worth a damn.'' So too when Agnes speaks of being ''burdened with the ability to view a situation objectively while I'm in it,'' when she apologizes for ''being articulate'' and adds ''if I shout, it's merely to be heard . . . above the awful din of your privacies and sulks,'' this too can ultimately be seen as an expression of Albee's own sense of artistic martyrdom.

Critical response to *A Delicate Balance* was largely hostile. Robert Brustein, writing in *The New Republic,* found the play to be little more than ''an old house which an interior decorator has tried to furnish with reproductions and pieces bought at auction''; while Richard Gilman, in *Newsweek,* attacked what he saw as the ''inflated dialogue,'' the ''kind of cliché that is all too prominent in Albee's rhetoric.'' Certainly Albee's use of idiom lacks the control which it had evidenced in *Who's Afraid of Virginia Woolf?* More important, however, is the fact that his preoccupation with the metaphysical roles which he ascribes to his characters is in danger of eliminating that very humanity which lies at the center of his dialectic. As James Baldwin has said of Camus, one cannot help feeling at times that ideas mean more to him than people.

Albee is always at his weakest with minor characters who seem to drift through the plays and who appear to be there truly to act as butts for humor or as conscious symbols. In this play Claire, whose name emphasizes the clarity of her insight, seems to be little more than the stereotype wise drunk. Rather like that inevitable figure in the early films who wanders in and out of the action and manages to survive reasonably intact while fist fights and custard pies proliferate, she moves uncertainly through the play making wise remarks which can have little validity so long as she lacks credibility as a character. The same is essentially true of Julia and of Harry and Edna. Their symbolic functions take complete control and they give the impression of being manipulated puppets. While Albee's characters have largely forfeited their humanity through their persistent resort to illusion and their acceptance of defined roles in the social charade, one is never convinced that their hollowness is merely an expression of this. Rather, as Brustein remarks, it is a direct result of Albee's failure ''to give his characters life.'' This, then, is Albee's central dilemma. He needs to create characters who have made themselves social ciphers but whose fate must not be allowed to become a matter of indifference to the audience. It is his failure to resolve this dilemma which works to undermine the force of the play.

To an audience becoming increasingly alienated from Albee's experiments, *A Delicate Balance* appeared to be a move towards the naturalistic style familiar on Broadway. To several critics, however, the play's chief fault lay in its mixture of styles. For one, the play moved from ''realism to fantasy,'' while to another, perhaps more surprisingly, from ''symbolism'' to ''naturalism.'' In fact one of the most important lessons which Albee has to offer to the American theater is that distinctions such as these no longer make any sense. *A Delicate Balance* like *Who's Afraid of Virginia Woolf?*, defies such classification. Perhaps the most that can be said is that it represents an attempt to achieve in prose what Eliot had sought to achieve in verse in *The Family Reunion.* It is an attempt to invest a modern setting with metaphysical significance. These metaphysical overtones are present from the very beginning. The only variation is one of emphasis and intensity. The ordered nature of the dialogue at the beginning of the play reflects the balance which is still being stubbornly maintained; the stylized language towards the end is an expression of a growing loss of control. The balance has been finally upset. If Albee's constant aim is to penetrate beneath the exterior of modern society to the fears which exist below the surface, it is because he considers this to be both the chief function of the dramatist and the main responsibility of the thinking individual. With T. S. Eliot's Agatha, indeed, he would insist that

> we cannot rest in being
> The impatient spectators of malice or stupidity.
> We must try to penetrate the other private worlds
> Of make-believe and fear.

Source: C. W. E. Bigsby, ''The Strategy of Madness: An Analysis of Edward Albee's *A Delicate Balance*,'' in *Contemporary Literature*, Vol. 9, No. 2, Spring 1968, pp. 223–35.

SOURCES

Adcock, Joe, ''Production a 'Delicate Balance' of Dreadful Characters, Excellent Acting,'' in *Seattle Post-Intelligencer,* January 26, 2001.

Amacher, Richard E., ''A Success Story,'' in *Edward Albee,* Twayne Publishers, 1969, pp. 15–25.

Berson, Misha, ''*Balance* Filled with Angst over Drinks,'' in *Seattle Times,* January 17, 2001.

Brustein, Robert, ''A Question of Identity,'' in *New Republic,* August 30, 1999.

Canby, Vincent, ''Theater Review; An Albee Horror Story, Set in a Drawing Room,'' in *New York Times,* April 22, 1996.

Clurman, Harold, ''Albee on Balance,'' in *New York Times,* November 13, 1966.

DeVine, Lawrence, Review of *A Delicate Balance,* in *New York Times,* August 15, 1999.

Drukman, Steven, ''Won't You Come Home, Edward Albee?'' in *American Theatre,* December 1998.

Farr, Richard, ''Edward Albee,'' in *Progressive,* August 1996.

Kerr, Walter, ''The Theater: Albee's *A Delicate Balance* at the Martin Beck,'' in *New York Times,* September 23, 1966.

Kolin, Philip C., ed., *Conversations with Edward Albee,* University of Mississippi Press, 1988.

McCarthy, Gerry, ''*A Delicate Balance,*'' in *Edward Albee,* St. Martin's Press, 1987, pp. 79–97.

Review of *A Delicate Balance,* at http://www.circletheatre.com (March 1999, archives; last accessed September 2001).

FURTHER READING

Bloom, Harold, ed., *Edward Albee,* Modern Critical Reviews, Chelsea House Publishers, 2000.
    Edited by literary critic Harold Bloom, this book gives readers a well-collected and comprehensive history of the literary interpretations of Albee's work.

De La Fuente, Patricia, ed., *Edward Albee: Planned Wilderness—Interview, Essays and Bibliography,* Pan American University Press, 1980.
    For a comprehensive background of Albee and his work, this book is a great resource.

Gussow, Mel, *Edward Albee: A Singular Journey: A Biography,* Applause Theatre Book Publishers, 2000.
    This book has been heralded as a very clear and objective piece of writing in which Gussow observes much of Albee's personal and professional journey through the lens of a theater critic as well as a personal acquaintance. The biography is based on research and interviews with Albee and Albee's colleagues and friends, and it provides very good insights into the long career of this American author. Gussow has also written books on Harold Pinter and Samuel Beckett, two playwrights who have influenced Albee's work.

McCarthy, Gerry, *Edward Albee,* St. Martin's Press, 1987.
    McCarthy provides an in-depth study of Albee's plays.

How I Learned to Drive

PAULA VOGEL

1997

Paula Vogel's play *How I Learned to Drive* opened in New York in February 1997. The play concerns an affair between its protagonist, named Li'l Bit, and her uncle Peck. The affair takes place over the course of years, with the character of Li'l Bit maturing from age eleven to eighteen before she puts an end to it. In spite of the serious situation, there are many comical elements of the play, which avoids the expected condemnation of this situation to look at the basic humanity that binds these two characters. It uses innovative staging techniques to fade from one time frame to another and one place to the next. It also uses just three actors, in addition to those playing Li'l Bit and Peck, to represent all of the other characters who affect their lives, especially their quirky, intimidating rural Maryland family. The addition of popular music from the early- and late-1960s, such as "Dream Baby" and "Little Surfer Girl," helps audiences understand the prevailing mood of the era that Vogel covers in this play: it is romantic and sexist, emphasizing youth and fun, the sort of social message that would make a girl like Li'l Bit, who has many feelings of insecurity, turn to a flawed relationship where she can bask in the reverence of an older man.

How I Learned to Drive is noteworthy for the many awards that it won, including the 1998 Pulitzer Prize for drama. Its initial off-Broadway run lasted for fourteen months. In addition to the Pulitzer, the play also was awarded an Obie, a Drama

Desk Award, a New York Drama Critics' Award, an Outer Circle Critics Award, and the Lucille Lortel Award.

AUTHOR BIOGRAPHY

Paula Anne Vogel was born on November 16, 1951, in Washington, D.C., and lived there throughout most of her early life. She attended Bryn Mawr College on a scholarship in 1969 and then went back to Washington, where she attended Catholic University of America, earning her Bachelor of Arts degree in 1974. She went to graduate school at Cornell University in Ithaca, New York, earning enough credits for a Ph.D. but leaving with an A.B.D. in 1977 after failing to submit her thesis. From 1979 to 1982, she was a lecturer in Women's Studies and Theater Arts at Cornell; she was fired in 1982 for political reasons. Leaving Cornell gave her time to work on theater projects including guest lectureships at McGill University and University of Alaska. In 1984, she took a position as the director of the graduate playwriting program at Brown University in Providence, Rhode Island, where she stayed until the fame she earned from *How I Learned to Drive* allowed her the financial independence to leave there in 1997. Throughout her playwriting career she has been associated with numerous programs, including Theatre With Teeth in New York, Theater Eleanor Roosevelt in Providence, and Perseverance Theater in Juneau.

Vogel's plays have been produced since 1974. Her themes have generally centered around imaginatively making sense of subjects that mainstream society finds taboo. *And Baby Makes Seven*, for instance, deals with a same-sex couple using the occasion of their impending childbirth to clear out the imaginary children that they already have. *Hot 'n Throbbing* has a divorced mother raising her children with the money she makes writing pornographic novels. In *The Oldest Profession*, senior citizens fight against their slide into poverty during the Reagan era by working as prostitutes. One of the most personal of Vogel's plays, and the most successful before *How I Learned to Drive*, was *The Baltimore Waltz*, written in 1989 and produced in 1992. In it, a woman tours Europe with her brother, seeking a cure for the fictitious Acquired Toilet Disease, or ATD. Vogel wrote it soon after watching her brother Carl, with whom she shared a close bond throughout life, die of AIDS. The play uses the prejudices and misconceptions about the imaginary

Paula Vogel

disease to highlight societal attitudes about AIDS and its victims. That play won numerous writing awards and was produced by over sixty theater companies in the United States, Europe, and South America.

With the acclaim that she has garnered for *How I Learned to Drive*, Vogel has been able to leave teaching and concentrate on writing. She is only the tenth woman to win the Pulitzer Prize for playwrighting and the first openly gay woman to do so. Among the projects that she has been involved in is adapting *How I Learned to Drive* to a movie and bringing John Barthes' novel *The Sot-Weed Factor* to the stage.

PLOT SUMMARY

How I Learned to Drive is not told with a straight-forward plot but is instead an uneven mixture of flashbacks, narration, monologues, and the kind of impersonal voice-over that accompanies driver education films. It starts with Li'l Bit as an adult, addressing the audience, as if she is giving a lecture about how to drive. She describes Maryland during her youth in the 1960s, and then the setting dissolves into 1969, with her uncle Peck sitting in a

Buick Riviera. Seventeen-year-old Li'l Bit climbs in next to him. He takes the role of a child, telling her that he has been good, and she acts like an authority figure to him. When he says that he has not had a drink all week, she allows him the "small reward" of undoing her bra. When they leave their parking spot, Li'l Bit drives.

At a family dinner in 1969, the conversation focusing on the size of her breasts is embarrassing to Li'l Bit. Her grandfather makes one wise crack after another about her breasts being big, until Li'l Bit flees the room for some privacy. Peck is the one who follows her and consoles her. Feeling better, Li'l Bit arranges to meet him later that night.

Grown-up Li'l Bit, as narrator, explains to the audience that she was kicked out of school in 1970 for constant drinking and then took a job in a factory and spent her nights drinking and racing through the streets in her car.

The scene fades to Li'l Bit and Peck at an inn far from home along the Maryland shore in 1968 (a year before the family dinner portrayed earlier). The occasion is a celebration of Li'l Bit having received her driver's license. Peck, who has had a drinking problem, does not order a drink, but he tells Li'l Bit to have one, even though she is only sixteen. Li'l Bit's mother shows up at the side of the stage to give the audience "A mother's guide to social drinking," which includes such advice as to eat much bread and butter and never to order sugary "ladies" drinks. Li'l bit orders a martini and quickly becomes drunk. When they leave, she is hardly able to walk, and she expects Peck to try to take advantage of her. She objects to their relationship, and he tells her not to worry, that he is a man and will not do anything sexual until she wants to.

There is a brief scene of Uncle Peck teaching Li'l Bit's cousin Bobby to fish, just as he has taught her to drive. At the end of the scene, Peck offers to show Bobby "a secret place" in the trees, where they can be alone and drink a beer: "this is something special just between you and me," Peck says, reminiscent of his friendly seduction of Li'l Bit.

The next scene has Li'l Bit, her mother, and her grandmother seated in a kitchen and is titled, "On Men, Sex and Women: Part I." The grandmother explains that her husband always wanted to have sex several times every day. As the grandmother and mother talk about what crude beasts men are, they become increasingly aroused.

The grown-up Li'l Bit narrates the story of a bus trip in 1979, when she was in her twenties. A high school boy sat down by her and struck up a conversation. She made herself attractive enough that he followed her when the bus stopped and continued his conversation until she invited him up to her room, where they had sex.

"On Men, Sex, and Women: Part II" has fifteen-year-old Li'l Bit asking her mother and grandmother about sex. Her mother tells her that it hurts just a little, at first. Her grandmother tells her that the first time a girl has sex is very painful and bloody. The mother is resentful about the misinformation that her own mother gave her, feeling that it is responsible for her having gotten pregnant young with Li'l Bit, leading to her awful marriage to Li'l Bit's father.

Then Uncle Peck is giving Li'l Bit a driving lesson. She is light-hearted and joking around. Instead of indulging her, as he has before, Peck is strict, demanding that she take driving seriously. Li'l Bit makes a brief joke about the need to "defend" herself, implying that Peck has already made advances toward her, but he promises that he would never try anything while she is driving.

Li'l Bit recalls a time when she was in the ninth grade and a boy embarrassed her by pretending to have an allergic reaction to foam rubber, grabbing her breast. In the locker room after gym class, female classmates took note of the fact that her breasts were indeed real and not foam rubber. At a sock hop, a shy boy approached Li'l Bit several times to dance. A radar-like beeping, supposedly emerging from her breasts, indicated the way that boys were drawn to them, making Li'l Bit wary of their attention.

In 1965, in his basement, Peck has a camera, and he has Li'l Bit pose for pictures in his "studio." He tells her that she is beautiful and urges her to respond to the music with her body. She loses herself in the moment but is shaken back into reality when he mentions that these pictures will help her compile a good portfolio in five years, when she is eighteen and can pose for *Playboy*. Li'l Bit is horrified at the realization that her pictures could be seen by someone else.

Christmas 1964, when Li'l Bit is thirteen, she has a conversation with her uncle about why he drinks so much, and he tells her how much it helps him to talk to her. She suggests that they could meet once a week to talk, that they would keep their meetings a secret from her mother and his wife. The meetings have to be in public, she says: ''You've got to let me—draw the line.'' She is aware from the start of the possibility of a sexual relationship.

In 1969, while Li'l Bit is away at college, Peck sends her a series of gifts, with notes that include a count of the days until she is eighteen, the age of legal consent. When he shows up on her eighteenth birthday, Li'l Bit explains that his notes have been so crazy they frighten her. She does drink the champagne that he has brought: as explained in an earlier scene, her first year at college was spent drinking constantly. She tells him that they should not ''see'' each other any more, and his offer to divorce Aunt Mary and marry her just makes her more frightened of him and more resolute that their relationship should end. He goes directly to a bar and starts drinking again. ''It took my uncle seven years to drink himself to death,'' the adult Li'l Bit tells the audience.

The play continues with ''On Men, Sex, and Women: Part III,'' which takes place in 1962. Peck wants to take her to the beach, and her mother refuses: ''I am not letting an 11-year-old girl spend seven hours alone in the car with a man. . . . I don't like the way your uncle looks at you.'' In the end, though, she gives in. It is on this car ride that Peck asks Li'l Bit for the first time if she would like to learn to drive, and he lifts her up on his lap behind the wheel.

The last scene is the adult Li'l Bit preparing to go driving. She climbs into the car and makes the necessary adjustments. When she adjusts the rearview mirror, she sees the image of Uncle Peck in the back seat, before she takes off.

CHARACTERS

B. B.

See Cousin Bobby

Big Papa

Li'l Bit's grandfather, the father of her mother and Aunt Mary, is a crude, offensive man who expects to be waited on by his wife. He is proud of the fact that he came and took his wife away, when she was fourteen, against her family's objections. His wife describes him as a big bull, wanting sex every morning and every evening and even coming home at lunch for it. Early in the play, the family

MEDIA ADAPTATIONS

jokes about Li'l Bit's developing breasts when she is seventeen, and her grandfather keeps making derogatory comments about what a waste it is for her to go to college: ''What does she need to go to college for?'' ''She's got all the credentials she needs on her chest—'' and ''How is Shakespeare going to help her lie on her back in the dark?''

Cousin Bobby

He has no spoken lines and does not appear onstage, but the actor playing Uncle Peck speaks to him in a monologue. In a scene announced as ''Uncle Peck teaches Cousin Bobby how to fish,'' Bobby pulls in a pompano and then cries until Peck cuts the fish loose and releases it. Then Peck asks if Bobby would like to go to a secret tree house with him, drink beer, and eat crab salad. Peck's behavior toward Bobby is similar to how he treats Li'l Bit in that he gives her liquor and driving lessons and swears her to secrecy. There is no indication of where this scene fits chronologically with the rest.

Bobby is first mentioned early in the play, as an example of how nicknames in the family center on genitalia. His nickname is ''B. B.'' for ''Blue Balls.''

Grandmother

Li'l Bit's grandmother is accustomed to serving her husband, Big Papa, which she does with bitterness. Although he constantly has sex with her, she has never had an orgasm and believes that her daughters made the concept up; when they talk with her about sex, she becomes almost violently irritable, suggesting that her sex drive is repressed. She makes it a policy to make sex sound dirty, painful, and disgusting to Li'l Bit, with the hope that the girl will not want to try it, even though the same tactic did not help keep her daughter, Lucy from getting pregnant.

Greg

Greg is a short, shy, courtly boy who frequently asks Li'l Bit to dance at the sock hop at Francis Scott Key Middle School. She is afraid to dance with him, suspicious that he just wants to dance with her so that he can watch her breasts.

High School Senior

On a bus trip to Upstate New York in 1978, when she is nearly thirty, Li'l Bit is approached by a boy who introduces himself as a senior at Walt Whitman High. He is awkward, with large ears and a high-pitched voice. After some conversation, she takes him to her hotel room and has sex with him, which reminds her of the way Uncle Peck seduced her when she was young.

Jerome

In ninth grade, when Li'l Bit's breasts are developing, Jerome, with the help of a female classmate, feigns an allergy attack and falls to the floor. When Li'l Bit bends down to help him, he says that his allergy is to foam rubber, and he squeezes her breast. Later, after gym class, a female classmate stares at Li'l Bit's breasts in the shower and, determining that they are real, tells her that this means Jerome owes her fifty cents from a bet.

Li'l Bit

This play focuses on Li'l Bit, following her life from age eleven to nearly thirty-five. It centers on her relationship with her uncle by marriage, Peck, showing how that relationship grows closer and closer to a sexual one and how Li'l Bit's life becomes increasingly disorderly as she matures. When she is eleven and her mother does not want her riding in a car alone with Peck, she assures her mother confidently that she "can handle" him. She basks in the attention that he gives her throughout the years, posing for pictures for him and accepting gifts. When, at puberty, her breasts develop, her mother and grandparents make her self-conscious, and other children at school make her feel like an outcast, but Peck speaks to her sympathetically. When she goes away to college, Li'l Bit stops going to class and develops a drinking problem; removed from Peck, she can see their relationship for what it is, and she tells him they can't see each other anymore, even though it destroys him. In late her

twenties, she picks up a high school boy on the street and has sex with him to feel the power over a younger person that Peck felt. In the end, as she drives off, she sees the image of Peck, long dead, in her rearview mirror.

Lucy

See Mother

Aunt Mary

Aunt Mary is the sister of Li'l Bit's mother and the wife of Peck. Li'l Bit describes her as "beautiful." In a monologue announced as "Aunt Mary on behalf of her husband," she speaks to the audience, explaining Peck's good qualities: he is always willing to help out the neighbors, and he works hard to provide for her and even brings her furs and diamonds. She explains the psychological trauma that he must have experienced in the war. She is well aware of the relationship between Peck and their niece, she says. She blames Li'l Bit: "She's a sly one, that one is. She knows exactly what she's doing; she's twisted Peck around her little finger and thinks it's all a big secret." Her response to this is to wait until Li'l Bit goes away to school, so she can get her husband back.

Mother

Li'l Bit's mother, Lucy, is skeptical of men. While giving Li'l Bit advice about how a lady should drink, she warns against particular drinks, stating vaguely, "Believe me, they are lethal . . . I think you were conceived after one of those." When she and her mother are talking about sex with Li'l Bit, she is the one to contradict the grandmother's warnings that sex is frightening. "It won't hurt you—" she tells Li'l Bit, "if the man you go to bed with really loves you. It's important that he loves you." She is angry at her parents for turning their back on her when she became pregnant, for telling her, "You Made Your Bed; Now Lie on It." She does practically the same thing, though, when Li'l Bit is eleven and wants to go on a long car ride with Uncle Peck. The mother gives in, even though she suspects Peck of having sexual intentions, telling the girl, "All right. But I'm warning you—if anything happens, I hold you responsible."

Uncle Peck

Uncle Peck is the only one in the family who takes Li'l Bit seriously when the others make fun of her, and she is the only one to take him seriously. His wife, Aunt Mary, says that she understands his suffering but that she does not talk to him when he is feeling bad. When Li'l Bit is thirteen, he says that talking to her makes him feel better and gives him the strength to battle his alcoholism. When she agrees to meet with him to talk regularly, a quasi-sexual relationship is established: their meetings must be secret, and she must be allowed to "draw the line." All future meetings between them lean toward sexuality. He takes pictures of her in his basement, planning for the day when she will be old enough to pose for *Playboy*. When she receives her license, he takes her to a restaurant that will serve her liquor. As she approaches her eighteenth birthday, when she can have sex legally, Peck sends letters, each with the number of days until her birthday, showing his excitement. When he visits her on her birthday and she breaks off their relationship, he starts drinking again. "It took my uncle seven years to drink himself to death," Li'l Bit tells the audience. "First he lost his job, then his wife, and finally his driver's license."

Waiter

The waiter at a restaurant on the Eastern Shore is the only character in the play to interact with Peck and Li'l Bit when they are together as a couple. He is skeptical about serving alcohol to a sixteen-year-old girl, especially when she orders a martini, but he does it, hoping that he will receive a big tip.

THEMES

Growing Up

Audiences can sometimes miss the fact that *How I Learned to Drive* is a play about growing up. One reason for this is that the main character, Li'l Bit, already has grown-up attitudes and responsibilities when she is young. The earliest chronological scene takes place in 1962, when Li'l Bit is eleven. Warned against the danger of riding in a car with her uncle, she not only shows an awareness of the possibility that he will take a sexual interest but also a cool confidence that she can control the situation. In addition, at the age of eleven, she is intelligent enough to understand her own psychological motive for being attracted to Peck: "Just because you lost your husband—" she tells her mother, "I still deserve a chance at having a father! Someone! A man who will look out for me! Don't I get a chance?" Even this young, Li'l Bit is intellectually mature, understanding her situation more

clearly than many adults would. The fact that she has an adult perspective about sex throughout the play helps to obscure the fact that she still needs to grow up emotionally, to distance herself from her family, especially from Uncle Peck.

Another reason that this play does not seem like a story about growing up is its structure. The play starts with Li'l Bit as a grown woman, nearly thirty-five, and it moves backward through her life, reaching the earliest time frame at the end. The action all reveals details of the relationship between Li'l Bit and Peck, but not in the way that Li'l Bit experienced it. She seems mature from the very first scene, when she is seventeen, and the narrator explains, "I am very old, very cynical of the world, and I know it all." The play questions assumptions that often connect growing up to chronological development, which is actually not such an important part of maturity.

What does make this a play about growing up is the emotional development that takes place in Li'l Bit, leading up to the point near the end at which she is able to end her unhealthy relationship with her uncle. To reach this point, she needs to understand the elements of her life that drove her to that relationship, including the mocking from classmates and other family members that lowered her self-esteem and increased her desire to take care of Peck, to help him stop drinking, to defend him from gossip, and so forth. To reach this point with her, the audience needs to see how the relationship developed, but they do not need to see its development in actual chronological order. For Li'l Bit, growing up means understanding, not just accumulating experience, and understanding does not follow a straight path.

Incest

Legally, the relationship between Peck and Li'l Bit is not an incestuous one, because he is only related to her by marriage and not by blood. He is right when he points out that once she is eighteen, they could be married if he divorced his wife. Morally, however, it is an incestuous relationship because of the social roles that they have. He has been present since Li'l Bit's birth—"I held you, one day old, right in this hand" is a line that is repeated several times throughout the play. Although they do not have a blood relationship, he has been a father figure to Li'l Bit throughout her entire life, and it would be impossible to push this emotional bond aside after eighteen years. When Li'l Bit expresses her horror at his proposal of marriage, she

TOPICS FOR FURTHER STUDY

- Research some of the songs that Vogel suggests could be used in staging *How I Learned to Drive* and report on what you think makes them appropriate for using in this play.

- Do you think that Li'l Bit and Uncle Peck would have developed a physical relationship if he had not given her driving lessons? Explain what there is about driving lessons that would lead to such intimacy.

- At one point in the play, Aunt Mary notes that ''The men who fought in World War II didn't have 'rap sessions' to talk about their feelings.'' Do you think that Uncle Peck's service in the war led to his becoming a child molester? Study what sort of psychological counseling is available to veterans today.

- Compare the role of the traditional Greek chorus to the roles that Vogel assigns to the Greek chorus in this play.

- At one point, Vogel implies that Uncle Peck is trying to draw Li'l Bit's cousin Bobby into the same sort of relationship that he has with her. Is it typical for child molesters to have several relationships with children of both sexes? Write about whether Uncle Peck would be typical or the exception to the rule.

- From her final speech at the end, do you think that Li'l Bit has come to grips with what happened between her and Uncle Peck, or is she trying to run away from the thought of it?

---

emphasizes this, stating, ''Family is family,'' echoing the fact that he told her the same thing in an earlier scene, showing that she is old enough to recognize the social ties that once seemed irrelevant to her.

Vulnerability

The relationship between Li'l Bit and Uncle Peck in this play is based on the vulnerability that each of them feels. The audience sees how Li'l Bit's family encourages her insecurities. They emphasize sex at a time when she is too young to understand it, and when she does ask about it, her grandmother tries to make her feel that it is disgusting and unpleasant for women but inevitable because men want it. Her mother's bitterness toward Li'l Bit's father makes her all that more determined to do better in love than her mother. With this social dynamic already established, Li'l Bit is made to feel even more self-conscious when she reaches puberty and her breasts develop. Her family draws attention to them, making them the topic of conversation at Sunday dinner; her classmates, both male and female, treat her breasts with awe, as if Li'l Bit is not

one of them but some other sort of creature. Her relationship with Peck counters this vulnerability and makes her feel a sense of empowerment. He is the only family member to go to her with calm, soothing words when everyone else is making her feel self-conscious. Even at a young age, she is able to dictate the terms of their relationship. When she is thirteen and agreeing to meet with him in secret, she is able to make him accept her demand, ''You've got to let me—draw the line. And once it's drawn, you mustn't cross it.'' Later in their relationship, she can make him beg like a child for the favor of unhooking her bra in exchange for ''being good.'' Uncle Peck's subservience makes up for the ways the world makes her feel vulnerable.

The relationship also helps Peck overcome his own feelings of vulnerability. He is aware of being out of his element, a Southerner. He feels most comfortable sitting barefoot at a South Carolina fishing hole. When Li'l Bit asks why he doesn't go back there to live, he responds, ''I think it's better if my mother doesn't have a daily reminder of her disappointment.'' During the same conversation, he tries to sidetrack her questions about fighting in the war, changing the subject at the earliest opportunity. Later, Aunt Mary refers to the trauma of his war experience as ''whatever has burrowed deeper than the scar tissue,'' and she explains that her way of dealing with it is to keep conversations superficial. It is clear that Peck is using his relationship with Li'l Bit to recapture some of his lost childhood, when he felt secure.

Gender Roles

''Rage is not attractive in a girl,'' a female classmate tells Li'l Bit when she screams at Jerome for grabbing her breast. Her statement reinforces the attitude that Li'l Bit has already learned at home, from her mother and grandmother, that women are expected to put up with being sex objects, that it is their responsibility. Her grandmother shows this attitude most clearly when she talks about her relationship with Li'l Bit's grandfather. Throughout their married life, they have had sex almost every day, because he demands it, even though she has never been interested in it. Though Li'l Bit's mother is not involved with anyone sexually at any point in the play, she still sends a similar message when she warns that men are only after sex and that women must stay sober and alert to fight off their advances. In her relationship with Peck, which gives her the upper hand over a grown man, Li'l Bit seems to be taking a different attitude than the one she was taught, but deep down she really believes in traditional gender roles. She accepts that cars are female after Peck explains that he calls his car a ''she'' because ''when you close your eyes and think of someone who responds to your touch—someone who performs for you and gives you just what you ask for—I guess I always see a 'she.'''

STYLE

Music

The music that Paula Vogel's script for this play suggests is music that spans two generations. The Motown music that she mentions several times, as well as songs by Roy Orbison, Jan and Dean, and the Beach Boys, are all historically correct for action that is taking place in the mid- to late-1960s. Stylistically, they are romantic songs with hints of sexuality and with roots in the harmonically rich doo-wop music of the 1950s. This is most important for understanding the playwright's point when, at the end of the discussion about sex, the chorus members who have been speaking for Li'l Bit's mother, grandmother, and grandfather break into song, singing in three-part harmony and evoking the kind of music that lovers would listen to on the radio, as the scene dissolves to Li'l Bit and Uncle Peck in his car. Though the play deals with child molestation, a subject that is generally treated with deadly seriousness, the music that Vogel suggests to accompany it is romantic, wistful, beautiful, and nostalgic. Using this music, the play is able to evoke the mood that surrounded Li'l Bit in her adolescent confusion, as opposed to the harsh facts of the case as the audience and the grown-up Li'l Bit can see them.

Form

The scenes of this play are presented, for the most part, in reverse chronological order from how they occurred in life. In the earliest scene, Li'l Bit is seventeen, driving, and already in a physical relationship with her uncle Peck, although intercourse has not taken place between them. Subsequent scenes show her at sixteen, when she receives her driver's license; at fifteen, when the other children at school notice that her breasts have developed; and at thirteen, when she agrees to meet in secret with Peck and he arranges to shoot photographs of her in his basement. The story reaches its climax when the results of this relationship come to fruition, on Li'l Bit's eighteenth birthday. They can finally have an adult relationship, and Peck eagerly anticipates the reward for the ''patience'' that he has mentioned over the years, but Li'l Bit puts an end to what has been going on instead, leaving him to destroy himself with alcohol. The last scene, with eleven-year-old Li'l Bit pestering her mother until she allows her to ride alone in the car with Peck and his subsequent first driving lesson with the girl, functions as an after-the-fact reminder of how their relationship developed, showing Li'l Bit as pursuing it from the beginning, even when he was not present to egg her on, and the start of Peck's obsession with her breasts.

One more element to the play's structure is the inclusion of dramatic monologues throughout. Most are from the grown-up Li'l Bit, who starts the play addressing the audience as if she is conducting a lecture in drivers' education. At various times in the play, different characters give titles to the scenes as they are being presented, such as the three ''On Men, Sex, and Women'' segments or ''Uncle Peck teaches cousin Bobby to fish'' and ''Aunt Mary on behalf of her husband.'' One of the most notable individual pieces is Li'l Bit's mother's lecture, "A mother's guide to social drinking," which is addressed to the audience while a scene is acted out of Peck getting Li'l Bit drunk. Like the drivers' education lectures, this serves to ridicule social formality, which conflicts with basic urges and emotions.

Symbolism

The main symbol in this play is, of course, Uncle Peck teaching his niece to drive, which represents an older man's attempt to initiate a young woman into a life of sex. It is a fitting symbol because the two, driving lessons and seduction, have so many points in common. The car has often been thought of as a sexual image, not only because of the power that its engine gives to its driver but also because it is a safe haven for lovers to meet in private, away from the attention of society. The relationship between Peck and Li'l Bit resembles a driving lesson in that he has experience and patience and she has power: the car is as much a powerful machine as her body. The day that she receives her driver's license marks a rite of passage, a celebration that is commemorated with another rite, her first drink. (This is paralleled later in the play when Peck drinks his life away, and Li'l Bit makes a point of mentioning that he lost, after his job and wife, his driver's license.) One of the clearest connections made between learning to drive and sexual initiation is in their final scene together, when Peck puts eleven-year-old Li'l Bit on his lap to drive the car. To her, the opportunity to control a car is awe-inspiring, racing down the highway, until he puts his hand inside of her blouse, forever uniting sex and driving in her mind. One last connection between the two, a bittersweet one, comes when Li'l Bit, a grown woman, takes off driving and sees Peck in her mirror. The rear view mirror is a fitting symbol for looking backward at the events of one's life, as Li'l Bit does in this play.

HISTORICAL CONTEXT

Intercourse between an adult and a child is called "statutory rape": that is, a rape that might not seem to fit the definition of the word because both participants consent in having sex but that is considered rape according to legal statute because children are considered unable to knowingly give such consent. The age at which a young person can legally consent to sex is different in different states but generally it is between the ages of sixteen and eighteen. In *How I Learned to Drive*, Uncle Peck anxiously counts the days leading up to Li'l Bit's eighteenth birthday, and she easily recognizes that he has been waiting for the opportunity to have sex with her legally, without fear of being put in jail for statutory rape.

Laws against sex with children have always been enforced in this country. In the 1960s, though, there was a sexual revolution that swept away much of the social stigma attached to many sexual practices. Starting in the 1950s, when *Playboy* magazine made pornography a mainstream commercial venture, and carrying on through the late 1960s and early 1970s, when there was a counter-culture revolution of college students who found their identity in social disobedience against the Vietnam War, sexuality came to be seen as a private matter, not a governmental one. Laws punishing homosexuality were challenged, in some cases successfully, and other laws were changed to make it easier to obtain divorces, giving people more leeway in determining what they could consider an unsatisfactory marriage. From the late 1960s to the mid-1970s, questions were constantly raised regarding which sexual practices were morally wrong and which were just deemed wrong by obsolete traditions.

The same social shift that powered the sexual revolution also drove the women's movement in the 1960s and 1970s. Feminists brought attention to subjects that had always been known but seldom talked about in public, subjects like rape, spousal abuse, and incest. In the 1970s, books began appearing that examined the psychological damage done by adults who sexually abuse children. One of the earliest and best-known of these was Louise Armstrong's *Kiss Daddy Goodnight,* which was about her being molested by her father throughout her childhood; it became a bestseller in 1978. In the wake of Armstrong's success, more and more women began to speak out about being sexually abused by older people, usually male relatives. Throughout the 1980s, the stigma attached to having been abused dwindled, as victims of the experience banded together, bolstering each other's pride in having had the strength to survive.

The support groups for survivors of childhood abuse grew so quickly and were so widespread that a backlash against them arose in the 1990s. To some extent, this backlash came from animosity toward celebrities who told their stories of being sexually abused during childhood. As Oprah Winfrey, Suzanne Sommers, Rosanne Barr, and others came out in public about their difficult origins, many Americans

COMPARE & CONTRAST

- **1960s:** Popular music, such as the songs referred to in the notes for this play, hints at sexual activity.

  Today: Many popular songs directly refer to couples having sex.

- **1960s:** Pedophilia is not spoken of. A child lodging a complaint about an older relative's improper conduct could expect not to be believed.

  Today: Pedophilia is talked about every day on daytime television. Support groups have been established to give serious attention to charges that family members might not want to admit.

- **1960s–1970s:** Alcohol use is considered an acceptable leisure activity. A "gentleman" is more likely to be able to buy a drink for a sixteen-year-old girl, as Peck does in the play.

  Today: After noting the correlation between alcohol and automobile fatalities, most states have become strict about enforcing underage drinking laws.

- **1960s:** America's reliance on mass transit falls to a third of what it had been during World War II, due to the availability of private automobiles and the thousands of miles of road that were built during the 1950s and 1960s.

  Today: Many people are abandoning cars in urban areas and switching to mass transit because the roads are too crowded.

---

sympathized, but others, finding no sympathy for the rich and famous, cast a cold eye toward the subject. The more it seemed that everyone had a story of childhood abuse, the more people tuned out the horror of the subject.

One extreme theory regarding sexual abuse of children was responsible for both the rapid growth of incidents reported and the growing firmness of skeptics. Repressed Memory Syndrome is based in the Freudian theory that a person suffering a traumatic experience is inclined to lose the memory of that event but that the memory can be accessed later to piece together what actually happened. Working with this idea, stories began making headlines during the 1990s of people suddenly "remembering" that they were abused by their parents. Suspicions rose when the stories became more and more outrageous. People claimed memories of having been forced to participate in Satanic sex and murder cults fifty years earlier; grown children accused parents and grandparents of abuses when no other physical or behavioral evidence backed up their claims. As news reports of cases relying on Repressed Memory Syndrome became more common, the methods that were used to bring these memories out were called

into question. In many cases, psychoanalysts led patients to claim that they remembered childhood sexual abuse by asking them guided, leading questions. (For instance, if a person remembered being given a bath by an older relative, the researcher might ask, "And where did his/her hands go on you?") Often, the repressed memories were brought out using techniques that have not been accepted as hard psychological science, such as hypnosis, visualization, and trance therapy. Sexual abuse is certainly a traumatic experience, and repression is recognized as the mind's way of dealing with trauma, but most researchers doubt the claims made by proponents of Repressed Memory Syndrome. The sensationalism and scientific dubiousness of this field has fueled the backlash against victims of sexual abuse, which in turn has encouraged writers like Paula Vogel to look at the situation from less traditional perspectives.

CRITICAL OVERVIEW

Critics have appreciated *How I Learned to Drive* since it was first produced in 1997, with general praise that only intensified when the play won the Pulitzer Prize in 1998. Writing about the original production at the Vineyard Theater, off-Broadway, Robert L. Daniels wrote in *Variety* that Vogel "paints a richly poetic and picturesque landscape," referring to the way that the playwright uses words to show things that cannot be presented on the stage. Daniels credited Vogel with her ability to deal with pedophilia in a way that was not distracting or off-putting, noting, "The play is a potent and convincing comment on a taboo subject, and its impact sneaks up on its audience." Stefan Kanfer, writing for the *New Leader* about the same off-Broadway production, found excellence all around: "Still," his review ended, after praise for the cast members, costumer, and scenarist, "as fine as these professionals are, the star of the evening remains Paula Vogel, a playwright who never gives in to the obvious. . . . Vogel is a major talent waiting for a big theater to display her wares." Kanfer's praise is built on the observation that, by 1997, the subject of incest was a familiar one on television and print. This review credits Vogel with being able to find something new in the material and presenting it with such style. "If *How I Learned to Drive* focused only on this roiled relationship it would still be an outstanding effort," Kanfer wrote. "But Vogel exhibits more than a talent for clinical analysis. She has also composed a comedy of bad manners, with a series of memorable riffs." Kanfer goes on to quote the "Mother's guide to social drinking" speech, which several reviewers referred to when discussing the play's humorous tone.

When Laurie Stone reviewed the play for the *Nation,* she acknowledged the acting, calling David Morse's Peck "brilliant" and observing of Mary Louise Parker's performance that "with her rabbit twitchiness, [she] seamlessly embodies a child whose nose sniffs for the hustle, the grope." Still, her review is mainly concentrated on Vogel's ability to carefully balance the complex psychology of the central relationship. "In this weirdly captivating play," Stone wrote:

> Vogel admits the psychological toll of intergenerational sex and the immorality of exploiting the weakness of children, but she stands apart from the advocates of victims' rights who don't grant the erotic allure of such connection—a given of our sexual natures, though one that responsible adults limit to fantasy. Perversion, *Drive* says, isn't in acts and wishes but in burying a piece of truth where it can leap out hungrily.

How I Learned to Drive remained in New York for over a year. After it received the Pulitzer Prize in 1998, it expanded to theaters across the country, as well as to places as diverse as Japan, Scandinavia, Germany, and South Africa. With her newfound fame, Vogel was able to take an extended leave from her teaching job and to concentrate on writing. Although there has not been much time to see what she can do to match the success of this play, it is clear that, at least in the short-term, she is not locked into following the award-winning formula but instead is exercising her creativity and branching out with new styles. She has been commissioned for an historical Christmas drama and for a screen treatment of *How I Learned to Drive*, which has yet to be produced.

Vogel followed *How I Learned to Drive* with *The Mineola Twins* in 1999. It is a comic, camp vehicle that uses clichéd; characterizations and settings while it follows two twins, one good and one evil, through the Republican administrations of Eisenhower, Nixon, and Reagan. While this play touched upon social extremes, it was not nearly as serious about its subject matter as its predecessor. Charles Isherwood, writing in *Variety,* called *The Mineola Twins* "a bright cartoon of a play" and took time to mention the earlier play by comparison: "It certainly lacks the depth and complexity of Vogel's *How I Learned to Drive*, but its go-for-broke adventurousness is endearing, and it's a divinely funny vehicle for [its star]."

CRITICISM

David Kelly

Kelly is an instructor of creative writing at Oakton Community College. In the following essay, he examines the ways Vogel makes the character of Uncle Peck, the child molester, bearable by making him understandable.

The focal characters of Paula Vogel's 1997 play *How I Learned to Drive* are Uncle Peck, a grown man who orchestrates a seven-year-long sexual assault against his niece, and Li'l Bit, the object of his fixation who encourages his lust. On their own, the facts of the case qualify the play as a drama, more specifically a tragedy. A good case can be made that such subject matter could never be anything but inherently and irrevocably tragic. But the play has comic elements, and all turns out well for Li'l Bit, its narrator and protagonist, who, fifteen or twenty years after the action, can look back on her

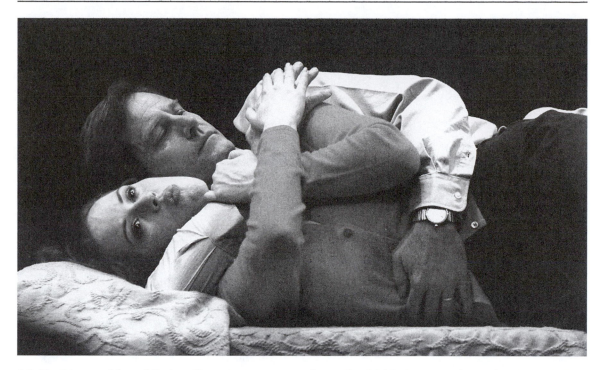

Molly Ringwald and Brian Kerwin in a scene from the 1999 theatrical production of How I Learned to Drive

relationship with her uncle, scrutinize it, and then get on with her life. These elements support the interpretation, made by the author herself, that the play is actually a comedy with tragic elements. The fact that there is no definitive answer, that the work remains suspended between the two categories, is one of the sources of its power.

A character like Uncle Peck is not one that can be found likeable, in theory. Morally, he has no ground to stand on. In the beginning of the play, Li'l Bit is, as she describes herself, ''very old, very cynical of the world, and a know it all. In short, I'm seventeen years old.'' There might be some room for moral equivocation when Peck fondles and kisses her breasts. Audiences just may think that Peck accepts the girl for the age she feels, pushing her age upward by just a few months, and that he is a hopeless romantic who views love as a moral imperative more compelling than the legal age of consent. It is a shaky argument at best, one that is probably used by pedophiles all of the time; with her nearness to the magic eighteenth birthday and her permission to his touch, he at least has a case to argue. The play only starts with that situation, though: where it builds to, even after the news of Peck's death while Li'l Bit is in her twenties, is a

scene of the same man fondling the same girl's breasts when she is eleven. There is no argument that could make this acceptable.

In spite of the horror that he is responsible for, the potential psychological destruction of his niece, Peck cannot be written off by audiences as a monster. He can't be seen as a decent man with the one small flaw of child molestation: the best that can be said about him is that he is a complex character. Vogel creates his complexity with an even hand that makes it difficult for audiences not to care about what he is going to do every moment he is onstage. Li'l Bit is complex, too, but audiences are not as resistant to feeling what she feels: because she is a child, the presumption of innocence is hers. Peck is guilty from the start. The greatest challenge that *How I Learned to Drive* faces is the challenge to invest Peck with enough innocence that audiences will leave the theater accepting his basic humanity.

It would be more difficult to accomplish this if innocence were a peripheral matter to this play, one that could only be hinted at symbolically. As it stands, however, innocence is a central issue, which allows Vogel to address it directly. The protagonist, Li'l Bit, can remember her early sexualization with nostalgia because, as an adult, she knows how

WHAT DO I READ NEXT?

- *How I Learned to Drive,* published in 1997, is available by itself from Dramatists Play Service, Inc. It is also bound with Vogel's follow-up play, *The Mineola Twins,* in a 1998 book called *The Mammary Plays* from Theatre Communications Group.

- Vogel's earlier plays are available from Theatre Communications Group in a 1996 book called *The Baltimore Waltz and Other Plays.* In addition to the title work, this book includes *Hot 'N' Throbbin, And Baby Makes Seven, The Oldest Profession,* and *Desdemona.*

- Paula Vogel has said in interviews that this play is an attempt to look at *Lolita* from the other side. The 1954 novel *Lolita,* by Vladimir Nabakov, has become a modern classic. It is about a middle-aged European man who becomes obsessed with a twelve-year-old American girl. The book is currently available in several editions, including Vintage Press's *The Annotated Lolita,* with notes by Alfred Appel, published in 1991.

- Moises Kaufman's play *Gross Indecency: The Three Trials of Oscar Wilde* concerns Wilde's relationship with a young man. It was performed off-Broadway at the same time as *How I Learned to Drive,* and several reviewers noted similar themes. The play is available in a 1998 paperback edition from Vintage Press.

- *The Kiss,* by Kathryn Harrison, is a memoir about her four-year affair with her father, whom she did not meet until she was twenty. Published by Bard Press in 1998, it covers much of the same psychological ground as the play.

- Finalists for the Pulitzer Prize for drama in the year that this play won were *Freedomland* by Amy Freed (published by Dramatists Play Service, 1999), and *Three Days of Rain* by Richard Greenberg (Dramatists Play Service, 1998).

- The book *Plays and Playwrights for the New Millenium* contains eight experimental plays that ran in off-off-Broadway theaters at the end of the 1990s. It includes works by up-and-coming authors, including Edmund De Santis, Lynn Marie Macy, and C. J. Hopkins. This collection was edited by Martin Denton and published in 2000 by New York Theater Experience, Inc.

- The comic novel *Roger Fishbite,* by Emily Prager, concerns a twelve-year-old-girl's relationship with a man who rents a room in her mother's house, leading to mayhem and murder. Told from the girl's point of view, this 1999 book was published by Random House.

---

wrong it was to want to give up her innocence so quickly, but at the same time, she understands why she wanted to do it. Even without the presence of Uncle Peck, Li'l Bit's family life is warped, a fact made clear early in the play with the information that family nicknames are based on genitalia, giving her an awareness of sex at an age when she was too young to cope with the knowledge. She sees her grandmother lead a miserable life because of her efforts to deny her own sexual urges, while her mother tells her that there is nothing wrong with sex, so long as it is intertwined with love. Her grandfather, ''Big Papa'' (audiences are told that his is one of the genitalia-inspired nicknames), is a bully who uses his wife as a receptacle for sex and who has no patience for anyone who is not a sex object for him. Sexuality equals maturity and power in Li'l Bit's home; innocence is to be ridiculed.

The same pattern continues at school, where, in a quick trio of scenes, audiences see Li'l Bit mocked, then alienated, then, finally, revered. This sequence starts with Li'l Bit naïvely unaware of the importance of the breasts that have grown on her, not expecting Jerome to ridicule her for them as he does. Even among other girls, she is an outcast, first because of her intimidating physical development and then because of the uninhibited sexual humor she brings from home. The last high school scene, with Greg, shows her dawning awareness of the way her breasts give her control over boys and men. The message throughout her childhood is that innocence is a problem, sexuality a cure.

Peck is a man who has seen some suffering, which he is too stoic to admit to himself. It is his wife, Aunt Mary, who tells the audience that his stint in the Marines affected him. In a display of considerable denseness, she explains that he will hang around her when troubled and that her well-meaning response is to avoid talking about anything substantial, leaving Peck to swallow his sorrows and deal with them alone. His ideal life is fishing barefoot, as he explains to Cousin Bobby in their scene together at the fishing hole. It is what he misses most of all about South Carolina, and, by extension, about his past. In that scene, the basic guidelines of his relationship with Li'l Bit show themselves. He starts the scene as a boy himself, fishing alongside Bobby, then eases into the role of the mature participant with his fishing advice, and finally he is forced, when Bobby is upset about the fish's pain, to take a paternal position to comfort him. His offer of beer at the end of the scene, apparently a seductive tactic (as it is when he buys Li'l Bit martinis), can be seen as an attempt to pull Bobby over the line into adulthood, so that he will not be alone.

With Li'l Bit, Peck goes even further, trying to bump her up ahead of him in maturity, putting her into the adult role so that he can reclaim his youth. He begs her for sex; he backs away when she shows her annoyance and promises that he will wait chivalrously until such time as she might be ready. Far from being the type of predator that usually comes to mind when the subject of grown men and young girls is raised, Peck acts like he is a young boy who has every reason to expect Li'l Bit's rejection and to dream of her attention. He acts like Greg, just as Big Papa is a grown Jerome, and, in fact, their overlapping scenes responding to the mystery signals from Li'l Bit's breasts merge Peck's and Greg's personalities into one.

If the situation were just left like this, with raw psychological motivations—Li'l Bit rushing to undo her innocence as Peck struggles to regain his—it might make a convincing paradigm, but audiences could be left to appreciate such a situation intellectually, instead of falling into the world of the work.

> IN SPITE OF THE HORROR THAT HE IS RESPONSIBLE FOR, THE POTENTIAL PSYCHOLOGICAL DESTRUCTION OF HIS NIECE, PECK CANNOT BE WRITTEN OFF BY AUDIENCES AS A MONSTER."

The setting cannot be ignored. It accounts for much of what makes these people and what they make of themselves. A rural setting might give Peck and Li'l Bit too much free reign to work out their own psycho-social dynamic between themselves, as occurs in countless Southern gothic stories, in which the characters' environment is more symbolic than real. An urban setting would be too real, though, making it unbelievable that they could stay the focus of one another's attention year after year. Instead, Paula Vogel has placed them in an artificial environment; they live in the suburbs, but when they need to be alone, they drive to the farms run by the Department of Agriculture, or else they go far away, to the shore, where attitudes are described as "European."

Vogel actually relies less on the physical place to tell audiences about the world these characters occupy than she does on the music that floats in the air around them. The songs that she suggests are for the most part sweet and melodic, celebrations of love and youth and the special synergy that the two create when they are blended together. Songs like "Come Back When You Grow Up, Girl," "You're Sixteen," and "Hold Me" might seem chosen to fit the specific details of the situation, but they all suppress their awareness of the danger of love. They are love songs with an edge. Pure, treacly love songs would not do for the story of Li'l Bit and Uncle Peck's illicit affair. They have a rock and roll attitude.

Rock and roll has always been known as the music of youth, especially when it was new and revolutionary in the 1950s and 1960s (when the songs that Vogel suggests were on the charts). The tension about this youth music is that it also has a reputation as the music of sexuality. As Bruce Springsteen explained in 1988 (quoted in Schultze):

When I was growing up, I got a sense of so many things from rock 'n' roll music. I got a sense of life. I got a sense of *sex*. But most of all, I got a sense of freedom. For me, the best rock 'n' roll always gave a sense of freedom and expanding awareness.

It is music that makes old people feel young and free and young people feel that they possess the wisdom of a hard-lived past.

Uncle Peck cannot be forgiven, but he also cannot be ignored. Vogel shows him and Li'l Bit in mutual agreement. The crime that Peck commits—and a considerable one it is—is in wanting so badly to be young again that he is willing to take the chance of causing his niece irrevocable harm. His wife drives him to it; his victim drives him to it; the music drives him to it; and, in the end, Li'l Bit comes away wiser and content: still, none of these extenuating circumstances absolves him of moral responsibility. Nor is his guilt any reason for audiences to take him lightly. He is too well written for that.

Source: David Kelly, Critical Essay on *How I Learned to Drive*, in *Drama for Students*, The Gale Group, 2002.

Lois Carson

Carson is an instructor of English literature and composition. In this essay, she examines both modern and classical dramatic elements of Vogel's play and its themes.

How I Learned to Drive forces its audience to confront the tough issues of parenting, gender stereotyping, incest, and child abuse. More comic than tragic, it succeeds because of Vogel's innovative handling of her subject matter. The play opens with the main character, Li'l Bit, speaking directly to the audience. "Sometimes to tell a secret, you first have to teach a lesson," she says. What follows is her stream-of-conscious monologue told in flashbacks. The action is circular, often looping back in time or jumping ahead to the future like incidents in a dream. The Li'l Bit who opens the play is a confident, self-possessed woman in her thirties, a teacher who begins by explaining the historical context of her lesson. With only her voice, she conjures up a warm summer night, thick with the smells of farm animals and the leather dashboard of the parked car. Both she and her audience are in the parking lot of the Beltsville Agricultural Farms on a warm summer evening in suburban Maryland. A hundred years before, farmers on the same spot might have

sat watching Civil War battles. Tonight, however, the audience will witness a different, far more personal and secret civil war between an eleven-year-old Li'l Bit and her middle-aged uncle Peck—a war that lasts for seven years.

Minimalist staging allows Vogel to create the bland bareness of a lecture hall. Two chairs facing the audience serve as the front seats of various cars. Sitting in the chairs, Li'l Bit and Peck do not touch. Pantomime suggests sexual behavior rather than overtly acting it out. Pop music of the sixties, automobile sounds, and road signs continually remind the audience of its participation in a driving lesson. The only actors other than Li'l Bit and Uncle Peck are the flat, static characters of the three-member Greek chorus that is actually part of the staging. Composed of a male, female, and teenager, the chorus members fulfill a variety of roles in the play. As individual family members, high school girls, high school boys, and a waiter, they assume roles in various scenes, as well as observing and commenting on the action. At times they provide a background musical score of 1960s' songs sung in three-part harmony. At crucial moments, they offer comic relief between the audience's moments of insight into Li'l Bit's family background. Throughout the play, the voice of the instructor announcing the next lesson topic drives the play from scene to scene, easing the audience over what might otherwise be too bumpy a road.

Because the lesson she wishes to teach is inseparable from her secret, Vogel deliberately begins the play *in medias res* (in the middle of the action) with an already old and cynical seventeen-year-old Li'l Bit parked in a dark lane with an older married man. Their conversation indicates that they know each other well, that such occasions are regular in their lives. In exchange for his not drinking all week, she permits him to kiss her breast but draws the line at anything more. It is not until she calls him Uncle Peck and reminds him that he needs to get home to Aunt Mary that the audience realizes the relationship of the two. Since clearly she is the one in the driver's seat, the one calling the shots, the audience tends to see her not as a victim but as a willing participant. Vogel's structuring of Li'l Bit's flashbacks throughout the play reverse that perception, ending the play with two unforgettable images: Peck's initial abuse of the eleven-year-old Li'l Bit and the soon-to-be thirty-five-year-old Li'l Bit. The former is an innocent victim; the latter, a whole woman who has learned a tough lesson, healed herself, and moved on to forgiveness.

Li'l Bit lives with her mother and maternal grandparents. Her mother's sister Mary and Mary's husband, Peck, are frequent visitors in the home. Conversation almost always centers on the discussion of men and women and sex. "In my family," Li'l Bit says, "folks tend to get nicknamed for their genitalia." Her remark provides the occasion for the first comic performance from the chorus as her mother explains how Peck, Li'l Bit, and her cousin Bobby got their names. Li'l Bit's grandmother was a child bride who still believed in Santa Claus and the Easter Bunny. She has never experienced an orgasm and does not believe such a thing exists. She warns her daughter that telling Li'l Bit the truth about sex will result in her ruination. However, Li'l Bit's mother blames her mother for not telling her the facts of life so that she could protect herself from pregnancy. The scene "A Typical Family Dinner" begins with Mother observing that Li'l Bit's bust is getting as big as her grandmother's. Li'l Bit's attempts to steer the conversation into another direction only encourage her grandfather, whose jokes perpetuate the stereotype that a female does not need an education. "She's got all the credentials she'll need on her chest," he says. His jokes only confirm what Li'l Bit is already discovering at school. To the teenage boys, she is no longer a person, only an object of sexual fantasy. Their innuendoes and jokes strip her of her self-confidence. She is embarrassed to dance, to participate in sports, or to be part of any activity that calls attention to her breasts.

Peck, Li'l Bit's uncle by marriage, is childless. He is a veteran of World War II and a Southern boy whose mama wants him to be more than his father, to amount to something in the world. A hard worker and a jack-of-all-trades, he is a gentle, kind man, but he is also an alcoholic and a pedophile. He goes back to South Carolina once or twice a year to see his mother and family but most of all to fish. His real prey, however, is his timid cousin Bobby, who cries at the baiting of a hook. He and Bobby keep secrets. He promises not to tell anyone that Bobby cries over the pain a fish might feel if Bobby won't tell anyone what happens in the tree house afterwards. He has truly loved his niece Li'l Bit all her life, ever since he first held her tiny body in his hand. She is only eleven, alone with him and completely at his mercy, when he first touches her in a sexual way. His wife Mary is an enabler who convinces herself that her husband is a good man. She complains that all the women in the neighborhood "borrow" him to shovel sidewalks, jump-start a car, or provide a ride. She

> IN 'THE PHOTO SHOOT,' VOGEL FORCES HER AUDIENCE TO CONFRONT THE TOUGHER ISSUES OF VOYEURISM AND SEXUALIZING OF YOUNG CHILDREN."

knows he has "troubles" but blames them on the lack of "rap sessions" to help men talk about their troubles after the war. She also knows that something is going on between her husband and Li'l Bit but chooses to blame her niece.

Unquestionably a very modern and innovative play, *How I Learned to Drive* succeeds in great part because of its classic elements. Although it is more comic than tragic in tone, the play focuses on a series of causally related events in the life of a person. Its two main characters, Li'l Bit and Peck, are observed and analyzed by a Greek chorus. Its purpose is to provide a catharsis for the audience. Its protagonist is superior to the people around her. Her own error in judgment results in her downfall. A sharp recognition of that error is immediate, but she does not move to reverse her actions for seven years. Li'l Bit is, after all, only eleven when her overconfidence leads her to ignore her mother's warnings and willfully persuade her mother to let her travel alone with her uncle Peck. When Peck invites her to sit on his lap and drive, she is at first surprised and then delighted by being treated as a grown-up. Peck instructs her to keep her hands on the wheel and her eyes on the road. Her delight in actually steering the car gives way when he places his hands on her breasts. She realizes that her mother's warnings were justified, that what he is doing is wrong, but she is a vulnerable child at the mercy, not only of an adult family member but also of her own innocent love for him. It is not until Peck attempts consummation of the relationship on her eighteenth birthday that Li'l Bit finally has the courage to end their relationship. For the first time in seven years, she takes back her body and her life. Peck goes home to drink himself to death. When the adult Li'l Bit drives off at the end of the play, once more able to believe in forgiveness and family, the catharsis for both Li'l Bit and the audience is complete.

Moreover, Vogel, like the ancient Greek playwrights, warns her audience of its own fallibility. She does not ignore omens that presage moral disaster but meets them head on. In ''The Photo Shoot,'' Vogel forces her audience to confront the tougher issues of voyeurism and sexualizing of young children. In dramatizing the different perspectives of Li'l Bit and Peck, by extension she dramatizes those of every member of her audience and its larger society. At thirteen, Li'l Bit is uneasy about being in the basement alone with her uncle but responds to his direction after being reassured that her aunt Mary is not at home. He tells her that she ''has a body that a twenty-year-old woman would die for,'' that in five years she'll have ''a really professional portfolio.'' She is horrified by the realization that he is building a portfolio of photos to submit to *Playboy* when she becomes eighteen, but he shrugs off her response. After a heated argument, the scene ends with her choosing to accept his promise that the photos will never be seen by anyone but him, a person who has loved her all of her life. Yet even as he is making his promise, his actual photos of the thirteen-year-old Li'l Bit and those of real contemporary models are being flashed on the stage in a slide montage.

Ironically, the family member that does the most harm to Li'l Bit is also the one who teaches her how to navigate life's roadways successfully, warning her that driving like a woman ''can be fatal'' because women ''tend to be polite'' and are likely to hesitate. ''Men are taught to drive with confidence—with aggression,'' Peck tells a fifteen-year-old Li'l Bit. ''They drive defensively—always looking out for the other guy.'' He teaches her how to drive like a man so that she will be capable of handling whatever road disaster she encounters—even a ten-car pile-up. When she checks her rearview mirror before driving off in the final scene of the play, she sees the spirit of Peck sitting in the backseat. At thirty-four, able once more to believe in family and forgiveness, she has made peace with the past.

Source: Lois Carson, Critical Essay on *How I Learned to Drive,* in *Drama for Students,* The Gale Group, 2002.

Stefan Kanfer

In the following essay, Kanfer examines Vogel's treatment of sexual predation in How I Learned to Drive.

The subject of childhood sexual abuse has gone from tabu to prime time. It has been explored on television shows like *NYPD Blue* and *Law and Order,* exploited on Oprah and Sally Jessie Raphael, given hours of carefully lascivious attention on network and local news. The current best seller, *The Kiss,* makes much of a deeply disturbed father-daughter relationship, and piles up royalties in the process.

Serious theater, usually the first art form to deal with difficult topics, is behind the curve in this matter. Still, *How I Learned To Drive,* at the Vineyard Theater, more than compensates for lost time. Paula Vogel's play begins as a diverting lecture in driver education as a high school student might perceive it—tips on how to hold the wheel, how to watch for on-coming traffic, how to turn and park. All too soon, however, we learn that this is a metaphor for the life and times of a toxic family.

In the sticks of Maryland the narrator, Li'l Bit (Mary-Louise Parker), grows out while she grows up. Her burgeoning figure becomes the star attraction for Uncle Peck (David Morse), who spends hours, days, weeks, and finally years, attempting to gain his niece's confidence. Peck's interest is hardly a secret. Li'l Bit's mother (Johanna Day) is well aware of what runs beneath the surface of her brother-in-law's avid, overly polite concern. ''I don't like the way he looks at you,'' she warns her daughter. But when Li'l Bit demurs, Mama cautions that ''if anything happens, it will be *your* responsibility!''

Meantime, Grandma (Kerry O'Malley) speaks of sex as a miserable burden carried by women down through the centuries. Constantly beleaguered by Grandpa (Christopher Duva), she has never had an orgasm and doesn't believe that such a thing exists. As for her Neanderthal husband, much of his dinnertime conversation consists of tormenting Li'l Bit by commenting on the increasing size of her breasts. (''You'll need a wheelbarrow to carry them soon.'') Manifestly this situation is rife with disastrous possibilities, and most of them occur. Despite the colorful characters and southern locale, however, Paula Vogel is not some Erskine Caldwell for the '90s.

How I Learned To Drive is in fact a scrupulous attempt to anatomize the drama of the abuser and the abused, and to see how such incidents occur *en famille.* To accomplish this most difficult task, the playwright tells her story in mosaic form—an accretion of small scenes leading to the truth. Sometimes it is 1969, and the girl is a mere child; at others it is her high school years, or her freshman college semester. The only person in her family ever to go on beyond high school, the restive and confused Li'l Bit finds it impossible to concentrate on her studies, drinks to excess, becomes the subject of campus gossip and innuendo, and finally gets expelled. Time moves back and forth like sand in an hourglass, the light and emphasis constantly shifting. One moment we may see the teenager squirm at a dinnertime confrontation; another moment we may be listening to her mother's moral lectures or her Uncle's continuing pleas for intimacy.

It is from the scenes of verbal seduction that the play derives its greatest strength. For Uncle Peck is not the kind of heavy-breathing seducer who populates so many Movies of the Week. He is a plausible soul with a good job and an attractive wife. "I've loved you since I could hold you in one hand," he confesses to his niece, and there is no reason to doubt his word. He does indeed love the girl—and not just carnally. His is an affection mixed with lust and insecurity and, as things progress, a fatal self-loathing. Alternately terrified and intrigued by his advances, Li'l Bit is a mixture of victim and unwitting temptress, not quite complicit in the affair—but not entirely blameless either.

If *How I Learned to Drive* focused only on this roiled relationship it would still be an outstanding effort. But Vogel exhibits more than a talent for clinical analysis. She has also composed a comedy of bad manners, with a series of memorable riffs. Watching an outstanding cast perform them is comparable to sitting in on a session of fine jazz soloists, each waiting for a turn at the microphone. In particular, "A Mother's Guide to Social Drinking," spoken by Mama to Li'l Bit, is a classic advisory to white-trash debutantes:

A lady never gets sloppy—she may, however, get tipsy and a little gay.

Never drink on an empty stomach. Avail yourself of the bread basket and generous portions of butter. Slather the butter on your bread.

Sip your drink, slowly; let the beverage linger in your mouth—interspersed with interesting, fascinating conversation. Sip, never slurp or gulp. Your glass should always be three-quarters full when his glass is empty.

Stay away from ladies' drinks: drinks like Pink Ladies, Sloe Gin Fizzes, Daiquiris, Gold Cadillacs, Long Island Iced Teas, Margaritas, Piña Coladas, Grasshoppers, White Russians, Black Russians, Red Russians, Melon Balls, Blue Balls, Blue Hawaiians, Green Arkansans, Hummingbirds, Hemorrhages and Hurricanes. In short, avoid anything with sugar or anything with an umbrella. Get your vitamin C from fruit. Don't order anything with Voodoo or Vixen in the title or sexual positions in the name like Dead Man,

> " ALTERNATELY TERRIFIED AND INTRIGUED BY HIS ADVANCES, LI'L BIT IS A MIXTURE OF VICTIM AND UNWITTING TEMPTRESS, NOT QUITE COMPLICIT IN THE AFFAIR—BUT NOT ENTIRELY BLAMELESS EITHER."

Screw or the Missionary. Believe me, they are lethal. I think you were conceived after one of those.

Drink, instead, like a man: straight up or on the rocks, with plenty of water in between. You're less likely to feel hung over, no matter how much you've consumed, and you can still get to work the next morning even on little or no sleep. Oh, yes, and never mix your drinks. Stay with one all night long, like the man you came in with: bourbon, gin, or tequila 'til dawn . . . If you feel you have had more than your sufficiency in liquor, do go to the ladies room—often. Pop your head out-of-doors for a refreshing breath of the night air. If you must, wet your face and head with tap water. Don't be afraid to dunk your head if necessary. A wet woman is still less conspicuous than a drunk woman.

The tragedy that lies behind these admonitions, of course, is that while Mama is an encyclopedia on the subject of boozing, she knows next to nothing about sexual predation—a lack that is to have dire consequences.

In telling a story that might easily have slipped into prurience, Vogel and director Mark Brokaw have taken a discreet, almost chaste approach. Uncle Peck lies down on a hotel bed with Li'l Bit but we never see him do anything more than put an arm around her shoulder. Indeed, the sole time his hand comes in contact with her torso is toward the end, and then only briefly.

When the seducer and his quarry converse, his voice emanates from his mouth. Yet Li'l Bit's responses are given by other members of the cast, giving the scene the quality of a dream happening to someone else.

At the epicenter of *How I Learned To Drive*, Parker is superb as a wide-eyed child, smoldering adolescent and marred adult. Morse gives such a well-rounded performance as her uncle that the play has been criticized for being overly sympathetic to an immoralist. Such carping misses the point: The kind of men who pursue the young are seldom testosterone-driven maniacs who advertise their intent. They may very well be the man next door, the uncle who dispenses driving lessons.

Moreover, in presenting what she calls a ''Male, Female and Teenage Greek Chorus'' (played by the supporting cast of three), Vogel shows how friends and family members can be, in the jargon of the moment, ''enablers,'' people who either look the other way or bewilder the young with ignorant counsel. The idea of love is treated as a four-letter word in these families, and children guiltily search for it the rest of their lives.

As complicit choristers, Duva, Day and O'Malley inhabit a variety of parts, ranging from juveniles to old folk. In every role they remain the same: that is to say, superb. Jess Goldstein's deliberately tacky costumes, and Narelle Sissons' minimalist scenery lend an acute sense of time and place.

Still, as fine as these professionals are, the star of the evening remains Paula Vogel, a playwright who never gives in to the obvious. Neither her plot nor her people are predictable; in the middle of the saddest scenes she evokes a laugh, and just when a moment seems to be edging on hilarity she introduces a wistful note that leaves the smiles frozen on the audience's faces.

Vogel is a major talent waiting for a big theater to display her wares. For now, try the small off-Broadway venue that houses *How I Learned To Drive*. She won't steer you wrong.

Source: Stefan Kanfer, ''On Stage: L'il Bit o' Incest,'' in *New Leader,* Vol. LXXX, No. 11, June 30, 1997, pp. 21–22.

SOURCES

Daniels, Robert L., Review of *How I Learned to Drive,* in *Variety,* March 24, 1997, p. 42.

Isherwood, Charles, Review of *The Mineola Twins,* in *Variety,* February 22, 1999, p. 159.

Kanfer, Stefan, Review of *How I Learned to Drive,* in *New Leader,* June 30, 1997, p. 21.

Schultze, Quentin J., et al., ''The Heart of Rock and Roll: The Landscape of a Musical Style,'' in *Dancing in the Dark: Youth, Popular Culture, and the Electronic Media,* William B. Eerdmans Publishing Company, 1992.

Stone, Laurie, Review of *How I Learned to Drive,* in the *Nation,* July 28, 1997, p. 34.

Vogel, Paula, *How I Learned to Drive,* Dramatists Play Service, Inc., 1998.

FURTHER READING

Armstrong, Louise, *Rocking the Cradle of Sexual Politics,* Addison-Wesley, 1994.
    Armstrong, whose book *Kiss Daddy Goodnight* opened a new era of open talk about pedophilia, discusses how the culture's view of offenses against children changed from the 1970s to the 1990s.

Holtzman, Linda, *Media Messages: What Film, Television and Popular Music Teach Us about Race, Class, Gender, and Sexual Orientation,* M. E. Sharpe, 2000.
    Holtzman, a former chair of the Department of Communications at Webster University, dissects the ways in which people like Li'l Bit have derived their self-images from mass culture throughout the years.

Kincaid, James, *Erotic Innocence: The Culture of Child Molesting,* Duke University Press, 1998.
    Kincaid's premise is that Western culture, while pretending to protect children from the complexity of sex, actually makes them sexual objects by making their purity an erotic trait.

Marsh, Peter, and Peter Collett, *Driving Passion: The Psychology of the Car,* Faber and Faber, 1987.
    This book examines some of the attitudes about driving, including feelings of power and control and freedom, that Li'l Bit discusses in the play.

Love for Love

WILLIAM CONGREVE

1695

Love for Love, by the well-known Restoration dramatist William Congreve, is a racy, broad, farcical comedy, which relies on mistaken impressions, disguises, and deception for much of its humor. Yet it is not the kind of silly drawing-room drama of wit many people imagine Restoration comedies to be. Underlying its complicated plot and clever dialogue is a serious exploration of such themes as good government, sexual ethics, gender roles, the complications of sophisticated society, and the difference between being and seeming.

Love for Love is one of Congreve's two best-known plays, the other being *The Way of the World* (1700). In each play, Congreve uses sexual gamesmanship to explore and satirize the complexities and duplicities of his society. The play is also ''metatheatre,'' or theatre that is a comment on theatre itself. Many of the characters are playacting parts to each other, and the dialogue negotiates the arena of sexual conquest, gender relations, and the exchanges inherent when marriage is part of a play. Moreover, Congreve's play enters into a conversation with the theatre of its time; *Love for Love* is a response to an earlier popular play, *Love for Money*. Arriving as a writer late in the Restoration period, Congreve uses the stage to comment upon an increasingly complex society and class structure that often seemed frivolous.

AUTHOR BIOGRAPHY

William Congreve was born on January 24, 1670, in the town of Bardsey in Yorkshire, England. By 1672, the family had moved to London; in 1674, the family relocated to the Irish port town of Youghal, where Congreve's father served as a lieutenant in the British army. Growing up in Ireland, Congreve attended Kilkenny College, where Jonathan Swift was a few years ahead of him. In 1686, Congreve matriculated at Trinity College in Dublin, where he developed an interest in the sensual pleasures of life. Perhaps more importantly, it was while at Trinity that Congreve became a devotee of the theatre. He likely attended the Smock Alley Theatre, which ran plays that recently had success in London.

In 1689, Congreve left Trinity and Dublin for London. He entered the Middle Temple, an institution that allowed men to study the law and, significantly, to enter into London society. At the time, coffeehouses were the rage in London. Fashionable men congregated there to read pamphlets, broadsides, and other publications about news and politics; they also came there to socialize and to form salons and circles. Congreve quickly became a member of one of the literary circles that met at Will's Coffeehouse, in the Covent Garden district (famous to this day for its theatres). In this group, Congreve met the eminent poet, critic, and playwright John Dryden.

Having decided to pursue writing, Congreve quickly finished his first play, *The Old Bachelor*, and it was first produced at the Drury Lane Theatre in 1693 before being produced by the Theatre Royal. Two other similarly successful plays followed: *The Double Dealer* (1693), and Love for Love (1695). His later plays, including *The Mourning Bride* (1697) and his masterpiece *The Way of the World* (1700), met with less success; critics have suggested that the satire of these plays was too sharp and made audiences uncomfortable. After 1701, he wrote no more plays (except for an adaptation of a Molière play he undertook with John Vanbrugh and William Walsh in 1704).

For his remaining years he lived, in the words of Voltaire (who met him and wrote about him in his *Letters Concerning the English Nation*), "upon no other foot than that of a gentleman, who led a life of plainness and simplicity." He invested in two theatre companies, neither of which brought him much money, and he had a small income from government sinecures (posts that require little work but secure a salary). Finally, in 1714, George I named him Secretary to the Island of Jamaica, a post that paid over 700 pounds a year. In his final years he remained an active member of his literary circle, the Kit-Cat Club, but wrote no more. He died in January, 1729, and was buried in Westminster Abbey.

PLOT SUMMARY

Act 1

The play opens in the chamber of Valentine, a young libertine who is lounging and attempting to avoid his creditors who besiege him with requests for the money he owes them. Valentine and Jeremy, Valentine's servant, banter briefly about the value of reading philosophy, introducing by the vocabulary they use the theme of economics and exchange that will recur throughout the play. Jeremy complains that the life of the wit and idler has ruined Valentine, but Valentine suggests that he might use his verbal talents in order to write. Scandal, Valentine's best friend, enters and tells him ironically that using his talents and wit would have him end up more penniless than he is already.

As the scene in Valentine's chambers continues, Jeremy is called to the door by a series of knocks. When he returns, he informs Valentine that he has turned away creditors, including the nurse of one of Valentine's illegitimate children. One of the creditors, however, enters. Trapland is a scrivener (a professional writer or scribe) to whom Valentine owes 1,500 pounds, and he is quite eager to be paid. Valentine attempts to distract him by drinking with him. When he insists on pursuing the debt, Scandal threatens him for insulting Valentine's hospitality. When Trapland leaves, Valentine informs Scandal that he has a solution for his debts: his father has promised him money immediately if he will sign over all of his future inheritance to his brother, Benjamin, a sailor.

Valentine's acquaintance Tattle arrives, and Scandal and Valentine make fun of his luck with women, eventually lying to him that they know he has had some experience with Mrs. Frail, who is about to arrive. Tattle, to their surprise, admits this, then insists on being sneaked out of the chamber before Mrs. Frail arrives. Scandal agrees, but only on the condition that Tattle tell him the names of six other women with whom he has been involved. When Mrs. Frail arrives, she informs the men that Valentine's brother Benjamin has arrived and that Miss Prue, her niece and Foresight's daughter, is coming up from the country, for she has been promised to Ben. The act ends with Scandal escorting Mrs. Frail while shopping. He promises to tell Angelica, Valentine's love interest, that Valentine is considering giving up his inheritance for her sake.

Act 2

The second act opens in Foresight's house, where Foresight (Angelica's uncle) asks his servant where the women of the house might be. Angelica arrives in the room, asking to borrow Foresight's coach, and Foresight tells his servant to inform Sir Sampson (Valentine's father) that he will soon call on him. Irritated at Angelica's desire to ride around town in the carriage, he tells her that her habit of "gadding about" will result in a bad reputation. She responds by intimating that he is practicing witchcraft with the nurse. Angered, he tells her that, although he cannot take her money away, he will ensure that Valentine, her beloved, will be made a pauper. She continues to make fun of him and he responds with his astrological predictions, eventually talking himself into a corner before Angelica leaves.

Sir Sampson enters holding the "deed of conveyance" (the papers that would take away Valentine's inheritance) in his hand. Sir Sampson and Foresight argue briefly, Foresight maintaining the validity of astronomy and Sir Sampson boasting about his travels around the world. Jeremy enters the room, followed by Valentine. Valentine informs Sir Sampson that he has received the 4,000 pounds but that it is barely enough to pay his debts and asks for more. This infuriates Sir Sampson, who roars that he hopes to see his son hanged. Valentine argues that it was his upbringing that caused him to be prodigal, and for that reason Sir Sampson should support him.

All four men exit just as Mrs. Foresight and Mrs. Frail enter. The two discuss how promiscuous Mrs. Frail appears to society. Mrs. Frail allows that she would like to break up the impending marriage between Benjamin and Miss Prue in order to marry Benjamin herself (she has heard of his imminent fortune). When Tattle and Miss Prue enter, the

William Congreve

sisters attempt to get the two to flirt, which they proceed to do. Tattle is chasing Miss Prue to her bedchamber when the act ends.

Act 3

When the third act opens, a nurse is banging on Miss Prue's door, trying to get her to come out. Miss Prue is on the other side of the door with Tattle, who is disgusted that he might have to lie about something he never did. He quickly leaves just as Valentine, Angelica, and Scandal come on stage. Angelica is acting indifferently to Valentine. Tattle enters, and Angelica begins teasing him about his success with women. Sir Sampson, Mrs. Frail, Miss Prue, and a servant enter, announcing that Ben has arrived; in an aside, Miss Prue tells Mrs. Frail that she is not interested in him. Hearing that Benjamin is about to arrive, Valentine leaves with Scandal, who has a plan for him.

Ben enters with a servant and greets his father and all present. Sir Sampson tells Ben that he will be getting married, but he shows little enthusiasm for anything but sea life. All exit except Ben and Miss Prue; he tries to be polite to her, accepting their arranged marriage, but she is not interested in him. When she continues to be rude to him, he curses her.

Mrs. Frail and Mrs. Foresight enter to take advantage of the quarrel. Mrs. Foresight escorts a weeping Miss Prue to the parlor and Mrs. Frail takes Ben to her bedchamber, ostensibly so that Sir Sampson and Foresight will not know that the betrothed do not get along.

The two men enter, wondering about the absence of Miss Prue and Ben, when Scandal enters to tell them that Valentine appears to have gone mad. Scandal makes fun of Foresight for his belief in astrology until Mrs. Foresight enters, urging Foresight to come to bed. Scandal whispers to Mrs. Foresight that he has great passion for her; she acts offended but immediately starts telling Foresight that he looks terrible and should take to bed. As he leaves, Mrs. Foresight and Scandal discuss whether a woman can be virtuous. Scandal says that, while it is possible, it is not particularly worth the trouble. As they talk, Mrs. Frail and Ben enter. He sings her a song before they all go off to bed.

Act 4

Scandal and Jeremy are in Valentine's chambers, making sure he is ready to appear mad before his father. Angelica and her servant enter, and Jeremy tells them that Valentine has gone mad, but Angelica senses that this is a trick. She pretends to be extremely concerned before exiting. Sir Sampson enters with Buckram, a lawyer, preparing to have Valentine acknowledge the deed of conveyance he has signed. As Jeremy tells Sir Sampson that Valentine is out of his wits, Buckram informs him that this unfortunate circumstance invalidates the deed. They enter Valentine's room and Valentine pretends to be insane until Buckram leaves. Valentine teases his distraught father, then leaves with Jeremy.

Foresight, Mrs. Foresight, and Mrs. Frail enter, and Scandal and Sir Sampson inform them that Valentine is out of his wits and, consequently, that the deed of conveyance is no longer in effect. Scandal banters with Mrs. Foresight about their encounter of the previous night before he and the Foresights leave. Ben enters, and in his conversation with Mrs. Frail she concludes that he is a fool, utterly devoid of sophistication. As Ben leaves, Mrs. Foresight enters, saying that Foresight has now rejected her and she is setting her sights on Sir Sampson. For her part, she tells Mrs. Frail that she has made a deal with Jeremy: they will bring Mrs. Frail to Valentine in disguise and tell him that Mrs. Frail is Angelica, ensuring a marriage between the two.

Valentine, Scandal, Foresight, and Jeremy enter, Valentine raving insanely. Mrs. Frail pretends to be Angelica. Then Angelica herself enters, followed by Tattle. Jeremy continues pretending to advance the plan of marrying Mrs. Frail to Valentine, but Valentine asks him to encourage everyone to leave so that he can tell Angelica of the plan. The room now empty, Valentine tells Angelica of his design; but Angelica pretends to think he is still mad.

Act 5

Act 5 opens at Foresight's house. Angelica is talking to her maid when Sir Sampson enters. The two flirt, and Angelica makes him believe that she is interested in marrying him. Tattle and Jeremy enter; Jeremy suggests that he would like to go to work for Tattle now that Valentine is insane. Miss Prue comes in and attaches herself to Tattle, who attempts to get rid of her. Foresight enters and attempts to interest Tattle in marrying Miss Prue, but Tattle resists. When Tattle leaves, Miss Prue resolves to marry Robin, the butler; Foresight has her locked in her room. Ben enters and informs the company that Angelica and Sir Sampson are to be married. Sir Sampson and Angelica enter with their lawyer, Buckram. When Ben is not sufficiently supportive of his marriage, Sir Sampson curses him.

Tattle and Mrs. Frail enter suddenly, bemoaning that Jeremy has tricked them and that they have unwittingly married each other. Valentine enters, learns of his father's impending marriage to Angelica, and comes clean, telling Sir Sampson that his insanity was nothing but a sham. Sir Sampson still wants his son to sign the deed of conveyance. Valentine refuses to do it until Angelica certifies that she does, indeed, want to marry Sir Sampson; when she does, he agrees to sign his inheritance over for the sake of her greater happiness. When he does so, she immediately tells him that she was pretending, and that now that he has proven his true love for her she wants to marry him. She upbraids Sir Sampson for being a terrible father and ends the play by speaking to men's unfair criticisms of women as inconstant and unreliable.

CHARACTERS

Angelica

Angelica is Valentine's beloved, a saucy, independent young woman possessed of "a considerable fortune." We first see Angelica in her uncle's house, asking her uncle for the loan of his carriage so that she can "gad about" town. During the play, we see her in no affectionate or loving exchanges with Valentine; rather, their scenes together reveal her wit and self-assuredness. She tests Valentine's love by pretending to desire his father, Sir Sampson, who assures her of his youthful vigor. Like a perfect coquette, she commits to no man, feigning indifference to all.

At the same time that she demonstrates her own wit, Angelica is suspicious of the motivations of witty men, telling Valentine that "She that marries a very Witty Man submits both to the Severity and insolent Conduct of her Husband. I should like a Man of Wit for a Lover, because I would have such a one in my Power; but I would no more be his Wife than his Enemy." Her role in the play is to "unmask" or reveal the characters' true natures that lie beneath the pretenses they put on. Through her, we learn that Sir Sampson cares for neither son; because of her, Valentine's genuinely loving side comes out; her conversation shows Foresight's astrological ideas to be idiotic. She is by no means "angelic," but in many ways she is the moral center of the play, for her actions reveal the dishonesties of the other characters.

Jeremy Fetch

Jeremy is Valentine's servant, who jokes about wishing to be released from his contract. Jeremy feels himself to be above servant status and mentions twice that he has been "at Cambridge" (albeit as a servant) and has picked up some education from his master there. Valentine confides in him and uses him to advance his plans. In the first act, he is quite impudent to Valentine, making fun of him and even criticizing his master's refusal to pay his debts. In act 4, though, it is Jeremy who is the intermediary between Valentine and the people to whom Valentine wishes to appear insane. Jeremy's purported intelligence and education are generally undercut by the other characters, who scoff at his pretense. In a scene not depicted on stage, we learn that Jeremy is quite clever, indeed: he tricks Tattle and Mrs. Frail into marrying each other, when they both were attempting to trick others into marrying them (Tattle sought Angelica's hand, while Mrs. Frail pursued Ben).

Mr. Foresight

Foresight is Angelica's uncle. He is a blowhard obsessed with astrological omens and other such

MEDIA ADAPTATIONS

- *Restoration* is not a filmed adaptation of *Love for Love*, but it is a fascinating portrayal of life in the Restoration period. The film stars Robert Downey Jr., Meg Ryan, and Ian McKellen and was directed by Michael Hoffman, for Miramax, 1995. The film is available from Miramax Home Video.

- An audio recording of *Love for Love* was made by the National Theatre of Great Britain in 1966 and was produced by the RCA Victor Corporation.

pseudoscience. From the second act on, he interprets everyone's comments as veiled knowledge about Mrs. Foresight's infidelities. His name is clearly ironic: all of his astrological readings and divinations are aimed at providing him with foresight, or a knowledge of the future, but he is probably the least perceptive character in the play.

Mrs. Foresight

Mrs. Foresight is Angelica's aunt. She and Mrs. Frail, who are sisters, attempt to break up the impending marriage between Ben and Miss Prue in order to marry Mrs. Frail to Ben. Like her husband's name, hers is meant to be ironic, for her plot to marry Mrs. Frail to Ben falls apart because she lacks a sufficient understanding of human nature.

Mrs. Frail

Mrs. Frail is Mrs. Foresight's sister. She is unmarried and in the market for a husband, and, before the play opens, she has already had an affair with Tattle. However, Mrs. Foresight feels that she behaves much too promiscuously to land a worthy husband. As a result, the two of them hatch a plan to land Ben as a husband for Mrs. Frail. Their plan fails, however, and Mrs. Frail ends up married to Tattle. She is hardly "frail"; she is a calculating and headstrong woman who is not timid about going after what she wants: Ben's fortune.

Benjamin Legend

Benjamin is Valentine's brother, a sailor just returned from a three-year voyage. Benjamin is primarily a plot device and an object of fun. His role is that of the "good brother" whom Sir Sampson contrasts with "bad brother" Valentine, who is asked to sign over his future inheritance to Ben. Ben has been directed to marry Miss Prue but has little affection for her. Instead, Mrs. Frail develops a liking for him when she discovers his future fortune. Ben's primary personal characteristic is his simplicity: he cannot fathom the duplicity, game playing, and plots that underlie all personal relationships among these urban sophisticates. His other important characteristic is his "sea-dog" language, which is a constant source of humor for the audience.

Valentine Legend

Valentine is a young "rake," or idle upper-class gentleman. His name alludes to his attraction to the ladies and their attraction to him. He owes a great deal of money to various creditors and has exhausted his father's patience with his spending. In addition, the play makes it clear that Valentine has done his share of corrupting young women. His most immediate motivations are to avoid paying his debts and to marry the young lady Angelica.

As the play opens and closes with Valentine as the central focus, he is the character most likely to be considered *Love for Love*'s "protagonist." He is also the character who comes closest to changing or developing. However, he is absent for much of the play. We see him in his chamber at the beginning, avoiding "duns" (debt collectors)—one of which is a young nurse who attempts to obtain money from him to support one of his illegitimate children—and bantering with his manservant and hatching plans with his friend Scandal. During the course of the play he tries to avoid seeing his father (who wants him to sign his inheritance over to his brother Benjamin) and eventually feigns madness in order to avoid his responsibilities. But at the opening of the play, he is not the typical "rake" character, for he wishes to drop out of society and live as a writer and thinker. His servant Jeremy and his friend Scandal persuade him that this route would be fruitless, however.

By the end, he seems to change. Only at the last minute, when he learns of Angelica's intent to marry his father, does Valentine abandon his scheme to get as much money as possible from his father, telling Angelica that he is willing to let her go and sign over his inheritance in order to secure her

happiness. While his earlier credo may have been "Love for Money" (to quote the title of a contemporary play), when *Love for Love* ends, Valentine demonstrates that he is indeed willing to pursue love as an end in itself.

Miss Prue

Miss Prue is Foresight's daughter by a previous marriage. She is young, naïve, "a silly, awkward, country girl." Not being sophisticated enough to understand the complicated plots and schemes of the people around her, she falls in love with Tattle, whom she wishes to make her husband. Her father refuses to arrange this, and when she then demands to be married to Robin, the butler, her father locks her in her room. Despite her name, she is neither prudent nor prudish. At the end of the second act, she allows herself to be seduced by Tattle, and, in terms of prudence, she has none, making snap decisions without any concern for their long-term consequences.

Sir Sampson

Sir Sampson is Benjamin and Valentine's father. He has a considerable amount of money and resents the fact that Valentine has been running through his estate with his fast living. In response, he offers Valentine a deal: sign over his future inheritance to his brother and Sir Sampson will give him four thousand pounds on the spot. Valentine takes the four thousand pounds in advance but feigns insanity to avoid signing the papers, which infuriates Sir Sampson.

Although at first Sir Sampson seems to feel affection for his son Ben, we learn as the play goes on that he really loves neither son. When Angelica begins to show interest in Sir Sampson, he is ready to write off both sons and spend their money himself. He is a selfish and arrogant man. Sir Sampson's name puns on the Biblical Samson, who destroyed a house by knocking down its pillars; Sir Sampson is willing to destroy his own house by his utter lack of care and affection for his sons.

Scandal

Scandal is Valentine's closest friend. He is a rake like Valentine but less coldhearted than Valentine at first is. When Valentine expresses disgust that the mother of one of his children did not smother the child, Scandal merely expresses his best wishes for his "Godchild" and sends money. Scandal helps Valentine appear insane for the purpose of winning Angelica. His function is to provide a mellowing influence on Valentine, who, without the presence of Scandal, would be a truly reprehensible character until the final scene of the play. Like most of the other names in the play, his is ironic; of the two friends, Scandal and Valentine, Scandal is by far the less scandalous.

Tattle

Tattle is largely an object of fun in the play. He brags constantly about his success with the ladies; however, his rhetoric is always undercut by reality. He develops an affection for Miss Prue and, by the end of the second act, attempts to seduce her. At the end of the play, he accidentally marries Mrs. Frail, whom he has already debauched.

Trapland

Trapland is a scrivener, or a professional scribe, to whom Valentine owes money. He shows up in Valentine's chamber in the first act when Valentine and Jeremy attempt to distract him from his mission.

THEMES

Gender Roles and Sexual Behavior

Throughout *Love for Love*, Congreve plays with the limited roles assigned to the genders in upper-class society. Men can be cuckolds, cruel masters, rakes, or provincials, while women can be scheming meddlers, whores, or (rarely) good wives. The crucial characteristic for women is how permissive they are in terms of bestowing their sexual favors; men, however, are judged less by their sexual behavior and more by their "mastery" of the world: their children, finances, servants, and love affairs.

For the contemporary reader approaching Restoration drama for the first time, what is most striking is the "double standard" applied to sexual behavior. Men were encouraged to seduce virgins or other men's wives, while women who were too promiscuous sexually were considered disreputable. Valentine, for instance, is visited by the nurse of one of his illegitimate children and curses the mother for not killing the child and sparing him the expense of supporting it; Tattle and Scandal both boast of their success with women. The women of the play, however, know to keep their experiences quiet. Ironically, in the comedies of this period, women's promiscuity is less serious and damaging than it

would be in later decades. After the two decades of strict Puritan rule (which strictly enforced conservative sexual behavior), the Restoration witnessed a return to relaxed attitudes about sexual behavior. The underlying joke of most comedy in this period is that men may not be having sex but are always talking about it, while women do the exact opposite.

Dissembling / Role Playing

The Puritans, who took over England in the 1640s, sought to establish God's rule on earth. Part of the Puritan ethic was a deep mistrust of costumes, disguises, and appearances; for this and other reasons, the theatres were all closed during Puritan rule. But the Puritans were also deeply suspicious of the intrigues, game playing, and stratagems that dominated court and upper-class life in the monarchical system. They wished things to be open to their scrutiny.

The Restoration of 1660 changed all of this. Attempting to make up for twenty years of lost fun and intrigue, courtiers immediately reestablished the complicated and sophisticated society they had enjoyed before. Playwrights, in turn, depicted their intrigues with irony and hyperbole. In *Love for Love*, only the provincial characters of Miss Prue and Ben are what they seem. All of the urbanites pretend to be what they are not in order to benefit themselves. Valentine's sham madness is only the most obvious example of this, and his own "dissembling," or seeming to be what he is not, is met by Angelica's. Other characters who dissemble are Jeremy (who fools any number of characters with phony plans), Sir Sampson (who pretends to be a loving father to Ben but really is antipathetic to his parental duties), Mrs. Foresight (who cheats on her husband), Tattle (who pretends to be interested in Miss Prue), and Mrs. Frail (who plays games in order to marry into Sir Sampson's estate). In act 2, Mrs. Frail and Mrs. Foresight encourage Miss Prue to act in a manner that is contrary to how she actually feels. Things are never what they seem in this society, Congreve tells the audience that only the best gameplayers will succeed in obtaining their desires.

Father/Son Relationships and Good Governance

Many critics have pointed out the potential political ramifications of Congreve's play. The model of governance he presents is that of Sir Sampson,

TOPICS FOR FURTHER STUDY

- Research the "Glorious Revolution" of 1688. Who was the king who was deposed? Why were people unhappy with him? Who replaced him? What lasting changes came about as a result of the revolution?

- As a group, direct part of one of the acts of *Love for Love*. How do you make sure the audience understands the jokes? How do you handle the actors' fast-paced entrances and exits? How do you interpret the characters of Angelica and Valentine?

- The late seventeenth and early eighteenth centuries saw many important scientific discoveries in engineering, astronomy, physics, biology, medi-

cine, and chemistry. What were some of these discoveries? Who were the important scientific figures of the time?

- Research the lives of upper-class women in English society during the late 1600s. What avenues were open to them in terms of education, careers, marriage, and owning their own property? When and why did these situations change?

- The Restoration restored the royalist government after a brief period of Puritan religious rule. Who were the Puritans? What relation did they have to the Pilgrims and Puritans in America? What became of the Puritans in England?

Ben and Valentine's father. Such critics have argued that Congreve is making a claim against government based solely on blood or lineage and that he stands for government based on the welfare of the governed. Sir Sampson pretends to have the welfare of his subjects in mind, but in reality he could care less about them; once Angelica shows interest in him he is more than happy to cut both sons off. Congreve must portray this idea with subtlety, for to argue against hereditary monarchy in seventeenth century England could have resulted in imprisonment.

Urban Sophistication

One of the most common and widespread themes in English-language literature has historically been the difference between sophisticated urbanites and country bumpkins. This theme is rarely a serious one; it is generally used for humorous purposes. An early example of this theme can be found in Chaucer's *Canterbury Tales,* where the pilgrim with the notably provincial accent tells a crude and naïve tale. To this day, humorous encounters between urbanites and provincials are a mainstay of many movie comedies.

In the Restoration period, the intrigues of London's high society were the primary concern of

popular drama (partly because the inhabitants of London's high society were the primary audience for such theatre). *Love for Love* uses the contrast between two provincial characters—Ben and Miss Prue—and the complicated urbanites of the rest of the play to underscore the differences between the social classes. Ben cannot understand, or "fathom," the dissembling and intrigues going on around him. His language refers always to maritime life, and he knows nothing of society or city life. Miss Prue, a country girl, cannot comprehend that people marry for reasons other than immediate attraction. She is betrothed to Ben (who, for reasons of their structural similarity, would probably be her ideal match) but rejects him immediately for the charms of the libertine Tattle. When Tattle shows no interest in actually marrying her, she decides that she wants Robin, the butler.

Although this theme is played for laughs, there is often a serious, satirical undertone. Urban life, as depicted by such writers as Congreve, is a complicated, subtle minefield of game playing and deception. Often these comedies criticize the Baroque constructions of the schemes hatched by the characters. Why, the playwrights seem to ask, can people not be honest? Why must sophistication equate with dishonesty? Why can't urbanites adopt the simple, unbeguiling ways of country people? But these questions are rarely serious, posed as they are by people who could not imagine living anywhere but in urban society.

STYLE

Irony

Wit, the skill most valued by the Restoration, depends upon a masterful use of irony if it is to convey an author's message. Many of the characters engage in wordplay and double entendre as they converse with each other. Though Congreve uses verbal irony to great effect in this play, his use of structural or dramatic irony is even more evident. Characters scheme to get things only to have their plans backfire in particularly ironic ways. Tattle's plan to marry Angelica while they are in disguise, for instance, ends with him being married to Mrs. Frail, who is pursuing a similar plot. But the characters' fates are themselves ironic. When Valentine first appears, he wishes to be a poor philosopher/poet with no worldly connections. By the end of the play, he is again willing to give up his fortune, only this time for love. Tattle's prowess with women, his ability to see three steps ahead in the game of seduction, leads him to ''blindly'' marry Mrs. Frail. Even the names of the characters are ironic: Angelica is hardly angelic, and Foresight utterly lacks the quality designated by his name.

Pace

The humor of *Love for Love* depends largely on the pacing of the work. Farcical comedies are light, frothy, and often silly works, and as such the director must pace the action quickly in order to sustain the comedy and prevent the audience from dwelling too much on the improbability of the plot. That sense of immediacy is lost, however, reading the play. As you read the play, try to imagine how it would be staged. The characters must enter and exit quickly; plots are hatched, secrets are revealed and betrayed, and characters are lied to and misdirected. The humor derives in part from the complexity of the plot. Even the audience becomes confused as to which characters know what and who is the target of seduction.

HISTORICAL CONTEXT

The Restoration

England is one of the world's most politically stable countries. It has been ruled in substantially the same way (by a monarchy and a Parliament) for almost a thousand years. The country's most traumatic political event, though, occurred in 1640, when Puritan forces overthrew King Charles I, executed him, and ruled under Lord Protector Oliver Cromwell for almost twenty years. In 1660, however, the monarchy was restored, King Charles II assumed the throne, and the complicated system of obtaining power by cultivating royal favor was reinstituted.

The Puritans attempted to radically change English society. They closed the theatres, feeling that they were immoral and promoted promiscuity, blasphemy, and prostitution; they destroyed such religious art as statues and stained glass because they felt they promoted idolatry; they discouraged the freewheeling, daring, sexually playful literature and social organization of the upper classes. Since Puritan theology was centered on man's sinfulness and on the doctrine of predestination, Puritan society was grim and focused entirely on religion and the world to come. For Puritans, enjoyment and sensual pleasures were not only suspect; they were sinful.

Consequently, when the monarchy was restored the hedonistic energies that had been suppressed over the previous decades surged forth powerfully. Early Restoration society was exuberant and risqué, and, as the theatres reopened, playwrights produced works centered on sexual intrigue, social game playing, and duplicity—all themes anathema to the Puritans. The upper classes, whose actions were depicted by these plays, enjoyed seeing their lives dramatized and appreciated verbal wit, and the lower classes, who also attended the theatre, loved the sexual innuendo and occasional slapstick humor. By Congreve's time, the excitement had diminished, and playwrights were beginning to satirize the complicated and often cruel games of London society.

This is not to say that England was without turmoil in the latter half of the seventeenth century. When James II took the throne upon the death of his brother Charles II in 1685, he sought to reestablish Catholicism as the official religion of the realm. Religious conflict, first between Catholics and the

COMPARE & CONTRAST

- **1690s:** England is ruled by King William III; the near-absolute power of the monarchy enjoyed by Queen Elizabeth I and King James II has just been limited by the acts of William. Parliament takes on new importance as England grows slightly more democratic.

  Today: England is ruled, in name, by Queen Elizabeth II, although in reality she has no political power. Tony Blair, the prime minister, is re-elected for a second term.

- **1690s:** Women cannot vote or run for political office in England or England's American colonies. Their only hope for influence in society is to enter into the royal court and curry favor from powerful people.

  Today: Women can vote and run for office in the United States and England. Although the United States has never had a female chief executive, England had a female prime minister (Margaret Thatcher) for much of the 1980s.

- **1690s:** In the New World, the country that will become the United States is just a collection of English settlements on the Atlantic coast. French trappers explore the interior of the continent, while Spain is the continent's most important power, holding all of Central America, Mexico,

and territories that comprise much of what is now the present-day United States.

  Today: The nations of Mexico, the United States, and Canada draw ever closer together as national borders become less important. The North American Free Trade Agreement (NAFTA) encourages trade among the nations, and millions of people of Mexican descent live in the United States, transforming the cultures and economies of both countries.

- **1690s:** Public schooling in England is far from a reality, and a university education is a reality for very few. Although literacy is widespread, it is by no means universal.

  Today: In England and the United States, literacy rates approach 100 percent, and primary education is compulsory. College attendance is at an all-time high.

- **1690s:** News travels via pamphlets and horse couriers.

  Today: Because of the telecommunications industry and its technology, information can travel instantaneously. Access to computers and televisions is widespread in England and the United States.

Church of England and then between High Church Anglicans and Puritans, had marked the previous century, and Britons were eager to avoid it. In 1688, a group of nobles invited William of Orange, a Protestant, to take the throne. He landed on the English coast, encountered little resistance from the king's forces, and took the throne. However, he refused to do so as an absolute monarch. Instead, he stipulated that he would only assume power under a bill of rights that limited royal privilege and guaranteed a number of basic rights to citizens. England became a constitutional monarchy. Perhaps most importantly for writers such as Congreve, the bill of rights allowed for a free press in England, which

made it more difficult for writers to be suppressed by the king or by religious authorities for sedition, immorality, or blasphemy.

The Rake / The Wit

The best-known stock character of Restoration comedy is the wit. The cult of wit and verbal wordplay was at its height in the late seventeenth and early eighteenth centuries, and such writers as Alexander Pope, Oliver Goldsmith, and Samuel Johnson are known as much for their wit and skill in conversation as for their writings. Since power and influence was often obtained through social settings, an ability to use words articulately and with flair could not only gain a person prestige and respect but tangible benefits as well.

Reflecting this aspect of society, Restoration plays often have as their primary characters men and women who succeed by their wit. Often the humor in such plays come from two sources: first, the ridiculous, often sexual, predicaments in which the characters find themselves (this humor was meant to appeal to lower-class audiences); second, from the eloquence, subtlety, and wit shown by the characters as they subtly insult each other and tie their opponents in verbal knots. In *Love for Love*, the main wit is Angelica—which is ironic, for in these plays the wits are generally men. Many of the male characters—Scandal, Sir Sampson, Valentine, and even Jeremy—use their wit to ridicule others or to get what they want.

Closely related to the character of the wit is the rake. The rake was another stock character of Restoration comedy—a male who took pride in seducing the women around him. The women seduced by rakes could range from servants to the wives of important men, but the rake does not care about the consequences of his actions. In *Love for Love* three rakes all appear together in the first act: Valentine, Scandal, and Tattle. Valentine shows himself to be utterly amoral when the nurse of his illegitimate child asks him for money and he says, with disgust, that she should have "overlaid," or smothered, the child. At the end of the play, Valentine (defeated by Angelica's superior wit) gives up his rakishness for his lady's love. Tattle is an unsuccessful or classless rake, for he brags about his conquests. In the first act, Scandal, using his command of language to his advantage, tricks Tattle into admitting an affair with Mrs. Frail. With an insatiable appetite for gossip, Scandal gets Tattle to name six other conquests in exchange for keeping silent about the affair. A true rake keeps his seductions to himself, to better create an air of mystery and allure about him. Scandal is the true rake here, for he not only seduces a married woman (Mrs. Foresight), he does so secretly.

CRITICAL OVERVIEW

As a member of some of the most eminent literary circles in London, Congreve had the support of the era's leading literary figures by the time he wrote his first play, *The Old Bachelor*. John Dryden, the most important poet and critic of the Restoration, said of Congreve "in Him all Beauties of the Age we see . . . all this in blooming Youth you have achieved." Colley Cibber, an important actor and writer of the period, also praised Congreve in the 1690s. *Love for Love* also won great approval from Congreve's circle, but Congreve was increasingly unhappy about the public's reception of his work. A tepid enthusiasm greeted *Love for Love*, and Congreve's later masterpiece, *The Way of the World* (1700), was positively rejected by audiences, probably because of its sharp criticisms of society.

Ironically, while sophisticated audiences resented Congreve's criticisms of social shallowness and libertinism, more religious audiences were beginning to react against the libertine attitudes and sexual playfulness of the Restoration. In 1698, the Rev. Jeremy Collier condemned Congreve and *Love for Love*, calling the play "blasphemy" and arguing that, for Congreve, "a fine Gentleman is a fine Whoring, Swearing, Smutty, Atheistical Man." (Congreve himself responded to Collier, arguing that the end of the play contained a virtuous message, since Valentine gave up his rakish ways for true love.) In 1748, Edmund Burke condemned the immorality of the play, writing that "the Rankness of [Angelica's] ideas, and her Expressions . . . are scarce consistent with any Male, much less Female, Modesty." The writer Fanny Burney commented in 1778 that "though it is fraught with wit and entertainment, I hope I should never see it represented again; for it is . . . extremely indelicate." Not all eighteenth-century viewers were of the same opinion, however. A reviewer in the *London Chronicle* of 1758 remarked upon the revival of the play that it was "the best comedy, either ancient or modern, that was ever written to please upon the stage." Victorian critics of the nineteenth century praised the play's wit, but, like their predecessors, regretted its "indelicacy" and immorality.

Modernist critics and writers of the early to mid-twentieth century paid little attention to the Restoration period, adhering to the belief, espoused by T. S. Eliot, that Milton and Dryden had weakened English literature by injecting too much Latin into the language. London productions of the play appeared occasionally, most notably one directed by and starring John Gielgud in 1943. But the revival of interest in the seventeenth and eighteenth century that began in the 1980s and 1990s increased the study of Congreve greatly. Recent examination of the play has focused on everything from

A scene from the 1985 theatrical production of Love for Love, *performed at the National Theatre in London*

CRITICISM

Greg Barnhisel

Barnhisel teaches writing and directs the Writing Center at the University of Southern California. In this essay, he discusses the varieties of love and ways in which love transforms people in Congreve's play.

In January of 1691, London saw the premiere of a new play by the popular playwright Thomas Durfey. *Love for Money,* in the words of theatre historian Derek Hughes, "uses the sexual and monetary intrigues of comedy as a way of praising the new political order . . . [it] affirms the power of law and the triumph of justice, with explicit reference to the struggle against James II and Louis XIV." By the "new political order," Hughes refers to the Glorious Revolution and overthrow of James II (who was allied, in his drive for absolute monarchical power,

with France's Louis XIV) and his replacement by William of Orange and a constitutional monarchy. *Love for Money* also depicts "mercenary relationships" vying for supremacy with relationships based on real love and loyalty. In Durfey's play, mercenary relationships—love for money, in other words— are condemned and the libertine character (who embodies these relationships) is condemned to be hanged.

In many ways, *Love for Love* (1695) is a response to Durfey's play. Whereas in Durfey's play the libertine must pay the ultimate price, in Congreve's play the libertine willingly reforms himself, not by judicial order but by the power of love. Congreve, by answering Durfey's play in such a public fashion (theatregoers would have recognized the similarity in the plays' titles), enters into a conversation with his fellow playwrights and with the public about the meaning and importance of love in a society increasingly based on the exchange of money.

Love for Love gives us many sorts of love. There is love between a husband and a wife (the Foresights); love between a father and his sons (Sir Sampson, Ben, and Valentine); love between a father and daughter (Foresight and Miss Prue); love

Congreve's political stances to the presence of feminist themes in the play to an attempt to rediscover Restoration stage engineering.

WHAT DO I READ NEXT?

- *The Way of the World,* originally produced in 1700, is Congreve's best-known play. In this play, many critics feel, Congreve created the highest accomplishment of Restoration comedy and of contemporary social criticism.

- Alexander Pope is, to many peoples' minds, the greatest wit that England ever produced. He generally wrote his works in ''heroic couplets,'' or rhymed couplets of iambic pentameter. Although he expressed his serious ideas about religion, philosophy, and literature in his *Essay on Man* and *Essay on Criticism,* his long poem *The Rape of the Lock* is a sophisticated, funny, rewarding satire of the upper-class morals of his—and Congreve's—time.

- The best and most comprehensive picture of daily life in Restoration London is not a play or a poem but a long journal. The diaries of Samuel Pepys describe in vivid and entertaining detail the social and political life of his time. Especially interesting is his portrayal of the London theater, its audiences, and conventions.

---

between sisters (Mrs. Frail and Mrs. Foresight); love between friends (Scandal and Valentine); even love between a servant and his master (Jeremy and Valentine). But the primary form of love examined in this play is romantic love, and this is exemplified in numerous false incarnations and in one valid instance. Valentine and Angelica represent in many ways the one true example of love—any kind of love—for all of the other relationships are, at their core, based on self-interest.

When we first see Valentine, he is plotting stratagems. Realizing that his financial situation has made him unable to continue his life as a rake and libertine, he resolves to give up the materialistic life and devote himself to study, writing, and the pursuit of his beloved, Angelica. ''So shall my Poverty be a Mortification to her Pride,'' he says in act 1. He will, he feels, be more appealing to her as a poor suitor than as a wealthy one; he will stand out, if nothing else. But his pretensions to morality and a rejection of his earlier behavior are immediately undercut by his callous response to the pleas of his illegitimate child's nurse. For a rake, love and lust are essentially synonymous, and Valentine is still an adherent of the rake's philosophy, for he aims at nothing more than ''getting'' Angelica. Harold Love argues that ''Valentine is still in this speech picturing Angelica as a quarry to be hunted, not as a human equal to be loved.''

In much of the rest of the play, the intrigues between Valentine and Angelica occur in the background. Rather than following their story in a detailed anatomy of one rake's progress toward true love, we watch any number of examples of untrue love. Congreve first examines lust-as-love through rakes like Scandal and Tattle. Tattle, we learn, is a successful seducer and has many notches on his bedpost. However, lacking wit, Tattle is tricked by Scandal into revealing the names of one of his lovers, Mrs. Frail. In order to prevent Scandal from revealing his knowledge to Mrs. Frail, Tattle must give Scandal the names of six additional conquests. Love, for these men, is simply a game, a way to gain prestige. No real affection whatsoever is expressed (except, ironically, by Scandal toward Valentine's rejected child).

The remainder of the cast that parades before the audience in the first two acts all add to the overwhelming portrayal of love as a sham and a joke. Mrs. Frail, who arrives in Valentine's chamber just as Tattle is attempting to avoid her, provides a disquisition on how a husband is the most pleasant person in the world because he saves all of his hostility for his wife. As act 2 opens, Angelica treats her uncle rudely and mercenarily, and he grouses about how he has been made a cuckold just before he vows to ruin her lover, Valentine. Sir Sampson enters and boasts vengefully, ''I warrant my son

> BY SHOWING THAT HE IS WILLING TO GIVE UP HIS INHERITANCE, VALENTINE NOT ONLY WINS ANGELICA'S LOVE BUT GETS TO KEEP THE MONEY AS WELL."

thought nothing belonged to a father but forgiveness and affection.'' He will change his son's tune, he blusters. When Mrs. Foresight and Mrs. Frail appear, they banter coquettishly and plan to break up an arranged marriage by introducing the prospective bride to Tattle (who, as we have learned, has already bedded Mrs. Frail).

Where the first two acts present the characters and allow them to each put forth their cynical attitudes about love, the third and fourth acts allow time for the various games and schemes that form the play's main plot to materialize and develop. After the nurse prevents Tattle from actually seducing Miss Prue, Angelica enters on the stage, and we finally see her with Valentine. But instead of a tearful reunion of lovers, Congreve gives us a deferral of love. ''You can't accuse me of inconstancy,'' Angelica says as she walks in. ''I never told you that I loved you.'' Angelica's defense against Valentine's rakish nature is typical of the society woman—hiding, not committing, playing games. Valentine, of course, is just as guilty of dishonesty and game playing, for he, with Scandal's help, is about to feign insanity.

After Angelica's appearance, the love between Valentine and Angelica fades into the background while further examples of false love occupy the stage. Sir Sampson appears genuinely happy to see Ben, but when he proposes a marriage Ben shows that his affections are not for women but for sea life (a suggestion of homosexuality, emphasized by Ben's lack of interest in marriage, would have been quite apparent to contemporary audiences). Additional examples of false love follow: Sir Sampson shows no concern when Scandal tells him about Valentine's insanity; Scandal and Mrs. Foresight scheme to get in bed together; Jeremy schemes to marry people without their knowledge or consent.

Although Angelica and Valentine's relationship is not depicted among them, these scenes provide examples of what the couple does not want. Scandal and Tattle show themselves to be the kind of dishonest, narcissistic, game playing men that Angelica does not want to be with, while Valentine discovers from his father's lack of concern that he needs someone willing to make sacrifices for him.

At the end of the play, then, both Angelica and Valentine give something up, accept a degree of vulnerability that is dangerous for inhabitants of such a complex and subtle society, to obtain love. As the play starts, both Angelica and Valentine view love as something with a quantifiable value. It is exchangeable; it is something with which they can barter; it is something that can be measured in terms of its worth. But Valentine is forced, because of the genuine feelings that he discovers he has for Angelica, to agree to give up everything in his life that has value (his inheritance and her) so that she can be happy. And although Angelica ''wins'' this encounter, in that her wit and her superior strategy get her what she wanted (a loving husband), she also has to give something up: her independence, her mistrust, her cynicism about the world of love and lovers. By showing that he is willing to give up his inheritance, Valentine not only wins Angelica's love but gets to keep the money as well.

Source: Greg Barnhisel, Critical Essay on *Love for Love,* in *Drama for Students,* The Gale Group, 2002.

James Thompson

In the following essay, Thompson explores themes in Love for Love, *particularly reading and it's influence on the characters' actions and the roles they assume.*

In *Love for Love* Congreve turned to Jonsonian humors characters and a romance plot that is quintessential New Comedy. This conservatism appears to be quite deliberate, as the playwright displays his mastery of the history and techniques of the stage in this particularly literary play. The characters and action come not so much from life as from literature, which makes *Love for Love*, as Arthur Hoffman notes, highly allusive; Valentine's madness, for example, recalls Achilles, Ajax, Hercules, Amadis, Orlando, Quixote, Hamlet and Lear. Congreve also invests his characters with self-conscious theatricality, for they talk about acting, while they adopt and abandon various roles, patterning their behavior on models that are often explicitly literary.

Literary models appear in the opening scene of the play, where Valentine is discovered "in his Chamber Reading" Epictetus, whose work eventually provides him with a moral ideal. The initial act of reading is doubly significant because the scene is patterned on *Don Quixote,* a fiction about reading. Like Quixote, Valentine misinterprets what he reads: Epictetus is to Valentine what the chivalric hero Amadis is to Quixote, an ideal or model which is initially misunderstood and improperly imitated, but eventually understood and validated. Reading leads to acting, and thus Epictetus and *Don Quixote* initiate two major occupations of *Love for Love.*

Few of Congreve's readers have been interested in his use of Epictetus in this play. Charles Lyons writes that Valentine is attracted to the Stoic's asceticism and "indifference to physical pleasure and pain." Aubrey Williams goes further, connecting the opening Epictetan contempt for riches with the whole strain of paradox in the play, paradoxes which prefigure Valentine's climactic renunciation. The *Enchiridion* serves as a manual or index to proper values in this play. Some of these values are explicitly Stoical, but the three Restoration translators of Epictetus praise him as a moralist who anticipates the Christian emphasis on humility, patience, resignation and renunciation, the virtues which become centrally important to Valentine. Valentine's progress may be seen in his gradual understanding and acceptance of Epictetus's message, for he initially misunderstands the Stoic, who sets forth at the beginning of the *Enchiridion* the difficulty that Valentine must face:

> Respecting Man, things are divided thus:
> Some do not, and some do belong to us.
> Should you suppose what is not yours, your own,
> Twill cost you many a sigh, and many a groan;
> Many a dissapointment you will find,
> Abortive hope, and distracted mind.

Love for Love dramatizes many such disappointments, particularly Valentine's vain attempts to control or manipulate people and objects not within his power; but when he humbly resigns his pretentions to an estate which is not his own, and when he allows Angelica the independence to choose for herself, he finally demonstrates his assimilation of Epictetus's moral lesson.

Valentine, however, is far from humble at the start of the play, when, setting down his book, he proposes to "follow the Examples of the wisest and wittiest of Men of all Ages; these Poets and Philosophers." According to Epictetus, this course of action can be more foolish than wise:

> BOOKS HAVE AN INORDINATE INFLUENCE HERE. THROUGHOUT THIS PLAY, READING AND ROLE-PLAYING BECOME INTERTWINED AS CHARACTERS LIKE VALENTINE ENACT WHAT THEY HAVE READ."

> Wisdom, you say, is what you most desire,
> The only charming Blessing you admire;
> Therefore be bold, and fit yourself to bear
> Many a taunt, and patiently to hear
> The grinning foolish Rabble laugh aloud,
> At you the sport and pastime of the Crowd,
> While in like jeers they vent their filthy spleen,
> Whence all this gravity, this careless mien?
> And whence, of late, is this Pretender come,
> This new Proficient, this Musheroom,
> This young Philosopher with half a Beard:
> Of him, till now, we have no mention heard.
> Whence all this supercilious pride of late?
> This stiff behavior, this affected gate?
> This will perhaps be said; but be not you
> Sullen, nor bend a Supercilious brow,
> Lest you prove their vile reproaches true.

Both Jeremy and Scandal try to dissuade Valentine from turning railing poet, an occupation symptomatic not of the philosopher but the "Musheroom"; and Scandal's words, "impotent and vain," suggest the countless broken-fortuned libertines of Restoration comedy who resort to poetry and the stage for revenge. Above all, the "supercilious pride" of Valentine's proposals indicates how imperfectly he understands the philosopher; he would preach a lean diet of books, but Epictetus advises against this, too:

> If you have learn't to live on homely Food,
> To feed on Roots, and Lupine, be not proud.
> Since every beggar may be prais'd for that,
> He eats as little, is as temperate.

Epictetus provides, moreover, an even more explicit condemnation of Valentine's proud new role:

> When you in ev'ry place your self profess
> A deep Philosopher, you but express
> Much Vanity, much self-conceit betray,
> And shew you are not truly what you say.
> Your knowledge by your way of living shew,
> What is't, alas, to them, how much you know?
> Act as your Precepts teach, as at a Feast,
> Eat as 'tis fit, 'tis vain to teach the rest.

Valentine's finding Epictetus a source of pride rather than humility, in short, his misreading, may have its analogue in *Don Quixote,* because this first scene appears to be a conscious imitation of Thomas D'Urfey's play, *The Comical History of Don Quixote.* According to Colley Cibber, Congreve's play was ready before the dissolution of the United Company, that is, in early December, 1694. Parts I and II of D'Urfey's play were produced in mid and late May, and were published July 5 and July 23, 1694. D'Urfey's play was consequently on stage and in print when we may presume that Congreve was writing *Love for Love.*

Congreve certainly had an interest in Cervantes, for his library contained two editions of *Exemplary Novels* and five editions of *Don Quixote*; and he had alluded to "the Knight of the Sorrowful Face" in his first play, *The Old Batchelour.* He probably took particular notice of D'Urfey's *Don Quixote* because the female lead, Marcela, was the last role Anne Bracegirdle performed prior to playing Angelica, and Congreve is said to have been devoted to this actress and to have written parts specifically for her. Marcela was the occasion of notable success for Bracegirdle. It has been suggested that the success of D'Urfey's play is due to the music of Eccles and Purcell, and D'Urfey himself supports this view in his preface where he writes of "a Song so Incomparably well sung and acted by Mrs. Bracegirdle." She performed so well as to have a print engraved of her as Marcela; and in his review of a revival of the play in 1700, the only player whom John Downes mentions is Bracegirdle, indicating that Marcela and Bracegirdle had become identified in the way that Thomas Dogget became known for his portrayal of Ben. It thus may well be that D'Urfey's play was not far from Congreve's mind as he was writing *Love for Love.*

As we might expect, Bracegirdle's two roles, Marcela and Angelica, are quite similar. Marcela is described in the dramatis personae as "a young Shepherdess who hates Mankind, and by her Scorn occasions the Death of Chrysostem." When she is introduced at Chrysostem's funeral, Marcela is brazenly unrepentant for having caused his lovesickness:

> Marcela . . . and could he die for love? Fie! 'tis
> impossible!
> Who ever Knew a Wit do such a thing?
> Ambrosio. Triumphant Mischief: have you no
> Remorse?
> Marcela. I rather look on him as a good Actor;
> That practising the Art of deep deceit,
> As Whining, Swearing, Dying at your Feet,
> Crack'd some Life Artery with an Overstrain

> And dy'd of some Male Mischief in the Brain.

Angelica is similarly undaunted at having sent Valentine mad for love, for she "comes Tyrannically to insult a ruin'd Lover, and make Manifest the cruel Triumphs of her Beauty." In the end, both heroines are won by generosity, not wealth or empty protestations; in Part II, when Ambrosio saves her from rape, Marcela falls madly in love with him. She exclaims, "What Beauty, Riches, or Gloss of Honour, with all th'Allurements never could subdue, is conquer'd by this great, this generous action," just as Angelica yields to a "Generous Valentine."

It is, however, in the beginnings rather than the endings of the two plays, where the parallel is most suggestive. D'Urfey's Part I opens with a hungry Sancho Panza and a learned Don Quixote, and Sancho responds to his master's caution against unchivalric gluttony with the following aside: "Now I am to be fed with a tedious Tale of Knight-Errantry, when my guts are all in an uproar within me for want of better provision." The literally hungry servant in both plays is metaphorically fed learning by the master, and neither servant is satisfied with his intellectual feast. Compare Sancho's "Oons, this is a choice Diet, I grow damnable fat upon't" in *Don Quixote* to Jeremy's "You'll grow Develish fat upon this Paper-Diet" in *Love for Love.*

If Valentine and Jeremy are a transformation of Knight and Squire, then Valentine's misreading of Epictetus is quixotic; where Quixote's misreading of Amadis de Gaul prompts the adaptation of an inappropriate role as chivalric hero, Valentine's misreading of Epictetus prompts his adaptation of an inappropriate role as wit/poet/philosopher. Quixote, too, may be one of the many literary sources of Valentine's feigned madness; because Orlando and Amadis went mad for love, Quixote does so, too; and in his mad scenes, Valentine similarly imitates the best literary heroes, ancient and modern. Valentine's various poses are commonly connected with Theseus's exposition of madness in *A Midsummer Night's Dream,* drawing together the lunatic, the lover and the poet. So, too, the play's Horatian motto indicates another literary source of methodical madness. Books have an inordinate influence here. Throughout this play, reading and role-playing become intertwined as characters like Valentine enact what they have read.

Reading and misreading in *Love for Love* are not, however, confined to literature. Like Puritans seeking signs of their salvation, all of Congreve's characters also read the book of nature, from signs and stars to faces and people. The most obvious reader is the astrologer Foresight: ''A wise Man, and a Conscientious Man; a Searcher into Obscurity and Futurity.'' A man supposedly expert in physiognomy, Foresight misreads sickness in his own face on the suggestion of Scandal. Sir Sampson, on the other hand, reads not the heavens but human nature: ''I that know the World, and Men and Manners . . . don't believe a Syllable in the Sky and Stars, and Sun and Alamanacks, and Trash.'' In the end, they both fail reading comprehension; as Sir Sampson concludes, ''You're an illiterate Fool, and I'm another.''

The complexity of reading is nicely condensed in Congreve's ''hieroglyphick'' metaphor. Scandal first uses ''hieroglyphick'' in its relatively new metaphorical sense, in reference to emblematic pictures, while Sir Sampson characteristically uses the term in its concrete, physical sense, claiming to possess ''a Shoulder of an Egyptian King, that I purloyn'd from one of the Pyramids, powder'd with Hieroglyphicks.'' In the Restoration, hieroglyphs were the subject of endless speculation among virtuosi; but to Sir Sampson, the Egyptian symbols have no meaning. They are only a useless possession, a collectable. To placate Foresight, Sir Sampson desires that his son ''were an Egyptian mummy for thy sake''; children also are objects in his collection. To Foresight, hieroglyphs are mystical, arcane and indecipherable; Valentine's mad ravings ''are very Mysterious and Hieroglyphical.'' The metaphor reaches its climax when Valentine likens Angelica to a hieroglyph:

> Valentine. Understand! She is harder to understand than a Piece of *Aegyptian* Antiquity, or an *Irish* Manuscript; you may pore till you spoil your Eyes, and not improve your Knowledge.

> Jeremy. I have heard 'em say, Sir, they read hard Hebrew books backwards; may be you begin to read at the wrong end.

> Valentine. They say so of a Witches Pray'r, and Dreams and Dutch Almanacks are to be understood by contraries. But there's Regularity and Method in that; she is a Medal without Reverse of Inscription; for Indifference has both sides alike. Yet while she does not seem to hate me, I will pursue her, and know her if possible, in spight of the Opinion of my Satirical Friend, *Scandal,* who says,That Women are like Tricks
>   by slight of Hand,

> Which to admire, we should not understand.

Despite Valentine's protestations, it is not Angelica but Valentine who is obscure. As Jeremy suggests, Valentine may have begun at the wrong end, because if he cannot understand himself, how can he expect to understand Angelica? His attempts to bully or shame or trick her into loving him indicate that, as yet, he does not know his own mind, and he must make himself understood before he can try to understand others. In his mad scene, he tells Angelica, ''You are all white, a sheet of lovely spotless Paper, when you first are Born; but you are to be scrawl'd and blotted by every Goose's Quill.'' But Angelica would not be so incomprehensible had not Valentine, in effect, scrawled upon her; he has complicated her, made her wary and defensive, with all his intrigues and stratagems. Valentine has turned Angelica into a hieroglyph, and his desire to ''know her if possible'' implies a certain misplaced pride. Scandal's view that one ''should not understand'' may be more admirable than Sir Sampson's, Foresight's, and Valentine's pride in their interpretive powers, for they reduce people to emblems to be deciphered. Angelica refuses to be read, just as Hamlet refuses to be played upon and mastered. Angelica, like Millamant, appears to be serious when she asks Valentine to preserve a little mystery: ''Never let us know one another better.'' Reading in this respect is an imposition or intrusion upon another's privacy and independence. Once again, Valentine must distinguish between what is and what is not within his power and further renounce his efforts to master that which he cannot and should not control.

Reading or knowing others and reading oneself are reflexive and interdependent: Valentine cannot read or know Angelica partly because he ''does not know his Mind Two Hours.'' He is changeable from the very start of the play; as his father says, ''You are a Wit, and have been a Beau, and may be a—,'' an ellipsis which is suggestive of Valentine's protean nature. He tries fop, philosopher, poet, wit, madman—whatever will win Angelica. A word that Jeremy and Scandal apply to Valentine is ''turn''; he is forever ''turning Poet,'' or ''turning Soldier,'' or he should ''turn Pimp'': ''He that was so neer turning Poet yesterday morning, can't be much to seek in playing the Madman to day.'' ''Playing'' implies that Valentine's various fronts are actor's parts, just as his opening role of wit/poet/philosopher is an enacting of the precepts he has (mis)read in Epictetus. Here acting is but another aspect of misreading, the result of improper or partial understanding; Valentine does not know the whole play in which he is performing, and, like an actor in rehearsal, he is learning to read his proper role. Other characters are also conscious of the roles they play, often achieving their ends by adopting new parts and costumes. Frail, Scandal, and Sir Sampson are all said to be "Players" or to have "Parts." We are shown an actors' "nursery" as Prue carefully learns a new part at the prompting of Tattle. Nor is Valentine the only one to adopt a role from his reading, for his father's behavior in his first scene with Foresight is clearly based on travel literature. Conscious playing is hardly unique in seventeenth-century drama, and would not be of interest here but for the fact that the efficacy and propriety of acting, involving matters of social adaptability, expediency and constancy, are questioned throughout.

Like so much of Restoration comedy, *Love for Love* contrasts those who can and cannot change. The fixity of humors characters like Ben, Prue, or Foresight is epitomized by Foresight's resignation: "if I were born to be a Cuckold, there's no more to be said." Still fixity is not always viewed so negatively; even though Ben is most often a comic butt, his stolidity contrasts favorably with the chameleon sisters, Mrs. Frail and Mrs. Foresight. Ben's simple loyalty is set against the worldly Frail, who changes roles and attitudes at a moment's notice. Similarly, Scandal, almost at the same time, plays astrologer to Foresight and lover to his wife, while she can summon up interest or indifference to Scandal on the spur of the moment; such extreme flexibility seems motivated by self-interest. Sir Sampson is only too willing to adopt a new role or a new attitude, and can change at will from despotic to doting father. He switches his family around, making each of his sons eldest for a time and subsequently abandoning both; the only constant in Sir Sampson's characters is his selfishness.

Constancy is, indeed, a major theme in *Love for Love*, one that is always before us from the song, "I tell thee, Charmion," to the images of "inconstant Element(s)"; "the Tide turn'd"; and the "Inconstancy" of the moon. Of all these traditional emblems, changeability or inconstancy is most beautifully expressed in the wind metaphor, a nautical figure that originates with Ben. Frail explains her sudden reversal towards Ben by claiming "Only the Wind's chang'd," and when Angelica rejects his father, Ben consoles him with the same phrase. While fickle characters, like ships, turn with the wind, Frail introduces the opposite metaphor: "What, has my Sea-Lover lost his Anchor of Hope." The anchor, an emblem of constancy, stability and hope, is common to Stoics, including Epictetus, who

likens the constant man to a ship at anchor: "Nor rowling Seas, nor an impetuous Wind, / Can over set this Ballast of the mind."

Valentine remains constant to Angelica, his anchor of hope, but in his intrigues and poses, he is as changeable as all the other schemers. Nevertheless, though these poses designed to win Angelica are unsuccessful, it does not follow that role-playing per se is condemned. Angelica herself pretends indifference in order "to make this utmost Tryal of Valentine's Virtue," for she must test or try Valentine in order to distinguish his love from the self-interest displayed by every other character in the play. Role-playing is not only useful but also necessary and inescapable according to the *topos theatrum mundi*. This figure is a commonplace from Democritus to John Bunyan, but if there was a *locus classicus*, it was Epictetus, who was most famous for his elaborate, moralized analogy between the world and the stage:

> While on this busie Stage, the World, you stay,
> You're as it were the Actor of a Play;
> Of such a Part therein as he thinks fit,
> To whom belongs the power of giving it.
> Longer or shorter is your Part, as he,
> The Master of the Revels, shall decree.
> If he command you act the Beggar's Part,
> Do it with all the Skill, with all your Art,
> Though mean the Character, yet ne're complain;
> Perform it well, as much applause you'll gain
> As he whose Princely Grandeur fills the Stage,
> And frights all near him in heroick Rage.

Although this comparison is ubiquitous, it has various interpretations; it is one thing to play the role assigned by the heavenly playwright or director and quite another to play an actor in repertory, switching from one role to the next all season. Epictetus's analogy continues,

> Say you a Cit or Cripple represent,
> Let each be done with the best management.
> 'Tis in your power to perform with Art,
> Though not within your pow'r to chuse the Part.

Role-playing can be seen as fundamentally artificial and unnatural, as did the Puritans in their antitheatrical writings, or as an accurate metaphor for the unalterable condition of this world. Jonas Barrish demonstrates that the player can even function as a metaphor for potentiality; in the Neoplatonism of Pico and Ficino, the protean actor, switching from role to role, represents all that men are capable of becoming.

Congreve sees acting as somewhere between the folly as it was seen by the Puritans and the glory as it was seen by the Neoplatonists; and his creation

Valentine must find a middle way between his fickle father and his inflexible brother. The play suggests that role-playing is necessary but that there are proper and improper roles for each character. In his disputation with his father and Jeremy, Valentine argues that he has been brought up to accept a rightful place, which is not a natural calling so much as a specific role to which he has been raised, a role which is as different from Ben's as it is from Jeremy's. Ben can no more be turned into the eldest son than he can be turned into a beau, and it is unnatural for Sir Sampson to try to change him into either.

If Valentine has a proper role to play, it therefore follows that his contrived roles are improper, something which he himself comes to realize; but unfortunately he grows accustomed to his acting. When he tells Angelica, ''The Comedy draws to an end, and let us think of leaving acting, and be our selves,'' she willfully refuses to understand him, and he finds himself cast in a role he no longer wishes to play. As he himself says, ''I know no effectual Difference between continued Affectation and Reality.'' Even by the end of Act Four, Valentine has still not accepted the humility and resignation that he should have learned from Epictetus. It is Scandal who charts the correct path for his friend: ''he may descend from his Exaltation of madness into the road of common Sense, and be content only to be made a Fool with other reasonable People.'' Instead of trying to make fools of others, he must consent to be one, and in Act Five he calls himself a fool. As Montaigne writes, ''To learne that another hath eyther spoken a foolish jest, or committed a sottish act, is a thing of nothing. A man must learne, that he is but a foole: A much more ample and important instruction.'' Epictetus also regards the acceptance of one's folly as a mark of wisdom:

> Wou'd you be wise? ne're take it ill you're thought
> A Fool, because you tamely set at Nought
> Things not within your pow'r.

Paradoxically, Valentine's success can only be achieved through failure, the game of ''Losing Loadum,'' wherein he can ''win a Mistress, with a losing hand.'' The resolution of dispossession, of renunciation, and of humility can only be effected by throwing over his plots and his roles and admitting failure; he must accept the ''Ruine'' with which his father threatens him. In the first scene, Valentine says, ''I'll pursue *Angelica* with more Love than ever, and appear more notoriously her Admirer in this Restraint, than when I openly rival'd the rich Fops, that made Court to her; so shall my Poverty be

a mortification to her Pride.'' Instead of her mortification, it is he who is shamed and humbled; the biter is bit, and he receives poetic justice. This plot is surely one of the world's oldest, and what Walter Davis has written of the *Arcadia* is as appropriate for Congreve's Valentine as it is for Sidney's Musidorus and Pyrocles; like them, he must undergo a trial and willingly accept the proper role assigned to him by the divine playwright: ''For failure becomes the necessary condition for submission to Providence; the hero must be released from all external controls or pressures in order to act out all his tendencies to lust, lassitude, deceit, and despair and so come to know his own weaknesses, to trust God to repair them, and hence to purify himself to them.''

Valentine wins Angelica through his constancy; and the answer to Scandal's central question, ''Who would die a Martyr to Sense in a Country where the Religion is Folly?'' is, of course, Valentine. ''How few, like Valentine,'' concludes Angelica, ''would persevere even unto Martyrdom, and sacrifice their Interest to their Constancy.'' Earlier, when pressed to decide, she replied, ''I can't. Resolution must come to me,'' but in the end, Valentine brings resolution, firmness, conviction and constancy to her, the lesson he has finally learned of Epictetus. His course contains elements of both gradual improvement and abrupt conversion. The sequence of his roles suggests improvement, for wit appears better than fop, and his feigned madness does lead to his final, true madness. At the same time his final act is predicated on the recognition that all his previous roles have been wrong; it is not that playing is condemned, but that he does not, until Act Five, know what his right role is. When Valentine is willing to give up his own good for another, when he willingly ''plays the fool,'' he has transcended self-interest, reaching the ideal goal of love and the ideal role of lover.

Source: James Thompson, ''Reading and Acting in *Love for Love*,'' in *Essays in Literature*, Vol. 7, No. 11, Spring 1980, pp. 21–30.

Harold Love

In the following essay excerpt, Love explores the relationship between Valentine and Angelica, and how the townspeople affect that romance in Congreve's Love for Love.

II

The climax of *Love for Love* is Angelica's acceptance of the reformed Valentine. It comes in two words, 'Generous *Valentine*', which, although they were written for the mouth of Anne Bracegirdle, not Elizabeth Barry, call for all the eloquence of an 'Ah! poor *Castalio*!' 'Generous' here is a Virgilian characteristic epithet expressing to us the significant truth of Valentine, his singularity and distinction as a human being. It is also, as the concluding point of his education, our chief clue to what the substance of that education has been. The meaning of the word in the seventeenth century was more complex than its normal sense in modern English would suggest, but seeing Angelica's words were prompted by the speech of Valentine immediately preceding them, we can assume that it is here that the nature of Valentine's generosity will be most clearly displayed:

> *Valentine.* I have been disappointed of my only Hope; and he that loses hope may part with any thing. I never valu'd Fortune, but as it was subservient to my Pleasure; and my only Pleasure was to please this Lady: I have made many vain Attempts, and find at last, that nothing but my Ruine can effect it: Which, for that Reason, I will sign to—Give me the Paper.

The basic thing is that Valentine has learned to trust and to give, absolutely and without reservation. When Angelica sees this she is prepared to give herself just as unconditionally in return. But for her to have done so without this assurance would have been disastrous. It is therefore Valentine who has taken the crucial step in resolving the relationship, and he has done this by challenging the first principle of town morality on a scale that even the trusting Ben and pliable Prue might have baulked at.

When we first see Valentine in Act I he is in every sense a creature of the town. He has exhausted his money in his pursuit of Angelica (the interpretation of the other characters would be no doubt that she has milked him of it) but without securing any profession of love in return. This is hardly surprising: his extravagant spending has been an attempt to buy her and she has been perfectly aware of this and is not prepared to be for sale. His next plan, and one that is open to much the same objections, is to shame her:

> *Valentine.* Well; and now I am poor, I have an opportunity to be reveng'd on 'em all; I'll pursue *Angelica* with more Love than ever, and appear more notoriously her Admirer in this Restraint, than when I openly rival'd the rich Fops, that made Court to her; so shall my Poverty be a Mortification to her Pride . . .

Valentine is still in this speech picturing Angelica as a quarry to be hunted, not as a human equal to be loved. It is also clear that his courtship is not

directed at her alone, but is simultaneously a performance put on to gain the approbation of the town. In compensation for these imperceptive and rather narcissistic attitudes, we are also made aware of an agreeable impulsiveness, a determination to make the best of whatever his situation offers, and a general openness to new possibilities, which raise him well above the usual pitch of the town. (Being unable to afford breakfast he has been edifying himself with a study of the Stoics.) He still has a chance to change. A visit from the nurse of one of his illegitimate children gives him a chance to display generosity in the limited modern sense by somehow finding her some money and his residual ill-nature by a quip about infanticide. The next visitors are Trapland, a creditor, accompanied by two officers, and, on another errand, Valentine's father's steward. Between them the choice is put to Valentine of accepting his father's proposal for the payment of his debts, which is to surrender his right in the family inheritance, or to go to prison. Valentine consents, as the arrangement will also permit him to leave his lodgings and go in search of Angelica, although here Scandal is pessimistic about his chances:

> *Scandal.* A very desperate demonstration of your love to *Angelica:* And I think she has never given you any assurance of hers.
>
> *Valentine.* You know her temper; she never gave me any great reason either for hope or despair.
>
> *Scandal.* Women of her airy temper, as they seldom think before they act, so they rarely give us any light to guess at what they mean: But you have little reason to believe that a Woman of this Age, who has had an indifference for you in your Prosperity, will fall in love with your ill Fortune; besides, *Angelica* has a great Fortune of her own; and great Fortunes either expect another great Fortune, or a Fool.

From the town's point of view his reasoning could hardly be faulted.

In the following act we receive our first sight of Angelica and are given no reason to question Scandal's diagnosis of her 'airy temper.' She comes in to demand her uncle's coach, ridicules his harmless obsession with astrology, taunts him openly with his wife's infidelity, confesses to spying on him through a keyhole, and threatens to denounce him to the magistrates as a wizard. None of this is at all serious, but there is still a strong air of gratuitous bullying about it. Our hero has not given very many signs of promise, and neither at this stage does our heroine. Valentine is a town rake and she, to all appearances, is little better than a town miss, superbly adroit in the skills of social manipulation, and not above keeping these skills razor-sharp by a little practice in the domestic circle. What is not clear is whether the purpose of this formidable conversational armoury is offensive or defensive, whether there is an Araminta behind the mask or just another Belinda.

When we see Angelica next she is together for the first time in the play with Valentine and once again she is giving nothing away:

> *Angelica.* You can't accuse me of Inconstancy; I never told you, that I lov'd you.
>
> *Valentine.* But I can accuse you of Uncertainty, for not telling me whether you did or no.
>
> *Angelica.* You mistake Indifference for Uncertainty; I never had Concern enough to ask my self the Question.

Later in the play, at the moment of self-revelation in Act V, we are to discover that she did love him after all; but in the present scene there is no sign of this. And it is not hard to fathom the reasons for Angelica's wariness. Living in a world of Tattles and Frails, she has had to learn to handle their weapons even better than they do themselves. To be in love is to be in a position of vulnerability. The rule of the town is to take advantage of the vulnerable. To be in love, and to reveal this love, is to invite the person you love to take advantage of you. The only safe course, therefore, is to conceal love under the affectation of indifference or dislike. This was Tattle's first lesson to Prue, and an identical principle guides Angelica's behaviour towards Valentine. The problem with Valentine is not simply that he is a town rake and lives by the assumptions of a town rake: that love is a hunt or pursuit, that women are mercenary simpletons to be bought or tricked into submission, that 'He alone won't Betray in whom none will Confide/And the Nymph may be Chaste that has never been Try'd.' If that were all that there was to him, Angelica would not have fallen in love with him in the first place. Valentine in fact has a number of very good and un-town-like instincts. He is not, for instance, interested in money for its own sake but only as a means of helping him to Angelica. (Though this still, of course, makes him guilty of the assumption that she is available to be bought.) His real trouble is that he insists on interpreting other people's behaviour, including Angelica's, according to the cynical principles of the town and Scandal. He is therefore in the grip of two wrong images, one of himself and one of Angelica, each reinforcing the other. For Angelica to reveal the wrongness of his image of her, which would not be hard as it is largely of her own creation, would be of no use until he had learned to

> " IF THEY WERE TO LIVE THEIR LIVES ACCORDING TO THE TOWN'S TERMS THERE WOULD ALWAYS HAVE TO BE SOME KIND OF MASK IN PLACE."

interpret such an action according to principles other than those of the Age. It is only when he has made the breakthrough of his own accord and come to see himself in completely new terms that it will be safe for her to reveal that she is not what he thought she was. It is this which Angelica is trying to explain to him when at the end of the scene he asks her whether she is going to 'come to a Resolution' and she replies 'I can't. Resolution must come to me, or I shall never have one.' It is Valentine who has to find both their ways out of the vicious circle.

At this stage in the play, however, the probability of such a breakthrough does not seem very high. The immediate task of Scandal and Valentine is to test the genuineness of Angelica's indifference, with the aim, should they find any evidence of feigning, of exploiting the revealed vulnerability as ruthlessly as possible. Scandal, whose power to fathom the masks and stratagems of the town has already been presented for our admiration in Act I, is clearly of the opinion that there is more to her behaviour than meets the eye. Taking up her 'I never had Concern enough to ask my self the Question' quoted earlier, he inserts a sly hint of his disbelief:

> *Scandal.* Nor good Nature enough to answer him that did ask you: I'll say that for you, Madam.
>
> *Angelica.* What, are you setting up for good Nature?
>
> *Scandal.* Only for the affectation of it, as the Women do for ill Nature.

Scandal's insight here amounts to nothing more than the normal town assumption that things are probably the reverse of what they seem, or, as Tattle enlarges, 'All well-bred Persons Lie! . . . you must never speak what you think: Your words must contradict your thoughts . . .' In reply to this, Angelica is rather surprisingly prepared to concede that he may be right but challenges him to persuade Valentine of this. For Angelica knows that Valentine has no real understanding of her and to this extent cannot seriously threaten her. And Valentine, again rather surprisingly, is perfectly prepared to confess to his ignorance both of her and mankind: 'I shall receive no Benefit from the Opinion: For I know no effectual Difference between continued Affectation and Reality.' This passage is sometimes quoted out of context as if it were a statement of Congreve's personal attitude towards social role-playing, but this is not so. The point of the lines is to show the inadequacy of Valentine's understanding both of himself and of others, for there *is* a difference between reality and continued affectation, a difference which Angelica understands perfectly because it is something she has to live with all the time.

The same issues, along with one or two new ones, inform the comedy of the subsequent scene between Angelica, the two men, and Tattle. Tattle embodies the values and expectations of the town in their purest state. Where Valentine had felt unable to distinguish between continued affectation and reality but was not prepared to deny that there was such a difference, Tattle is so far gone as to have mistaken his own affectations for reality. His conversation is a long romance on the theme of his prowess as a lover. At the same time, as we saw in Act I, he is inordinately proud of his reputation for discretion. This is partly an effect of his desire to be thought a wit and partly a technique of seduction in its own right, on the principle that women would be more inclined to have affairs with a man who could be relied on to keep it a secret. At the present juncture he is exhibiting his accomplishments, secrecy among them, for the benefit of Angelica. The fun of the scene lies in the careful manœuvring by which Valentine and Scandal set his two reputations at odds with each other, a subtle exercise in the art which Wilkinson calls 'enjoying the fool.' In trying to defend his reputation for secrecy he is forced to assert that he had 'never had the good Fortune to be trusted once with a Lady's Secret.' This brings the objection from Angelica 'But whence comes the Reputation of Mr. *Tattle*'s Secresie, if he was never trusted?,' putting him in the position of having to betray his reputation in order to defend it:

> *Tattle.* Well, my Witnesses are not present—But I confess I have had Favours from Persons—But as the Favours are numberless, so the Persons are nameless.
>
> *Scandal.* Pooh, pox, this proves nothing.
>
> *Tattle.* No? I can shew Letters, Locketts, Pictures, and Rings, and if there be occasion for Witnesses, I can summon the Maids at the Chocolate-Houses, all the Porters of *Pall-Mall* and *Covent-Garden,* the Doorkeepers at the Play-House, the Drawers at *Locket's, Pontack's,* the *Rummer, Spring Garden;* my own

Landlady and *Valet de Chambre;* all who shall make Oath, that I receive more Letters than the Secretary's Office; and that I have more Vizor-Masks to enquire for me, than ever went to see the Hermaphrodite, or the Naked Prince. And it is notorious, that in a Country Church, once, an Enquiry being made, who I was, it was answer'd, I was the famous *Tattle,* who had ruin'd so many Women.

> *Valentine.* It was there, I suppose, you got the Nick-Name of the *Great Turk.*
>
> *Tattle.* True; I was call'd *Turk-Tattle* all over the Parish—

Tattle's narcissistic male egotism is exactly what Angelica is trying to protect herself from. However, his situation is also relevant to hers in another way. As he has destroyed his reputation for secrecy in defending it; so she is still in the position where to reveal her love to an unregenerate Valentine would be to resign herself forever to the role of conquered quarry. Hers is a genuine secrecy, unlike Tattle's fraudulent one, but is just as self-defeating.

By this time Scandal has a strong suspicion that Angelica is more kindly disposed than she would have the men believe. When he exits it is with the promise to Valentine 'I've something in my Head to communicate to you'—presumably the pretence of madness which is to be Valentine's last and most daring throw in his attempt to confound his father and to extract a capitulation from Angelica on his terms rather than hers. Angelica is the first to call on him after his supposed condition has been proclaimed, and on her entrance comes close to betraying her real feelings. 'She's concern'd, and loves him' is Scandal's diagnosis. But Scandal has forgotten, or perhaps never realized, that she is quite as brilliant a penetrator of pretence as himself, and he betrays his own game by an unguarded wink to Jeremy. Having gauged the true situation, Angelica's responsibility is to repay trick with trick, which she does by denying outright that she loves Valentine and then announcing on the basis of excellent London reasons that she will not see him after all:

> But I have consider'd that Passions are unreasonable and involuntary; if he loves, he can't help it; and if I don't love, I can't help it; no more than he can help his being a Man, or I my being a Woman; or no more than I can help my want of Inclination to stay longer here. . .

Angelica here is doing no more than give the men the treatment appropriate to the role in which they insist on casting her. She sweeps out leaving Scandal undisturbed in his belief in the weathercock nature of 'this same Womankind.' Later she will be back to put Valentine through his paces more thoroughly.

Angelica resents the situation because it shows that Valentine is still seeing the world in terms of Scandal's bitter satiric vignettes at the close of Act I, among them 'Pride, Folly, Affectation, Wantonness, Inconstancy, Covetousness, Dissimulation, Malice, and Ignorance' as the image of a 'celebrated Beauty.' But it is now Valentine's turn to grow satirical: his 'madness' takes the form of ringing denunciations directed at such targets as lawyers, citizens, and elderly husbands; when he comes to address Angelica, however, the tone changes and the accents of simulated madness give way to a perfectly composed beauty:

> *Angelica.* Do you know me, *Valentine*?
>
> *Valentine.* Oh very well.
>
> *Angelica.* Who am I?
>
> *Valentine.* You're a Woman,—One to whom Heav'n gave Beauty, when it grafted Roses on a Briar. You are the reflection of Heav'n in a Pond, and he that leaps at you is sunk. You are all white, a sheet of lovely spotless Paper, when you first are Born; but you are to be scrawl'd and blotted by every Goose's Quill. I know you; for I lov'd a Woman, and lov'd her so long, that I found out a strange thing: I found out what a Woman was good for.
>
> *Tattle.* Aye, prithee, what's that?
>
> *Valentine.* Why to keep a Secret.
>
> *Tattle.* O Lord!
>
> *Valentine.* O exceeding good to keep a Secret: For tho' she should tell, yet she is not to be believ'd.

The speech is one of the few in the play where Congreve's language achieves a genuine richness of poetic implication, yet once again the images are expressions of an imperfect understanding: Angelica had asked Valentine if he knew her, and he reveals very clearly in his reply that he knows only the false self she shows to the town. He does not see that the scrawls and blots are of his own imagination: that were he to leap, he would not be sunk at all. Yet the closing lines do suggest that he has intimations of a truth unknown to him before the experiment with madness. Angelica has indeed kept a secret, two secrets in fact: that she is in love with him, and that she is not the person he and the town take her for. He is beginning to know this without knowing that he knows.

There is still, however, a long way to go. Angelica is not yet won; she is still resentful of the contemptuous shallowness of his artifices; and when

he trustingly confesses the stratagem, she will not yield an inch in return. His request is that, as he puts off his pretence of madness, so she should suspend her affectation of disregard:

> Nay faith, now let us understand one another, Hypocrisie apart,—The Comedy draws toward an end, and let us think of leaving acting, and be our selves; and since you have lov'd me, you must own I have at length deserv'd you shou'd confess it.

This is too simple altogether. For one thing it shows that he still regards courtship as a matter of trickery and charades. So Angelica repays him in kind by pretending that she still believes him to be mad and treating his protestations of sanity as a madman's self-delusion. She is also quick to take him up on his reasons for adopting the stratagem:

> *Valentine* . . . my seeming Madness has deceiv'd my Father, and procur'd me time to think of means to reconcile me to him; and preserve the right of my Inheritance to his Estate; which otherwise by Articles, I must this Morning have resign'd: And this I had inform'd you of to Day, but you were gone, before I knew you had been here.
>
> *Angelica.* How! I thought your love of me had caus'd this Transport in your Soul; which, it seems, you only counterfeited, for mercenary Ends and sordid Interest.
>
> *Valentine.* Nay, now you do me Wrong; for if any Interest was considered, it was yours; since I thought I wanted more than Love, to make me worthy of you.
>
> *Angelica.* Then you thought me mercenary—But how am I deluded by this Interval of Sense, to reason with a Madman?

Valentine's frankness has been returned with a town miss's trick which, of course, he knows to be a town miss's trick. But he is also to be given a clue to the secret which still eludes him. Before she leaves, Angelica speaks to him in words which have some of the elegiac quality of his own mad language, and which are her most explicit statement of her sense of the situation:

> *Valentine.* You are not leaving me in this Uncertainty?
>
> *Angelica.* Wou'd any thing, but a Madman complain of Uncertainty? Uncertainty and Expectation are the Joys of Life. Security is an insipid thing, and the overtaking and possessing of a Wish, discovers the Folly of the Chase. Never let us know one another better; for the Pleasure of a Masquerade is done, when we come to shew Faces; But I'll tell you two things before I leave you; I am not the Fool you take me for; and you are Mad and don't know it.

In returning him the unmasking image Angelica is conceding what is after all a central fact of the play—that the world of masks, of illusion, of inconstancy, of trickery, of unceasing psychological combat, of the rake's pursuit and the woman's hypocritical refusal, the world in which 'Love hates to center in a Point assign'd, / But runs with Joy the Circle of the Mind', is in its way an exciting, testing world. Valentine has thoroughly enjoyed his life in it, and so far he has resisted all her attempts to make him leave it. But now that Angelica has seen beyond it she is not to be drawn back. For all its dazzle and movement it is a world in which it is impossible to trust or to love. The relationship of Angelica and Valentine has been conducted along the lines prescribed by the world and behind the masks of its making. When Valentine asks her to take off her mask it is in the expectation of finding a face beneath which will be not very different from the mask. Appreciating this, Angelica is only being fair in warning him that 'the Pleasure of a Masquerade is done, when we come to shew Faces.' If they were to live their lives according to the town's terms there would always have to be some kind of mask in place. But what if the face beneath the mask were itself a mask and the face beneath that second mask one that Valentine had never dreamed of? If this were so it is possible that she might after all not be a fool, which is the rake's basic assumption about the women he pursues by trick and bribe, and that Valentine might well be led into actions which by all the standards of the town (and when the moment comes Scandal is to use exactly this word) are 'mad' ones. If she does not succeed in enlightening him she is at least able to puzzle him. 'She is harder to be understood than a Piece of *Ægyptian* Antiquity, or an *Irish* Manuscript; you may pore till you spoil your Eyes, and not improve your Knowledge.' Yet he has at least recognized that there is a mystery and that his 'Lesson' must have a 'Moral'; which is a start. And at the close of the scene he is even prepared to query one of the dicta of the hitherto infallible Scandal. By the time we see him again he has discovered the answer which, all things considered, is a very simple one. For Scandal's principle of 'trust to no one' he has substituted another—'if you do trust, trust absolutely'—and his trust is rewarded. At the very moment he is about to give assent to the deed of disinheritance, Angelica tears the earlier bond and in the same breath renounces the marriage with Sir Sampson. What is it that he has discovered to bring about this change? His preparedness to sacrifice himself is the most obvious thing; but this is itself the fruit of a deeper awareness. The solution is in her answer to the question he asks her before he proceeds to sign to his own undoing:

> 'Tis true, you have a great while pretended Love to me; nay, what if you were sincere? still you must pardon me, if I think my own Inclinations have a better Right to dispose of my Person, than yours.

The notion that other people's persons should be in their own disposal, and not one's own, is not particularly original, but the difficulty that Valentine has had in reaching it should caution us against imagining it to be self-evident. For the whole system of the town had been built on an explicit denial of it. Valentine has at last emerged from the delusion, and through this from his poverty. Ironically enough the second part of the benison has been brought about by the most arrant town trick of all—and its perpetrator has been Angelica.

III

We have followed the action of *Love for Love* through to the point of resolution. The question still has to be asked whether that resolution is a satisfactory one. Triviality and self-seeking are to be countered with idealism; but how valid is the countering? May it not be open to the accusation of sentimental unreality just as Congreve's presentation of the world may be to the charge of immature cynicism? Both these suggestions have been made.

Part of the trouble here lies in the abstract, externalized way in which Congreve presents his resolution. Assuming that the real climax of the play is Valentine's acceptance of Angelica not as a quarry or an opponent but as a fellow human being with exactly the same rights as himself, it can still be argued that we do not actually experience what this realization means for Valentine. The crucial stage in his growth to realization comes between his exit in Act IV and his entrance in Act V. By the time he reappears he has discovered what previously eluded him; but we are not shown how this happens or what it feels like to have it happen; we simply have to accept it as it is stated. The same holds for Angelica. The assumption of the play is that behind the façade of the town jilt there is a profound longing for those human satisfactions that the town ignores and a genuine capacity for unselfish love; but it is only in isolated speeches that we have any direct sense of this part of her; the rest has to be deduced from things that she states in a fairly abstract way and the nature of her reactions to the stratagems of Valentine and Scandal.

I would suggest that this effect was quite deliberate on Congreve's part and is an important clue to the kind of comedy he is writing. Here we need to remember that the immediate ancestor of Restoration comedy is not Jacobean comedy but that phase of Caroline comedy when it was most under the influence of the court masque. The essence of a masque, to borrow a phrase from Chapter I, is that it should give 'sensuous life to abstract formulations.' In comedy under the influence of the masque the playwright's primary interest will be the profile of the idea rather than depth of characterization and we should not complain if the persons of the drama are occasionally allowed to dwindle into cut-outs. One could argue that this kind of comedy is more restricted in its possibilities than the kind which takes personality as its starting point and allows us not only to observe the actions of the characters, but to share in their inner growth; yet having conceded this, one is not entitled to judge one kind as if it were an unsuccessful attempt at the other. (If we object to Congreve's methods we should remember that they are also Molière's and Shaw's.) The minuet of ideas which is the structural basis of Congreve's play is there to be appreciated as a minuet, the theatrical articulation of an abstract ideal of love and gentility. Congreve is not particularly interested in how these ideals are to be made workable at the level of individual, everyday living, or at least not in *Love for Love*.

For these reasons, the criticism of the play which claims that its values are arbitrary and unrealized seems to me a little beside the point. There is still, moreover, the question of whether the abstract ideals so elegantly traced out in the course of the minuet are the true informing values of the comedy. I would suggest that they are probably not, and that the most valuable thing the play has to give us is much simpler. Despite its preoccupation with the least sublime of human passions, its singularly unsatisfactory gallery of characters, and Congreve's insistence on showing us just why these characters are unsatisfactory, the overall sense given by *Love for Love* is of an immense and heartening liveliness— one is tempted to say a joy. Squalid and selfish as the creatures of the town are, they do not repel us in the way the corresponding characters in Jonson do and we may even envy them their unconquerable bravura and their outrageous and wholly unjustified self-admiration, much as on a larger scale we do Falstaff's. I suggested earlier that *Love for Love* was the most Shakespearean of Congreve's plays. In an influential essay contrasting the Shakespearean and Jonsonian styles in comedy Nevill Coghill suggested that the essence of the former lay in the assertion 'that life is to be grasped.' This is surely the reason why Congreve's characters remain attractive. Despite the fact that the life they possess is

by any objective standard paltry, dishonest, and trivial, they are prepared to lay hold of it with every atom of energy in their beings. There can be a vividness, an elevation, even to being a fop, a tyrannical braggart, or a temporarily stranded porpoise, as long as one is prepared to take possession of the role with the self-proclaiming gusto of a Tattle, a Sampson, or a Ben. There may even be a sublimity of sorts in being a cuckold philosopher if one can say with the heroic fatalism of Foresight, 'Why if I was born to be a Cuckold, there's no more to be said—.' In the case of Valentine the spectacle is one of a character who has succeeded in extracting 'a quintessence even from nothingness'— understanding from madness, truth from jest, love from despair, generosity from selfishness. It is our sense of this miracle, this heroic laying hold of every possibility of even the most tawdry and unsatisfactory existence which allows us to claim for *Love for Love* a rank among Restoration comedies only just beneath that of *The Way of the World*.

Source: Harold Love, "*Love for Love*," in *Congreve*, Rowman and Littlefield, 1974, pp. 60–84.

F. P. Jarvis

In the following essay, Jarvis discusses how the ideas of John Locke and other philosophers informed Congreve's writing of Love for Love.

I

Criticism of Congreve's *Love for Love* prior to Norman Holland's publication of *The First Modern Comedies* in 1959 is relatively unimpressive. Writers of articles appearing in scholarly journals have studiously avoided the larger concerns of the play by focusing their microscopes on such minutiae as the attribution of the ballad "A Soldier and a Sailor" in Act III; Sailor Ben's literary genealogy; the identification of the scene in Act III that Congreve in his dedication to the Earl of Dorset claims to have omitted from the first public performance of the play on April 30, 1695, at Lincoln's Inn Fields; and Congreve's possible indebtedness to Dryden's *Wild Gallant* for scenes in Acts III and V.

Scarcely more impressive are the perfunctory and largely repetitious readings of the play as a proto-sentimental comedy, which one finds in most of the standard studies of Restoration comedy. Bonamy Dobrée, for instance, in 1924 and again in 1963, discovers in *Love for Love* an expression of Congreve's deepest aspiration—his longing to find the world nobler than it really is. "The fear of lost illusion haunts him," Dobrée writes in 1924. "Like

> CONGREVE, IN THE END, PROVES SOMETHING OF A SKEPTIC IN TERMS OF HIS CONFIDENCE IN THE ABILITY OF REASON TO DISCERN MAN AND CONSEQUENTLY REGULATE HUMAN AFFAIRS."

Valentine, in *Love for Love*, Congreve is melancholy at the thought of spoiled ideals and spoiled beauty." In a similar vein, he writes again, in 1963, "The love-affair between Valentine and Angelica brings out his [Congreve's] fear of disillusion, his insistence that the precious thing in life, affection in human relations, must be preserved at all costs."

Thomas Fujimura, ostensibly focusing his attention exclusively on the play rather than on the playwright's psyche, nearly falls victim to the same error as Dobrée. After observing that Congreve was "too warm-hearted and moral to be a Truewit," he implicitly identifies the playwright with his protagonist several pages later by analyzing Valentine in the same terms he used for Congreve. Rather than the libertine he professes to be, Fujimura writes, Valentine is a "reformed libertine, and he reveals a fundamentally sound (and even moral) character . . . He is also more introspective and thoughtful than most Truewits . . . What makes Valentine a more subtle and attractive figure . . . is the suggestion of this latent reflectiveness, of a mind sensitive enough to have some apprehension of the undercurrents of human existence."

Both of the foregoing approaches to *Love for Love*—on the one hand, investigation of the facts behind the play, and on the other, appraisal of the play in the light of Congreve's life and the changing tastes of the late 1690's—have a legitimate place in Congreve scholarship, especially since the facts of Congreve's life and career as a dramatist are relatively obscure, and since his position as a playwright in relation to the high Restoration comedy of the 1670's and the sentimental comedy of the early eighteenth century is still in dispute. Nevertheless, the narrow range of interests of the one approach and the broad, often tangential interests of the other left something of a vacuum in *Love for Love* criti-

cism until Norman Holland's book appeared in 1959, which for the first time provided students of Restoration comedy with a thorough and penetrating analysis of the play *qua* play. Since the publication of Holland's work three additional studies have appeared: Charles Lyons' article, "Congreve's Miracle of Love," and W. H. Van Voris' analysis of the play in a volume entitled *The Cultivated Stance: The Design of Congreve's Plays,* both of which are heavily indebted to Holland's seminal essay; and, most recently, Aubrey Williams' cursory but highly suggestive treatment of the play in a study entitled "Poetical Justice, the Contrivances of Providence, and the Works of Congreve," an independent analysis of Congreve's drama in the light of popular religious assumptions of the day, wherein the author effectively questions Lyons' premise concerning "the naturalistic perspective of *Love for Love.*"

The vital importance of Holland's study lies in his recognition of John Locke's *Essay Concerning Human Understanding* (1690) as the informing source of *Love for Love* (1695). It is an "epistemological comedy," Holland writes, the theme of which is contained in Valentine's statement, "I know no effectual difference between continued affectation and reality": "His [Valentine's] failure to realize that outside society there is a difference and his related failure to seek Angelica through something other than show or "affectation" are what keep him from winning her . . . Valentine needs education: that there is a reality which is higher and larger than 'continued affectation.'"

In schematizing the play, Holland draws an elaborate diagram that shows the relationships among the chief characters and in turn their relation to three different levels of knowledge that man is capable of attaining: presocial or sensitive knowledge; social or rational knowledge; and supra-social or intuitive knowledge, the last two of which are especially relevant to Valentine in his pursuit of Angelica. "The action of the play," Holland writes,

> is to make Valentine bring his real nature out from under the shell of pretenses he has drawn round himself. In doing so, Valentine grows out of the limited social world into something larger . . . Valentine's problem in winning Angelica is that he is still too close to social pretense; he is trying to win her by putting on a show . . . He must learn to transcend his social habits through an action completely asocial, resigning both his fortune and his love; he must learn that the intrigue is not effective on the supra-social level. It is to the education of Valentine that the title *Love for Love* refers: Valentine learns to substitute real love for showy love. In return Angelica gives him

real love for real love, a response not possible for love merely social . . .

Writing in the wake of Holland, Charles Lyons and W. H. Van Voris reinforce his major claims. Van Voris' study shows Congreve's indebtedness not only to *An Essay Concerning Human Understanding,* but to the *Two Treatises of Civil Government,* also published in 1690. Lyons' article, on the other hand, carries Holland's argument one significant step further by showing how the imagery of the play supports Holland's notion of the ideal, "suprasocial" relationship of Valentine and Angelica. He refers to what he terms the "Christian images of grace and blessing" in the last scene of the play. According to Lyons, the final statement of value in the play is Angelica's concluding couplet: "The miracle today is that we find / A lover true: not that a woman's kind." The passage is significant, Lyons writes, because "it is the final answer to Scandal's cynicism, a lack of faith which is considered to be the despair of the infidel. In opposition to this infidelity is Valentine's constancy, conceived in . . . religious terms . . . ''

II

While the efforts of these critics might seem at first glance to preclude the necessity for further comment on *Love for Love,* Professor Holland's suggestion of Congreve's indebtedness to Locke's *Essay* for the philosophical framework of the play leaves yet unanswered the question of the extent of his indebtedness: Is the *Essay* serviceable to Congreve only insofar as it provides him with the categories of knowledge—social and supra-social—through which Valentine must necessarily migrate before union with Angelica is possible? Or does the play perhaps deal in social terms with the fundamental problem that Locke poses in the *Essay,* that is, the certainty and extent of human knowledge? The point worthy of speculation is that perhaps Congreve made more extensive use of *An Essay Concerning Human Understanding* in *Love for Love* than even Holland intimates in his essay when he pigeon-holes the major characters in the play according to the kinds of knowledge they have or attain; that perhaps the play is not only a dramatic rendering of the levels of knowledge possible in human experience, but also a live demonstration, in part at least, of *how* one arrives at such knowledge.

That Locke's *Essay* may well have been in the forefront of Congreve's mind at the time he wrote *Love for Love* is evident in the letter he sent John Dennis on July 10, 1695, a little more than two months after the play was initially performed at Lincoln's Inn Fields, on April 30. This letter, sometimes referred to by the title "Concerning Humour in Comedy," has a twofold importance as far as the play is concerned. First, it is in part an outline of Congreve's notion of a stage character as a composite of what he calls "humour," "habit," and "affectation." Second, his analysis of humor proves beyond doubt that he had fairly digested Locke's *Essay* at least by July of 1695, and very likely by the time he had written *Love for Love,* if one can accept as proof Professor Holland's citation of Valentine's lines toward the end of Act IV as a covert allusion to the *tabula rasa:* "You are all white, a sheet of lovely, spotless paper, when you first are born; but you are to be scrawled and blotted by every goose's quill."

In the letter to Dennis, Congreve uses the term "Humour" in two different senses: first, in a specialized sense to qualify a type of character proper to comedy, the excess of whose humor makes him appear "ridiculous upon the stage"; and second, in a looser sense, to indicate simply a man's nature, character, or identity. Humor, according to Congreve, "*shews* [italics mine] us as we *are.*"

> Our Humour has relation to us, and to what proceeds from us, as the Accidents have to a Substance; it is a Colour, Taste, and Smell, Diffused through all; thô our Actions are never so many, and different in Form, they are all Splinters of the Same Wood, and have Naturally one Complexion; which thô it may be disguised by Art, yet cannot be wholly changed: We may Paint it with other Colours, but we cannot change the Grain. So the Natural sound of an Instrument will be distinguish'd, thô the Notes expressed by it, are never so many. Dissimulation, may by Degrees, become more easy to our practice; but it can never absolutely Transubstantiate us into what we would seem: It will always be in some proportion a Violence upon Nature.

The words "Substance" and "Accidents," which Congreve uses in this passage to define the relationship between a person and his humor, are nearly identical to those used by Locke in the *Essay* to explain the relationship between a "body" and its "qualities." Just as one's humor, therefore, shows a man as he actually is, so the qualities of a substance or a body show that object as it is. When Congreve further defines humor as a "Colour, Taste, and Smell, Diffused through all," he indicates, in effect, that one's humor is the equivalent of what Locke calls a "secondary quality," or the "power" that a body or a substance has to produce ideas in someone who perceives it. Humor, then, which shows a man as he is, is what gives him his identity in the minds of other people: ''I take it [humour] to be, A singular and unavoidable manner of doing, or saying any thing, Peculiar and Natural to one Man only; by which his Speech and Actions are distinguish'd from those of other Men.''

Unfortunately, however, man rarely appears as he actually is. He and his humor are often obscured by additional qualities that make him a substance or body difficult to know, that is, habit and affectation. ''Habit,'' Congreve writes, ''*shews* [italics mine] us as we appear under a forcible Impression.'' Habits are, in other words, involuntary accretions ''contracted by Use or Custom,'' that the personality takes on: ''Under this Head may be ranged all Country Clowns, Sailers, Tradesmen, Jockeys, Gamesters and such like, who make use of *Cants* or peculiar *Dialects* in their several Arts and Vocations.'' Affectation, on the other hand, ''*Shews* [italics mine] what we would be, under a Voluntary Disguise.'' In this category fall pretense, deceit, and other forms of dissembling.

In the end, therefore, man is a fairly complicated being whose veneers of habits and affectations make him a difficult, if not impossible, object of knowledge. This multi-dimensional concept of character that Congreve outlines in his letter to Dennis is what gives *Love for Love* its richness as a play. All of the characters, even the stock-types of comedy, like the *dromo* (Jeremy and Angelica's Nurse) and the *senex* (Sir Sampson and Foresight), are considerably removed from the level of stereotype and are, instead, highly individualized.

III

If, as I have indicated, Congreve's letter to Dennis contains more than ''such unpremeditated Thoughts, as may be Communicated between Friend and Friend,'' and if indeed the question of the certainty and extent of human knowledge was immediate to Congreve's mind when he wrote *Love for Love*, then the question yet remains, to what degree does Congreve's art translate the psychology and philosophy to effective dramatic action? Professor Holland correctly maintains that the focus of the play is Valentine's education, his final recognition of a reality higher and larger than continued affectation. In another sense, however, an equally important issue raised in the play is the ability or inability of the several characters to arrive at a rational understanding of the social universe, their microcosm, and of the inhabitants who people it. From this perspective, each of the characters may be regarded as a representative or symbol of an approach to knowledge, each offering his formula or prescription for registering and ordering his social experiences.

Some of the characters, like Tattle, Mrs. Frail, and Mrs. Foresight, abrogate entirely their responsibility to come to terms intellectually with the external universe. For these closed-eyed characters the broad distinctions of truth and falsity do not exist, and, consequently, they have no sense of obligation to look for an agreement between their ideas and the substances from which these ideas emanate. Appearance for them in effect has become reality, as Holland maintains. In terms of Locke's epistemology, the mental and verbal propositions they formulate from the ideas in their minds have no agreement with the reality of things. Thus Tattle, without qualm of conscience, can teach Prue in Act II that to lie and dissemble is better than to tell the truth and be honest. And similarly, Mrs. Foresight in Act IV can, without compunction, profess her virtue the very morning after she cuckolds her husband.

The prescriptions for understanding offered by Sir Sampson, Foresight, and Ben, three legitimate humors characters, are likewise tangential to the reality of things, yet the error of their respective ways lies not so much in the voluntary confusion of truth and falsity as in the frames of reference these characters use to screen experience. In other words, the propositions they formulate are made to conform to preconceived notions of how ideas and experience are ordered. For Sir Sampson the frame of reference is paternal authority, arbitrary edict, and fiat: ''I warrant my son thought nothing belonged to a father, but forgiveness and affection; no authority, no correction, no arbitrary power ...'' For Foresight the frame of reference is even further removed from the world of the play than it is for Sir Sampson. He sifts all experience through the sieve of prognostication, and, as a result, the mental and verbal propositions he formulates have little or no relevance to social reality:

> But I tell you, I have traveled, and traveled in the celestial spheres, know the signs and the planets and their houses. Can judge of motions direct and retrograde, of sextiles, quadrates, trines, and oppositions, fiery trigons and aquatical trigons. Know whether life shall be long or short, happy or unhappy, whether diseases are curable or incurable. If journeys shall be prosperous, undertakings successful, or goods stolen recovered, I know.

Like Sir Sampson and old Foresight, Sailor Ben is a humors character, but unlike them he is also a character of habit. In keeping with his habit, Ben's frame of reference is the sea, which he uses to screen experience and in a sense transmute it to a kind of nautical poetry. Although technically the sea has as little relevance to Valentine's social world as either prophecy or fiat, Congreve uses Ben as a sounding-board by which to judge and criticize that world: "You don't think I'm false-hearted, like a landman. A sailor will be honest, tho'f mayhap he has never a penny of money in his pocket." Ben, therefore, by virtue of his frame of reference outside of the world of the play, is the best qualified of the characters to pass judgment upon that world.

Just as there are three characters in the play who look at the world closed-eyed, and three whose judgments of it are distorted to varying degrees by their frames of reference, so there are three who make a serious attempt to understand it through close scrutiny and analysis. Jeremy Fetch, whose locus of reality is the tangible and the concrete, is skeptical of those areas of experience he cannot refer to immediate and practical use: "Was Epictetus a real cook, or did he only write receipts?." He registers sense experience but seems alien to conceptual thought, and when confronted with an abstraction, he is prone to make it concrete:

> Ah, pox confound that Will's Coffee-House . . . For my part, I never sit at the door that I don't get double the stomach that I do at a horse race . . . I never see it, but the Spirit of Famine appears to me; sometimes like a decayed porter, worn out with pimping and carrying billet-doux and songs; not like other porters for hire, but for the jest's sake; now like a thin chairman, melted down to half his proportion with carrying a poet upon tick to visit some great fortune; and his fair to be paid him like the wages of sin, either at the day of marriage, or the day of death . . . Sometimes like a bilked bookseller, with a meager, terrified countenance, that looks as if he had written for himself, or were resolved to turn author, and bring the rest of his brethren into the same condition. And lastly, in the form of a worn-hout punk, with verses in her hand, which her vanity had preferred to settlements, without a whole tatter to her tail, but as ragged as one of the Muses; or as if she were carrying her linen to the paper-mill, to be converted into folio books of warning to all young maids, not to prefer poetry to good sense, or lying in the arms of a needy wit, before the embraces of a wealthy fool.

Holland is right when he refers to Jeremy's knowledge as mere "belly knowledge"; Sir Sampson's impression of him is surprisingly accurate: "And if this rogue were anatomized now, and dissected, he has his vessels of digestion and concoction, and so fourth, large enough for the inside of a cardinal . . . "

In the play, Angelica is perhaps the most elusive and enigmatic of the major characters, and yet she is the object of knowledge for both Valentine and Scandal. The abortive attempts these characters make to comprehend or understand her reflects both Congreve's and Locke's conviction about the difficulty and perhaps the impossibility of arriving at perfect knowledge of a substance, whether it be an object in nature, as it is for Locke, or the human personality, as it is for Congreve.

While Jeremy invariably reduces an abstraction to a concrete particular, Scandal's habit of thought is the reverse. He looks at the particular in terms of the category it falls under, and, as a result, the abstraction is more valid for him than the concrete thing that first suggested it: "I can show you pride, folly, affectation, wantonness, inconstancy, covetousness, dissimulation, malice, and ignorance, all in one piece. Then I can show you lying, foppery, vanity, cowardice, bragging, lechery, impotence, and ugliness in another piece . . ." Scandal's effort to understand Angelica is colored largely by his knowledge of other women, and yet his "conversion" at the close of Act V indicates that the propositions he had earlier formulated have been abandoned. Through the first four acts Scandal looks at Angelica in terms of the category of which she is a member—woman:

> All women are inconstant and unkind.
> Angelica is a woman.
> Angelica is inconstant and unkind.

Typical of his mode of judging Angelica is a passage in Act I:

> Women of her airy temper, as they seldom think before they act, so they rarely give us any light to guess at what they mean. But you have little reason to believe that a woman of this age, who has had an indifference for you in your prosperity, will fall in love with your ill fortune; besides, Angelica has a great fortune of her own, and great fortunes either expect another great fortune, or a fool.

Scandal's logic obviously suffers from a faulty premise (though his experiences with Mrs. Frail and Mrs. Foresight would seem to confirm it as true). He cannot distinguish Cow (1) from Cow (2), to borrow Hayakawa's metaphor. His error in judgment is simply that he fails to see distinctions, an error that Locke anticipates in the *Essay:*

> He that has an idea made up of barely the simple ones of a beast with spots has but a confused idea of a leopard; it not being thereby sufficiently distinguished from a lynx, and several other sorts of beasts that are spotted. So that such an idea, though it hath the peculiar name "leopard," is not distinguishable from

those designed by the name ''lynx'' or ''panther,'' and may as well come under the name ''lynx'' as ''leopard.'' How much the custom of defining of words by general terms contributes to make the ideas we would express by them confused and undetermined I leave others to consider. This is evident, that confused ideas are such as render the use of words uncertain, and take away the benefit of distinct names.

Scandal's conversion at the end of the play from infidel to believer necessarily entails a revision of the major premise under which he has been laboring. In other words, Angelica as an exception to the rule compels him to abandon the universal affirmative proposition that all women are inconstant and unkind for a proposition that is particular: some women, not all, are inconstant and unkind.

Each of the major affectations that Valentine assumes in the course of the play—his postures as poet-satirist and madman—is a tactical maneuver designed to afford him knowledge of Angelica's heart. The possibility of such knowledge, however, is necessarily predicated on his ability to penetrate intellectually the concentric layers of affectation that obscure her substance and humor. But, in spite of his efforts, Angelica continually eludes him and remains outside his intellectual grasp:

Jeremy. What, is the lady gone again, sir? I hope you understand one another before she went?

Valentine. Understood! She is harder to be understood than a piece of Egyptian antiquity or an Irish manuscript. You may pore till you spoil your eyes, and not improve your knowledge.

Jeremy. I have heard 'em say, sir, they read hard Hebrew books backwards. Maybe you begin to read at the wrong end.

Valentine. They say so of a witch's prayer, and dreams and Dutch almanacs are to be understood by contraries. But there's regularity and method in that. She is a medal without a reverse or inscription, for indifference has both sides alike. Yet while she does not seem to hate me, I will pursue her, and know her if it be possible, in spite of the opinion of my satirical friend, Scandal, who says,

That women are like tricks by slight of hand,
Which, to admire, we should not understand.

It is not surprising, then, that Valentine's impersonation of a madman is thematically appropriate in the play, as is his refrain in Act IV, ''I am Truth''; for in a world where certain knowledge of the object in nature is problematical, Valentine has little recourse but to retreat to the subjective world, the private inner world, the only world that seems to have coherent meaning.

Valentine never does arrive at a human understanding of Angelica. She remains a perplexity even when she relents and gives her heart to him in the last act. Holland is right when he claims that Valentine arrives at intuitive knowledge at the end of the play, and when Valentine says, ''Between pleasure and amazement, I am lost—but on my knees I take the blessing,'' the emphasis falls on *amazement* as an indication of his intellectual confusion. The knowledge he attains is intuitive, apprehended immediately without the mediation of his rational powers. It is, in effect, not unlike the mystical experience that the image ''blessing'' suggests.

IV

While the foregoing analysis of *Love for Love* indicates Congreve's heavy indebtedness to Locke's concept of knowledge and his explanation of how it is attained, the final effect of the play is to undercut much of what the philosopher has to say about the extent and certainty of that knowledge, particularly when the perceived object is as elusive as the human personality and the faculty for judging it is as unreliable as the human reason. One of the important implications of Congreve's letter to Dennis is that people, as objects of knowledge, defy rational understanding in a way that stones do not. Thus, the extent of one's awareness and level of perception prevents him in most cases from properly judging the social world, and this incapacity in turn often accounts for the aberrations in his own social behavior. In a sense, the play may be read on more than one level. It is, in part at least, a variation on the time-worn theme of woman's inscrutability. More importantly, however, it is a critical examination of the adequacy of rational knowledge to assess man and his behavior in society. Congreve, in the end, proves something of a skeptic in terms of his confidence in the ability of reason to discern man and consequently regulate human affairs. He would agree with Locke that there is an area of experience outside the scope of human ken and, in terms of this particular play, that area is the human personality— ever indefinable, elusive, and enigmatic. With Locke, Congreve might say:

Thus, men extending their inquiries beyond their capacities, and letting their thoughts wander into those depths where they can find no sure footing, it is no wonder that they raise questions and multiply disputes, which, never coming to any clear resolution, are proper only to continue and increase their doubts, and to confirm them at last in perfect scepticism. Whereas, were the capacities of our understandings well considered, the extent of our knowledge once discovered, and the horizon found which sets the bounds between the enlightened and dark parts of things, between what is and what is not comprehensible by us, men would perhaps with less scruple acquiesce in the avowed ignorance of the one, and employ their thoughts and discourse with more advantage and satisfaction in the other.

The tendency to date, among critics, has been to sentimentalize *Love for Love*, and, to be sure, Congreve's drama, unhappily, is responsive to the forces set in motion by the lugubrious comedy of Colley Cibber at the close of the seventeenth century. But in another sense, the play is a genuine comedy of errors, albeit sober and reflective in the last act. In the final analysis, *Love for Love* is a sophisticated and somewhat skeptical statement of the limitations of human reason. Neither Scandal's mental gymnastics nor Valentine's trial-and-error courtship avails the hero or his friend of an adequate knowledge of Angelica. She escapes formula and definition, as does every human being, and Valentine at the close of the play, dumbfounded by her unexpected benevolence, is confronted with the comic absurdity of man's condition: his inability to fathom, by reason at least, the people upon whom his happiness in life depends.

Source: F. P. Jarvis, ''The Philosophical Assumptions of Congreve's *Love for Love,*'' in *Texas Studies in Literature and Language,* Vol. XIV, No. 3, Fall 1972, pp. 423–34.

SOURCES

Hughes, Derek, *English Drama 1660–1700,* Clarendon Press, 1996.

Love, Harold, *Congreve,* Basil Blackwell, 1974.

Lyons, Patrick, *Congreve: Comedies. A Critical Casebook,* Macmillan, 1982.

Stieber, Anita, *Character Portrayal in Congreve's Comedies: ''The Old Bachelor,'' ''Love for Love,'' and ''The Way of the World,''* Edward Mellen Press, 1996.

Thomas, David, *English Dramatists: William Congreve,* Macmillan, 1992.

Young, Douglas M., *The Feminist Voices in Restoration Comedy,* University Press of America, 1997.

FURTHER READING

Hughes, Derek, *English Drama 1660–1700,* Clarendon Press, 1996.

In this book, Hughes provides a brief discussion of almost every play to have been produced on the London stage during this period. The book is an excellent resource for discovering what kinds of plays were popular and what the conventions of playwriting, production, and theatre attendance were like during the Restoration.

Scouten, Arthur H., and Robert D. Hume, '''Restoration Comedy' and its Audiences,'' in *The Rakish Stage: Studies in English Drama 1660–1800,* edited by Robert D. Hume, Southern Illinois University Press, 1983.

Reading and analyzing plays, even accessing records of how they were produced, can foster a better understanding of their meaning. Knowing the composition and expectations of audiences during this early period of modern theater, is, however, much more difficult. Scouten and Hume have researched the subject thoroughly in an effort to reconstruct a picture of Restoration theatre's audiences.

Quinsey, Katherine M., editor, *Broken Boundaries: Women and Feminism in Restoration Drama,* University Press of Kentucky, 1996.

This collection of twelve original essays is noted as being the first direct study of feminism in the plays of the Restoration period. The essays discuss gender roles in Restoration drama, and in doing so, examine the place of women and men in both family and society during this period.

The Man Who Turned into a Stick

KOBO ABE

1967

The first performance of *The Man Who Turned into a Stick* was staged at Kinokuniya Hall in Tokyo in 1967. However, it was not until Kobo Abe directed the play in his own Kobo Abe Studio in 1976 that the play reached, in Abe's mind, a level of completion. Whenever Abe presented *The Man Who Turned into a Stick*, a short, one-act play, he joined it to two other short plays; but in the 1976 version, a new and more specific sequence came to Abe's mind, one he believed made the three-play set more comprehensive. The individual plays in the revised series were then given subtitles. The first play of the set, *The Suitcase*, was subtitled *Birth;* the second play, *The Cliff of Time*, was subtitled *Process;* and the third, *The Man Who Turned into a Stick* was given the subtitle *Death.*

Even with the subtitle suggesting a theme, *The Man Who Turned into a Stick* is not a play that is easily understood, and many people believe that that is exactly how Abe wanted it. Abe did not like to write plays for passive audiences. He wanted his audiences to work. He liked that his plays made people feel uncomfortable because he believed that it was through this discomfort that people would begin to question their own lives rather than perfunctorily accept their fate. In *The Man Who Turned into a Stick*, he not only presents obscure characters and dialogue that demand attention, he deliberately ends his play with one of the characters pointing directly at the audience and telling the people sitting

there that they all resemble sticks. The audience must therefore participate in the play and consider its meaning on a more personal level.

Abe enjoyed complexities and ambiguities because he believed that it was through confronting uncertainty that people would break out of their rigid (or stick-like), preprogrammed thoughts. His plays are built upon dreamlike images, uneasy to grasp. As Abe told Nancy Shields in her book *Fake Fish,* ''The more we become free from the framework of reality the more clearly we get the real experience which corresponds to the fake experience in a dream.'' That this statement is not easy to comprehend is also typical of Abe. In essence, however, these sentiments are the backbone upon which *The Man Who Turned into a Stick* was built. In Abe's metaphor, the rigidity of staunchly held beliefs that contradict one's existence causes people to turn into sticks. A stick is dead and inflexible. By taking the ordinary object of a stick and personifying it, Abe hoped to shake his audiences out of their ''fake dreams.''

Kobo Abe

AUTHOR BIOGRAPHY

On March 7, 1924, while his father was conducting research in Tokyo, Japan, Kobo Abe was born. Abe's father, Asakichi, a citizen of Japan and a physician, had a medical clinic in Mukden, Manchuria, where he would return with his family one year after his son's birth. Abe spent most of his youth living in a Japanese colony in Mukden with his father and his mother, Yorimi. According to Shields, who interviewed the playwright for her book *Fake Fish*, Abe remembered this city of his youth as a ''terrifying place.'' Abe reportedly told Shields that there were no laws in the streets of the city, and ''sometimes children were sold as slaves.'' This Manchurian city, as Abe describes, was made up of ''barren spaces, city mazes, and solitary human figures.'' These images, thrown together inside high, dirty walls that were built to keep the drifting sand of the surrounding desert from overtaking the buildings and the people who dwelled inside them, would forever mark the imagination of this future author of surrealistic fiction and drama.

In 1931, when Abe was seven years old, Japan invaded Manchuria. Fearing for his family, Abe's father sent Abe and his mother to Hokkaido, the northernmost island of Japan. There, mother and son lived with Abe's maternal grandfather, while Abe's father accepted a medical grant to conduct research in Hungary. Upon his grandfather's death, Abe and his mother returned to Manchuria, which was still in the throes of war. It was in Manchuria, while Abe was still an adolescent, that he discovered the magic of storytelling. Abe tells the story of how the winters were so cold in Manchuria that the students could not go outside. At first to entertain himself and then later the whole class, Abe recited the stories of Edgar Allan Poe. When Abe ran out of Poe stories, he began writing his own. ''That was the first time I began to write the kind of story that could entertain other people,'' he states in *Fake Fish.*

For his high school years, Abe once again returned to Japan. Upon graduation, he entered Tokyo University Medical School, partially as a response to following in his father's footsteps but equally in response to the war. ''The specific situation in Japan at that time,'' Abe states, was that ''those students who specialized in medicine were exempted from becoming soldiers.'' In 1944, before attaining a medical degree, Abe left Tokyo and returned to Manchuria to work in his father's clinic. A few months later, Abe's father died of typhus. Abe's last memories of Mukden were of a city ''lined with coffin shops.'' Abe would return to

Japan with his father's ashes and soon afterward complete his medical degree, which he would never use.

In 1945, Abe moved to a bombed-out part of Tokyo with his new bride, Machi Yamada, an art student and stage designer. In accordance with his pacifist views on war, Abe joined the Japanese Communist Party, believing that its philosophy matched his more precisely than any other political ideology. Although he would later denounce the Party for the disparity between its abstract principles and practical applications (as well as the censorship it placed on his creativity), his communist membership would later prevent Abe from gaining easy entry into the United States.

Abe is best known for his novels and short stories. His most popular and critically acclaimed work is *Suna no onna* 1962 (translated as *The Woman in the Dunes*, 1964), a story set in a nightmarish setting reminiscent of the barren Manchurian desert.

However, it was the writing of plays that consumed most of Abe's later years. In 1973, dissatisfied with the production of his plays, Abe founded his own theater group that was named the Kobo Abe Studio. It was here, in 1976, that Abe produced the more familiar version of his play, *The Man Who Turned into a Stick*. As with many of his other productions, Abe's wife created the set designs.

In Tokyo on January 22, 1993, Abe, at the age of sixty-eight, died of a heart attack. His wife died nine months later. He is survived by his daughter, Neri Mano, and three grandchildren.

PLOT SUMMARY

Beginning

The Man Who Turned into a Stick is a short, one act play. It is set on a busy city street in front of a department store in the middle of summer. Two characters are on stage, Hippie Boy and Hippie Girl. Abe's script directions suggest that the hippie couple may be shown sniffing glue. Suddenly, a stick falls from above. The stick is an actual stick as well as an actor who plays the man who turned into a stick. Abe indicates that the actor playing the stick should manipulate the actual stick upon its falling. Man from Hell enters stage-left and Woman from Hell enters stage-right.

Hippie Boy is startled when he realizes how close he came to being hit by the falling stick and declares that even standing on the sidewalk can be dangerous. Man from Hell and Woman from Hell recite poetic lines referring to fate and the fact that another man has turned into a stick while Hippie Girl reflects on the incident philosophically, almost as if reading a Buddhist text. "Which do you suppose is the accident—when something hits you or when it misses?" she asks. Then Man from Hell and Woman from Hell continue reciting their poetic verses.

Hippie Boy picks up the stick and begins to tap out a rhythm. Hippie Girl tries to guess the song that goes along with that rhythm, then she looks up and notices a child on top of the department store (where, in Japan, there often is a type of playground). Both Hippie Girl and Hippie Boy guess that it was the boy who threw the stick down, with Hippie Girl believing it was an accident and Hippie Boy thinking the child threw it on purpose, trying to see if he could hit someone with the stick. At this point, Stick speaks his first lines. It is through these lines that the audience realizes that the stick is the father of the boy and that the boy is calling to him.

Middle

Man from Hell and Woman from Hell continue to talk in poetic stanzas until they meet at center stage. They both begin to question Hippie Boy and Hippie Girl about the stick. They want to know where the hippies found the stick. The hippies in turn want to know if the man and woman are police. The man and woman assure them that they are not with the police and ask the hippies to give them the stick.

It is clear that Hippie Boy does not trust the man and woman. He calls them liars and accuses them of being the ones who threw the stick at him and now want to suppress the evidence. Hippie Girl intervenes, reminding Hippie Boy of the child on top of the roof. Woman from Hell confirms that there was a child on the roof and that the child was calling for his father. When Man from Hell attempts to explain why they need the stick and asks for the hippies' understanding, Hippie Boy replies: "I don't understand nothing." To which Hippie Girl makes it clear that Hippie Boy is commenting on the gap between the two generations, then adds: "We're alienated."

While the man who turned into a stick bemoans his fate, the hippies and Man and Woman from Hell have a brief philosophical discussion on the topic of aims (or goals) in life. Man from Hell asks what Hippie Boy intends to do with the stick, to which the boy responds that he is "not interested in aims." Hippie Girls adds: "Aims are out of date." Man from Hell counters that since aims are out of date there is no reason for Hippie Boy to keep the stick. After circling around the theme of ambition to the point of confusion, Man from Hell concludes that it is "bad for your health to want something that doesn't really exist."

The hippies become distracted. To bring them back to the subject of the stick, Man from Hell offers them money for the stick. Hippie Boy refuses the offer, stating, "Me and this stick, we understand each other."

The hippie couple then begin a dialogue about Hippie Girl's sister, who has died. At the end of their conversation, Hippie Girl becomes confused and states, "Everything is wrapped in riddles." Man from Hell interrupts them, once again bringing them back to the stick. Woman from Hell, who had briefly left the stage, returns, urging Man from Hell to hurry because the child is coming. She also informs him that the child saw his father turn into a stick and has told the officials in the department store, although no one believes him. At this news, the stick begins a monologue, reflecting on how he fell and questioning why he turned into a stick. At the end of the monologue, Hippie Boy suddenly drops the stick and looks at it nervously. He claims: "It twitched, like a dying fish."

Woman from Hell points out the small child in the crowd. She tells Man from Hell that he is coming closer. Stick, speaking to himself, says that he can hear his son's footsteps. Hippie Boy, meanwhile, remains scared of the stick. He thinks the stick looks a lot like him. He is uneasy and finally tells Man from Hell that he will give him the stick for five dollars. Before Hippie Boy leaves the stage with his money, he tells Man from Hell that the only reason he is selling the stick is because he doesn't want to sell the stick. He then says: "That's a contradiction of circumstances. Do you follow me?" Hippie Girl then repeats: "It's the generation gap," and the two hippies leave the stage.

End

From this point on, Woman from Hell and Man from Hell discuss the forms and regulations that govern their investigation of yet another person who has turned into a stick. They write notes on the incident, contact their headquarters in Hell, briefing them on their findings. When Woman from Hell confesses that she feels sorry for the stick, she is told by the man that "sympathy has no place in our profession."

In the process of recording the event, the man and woman begin a philosophical conversation. The man refers to the stick as being capable and faithful. "In short," he says, "the stick is the root and source of all tools." He later adds that, "A stick remains a stick, no matter how it is used .... You might almost say that the etymology of the word faithful is a stick." When Woman from Hell relates that this is the first time she has seen a specimen in the form of a stick, the Man from Hell reminds her that this is due to the fact that they never save stick specimens because they are so common. Then he continues by telling her that in the last thirty years the percentage of people turning into sticks, as compared to people turning into other objects, has increased. "I understand that in extreme cases," he adds, "98.4 per cent of all those who die in a given month turn into sticks."

The woman again feels an attachment to the stick when the man tells her to discard it. She wonders if it has feelings. She also thinks that maybe they should give the stick to the young boy so he can reflect on what has happened to his father. The man, contrasting her concerns, laughs at the thought of reflection on the part of the son. The man claims that the child is satisfied, as was his father, and that is the reason the father turned into a stick.

Man and Woman from Hell slowly leave the stage, on their way to another incident of a person turning into a stick. Stick then begins another monologue, with Man and Woman from Hell standing behind a curtain, seen only in silhouette. They return, once again, to speaking in poetic stanzas as Stick reflects on what has happened. Stick questions their presumptions that he was satisfied. Man from Hell then steps out from behind the curtain and points out that there is "a whole forest of sticks" in the audience. Woman from Hell goes over to Stick and tells him that he is not alone.

CHARACTERS

Hippie Boy

Hippie Boy is standing on the sidewalk outside a department store when a stick falls, barely missing

MEDIA ADAPTATIONS

- Although Abe's *The Man Who Turned into a Stick* was never made into a movie, several of his other works were. Abe wrote the screenplays for each of these movies, all of which were directed by Hiroshi Teshigahara: *The Woman in the Dunes* (1964), which received a special jury prize at the Cannes Film Festival. His *Face of Another* was produced in 1966, and *The Ruined Map* was produced in 1968 as *The Man without a Map*. *The Woman in the Dunes* is available on videocassette.

him. At first he is angry at whoever threw the stick down, then, as the play progresses, he becomes simultaneously attached to the stick and repulsed by it because it reminds him too much of himself. He thinks he looks like the stick and believes that the stick understands him.

In the beginning, Hippie Boy does not want to part with the stick, but in the end he sells the stick to the Man from Hell. Hippie Boy tells Man from Hell that the only reason he is selling the stick is because he doesn't want to sell it. Hippie Boy represents the alter ego, or opposite, of Man from Hell. He is a symbol of rebellious youth, and he makes decisions based on emotions.

Hippie Girl

Hippie Girl is partnered with Hippie Boy, much like Woman from Hell is partnered with Man from Hell. She is somewhat subservient to Hippie Boy, who at one point tells her she is stupid and at another time tells her to shut up. Hippie Girl does not respond. She is also more emotionally involved with the little boy on top of the department store, whereas Hippie Boy is only angry with him, declaring that he hates kids. She also tries to explain Hippie Boy, in some ways, to the older couple. She reinforces Hippie Boy's thoughts, for instance, by explaining Hippie Boy's attitude by telling Man and Woman from Hell that the younger generation is

alienated. At one point in the play, Hippie Girl asks Hippie Boy for a kiss, which he refuses. She then stands up for herself after the rejection, telling him that he needn't put on airs. She then asks him to scratch her back with the stick, which he does reluctantly. When Hippie Boy becomes upset about his resemblance to the stick, Hippie Girl is very consoling, showing her emotional connection with Hippie Boy.

Man from Hell

Man from Hell works with his partner, Woman from Hell, reporting cases of people turning into objects (apparently upon death). Man from Hell stresses rationality, and he appears to be a mentor of the woman, who is in training. In his communications with the hippies, Man from Hell comes across as a parent, or authority, figure. However, when Woman from Hell suggests that they give Stick to the young boy, Man from Hell expresses no sentiment whatsoever. He represents logic and discipline. He is detached from the people with whom he must associate. The only hint of softness in his tone occurs when he calls headquarters and asks the person on the other end of the line to deliver a message to his wife. It is Man from Hell who, at the end of play, stands before the audience and tells them that he hopes they don't think he is rude by pointing out that they are all sticks. "It's just the simple truth," he says, "the truth as I see it." Man from Hell represents bureaucracy and the status quo.

Stick

Stick is the man who falls off the roof, leaving his son above, as he turns into a stick. He is dying. He displays his emotions when he thinks about his son, who has been crying out for him from atop the department store. Almost all his comments are emotional. He hears the conversations of Man and Woman from Hell as well as of Hippie Boy and Hippie Girl. When he observes what they are saying, he reacts emotionally. He does not understand why he has turned into a stick, or even why he fell off the roof. When Man from Hell suggests that Stick was satisfied, Stick questions this, claiming that he never felt satisfied.

When Stick is thrown into the wet gutter, he exclaims that he would be surprised if he didn't catch a cold, thereby acknowledging that he doesn't fully realize his own condition: first, that he has been turned into a stick; and second, that he is dying. He also questions his condition when his son almost discovers him in his new stick form. The stick asks:

"There was nothing I could have done anyway, was there?" Woman from Hell describes a stick as something that is used by people for some particular reason. To this comment, Stick replies to himself: "That's obvious, isn't it? It's true of everybody."

Stick represents people who are too rigid, who get stuck in certain patterns in life and cannot break free of them. Stuck in this way, they might as well be dead, for they no longer experience life with a fresh view.

Woman from Hell

Woman from Hell's job is to record, in an unemotional way, the occurrences of people turning into objects. Woman from Hell is in training and at times must be reminded what to do. Woman from Hell also tends to become emotionally involved with the people she studies, as contrasted with her partner and mentor, Man from Hell, who is pure logic. Woman from Hell empathizes with the man who has turned into a stick and with his son. She feels badly about throwing the stick in the gutter and wants to give it to the young son. When Man from Hell expresses doubt that he or she really exists, being no more than the dreams of dying people, Woman from Hell states: "If those are dreams, they are horrible nightmares." At the end of the play, Woman from Hell tries to comfort Stick, telling him (after Man from Hell points out an audience full of sticks) that he is not alone. "You've lots of friends," she tells him. Woman from Hell represents the formation of bureaucracy. She registers details but maintains empathetic relationships with the things she studies.

THEMES

Alienation

Alienation is a theme that runs through most of Abe's work. In *The Man Who Turned into a Stick*, alienation is represented as Hippie Girl and Hippie Boy, the younger generation. Their alienation is specifically expressed by Hippie Girl when she declares that there is a generation gap between her and Hippie Boy and the man and woman from hell. Hippie Girl also delivers the line: "We're alienated."

These are obvious examples of Abe's theme. There are more subtle ones, however. There is the problem of communication between the father (the stick) and his son. The father has fallen away from

the son and turned into something unrecognizable. The son calls out to his father, but the father cannot respond because he has turned into a stick.

As a stick, the man can hear the other characters speaking but they cannot hear him. When Man from Hell states that the man was turned into a stick because he was satisfied, Stick disagrees but cannot protest. Taking this further, Stick cannot elucidate a comprehensive evaluation of his life even to himself. He questions Man from Hell's assumptions, but does not offer any answers. This represents alienation in the sense of being separated from one's own thoughts.

This kind of alienation from self is also depicted when Hippie Girl tries to remember her sister and the nicknames her siblings called her. She becomes confused when she tries to bring up memories, suggesting that she is confused about her own identity. She says that everything is wrapped in puzzles, intimating that this also includes herself.

Another form of alienation is the conflict between inner and outer realities. This is conveyed in the dialogue between Man from Hell and Woman from Hell. Man from Hell is determined to record only the facts of reality. He trains Woman from Hell to take down the time of day, details of location, the identification number of the latest victim, and what he describes as truthful descriptions of the objects they examine. Woman from Hell, on the other hand, is torn between recording these rational descriptions in order to do her job well and expressing her emotions, which make her empathize with the people she meets in the course of her work. Man from Hell believes that her emotions are a distraction and that she should learn to control or eliminate them.

Satisfaction

Man from Hell states that people turn into sticks because they are satisfied. This suggests that Abe believes satisfaction to be a negative thing, as sticks are stiff and lifeless. For Abe, satisfaction represents the status quo or, worse yet, stagnation. It is a state of mind that is frozen, accepting things as they are without searching for improvement.

Whereas Man from Hell states that the man was changed into a stick because he was satisfied, it is interesting to note that the Man from Hell also appears satisfied. He is very rule-oriented and teaches

TOPICS FOR FURTHER STUDY

- Abe stages his play *The Man Who Turned into a Stick* as a series of three one-act plays. Read the other two plays (*The Suitcase* and *The Cliff of Time*) and write an analysis of how these plays fit together. Do you find a common theme? Do the plays reflect the subtitled themes of birth, process, and death? In reading the plays together, does it give you a better grasp of what Abe was doing in *The Man Who Turned into a Stick*?

- At the end of his play, Abe has the Man from Hell character turn to the audience and state that he sees a forest of sticks out there. If you were sitting in the audience, how would you respond? Write a letter to Abe stating how you interpret this accusation. How does it make you feel? Do you agree with the assessment? Does it waken you to some new realization about your life?

- Two of Abe's characters are described as hippies. Change the description of these characters to bring them up to date. What would their names be? How would their attitudes differ in their communications with the other characters? Rewrite the portion of the play where these two

characters are on stage, using a modern definition of rebellious and alienated youth.

- Abe is often compared to Franz Kafka. Read Kafka's *The Metamorphosis,* in which a man turns into a bug. What are the themes of Kafka's story? Are these themes similar to any of the themes in Abe's *The Man Who Turned into a Stick*? Enlist a few volunteers to sit on a panel to discuss the two works. Research the backgrounds of these writers, the overall themes of their writing, and how these factors influenced their respective stories.

- Research the history of Japanese imperialist rule in Manchuria. Then write a fictionalized account of Abe's adolescence as if it were true. You may want to focus on one week in his life, covering what it must have been like to walk through the streets in constant fear of being kidnapped or to ride on the train and see heads stuck on the ends of poles. Find out what the landscape was like. Decide if you want this story to take place during the harsh winter or another season. Remember that Abe was a loner, so you might want to include interior dialogue.

Woman from Hell not to deviate from the rules. He does not question what he and she are doing and goes about his business with no inclination to change anything. While Man from Hell points at the audience and judges it as a forest of sticks, he does not consider himself to be part of it. Man from Hell also scoffs at the idea that either the man (who turned into a stick) or his son were capable of reflection, and yet there is nothing in the play that suggests that Man from Hell has reflected on his own life. If, on the other hand, he has, there are no signs that he is anything but satisfied with what he has seen.

Aimlessness

Hippie Boy and Hippie Girl launch into a discussion about aims in the play. They state that

they have no aims. ''Aims are out of date,'' states the girl. Man from Hell tries to use their aimlessness to his advantage by persuading the hippie couple to give the stick to him.

Having an aim is one of Man from Hell's more positive attributes. He has a job to do and his aim is to make sure that that job is completed according to regulations. Whether this is a positive attribute in Abe's mind is unclear. By his name alone, Man from Hell does not fit a positive description. Yet, it is Man from Hell who tries to awaken the audience by pointing out their lack of idealistic aims, thus assuring that they will be turned into sticks.

In the conversation with Hippie Girl, Man from Hell appears to contradict his own goal-oriented personality. He tells Hippie Girl that she is making too much of nothing when she starts daydreaming about the potential advantages of having aims (thus contradicting her original statement against them). Man from Hell refers to aims as ''nothing.'' He then concludes, ''it's bad for your health to want something that doesn't really exist.'' Rather, Man from Hell suggests, it is better to feel uncertainty and anguish about not having aims, for ''they're a lot better proof that you are there, in that particular spot, than any aim I can think of.''

Once again, it is unclear if Man from Hell is delivering this rhetoric for the girl's benefit or for his own. If he succeeds in confusing the girl, he might also succeed in attaining his aim, which is to gain control of the stick.

Death

Abe has subtitled this play *Death.* In the play, there is the imminent death of the man who has turned into the stick, but there is also an overtone of imminent mortality for everyone. It is through the awareness of death that Abe hopes to awaken his audience. Abe's own life was marked with many scenes of death, from the war in Manchuria to his father's death, and the aftermath of bombing raids on Tokyo, Hiroshima, and Nagasaki. His awareness of death prompted him to see life with fresh eyes. Shields writes, ''Abe's ability to see ordinary things in extraordinary ways enabled him to suggest to his audience that they could do likewise.'' By having a man fall off the top of a building and turn into a stick, and then have the audience watch as the man (now a stick) slowly succumbs to death, forces the audience to consider their own mortality. In considering their own deaths, people are compelled to look at the nature and condition of their lives, to reflect on the quality of their life choices.

STYLE

Abe's youth outside of Japan in the stark and war-ravaged deserts of Manchuria, his background in medicine, and his residence in a bombed-out section of Tokyo have all influenced the way he looks at the world, and thus the way he writes and

constructs his plays. Unlike many of Japan's previously noted authors, as well as some of his contemporaries, Abe presents images that are urban, desolate, and somewhat distrustful of traditional Japanese society.

Much like a surgeon who must distance himself from his patients, Abe removes himself from the emotions of his characters to the point of seldom giving them personal names. Although Abe lived most of his adult life in Japan, his plays are written without specifically identifiable settings—they are non-descriptive and could occur anywhere in the world. In this respect, J. Thomas Rimer, writing in *Dictionary of Literary Biography,* compares Abe's approach to the style of Russian dramatist Anton Chekhov, who, coincidentally, was also trained as a doctor.

There are many different descriptions of Abe's style of writing. It has been called avant-garde, which in his day referred to the alienated characters he created who were forever seeking meaning in a seemingly apathetic world. His writing has also been labeled science fiction, in terms of his creating futuristic settings that address questions that concerned him in the present. Early in his career, Abe became fascinated with the promises of Marxist philosophy, and his work was subsequently imbued with a propagandist tone. Abe's novels and his plays also possess absurd or surreal elements, creating hallucinatory, or dreamlike, images. He has also been called an existentialist, his works displaying, as Rimer states, ''an ironic questioning of all established values.''

A consistent pattern in Abe's work is the use of metaphor. Almost all of his narratives are built around a single metaphor and, as William Currie describes, ''are developed with a kind of dream literalism.'' Abe presents the metaphor in somewhat realistic terms, but, as the play unfolds, the only thing that holds everything together is a sense of the irrational. ''I [Abe] tend instinctively, in a sense, to make the ordinary the starting point of all my thoughts. But at the same time, I dislike that as well, so I create monsters, to surprise.''

Later, in an interview with Shields, Abe mentions that he enjoys Anton Chekhov but believed that Chekhov's plays were also ''satisfying as literature.'' They could be enjoyed without seeing them in performance. For Abe's play, this was not true. "I write novels, so I have the means of expressing what can be expressed in novels. I want to express on the stage something which is at once original and can only be expressed on the stage." Toward this end, Abe added elements to his plays that could only be presented in live performance. These components were added not only to enhance the flavor of a live performance but also to shock his audience. Often included were the sounds of someone going to the bathroom or the noises of a gurgling stomach. "Smells, too, are significant in Abe's oeuvre," writes Shields, "and tend to be disgusting."

Abe's style is not easy. His plays are puzzles that are difficult to understand; better yet, they are more like dreams that no one fully understands. Abe's philosophy of drama was not to present everyday images that would entertain his audiences. His style was to make his audiences think. "Unless the theater regains the power to realize on stage those more abstract things which are impossible to see in everyday reality," Abe tells Shields, "audiences will find theatrical productions more and more boring." Abe elaborates on this challenge in an afterword to the published script of his play: "In performance it is essential that the style, rather than the words, be emphasized."

HISTORICAL CONTEXT

Manchuria

During the almost twenty years that Abe lived in Manchuria (from approximately 1925 to 1944), Japan's imperialist expansion in Asia achieved one of its most infamous moments. Having defeated Russia in the Russo-Japanese War (1904–1905), the Japanese established themselves in China and began transforming Manchuria by first setting up a puppet Chinese government, then building an industrial and military complex there. By the end of World War II, Manchuria had become the most industrialized region in China.

This transformation was not a humanitarian effort. There were horrific atrocities that occured in a hostile take-over of one cultural group by another,

with severe physical punishment and torture used to control dissent. Abe recounts one childhood memory of riding in a train, looking out of the window, and seeing a large dump ground that was surrounded by stakes on which heads of dead people had been placed as a reminder to others of what would happen if they were deemed criminals. Abe, in Shields's book, referred to these heads as "'anonymous figures,' whose stories would never be told." These images of death would stay with Abe, informing his plays as well as his life, by constantly reminding him of his own mortality. "I feel that both novels and the stage offer an opportunity to give voice to the shouts that I heard from the dump ground," Abe adds.

Japanese Theatre

One of Abe's contemporaries, Koreya Senda, once complained about the influence of traditional theatre on drama in Japan, stating, in Shields's book, that "all we had to work with was a group of actors who could only deliver lines in chanting, Kabuki fashion." This reference was made in the name of the traditional Japanese form of theatre, which was so different from Western drama to which Abe was most attracted. Japanese theatre is a very old tradition, going back to the fourteenth century, and the form is very rigid, especially when compared to modern European and American drama.

For example, the first Japanese theatre form, Noh, is a stylized and prescribed performance that combines music, dance, poetry, and drama. The characters in Noh plays, as well as their movements and gestures, are specifically dictated by an ancient form and structure. The actors are highly trained to represent an artistic expression of quiet elegance and grace, as they play out the roles of gods, warriors, beautiful women, and supernatural beings. Accompanying the actors is a chorus of eight people who sit to one side of the stage narrating the story, expressing the thoughts and emotions of the characters, and singing the characters' lines. Although not as popular as it once was, Noh theatre continues to flourish in Japan and around the world.

In the seventeenth century, a more relaxed form of drama evolved from the Noh tradition. Sometimes likened to vaudeville or burlesque, Kabuki theatre presents stories of larger-than-life heroes as well as ordinary people in more comic (and often more sensual) settings. As a matter of fact, sensual-

COMPARE & CONTRAST

- **Early 1900s:** Korean, Russian, and Japanese forces fight over Manchuria in a series of wars. In the decade prior to World War II, Japan exerts military control over the land and establishes Manchuria as the most industrialized section of mainland China.

  Middle 1900s: Japan loses its rights to Manchuria after World War II. Chinese Communist forces take control of the area when Russia threatens to invade.

  Today: China's interest in Manchuria wanes and large-scale unemployment ensues as state-controlled businesses stagnate.

- **Early 1900s:** Japan's economy is largely based on textile goods. Later, as imperialist ambitions increase, the Japanese economy becomes even stronger with the manufacture of heavy war machinery.

  Middle 1900s: After a total collapse of its economy coming as a result of its defeat in World War II, Japan emerges as a major industrial power, manufacturing machinery, automobiles, and steel.

  Today: Japan is the most industrialized country in Asia and is the second-greatest economic power in the world, second only to the United States. Japan's economy is now based on technological goods such as electric and electronic appliances.

- **Early 1900s:** Expressionist playwrights like Karel Capek (Czechoslovakia) and Eugene O'Neill (U.S.A.) influence dramatists around the world with their use of minimal scenery, talking machines, and characters as types, rather than as real people, to convey the dehumanizing aspects of a technological society.

  Middle 1900s: The Theatre of the Absurd reflects a widespread sense of the utter meaningless in life through the work of such dramatists as Samuel Beckett (Ireland), Eugene Ionesco (France), and Edward Albee (U.S.A.), who influence many young, international playwrights.

  Today: There is a trend in modern plays to reflect realistic themes such as gay lifestyles, multicultural interests, reflections of Holocaust and Hiroshima survivors and their children, the political struggles of Apartheid, the devastation caused by AIDS, and cultural conflicts of post-Colonialism.

ity became such a dominant theme that, in 1629, women were eventually banned from appearing on stage, as government officials noted that some of the actresses were using the stage to promote prostitution. Thereafter, young boys took on the female roles until 1652, when they too were banned for the same reason. After that point, only mature men were allowed to play all the roles, a practice that, although no longer enforced by law, continues into modern times. Kabuki remains very popular in Japan, with Kabuki actors enjoying the same popularity as Hollywood movie stars.

Although Kabuki plays have evolved to address more contemporary themes, with dramatists such as Mishima Yukio (1925–1970) adding modern innovations, the structure is still highly stylized and the elements of music and dance, exaggerated movements, and extravagant makeup confine the type of drama it produces. William Currie, in his article ''Abe Kobo's Nightmare World of Sand,'' confirms the conflicts Abe felt in trying to adapt his style of writing to the traditional theatrical form: ''in range, depth and style, the works of Abe Kobo represent a considerable departure from the writing of almost all the Japanese novelists and dramatists who preceded him.''

Effects of World War II

Hiroshima lost over 200,000 people when the atomic bomb was dropped on August 6, 1945.

Another 70,000 people died three days later, when an atomic bomb was dropped on Nagasaki. These incidents marked more than the end of the war. They marked the people of Japan as helpless victims, both physically (in the form of radiation burns from the bombs) and psychologically (with the awareness of their own mortality).

Besides the devastation and destruction caused by the bombs, Japan also came under the cultural and economic influence of the United States. Western culture infiltrated Japan, causing the younger generation, which included Abe and his peers, to stray from the rites of traditional Japan and embrace the new—and more individualistic—concepts of the West. Along with the influence of Western culture came the anguish of alienation, the search for self-identity, and the sense of living the inauthentic life—concepts that were very foreign to traditional Japanese culture. After World War II, the experience of cultural dislocation and problems of identity were addressed by a new generation of leftist writers such as Abe, who used narrative and dramatic techniques developed from Western modernism.

CRITICAL OVERVIEW

Abe's *The Man Who Turned into a Stick* received very little attention outside of Japan. Although it was not a hit with the traditional theatergoing crowds in Japan, the play did receive an outstanding reception, given its surreal and avant-garde themes, settings, and style, as well as it having its main production held in Abe's small studio that seated only sixty people. Despite the fact that the play was used by Abe at his Kobo Abe Studio "as a studio exercise by the most junior members of the troupe," it still played to over one thousand spectators.

Donald Keene, writing the Introduction to Abe's play *The Man Who Turned into a Stick*, states, "The play was a popular as well as an artistic success." Keene then relates, in a more general statement about Abe, that besides being respected as a writer

> Abe's commitment to the theatre has gone far beyond creating plays of literary excellence; he is profoundly concerned with techniques of acting, the effectiveness of gestures and speech, even the mechanisms of stage

lighting and sound effects[.] He is, in short, a truly professional dramatist.

There are no specific reviews of this play written in English. However, there are studies of Abe's work written by academics. J. Thomas Rimer, in his book *Modern Japanese Fiction and Its Traditions: An Introduction,* writes that "Abe has always been a fashionable writer. His early work, especially in the theater, shows the powerful influence of Marxism, so important in the Japanese intellectual scene during the early postwar years." Rimer also compares Abe's writing to Franz Kafka's and further states that it is "most conspicuously 'avant-garde,'" and adds that his "literary strategies emphasize wit and satire." Rimer, this time writing in the *Dictionary of Literary Biography,* credits Abe with not only changing the face of Japanese theatre but also, through his plays, attracting international attention.

> Abe's protean literary activities during complex postwar times in Japan helped strengthen creative currents drawn from international developments in literature rather than from purely Japanese sources . . . [and] helped attract international attention to issues in postwar Japanese life.

However, Rimer also brings up the fact that, because Abe shed "too much of the Japanese literary tradition," Japanese audiences regarded him as an inauthentic mirror of their culture. Meanwhile, Western critics paid little attention to Abe's writing for basically the same reason: "Abe's concerns and obsessions resemble those of other contemporary writers around the world." In other words, Western critics expected Japanese writers like Abe to reflect a more specifically Japanese world. Rimer concludes his article by stating that, although Abe may not have received a lot of critical attention in his time, his influence is being felt in a new generation of Japanese writers, thus making Abe's work a "harbinger of a broad new Japanese sensibility."

Currie compliments Abe's use of metaphor. He writes that Abe

> uses strong, universal metaphors in such a way that they become a basis for his narrative art. By using metaphors, Abe expresses complex ideas not by analysis, nor by making an abstract statement, but by a sudden perception of an objective relation. This relation is expressed in one commanding image.

Many of Abe's other plays received critical acclaim and won awards. One such play, *The Ghost*

Is Here (1958, 1967), even traveled to East Germany where it played for two years. *The Man Who Turned into a Stick* was the first play that Abe himself directed.

CRITICISM

Joyce Hart

Hart has degrees in English literature and creative writing and is a freelance editor and published writer. In this essay, she examines the dramatic and psychological techniques Abe uses in his play to enthrall his audience.

Kobo Abe's *The Man Who Turned into a Stick* is a play that, despite its idiosyncratic features, its nameless characters, and practically nonexistent plot, has the power to not only capture its audience but to touch upon issues that merit attention even forty years after it was written. There is something very personal about Abe's writing that makes members of his audience pay attention to every line and sometimes even squirm in their seats as they recognize themselves in his play. Abe is a master of knowing how to grab his audience's attention and then exposing some of their more intimate thoughts and emotions. He accomplishes this without their knowing what he has done or how he has done it.

Anyone who has read Abe or attended one of his plays does not have to be told that they are difficult to understand. However, in spite of the challenge of his disjointed plots and obscure meanings, his audiences tend to leave the theatre excited about what they have just seen. As Shields writes, ''Abe's fervor infected everyone with a sense of contagious excitement. It did not matter if the actors, audience, or even Abe himself did not completely comprehend his creation.'' Abe's drive to create plays that are completely new, so new that even *he* might not understand their meaning, is an act of courage. That might be part of the reason why his plays attract attentive audiences, but there is more going on in his plays than new angles and perspectives, innovative tricks, and far-fetched characters. Although the overall ambiance of an Abe play makes the audience feel like they have entered a dream, Abe has put a lot of rational thought into the creation of his fantasies. He knows how to keep his audience tuned in to the action on stage. He is more than a writer. He is a combination of orchestral conductor, dramatist, and psychologist: wooing his audience with his charm, he pretends to entertain them while he divulges some of their deepest secrets.

Abe begins his play *The Man Who Turned into a Stick* with stage directions that suggest that the young hippie couple (Hippie Boy and Hippie Girl) could be shown sniffing glue. So the curtain opens with an image of rebellion, risk-taking, and somewhat disorienting recklessness. Granted, a glue-sniffing scene in the twenty-first century might seem a bit tame, but modernize the element to a more radical, modern drug, or cheap high, and the impact is there. With this first image, before any dialogue has been spoken, Abe broadcasts more than could be explained in several minutes of conversation. Of course, Abe did not know how his audience might interpret this opening scene, but he knew it would grab their attention and set them on edge, ready for a night of theatre unlike any they had experienced before.

From this opening scene, Abe then has a four-foot-long stick ''hurtling down from the sky,'' and crashing to the stage, nearly hitting Hippie Boy. Not only does the stick startle the young hippie couple, it assuredly startled the audience. As the audience ponders what the stick might represent, Man from Hell enters from stage-left and, in a poetic, chant-like voice, recites lines about the moon being a knife that is ''peeling the skin of fate.'' Abe wastes no time garnering the audience's attention. Before easing his audience into a slightly more comfortable mode, however, Woman from Hell announces, almost like a town crier, the somewhat startling news that yet another man has turned into a stick. There is, in fact, a man (referred to as Stick) on stage who matches his movements, as best he can, to those of the real stick that is now in Hippie Boy's hands. With this introduction, Abe has arrested his audience's curiosity. They are now wide awake with anticipation. They are primed and ready for the drama to unfold.

Next, Abe eases back into his chair, allowing his audience to catch its breath, as the hippie couple exchange lines about the rhythm the boy is tapping on the sidewalk with the stick. Then the girl looks up and exclaims, ''Look!'' and points to a young

WHAT DO I READ NEXT?

- Abe's work and style are often compared to Franz Kafka, a writer born in Prague in 1883. Two of Kafka's better known works include *The Metamorphosis* (1915; English translation 1937), in which a young man wakes up one morning to find that he has been changed into a large bug. The theme of this book, as with most of Kafka's work, is the individual's feelings of inadequacy and isolation in modern civilization. The other book, *The Trial* (1925; English translation 1937), involves a young man accused of a crime he did not commit, much less understand. He is eventually released but must return to court to repeatedly prove his innocence. Both novels explore the psychological terrors that many people experience in modern-day life.

- Another writer to whom Abe is compared is Alain Robbe-Grillet, who was born in Brest, Brittany, in 1922. Robbe-Grillet wrote about characters who had little or no previous history and no conventional names to identify them, as do the characters of Abe's plays. Robbe-Grillet's most famous work is the novel *Les Gommes* (1953; translated as *The Erasers,* 1964). This book is a type of murder mystery, which covers a supposed twenty-four-hour period that begins when a bullet is fired from a gun and ends with the bullet entering and killing its victim.

- Three other popular plays by Abe include *Fake Fish* (1973), a play about fish who dream of being men and men who dream of being fish; *Friends* (1965), in which a smiling but unidentified family invades a man's life and drives him to suicide—Abe's statement against the traditional Japanese communal values; and *Green Stockings* (1974), a play about a man who, in an attempt to transcend his everyday existence, steals stockings, panties, and brassieres from other people's clotheslines.

- Abe's most popular work of fiction is *The Woman in the Dunes* (1964). In this story a schoolteacher, who is also an amateur entomologist, sets out to find a rare insect. While searching in vast, unnamed sand dunes, the protagonist comes across a primitive colony of people whose daily task is to haul sand out of their submerged living quarters. The schoolteacher eventually becomes entrapped and is kept prisoner there. When he finally escapes, he no longer has the desire to return to his former life.

- Jacob Golomb's *In Search of Authenticity: Existentialism from Kierkegaard to Camus (Problems of Modern European Thought)* (1995) is a study of the writings of Søren Kierkegaard, Friedrich Nietzsche, Jean-Paul Sartre, and Albert Camus, existential philosophers and novelists who examined mankind's responsibility in determining what is right and wrong, a subject (and philosophy) that Abe often referred to.

(unseen) boy, on the roof of a tall building. She surmises that the boy threw the stick. Hippie Boy responds derogatively, stating that he hates all little boys, while Hippie Girl is concerned that the young boy might fall over the edge. Abe has caught the audience's attention again. He had lightened up for a couple of lines, but now he introduces more tension: first, the Hippie Boy's straightforward announcement that he hates little boys, an unpopular sentiment; second, there is the idea that the little boy might fall, arousing concern in the audience. At this point, with everyone looking up, hoping for the young boy's safety, Stick speaks. As his monologue progresses, the audience begins to relate to him. He is sensitive, concerned, confused, and loving. He is, in other words, like most members in the audience. He is the quintessential Everyman.

When Man and Woman from Hell meet at center stage (they have been slowly walking in from opposite sides of the stage) they begin a dialogue with the hippies. Through their exchanges, Abe hints at his themes of alienation, death, passivity, and aimlessness. He creates short conversations that focus on these themes, but he intersperses slightly off-balanced dialogues that don't make a lot of sense. For instance, immediately following a somewhat lengthy description of Man from Hell's sentiments about the benefit of uncertainty and anguish in one's life, Hippie Girl turns to Hippie Boy and asks: ''How about a kiss, huh?'' It is as if Abe wants to catch the audience off-guard. He has turned and caught them catnapping, something he cannot allow them to do. So he throws out a line that will again wake them up. After all, who can resist the mention of a kiss?

Apparently, Hippie Boy can—and does. Hippie Girl is put off, but offers a compromise. Why doesn't Hippie Boy scratch her back with the stick? By now, the audience has associated the male actor with the stick. The man has been talking for the stick and has matched the stick's motions as best he can. The audience has identified the stick with the man and must wonder how the boy will scratch the girl's back with Stick? Will he use the stick or the male actor? The audience must figure this out. Again, Abe lures the audience into the act, forcing them to think through the motivations of the characters and anticipate what the author has planned next.

The girl bends over in Hippie Boy's direction, implying that she is ready for him to scratch her back. Hippie Boy inserts the stick (the real stick) down the back of her dress. In likewise fashion, Hippie Girl then scratches Hippie Boy's back with the stick. Hippie Boy enjoys the scratching so much he emits strange, ecstatic noises and announces that he hasn't had a bath in a long time. Here Abe inserts humor. It is used as a respite, an opportunity for the audience to relax and laugh at nonsense. However, it does not last long. As soon as the audience begins to laugh, Abe turns their emotions around and makes them confront anger. Hippie Girl throws the stick down in disgust and exclaims: ''You egoist!'' Just when the audience thought that Abe was letting up the pressure, he catches them again. This time he catches them in a puzzle. What is wrong with Hippie Girl? What does she mean by calling Hippie Boy an ''egoist''? What is going on? In throwing out questions at his audience, Abe keeps them connected to his play. Nothing is answered or explained, of course, leaving the audience to work through the confusion, creating their own answers.

> **"THE PLAY PROGRESSES, WITH ABE CLENCHING AND SQUEEZING THE NERVES OF HIS AUDIENCE, THEN RELEASING THEM FOR SHORT PERIODS OF TIME, ONLY TO GRAB THEM AGAIN WITH NEW, UNSETTLING ELEMENTS."**

The play progresses, with Abe clenching and squeezing the nerves of his audience, then releasing them for short periods of time, only to grab them again with new, unsettling elements. Stick speaks. He is very emotional. His son is crying out for him. Stick knows that this is the last he will see of his son. Interspersed between the monologues of the dying stick are Abe's reflections on modern life, as expressed by the other characters in the play. The audience, now completely rapt with anticipation, wonders why the Man from Hell has asked for their attention. Their minds are open, and Abe is about to leave them with a message that will remain with them for quite some time.

Toward the end, the play takes a turn toward the serious. Hippie Boy, while holding the stick, senses his own resemblance to it. He feels the life flowing out of it, and it startles him. The reflection on the boy's part is flitting, at first, for the conversation quickly changes direction, returning briefly to comedy, with Abe orchestrating a discordant rhythm that keeps the audience perturbed as the characters switch from jokes to irrational actions to moments of reflection. Hippie Boy's identification with the stick continues to weave its way through the play until, in astonishment and confusion, Hippie Boy gladly hands over the stick to Man from Hell. Hippie Boy, Abe demonstrates, does not like what he feels. He does not want to see himself as a stick.

It is during the last section that the play delivers most of Abe's message. The dialogue is fairly straightforward, with no comedic interruptions. Abe partially explains the metaphor of the stick and the reasons why the man has turned into one. Then he has everyone but Stick leave the stage, with the Man and Woman from Hell seen in silhouette as they stand behind a curtain. They begin reciting poetic stanzas again as Stick contemplates the reasons for his present condition. Without stepping out from behind the curtain, Woman and Man engage in a brief dialogue, wondering how a stick would scratch himself if he had an itch. The audience is lulled into believing that the play has reached its conclusion. However, Abe has a few more tricks up his sleeve. The audience is in for another surprise. Abe is not quite finished with them.

Man from Hell suddenly reappears on stage and walks over to the audience. He stands, pointing his finger at individuals in their seats. Then he says: "Look—there's a whole forest of sticks around you." With this, Abe has done it again. The play, in essence, has finished, but the final message has yet to be delivered. Abe is not going to let the audience go home, believing they can sneak out of the theatre unnoticed. Abe is like a teacher, and Man from Hell is handing out Abe's take-home exam. The play has delivered Abe's message, only now he wants to make sure that the audience understands that he was talking directly to them. There was only one man in this play who turned into a stick, but in the audience there are many more potential victims. Man from Hell then delivers his last lines: "I wouldn't want you to think I'm saying these things just to annoy you . . . . It's just the simple truth."

Just in case the audience didn't get Abe's message, he has Woman from Hell console Stick by telling him, just before the curtain falls, that he is not alone. "You've lots of friends," she says. With these words, Abe leaves his audience alone. At least he leaves them in the physical sense. His play, his thoughts, his quirky images, and his disturbing questions go home with every member of the audience. If there are questions in their minds, and most assuredly there will be questions, Abe leaves the members of the audience to answer them on their own.

Source: Joyce Hart, Critical Essay on *The Man Who Turned into a Stick,* in *Drama for Students,* The Gale Group, 2002.

Erik France

France is a librarian and teacher of history and interdisciplinary studies at University Liggett School. He also teaches basic writing at Macomb Community College near Detroit, Michigan. In the following essay, he discusses elements of existentialism and the Theatre of the Absurd in Abe's play.

In a darkly playful and bizarre manner, *The Man Who Turned into a Stick* forces its audience to think about the purpose of life in a crowded, technology-

saturated society. Subtle conflicts between characters inspire one to explore the meaning of life and death as an essential aspect of the human condition. As the play opens, the title character jumps off the roof of a department store located above a busy subway or train station in Tokyo. His suicide creates the play's situation and plot. However, one cannot determine whether the ensuing action and dialogue are "real." As the Man from Hell suggests, it is possible that he and his partner-in-training "constitute no more than the dreams that people have when they are on the point of death." Such ambiguity gives the play disturbing and unsettling force. Conceptually, the bleak themes of existential despair and death in Kobo Abe's *The Man Who Turned into a Stick* can be placed within a historical context.

The philosophy of modern existentialism and the closely related Theatre of the Absurd came into their own in the wake of the destruction and trauma caused by World War II. This horrendous conflict, raging from 1939 to 1945 in Europe and the Pacific, killed millions of men, women, and children. It left the survivors, particularly those who lived in areas where the fighting was most intense, disoriented and devastated, in a state of shock. For many, religious leaders seemed incapable of explaining why or how God or a Supreme Being could allow such an atrocity to occur. Many intellectuals and artists lost faith in either God or the idea of rational human progress. Existentialism flourished in the wake of such twentieth century horrors as the European Holocaust and the atomic bombings of Hiroshima and Nagasaki in Japan, events that provided ample evidence of mankind's capacity for inflicting—and enduring—tremendous suffering. Emerging in Paris, which had been occupied by Nazi forces from 1940 to 1944, existentialist writers such as Jean-Paul Sartre (1905–1980) and Albert Camus (1913–1960) stated that modern life is pointless and absurd, without real meaning. In their view, God or a Supreme Being has apparently abandoned humans to their own devices. The best one can do is bravely face the absurdity of life and act accordingly.

Following World War II, the Theatre of the Absurd developed and explored the theme of existentialism. Sartre and Camus wrote plays as well as novels and essays and books of philosophy, but Samuel Beckett's *Waiting for Godot* (1954) is probably the best-known example of Theatre of the Absurd. In this genre, characters frequently experience alienation, a feeling of separation from society and place. They often come to realize that their lives are pointless. Once they reach this conclusion, they either continue on without much hope or try some desperate and often irrational act such as suicide. To keep audiences from fleeing to the exits in despair or denial, Theatre of the Absurd playwrights often use humor—usually bizarre and often nonsensical—to provoke laughter, even if the laughter is nervous or anxious. The Theatre of the Absurd made its maximum cultural impact in the 1950s and 1960s, a period of recovery from World War II. Tellingly, Samuel Beckett (1906–1989) won the Nobel Prize for Literature in 1969. Kobo Abe's *The Man Who Turned into a Stick*, first staged in 1967, fully resonates with elements of both modern existential philosophy and the Theatre of the Absurd.

Modern Japan, the setting of Abe's play, has undergone radical and startlingly rapid change in less than thirty years. Once the principal Asian military power, Japan suffered firebombings of its major cities, atomic attack, and military occupation by the United States and its allies. It then became transformed into a technologically advanced and rapidly developing economic power. Throughout this time, Japan was served by a disciplined workforce that accepted personal sacrifice as a rule. The Man Who Turned into a Stick represents this workforce, the necessary ingredient that made modern post-war Japan possible. He, like most Japanese workers, pays a heavy price for Japan's ''success.'' The Man from Hell explains that the Stick ''has put up with every kind of abuse, until its whole body is covered with scars, never running away and never being discarded'' and therefore ''should be called a capable and faithful stick.'' Similar characteristics could also describe those who led and served under the Japanese war machine of the 1930s and 1940s. From Abe's point of view, as expressed by the Man from Hell, capability and faithfulness are not particularly enlightened attributes for humans. Indeed, when placed entirely at the disposal of others without question, they eventually contribute to one's sense of alienation from the world. In the Stick Man's case, it leads him to such despair and desperation that he flees his son and leaps off a roof. Life has become so unbearable that an act of suicide seems heroic and liberating by comparison. For once he does something for himself. This seems irrational, perhaps, but taking responsibility for one's actions despite the absurdity of life is a heroic gesture, an act that constitutes one of the hallmarks of existentialism and Theatre of the Absurd. In life, one makes self-defining choices, even if they lead to one's own death.

> ''LIKE A STICK PRODDING THE AUDIENCE TO EXAMINE ITS BELIEFS AND VALUES, THE PLAY FORCES DIFFERENT GENERATIONS TO BECOME AWARE OF HOW THEY LIVE THEIR LIVES.''

Free will is an essential aspect of existentialist thought. The very act of transforming a man into a stick seems absurd on a rational level, but this transformation makes more sense on a subconscious and symbolic level. The quality of workers' lives is so poor that they are worth no more than sticks to be used as tools. The outlook is bleak. The Man from Hell points out to his partner that ''the percentage of sticks has steadily gone up.'' Workers' lives have become so dehumanized that they require no judgment or punishment when they die. Without hope while they live, they have no faith in Heaven or a redemptive afterlife. Yet Hell exists, at least in a dying man's consciousness. If there is a God or Supreme Being, he has abandoned humankind to its own devices. According to Hell's textbook: ''The Master has departed and the earth has become a grave of rotten sticks. That's why the shortage of help in hell has never become especially acute.'' Here and throughout the play are echoes of Sartre, Camus, and Beckett.

Two other characters provide an alternative to the Stick Man's way of life. Hippie Boy and Hippie Girl represent the counterculture that developed throughout the 1960s in reaction to the established values of the time. The counterculture movement made a lasting impression on the United States during the Vietnam War and soon became a worldwide phenomenon. Hippies defied the accepted social norms, yet they defined themselves simply by being against these norms rather than offering an alternative. Hippie Girl says blithely, ''This is the age of the generation gap. We're alienated.'' With this pronouncement, the playwright indicates that hippies are just as alienated as people who live by the more accepted social rules and expectations. The hippies live aimlessly, which bothers Hippie Girl somewhat. Her sister has died recently and she feels unsettled. She suggests that some aims in life would be a good thing. The Man from Hell replies in typical existentialist fashion. ''The uncertainty you feel at the thought you have lost track of whatever aims you once had—they're a lot better proof that you are there . . . than any aim I can think of,'' he tells her. In existentialism, mental anguish is a necessary part of understanding the absurd nature of human life no matter how it is lived. Hippie Boy acts disagreeably, trying to assert his uniqueness. But he feels anxious after Hippie Girl tells him that he resembles The Man Who Turned into a Stick. Hippie Boy cannot help but feel more disturbed when the Man from Hell follows up her observation: ''Let's suppose for the moment you do look like the stick—the meaning is not what you think it is.'' Hippie Boy thinks he's been clever by selling the stick for five dollars, but immediately after he makes the deal the Man from Hell says rather menacingly, ''It wasn't just a stick you sold, but yourself.'' In folklore, making a bargain with the Devil or his minions frequently leads to the surrender of one's soul. Later, when the Woman from Hell asks her partner what will become of the hippies, he says: ''If they don't turn into sticks maybe they'll become rubber hoses.'' He seems to be saying that, in the end, it makes no difference.

Much of the subtle conflict in *The Man Who Turned into a Stick* results from the interaction between Hippie Girl and Hippie Boy and between the Man and Woman from Hell. The girl and woman show more compassion and hope, which their male counterparts try to dash through quips and commentary. Hippie Boy calls Hippie Girl ''just plain stupid,'' while the Man from Hell chides his partner for being too compassionate, too sentimental. Hippie Girl thinks that some aims in life would be worthwhile. The Woman from Hell thinks that The Man Who Turned into a Stick should be given to his son. ''Don't you think that's the least we can do?'' she asks. ''At least it ought to serve as a kind of mirror. He can examine himself and make sure he won't become a stick like his father.'' But her partner refuses to do so. Still, their own fate is no better. After all, they reside in Hell—or in a figment of the dying Stick Man's imagination. The Man from Hell even has problems back at Headquarters. He's forgotten his keys and his wife might be mad at him. The Voice from Hell tells him over the walkie-talkie that he's ''hopeless.'' Elements of existentialism and Theatre of the Absurd are found throughout *The Man Who Turned into a Stick*. Kobo Abe bluntly and repeatedly announces that no one can escape the human predicament. Like a stick prod-

ding the audience to examine its beliefs and values, the play forces different generations to become aware of how they live their lives. As if this is still not clear enough, in the final moments before the curtain falls, the Man From Hell advances toward the audience and says ''Look—there's a whole forest of sticks around you . . . All those sticks. You may never be judged, but at least you don't have to worry about being punished.'' This pronouncement is merely ''the simple truth, the truth as I see it.''

Source: Erik France, Critical Essay on *The Man Who Turned into a Stick,* in *Drama for Students,* The Gale Group, 2002.

SOURCES

Abe, Kobo, *The Man Who Turned into a Stick: Three Related Plays,* translated by Donald Keene, University of Tokyo Press, 1975.

Currie, William, ''Abe Kobo's Nightmare World of Sand,'' in *Approaches to the Modern Japanese Novel,* edited by Kinya Tsuruta and Thomas E. Swann, Sophia University, 1976, pp. 1–3.

Iwamoto, Yoskio, Review of *Kangaroo Notebook,* in *World Literature Today,* Winter 1997.

Keene, Donald, Introduction, in *The Man Who Turned into a Stick: Three Related Plays,* translated by Donald Keene, University of Tokyo, 1975, pp. vi–x.

Rimer, J. Thomas, ''Abe Kobo,'' in *Dictionary of Literary Biography,* Volume 182: *Japanese Fiction Writers Since World War II,* Gale Research, 1997, pp. 3–10.

Rimer, J. Thomas, ''Tradition and Contemporary Consciousness,'' in *Modern Japanese Fiction and Its Traditions: An Introduction,* Princeton University Press, 1978, pp. 261–65.

Shields, Nancy K., *Fake Fish,* Weatherhill, Inc., 1996.

FURTHER READING

Goodman, David. G., trans. and ed., *After Apocalypse: Four Japanese Plays of Hiroshima and Nagasaki,* Cornell University Press, 1994 (reprint).

   A collection of modern Japanese plays that looks into the spiritual, political, and moral questions that faced most Japanese during the postwar era.

Iles, Timothy, *Abe Kobo: An Exploration of His Prose, Drama and Theatre,* European Press Academic Publishing, 2000.

   This is one of a very few books written in English that is totally focused on Abe's work. Iles offers a comprehensive study, interpretation, and criticism of both Abe's fiction and his plays.

Keene, Donald, *Dawn to the West: Japanese Literature of the Modern Era,* Columbia University Press, 1984.

This book, written by the noted scholar and translator of Abe's works, offers an extensive study of Japanese literature, including drama. Keene has translated the works of many major contemporary Japanese writers.

Mishima, Yukio, *Five Modern Noh Plays,* Charles E. Tuttle Co., 1981.

Using the traditional form of the Noh play, Mishima, a famous novelist, explores modern existential questions. Modern audiences often state that Mishima's work haunts them long after they have experienced his plays.

Takaya, Ted T., ed., *Modern Japanese Drama: An Anthology,* Columbia University Press, 1979.

This collection offers an overview of modern Japanese plays that were written and produced in Abe's time. Included are plays by Abe, Yukio Mishima, and other contemporary Japanese dramatists.

The Marriage of Figaro

PIERRE-AUGUSTIN DE BEAUMARCHAIS

1784

Like its author, Pierre-Augustin Caron de Beaumarchais, *The Marriage of Figaro* had a long, illustrious history. Completed in 1780, the play would not be acted on the French stage until 1784. Beaumarchais faced many obstacles in producing his comedy. The official French censors, as well as King Louis XVI, opposed the play. The comedy was scandalous in its depiction of a pleasure-seeking, incompetent nobleman who is upstaged by his crafty, quick-witted servant in their quest for the same woman. In its questioning of France's long-standing social class system, which stood as the very basis of France's governing body, it was also revolutionary. The aristocracy who made up the play's appreciative audience understood its subversive nature, yet continued to attend showings in record numbers.

The Marriage of Figaro deserves praise for its important social messages, its subtle wit, comic mastery, and vivacious dialogue; many scholars believe that this play is Beaumarchais's masterpiece. However, the play also holds an important place in the development of French theatre. It is a play in which the aristocracy face their impending decline. The triumph of Figaro, valet to a nobleman, signifies the victory of ability over birthright. As such, Beaumarchais presages the tumultuous events of 1789, the year that brought the French Revolution and the downfall of France's established class system.

AUTHOR BIOGRAPHY

Beaumarchais was born in Paris, France, on January 24, 1732. In 1753, working as an apprentice to his watchmaker father, Beaumarchais devised a mechanism that was recognized by the Academy of Sciences. Two years later, he was appointed watchmaker to the royal court of Louis XV. Upon marrying a widow, he became Clerk Controller and also inherited the property of Beaumarchais, from where he took his name. He became wealthy through business associations and purchased the title of Secretary of the King, which made him a member of the French nobility.

Beaumarchais traveled to Spain in 1764, after his sister's fiancé refused to marry her, where he revealed the fiancé's treachery. This trip gave him the opportunity to observe Spanish life and culture, including the wastefulness of the nobility and the abuses of the government. He returned to Paris in 1767 to present his play *Eugénie*, which made use of these experiences. His next play, *Les Deux Amies*, appeared three years later, in 1770. That same year, Beaumarchais became involved in a lawsuit. Although he eventually won his case, he was stripped of the civil rights belonging to French citizens, and these rights were not reinstated until 1776.

During this period, King Louis XV hired Beaumarchais as a secret agent. On frequent trips to England, he became interested in the cause for American independence. With the support of the French government, he helped provide unofficial money and arms to the American colonists.

He continued to work on his writings. *The Barber of Seville*, which first introduced Figaro, was produced in 1775. He completed *The Marriage of Figaro* in 1780, but it was not produced until four years later. The liberetto *Tarare* came out in 1787, and again in 1790 with a new ending adapted to the political changes that had taken place because of the French Revolution. *La Mere Coupable* was presented in 1792. Between 1783 and 1790, Beaumarchais published a complete edition of the works of Voltaire. In 1777 he also founded the Society of Dramatic Authors, one of the first organizations that protected an author's rights.

Beaumarchais continued to pursue his business interests, undertaking arms negotiations in 1792 on behalf of the French revolutionary government. Accused by the government of hiding the guns, he was imprisoned but freed from jail in time to escape the September massacres that took place that year.

Pierre-Augustin Caron de Beaumarchais

Beaumarchais fled to England and then to Hamburg, Germany. The French government declared him an émigré, which barred his return to France, before imprisoning his family and seizing his property. He remained in exile in Germany until 1796, when the new government allowed him to return. He died of a stroke in Paris on May 18, 1799.

PLOT SUMMARY

Act 1

The Marriage of Figaro opens on the day of Figaro and Suzanne's marriage. Suzanne informs her fiancé that the Count has offered her a dowry if she spends the first night with him. Figaro realizes that he must take quick action to thwart the Count's desires. He vows to mislead the Count by moving ahead the time the wedding will take place. At the same time, he must ward off Marceline, who wants to marry him. Marceline has involved Bartholo in her plans to win Figaro, which include encouraging the Count to oppose the marriage between Suzanne and Figaro.

Alone in her room, Suzanne is visited by Cherubino, whom the Count has dismissed upon catching him in Fanchette's room. Cherubino wants Suzanne to persuade the Count to reinstate him. The Count's arrival forces Cherubino to hide behind the chair and thus overhear the Count asking Suzanne to meet him later to discuss spending the night together. Basil's entry into the room, however, forces the Count to hide behind the chair and Cherubino to hide atop the chair. Basil counsels Suzanne to give in to the Count. He also reveals Cherubino's love for the Countess, which forces the Count to announce himself. He orders the page dismissed for good. Under pressure from the household, however, he declares that he will give Cherubino a commission in the army instead of merely casting him out. Figaro needs Cherubino for his scheme to thwart the Count, so he tells the page to return to the castle right away. The Count, meanwhile, hopes that Marceline will help him prevent the marriage.

Act 2

The Countess, Suzanne, and Figaro agree upon a two-fold plan to thwart the Count and return his affections to his wife: Figaro provokes the Count's jealousy by giving him an anonymous note warning that the Countess has a lover; Figaro also proposes that they send Cherubino, disguised as Suzanne, to meet the Count that evening. Cherubino arrives, but when the Count knocks on the door, he hides in the closet. The Count is upset by the note he has just received, and his suspicions are raised further when Cherubino makes a noise in the closet. Although the Countess says it is only Suzanne in the closet, the Count does not believe her. He leaves the room, accompanied by the Countess, to get tools to break down the door. While they are gone, Suzanne takes Cherubino's place in the closet, and he jumps out the window. When the Count opens the door, he finds only Suzanne.

Figaro comes in and is forced to cover himself when the Count finds out that he was behind the note. Marceline arrives on Figaro's heels, proclaiming that she has a note that says that Figaro must either repay a debt or marry her. The Count declares that the matter will be heard by the court.

Alone, the Countess and Suzanne reject Figaro's plan. They decide that the Countess will dress up as Suzanne and go meet the Count. The Countess forbids Suzanne to tell Figaro of the new plot.

Act 3

At the beginning of act 3, the Count wavers back and forth over whether he will rule in Marceline's favor or in Figaro's. Although Suzanne agrees to meet him that night, the Count does not trust her motivation because he realizes that she has told Figaro of his seduction plan. He decides instead to champion Marceline's cause.

At the trial, a blot over a crucial word renders unclear the exact meaning of the contract between Marceline and Figaro. After numerous readings, the Count decides that Figaro must, within the day, repay Marceline or marry her. Figaro tries to escape the verdict by arguing that he cannot marry without his parents' permission. However, he was stolen by gypsies at birth, so he does not know their identity. He reveals a mark on his arm, leading Marceline to realize that he is her and Bartholo's illegitimate son. Marceline embraces her long-lost son, but Bartholo is disgusted because he dislikes Figaro. Suzanne rushes in with money the Countess gave her to enable Figaro to repay the loan, but Marceline returns it to Figaro as his dowry. The Countess, Suzanne, and Figaro then urge Bartholo to marry Marceline.

Act 4

Figaro asks Suzanne not to meet the Count, and she agrees. However, when she tells the Countess of her intention, the Countess points out that she needs Suzanne's help so she can have the opportunity to win back her husband's love. The two women write a note to the Count, asking for a meeting under the elm trees. During the double wedding ceremony, Suzanne passes her note to the Count. Figaro observes the Count reading it but does not yet know it is from Suzanne. However, a chance comment alerts him to this fact and the location of the meeting. Figaro grows jealous and angry but, at Marceline's advice, decides to attend the rendezvous secretly.

Act 5

The Countess, disguised as Suzanne, meets the Count, Cherubino, and Fanchette, who had arranged their own meeting. They hide in the pavilion on the left, where Marceline has also ensconced herself. The Count attempts to seduce ''Suzanne,'' and her complicity angers Figaro, who is observing the pair from afar. He steps forward to stop the Count, the Count flees, and the Countess enters the pavilion on the right. Figaro then meets Suzanne, disguised as the Countess, but he quickly recognizes his bride's voice. To get back at Suzanne, he proposes a sexual liaison to the Countess. When Suzanne realizes that Figaro has recognized her, she explains why she made the rendezvous with the Count. When the Count returns to find "Suzanne," he becomes irate upon seeing his "wife" with Figaro. Suzanne flees into the pavilion on the left, while the Count seizes Figaro and places him under arrest. Figaro pretends that he was about to have an affair with the Countess. The Count goes into the pavilion to drag his wife out and force her to admit her infidelity in front of the household. However, Cherubino, Fanchette, and Marceline are dragged out instead. Then Suzanne herself comes out, but she hides her face so the Count will still think she is the Countess. The company all fall on their knees in front of the Count, begging him to forgive his wife. While he steadfastly declares that he will never do so, the disguised Countess emerges from the other pavilion and joins the others. Seeing both Suzanne and his wife, the Count realizes that he has been tricked. The play ends with Figaro and Suzanne married and rich with a triple dowry.

CHARACTERS

Count Almaviva

The Count's main interest in the play is fulfilling his amorous desires, and intrigue surrounds his efforts to seduce Suzanne. To this end, he promises her money if she will spend her first night as a married woman with him. Although he places a monetary figure on the situation and also holds the power to prevent Suzanne and Figaro's marriage, the Count views his designs as merry and lighthearted; as Beaumarchais describes the character of the Count in the playscript, "In keeping with the morals *of those days,* the great regarded the conquest of women as a frolic." While he actively pursues women, the Count becomes extremely angry when he suspects his wife of infidelity, thus demonstrating the double standards of his day.

The Count holds the ultimate authority on his estate, even deciding the outcome of Figaro and Marceline's court case. He demands the respect of those who surround him but does not realize that his own actions, at times bordering on the ridiculous or petty, make this difficult. At the end of the play, however, he laughingly accepts that he has been outwitted.

Countess Almaviva

The Countess is the Count's wife. She is torn between two conflicting feelings for her husband:

MEDIA ADAPTATIONS

- Mozart wrote a four-act opera, *Le Nozze di Figaro,* based on *The Marriage of Figaro.* It was first performed in 1786. Numerous recordings of it are available.

anger and love. She seeks to regain his affections and, to this end, secretly hatches a plan with Suzanne. Unlike her husband, the Countess is a very human, likable figure. She is clever enough to devise the plot that ends in success for her, Suzanne, and Figaro. She is a good friend to Suzanne, despite the vast difference in their classes, doing what she can to bring about the maid's marriage. Also, as further demonstration of her humanity, she cannot help but be drawn to Cherubino who shows her affection at the very time her husband has withdrawn his.

Antonio

Antonio is the castle's tipsy gardener. He is also Suzanne's uncle and guardian as well as Fanchette's father. Antonio is prepared to oppose Suzanne's marriage to Figaro. Antonio is the one who reports on the man who jumped into the flowerbed, causing Figaro to devise a story about what happened so the Count will not learn of Cherubino's presence.

Dr. Bartholo

Bartholo is a doctor from Seville. He helps Marceline, his former mistress, attempt to win Figaro for her husband. After they discover that Figaro is their son, he marries Marceline.

Basil

Basil is the Count's music master. He loses the Count's favor when he delivers the note from Figaro that falsely accuses the Countess of infidelity. Basil dislikes Figaro greatly. Although he wanted to marry Marceline, he loses all interest in her once he discovers she is Figaro's mother.

Don Guzman Bridlegoose

Bridlegoose is the judge of the district. However, in this role he is generally ineffective, failing to understand the cases that are put before him as well as the events that have taken place during the day.

Cherubino

Cherubino is a page in the Count's household. A prepubescent youth, he is beginning to feel sexual stirrings, and he is infatuated with many of the females on the estate, including the Countess, Suzanne, Fanchette, and even Marceline. Dismissed from the household after the Count finds him in Fanchette's bedroom, he becomes a part of Figaro's plan; he is the one initially chosen to meet the Count, dressed as Suzanne.

Fanchette

Fanchette is the twelve-year-old daughter of Antonio. As befits her youth and inexperience, she is naïve, not understanding the Count's true desires toward her. She is also important to the plot, being the person who reveals to Figaro the rendezvous between the Count and ''Suzanne.''

Figaro

Figaro is the Count's faithful servant as well as his competition. The Count's pursuit of Suzanne requires that Figaro conspire against his master. He must rely upon his wits to carry out a plan for keeping Suzanne out of the Count's hands that still allows the couple to marry. Because the plot that he devises is complex and even backfires in key instances, the Count's suspicions are raised, and Figaro is unable to make it work. Figaro further jeopardizes the situation by deliberately playing with the Count. In this respect, his belief that he is more resourceful and smarter than the Count, though borne out by the play, fails to serve him well, for he increases the Count's wrath.

Suzanne and the Countess come up with their own plan for thwarting the Count but do not inform Figaro about it. His isolation contributes to a jealous rage that overtakes him when he believes Suzanne is unfaithful. His monologue in act 5 asserts his rights, despite a lack of parentage, fortune, or social rank.

Marceline

Marceline is the housekeeper of the castle. She has strong feelings for Figaro. Not realizing that it is maternal love, she conspires to marry him, even if it means forcing him to do so against his will. Upon finding out the truth, however, she embraces her long-lost son and helps him to find happiness with Suzanne. At the end of the play, she marries Bartholo.

Rosine

See Countess Almaviva

Suzanne

Suzanne is the maid to the Countess. ''In her role . . . there is not a word that is not inspired by goodness and devotion to her duty,'' writes Beaumarchais of her in his character descriptions. She is also intelligent, honorable, and full of wit. She has the good sense to tell the people she trusts the most—Figaro and the Countess—of the Count's intentions toward her. As the object of the Count's lust, Suzanne must be careful to protect herself without alienating the Count to such an extent that he will forbid her marriage. Suzanne and the Countess, her friend and confidante, conspire secretly against the Count. It is their plan that ends in success, bringing Suzanne her happy marriage.

THEMES

Social Classes

From its earliest readings in France, *The Marriage of Figaro* raised concerns over Beaumarchais's criticism of the social class system. This system, in place since the Middle Ages, put members of the aristocracy in positions of governmental and military power even if they did not merit it. It also allowed for little upward mobility. Figaro's plotting against his master is a usurpation of aristocratic authority. His actions literally demonstrate several bold assertions: that such authority is designated merely by virtue of birth and not by worth, and that his own desire is paramount to the Count's. He and the Count then compete for Suzanne, and Figaro— the worthier man—wins. Figaro also continuously expresses his disdain for the aristocracy, letting no opportunity pass for criticizing the upper class. Among other things, he points out their lack of intelligence and their lax morality.

Figaro's monologue contains the most biting criticism of the aristocratic class. In this speech, he specifically points out the randomness that places some people in power over others. ''What have you done to earn so many advantages?'' he wonders. He provides the only accurate answer: ''You took the

TOPICS FOR FURTHER STUDY

- Beaumarchais originally set *The Marriage of Figaro* in France in the 1780s. Do you think changing the setting to Spain lessens any of the issues he raises about social classes and rebellion against it? Write a paper comparing the social and political environments of these two countries.

- Critics disagree as to whether Figaro's monologue in act 5, in which he chronicles the abuses of the nobility against the lower classes, forecasts the French Revolution and the end of the French aristocracy. Write a persuasive essay supporting this belief or attacking it.

- Read *The Barber of Seville*. Compare Beaumarchais's characterizations of the Count, the Countess (Rosine), and Figaro in the two works.

- Conduct research to find out more about the social abuses of the aristocracy in the years prior to the French Revolution. Does Beaumarchais do a good job of presenting these issues? Explain your answer.

- Learn more about Beaumarchais's life. In what ways do you think his own experiences affected his creation of *The Marriage of Figaro*?

- Conduct research about the development of either the comedic play or the French theatre. Comment on the importance of Beaumarchais's contribution.

---

trouble to be born, nothing more. Apart from that, you're a rather common type.'' Figaro then asserts that members of the servant class, such as himself, must use their wits, strategy, and skill merely to get by; therefore, they clearly have more natural abilities.

Fidelity and Adultery

The play's intrigue centers around the Count's adulterous desire for Suzanne. Bored with his wife, the Count has set his sights on Figaro's betrothed. That she is the fiancée of his loyal servant does not divert him in the slightest, which clearly depicts how noblemen such as himself regarded affairs with their underlings. Indeed, this experienced philanderer pursues other young, attractive women on his estate in addition to Suzanne.

Despite his own lapse of fidelity, the Count becomes furious when he believes that his wife is, or may be in the future, unfaithful. He banishes Cherubino from the estate because the page reveals his love for the Countess. He assumes that the reason his wife won't open the closet door is that a man is in the room. When he views Suzanne dressed in his wife's clothing, having apparently succumbed to Figaro's seduction, he rushes out to attack the servant. He refuses to forgive his ''wife,'' and fails to see the hypocrisy within himself, even though his wife forgives him.

Figaro also questions his beloved's fidelity. Although he told Marceline that he would forgive Suzanne anything, even unfaithfulness, he becomes furious when he believes she is accepting the Count's favors. His jealously leads him to the elm grove so he can see what happens. In this instance, he comes to resemble the Count in his quick acceptance of his lover's infidelity.

Women and Gender Roles

The way the men in the play treat the women demonstrates how society in Beaumarchais's time regarded gender roles. Women faced great inequality. They were often subject to the whims of their husbands or guardians. For example, Suzanne cannot marry Figaro unless her uncle Antonio allows it, and the Count threatens to banish the Countess to her room ''for a long time!'' as punishment.

Most significantly, although the Count happily and casually engages in extramarital affairs, his wife can ''never'' be forgiven for doing the same thing. The Count's attitude toward his wife—and

Figaro's attitude toward Suzanne when he believes she is about to have an affair—shows that women were perceived as objects that belonged to their lovers. In this view, women lose ''value'' when they commit an infidelity. On the basis of circumstantial evidence, Figaro even considers ''dropping one wife and wedding another.'' Such threats show that a woman's value—derived exclusively from her faithfulness and virtue—reflects on the man who possesses her.

The plot hatched by the Countess and Suzanne, however, show women attempting to subvert this narrow gender role, and the Countess specifically forbids Suzanne from telling Figaro about the plan. Indeed, all the key players in the plan are female. Significantly, Figaro's plan to outsmart the Count does not work, but the Countess's does; she and Suzanne alone devise and execute a plan to save the maid's virtue and return the affections of the Count to the Countess.

STYLE

Monologue

Figaro's lengthy monologue in act 5 breaks up the quick pace of the comedy. In the first part of the monologue, Figaro reflects upon Suzanne's faithlessness and deceit as well as the arbitrary nature of the aristocracy's power. In the second part, he recounts the numerous jobs he has held as a means of exploring his future. In the third and final part, Figaro reflects upon the course his life has taken.

While Figaro's monologue slows down the pace of the play at a crucial juncture, it serves to demonstrate that he possesses greater depth than his previous comic antics, as well as his irrational jealousy, might otherwise suggest. On a larger thematic level, the monologue challenges French society's tradition of honoring wealth and rank above merit. Some critics have interpreted Figaro's commentary on the social abuses of the aristocracy as a forecast of the impending French Revolution and the end of the class system.

Satire

A satirical play is one that uses humor and wit to criticize human nature, society, and institutions.

Beaumarchais's play, though comic, never shies away from pressing social issues. However, he uses indirect satire, relying upon the ridiculous behavior of his characters to make his point. An example of indirect satire is when the Count is forced to hide behind the chair in Suzanne's room.

Beaumarchais's main objects of satire are the members of the aristocracy. Embodied in the person of the Count Almaviva, the aristocracy is seen as vain, foolish, self-centered, dissolute, and dishonest. The character of the judge, Bridlegoose, provides another good example of how Beaumarchais uses satire, in this case, to attack the judicial system. The stuttering Bridlegoose is completely ineffective and stupid. He has great difficulty understanding the facts of Figaro's case as put before him. The only thing that is clear to him is that Marceline, Figaro's mother, will not marry her son. Though his position as a judge—a position that he purchased—would seem to require that he render opinions, he constantly refuses to do so. In fact, his opinion is not needed at all, for the Count is the final authority in the court; he delivers its decision, thus devaluing Bridlegoose by taking away what should be his primary function.

Trilogy

Beaumarchais's plays *The Barber of Seville*, *The Marriage of Figaro*, and *A Mother's Guilt* comprise his trilogy about Count Almaviva. *The Barber of Seville*, the first play of the trilogy, focuses on Figaro's successful plan to win Rosine (the Countess Almaviva) for the Count. *A Mother's Guilt* finds the Count and Countess, and their loyal servants Figaro and Suzanne, living in France.

Beaumarchais makes use of the first play in his second. For instance, he neglected to write new descriptions for some characters in the playscript of *The Marriage of Figaro*; instead, he describes them as ''the same as in *The Barber of Seville*.'' However, Beaumarchais also breaks away from the earlier play in significant ways. Most notably, he reverses the character of the Count from a gallant romantic to a deceitful lech. The Count abolished the ''rights of the nobleman''—the right dating from feudal times that allowed the lord of the manor to deflower his vassal's wife on her wedding night— upon his marriage to Rosine in the first play, but he attempts to take advantage of this outmoded right in *The Marriage of Figaro*.

COMPARE & CONTRAST

- **1780s:** In the mid-1780s, France is a monarchy ruled by King Louis XVI. The king holds absolute power.

  Today: France is a republic headed by a president who is elected by popular vote for a seven-year term.

- **1780s:** French women lack the same rights as men. For instance, the father is the absolute authority of the family and males usually supersede females in inheritance rights.

  Today: Although laws guarantee women political, economic, and social rights equal to men, French women still are discriminated against. For example, they earn on average twenty percent less than men and make up less than five percent of senior managers in France's two hundred largest companies. An unequal division of labor still exists at home, where women complete eighty percent of domestic tasks and working women spend two hours more each day on such tasks than working men do.

- **1780s:** The nobility, who make up less than two percent of the population, enjoy special privileges such as the right to collect feudal dues from peasants. The nobility holds the highest positions in the army and government. Members of the Third Estate, however, may purchase titles and thus enter the aristocratic class.

  Today: A French aristocratic class still exists, but many members of this class work for a living. Class distinctions are generally accepted in France, and many class divisions remain rigid. Children of all classes attend state schools together, but there is little sense of a classless meritocracy.

HISTORICAL CONTEXT

France on the Brink of Revolution

Throughout the 1700s, France was the largest and most powerful nation in Europe. French society was divided into three estates. The First Estate consisted of the clergy of the Roman Catholic Church and made up less than one percent of the population. The Second Estate, the nobility, made up less than two percent of the population. People were born into the Second Estate, but they could also purchase titles. Neither the First nor the Second Estate paid any significant taxes. The Third Estate consisted of everyone else in France, from the peasants to the bourgeoisie, and constituted about ninety-seven percent of the French population.

Around the mid-1700s, discontent in France began to grow among the members of the Third Estate. Peasants were charged higher rents, and laborers' wages did not match the rising cost of food. The bourgeoisie, the urban middle class, wanted political power equal to their economic strength, less governmental interference in business dealings, and their sons to have important positions in the church, government, and army. The Third Estate also resented being the only group to pay taxes.

France was also undergoing a serious financial crisis. Left with huge debts after fighting the Seven Years' War, Louis XV, who ruled France from 1715 to 1774, raised taxes, borrowed more money from bankers, and refused to economize. His successor, Louis XVI, saw France's debts rise as the country aided the colonists in the American Revolution. Louis's financial advisers advocated taxing the First and Second Estates. When such taxes were proposed, the nobles protested and refused to cooperate; some even took part in riots. By 1787, the country stood on the brink of financial ruin.

Having little choice, Louis called representatives of all three estates to the Estates General at the Palace of Versailles in May 1780. He hoped that the group would approve his new plan of imposing taxes upon the wealthy. However, the Third Estate refused to follow the old custom that called for each of the three representative bodies to cast one vote. When the king did not take action, the Third Estate, on July 17, 1789, declared itself the National Assembly. This action began the French Revolution, which brought an end to the French monarchy.

The American Revolution

The American Revolution started in 1776 with the American Declaration of Independence. For several years, colonists were angry over the fact that they were forced to pay increasingly higher taxes without having representation in the British Parliament. France, Britain's longtime enemy, was pleased to see the Revolution start. France formed an alliance with the patriots, signing a treaty in 1778, and French emissaries such as Beaumarchais supplied the American forces with weapons. Individual French citizens also contributed to the patriot cause. The Marquis de Lafayette arrived in America in 1777 to fight alongside the patriots. He also gave large sums of money to aid the American forces. The fighting lasted until 1781, when the British surrendered. A new democracy was born. The success of the American Revolution was an inspiration for the leaders of the French Revolution.

The French Theatre

French drama developed greatly in the 1600s and 1700s. The seventeenth century was France's neoclassical period. Pierre Corneille wrote more than thirty plays, most of which followed Aristotle's precept of unity of time, place, and action. Jean Racine introduced a simpler style and more realistic characters and plot structures. The comic genius of Molière explored social, psychological, and metaphysical questions. The works of these playwrights remain mainstays of the French theatre. Other playwrights who contributed to the development of French drama during his period include Scarron, whose comedies were based on absurdity, and Marivaux, who focused on love instead of social realism. The 1700s witnessed fewer landmark developments in the theatre. Although French comedy reached its height in Molière's day, Beaumarchais offered many bold and exciting changes for the stage. He introduced social discourse into French comedy, along with rapid action, lively dialogue, and complex plots. His plays used comedy to highlight social abuses and subtly protest them.

CRITICAL OVERVIEW

Beaumarchais first completed *The Marriage of Figaro* in 1780. Although the Comédie Française accepted it for production in September 1781, the play took several years to gain the approval of the official censors because of its theme of rebellion. During this period, however, it was played in salons and at court, where it brought out conflicting opinions among the audience. Madame Campan reported in her *Mémoires* that King Louis XVI denounced the play, proclaiming: "It is hateful, it will never be played . . . . That man mocks everything that is to be respected in government." After a private performance of the play was given in honor of his brother, the king relented. Beaumarchais also had made several edits to the play, including changing the location of the play from contemporary France to old Spain, which made the comedy less objectionable.

The premiere of *The Marriage of Figaro* finally took place in April 1784 at the Comédie Française, though the struggle to get the play produced was not quite over. Suard, one of the censors who refused to give his approval, continued to attack Beaumarchais. When Beaumarchais made it known that he planned to ignore Suard, having had to fight "lions and tigers" in order to win the play's approval, the king, believing that Beaumarchais included him in this characterization, sent him to prison. However, Beaumarchais was freed on the fifth day with the king's apologies.

The Marriage of Figaro was an immediate, resounding success among its aristocratic audience. In *French Comic Drama from the Sixteenth to Eighteenth Century,* Geoffrey Brereton sums up the play upon its opening as having "quite enough dynamite . . . to make this appear a dangerously, or excitingly, revolutionary play." Despite its criticism of the class order, the play enjoyed a record run at the theatre. However, as Joseph Sungolowsky writes in *Beaumarchais,* "Eighteenth-century audiences did not fail to see the far-reaching social and political implications of the *Mariage* amid its joyfulness." Baronne d'Oberkirch was one aristocrat who went to see the play and was angry at herself for laughing at it. Cynthia Cox quotes the Baronne in *The Real Figaro* as writing that the "nobility showed a great want of tact in applauding it, which was nothing less than giving themselves a slap in the face. They laughed at their own expense . . . They will repent it yet . . . . "

Sylvester McCoy, as the Count, and John Bowe, as Figaro, in a scene from the 1991 theatrical production of The Marriage of Figaro, *performed at the Palace Theatre in Watford, England*

Despite its popularity, the play and its author still drew criticism based on the astonishing themes that ran through this long play. After it had been running for a year, Beaumarchais wrote a lengthy preface to the work in which he defended its morality. Among other declarations, Beaumarchais asserted that he never intended to criticize the French aristocracy, justices, or military.

One of the most shocking ideas that the play raised was that a nobleman and a commoner could come into a conflict that was eventually won by the member of the lower class. Critics over the years have considered the play's illustration of class struggle. Annie Ubersfeld notes in her introduction to *Le Mariage de Figaro* Napoleon Bonaparte's opinion of the play: it portrayed "the Revolution in action." However, Sungolowsky notes that while "[C]ritics have carefully weighed the theory of Beaumarchais as a revolutionary . . . most of them discard it."

While Beaumarchais has consistently enjoyed a high critical stature in France, where he is seen as instrumental in transforming the comedic play, his work is far less known in the English-speaking world. Although Thomas Holcroft first translated *Le Mariage de Figaro* into English at the time the play appeared in France, no modern English edition appeared until 1961, when Jacques Barzun published a new translation. Since then, several other editions have been published, but there is still little English criticism of Beaumarchais's work. Those critics who do exist, however, praise *The Marriage of Figaro* robustly. Sungolowsky calls it a "sublime masterpiece" whose message about the rights of the individual "remains eternally universal."

CRITICISM

Rena Korb

Korb has a master's degree in English literature and creative writing and has written for a wide variety of educational publishers. In the following essay, she explores how Beaumarchais uses comedy to raise social issues.

The subtitle of *The Marriage of Figaro*, "A Single Mad Day," indicates the complexity of the intrigue that faces Figaro and the other characters on the day of his proposed marriage. What neither the title nor the subtitle indicate, however, are the more serious issues that Beaumarchais raises in his play. One of the most significant messages, and the one that led to the play's initial censorship, is that the lower classes should be given the opportunity to resist and even compete with the upper classes. Writes Joseph Sungolowsky in *Beaumarchais,* "Insofar as it [the play] claims the rights of the illegitimate child, of women, and of the individual to enjoy his freedom and to obtain a fair trial, it remains eternally universal."

On one level, despite the ever-changing plot machinations, the intrigue is very simple: Figaro, servant to the Count, wants to marry the woman he loves, Suzanne, who is the Countess's maid. The Count, however, is determined to seduce Suzanne. These two men come into conflict as each strives to thwart the other and achieve his desire. The Countess, upon learning of her husband's faithlessness, decides to teach him a lesson and plans with Suzanne to trap him. Meanwhile, Suzanne, who knows that Figaro is busy trying to foil the Count, does not alert him to the Countess's plans. Thus, deception is crucial to the plot. The ways the characters deceive each other, and the extents to which they go, render the play comic. Despite the frivolity, the play does not lose sight of the crucial social issues it raises. Most shocking to the eighteenth-century audience, writes Brereton in *French Comic Drama from the Sixteenth to the Eighteenth Century,* was the

> struggle between two males for a desirable woman . . . [and] however it . . . is surrounded with gaiety, spectacle and song, there is no question that it is won by the better man, who is a commoner.

The physical act of hiding is most pronounced in act 1 as Suzanne receives many unwanted male visitors in her room. Not wanting to be seen by the Count, Cherubino hides behind the armchair. When the Count fears discovery by Basil, he throws himself behind the armchair, and Cherubino throws himself atop the armchair while Suzanne hides him under a dress. This series of movements is carried out gracefully yet is still largely comic because the Count is completely unaware of the page's presence. Additionally, the Count is ridiculed as he is forced to hide, crouching, in his own domain. In a further bit of comic irony, his ignominious position comes at the heels of his using his social position as leverage to demand that Suzanne sleep with him. The comic tension in the scene is further heightened

when the Count, having revealed himself, reenacts how he earlier discovered Cherubino hiding in Fanchette's room.

> I grow suspicious while I talk to her and as I do so I case an eye about. Behind the door there was a curtain of sorts, a wardrobe, something for old clothes. Without seeming to I gently, slowly lift the curtain . . .
> *He illustrates by lifting the dress off the armchair.*
> And I see . . .
> *He catches sight of Cherubino.*
> . . . I say!

In this scene, the literal act of hiding provides comic release for the audience along with the opportunity to learn about the dynamics of the castle's inhabitants. At the same time, however, the scene alludes to the social relationship between the upper and lower classes. Suzanne, as a servant in the Count's household, is subject to his desires. The Count touches Suzanne and pressures her to meet him that evening. She also sees her wedding plans grind to a halt at the Count's whim. Thus, she, as well as Figaro, is hardly able to assert individual will. Any amount of liberty they can attain must come through trickery, even when their own behavior is deserving of such liberty.

Act 2 mixes physical deception with an idea that is key to the success of both Figaro's and the Countess's plans to unmask the Count: taking another's place. The Count surprises the Countess, who has been visited by both Suzanne and Cherubino. With nowhere to go, the page ducks into the closet, but when the Count is away from the room, Cherubino slips away and jumps out the window. Suzanne takes his place in the closet, but the Countess is unaware of the exchange. She is forced to admit that the page is hiding, however, when the Count opens the door, for the stage directions indicate that Suzanne comes out laughing. Suzanne's laughter shows that she has the upper hand in this situation, if only for a brief moment. Of the three people now in the room, she alone knew the truth about what the Count would find when he opened the closet door. Here Beaumarchais underscores the idea of rebellion against the upper classes. Suzanne, a mere maid, holds power—in the form of knowledge—over her superiors. Later in this act, the Countess and Suzanne conspire to outsmart the Count. The Countess forbids Suzanne from telling Figaro about the plan, which Suzanne believes to be "delightful," one that will ensure that her marriage will take place. This interlude upends the subjugation of women in Beaumarchais's society. It pits the women against the men, even Figaro, who is certainly sympathetic to the cause. The women have taken control of their own destinies, and as the play bears out, it is their plan that results in happiness and triumph for both of them.

Another type of deception that is used throughout the play is the tactic of speaking in asides. The characters are continuously having conversations in which they try to determine how much knowledge the other person has and what his or her intentions are. As well, they attempt to mislead the other person about their own knowledge and intentions. A prime example of this occurs in the conversation between Figaro and the Count in act 3. The Count wants to know if Suzanne has told Figaro about his designs on her, while Figaro deliberately leads him to believe first one thing and then its exact opposite. In a series of asides, both the Count and Figaro announce their perceptions to the audience. The Count first believes that Figaro "wants to go to London; she hasn't told him." Shortly thereafter, he notes, "I can see she's told him everything; he's got to marry the duenna [Marceline]." These asides are comic because the characters remain oblivious to the irony of their words and actions, yet these scenes serve the important function of alerting the audience to plot developments. The importance of speaking secretly is emphasized at the end of this exchange. Suzanne, believing the Count has already exited, speaks aloud to Figaro: "You can go to court now, you've just won your suit," meaning that the Count will allow the marriage between Figaro and Suzanne to take place because he thinks that Suzanne will give in to his demands for sex. However, the Count overhears, which leads to the next major plot twist— the court hearing that ends in Figaro being ordered to either pay Marceline back or marry her before the day is through.

On another level, this dialogue between the two men reveals the class conflict that was an integral part of Beaumarchais's society. Figaro acts insubordinately by refusing to be honest with his master. Additionally, he deliberately tries to needle the Count. As he reveals in an aside, "Let us see his game and match him trick for trick." In truth, there is no logical reason for Figaro to let the Count know that Suzanne has revealed the seduction plan, and it is when the Count thinks thusly that he decides Figaro must marry Marceline. One plausible explanation for Figaro's actions, however, is his desire to place himself on the same level as the Count. He can tussle with the Count as the man's equal, not as a

> ONE PLAUSIBLE EXPLANATION FOR FIGARO'S ACTIONS . . . IS HIS DESIRE TO PLACE HIMSELF ON THE SAME LEVEL AS THE COUNT. HE CAN TUSSLE WITH THE COUNT AS THE MAN'S EQUAL, NOT AS A SUBORDINATE."

subordinate. This dialogue shows that members of the lower classes have the same abilities as members of the upper classes.

Act 5 culminates in these two types of deception—physically hiding and speaking falsely— as the Countess, dressed as Suzanne, meets the Count. This rendezvous has attracted a large audience; Marceline, Fanchette, and Cherubino all are hidden in one of the pavilions. They observe the Count's attempts to seduce "Suzanne." His efforts are comical partly because they show him to be a practiced seducer who relies on clichés, like how her "little arm [is] firm and round" and her "pretty little fingers full of grace and mischief!" The comedy also derives from his comparison of "Suzanne" to the Countess; "Your hand is more lovely than the Countess's," he avows. Figaro and Suzanne are right in laughing at the Count, for all the trouble he takes to seduce his own wife.

In Act 5, Figaro and Suzanne also act out their own drama for the Count, pretending that the "Countess," really Suzanne, is allowing Figaro to seduce her. The Count then chastises his wife, elevating the comedy to an even higher pitch. Condemning his wife as "an odious woman," the Count proclaims that he can never forgive her, even though what he castigates her for is exactly what he wanted to do with Suzanne and has suggested to Fanchette. The Countess appreciates the ridiculous position in which her husband has placed himself in front of a large audience of his underlings—which now includes Basil, Antonio, Bartholo, and Bridlegoose—as she grants him forgiveness, she is laughing.

As with the rest of the play, however, the comedy masks serious issues. The Count's behavior demonstrates that women are merely the chattel of their husbands or the men who hold power over them. The Countess's words make this clear: "In my place, you would say 'Never, never!' whereas I, for the third time today, forgive you unconditionally." This idea that women may be regarded as nothing more than property is further supported by Figaro's rampant jealousy when he believes that Suzanne will actually have an affair with the Count. It is only after heeding Marceline's advice that they go witness the rendezvous that reins in his emotions and anger.

The play closes with a series of ten short verses. Though this segment is dubbed as "entertainment," thus implying that its purpose is merely to amuse the audience, Beaumarchais has imbued the short songs with important messages. Suzanne sings the second verse, decrying the society that allows a husband to betray his wife but mandates that, if she similarly "indulge her whim," she will be punished. Suzanne concludes that this double standard exists only because men, who are the dominant sex, have brought it about. The Countess's verse puts down false virtue and recommends that women should be judged by their honesty. The two final verses remind the audience to pay attention to the moral issues raised in the play. Suzanne acknowledges that, though this play is "mad yet cheerful," the audience should "accept it as a whole"; that is, enjoy the "gaiety" of the play, yet recognize the truths it speaks. Bridlegoose, upon whom the play closes, reminds the audience that the "c-comic art / . . . Apes the life of all of you." Thus does Beaumarchais beseech the audience to pay attention to their own moral behavior.

Source: Rena Korb, Critical Essay on *The Marriage of Figaro,* in *Drama for Students,* The Gale Group, 2002.

Elizabeth J. MacArthur

In the following essay, MacArthur discusses how the body and its desires contribute to the public sphere in the Marriage of Figaro.

On 27 April 1784, the most successful play of eighteenth-century France opened at the Comédie-Française: Pierre Augustin Caron de Beaumarchais's *Mariage de Figaro.* Although the play had been accepted for performance by the theater's actors nearly three years earlier (September 1781), only after reports by six official censors, interdiction, a vigorous campaign of letters and readings by Beaumarchais, and finally approval by Louis XVI, could it at last be staged publicly. Friedrich Melchior Grimm's celebrated description of opening night, in

the *Correspondance littéraire,* captures the public's enthusiasm for this controversial play:

> Never has a play attracted such crowds to the Théâtre-Français; all Paris wanted to see this famous *Wedding,* and the theater was filled almost at the moment when the doors were opened to the public; barely half of those who had been waiting since eight in the morning were able to find seats; most entered by force, throwing their money to the porters . . . more than one duchess considered herself too lucky, on that day, to find in the balconies, where proper women rarely sit, a wretched little stool.

Finally the public itself was allowed to judge Beaumarchais's play for themselves rather than accept the king's judgment that it must be suppressed. Finally their desire to watch this infamous entertainment could be satisfied.

Of course all playwrights want their works to be staged successfully. But for Beaumarchais, this opening night was the culmination of a campaign to have his play performed during which he appealed to the public, and to the abstract notion of a public, in a struggle to overturn the king's prohibition. What makes this appeal to the public in a struggle against the king particularly fascinating is that it is also the subject of the *Mariage de Figaro* itself. Within the play, too, characters appeal to public opinion and public pressure to force an authority figure to modify his behavior. Thus both as a text and as an event, the *Mariage de Figaro* is about the relationships between the individual, the State, and a new kind of public that is invoked to challenge the authority of the State.

Le mariage de Figaro is the second play in a trilogy, preceded by *Le barbier de Séville* (1775) and followed by *La mère coupable* (1792). In the *Barbier de Séville* Beaumarchais shows how his heroine, Rosine, becomes a self-determining subject by "freely" choosing a husband, the Count Almaviva, thereby subverting the commands of a despotic parental figure, Bartholo. Rosine's preference for Almaviva takes her outside the bounds of Bartholo's authority, which he has abused by trying to force her to marry him. Rosine repeatedly makes it clear that she loves the Count simply because he will liberate her from her prison in Bartholo's house ("I will give my heart and my hand to whoever can rescue me from this horrible prison"); the very act of choosing her own marriage partner symbolizes her accession to the status of self-willed individual.

In the second play of the trilogy, *Le mariage de Figaro,* Beaumarchais situates several desiring subjects within a larger social context and shows how they create what Jürgen Habermas might term an authentic public sphere in order to critique and control an abusive state authority. Rosine and the Count are now three years into their marriage, but the Count has become promiscuous and neglects his wife. Most seriously, he hopes to obtain sexual favors from Suzanne, the fiancée of Figaro, who had been the Barber of Seville and is now the Count's concierge. In his official capacity as corregidor, or first magistrate, of Andalusia, the Count wants to reinstate a former seigneurial right, the *droit de cuissage* or the right to sleep with any woman in his domain on her wedding night. The Count's status as state authority and representative of the king is most apparent in act 3, when he serves as judge for his domain in a ''throne room'' with a portrait of the king above the judge's seat. Although the Count had renounced the *droit de cuissage* on marrying Rosine, he now hopes to buy it back secretly through a generous wedding gift to Suzanne (note the transition from a system based on noble privilege toward a monetary economy). Figaro and Suzanne are acutely sensitive to the injustice of this intrusion of the Count's authority into their private lives, so during the course of the play they mobilize what could be called public opinion. By the play's final scene, the Count has been humiliated and forced to renounce publicly and officially both his seigneurial rights and his attempt to buy Suzanne (though Figaro and Suzanne still pocket the money). As Jean Goldzink writes, ''The central conflict of the *Mariage* concerns the status of private space under a seigneurial regime . . . . In order to defend this private space, that is, his right . . . Figaro has double recourse to the public order . . . . Thus the play mobilizes two authoritative bodies for appeals against the abuses of power: the law . . . [and] opinion.'' Or, to use Habermas's terminology, Figaro appeals to the law and to the public sphere to attack and modify the will-based state authority of the Count. (It is worth noting, however, that Almaviva remains in power; there is no Revolution.)

The play opens with a spatial emblem of the intimate sphere: the room in the château that is to be Suzanne and Figaro's bedroom following their marriage. Figaro is happily measuring the dimensions of his property, his private sphere, until Suzanne warns him that the Count intends to penetrate regularly into that private domain and into the body of Suzanne. Part of what Figaro and Suzanne are seeking, then, is what we now call the right to privacy: their sexuality should be their own affair and not the province of state authority and intrusion.

> BEAUMARCHAIS'S MOBILIZATION OF PUBLIC OPINION REVEALS NOT ONLY THE RESEMBLANCE BETWEEN LITERARY AND SEXUAL DESIRE BUT ALSO A DISTURBING CONNECTION BETWEEN THE PUBLIC SPHERE AND PUBLICITY OR ADVERTISING.''

But Figaro and Suzanne have larger aims too, for they also want to force the Count to rein in his own wayward desires and return to his devoted wife (whose bedroom is the setting for act 2). The Count learns that he must exercise his mastery not over his subjects' sexuality, but over his own. As Figaro comments to the enraged Count in act 5, ''You are in command of everything here, except yourself'' *Le mariage de Figaro* suggests that society functions best when individuals not only have the *right* to use their own reason and desire to make sexual choices but also assume the *responsibility* for doing so. In addition, the play suggests that the rights and responsibilities of sexuality are best negotiated through ongoing public exchange, involving both sexes and all classes, from the noble Countess, through bourgeois Figaro, to the gardener Antonio and his daughter Fanchette. After the bedrooms of acts 1 and 2 and the public spaces of judgment and ceremony of acts 3 and 4, the final scenes of the play take place in a third kind of spatial setting: in act 5, the characters circulate in the darkened garden of the château, from a ''room of chestnut trees'' to two bedroom-like pavilions to a wood in the back. Since we never see the interior of the pavilions, it is as if the characters have succeeded in creating a private space protected from public view, whether that of the State or that of the theater audience. By contrast, the Count's attempted rendezvous with Suzanne takes place center stage, where it is submitted to the scrutiny and judgment of all the other characters.

Because one of the central problems of the play is the Count's uncontrolled desire, critics have often read *Le mariage de Figaro* as a parable about the need to regulate sexuality with laws; as Jean-Pierre de Beaumarchais—not to be confused with Pierre

Augustin Caron de Beaumarchais!—writes, "But this freedom, the freedom to take pleasure undisturbed both from and in one's own domain, presupposes that everyone recognize henceforth the power of the *law* as regulating principle of individual appetites." This interpretation seems to me to miss one of the play's most important and original insights, that individual appetite should not be regulated only by law, but by the individual him- or herself, who must learn to recognize and shape his or her own desires. In fact, the one point in the play where the State tries to legislate desire skirts disaster, for the trial on Figaro's contractual agreement to marry Marceline if he can't reimburse the money she has lent him ends in the Count's decision that they should indeed marry; yet the characters then discover that Marceline is Figaro's mother, so that the law's intervention would have resulted, inadvertently of course, in incest; as Figaro exclaims, "It was going to make me do a splendid stupidity, justice was!". Just as in *Le barbier de Séville* Rosine becomes a public-sphere-ready individual by choosing her own love object, so in *Le mariage de Figaro* all of the characters' identities depend on their recognizing their own desires and regulating those desires themselves.

This link between desire and identity becomes most apparent in Figaro's famous monologue of act 5, when he reflects on his whole past in an effort to understand who he is. Figaro's fear of Suzanne's infidelity, his failure to control events as he had in the previous play, and his newly discovered parentage have destabilized his sense of who he is. His confusion reaches a kind of paroxysm at the end of the speech, when he exclaims,

> One struggles, it's you, it's him, it's me, it's you, no, it's not us; ah! but who then? . . . . Oh bizarre series of events! How did this happen to me? . . . and still I say my gaiety without knowing if it is mine more than the rest, nor even what is this "me" with which I'm concerned: an unformed assemblage of unknown parts . . . a young man ardent in pursuit of pleasure . . . master here, valet there . . . I have seen everything, done everything, used up everything . . . . This is the moment of crisis.

Uncertain of Suzanne's love, Figaro cannot make his beliefs and experiences add up to a coherent identity, a "me." It is of course not an accident that this speech is followed by a series of scenes of confused identity: Suzanne and the Countess disguised as one another, Figaro receiving a blow meant for Chérubin, the Count receiving a kiss meant for the Countess, who is dressed as Suzanne, and several moments when the characters' feelings

overlap to such an extent that they repeat each other's words (as the Count observes, "There is an echo here, let's speak more quietly". Only when all the characters' desires have been sorted out can they also recognize their own identities and the identities of the others.

If the play as a whole stages a crisis in identity linked to a crisis of desire, Chérubin, the Count's page, is the very emblem of these interrelated crises. For Chérubin, aged thirteen, is poised between childhood and adulthood and just learning to recognize both his desires and his identity. As he explains to Suzanne:

> I no longer know what I am; but for some time my chest has been agitated; my heart palpitates at the very appearance of a woman . . . . Finally the need to say to someone "I love you," has become so pressing to me, that I say it all alone, as I run in the park, to your mistress, to you, to the trees, to the clouds, to the wind that blows them away with my lost words.

He is not sure *who he is* because he is not sure *who he desires,* but expressing his desire in language, saying "I love you," is crucial to the process of self-discovery. At this stage in the construction of his identity, Chérubin is both female and male, or perhaps more accurately, he is not fully either, since he is an adolescent: he desires the female characters (or nature!) rather than the males; he is ostensibly of the male sex, but Beaumarchais insisted that the part be played by a woman; twice during the play Chérubin dresses in women's clothes, once even passing himself off as a peasant girl; and the women make much of his beauty (soft white skin, long eyelashes, and so forth). This transitional identity is expressed spatially by Chérubin's suspension between two places, the château and the army; in the first act the Count sends him away, but although throughout the remainder of the play he is always supposed to have left, he never has. In a sense he is nowhere, or in a space between spaces. His status in the social hierarchy is equally suspended, since he is young enough to be called "tu" by Figaro, but of a rank to merit "vous" when he grows up. One can explain the ambiguity of his character by asserting that he represents adolescence, the age when a person creates or recognizes his or her identity, notably in the process of orienting (or recognizing the orientation of) his or her sexual desires. As Beaumarchais writes in his description of the character, "He is rushing into puberty". Chérubin's combination of masculine and feminine traits and his spatial suspension between château and army can thus be explained as a phase, part of the passage from childhood to adulthood that enables people to become individual subjects and enter into the public sphere. At the end of the play he will leave for the army and become an adult, and central to becoming adult will be becoming definitively male.

However, the Chérubin of the *Mariage* never completes this transition to adulthood; the play shows him in perpetual transition. Thus Beaumarchais stages a subject in the process of becoming a subject. And Chérubin bears out Judith Butler's argument, in *Bodies That Matter,* that subjects become subjects by assuming a sex; as she explains, "'Sex' is, thus, not simply what one has, or a static description of what one is: it will be one of the norms by which the 'one' becomes viable at all, that which qualifies a body for life within the domain of cultural intelligibility." According to Butler, then, "The subject, the speaking 'I,' is formed by virtue of having gone through such a process of assuming a sex" ("the process by which a bodily norm is assumed, appropriated, taken on,"). Chérubin, in the *Mariage de Figaro*, is in the process of assuming the bodily norm of (male) heterosexuality and becoming a subject. But because Beaumarchais focuses his gaze, and ours, on the process rather than its presumed outcome, on the phase when Chérubin is "appropriating" and identifying with both female and male norms, rather than the time when he has fully assumed his male sex, he draws our attention to what is destabilizing about the construction of identity. Chérubin fascinates and repels the characters within the play as well as the audience outside it because he reveals the threat to heterosexual norms, and more broadly to the social order, in the very process by which subjects are constituted. The male characters in the play, especially the Count, want nothing better than to eliminate the danger Chérubin represents to their social world by inserting him securely into a masculine role as soldier; the female characters, conversely, find his freely circulating, cross-dressing desire fascinating. Apparently the audience repeated this differential reaction, men objecting to Chérubin as immoral, and women falling in love with him (even though the part was played by a woman). Beaumarchais captures the ambiguous erotics of the audience's reaction to Chérubin when he writes in his preface, which was published with the first edition (1785): "He's a child, nothing more. Didn't I see our ladies, in the boxes, love my page madly? What did they want with him? Alas! nothing: it was interest, too; but, like that of the Countess, a pure, naive interest . . . an interest . . . without interest."

Conversely, Chérubin may fascinate and repel some of us in the 1990s because he (she?) also exposes the power of the "regulatory apparatus of heterosexuality" working to suppress the threat he represents. Those who know the third play in Beaumarchais's trilogy, *La mère coupable*, know that this liberty cannot last, that Chérubin will get a name, a baby by the Countess, and death in battle, thus acceding to a norm of masculinity.

In both *Le barbier de Séville* and *Le mariage de Figaro*, the characters' explorations of the connections between desire and identity are conjoined by explicit discussion of the value of freedom of expression. In each case the protagonists struggle for the right not only to regulate their own desire but also to choose their own readings; they are as against the intrusion of state authority into what they can write and read as into whom they can love and marry. Beaumarchais suggests that the fight against censorship and the fight against Bartholo's despotic control over Rosine's sexuality, or against the Count's despotic intervention into Figaro and Suzanne's sexuality, are the same, a fight for freedom of expression in the broadest sense. For in *Le barbier de Séville*, it is the same character, Bartholo, who both attempts to control Rosine's desire and speaks out against freedom of the press; his efforts to block Rosine's love for the Count are predominantly efforts to block the circulation of letters between them. And in *Le mariage de Figaro*, Figaro's monologue about his desire and identity also becomes the occasion for overt attacks on abusive acts of state authority, especially censorship. "How I would like to get hold of one of these men who are powerful for four days," exclaims Figaro, "I would tell him . . . that printed stupidities are only important in places where their circulation is blocked; that, without the freedom to blame, there can be no flattering praise; and that only small men are afraid of small writings." These attacks were supposedly what most aroused the king's wrath and led him to ban the play. According to Mme Campan's (probably apocryphal) account in her 1822 *Mémoires,* Louis XVI leapt up during the reading of this scene and exclaimed, "It would be necessary to destroy the Bastille for the performance of this play not to be a dangerous contradiction."

Beaumarchais communicated this conception of individual freedom of expression as much through the relationship he created between the play and its readers or viewers as through the play's plot and themes. For Beaumarchais wanted to incite in his audience both a desire to see his play and a sense that they had a right to judge it for themselves. This dual purpose shaped his campaign to get the play performed. He had to struggle for three years for the king's permission to have the play staged publicly; one of his principal claims to all the court and government officials to whom he pleaded his case is that the public should be allowed to judge the play for themselves, rather than submit to the authority of the king's or the censor's interpretation. As Beaumarchais explains to the Lieutenant de Police, "This trifle only became important to me because of the tenacity with which it was treated as a public wrong of mine, without the public being allowed to judge it for themselves". Similarly, to the Baron de Breteuil (minister of the Maison du roi) he writes, "I persisted in asking that the public be judge of that which I had destined for the public's entertainment." Beaumarchais even urges the king to judge for himself rather than be swayed by others' opinions. In the prefatory material accompanying the publication of both the *Barbier* and the *Mariage*, Beaumarchais stresses the public's role of judging his work. "You must be my judge absolutely, whether you want to or not, for you are my reader" he warns in the *Lettre modérée*; "You cannot avoid judging me except by becoming null, negative, annihilated, by ceasing to exist in your capacity as my reader". And in the epistle dedicated "to the people mistaken about my play [*Mariage de Figaro*] and who have refused to see it", he reminds readers "that one knows men and works poorly when one has faith in other people's judgments", and that the only pure basis for judgments is "the advice . . . of their own enlightenment".

In order to counteract the king's state authority and give people the right to judge his play for themselves, Beaumarchais mobilized public opinion by giving many private readings of the play in salon and court circles. Beaumarchais tried to use even the royal censors to help garner support for his play. Before he would allow a private, court performance at Gennevilliers, for example, he writes that first he "wished absolutely to fix public opinion with this new examination [by another censor]", and later he explains to the king that he had hoped to justify his play by forming a kind of public tribunal that would include the royal censors but also people of letters, men of the world, and court personages:

> Wishing more and more to justify a work so unjustly attacked, the author begged M. the Baron of Breteuil to agree to form a kind of tribunal composed of members of the French Academy, censors, people of letters, men of the world, and persons of the Court,

both just and enlightened, who would discuss in the presence of this minister the basis, the content, the form and the diction of this play.

Apparently such a meeting did take place, following the favorable report of the sixth censor, but this passage could also be taken as a broader characterization of Beaumarchais's way of manipulating court and salon social circles as well as various administrative authorities. And challenged by this "public sphere," Louis XVI's prerogative authority succumbed.

In order to mobilize the public in favor of his play, Beaumarchais needed to arouse their desire to see the play performed. Gifted publicist that he was, Beaumarchais succeeded in seducing large sectors of the court and salon public, and evidently, given the ultimate success of the play, the lower sectors of society as well. He gave many private readings, but never so many as to satiate his audience; as Félix Gaiffe remarks, "He wasn't slow to give in, though with some coquetry, to the numerous demands for private readings which came to him from all sides; there was general curiosity about this work that had had the gift of exciting the actors and scandalizing the king." The sexual component in this coquettish seduction of the public is blatant in the statement with which Beaumarchais prefaced his salon readings of the play:

> A young author supping in a house was asked to read one of his works . . . he resisted. Someone became angry and said to him: You resemble, Monsieur, the clever coquette, refusing to each that which underneath you are burning to grant to all.
>
> —Coquette aside, replied the author, your comparison is apter than you think, beauties and authors often having the same fate of being forgotten after sacrificing ourselves. The lively and pressing curiosity a heralded work inspires resembles in a way the ardent desires of love. Once you have obtained the desired object, you force us to blush for having had too few charms to make you settle down.
>
> . . . but (added the young author), in order that nothing be lacking in the parallelism, having foreseen the result of my action, inconsistent and weak as beauties are, I give in to your entreaties and will read you my work.
>
> He read it, people criticized it; I am going to do the same, and so are you.

In this prefatory image, Beaumarchais and his text become a blushing young woman, wildly desired by the public but perhaps insufficiently attractive to hold their interest once sexual favors have been granted. Thus Beaumarchais had to manage his public, to awaken and sustain their lust. He was so successful that when the first scheduled private performance, at the *Salle des menus plaisirs* at court, was canceled by the king literally at the last minute, the desiring spectators were outraged; as Mme Campan describes it in her *Mémoires,* "The King's interdiction seemed an attack on public liberty. All the disappointed hopes excited so much discontent that the words oppression and tyranny were never spoken, in the days preceding the fall of the throne, with more passion and vehemence." Surely Campan, writing after the Revolution, exaggerates, but her description shows how powerfully Beaumarchais had inflamed his public. Finally the king gave in to the desires of court and city, and on the night of the premiere, as I have already described, the play's success was spectacular.

But Beaumarchais's publicity campaign continued even after his play had reached the stage. On the night of the fifth performance, printed epigrams were thrown from the fourth loges; the verses criticized the immorality of the characters and attributed all of their vices to the author. From the start, it was suspected that Beaumarchais himself had written the verses to attract further publicity for his play. In celebration of the play's success, and to bolster lagging attendance, Beaumarchais also arranged that the proceeds of the fiftieth performance would be donated to nursing mothers. As the playwright explained to the actors of the Comédie-Française, "If no advantageous marriage is made without opposition, so too none lasts happily without a celebration of its fiftieth: this is what I am proposing today." This charitable scheme was announced in the *Journal de Paris* and on the night of the performance several couplets alluding to it were added to the play's final vaudeville. By the following day more epigrams were circulating, of which the following is a malicious example: "Nothing good comes from the evil, / Their good deeds are imaginary; / Thus Beaumarchais at our expense / Performs murderous charity: / He buys milk for babies / And gives poison to the mothers." The play might help feed babies, but their mothers, in the audience, are being corrupted by it. All of Beaumarchais's advertising paid off; in the year following the opening, the play was performed an unprecedented sixty-seven times.

Beaumarchais never forgets the role of desire in the relationship of reader to text or performance. Readers and viewers must feel an almost sexual lust for his work if they are to be willing and able to judge it for themselves. Two of the most fascinating images Beaumarchais uses to characterize the per-

formance of his play reveal his awareness of the centrality of the body in literary reception. In a letter to M. de La Porte, Beaumarchais characterizes the process of producing the play as childbirth, with the actors as midwives and the public as onlookers:

> When the time has come to give birth to a play before the public, one must, in faith, classify this operation as a serious matter . . . . So are the actors, my midwives, all ready? A censor who felt my stomach in Paris said that my pregnancy was going well. Several practitioners from Versailles have since claimed that the baby was coming out wrong: it has been turned around.

The play, like a baby, is conceived in physical desire: "It's a matter of life and death for the child conceived in pleasure." And several times in his correspondence and in the preface to the play Beaumarchais refers to the process of getting the play performed as a marriage; as he writes to Breteuil early in 1784, "And if it is true that no *marriage* takes place in this country without great opposition, in reading this description you will admit that if one judges the quality of a *marriage* by its obstacles, none has experienced so many of them as *the Marriage of Figaro.*" In a letter inviting the abbé de Calonne (brother of the minister) to dinner on opening night, Beaumarchais combines the images of marriage and childbirth into one:

> attend, attend, my andalusian barber does not want to celebrate his marriage without your official support. Like a sovereign, he will use placards to invite one hundred and twenty thousand people to his wedding. Will it be gay? That I don't know, I conceived this child in joy, may it please the gods that I give birth to it without suffering; I already feel some pains, and my pregnancy has not been happy.

If a play is a marriage between audience and actors or actors and text, as well as a child conceived in pleasure, it would be wrong to describe the audience's role as one of abstract, purely rational judgment. The public is expected to judge, but that judgment is inextricably intertwined with pleasure and desire. Beaumarchais's theatrical exploration of individual desire in its relation to the public sphere and the State, and his three-year struggle to ensure the performance and success of his work, reveal his recognition that the individual reader or spectator is constituted precisely by the interdependent abilities to *judge* and to *desire* for him- or herself.

In Beaumarchais's play the construction of the public sphere depends on the bodies as well as the minds of its participants (if any such rigorous distinction were even possible). Yet the notion of the public sphere has come under considerable attack recently, and the attacks tend to share the assumption that the public sphere requires subjects to become abstracted or disembodied. Because the public sphere does not grant a place to the body, it favors one particular social group: white males. This radical perspective is perhaps most intelligently argued by Michael Warner in his brilliant book on the public sphere in eighteenth-century America, *The Letters of the Republic*. Warner sees the public sphere as an outgrowth of "print capitalism," in which public discourse and the market are mutually articulated. For Warner, the private subject "finds his relation to both the public and the market only by negating the given reality of himself, thereby considering himself the abstract subject of the universal (political or economic) discourse". And not only must the subject negate his particularity, especially his body, in order to participate in this abstract, universal discourse but also some subjects have a privileged relation to what is supposedly universal. Educated white males may experience print culture as universal, but women, blacks, or illiterate men do not, and even those elite white males experience print differently if they are communicating with someone more powerful than themselves. As Warner explains, "No one had a relation to linguistic technologies—speaking, reading, writing, and printing—unmediated by such forms of domination as race, gender, and status." To reduce Warner's subtle and elegant argument to its bare outlines, then, one could say that he attacks the public sphere because, in his view, it requires people to become disembodied minds, and some people are in a better position than others to carry out this self-disembodiment.

It is indisputable that originally the public sphere did privilege educated white males, and that there will always be individuals with more cultural capital to facilitate their own participation. But even some of Warner's own examples belie his claim that people had to negate their bodies in order to communicate publicly about public issues. This claim rests on a belief that all language is alien to the body, that written language is further from the body than spoken language, and that printed language is further still than written. It is as if Warner were yearning for a time before we became alienated from ourselves through technologies of language— a yearning that in light of recent scholarship seems a nostalgic attempt to separate language from the body and get back to the "given reality" of ourselves. Our bodily experiences cannot be disentangled from the language through which we have

access to them and which helps make us sexed and raced human beings; language can never be purged of the body and transformed into an abstract, rational instrument. Warner also risks essentialism by suggesting that women and blacks are closer to their bodies and more alienated from language than men. Education, family background, and societal pressures certainly made and continue to make it more difficult for some social groups to have their writings published, or even master standard grammar, and thus to gain access to the public sphere, but these problems of access are contingent rather than constitutive.

It is not only critics of liberalism, however, who associate the public sphere with disembodiment; most twentieth-century liberals make the same association. The liberal position might be epitomized by Ronald Dworkin in his review of Catharine MacKinnon's 1993 book on pornography, *Only Words*. Although Dworkin argues that pornographic expression should be protected by the First Amendment, he wants to make his own abhorrence of pornography absolutely indubitable. In his critique of MacKinnon's antipornography position, he explains that we must grant everyone, even Nazis and pornographers, an equal right to attempt to influence the nation's policies and "moral environment." But Dworkin takes pains to distance himself from pornography ("almost all men, I think, are as disgusted by it as almost all women", and above all he asserts that pornography can never actually contribute to public debate:

> The conventional explanation of why freedom of speech is important is Mill's theory that truth is most likely to emerge from a "marketplace" of ideas freely exchanged and debated. But most pornography makes no contribution at all to political or intellectual debate: it is preposterous to think that we are more likely to reach truth about anything at all because pornographic videos are available.

Thus Dworkin implies that the body and its desires cannot possibly have a role in the public sphere.

My analysis of Beaumarchais's *Mariage de Figaro* suggests that, contrary to the claims of both today's liberals and their critics, people become public-sphere subjects through a process of assuming their corporality, especially their sexuality. Habermas's theory in fact implies a crucial role for the body because of the importance it grants to the conjugal family as site for the formation of individuals ready to enter into public sphere discussion.

For, as the example of Beaumarchais suggests, the public sphere can only come into being at times and places when people believe they are individuals, and the construction of individual subjects is inextricably bound up with sexuality. Free speech and liberalism were made possible in part, then, by the changes in marriage practices during the eighteenth century, whereby people increasingly chose their own love objects rather than obey parental authority. Choosing a marriage partner symbolizes the larger process of becoming aware of one's position in various networks of heterosexual and homosexual interaction and ultimately in the social order as a whole. Paradoxically, this apparent freedom to choose one's identity is also linked to an emptying out of identity. As J. G. A. Pocock has noted, "The citizen of the modern commercial republic enjoys unrivalled opportunities to diversify, to emancipate, to criticize, to transform his-and-her-self, but pays the price of not knowing what that self is or whether one has a self at all."

At the same time that sexuality began to be a domain of individualizing choices, analogous changes occurred in reading practices: increasingly, people decided for themselves what and how to read and questioned the authority of books. Roger Chartier, Rolf Engelsing, and others have argued that in Europe during the eighteenth century reading became more mobile and individualistic, less communal and obedient, as increasing numbers of less durable texts were produced. According to Roger Chartier, "A communitarian and respectful relation to the book, made up of reverence and obedience, gave way to a freer, more casual, and more critical way of reading . . . a new relationship between reader and text was forged; it was disrespectful of authorities, in turn seduced and disillusioned by novelty, and, above all, little inclined to belief and adherence." Once readers had many books to choose from, books, like lovers, needed to seduce readers, to arouse their readerly desire. Thus reading (or watching a play) contributed to the formation of individual subjects in several ways, as people chose what to read, made reading a pleasurable and solitary activity, fell in love with fictional characters, or identified with fictional feelings and situations. Although Chartier does not mention Beaumarchais, the relationship Beaumarchais encourages with readers and viewers, as I have described it above, exemplifies the new position of books and plays in late-eighteenth-century culture.

Beaumarchais's mobilization of public opinion reveals not only the resemblance between literary and sexual desire but also a disturbing connection between the public sphere and publicity or advertising. Readers and viewers desired Beaumarchais's play and demanded that it be performed partly because Beaumarchais had seduced and manipulated them into desiring it. One of the inevitable consequences of the new relationship in the eighteenth century between books and readers—as well as between lovers—was this need to mobilize desire: in short, to advertise. Nevertheless, although this hint of a similarity between Beaumarchais's publicity campaign and twentieth-century advertising may threaten any attempt to idealize the Enlightenment, it need not invalidate Beaumarchais's contribution to the public sphere. Whatever Beaumarchais's ideological or financial motives, his play still incited the desires and judgments of viewers and thereby helped engender public sphere subjects.

Paradoxically, while radical critics of today such as Michael Warner attack the public sphere for its alleged disembodiment, some eighteenth-century radical critics of Beaumarchais accused him of granting too large a role to the body. From what might be termed a republican perspective, the linguistic playfulness and eroticism in Beaumarchais's plays and other writings rendered him politically suspect. Such criticism might be seen to confirm the connection between liberalism and the body even while it complicates our understanding of Beaumarchais's political position. In his wonderful book *Painters and Public Life in Eighteenth-Century Paris,* Thomas Crow accepts the judgment of the eighteenth-century critics whom he studies, when he characterizes Beaumarchais as hopelessly mired in obsolete aristocratic values, such as sensuality, ambiguity, and stylishness. Again like the critics he cites, Crow admires the painter Jacques-Louis David, who becomes the book's hero and telos, for expressing the new values that were to produce the Revolution, such as virtue, truth, and severe rejection of the erotic. Crow criticizes Beaumarchais for favoring Mme Kornmann's liaison with an aristocrat rather than supporting the claims of her bourgeois husband and for writing a play that celebrated sexual immorality and linguistic playfulness, thereby losing touch with what the public wanted. As Crow explains,

> Play with meaning, the nuanced terrain of humor and sexuality, "les tons variés," no longer appealed to a public which had arrived at a precarious political consciousness attending to the dour single note sounded by Kornmann's defenders. The politically-aware element of the Parisian populace now indeed believed

that [to cite Jean-Louis Carra] "the language of virtue cannot allow, in the direct construction of its sentences, any vague and uncertain nuance."

David's paintings, exemplified by the *Oath of the Horatii*, appeal to that "largely bourgeois" public by rejecting "sensual appeal and emotional nuance", so that "everything is abstracted; no form calls on the complex, learned routines stored in our bodily memories", and "the effect of the [*Oath of the*] *Horatii* is to deny freedom to the play of the imagination, a play which . . . always has an erotic component." During the Revolution David's paintings become even more explicitly representative of the will of his audience, now the nation as a whole; he is commissioned to paint the *Oath of the Tennis Court,* and later his *Death of Marat* becomes a cult object. For Crow, then, Beaumarchais represents the corrupt aristocrat unable to bring about any political change, the villain playing opposite the heroic and revolutionary David.

But surely the playwright of the *Mariage de Figaro*, who pleaded for the rights of authors, provided arms to the American revolutionaries, and schemed to make money from every situation, is not best understood as an aristocrat. The values expressed in both his life and his most celebrated play are surely those of the exchange economy that was becoming increasingly pervasive in Europe by the 1780s. As Suzanne Pucci argues in a fascinating recent article, "The Currency of Exchange in Beaumarchais's *Mariage de Figaro*," the play portrays a monetary, exchange economy in which values are arbitrary and fluctuating. This fluctuation disrupts "the symbolic and representational system coextensive with the ancien regime." For Pucci, Beaumarchais's play is "innovative and subversive" precisely to the extent that it shows how individual identity is emptied out and rendered unstable by this exchange economy. As she concludes, "To signify promiscuously is not solely a trait of a decadent aristocratic culture but can be, as I believe it is in this case, a function of a different system at work that empties older structures of their value in favor of a new economy of signification."

If Beaumarchais's values were subversive of aristocratic culture, why then were Antoine-Joseph Gorsas, Jean-Louis Carra, and Jacques-Pierre Brissot so eager to label him as tainted by the aristocracy? In order to grasp Beaumarchais's position, both subversive of the Old Regime and threatening to radicals, it is useful to bracket the labels "bourgeois" and "aristocrat." The two sets of values

represented by David and Beaumarchais might better be termed classical republican and liberal. Neither of these categories aligns simply with the bourgeoisie or the aristocracy. In *Virtue, Commerce, and History,* J. G. A. Pocock argues that classical republicans, or civic humanists, privilege virtue, land as guarantor of personal liberty, and each citizen's participation in government (think of Jean-Jacques Rousseau as well as David); liberals, on the other hand, privilege exchange, property that is mobile or even purely speculative, people's rights, and manners. While Beaumarchais eludes the distinction between bourgeois and aristocratic, he can be quite fairly described by the term liberal. Pocock's terms in fact help explain what is otherwise obscure in Beaumarchais: the combination of claims to political rights with linguistic ambiguity and erotic sensuality. As Pocock writes,

> Economic man as masculine conquering hero is a fantasy of nineteenth-century industrialisation . . . . His eighteenth-century predecessor was seen as on the whole a feminised, even an effeminate being, still wrestling with his own passions and hysterias and with interior and exterior forces let loose by his fantasies and appetites, and symbolised by such archetypically female goddesses of disorder as Fortune, Luxury, and most recently Credit herself. Pandora came before Prometheus: first, because to pursue passions and be victimised by them was traditionally seen as a female role, or as one which subjected masculine *virtù* to feminine *fortuna*; and second, because the new speculative image of economic man was opposed to the essentially paternal and Roman figure of the citizen patriot. Therefore, in the eighteenth-century debate over the new relations of polity to economy, production and exchange are regularly equated with the ascendancy of the passions and the female principle. They are given a new role in history, which is to refine the passions; but there is a danger that they may render societies effeminate.

Republican values are seen as male and ascetic: masculine *virtù,* the paternal citizen patriot; the new liberal values, in contrast, are seen as female and sexualized: passion, luck, imagination. Although David's revolutionary republic requires disembodiment, liberal democracy was from its beginnings associated with sexuality and the body. Yet, as becomes clear during the French Revolution, both liberalism and republicanism were to have their part in challenging the Old Regime. Perhaps one could say that while David comes closer than Beaumarchais to expressing the national will in its most revolutionary phase, between 1792 and 1794, Beaumarchais may be closer to expressing the sexualized, pluralistic liberal ideology that came to dominate in France once the revolutions were over. Beaumarchais's appeal to individual rights, which disturbed the king, and his staging of sexuality, which disturbed the Left, should not be detached from each other. It is their perhaps surprising conjunction that enables us to see the centrality of embodiment to the liberal public sphere. If the *Marriage of Figaro* was censored by the king, considered revolutionary by its author and by Napoleon, and disdained by radicals, it was as much because of the relationship Beaumarchais developed with his audience as because of the content of the play; and within the play, as much because of the valorization of individual desire as because of the critiques of political authority.

It is my contention, then, not just that the body and its desires should contribute to the public sphere, but that in fact they always have. To return to my quotation from Ronald Dworkin, it may very well be the case that individuals in the twentieth-century United States are better able to constitute themselves as individuals and thus participate in public sphere debate because pornographic videos are available. Think, notably, of how gay and lesbian pornography might help individuals recognize and validate their own desires and thus take new political positions in the public sphere. In response to radical-left critiques of the public sphere, I have argued that the public sphere subject was never disembodied, and that it is precisely the presence of the body that made almost inevitable the historical changes we have been witnessing, whereby people of color, women, and now gays and lesbians fight for and obtain a place in the public sphere dialogue. The example of Chérubin reveals with particular explicitness the potential for change built into the way public sphere subjects are constructed. Chérubin ends up conforming to the sexual norms of his society once the play is over, but for the space of the play he threatens those norms and thus disturbs both characters and audience. Beaumarchais's prolonged gaze at the process by which subjects are constituted shows us the likelihood that the process will destabilize the norms even as subjects are assuming them. The arrival of every Chérubin and every Figaro in the public sphere means a potential disruption and modification of the public sphere, as their bodies and words enter the dialogue.

But Beaumarchais's play does not just portray the subject's entry into the public sphere, it also incites desire and language in viewers, and thus helps construct public sphere subjects in the external world. His text deliberately solicits an erotic reading. If David's paintings, as described by Crow, block all bodily and imaginative response through rigorous abstraction and univocality, Beaumarchais's play encourages such response through ambiguity and sensuality. His very language speaks to our bodies as well as our minds. The play itself and all the documents surrounding it, from the dedication and preface to letters written to actors and government officials, make clear that Beaumarchais worked hard to ensure this dual address. Thus *Le mariage de Figaro* demonstrates how body and language are mutually imbricated in the process of the desiring subject's entry into the public sphere and at the same time encourages practices of reading and viewing that embody that mutual imbrication. For the space of the play, every reader or spectator becomes Chérubin, choosing what to desire and who to be, suspended in the moment of assuming social norms.

Source: Elizabeth J. MacArthur, ''Embodying the Public Sphere: Censorship and the Reading Subject in Beaumarchais's *Mariage de Figaro*,'' in *Representations*, Vol. 61, Winter 1998, pp. 57–72.

Walter E. Rex

In the following excerpt, Rex discusses the idea of games and the convention of the monologue in The Marriage of Figaro.

a. Games

Beaumarchais' *Mariage de Figaro* is a mixture of ingredients so perfectly combined, it would be almost perverse to strain out any single element and call it the essence. The play is everything at once: situation comedy, farce, comic opera, *parade*, comedy of manners, erotic comedy, social satire, *drame bourgeois, comédie larmoyante*, revolutionary indictment of the system, plea for unwed mothers and women's liberation, and so on. The action shifts focus constantly, and each time a new strand comes by the audience must catch on as best it can. If we look behind the play to its literary ''sources'' we find likewise a pleasantly heterogeneous jumble of overlapping fragments. Behind the character of Figaro stands a virtually endless line of impudent theatrical valets stretching from the plays of Marivaux, Dancourt, Regnard, and Molière all the way back to the comedies of Terence and Plautus. Count Almaviva, that jealous thwarter of young lovers, also falls heir to an abundant theatrical ancestry, going back at least to those hindering and slightly ridiculous fathers of ancient Roman times.

Jacques Scherer reminds us that in the character of Suzanne we find something of the innumerable Dorines and Lisettes of Molière, Marivaux, and how many others in the eighteenth century. Plays by Vadé and Rochon de Chabannes may have suggested, in germ, the scenes between Chérubin and the Countess; the trial scene may look back to the *Wasps* of Aristophanes, or to Rabelais, or to *Les Plaideurs* of Racine, among other possibilities. When Chérubin hides in the Countess' *cabinet,* is he not reenacting the same situation we find in Scarron's *La Précaution inutile* and in Sedaine's *La Gageure imprévue*? The scene in which the Count makes love to his own wife, believing her to be someone else, may be borrowed from Dufresny's *Le Double veuvage* (1702) or Vadé's *Trompeur trompé*. As for the main plot of *Figaro*, W. D. Howarth has found records of no fewer than five plays antedating *Figaro*, all bearing the title ''Le Droit du seigneur.'' One of them is by Voltaire.

Certainly it is helpful to know about literary antecedents such as these. Yet, when one gets through reviewing the ''sources'' of *Figaro*, perhaps the most striking conclusion one reaches is how far short they fall of Beaumarchais. Voltaire's *Droit du seigneur* resembles the plot of *Figaro* only in the most general and mechanical way, with innumerable differences of detail There may be other plays in which a young page or *écuyer* makes love to an older woman during the absence of her husband; yet, in their cheapness, they only make us appreciate still more the gracious subtlety and discretion we find in Beaumarchais. Put all the valets of theatrical tradition together, even adding the Picaro progeny into the bargain, and how close are we to Figaro in his great monologue? Perhaps such a chasm between the ''sources'' and the emergent work is to be expected when one is dealing with a truly original author. Certainly the gap exists with Molière, as many scholars have observed.

We note, too, that for other plays by Beaumarchais literary sources are strikingly more important than they are for *Figaro*. *La Mère coupable* (1792), the last play of the Figaro trilogy, is literally dominated by Molière's *Tartuffe,* and Beaumarchais reminds us of this in the play's subtitle, *L'Autre Tartuffe*. *Le Barbier de Séville* (1775), the earliest of the Figaro trilogy, clearly looks back to the long line of comedies typified in Molière's *Ecole des femmes*. It is a conventional play in the best sense, bringing to a new perfection *données* that are quite traditional. In short, whereas the two other plays of the

Figaro cycle fall rather neatly into recognizable literary traditions, *Figaro* would appear rather as an exception.

We reach curiously similar conclusions if we compare *Figaro* and *Le Barbier* from the standpoint of the unities: whereas in *Le Barbier* the traditional unities of time, place and action are observed to perfection, forming an integral part of the play's structure and actually intensifying the comedy, in *Figaro* they really are not. Even though the play conforms to the letter of the rules, aesthetically *Figaro* never achieves unity, at least not in the way *Le Barbier* does. The locus of the play actually shifts, from the bedroom at the beginning, to increasingly larger rooms in the château, and finally into the *parc,* impelled as it were by the gathering energy and excitement of a plot that simply will not be contained within four walls. In a sense, the play is breaking out of the unity of place. The same is true of the action: though the theme of Figaro's marriage may provide a pivot around which most of the incidents revolve, aesthetically one is hardly aware of any unity. The plot unfolds as an endless series of surprises, adventures, novelties, and incredible happenings, worlds apart from the centered harmony one experiences in a play by Molière. And then, the character of Chérubin—unless one goes to desperate lengths to allegorize him as Eros—does not really belong anywhere in the main plot, though he is probably the author's most inspired creation and a frequent object of our concern and delight. The unity of time is also stretched beyond the point of credibility on this frantically crowded day. In short, whereas knowledge of both literary sources and structural conventions is quite helpful in enabling us to enjoy some of the finer and more original qualities of the two other plays in the trilogy, with *Figaro*, on the other hand, such knowledge really has little to do with the play's unique qualities, and sometimes it may actually hinder us from enjoying them: if one embarked on a determined search for the unities in *Figaro*, in the same way one finds them in a play by Dancourt, one might be forced to conclude—quite wrongly—that Beaumarchais was a less successful author.

The truth is, rather, that we have not been looking in the right direction. For, despite Beaumarchais' worship of Diderot and Molière, *literary* traditions are not the key to this particular play. The unique comic spirit of *Figaro* is not literary; it is something far less learned and more spontaneous. What actually gives the play its special qualities, while at the same time underpinning much of its structure and provoking most of its laughter, is a whole series of children's games. Of course, *Le Mariage de Figaro* observes the unity of place: it just moves from playroom at the beginning, to playground at the end. It observes the unity of action also, largely because, throughout the plot, the Count is "it."

The "game element" in *Figaro* makes it virtually unique not only in Beaumarchais' trilogy but in the tradition of the French theatre before him. In this connection, it is useful to observe as a point of contrast that in an author such as Molière laughter is usually associated with some insight the audience has into character: the blind infatuation we see in Orgon, for example, gives a sense of rightness, almost of inevitability, to the absurd line "Le pauvre homme!" Dorine's earthy directness, as against the vulnerable sensibilities of Mariane, is what makes "Vous serez, ma foi! tartuffiée" such a choice moment in the play. This is to say that Molière, in his great comedies, usually engages our maturity and our understanding while making us laugh: we are mirthful—in part at least—because we are wise about human character.

But let us now consider the first act of *Le Mariage de Figaro*, with Chérubin rushing to hide behind the chair as the Count comes in, and then the Count hiding behind the chair while Chérubin crouches on the seat underneath Suzanne's dress, and then the Count getting "caught" when he forgets to hide, and finally Chérubin getting "caught" too in the most droll and surprising way. Such terms as "comédie d'intrigue," or even "lazzi," are really quite inadequate to describe this situation, because the tension and laughter of this scene are the tension and laughter peculiar to a game of hide-and-seek: the suddenness of the movements, the daring and completely unexpected improvisations of hiding places, the complete seriousness of the players' efforts to escape the person who is "it," the near-discoveries, even the ironic feeling of inevitability connected with the catch at the end-all these things belong specifically to children's games. In contrast to Molière, the identity of the players, or the individual qualities they may possess, are of relatively minor importance. Indeed, the same person can completely change character during the game, as the Count does when, having been the "seeker," he turns suddenly into a "hider" and crouches in a rather undignified manner behind the chair, just as Chérubin had done, and for once actually gains a measure of sympathy from the audience. Nor are we here in the traditions of the

> " INSTEAD OF ACHIEVING A NEW IDENTITY THROUGH HIS NEGATIVE OUTBURSTS, HE REALIZES HE DOES NOT EVEN KNOW WHO HE IS."

farce: the *coups de bâton,* in fact all the punishments that bring on laughter when performed by clowns, have little to do with the universe of hide-and-seek. What causes the laughter in this scene of *Figaro* is simply the suspense connected with being caught, and when, finally, Chérubin *is* caught, the tension is broken and a new round can begin. *Coups de bâton* are not really the point of the game.

For Chérubin the game of hide-and-seek goes on throughout the entire play; he seems to be endlessly turning up in new and unpredictable hiding places: fleeing into the Countess' *cabinet,* disappearing into the *pavillon,* disguising himself as a girl, or even jumping out the window when all else fails. Occasionally, he becomes a chaser himself, running after Suzanne to snatch the Countess' ribbon, or to make her give him a kiss. No one else is a game player to this literal degree in the play, but then, no one else, except his partner Fanchette, is so young.

The games Figaro plays with the Count are more sophisticated and slightly more adult. They are mainly verbal, whereas Chérubin's are not. For example, in act II, scene XXI, the Count backs Figaro into a corner with question after question concerning the incriminating officer's *brevet* that Chérubin had dropped while falling from the window. Figaro runs out of inventions and seems to be on the verge of revealing the truth, when, in the nick of time, whispered help is relayed from the other members of the team; Figaro learns the magic phrase "le cachet manque" and is made safe. Or again, in act III, scene V, the Count attempts to find out whether Figaro knows of his designs on Suzanne. This time, not only do his thrusts fail to hit home, but, in a series of "turnabouts," they leave him wide open to half-disguised insults from Figaro . . .

Whenever the situation is reduced to a sort of verbal guessing game, the symmetry of the game tends to make the players equal, and, just so long as Figaro is able to invent responses that literally satisfy convention, the Count has no choice but to accept them. In fact, merely by asking the question the Count has tacitly agreed to let Figaro go free if he can come up with an answer to his *devinette*. In the world of children's games both the hiders and the seekers obey the rules as law.

This is the reason the trial scene fits so perfectly into the general ambience of the play, although to critics looking for the conventional unities or for *vraisemblance* this part of the action has proved something of an embarrassment. It is true that the scene fits awkwardly into the main plot; moreover, it is entirely legitimate to wonder, as critics have done, why a person as familiar with real courts as Beaumarchais should deliberately create a ''tribunal de fantaisie'' quite unrelated to actual judicial procedure. The answer may be that, from the start, the audience never takes the trial seriously as a trial. Realistic details would only impede our enjoyment of such marvels as the legal wrangle over the copulative conjunction ''et.'' It is a mock trial, of course, the merest *game* of ''courts of law,'' with a pasteboard Brid'oison as judge, and everyone enjoying Figaro's inventiveness as he talks his way around the absurd evidence. There are occasional political overtones of a very serious nature in this scene, as there are in many other parts of the play; yet, precisely because they are held in suspension, diffused, so to speak, in the atmosphere of the games being played, they may deepen the tone, but they never become obtrusive. Johan Huizinga has pointed out that even real court procedures involve many ''play elements,'' and in the trial scene of *Figaro*, play simply becomes the essence.

Reading the book on children's games by Iona and Peter Opie, one is tempted to conclude that the tension between the seeker and the hiders, between the one who is ''it'' and the others who are not, has a good deal of the tension between the old and the young about it: what is being played out by children in these games may be the fundamental contest between the parent and the child. In hide-and-seek the game's playful tone and the deliberately limited scope of the action imply that there can be no true heroes, or villains, among the players—even though the hiders have all our sympathies, since they are the ones who are vulnerable to being caught, while there is something almost inherently distasteful about the role of ''it.'' Likewise, in *Figaro* there is no truly heroic character, nor does the Count qualify

as a truly unpardonable villain, even though he is certainly unpopular enough: feared by Chérubin, taunted and jeered at by Figaro, mocked by Suzanne, and deceived even by the Countess. The audience enjoys all this because it disapproves of both the Count's determination to press an unfair advantage and the promiscuity of his marital infidelities. Yet this is surely not the whole explanation, for in his own way Chérubin is quite promiscuous also, and when we learn in *La Mère coupable* that eventually the Countess is supposed to have a child by Chérubin, we may revise our feelings somewhat about the Count's suspicions of him in the earlier play. Pomeau remarks that Figaro is not really so innocent either, and, given the ambiguous character traits he inherits from Beaumarchais himself, we may conjecture that were he in the Count's place he would not behave any better than the Count does. However, we are willing to forgive Chérubin and Figaro for practically anything they do, partly because they are so young, partly because they have so little while the Count, the establishment personified, has so much, and—perhaps most of all—because as hiders they are vulnerable to being caught, and the Count is after them.

But then isn't the play in many ways a celebration of childhood—with gay songs to sing, a march to walk in step to, a ''tableau vivant'' to pose in, costumes to dress up in and disguises to wear, and even a kind of seesaw as Marceline and Suzanne curtsey back and forth to one another? At the end, during almost the whole of act V, there is a grand game of blindman's buff, held just as it is getting dark—the time when the best hiding games are always played—with several players exchanging clothes to deceive the ''blindman,'' the way real children do.

Actually, this last game is the most elaborate, and the entire cast takes part; even Marceline and Brid'oison get into the act somehow. There are three main rounds, with darkness serving as a blindfold: first Chérubin plays with the Countess, thinking he has caught Suzanne; then Figaro plays with Suzanne, thinking he has caught the Countess; finally, the Count plays with his own wife, thinking her to be a mistress. Thus, in rapid succession each of the three principal masculine characters has been ''it,'' and has managed in a very short time to flirt with the wrong lady. Once there is even an extra layer of confusion as Figaro discovers that the person he took for the Countess is really Suzanne, and then turns the tables on her by feigning to have designs on the lady whose costume she wears. In the world of children's hiding games such "turnabouts" may occur with almost magical speed, and in *Figaro* swift surprises such as these account for a good deal of the hilarity of the play's dizzy pace which gets faster and faster as it approaches the end. But with blindman's buff, to watch the person who is "it" mixing everyone up is only half the fun; almost the best part comes when at last the light of torches brightens the stage and, one by one, the characters emerge from the dark *pavillons*. Then the Count learns how blindfolded he really has been, while we, the audience, just like the other players, have the pleasure of watching his dumbfounded amazement when he learns the true identity of those he has been trying to catch. Virtually everywhere in *Le Mariage de Figaro* we find the unifying spirit of child's play.

Even in the play's eroticism childhood, or adolescence—and Beaumarchais does not clearly distinguish between them—seems especially important: the Countess' feelings for Chérubin are aroused precisely because he is a child as well as a man. On a more comical level, we find a mixture, too, in Marceline as her desire for Figaro gives way to feelings that are mostly maternal, and she embraces him in as motherly a fashion as she can. If Figaro sheds his first tears, it is because, though a grown man, he finds himself like a lost child brought home to his mother. How often the characters in the play fall momentarily into a kind of reverie: the Count and the Countess both experience this, the former for reasons of jealousy, the latter for reasons of love. Figaro's monologue is the most striking example, as we will see.

And yet, all this changes at the end, when the numerous pieces of the topsy-turvy plot return once and for all to their right places; the Count is beaten, the game is won, and the marriage really will take place. Meanwhile Chérubin, that timid little boy with his girlish complexion, has, almost miraculously, grown up and become a man. His game is ended too, and instead of running to hide, he now stands and faces the Count, even starting to draw his sword when he feels threatened by him. Seeing this gesture, one is tempted to infer that in the case of Chérubin, the beginning of manhood is symbolically a moment of revolution. One might say something similar about the character of Figaro and about the general spirit of this play, that in many senses ushers in a new age.

Cervantes, writing with poignant irony of the great analogy between the theater and life, has observed that the end of a play, too, has its counterpart in our existences—in death itself. Perhaps this explains the tinge of sadness one feels during the final vaudeville of *Figaro*: the falling curtain is bringing to an end the part of life, and the time in history, when one knew the joys of hide-and-seek. There are other reasons, too, as the second part of this chapter will suggest.

b. The Monologue

Though the character of Figaro may be seen as deriving from a variety of stock theatrical types, the single one he relates to most obviously is the "impudent valet" in the classic "guardian and ward" plot—which is always the same: a beautiful girl is being held under lock and key by a ridiculous old man, a dragon, bent on matrimony. Enter a handsome young hero, who is smitten with love at the mere sight of her, and who then uses the devices of his ingenious valet to out-fox the old guardian, and get the girl for himself. This kind of play, as ancient as the Greeks and Romans, had crystalized into a sort of perfection in the modern Classical period, in Molière's hilarious farce, *Les Fourberies de Scapin*. When we first meet Figaro, in Beaumarchais' *Barbier de Séville*, he, too, is behaving rather like the wonderfully brash valet of Molière's comedy. Indeed, Beaumarchais' valet in the early play is so winningly clever he almost steals the first act of *Le Barbier* for himself. From then on, however, the Count comes more and more to dominate the action, and Figaro's function is reduced to the traditional one, that of conjuring away by his clever inventions the numerous impediments that keep the lovers apart. When Rosine's elderly guardian has been outsmarted, the play ends, naturally, in matrimony—an indispensable ingredient of the traditional plot. For in essence this play always celebrates the permanent triumph of love over the external hostilities that threatened it, even as youth wins out over old age. In one version of this ancient play, the impudent valet was actually a god in disguise.

If the valet's dominant trait was, typically, inventiveness, the lovers, by contrast, were at best characterized by near helplessness, and at worst by mental deficiency. The first pair of lovers in Molière's *Scapin* are a good example: their passion has apparently paralyzed their intellectual capacities, and their breeding has rendered them so exquisitely sensitive, so utterly lofty, that they can no longer cope with real life. This is why, in the classic situation, only a servant could help them, for by definition a servant is disengaged from true passion (a great help to his mental powers), and, theoretically at least, he has never done anything else in life but untangle its baser realities. The disparity between the elevation of the lovers and the dubious morality of the valet was translated also in the width of the social gap separating the two. Thus in *Scapin* the lowliness of the valet was counterbalanced by the wealthy bourgeois origins of his masters. In Beaumarchais' schema, such as we find it in *Le Barbier de Séville*, the gap was wider still, since the master was so pointedly a nobleman. And indeed, perhaps this plot, though it can exist in any period, was most at home in an aristocratic environment where the separation of functions, with feeling and nobility on one hand, and practicality and intelligence on the other, can be imagined most easily as reflecting the structure of society. No doubt this was why, having achieved such a lively perfection in the theatre of Molière and Beaumarchais, it became one of the temporary casualties of the French Revolution.

Le Mariage de Figaro is a far more complexly conceived play than *Le Barbier de Séville*; nevertheless it still features part of the classic plot: Figaro is still behaving very much like a traditional clever valet as he devises stratagems to bring off a marriage. Moreover, one of the results of his inventions is that, at the very end, the Count will be reunited in love with the Countess—no doubt a vestige of the classic situation. But of course the fact that the main matrimony Figaro is so busily improvising is his own completely upsets the original balance, leaving the traditional plot dangling in incompletion, in fact lacking the essential half that had always given it, morally, a sense of fulfilment: in the classic situation the audience gladly tolerated any amount of impudence, wiles and deceits on the part of Scapin, not merely because we all secretly envy someone who can so charmingly disregard the restrictive laws of society, but because his dubious activities at the same time are fully counterbalanced in the plot, indeed they actually help preserve the finer and more noble qualities we enjoy in the hero and heroine. Because he is so clever, they can remain pure. So it was absolutely inevitable that, despite all his *fourberies,* Scapin would finally be invited to join in the banquet at the end of Molière's play: everyone knew that it was only thanks to him and his dubious stratagems that virtue had won the day.

What we find in the first four acts of *Le Mariage de Figaro*, on the other hand, is a great deal of impudence and devious devices by the valet,

tricks and games of all sorts, but morally there is no counterpoise: instead of a noble hero we are given a corrupt Count, almost a villain. And the *valet de chambre* we are left with in these early acts clearly does not yet fill the bill as hero. Though he is constantly measuring himself against the Count, and sometimes besting him in their verbal fencing matches, he is still, in essence, behaving according to type, as the impudent valet. Moreover, these skirmishes are minor affairs, the main one, over the Count's attempts to seduce Suzanne, still remaining unresolved. Even the revolutionary implications of these contests may not, so far as we can tell, go beyond those we find in the first act of *Le Barbier de Séville*: for all we know, they may eventually fizzle out, submerged in some larger dramatic situation, just as they had done in the earlier play. Meanwhile, as we watch the progress of the action, our interest wanders almost at random from the romance between Figaro and Suzanne, to Chérubin's getting caught, to the Countess' unhappiness over her husband's negligence, to Figaro's lawsuit and the Marceline subplot, and so on. The play doesn't have a dramatic centre, and in a sense the many scholars who have criticized it for not being unified were quite right. But then, one could hardly expect the action to have much focus so long as the play lacked such a key piece as its hero.

Le Mariage de Figaro gets a hero and finds its centre only in act v, during garo's great monologue— a unique moment in eighteenth-century theatre, if only for its extraordinary length. No other monologue in a "regular" comedy even approaches its size. To find monologues so gargantuan in proportions, monologues that contained such astonishingly diverse elements they are virtually whole plays in themselves, as this one is, one has to look back to the *pièces en monologue* of Piron's time, and these, to be sure, since they were the direct result of a rather peculiar sort of theatrical oppression, were devised to serve other purposes and had a very different cast to them.

Figaro's monologue is outlandish in a way all its own. In this connection, it may be useful to report that in actual Parisian performances, the monologue sometimes becomes not merely an incidental mishap, but a general catastrophe that does in once and for all the entire production. The play is already so long—again breaking all eighteenth-century records for comedy in France—that to bring the action to a dead halt so near to (although it actually turns out to be so far from) the end, just so that this valet can indulge himself in streams of consciousness, rambling thoughts about one thing and another, broken by all those pauses, musings and vague ideas that finally decide not to go anywhere after all, leaving us with *trois points de suspension . . .* this is a strategy fit to strain the patience of even the mildest gods of retribution. It may be an act of self-preservation to grope for the exit without waiting for the end.

Obviously the monologue demands the kind of superlatively great actor that Dazincourt might have been, someone whose skill can make an audience oblivious to the midnight hour and charm them into finding him alone to be just as enthralling as a whole stageful of characters, someone worth breaking the momentum of the action for. And since there is, dramatically, so much at stake in Figaro's monologue, one can easily understand why it can lead to total *déroute,* as well as—I presume—to exhilarating success. For in this enormous scene the play either creates, or fails to create, its hero. That is the possibility—or the problem. There don't seem to be any other Classical *comédies* constructed in quite this way, although certain tragedies, notably the famous ones by Corneille, also have monologues, moments of deep reflection like this one, in which the budding hero determines whether he will, or will not, achieve his essence. In these plays by Corneille he always does; and, in retrospect, the right decision was inevitable, because, even though he did indeed have free choice, it was a question of remaining true to a nobility that was a birthright, and hence an inherent part of his character. With Figaro, in contrast, it is a question of turning a servant—someone often associated with clowns in theatrical tradition as we have seen, almost a sort of puppet in the eyes of his master—into a hero, even a man.

Sagacious Diderot once remarked that, in effect, the notion of identity in an individual depends totally on knowledge of the past (or memory): if we had no idea of who we had been, we wouldn't have any idea of the kind of person we are. Perhaps Beaumarchais was thinking along these lines as he composed his monologue, for, as he reinvents Figaro, refashioning him to be a three-dimensional human being, he endows him with a long and diverting past, full of drama and incident, and this serves first of all to deepen our sense of his identity. He also gives him a many-faceted personality, displaying him as someone capable of expressing a wide range of emotions, from impudence and good-humored defiance to deepest melancholy; someone whose

picaresque life—in and out of jails, knocking about from pillar to post—takes on new seriousness as we realize Figaro's keen sense of social injustice.

Now, Figaro is recreated here, not merely as some vague reflection of the author's own personality, as so many critics have maintained, but according to strict principle, and one that illustrates the attraction of the contrary to a kind of perfection. It is as if the intensity of this historic moment on the eve of the Revolution had imbued the familiar phenomenon of contrariness with all the potential force it had been accumulating in so many authors during the century. In this play the dynamism of opposition generates, momentarily, something like an explosion.

We have already been aware of the long theatrical tradition that represented noblemen and their valets as opposites—sometimes even to the advantage of the latter—but now Beaumarchais pushes this classic opposition to its extreme limits, so that it becomes a true antithesis. Figaro is triumphantly reconstructed to be an anti-nobleman: quite precisely everything that, according to the traditional stereotype, noblemen never are. Since noblemen by definition have noble lineage, Figaro has no family background at all—his wit replaces his genealogy; since they—as their noble particles imply—always come from a given place and are geographically fixed, Figaro comes from nowhere, constantly changes location, and is all the freer and more effective for not being tied down; they were never gainfully employed, therefore Figaro masters a dozen skills and occupations—clear proof of his superiority; they were pillars of the Church, therefore Figaro devotes himself to attacking religious abuses; they were hostile to freedom of the press and economic reform, therefore Figaro champions both, and becomes everyone's hero; they were soft and decadent, therefore Figaro is strong—vitality and youth personified.

This is no minor matter, for Figaro's energetic negations of nobility amount to a liberation: simply by coming into being as an antithesis he has denied the old order, deliberately cancelled out the *ancien régime,* and, in the freshness of his strength and intelligence, he embodies all that is most joyous in the Enlightenment's idea of life's possibilities. Since this emergent hero in his monologue has succeeded in imposing the values he represents, now in his triumph he threatens to take on all the aristocratic prerogatives of the character he has supplanted. The tables are turning decisively, the *renversement,* the

Revolution is on its way to completion. In short, Beaumarchais' *Mariage de Figaro* doesn't *have* a hero, it *acquires* one, and with him the play gains not only the shape and dramatic focus, but the revolutionary significance it lacked before.

Hopefully this interpretation will seem plausible and consistent, for it certainly is part of the message the author is seeking to convey. And yet, staggering thought, it is by no means the whole story. For in addition to all the taunting defiance and impudent self-assertiveness, this monologue also contains one moment of self-doubt so problematic as to bring all the rest, everything that has been asserted, into question. The fact is that just a few lines before the end of the monologue, we see our newly formed hero, his plumes barely dry, on the verge of losing confidence completely. The famous anti-aristocratic principle that, even a moment before, had given such zest to the recounting of his life, now wears so thin it just spins in the air, barely able to sputter, while the tale of his adventures, as it reaches the present, ends in something very much like meaninglessness. Coming down in his narration to the here and now, he discovers that his existence has no more illusions, that everything is worn out. Instead of achieving a new identity through his negative outbursts, he realizes he does not even know who he is . . .

The scandalous circumstances under which the play was originally put on, the incredible drama of Beaumarchais' efforts to get his comedy publicly performed in spite of, or because of, the King's interdiction, the mere fact that the great Revolution was only six years away, all this rightly politicizes our view of this work, for Beaumarchais was quite aware of how combustible the situation was in which he was so heedlessly striking sparks. Yet at the same time the exhilarating, giddy timeliness of *Le Mariage de Figaro* should not blind us to the strength of its ties to the past. This was the last great pre-Revolutionary, the last great Classical, comedy anyone would produce in France. And in the beautiful costumes so carefully indicated by the author, in the flirtations in the Countess' apartment, in the clever impudence of the valet, in all the things making up the lovely idleness that is the very stuff of Beaumarchais' play, we are enjoying the aristocratic pleasures of the social structure the author himself was helping to bring down.

Source: Walter E. Rex, ''The Marriage of Figaro,'' in *The Attraction of the Contrary,* Cambridge University Press, 1987, pp. 184–96.

SOURCES

Brereton, Geoffrey, *French Comic Drama from the Sixteenth to the Eighteenth Century,* Methuen & Co. Ltd., 1977, pp. 237–55.

Campan, Mme., *Mémoires,* quoted in Joseph Sungolowsky, *Beaumarchais,* Twayne Publishers, 1974.

Cox, Cynthia, *The Real Figaro: The Extraordinary Career of Caron de Beaumarchais,* Longmans, 1962, quoted in Joseph Sungolowsky, *Beaumarchais,* Twayne Publishers, 1974.

Sungolowsky, Joseph, *Beaumarchais,* Twayne Publishers, 1974.

Ubersfeld, Annie, ed., *Le Mariage de Figaro,* Editions Sociales, 1966, quoted in Joseph Sungolowsky, *Beaumarchais,* Twayne Publishers, 1974.

FURTHER READING

Hayes, Julie C., ''Rewriting Bourgeois Drama: Beaumarchais's Double Plan,'' in *The Age of Theatre in France,* edited by David Trott and Nicole Boursier, Academic Printing & Publishing, 1988, pp. 41–51.
   This volume collects essays about the French theatre in the seventeenth and eighteenth centuries.

Howarth, William D., *Beaumarchais and the Theatre,* Routledge, 1995.
   Howarth analyzes Beaumarchais's plays and their critical reception in the context of the political and theatrical events of the period.

Lally, Carolyn Gascoigne, ''Beaumarchais's *Le Mariage de Figaro,*'' in *The Explicator,* Vol. 58, Winter 2000, p. 75.
   This short piece discusses how Beaumarchais uses comedy to attack the civil justice system.

Le Maître, Georges, *Beaumarchais,* Knopf, 1949.
   Le Maître presents a basic account of Beaumarchais's life.

McDonald, Christie, ''The Anxiety of Change: Reconfiguring Family Relations in Beaumarchais's Trilogy,'' in *Modern Language Quarterly,* Vol. 55, No. 1, March 1994, p. 47.
   McDonald discusses the depiction of familial relations in *The Barber of Seville, The Marriage of Figaro,* and *A Mother's Guilt.*

Men in White

SIDNEY KINGSLEY
1933

Men in White, originally presented by the Group Theatre in New York in 1933, was Sidney Kingsley's first play. The drama focuses on the personal sacrifices required by the medical profession. The main theme of the play is summed up in one of the doctor's final utterances: ''It's not easy for any of us. But in the end our reward is something richer than simply living. Maybe it's a kind of success that world out there can't measure . . . maybe it's a kind of glory.''

Men in White grew out of Kingsley's long-standing interest in the medical field. As he explained more than fifty years later in *Sidney Kingsley, Five Prizewinning Plays*, ''I worked and spent an enormous amount of time in the hospitals of New York and was so impressed with the study of the history of medicine and the achievements made in the previous decade.'' Kingsley witnessed firsthand those doctors he applauded in his dedication, ''the men in medicine who dedicate themselves, with quiet heroism, to man.'' Kingsley's diligent research paid off in his writing; theatergoers, critics, and the medical community alike responded favorably to the realism and idealism that forms the backbone of *Men in White*.

The play also started Kingsley's tradition of dealing with significant social issues—issues that many other writers were unwilling to explore or even raise. A pivotal plot twist in which a young woman dies of a botched abortion gave Kingsley the

opportunity to speak out in support of legalized abortion, a practice that was not adopted in the United States until 1973. As Nena Couch points out in her introduction to *Sidney Kingsley, Five Prizewinning Plays*, ''In *Men in White* Kingsley did what was clearly characteristic of him and what has marked his long career—to present on the stage a major human concern boldly and without apology or disguise.''

AUTHOR BIOGRAPHY

Kingsley was born Sidney Kirshner on October 22, 1906, in New York, New York. While attending high school, he began writing one-act plays, directing, and acting. He won a scholarship to Cornell University, where he continued to write and direct plays. In 1928, the same year in which he earned his bachelor of arts degree, he won an award for the best student one-act play.

After graduation, Kingley acted with the Tremont Stock Company in the Bronx, New York. Deciding that he would never be a great actor, Kingsley moved in 1929 to California. He worked as a scenario reader in the movie business. At the same time, he continued working on a play called *Crisis*. This play opened in 1933 in New York under a new title, *Men in White*. The play was a critical and commercial success both in the United States and London, and it won the 1934 Pulitzer Prize in drama.

Throughout the rest of the 1930s, Kingsley wrote three more plays: *Dead End* (1935) was a Broadway success, but *Ten Million Ghosts* (1936) and *The World We Make* (1939) both were considered failures. In 1939, Kingsley also married the actress Madge Evans, who would appear in several of his later plays.

Kingsley wrote five more plays in the 1940s and 1950s. Both *The Patriots* (1943) and *Darkness at Noon* (1951) were given New York Circle of Critics Awards. *Night Life* (1962) was the last complete work that Kingsley presented on the stage. *The Art Scene* (1969) was part one of an unfinished trilogy.

From 1962 until his death in 1995, Kingsley remained an active participant in the theatrical community. He was a member of the influential Dramatists Guild, serving as its president and vice president. He also sat on the board of directors of the Cafe La Mama Experimental Theatre Club. Kingsley died on March 20, 1995, in Oakland, New Jersey, following a stroke. The Dramatists Guild Fund presented the first annual Evans-Kingsley Awards for significant achievement in 1999.

PLOT SUMMARY

Act 1

Men in White opens in the library of a metropolitan hospital where members of the staff are gathered. Hochberg, the chief of the surgical staff, and Ferguson, an intern, are discussing Mr. Hudson, a wealthy patient who is about to be discharged. Ferguson is engaged to Hudson's daughter Laura. After the couple marry, they plan to go to Vienna, where he will study surgery. The following year, he will return to work with Hochberg. Ferguson finds out that he needs to stay at the hospital with one of his patients. He agrees to break his evening plans with Laura. Then an emergency calls him to the operating room.

Scene 2 opens in Hudson's hospital room, which Hochberg and Laura soon enter, and they discuss the demands of the medical profession. Hochberg points out that the next five years are crucial to Ferguson's career as a surgeon. After Ferguson joins the group, he and Laura are soon left alone. When he tells her that he has to cancel their plans for that evening, she gets very upset. She tells him that she cannot put up with his demanding schedule much longer. She threatens to break their engagement if he does not promise to forgo his studies with Hochberg and instead open a private practice after returning from Vienna. Before they can discuss the situation in depth, Ferguson has to run off to attend to an emergency.

Ferguson has been called to see a young diabetic who has lost consciousness. When he arrives at her room, he finds the girl's own doctor, Cunningham, is already there. The two doctors disagree on the diagnosis. Cunningham believes the girl has slipped into a diabetic coma and orders insulin, but Ferguson thinks she has gone into shock. The men argue, and when Cunningham hesitates, Ferguson wrests the hypo of insulin from him and takes charge of the patient. His diagnosis proves correct and the patient recovers, but Cunningham threatens to report him nonetheless. After Cunningham leaves, Ferguson offers to give the nurse, Barbara, some medical notes for an exam. Before moving on to his next patient, he promises to leave the notes on the first floor for her.

Later that evening, Ferguson, who has retired to his room, has a brief conversation with Laura in which she asks him to make a decision about their future. A former student of Hochberg's named Levine, who is now in private practice, enters. He wants Ferguson to check on some specimens from his wife that he left with Hochberg. Ferguson arranges for the results to be sent down. While they wait, Levine tells the younger man that he once had the chance to work with Hochberg, but instead he married and went into practice to support his wife. His life since then has been exceedingly difficult, and he wonders if he made the right decision. Ferguson explains that being a doctor has always been the only thing he wanted to do, even if he has to put aside personal pleasures to accomplish this goal. The orderly then brings in the lab results, which confirm that Levine's wife has tuberculosis.

After Levine leaves, Barbara arrives for the notes, which Ferguson forgot to leave for her. Barbara volunteers to go speak with the hospital administrators if Cunningham tries to get Ferguson in trouble. They talk briefly about patients and the hard work the hospital requires. Ferguson kisses Barbara but then tells her that he is going up to the ward and she had better leave. However, after he has departed, she sits on the bed, waiting for him to return.

Act 2

Three months have passed when act 2 opens. The hospital committee is meeting to discuss the perilous financial situation of their institution. Hudson is prepared to join as a new trustee and will provide the hospital much-needed funds. In return for his donation, the hospital needs to offer Ferguson an associateship. Hochberg objects that such an appointment is not possible because Ferguson is not yet qualified for the job. The other members of the committee do not see the problem because, with Hudson's connections, they believe Ferguson can develop a lucrative practice. Much to Hochberg's surprise, Ferguson already has informed one of the committee members that he is delighted with the plan.

Coming from their wedding rehearsal, Ferguson and Laura enter the library in high spirits.

Sidney Kingsley

Ferguson tells Laura that he is looking forward to the associateship appointment. Although he hopes to talk to Hochberg before the committee brings it up, when Hochberg enters the library, Ferguson realizes that he is too late. Ferguson and Laura try to make Hochberg understand that they want to have time for each other, but Hochberg remains unhappy with the decision. Their conversation is interrupted by the news that Barbara is ill with a serious infection resulting from an illegal abortion. She may need surgery. Ferguson heads out for the operating room. After he leaves, Hochberg suggests that Laura observe the surgery. He hopes it may make her understand how important Ferguson's work is. She agrees.

As Barbara is being prepared for surgery, Ferguson asks one of the nurses why Barbara never came to him for help. He says that he would never have let her go to a dangerous abortionist. Barbara is now completely alone, for she has no family and she will be thrown out of the nursing program. After examining Barbara, Hochberg orders a hysterectomy as the only hope of saving her life. The doctors head for the operating room. One of the nurses brings Laura into the operating room, and then Barbara is wheeled in. When Ferguson approaches Barbara, she asks him to take care of her and tells him that she loved him. Laura realizes that Ferguson is the one who got Barbara pregnant, and Ferguson admits to the affair. Starting to cry, Laura leaves the operating room, and the operation begins.

Act 3

The next day Hochberg finds Ferguson in his room. Ferguson stayed up all night with Barbara, and now her temperature has fallen. Ferguson tells Hochberg that he plans to ask Barbara to marry him—Laura refuses to speak to him and Barbara is alone in the world with little future. Hochberg questions Ferguson's decision, pointing out the difficulties of going into private practice. Hochberg cannot convince Ferguson to change his mind, however. Ferguson even declares that he will give up medicine, if he must, to support Barbara. Then Laura comes in to see Hochberg. Ignoring Ferguson, she tells Hochberg that she is planning to sail to Europe that evening. Hochberg reveals Ferguson's plans to marry Barbara and then leaves. Ferguson and Laura talk about what has happened. Ferguson says he has no choice; he is responsible for the destruction of Barbara's life so he must help her. Laura admits that she was acting selfishly by making Ferguson give up his dreams of being a surgeon. She admits that she stills loves him. Then Hochberg returns with the news that Barbara has died. Laura wants Ferguson to go with her and talk things over. Ferguson refuses, saying that he belongs at the hospital. He has made the decision to devote himself to medicine.

CHARACTERS

Dr. Cunningham

Although he enjoys a roster of wealthy clients, Cunningham is a lazy, careless, and incompetent practitioner. His colleagues disparage him, but because of his influential friends, he still is granted hospital privileges for his patients. Ferguson draws his disfavor when he disagrees with Cunningham's treatment of a patient, even though Ferguson's actions save the patient's life.

Barbara Dennin

Barbara is a lonely student nurse at the hospital. She is infatuated with Ferguson and initiates a sexual encounter with him. When she becomes pregnant, instead of turning to anyone at the hospital for help, she goes to an illegal abortionist who botches the job. She is brought into the hospital with an infection. The news of her indiscretion means that her life is in ruins—she will be cast out of the nursing program, and no other hospital will take her. Ferguson vows to marry her, but, although she initially seems to be recovering, she dies.

Dr. George Ferguson

Ferguson is a promising young intern who struggles with conflict between his personal and professional lives. He is dedicated to his work and his patients, and hopes to better the lives of humanity through medical care and the development of new medical treatments. As the play opens, Ferguson is set to marry Laura—whom he deeply loves—and go with her to Vienna, where he intends to study surgery for a year. He then plans to return home to study under Hochberg at the local hospital. He wants this future despite the fact that his father, also a doctor, died at a young age of a heart attack brought on by overwork.

As the demands of his profession are so great, Laura forces him to choose between marrying her and going into private practice or continuing his studies and becoming a surgeon. Threatened with the demise of the engagement, Ferguson decides to give up his plans to become a surgeon. He decides to accept the hospital's offer of an associateship and agrees to go into private practice, though he realizes he may never fulfill his full potential as a doctor if he goes this route.

Free to pursue his medical career after Laura learns about his affair with Barbara, Ferguson again questions the importance of his medical career when he determines to marry Barbara. As before, this decision would end his dreams of becoming a surgeon. Ferguson is ready to give up medicine entirely to support Barbara. At the end of the play, however, with Barbara's death, he chooses a professional life over a personal life. Although Laura wants to reconcile, he rededicates himself to medicine, telling her, ''This is where I belong!''

Dr. Hochberg

Hochberg is the well-respected chief of surgery. His dedication to his profession is boundless; he appears to have no life outside of the hospital.

Hochberg believes that achieving potential in the medical field requires absolute sacrifice and that a doctor's reward "is something richer than simply living." As Ferguson's mentor, he urges the younger doctor to stay focused on his medical career. His call that Ferguson place his studies above all other demands, even those of honor or love, shows that Hochberg has little comprehension of such demands. At the end of the play, Ferguson chooses Hochberg and the ideals he represents over all others.

Hocky

See Dr. Hochberg

Laura Hudson

Laura, Ferguson's fiancée, is the daughter of a wealthy businessman. She wants Ferguson to give up his dreams of being a surgeon and go into a less-demanding private practice. When Ferguson says he will not do so, she threatens to break off their engagement. By the end of the play, however, she realizes how important medicine is to Ferguson. Although she wants to work out a compromise, Ferguson has decided not to let marriage sidetrack his medical aspirations.

Mr. Hudson

Hudson is a wealthy businessman, one of the few who continues to prosper during the Great Depression. A patient of Dr. Hochberg's, he declares his intention of becoming a trustee of the hospital in return for awarding his future son-in-law, Ferguson, an associateship.

Dr. Levine

Levine is a former intern of the hospital. Six years ago, he abandoned his opportunities to work with Hochberg in order to marry. Forced into private practice to support his wife, for the past six years he has barely eked out a living. His experiences have left him an unhappy, beaten man. By the end of the play, he and his wife, who is stricken with tuberculosis, have relocated, and once again Levine faces the formidable challenge of earning a living through private practice.

Dorothy Smith

Dot is a young diabetic patient of Cunningham's. She has gone into shock as a result of

MEDIA ADAPTATIONS

- *Men in White* was adapted for the screen in 1934 by Waldemar Young. It was directed by Richard Boleslawsky, produced by MGM, and starred Clark Gable, Myrna Loy, Jean Hersholt, and Elizabeth Allan.

Cunningham having ordered a too-large injection of insulin, but Cunningham thinks she is in a coma. Ferguson's correct diagnosis and treatment saves her life.

THEMES

Professional versus Private Life

At the center of Ferguson's dilemma is whether his professional or private life will take priority. Ferguson has spent his whole life dreaming of being a doctor. He wants this future despite the fact that his father, also a doctor, died at a young age of a heart attack brought on by overwork. The demands of the medical profession are made clear in the play. Hochberg points out that being a doctor is not about making money, but about working hard to save lives.

Laura presents a conflict for Ferguson. She is unsupportive of his professional work because it demands his almost complete concentration. She begs him to make time for their life together. She does not want him to be a man like her father and Hochberg, who have no interests outside of their careers.

Because Ferguson loves Laura so much and cannot imagine his life without her, he convinces himself that he can balance his career and his relationship. As a means of accomplishing this new

TOPICS FOR FURTHER STUDY

- Research the abortion issue in the United States from the 1930s to the present day. How did abortion come to be legalized? Which groups support and which oppose abortion today? What are the reasons given by each side for their viewpoints?

- The 1930s saw a number of important discoveries in the medical and surgical fields. Research what accomplishments doctors made during this period and explain how these accomplishments affected the quality of life and health.

- Kingsley's other plays also focus on important social issues. Read either *Dead End* or *Detective Story*. Then analyze the selected work in terms of what social problem(s) it presents and any solutions suggested.

- Nena Couch writes in her introduction to *Sidney Kingsley, Five Prizewinning Plays* that Kingsley's "pioneering work for the stage led the way for new genres," such as hospital and doctor dramas like *ER*. Compare *Men in White* to a modern hospital drama. How are the two works similar? How are they different?

- The doctors in *Men in White* make several references to potential changes in the government's relationship with the medical establishment. Research how Americans in the 1930s felt about reforming the country's health care system. How did members of the medical community feel about potential reforms? What, if any, reforms took place?

- *Men in White* raises many important social issues. Make a list of some of these and then determine if these issues are still relevant to today's society. Explain your assertions.

---

goal, he prepares to accept the associateship and enter private practice. With this decision, he is attempting to mold a future in which he can be both a doctor and a husband. The play ends, however, with Ferguson realizing how much medicine has yet to accomplish and preparing to give up any semblance of a personal life. He dedicates himself completely to his professional life and to the medical field.

Ethics

The play raises the ethical questions as it demonstrates the favoritism that exists even in as noble a profession as medicine. Ferguson is offered an associateship solely because of his relationship to Hudson, whom the medical board committee is courting to become a trustee. The members of the board openly admit to trading this position for Hudson's money, which they so desperately need. While Ferguson is a very promising intern, he is not prepared for the job, nor does he have the training to go into practice. The board further acknowledges that, even without the proper training, Ferguson will do well in private practice, because of the Hudson connection.

In a contrasting situation, however, the board refuses to award an internship to a medical student who is the nephew of a senator. The student has finished 297th out of 300 candidates who took the medical boards. Despite this abysmal performance, several of the doctors support his candidacy because of his family connections and background.

Duty and Responsibility

Ferguson is a man who wants to fulfill his duties and responsibilities to others. He believes that as a man of medicine his greatest duty lies with his patients. Although he loves his fiancée, she must take second place to people he does not even know. Ferguson briefly denies this sense of duty when he opts to accept the associateship and rejects further studies. At the end of the play, Ferguson reaffirms that a doctor's greatest responsibility is to humanity and to learning more about medical care.

Barbara is the only person toward whom Ferguson feels a strong sense of personal responsibility. When she faces disgrace and the loss of her job and reputation after the abortion, he determines to marry her. He does not love her but feels he has no choice but to do the honorable thing because he holds himself responsible for her predicament.

Law and Abortion

The denouement of the play comes after Barbara dies as the result of an infection brought on by a botched abortion. This incident points to a theme that is essential to the play, even if it is not emphasized: that the law sometimes does not reflect what is best for the people it protects. At the time the play was written, abortion was illegal, yet many women underwent them. The individual members of the medical community in the hospital do not support the criminalization of abortion. Hochberg refers to whomever performed the abortion on Barbara as a butcher and tells a colleague that it is a ''shame'' that ''some our laws belong to the Dark Ages!'' A footnote to the 1933 edition of the play further discusses views on abortion. It notes that a doctor and former president of the American Medical Association estimated that there were more illegal abortions performed in New York and Chicago than there were children born in those cities. The footnote advocates that the United States should follow a program of fostering birth control education (birth control was also illegal at the time) as well as run legal abortion clinics.

from the medical techniques to the instruments and the treatments. For instance, in the 1930s, insulin was just beginning to be used on diabetics and blood transfusions were starting to be performed. The characters also make many references to issues surrounding the medical community, mentioning actual doctors and surgeons, medical school education, and even illegal abortions. The committee members talk in blunt terms about the perilous financial situation that hospitals face because of the Great Depression. The doctors discuss their concern over the government's involvement in medical institutions, which caused many doctors of the period a great deal of worry. For its original 1933 production, the script of *Men in White* contained numerous footnotes to clarify many of the points and references raised throughout the drama, as well as the medical terminology.

Conflict

There are many conflicts with which Ferguson must deal. He confronts an older doctor, loses a patient, fights with Laura, and has an affair with a student-nurse. The most important conflict, however, is the conflict that takes place within him as he decides which is more important to him: a satisfying personal life or a challenging professional life. As Ferguson—and everyone around him, from Laura to Hochberg—sees it, he is unable to fulfill both his professional and personal needs. Ferguson is pulled in two directions as Laura threatens to break their engagement with him if he continues his studies with Hochberg, and Hochberg continuously reminds him of the noble work for which the doctor sacrifices his personal life. Ferguson's resolution of these conflicts comes three months after the dilemma first presents itself and after many dramatic events take place.

STYLE

Realistic Setting

Men in White takes place in a New York City hospital in the early 1930s. The hospital is typical of those found in large cities. The play presents this setting, and the characters who inhabit it, in an utterly realistic fashion. All of the details reflect the state of the medical profession in the early 1930s,

HISTORICAL CONTEXT

The Great Depression

By 1933, the United States had been suffering under the effects of the Great Depression—the worst depression in American history—for four years. During the Depression, with the loss of work

COMPARE
&
CONTRAST

- **1930s:** Three out of every four Americans polled in the mid- to late 1930s want the government to help pay for medical care.

  Today: A 1999 poll conducted by NBC and *The Wall Street Journal* shows that two out of three Americans believe the federal government should guarantee health care to all citizens.

- **1930s:** Only about 5 percent of all medical students are women.

  Today: Women make up close to half of all medical students, and more women than men are applying to medical school.

- **1930s:** Because many Americans cannot pay for their medical care, the U.S. government initiates changes in health insurance as well as changing its own role in providing money for health care.

  Today: Despite an effort led by President Bill Clinton to reform the health care system and provide medical coverage for all Americans, many Americans—nearly one in four—still lack health care and medical insurance. By the end of the decade, 42 million Americans have no health insurance while another 20 million Americans are under-insured.

- **1930s:** In 1933 the average hospital stay is two weeks.

  Today: In 1998 the average hospital stay is 5.1 days.

- **1930s:** In 1932 tax funds pay for 14 percent of the national medical bill.

  Today: In 1998 government funds pay for just over 50 percent of all hospital care and physician services expenditures.

- **1930s:** In 1931 there are 156,440 physicians in the United States, or about 12.74 physicians per 10,000 American citizens. Doctors are clustered in the cities and are rare in rural areas.

  Today: In 1998 there are 777,900 medical doctors in the United States, or about 29.03 doctors per 10,000 American citizens.

- **1930s:** Feminist Margaret Sanger, appalled by the deaths from self-induced abortions that she witnessed as a nurse in New York City, pioneers the birth control movement in the United States. Before a federal law legalized the dissemination of birth control information in 1938, one of every four maternal deaths is due to abortion. In 1933, 58 pregnant women out of every 1,000 die.

  Today: Birth control and abortion are legal, but there are continuing challenges to the laws governing these practices. In 1997, 1 pregnant woman out of every 1,000 dies.

---

and the lowering of wages, millions of Americans sank into poverty. Under the New Deal initiated by President Franklin Roosevelt, social welfare programs, including those that helped pay for health care for Americans, came under the federal government's auspices.

The Field of Medicine

In the 1930s, the United States faced a serious problem in medical care in that many Americans could not afford it. Many people responded to this financial situation by curtailing visits to physicians and hospitals. At the same time, those people forced to seek medical help often could not pay their bills. As a result, the income generated by physicians and hospitals dropped. Hospitals further suffered as charitable contributions fell. Private insurance, such as the Blue Cross plan for hospital costs, created in 1933, helped cover some costs for those Americans who could afford to purchase it.

In the 1930s, there were three types of hospitals—voluntary, public, and university. Voluntary hospitals (privately owned but nonprofit) attracted paying patients and added amenities such as private rooms and quality food and nursing care. In order to stay solvent, they reduced the amount of charity care they provided, and to attract more paying patients, they opened their facilities to private physicians; many extended surgical privileges to surgeons who were not properly qualified. Public hospitals began to conduct more medical school and specialty training and to establish affiliations with medical schools. While these developments helped improve the quality of care, hospitals continued to suffer from inadequate facilities and funding. The university hospital of medical schools also emerged at this time. These institutions accepted many charity patients, but focused on teaching and research or patients with special problems.

Medical school education and curriculum also became more standardized. Higher admission standards improved the quality of medical students. All medical school graduates were required to complete internships, a period of one to two years of unpaid postgraduate training. Most hospitals, however, did not have enough staff or facilities to train the interns. The residency system, consisting of a period of post-internship training in a specialty, also developed.

New Developments in Medicine

Many important discoveries in drug therapy took place in the 1930s, such as insulin injections for diabetics and cures for bacterial infections. Surgery also saw many significant improvements. American doctor Karl Landsteiner identified blood groups. This discovery allowed blood transfusions to take place and thus more complicated surgeries began to be performed. Surgeons also made use of intravenous replenishment of salts, fluids, and nourishment, as well as X-rays. While these innovations led to beneficial surgical operations, useless and even harmful surgeries were also performed.

Abortion and Birth Control Reform

In 1930, the drive to reform abortion and birth controls laws was beginning to gather momentum. At that time, abortion was illegal throughout the country, and women who sought them were undertaking a significant health risk. The Depression years saw a big surge in the abortion rate. Some doctors and clinics performed abortions, and "birth-control clubs" formed, wherein members could

draw from the club's fees to pay for an abortion as needed. Despite reform efforts, abortion remained illegal for decades.

Prior to 1930, existing obscenity laws outlawed anyone from circulating birth control information. People who merely possessed contraceptive articles could be fined or imprisoned. Margaret Sanger was a leading pioneer in the birth control movement. Despite the laws forbidding the prescription of contraceptive devices, she opened several birth-control clinics in New York. She also organized American and international birth control conferences in the 1920s. In 1930 the National Committee on Federal Legislation for Birth Control endorsed lifting such restrictions, and in 1936 the courts said birth control did not violate obscenity laws. Within a few months, the American Medical Association approved birth control as part of medical practice and education. All but three states struck down the laws against birth control (these states lifted their laws in 1938).

CRITICAL OVERVIEW

Men in White opened to rave reviews in 1933. In *The Nation,* Joseph Wood Krutch called it an "extraordinary production of an extraordinary play." This "genuine work of art," Krutch lauded, "furnishes an experience which is thrilling and absorbing." *New York Times* critic Brooks Atkinson wrote two glowing reviews of what he called "a good, brave play" within one week's timespan. He found that the play was "warm with life and high in aspiration." Arthur Pollock wrote in the *Brooklyn Daily Eagle* that the play "shines continuously with a steady intelligence." Most of these reviewers' contemporaries agreed; ten of twelve critics named *Men in White* as one of the best plays of the year, and it went on to win the Pulitzer Prize.

John Mason Brown was the primary voice of dissent, asserting in the *New York Evening Post* that the play was "piffling" and "mildewed in its hokum." While the play's advocates were not immune to its weaknesses—for instance, Atkinson questioned the play's "slavish fondness for medical terms" and Krutch admitted that "it can hardly be said that there is anything completely new in

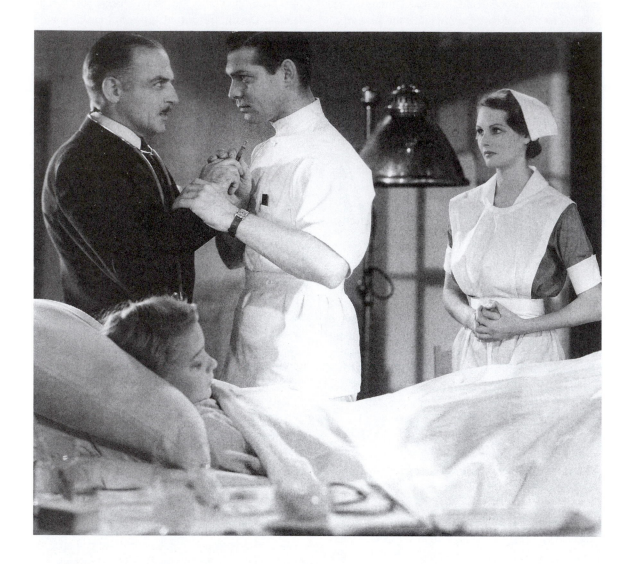

A scene from the 1934 film adaptation of Men In White, *featuring C. Henry Gordon, Clark Gable, and Elizabeth Allan*

[its] theme''—the vast majority of audiences responded favorably to the compelling social issues, human drama, and triumph of the dedicated medical profession.

Men in White quickly moved beyond New York, touring the United States and on to productions in London, Vienna, and Budapest, all to equally receptive audiences. The American medical community was particularly receptive to the play, which was reviewed in medical journals and bulletins. The *Medical Record* even recommended it for ''wives and fiancées of physicians and those who depend or

expect to depend on a physician's income . . . [and] every medical man, for it gives to the public a clearer idea of the ideals and the problems of our profession.''

The later years, however, were not as kind to *Men in White*. In a retrospective of Kingsley's career in the *Dictionary of Literary Biography,* Paul Bailey acknowledges that the ''play is dated''; Kingsley's dramatic techniques, which are ''frozen in the 1930s,'' have ''not aged well.'' Despite this weakness, however, Bailey asserts that because ''it is imbued with a sense of optimism in the future and in progress, and as a reflection of attitudes in the 1930s it remains historically significant.'' Other contemporary critics and scholars have pointed out that the social issues raised by Kingsley remain relevant, even more than six decades later. As Couch writes in her introduction to *Sidney Kingsley, Five Prizewinning Plays*, ''And in this time in which some form of all the humans rights issues and social problems dealt with in these plays are still, or again, with us, Sidney Kingsley has proven to be a playwright whose work is timely as well as timeless.''

CRITICISM

Rena Korb

Korb has a master's degree in English litera-ture and creative writing and has written for a wide variety of educational publishers. In the following essay, she explores how Kingsley uses characteriza-tion to explore different types of physicians.

Men in White was a critical and commercial success when it was first produced on the New York stage in 1933. Although it raises compelling social issues that are still of concern today, such as abortion and the conflict between personal and professional life, Kingsley's work generally has resonated much less loudly in the decades following his initial success. Paul Bailey notes in the *Dictionary of Literary Biography,* ''Many contemporary critics of drama and theatre . . . tend to dismiss him with a brief mention of his work and an acknowledgment that his plays are either dated or insignificant.'' The main reason for this dismissal is Kingsley's dra-matic style, which often strikes modern audiences as unrealistic, stilted, and underdeveloped. Writes Couch in her introduction to *Sidney Kingsley, Five Prizewinning Plays* this style ''dates his work more than do the issues he confronts in that writing.''

A prime example of the shortcomings of Kingsley's writing, from a contemporary point of view, is seen in the characters who populate the hospital in *Men in White*. Medical personnel and patients alike fail to truly emerge as flesh-and-blood people. However, this stylistic technique for creat-ing characters serves a more important purpose than presenting ''round'' characters: It illuminates Kingsley's message—that being a good doctor re-quires absolute dedication, and if necessary, self-sacrifice. Kingsley creates three doctors associated with the hospital, whom Bailey finds to be ''drawn

> AT THE END OF THE PLAY, WITH BARBARA'S SUDDEN DEATH, FERGUSON HAS THE CHANCE TO CHOOSE BETWEEN THESE THREE MODELS OR TO CARVE OUT HIS OWN STYLE OF DOCTORING.''

in bold and clear strokes,'' to demonstrate the options that Ferguson has before him as he is forced to choose between the demands of his fiancée, his mentor, and himself. These doctors—Cunningham, a successful but incompetent society doctor; Levine, a beaten-down doctor scraping by in private practice; and Hochberg, the well-respected, capable chief of surgical staff—all provide examples of whom Fer-guson might become in the future.

As a young, talented intern with a bright but busy future ahead of him, Ferguson is at a cross-roads in his life and career. He plans on becoming a surgeon but this path requires significant sacrifices. He is willing to make these sacrifices but his willful, spoiled fiancée, Laura, rejects all notion of them. Tired of Ferguson's unavailability and foreseeing this as the pattern of their life together, Laura tells him that she only will put up with his schedule for another year; after they return from Vienna she wants him to discontinue his studies in order to ''arrange our lives like human beings.'' Her solu-tion is for Ferguson to ''open up an office and have regular hours . . . specialize!'' Through the charac-ter of Cunningham, however, Kingsley makes it clear what kind of doctor—and man—Ferguson would become were he to choose this path.

With his flourishing Park Avenue practice, ''impressive equipment,'' and wealthy patients, Cun-ningham would seem the picture of a successful doctor. However, Cunningham is all image, and his success merely the result of his ''political influ-ence,'' which has also helped him secure the privi-lege of using the hospital facilities although ''his colleagues look down on him with scorn.'' In truth, Cunningham is a dangerous, incompetent quack. Having no interest in ''keeping up with the medical journals and the march of treatment,'' and believing that ''nine patients out of ten will be cured by nature anyway, and the tenth will die no matter what the physician does for him,'' he lacks the dedication that people expect from physicians. He is so unfamiliar with current medicine that, were it not for Ferguson's intervention, he would have killed his young patient, Dot, whom he had misdiagnosed and sent into shock with an overdose of insulin.

Kingsley makes it clear that if Ferguson accepts the hospital's offer of an associateship, he will end up like Cunningham, a doctor for whom he feels nothing but distaste. At the meeting of trustees, it is roundly acknowledged that if Ferguson goes into private practice, ''[W]ith his wife's connections, he ought to . . . er . . . do very nicely.'' But according to Hochberg, Ferguson ''doesn't know enough, yet; he's apt to make mistakes''; Ferguson is neither ready for an associateship nor private practice, but at Laura's behest, he is willing to ''sacrifice his career for a nice office and an easy practice.'' Ferguson well recognizes the mistake he is about to make in terms of his medical career. Though he claims to be ''delighted'' by the opportunity, in reality he ''looked so glum'' after speaking to one of the doctors about his acceptance of it. Already, with the decision he has made, Ferguson is becoming more and more like Cunningham.

This potential of developing into Cunningham is taken away after Laura breaks off the engagement, which means Ferguson loses the offer of the associateship and the chance to progress himself through the Hudson family connections. However, the chain of events instead offers Ferguson another alternate future: becoming a Levine. This once-promising intern gave up the chance to ''be somebody'' when he married. Disowned by his wealthy mother, he was forced to discontinue his studies in order to go into private practice to support his wife. The facts of his life since he left the hospital bear out his loss. When Levine first went into practice, he was sure and confident. He wouldn't allow Hochberg to help him even a little bit. However, without connections, as Ferguson now is, Levine was reduced to ''Tenements! Fifty-cent patients! Poverty! Dirt! Struggle!'' The past six years have been a struggle for Levine and his wife, who has since developed tuberculosis. When Ferguson first meets Levine, the former intern presents the picture of a man whom life has beaten down, with his shabby clothing and worry lines crossing his forehead. By the end of the play, desperately trying to build up a new practice in Colorado, he is reduced to begging Hochberg for the loan of a few dollars.

Levine has come to feel some sense of regret for the choices he made in the past. He considers Ferguson lucky to have the opportunity to study with Hochberg and sighs sadly when speaking of the same opportunities that he squandered. Kingsley makes the parallelism clear: If Ferguson follows through on his intention of marrying and going into private practice to earn a living, he will become like Levine, haunted by bitterness and the memories of what he gave up. Levine considers himself a ''human sacrifice,'' and Ferguson will undoubtedly become another sacrifice, with his ambitions and ideals destroyed.

One other future faces Ferguson, a future represented by Hochberg himself. Hochberg has devoted his life to his work and urges Ferguson, whom he believes has great potential, to follow in his footsteps. His dedication to the medical profession shows itself in his utter lack of personal life; with Ferguson, he talks only of patients and of the studies that lie ahead. The rest of the doctors, as well as discerning patients such as Hudson, greatly revere Hochberg. When he enters the library where they gather, he is immediately bombarded with requests and opinions. Hochberg has earned this position because he placed his medical career above everything else. He continually reminds Laura that Ferguson needs to concentrate on his studies, holding out as an example a doctor who works with him now who ''even has a cot rigged up in one of the laboratories'' to ease his 16-plus hour days. As Ferguson's mentor, Hochberg will undoubtedly sculpt the younger man into a version of himself.

While Bailey finds Hochberg a sympathetic character who is ''full of wisdom and patience,'' other readers may choose to question the surgeon's narrow focus and its accompanying lack of humanity. His attitude is most clearly seen when he learns of Ferguson's intention to marry Barbara. Calling Ferguson's desire to do the honorable thing ''[M]id-Victorian idealism,'' he urges Ferguson to reconsider letting this ''accident . . . ruin yourself—the rest of your life—destroy your ambition.'' He believes that in helping a woman whose ruin he helped bring about, Ferguson will merely be ''throwing his life away.'' With his admonitions, he reveals his essential belief that nothing is important but the medical profession. He puts the important work that good doctors do—saving lives—ahead of everything else.

At the end of the play, with Barbara's sudden death, Ferguson has the chance to choose between these three models or to carve out his own style of doctoring. After Laura rescinds her earlier demands that he give up his studies with Hochberg, declaring that she will marry him nonetheless, Ferguson has the opportunity to combine his professional love and his personal love. Instead, Ferguson decides to follow in Hochberg's footsteps. He affirms his commitment to the medical profession when he tells Laura ''This is where I belong!'' Ferguson has come to accept, like Hochberg before him, that for the physician the reward is in ''something richer than simply living''—it is in sacrificing his own life to the greater need of society.

Source: Rena Korb, Critical Essay on *Men in White,* in *Drama for Students,* The Gale Group, 2002.

Ray Warren

Warren is a freelance writer with a master of fine art's degree in writing from Vermont College. In this essay, he explores the deeper issues of this staged production as they contributed to its Broadway success.

Sidney Kingsley's three-act play, *Men in White*, is a mix of social commentary on moral issues and soap-opera drama. But more than this, it is a deeply felt philosophical treatise on humanity. The visible, driving emotional force of the play is a young intern's struggle to integrate his career with an upcoming marriage. Its hospital setting uses life-and-death issues, love, and betrayal to pull the audience toward a conclusion. The drama of the intern's tortured conscience over a sexual impropriety, which eventually causes the death of a young nurse, rakes the conclusion with profundity. The actual cause of her death, a botched, back-street abortion, becomes an underlying moral theme, seldom discussed in the 1930s. Beneath this veneer, however, many other serious issues are brought forth: medical ethics, the economics of medicine following the Depression, integrity in actions, and altruism in a most dedicated form.

Rather than using medicine as a mere setting for entertainment, Kingsley takes on the philosophical issues of ethics, truthfulness, compassion, altruism, and even greed, in a very simple, yet dramatic format. One line, brought into the body of the text through the remembered voice of the young intern's father, sums up Kingsley's theme for *Men in White*: ''My dad used to say, 'Above all is humanity!' He was a fine man—my dad.'' The intern goes on to say how his father died because he refused to give up medicine as a career in favor of his own health. Then

> THE PRINCIPLES OF A DEDICATED HUMANITY ARE EXTREMELY IMPORTANT TO THIS AUTHOR.''

he says, ''Above all else is humanity—that's a big thought. So big that alongside of it you and I don't really matter very much. That's why we do it, I guess.'' Kingsley's ideas about personal values come through in scene after scene. Had he not become a playwright and actor, he may well have become a physician or some other server of humanity.

Along with praise, reviewers and critics have found fault with *Men in White*, yet it was a triumph on stage and screen. In a review in *Sidney Kingsley: Five Winning Plays*, edited by Nena Couch, Thomas E. Luddy of Salem State College in Massachusetts says that the usual response of critics to Kingsley's plays has been that ''they practice outdated dramaturgy (19th-century naturalism), argue a suspect sociology (determinism), and embrace a dead politics (socialism).'' In the 1930s, ideas of the nineteenth-century may have become stale to the point of feeling outdated, but it was these elements that contributed to the success of *Men in White*. Kingsley's use of personal struggle and dedication in an unkind world gave its audience a point of identification. Luddy believes, however, that because of ''the writing power, the mastery of issues, and complexity of the stage vision,'' Kingsley's plays have a permanent place in the theatre. The themes and style of Kingsley's plays can be seen in many contemporary TV shows. Social elements and laws of nature, always present in society and often presented as dramatic themes, create an emotional impact for an audience.

One person who thought little of Kingsley's writing power in *Men in White* and of his mastery of issues was Elia Kazan. Kazan was a member of the Group Theatre company, as was Kingsley, that first performed *Men in White* in 1933. In his autobiography, *A Life,* published in 1988, Kazan wrote that it was ''the style of Lee Strasberg's production and their own [the Group's] ensemble playing [that] had provided Sidney Kingsley's bone-bare text with what it didn't deserve.'' What it didn't deserve, according to Kazan, was its great success on Broadway, and the Pulitzer Prize it won the following year. It was even the "first great success" for the Group, said Kazan, giving its members "a long flow of full salaries." In 1934, while still on Broadway, *Men in White* was released as a film by MGM, starring Clark Gable and Myrna Loy. It was a success, although Kazan never acknowledged its attributes. Its issues and emotional base did not make it a success for Kazan.

MGM recognized the opportunity for success with Kingsley's theme and issues, however; issues common to all societies, issues of substance, brought forth through love, death, and sacrifice. This is dramaturgy with naturalism that reaches across social boundaries. Beyond soap-opera dramatizing, the emotional impact of the issues thrives.

In reading only the script, it is true that the dialogue, settings, and characterizations are all quite average. The story is simple, the scenes minimal. Yet, when reading the original text as published by Covici Friede in 1933, with footnotes intact, it is apparent that Kingsley's purpose was not merely to create an actable play, with hopes of stardom, but rather to purport some profound philosophical ideas. His dedication of the play reads "To the men in medicine who dedicate themselves, with quiet heroism, to man." Following the dedication in the text, and before the opening scene of the play, Kingsley places a lengthy excerpt from the Hippocratic oath, which as Kingsley says, "physicians have bound themselves since the days of antique Greece." As an oath, it is a most serious commitment for men of medicine, meant to bind them with heart, mind, and spirit to the principles of altruism. They are sworn by "all the gods and goddesses" to do only good for the benefit of the sick and all men.

Through the play's dialogue, Kingsley speaks seriously about the nature of humanity, of the importance of man's humanity toward his fellows as being the most important element of their lives. In the hospital setting, it is the service of the physician to his patients—above all else—be it home, health, money, or personal need that he attempts to bring forth. However, it is in the footnotes of the original text where Kingsley records not only his own views on these issues, but backs them up with serious thought from respected sages of the past. Some footnotes are merely historical in nature or give medical definitions to the reader, while others are educational, regarding advances in anesthesia and sterilization techniques. Many of Kingsley's more serious concerns are brought out in the footnotes of the opening pages. A footnote on the first page of dialogue quotes the German born physician and researcher Hermann Nothnagel: "All knowledge attains its ethical value and its human significance only by the humane sense in which it is employed. Only a good man can be a great physician." He makes a footnote reference to the enormous bulk of information that had come to the science of medicine by then, and to the great task of the physician to absorb and use it. Another footnote quote is by Karl Marx, from Garrison's *History of Medicine:* "The education of most people ends upon graduation; that of the physician means a lifetime of incessant study." Throughout both footnote and text, Kingsley continues to make a strong case for the seriousness and dedication needed to succeed in medicine. The principles of a dedicated humanity are extremely important to this author.

Perhaps the play's most important issue, and the one it is most often remembered for, is abortion. While abortion plays a prominent part in the stage production, it is also discussed in the footnotes. Kingsley takes the issue seriously. He comments clearly on the criminal state of abortion: politically, ethically, and socially. Expanding on a footnoted quote by a former president of the American Medical Association on the number of abortions in New York and Chicago being greater than the number of children born, Kingsley says:

> Most of these operations are performed on otherwise respectable, law-abiding, married women. Proof enough that here is another social problem that can't be eliminated by legislation. No one wants to encourage the indiscriminate use of this grim practice. However, the lash of the law, instead of correcting the evil, only whips it into dark corners, creating a vicious class of criminal practitioner—bootleg doctors and ignorant midwives who work in dark, back-room apartments. A saner, healthier attitude is that adopted by the Soviet government, which is fostering birth control education, and instituting legal abortion clinics in a spirit best expressed by the motto inscribed over the door of one such clinic: 'You are welcome this time, but we hope you will never have to come here again.'

The Group Theatre ensemble produced plays that dealt with moral issues. When Kingsley presented his "bare-bones text" to the Group, he opened the door for the rest of the process to complete itself—that process being creativity. Kazan was right in this regard, that the play needed a skilled ensemble to present it. When a dramatic work is written as a play, it is never finished on the page. Not until it is interpreted and performed by its actors is it a completed work. Kingsley was able to, with his simple presentation and complex issues, give his players just the right formula for a successful performance. Its ingredients were: an altruistic and well meaning leading man; an obstacle for the leading man in terms of a fiancée who doesn't fully understand his need for dedication to medicine; a small but important outside love interest; a plot-driving mentor, always pushing for the hero's success; one less-than-competent wealthy physician; comic relief in the form of two rather less-than-serious interns; a serious sociopolitical issue of the day (i.e., the state of medicine and hospitals in a floundering society recovering from a major Depression); and a seldom discussed social issue, abortion. Without the depth and intensity of the emotional issues, this may well have been bare-bones. But it is not and was not bare-bones, not when the surface had been pierced by the accomplished actors of the Group, who were able to bring all of the background sentiments and seriousness of the issues to the foreground. They brought personal feelings and experience to the stage and created believable, flesh-and-blood characters.

Apart from the emotional intrigue of the play, Kingsley did a successful job with pacing to give it dramatic impact (even with its contemporary soap-opera flare). At the end of the first act the hero has an undescribed, but obvious, sexual liaison. At the end of act 2 he is in the operating room helping to undue the damage he had done at the end of act 1 (the girl with whom he had a sexual liaison had an abortion outside the hospital and was at the hospital due to complications from a botched underground procedure). Meanwhile, the hero's fiancée is also in attendance and discovers that her fiancé is the cause of the poor girl's condition. This is the major plot point of the entire play. At the end of act 3, all truth is revealed and actualized. The young nurse dies, from even more complications, the hero is sent into the world with a blessing to do his best for humanity and himself, and the fiancée has understood and accepted his need for dedication and service, somewhat forgiving him for his indiscretion. Her parting words are, "Maybe some day we'll get together, anyway." An audience loves the possibility of happily ever after.

Sidney Kingsley wrote a number of plays. Some were successful and some not, but the success of *Men in White* came from not only the drama of life, death, love, and sex, along with a talented ensemble and receptive audience, but also from the depth of the author's obviously heartfelt issues involving medicine and altruism. *Men in White* was a combination of elements that worked.

Source: Ray Warren, Critical Essay on *Men in White,* in *Drama for Students,* The Gale Group, 2002.

Laura Kryhoski

Kryhoski is currently working as a freelance writer. In this essay, she considers the social impact of Kingsley's play on his contemporaries.

Sidney Kingsley's *Men in White* had a profound impact on American audiences of the 1930s. The production was amongst only a handful of theatrical successes set against the backdrop of the depression era and Hitler's rise to power in Germany. The play earned Kingsley a Pulitzer Prize, remarkable for a work represented by stilted, or stiff, cookie-cutter character types and a rather predictable story line. It was an obvious victory, however, when noting the work's consideration of the medical profession. Kingsley specifically created Dr. Ferguson, a young rising star and physician, to illuminate this addiction to the medical profession. It is the audience which then becomes hooked, however, captivated by a young doctor's ineffectual struggle to separate his professional from his personal life.

Kingsley uses his characters to convey the progressive, powerful nature of modern medicine. At the outset of the play, Dr. McCabe is "worried" by all of the "new medical literature" that "keeps piling up," fearing "it will all end in confusion." Dr. Hochberg agrees, adding, "where the sciences in general are going to end, with their mass of detail—nobody knows." The practice of medicine is depicted by McCabe and Hochberg as an ever-changing frontier, a science constantly reinventing itself, creating new challenges for practitioners. There is never enough for a physician to observe, to learn, to accomplish.

Central to the play is Dr. Ferguson, a physician and rising star. He is a young doctor consumed by his passion for medicine. He too marvels at his dedication to medicine, admitting that "it wasn't much fun . . . but still . . . it's the only thing I really want to do." He later adds "above all else is humanity—that's a big thought. So big that alongside of it you and I don't really matter very much." According to Ferguson, medicine is a power far greater than he is, a force he cannot understand but

"IT IS ALSO EASY TO EMPATHIZE WITH FERGUSON BECAUSE HE OPERATES UNDER THE ILLUSION OF FREE CHOICE, WHEN IN FACT, THE AUDIENCE CAN ALREADY SEE HE HAS NONE."

to which he is compelled to respond. This idea is pivotal to understanding Kingsley's work—medical crises at the hospital prove to be uncontrollable life-changing events for his characters, both professionally and personally.

Evangeline Morphos, in her work "Sidney Kingsley's *Men in White*," discusses Kingsley's insistence on creating a realistic hospital environment as a factor in characterization and as a function of unity for the play. On the subject, she quotes Kingsley: "I take a long time developing a play because I am developing a whole environment, on the premise that a man's—or woman's—environment is enormously important to their life and their life's work." This statement gives credence to Morphos's idea that Kingsley's hospital environment creates unity and confines the action to a single location. The idea of confinement is of central importance to the struggle occurring throughout the work, that of a young doctor attempting to juggle his personal relationships with his professional duties. During the course of the play Ferguson's life is illuminated only within the walls of the hospital. Neither he nor any of the other characters are observed elsewhere. Kingsley, from the outset, successfully presents a view of medicine as being more than a profession—it is an all-consuming lifestyle.

Morphos comments on the subject matter of the work, stating "*Men in White* presents a series of crises set against the backdrop of hospital life. The ultimate crisis involves a young intern's choice between his fiancée and his research." Ferguson's personal struggle to create a balance between his relationship with his fiancée Laura and hospital life serves to create tension in the play. In several instances, Ferguson is called upon by the hospital staff and must choose between his personal plans

with Laura and his obligation to the hospital. Despite his desire for a relationship, Ferguson consistently makes choices that sabotage any efforts with Laura.

In act 1, scene 2, an intimate moment between lovers is interrupted by a loudspeaker call and Laura stating "don't move," only to be countered by Ferguson, who exclaims "It's no use, Laura! That's my call! Let me up!" Laura pleads her case with him, only to find out that he has also rejected her plans for the evening in order to perform a blood transfusion. This inspires yet another serious conversation and an ultimatum from Laura. What is of interest here concerns Ferguson's response to the situation. Laura has just threatened to "break off now and try to forget" him, yet he is once again distracted by the loud speaker. He forgoes any attempts to resolve the conflict and becomes instantly engrossed in the medical emergency at hand.

Ferguson's reaction to his argument with Laura is to take comfort in an affair with Barbara, a nurse who can understand his struggles as a doctor. It is Barbara's passion for medicine to which Ferguson is drawn. Ferguson's affair, however damaging, is little more than a predictable reflex action. The attraction medicine holds for him compels Ferguson to respond to crises in a particular manner. Based on his responses, it is easy to anticipate the failure of Ferguson's relationship with Laura, despite his desire for the relationship. Medicine is the ultimate force driving him, inhibiting his ambitions to pursue any life outside of the hospital. It is also easy to empathize with Ferguson because he operates under the illusion of free choice, when in fact, the audience can already see he has none.

It is a bizarre love triangle (Laura/Ferguson/ medicine) playing on a swell of emotion from the audience as tension rises and falls, scene by scene. Estelle Manette Raben, in her piece "*Men in White* and Yellow Jacket as Mirrors of the Medical Profession*," comments on Ferguson's commitment to medicine, claiming that "the hospital presents its demand for a type of almost religious celibacy." She continues, observing "doctors are thereby exhaulted to a position that the public seems to have wanted them to occupy and that doctors were all too willing to accept—namely, a total devotion to their profession." As Raben also points out, this is clearly apparent in the case of Dr. Levine, who chose marriage over medical training. The consequence of his decision, the audience comes to learn, is that he is left with both an ailing career as well as an ailing wife and has been disowned by his mother. In act 1, scene 4, Levine speculates on the opinion of one of his former professors, stating "I know just what he says: Levine—the fool!—wealthy mother—chance to work with Hochberg—to be somebody. Threw it all away . . . for a pretty face."

However understandable this devotion to medicine may be, the victims of Ferguson's professional devotion happen to be women. Women are on the periphery of this medical mayhem, their protests muted. Raben provides clarification on this point. She identifies within the body of the work the existence of what she calls "institutionalized sexism," which "manifests itself through every female character." This idea is readily observable—the main females characters of the play, whether nurse or fiancée, are portrayed as impediments to Ferguson's professional progress and are sacrificed for his sake.

Laura is characterized as being a selfish, impulsive child rather than a competent adult. Often Hochberg's interaction with Laura is that of an overbearing father chiding or scolding his ill-behaved daughter rather than a mutual discussion between respectful adults. Hochberg expends considerable effort to influence the course of Ferguson's professional career, not with Laura's help but despite what he clearly views to be her interference, without respect for the couple or their wedding plans. In act 2, scene 2, for example, Hochberg responds to Laura, who has just returned with Ferguson from their wedding rehearsal, saying "Laura, you deserve to be spanked! Don't you realize what that boy's work means?" Hochberg engages in this dialogue repeatedly throughout the course of the play. Laura is consistently portrayed as an impediment or roadblock to Ferguson's progress, not appreciated as a supportive figure in his life.

Barbara is the object of Ferguson's desires and a victim of an illegal abortion. While the audience is never privileged to learn the details of their one-night stand, the event does cost the nurse her life. Even more startling, as critic Raben is also quick to point out, is Hochberg's reaction in act 3, scene 1, to the news that Ferguson is responsible for the pregnancy. He immediately suggests to Ferguson that, if Ferguson did not force himself on the girl, he should not feel responsible for her unwanted pregnancy nor her dismissal from the hospital. Furthermore, when Ferguson comments on the fact that Barbara has been thrown out of the hospital, her life disgraced by the incident, Hochberg refutes Ferguson's idea to marry her and is quick to remark, "Don't worry.

We'll find something for her." Hochberg simply dismisses a grave situation as being a casual mistake rather than acknowledging what is really a terrible tragedy for one young woman.

It is easy to surmise or guess that the female characters only serve as impediments or roadblocks to medical progress. Ferguson, at the end of the play, has gone through several major crises—he has contemplated a loveless marriage, faced the deadly consequences of an irresponsible affair, and dismissed his fiancée—yet he returns to medicine, seemingly unchanged by this dramatic chain of events. Raben has a rather interesting theory behind this behavior, stating "the women in the play function essentially as props to emphasize the male doctors' superior social status and commitment." The main female characters in the play are presented as hurdles to Ferguson's professional success. Laura is portrayed as the self-centered, childish, demanding fiancée and Barbara as a life burden to Ferguson. Throughout the play Ferguson struggles with the idea of coupling his romantic life with his professional life, but by the play's end he is unable to synthesize both aspects of self, all attempts at compromise having failed. Ferguson's triumph is his return to medicine despite his personal challenges.

Scientific thought is presented as the superior rationale, an idea mirroring the work of one of Kingsley's contemporaries, Aldous Leonard Huxley, author of *Brave New World.* Huxley's novel is much like Kingsley's play, insomuch as it has been called a novel of concepts or ideas, the characters having little depth, not unlike Kingsley's characters. Nor is Kingsley's hospital terribly different, philosophically speaking, than Huxley's utopia. In utopia, babies are produced in a lab, born and classified by order of intelligence. The children are conditioned psychologically after birth to excel in a specific, predetermined profession based on their intelligence—not unlike Ferguson's environment, one fostered by his father and society at large. In utopia, Hypnopaedia is just one of the psychological techniques employed, by utilizing the power of suggestion. This method induces people to behave in certain ways. During the course of the play, Dr. Hochberg engages in a similar type of mental conditioning or priming when speaking to Ferguson of his future career objectives, and as a result retains him as an understudy. Utopia, not unlike Kingsley's world of medicine, also encourages reliance on the scientific, the rational, rather than a dependence on the emotional world. Finally, utopia is an emotionless world run entirely by men, not unlike St. George's Hospital.

Sidney Kingsley and Aldous Huxley had separate artistic agendas. Huxley's novel was a social commentary warning of world like utopia based on the nature of contemporary society, whereas *Men in White* celebrated it. Juxtaposing or comparing the works makes clear the climate and influences Kingsley was working under, and explains his success as a playwright with the completion of *Men in White*. The idealistic content of the play was responding to an audience enchanted with scientific advancement and captivated by the nobility, and also by the heroism of practicing medicine. This sentiment is perhaps captured best by the words of Hippocrates, who believes that ''where the love of man is, there also is the love of the art of healing.''

Source: Laura Kryhoski, Critical Essay on *Men in White,* in *Drama for Students,* The Gale Group, 2002.

SOURCES

Atkinson, Brooks, ''Men of Medicine in a Group Theatre Drama,'' in *New York Times,* September 27, 1933, p. 24.

Bailey, Paul M., ''Sidney Kingsley,'' in *Dictionary of Literary Biography, Vol. 7: Twentieth-Century American Dramatists,* edited by John MacNicholas, Gale Research, 1981, pp. 31–41.

Brown, John Mason, ''Hospitals and the Stage: Further Remarks on the Group Theatre's Production of *Men in White,''* in *New York Evening Post,* October 7, 1933, quoted in *Sidney Kingsley: Five Prizewinning Plays,* edited by Nena Couch, Ohio State University Press, 1995.

Couch, Nena, ed., ''Introduction,'' in *Sidney Kingsley: Five Prizewinning Plays,* Ohio State University Press, 1995.

Huxley, Aldous, *Brave New World,* Harper & Row, 1989.

Kazan, Elia, *A Life,* Alfred A. Knopf, 1988.

Krutch, Joseph Wood, ''An Event,'' in *Nation,* Vol. 137, No. 3562, October 11, 1933, pp. 419–20.

Luddy, Thomas E., ''Review: Sidney Kingsley,'' in *Sidney Kingsley: Five Prizewinning Plays,* edited by Nena Couch, Ohio State University Press, 1995.

''*Men in White,''* in *Medical Record,* February 7, 1934, quoted in *Sidney Kingsley: Five Prizewinning Plays,* edited by Nena Couch, Ohio State University Press, 1995.

Morphos, Evangeline, ''Sidney Kingsley's *Men in White,''* in *The Drama Review,* Vol. 28, No. 4, Winter 1984, pp. 13–22.

Pollock, Arthur, ''*Men in White,''* in *Brooklyn Daily Eagle,* September 27, 1933, quoted in *Sidney Kingsley: Five Prizewinning Plays,* edited by Nena Couch, Ohio State University Press, 1995.

Raben, Estelle Manette, ''Men in White and Yellow Jack as Mirrors of the Medical Profession,'' in *Literature and Medicine,* Vol. 12, No. 1, Spring 1993, pp. 19–41.

FURTHER READING

Abbott, Berenice, *New York in the Thirties,* Dover Publications, 1974.
　　This volume collects photographer Abbot's black-and-white shots of New York City during the Depression years.

Clurman, Harold, *The Fervent Years: The Group Theatre and the Thirties,* Da Capo Press, 1988.
　　Clurman, a member of the Group Theater (which first produced *Men in White*), chronicles the birth and development of this drama company.

''Conversations with . . . Sidney Kingsley,'' interview by John Guare and Ruth Goetz, in *Dramatists Guild Quarterly,* Autumn 1984, pp. 8, 21–31.
　　Two noted playwrights discuss Kingsley's plays, background, and theatrical history with Kingsley.

McElvaine, Robert S., *The Great Depression: America, 1929–1941,* Time Books, 1994.
　　McElvaine's revised edition focuses on the human consequences of the Great Depression.

Watkins, T. H., *The Great Depression: America in the 1930s,* Little Brown & Co., 1995.
　　In this companion piece to the PBS series of the same title, Watkins chronicles American life in the 1930s. The book includes many illustrations.

Mountain Language

HAROLD PINTER
1988

When *Mountain Language* opened at the National Theatre in London on October 20, 1988, the audience was shocked by the play's stark look at the machinations and effects of totalitarianism. Employing the characteristic structure and style of his previous plays, Harold Pinter focused on new subject matter. Drawing his inspiration from the long history of oppression the Kurds suffered under Turkish rule, Pinter centered his play in a prison controlled by unnamed guards in an unnamed country. As the Turkish did to the Kurds, the guards ban the prisoners' native language as they incarcerate them for unnamed crimes against the State. This enigmatic play employs the innovative techniques found in Pinter's earlier plays, blending absurdism and realism in illustration of the harsh reality of modern society and the individual's isolated and powerless state within that society.

Commenting on Pinter's distinctive style in his plays, Tish Dace writes in her article in *Reference Guide to English Literature* that his plays are "so rich" with "inscrutable motivations and ambiguous import that an international industry has arisen to explicate his art, and his name has entered the critical lexicon to deal with those derivative dramas now termed 'Pinteresque.'" While *Mountain Language* can definitely be labeled "Pinteresque," it also has been recognized for its author's compelling political subject matter.

AUTHOR BIOGRAPHY

Harold Pinter was born on October 30, 1930, in Hackney, a working-class neighborhood in East London, the only child of Hyman (a tailor) and Frances (Mann) Pinter. Although Pinter seemed to have a relatively happy childhood, he also experienced terror during World War II, during Germany's air attacks on London. Pinter's Jewish heritage also caused problems for him while he was growing up. Gangs would continually menace anyone with Jewish features. Pinter, however, often was able to talk his way out of these confrontations. Feelings of terror caused by an inescapable menace, along with the manipulative power of language later became prominent themes in his works.

Pinter's love for the theatre emerged in his grammar school days when he played the title roles in *Macbeth* and *Romeo and Juliet*. He also revealed his literary talents during this period. The *Hackney Downs School Magazine* published Pinter's essay on James Joyce and two of his poems that showed the beginnings of his distinctive literary style. In 1948 Pinter began his acting studies at the Royal Academy of Dramatic Art (RADA) but soon left. For the next ten years, he wrote poems and short prose pieces and acted on the stage and on television under the pseudonym David Baron. He has noted that his acting experience gave him valuable insight into how successful plays are structured and provided him with a sharp ear for dialogue.

In 1957, over a four-day period, Pinter wrote *The Room*, a one-act play, for a friend's student production. The successful production of the play sparked his interest in playwriting and soon after he wrote the full-length play entitled *The Birthday Party*. Although some reviewers took note of Pinter's innovative style in *The Birthday Party*, the initial popular and critical response was overwhelmingly negative. Two years later, he gained accolades from the public and the press with *The Caretaker*, which signaled his emergence as one of the British theater's new breed of playwrights. Pinter continues his successful writing career as a playwright, a scriptwriter for radio and television, and a screenwriter in the early twenty-first century. He has won several awards, including the *Evening Standard*'s drama award in 1961 and the Newspaper Guild of New York award in 1962, both for *The Caretaker*; the New York Film Critics Award in 1964 for *The Servant*; the British Film Academy Award in 1965 and 1971; and the New York Drama Critics Circle Award for *The Homecoming* in 1967. He has also received honorary degrees from many universities in Great Britain and the United States.

PLOT SUMMARY

Act I: Prison Wall

The play opens with a line of women standing up against a prison wall. An elderly woman cradles her hand while a young woman stands with her arm around her. A sergeant and an officer enter. The sergeant points to the young woman and asks her her name. The young woman replies that they have given their names. The two repeat this dialogue until the officer tells the sergeant to "stop this s——."

The officer then turns to the young woman and asks her if she has any complaints. The young woman responds that the older woman has been bitten. When the officer asks the elderly woman who bit her, she slowly raises her hand but remains silent. The young woman tells him that a Doberman pinscher bit her. Again he asks the elderly woman who bit her hand, as if he had never heard the young woman's reply. The elderly woman stares at him and remains silent. The younger woman, redefining her response, tells him "a big dog." When the officer asks the dog's name, he is met with silence, which agitates him to the point that he insists "every dog has a name" given by its parents. He informs them that before dogs bite, they state their name. He then tells the young woman that if the dog bit the elderly woman without stating his name, he will have the dog shot. When he is met again with silence, he barks, "silence and attention."

The officer then calls the sergeant over and asks him to take any complaints. When the sergeant again asks for complaints, the young woman tells him that they have been standing all day in the snow, while the guards have taunted them with the dogs, one of which bit the woman. The officer again asks the name of the dog. The young woman looks at him and answers, "I don't know his name."

The sergeant then abruptly changes the subject, informing the women, "your husbands, your sons, your fathers, these men you have been waiting to see, are s——houses" and "enemies of the State." The officer steps forward and identifies the women as "mountain people" and tells them that since their language is forbidden, it should be considered "dead." They are only allowed to speak "the language of the capital.'' He warns that they will be ''badly punished'' if they try to speak the mountain language. He reiterates that this is the law and that their language is dead, and ends by asking whether there are any questions. When the young woman responds that she does not speak mountain language, the sergeant puts his hand on her ''bottom'' and asks, ''What language do you speak with your a——?'' When the officer warns the sergeant to remember that the women have committed no crime, the sergeant asks, ''but you're not saying they're without sin?'' The officer admits that was not his point, and the sergeant concludes the young woman is full of sin, that ''she bounces with it.''

The young woman then identifies herself by name and tells them she has come to see her husband, which she claims is her right. When she presents her papers, the officer notes that she and her husband do not come from the mountains, and realizes that he has been put ''in the wrong batch.'' The sergeant concludes, ''she looks like a f—— intellectual to me.''

Harold Pinter

Act II: Visitor's Room

The scene opens with the elderly woman sitting next to a prisoner. When she speaks to him in a rural accent, the guard jabs her with a stick, insisting that the language is forbidden. The prisoner tries to explain to the guard that the woman doesn't know the language of the capital but is met with silence. When the elderly woman tells the prisoner that she has apples, the guard again jabs her and shouts that her language is forbidden. The prisoner admits that the woman does not know what the guard is saying. The guard refuses to accept responsibility and concludes, ''you're all a pile of s——.'' When the prisoner does not respond to the guard's questions, the guard calls the sergeant and reports, ''I've got a joker in here.''

The action freezes and, in a voiceover, the audience hears a conversation between the elderly woman and the prisoner, who identifies himself as her son. He voices concern for her bitten hand. She tries to encourage him, telling him that everyone is looking forward to his homecoming. The sergeant then appears, asking ''what joker'' and the scene abruptly ends.

Act III: Voice in the Darkness

The scene opens in a corridor where a guard and the sergeant are holding up a hooded man. When the sergeant sees the young woman there, he

demands to know who let her in. The guard answers that she is the hooded man's wife. The sergeant first asks whether this is a reception for ''Lady Duck Muck'' then apologizes to her, saying that there must have been ''a bit of a breakdown in administration,'' and so she was sent through the wrong door. He then asks if there is anything he can do for her.

The characters freeze again. In a voiceover conversation, the hooded man and his wife, the young woman, speak lovingly about their lives together and imagine they are on a lake holding each other. When the action starts again, the hooded man collapses, and his wife screams, calling him by name. He is then dragged off. The sergeant reiterates that she has come through the wrong door and informs her that if she has any questions, she can ask the ''bloke'' who comes in ''every Tuesday week, except when it rains.'' She asks whether ''everything [will] be all right'' if she has sex with this man, and the sergeant replies ''sure. No problem.'' The scene ends after she thanks the sergeant.

Act IV: Visitor's Room

This act returns to the visitor's room where the prisoner sits next to his mother, trembling with blood on his face. The guard informs them ''they've changed the rules.'' Until ''further notice,'' they can speak in their own language. When the prisoner translates this to his mother, she does not respond, as if she no longer understands her own language. The prisoner's trembling grows until he falls to his knees, shaking violently. The sergeant appears, sees him and says, ''you go out of your way to give them a helping hand and they f—— it up.''

CHARACTERS

Charley

Charley is one of the prisoners. His affection for Sara, his wife, becomes evident during a voiceover, when he and Sara talk lovingly about their union and imagine being together in the future. Toward the end of the play, he collapses in front of her, suggesting that he has been tortured.

Elderly Woman

The elderly woman is referred to as a mountain woman. She has come to the prison to see her son. While she is waiting in the snow for eight hours, a guard dog bites her hand so severely that her thumb is almost detached. She shows her capacity for compassion and nurturance when she brings food to her son. She also tries to comfort him and fill him with hope by telling him that everyone at home is looking forward to his return. Her inability to understand the official language, and therefore the warning against speaking her own language (mountain language), results in her being beaten by the guards.

She ends the play in silence, in an almost catatonic state. When her son tells her that the prison officials have changed the rules and they are now allowed to speak in their language, she does not respond. It is not clear whether she is too afraid to speak or has lost the ability to do so, perhaps due to her son's condition.

Guard

The guard exhibits cruelty when he repeatedly jabs the elderly woman with a stick when she speaks mountain language. He tries to justify his treatment of her by saying that he has responsibilities and that he has a family. The guard refuses to recognize that his prisoner also has a family, and in an effort to punish him, the guard informs the sergeant that the prisoner is a ''joker.''

Sara Johnson

Sara comes to the prison to see her husband, Charley. Although she is not a ''mountain woman'' and obviously is from a higher social class, she forms a bond with the elderly woman. She illustrates her compassionate nature when she comforts the older woman after she has been bitten by the dog and tries to get help for her. Sara reveals her courage when she stands up to the sergeant and officer on several occasions. She refuses an order to give her name a second time and often meets absurd questions with silence.

Sara is smart enough though to answer some of their questions patiently, as when the sergeant asks her again the name of the dog who bit the elderly woman, and she answers that she does not know, which of course should have been obvious to him. When the women are asked whether they have any complaints, she speaks up, noting that they have been standing all day in the snow, waiting to see the prisoners. She insists that it is her right to see her husband.

After accidentally coming across her hooded husband and realizing that he has been tortured, she breaks down. At the end of the play, she admits that she is willing to sleep with a prison official in order to save her husband.

Hooded Man
See Charley

Officer

The officer is the person in charge of the prison. At times, he appears to follow reasonable guidelines, but his behavior quickly dissolves into the absurd, along with that of the sergeant. Sometimes he chastises the sergeant for repeatedly asking the women the same question, and he seems to show concern for the elderly woman's hand. However, that concern quickly vanishes in a silly discussion of dogs' names. While he directs the sergeant to ask the women whether they have any complaints, he never acts on those complaints. He reminds the sergeant that the women are not criminals, but he cannot acknowledge that they have not sinned. When the officer discovers that Sara's husband is not a mountain person, he admits that he has been placed in the ''wrong batch'' but does not question his guilt. He tries to assert his authority, and points out the absurdity of his rules when he insists that if the dog that bit the elderly woman did not give his name, he will be shot. He reveals his need for control when, as the women are standing silently, he tells them to be silent.

Prisoner

The prisoner illustrates his compassion when he shows great concern about his mother's hand. He also tries to explain to the guard that she cannot understand the official language in the hopes the guard will stop hitting her. In an effort to encourage the guard to feel compassion and a sense of brotherhood, he explains that he too has a wife and three children. His boldness, however, is punished when the guard determines him to be a "joker." The blood on his face in the next scene suggests that he has been beaten. When, at the end of the play, his mother appears in an almost catatonic state, he collapses on the floor, gasping and shaking violently, seemingly experiencing a mental and physical collapse.

Second Guard

The second guard appears in the corridor, holding up Sara's husband.

Sergeant

His cruelty and desire for power is exhibited throughout the play. He repeatedly categorizes the prisoners as "s——houses," and he tries to demean Sara, whom he considers a "f—— intellectual." In order to assert his power over her, he puts his hands on her and claims, "intellectual a——s wobble the best" and that she "bounces" with sin. At other times, he professes to be carrying out the law, as when he tells them that mountain language has been forbidden. Later, he appears in the guise of a public servant when he asks Sara what he can do for her after she accidentally appears in the corridor where she sees her husband with a hood over his face. She does not respond, knowing he will do nothing to help her or her husband. He pretends to be magnanimous at the end of the play, suggesting he engineered the change in the rule forbidding anyone to speak in mountain language but then reveals his true nature when he shows no compassion as he watches the prisoner collapse, exclaiming "you go out of your way to give them a helping hand and they f—— it up."

Young Woman

See Sara Johnson

TOPICS FOR FURTHER STUDY

- Create a "Pinteresque" conversation between two people that employs language techniques similar to those found in Pinter's works.

- Read another play by Pinter and write a paper comparing its style and themes to that of *Mountain Language*.

- Research Pinter's political writings, especially noting his critique of British government. Do you think he was making a statement about Britain in the play? Why or why not?

- Investigate the lives of the Kurds. Why did the Turkish government ban their cultural practices? Did the Kurds give up their culture or find ways to hide expressions of their tradition? Explain.

THEMES

Meaninglessness

Pinter illustrates the play's major theme, meaninglessness, in his adroit construction of the play. In the absurd prison world, nothing makes sense. The prisoners, referred to as "s——houses" and "enemies of the state" are being held for unnamed crimes. The narrative suggests that they have been imprisoned because they are "mountain people" who speak an outlawed language. When the officials discover that Charley, Sara's husband, is not a mountain person, they decide he has been put into the "wrong batch" but do not question his guilt.

The play presents an existentialist vision of the condition and existence of men and women as it deconstructs the traditional view that humans are rational beings existing in an intelligible universe. The characters repeatedly question the prison rules, trying to determine a logical structure to the system but are continually thwarted because there is no logic behind a world that contains neither truth nor value. As they face this meaninglessness, they experience isolation and anguish.

Pinter illustrates this sense of meaninglessness in his presentation of the breakdown between language and meaning. Sara continually tries to communicate with the prison officials in order to convince them to treat her and the others humanely and to allow her to reunite with her husband, but her dialogue with them continually degenerates into pointless babble. For example, when she tries to get someone to tend to the elderly woman whose hand has been torn by a dog bite, the officer and sergeant begin a nonsensical discussion about the dog's name and never offer assistance.

Social Protest

Pinter constructs scenes like the one concerning the dog as a form of social protest. Through his characterizations and dramatic structure, he presents a compelling indictment of totalitarian regimes. Pinter has suggested the oppression the Kurds have experienced as a minority group in Turkey inspired his writing of the play (as mentioned by Charles Spencer in the *Daily Telegraph,* but his use of Anglo names like ''Sara Johnson'' and ''Charley,'' along with the indeterminate setting, suggests Pinter is condemning any government that oppresses its people.

Censorship

One of the main ways the prison officials oppress the characters in the play is to censor them. In order to strip them of their cultural identity, they decree that ''mountain language'' is forbidden, that it should be considered ''dead,'' and those who speak it will be severely punished. This censure not only denies the characters a sense of self but also serves to isolate each from the other because communication within the community becomes impossible.

Sexual Abuse

When the officials realize that Sara is not a mountain woman and so cannot control her due to her social status, they find another way to exercise their power over her. After the sergeant identifies her as a ''f—— intellectual,'' he abuses her to assert his power over her. When she admits to the sergeant that she does not speak mountain language, he puts his hands on her and asks, ''What language do you speak with your a——,'' thus effectively undermining her position in the prison hierarchy. Later, he insists to the officer that Sara is full of sin, that she ''bounces with it.''

Resistance

Sara makes attempts to resist the authority of the officials through her questions and her silences. She insists that something should be done to help the elderly woman after the guard dog bites her, and she insists it is her right to see her husband. She meets the officials' repeated, foolish questions (for example, ''What is the dog's name?'') with silence, refusing to participate in meaningless dialogue. Yet, by the end of the play, her spirit has effectively been broken by the totalitarian system. She finally sees her husband but is powerless to prevent his torture through rational means. As a result, she agrees to prostitute herself so that she can save him.

STYLE

Structure

Pinter fragments the structure of the play to illustrate the sense of isolation and alienation that the characters experience. The acts present separate vignettes of the women trying desperately to see their men. Act I centers on the women, who have stood in the snow for eight hours, and their interaction with the sergeant and the officer. The absurd dialogue in which Sara must engage with the two officials reinforces her sense of alienation as does the fact that the scene ends before she can see her husband. This opening scene sets the tone of the play and suggests that the women will not be able to be truly reunited with the men.

Acts II and IV center on the elderly woman and her son. In act II, the two try to talk to each other, but their communication is continually broken off by the guard, who jabs the elderly woman with a stick every time she tries to speak to her son. This sense of broken communication is reinforced in the last act, when the elderly woman does not respond to her son, either due to her fear of being beaten or to her son's shocking physical condition.

The third act takes place in a corridor where Sara accidentally comes upon her husband. The claustrophobic atmosphere of the entire scene suggests that neither Sara nor her husband, who has obviously been tortured by the guards, can escape the absurd world in which they find themselves.

Language

Pinter's unique use of language, or lack of it, also reinforces the play's themes. Most of the dialogue between the guards and the women and prisoners appears to make little sense, reflecting the play's focus on communication breakdown and the absurdity of their position. Pinter also uses silences throughout the play to illustrate this theme as well as his focus on the power plays that occur in the prison.

HISTORICAL CONTEXT

Theatre of the Absurd

This term, coined by Martin Esslin who wrote *The Theatre of the Absurd* (1961), is applied to plays that focus on and reflect the absurd nature of the human condition. The roots of this type of literature can be found in the expressionist and surrealist movements as well as in the existential philosophy that emerged from the theories of nineteenth-century Danish theologian Søren Kierkegaard, and German philosophers Martin Heidegger and Friedrich Nietzsche. Dramatists associated with this group include Samuel Beckett, Eugene Ionesco, Günter Grass, Jean Genet, Edward Albee, N. G. Simpson, and Pinter.

Absurdist plays portray a specific vision of the condition and existence of men and women and an examination of their place and function in life. They reject the notion that humans are rational beings operating in an intelligible universe that maintains a logically ordered structure. Absurdist playwrights present characters who strive but ultimately fail to find purpose and meaning in a world that contains no truth or value. As a result, the characters experience isolation and anguish in the face of the inherent nothingness in their world.

These plays typically lack a conventional structure. Often they incorporate silences and scenes of miscommunication to reinforce the sense of isolation and alienation experienced by the characters. A loose plot is often strung together as a series of fragmented scenes, disconnected images that reflect the characters' experiences.

Repression of the Kurds

Pinter has noted that *Mountain Language* is based on the oppression the Kurds have experienced as a minority group in Turkey. The Kurds, numbering about twenty–five million, are primarily located in a mountainous region in the Middle East, stretching from southeastern Turkey through northwestern Iran. They have had a long history of conflict with Turkey, heightened at the end of World War I with the Treaty of Versailles, which gave the Turkish government the right to rule over them. Tensions heightened in 1937, when Mustafa Kemal Ataturk decreed that religious and non-Turkish cultural expression would be outlawed in Turkey, including the word *Kurd*.

During the next decade, Kurdish schools, organizations, and publications were banned, and any references to Kurdish regions were removed from maps and documents. After the word *Kurd* was outlawed, the Kurds were officially referred to as "mountain Turks who have forgotten their language." They were denied government positions, and the Turkish government confiscated land and property. Kurds launched a series of revolts against the Turkish government, trying to gain widespread support by appealing to traditional religious beliefs and cultural practices. However, Kurdish leaders could not get the cooperation of the various Kurdish tribes. After the revolts were suppressed in 1925 and 1930, the government handed out harsher and more repressive measures. The Kurds remain an impoverished and culturally oppressed minority in Turkey.

In 1996, eleven Kurds, while rehearsing *Mountain Language* with plastic guns, were arrested by London police. They were held until authorities could establish what was actually occurring in the community center where they were rehearsing. Pinter suggests that this incident is a case of life imitating art.

CRITICAL OVERVIEW

When *Mountain Language* opened at the National Theatre in London on October 20, 1988, it earned mixed reviews. Some commentators praised the play's compelling subject and themes, while others found the play to be too political. In an overview of Pinter and his work in *Contemporary Dramatists,* Lois Gordon applauds the play's "frightening images" of totalitarianism. Douglas Kennedy, in his review of the play in *New Statesman & Society* writes that *Mountain Language* is "a highly condensed guided tour through state tyranny" presented through "a series of stark, rather atypical images of political repression." While he commends its "tight" construction, he considers it to be "uncomfortably hollow," arguing that it is "terribly predictable in its vision of state terror." Kennedy claims that the play "could be ultimately seen

COMPARE
&
CONTRAST

- **1930s:** In the new republic of Turkey, president Mustafa Kemal Ataturk works hard to "Europeanize" his people, including the adoption of surnames and giving women the right to vote. This change also includes the abolishment of religion within Turkey, which greatly affects Kurds.

  1980s: Torn by internal strife, Turkey's Council of National Security seeks to restore public order through the capture of terrorists, the confiscation of large caches of weapons, and a ban on political activity. A state of emergency is declared in 1987 to deal with the uprising the of the Kurdistan Workers Party (PKK).

  Today: The number of deaths from terrorism drops significantly as Turkey seeks involvement with the European Union. A state of emergency still exists in the six southeastern states that are native to Kurds.

- **1930s:** Theater sees enormous growth in Turkey after the formation of the republic. The first Children's Theater is opened. The *Halkevleri* (people centers), established by the State, play a large role in the spread and development of theater through publications, tours, and courses.

  1980s: Drama continues to be popular in Turkey as more theaters open all over the country.

  Today: The Turkish government is trying to provide financial support to private theaters in the interest of preserving artistic expression, but this backing is not regulated and is therefore subject to political whim.

- **1930s:** A latinized Turkish alphabet is now the basis of the official written language of Turkey, a nation recently assembled from the remains of the Ottoman empire and including a variety of ethnic groups.

  1980s: The constitution adopted in 1982 preserves democratic government and protects basic human rights, including freedom of expression, thought, and assembly.

  Today: Twenty percent of Turkey's population is ethnically Kurdish; the remaining eighty percent is Turkish. Ninety-nine percent of the population is Muslim. Turkish is the official language, but Kurdish, Arabic, Armenian, and Greek are also spoken.

---

as more of a pronouncement of Pinter's new-found political activism than as a polemical statement about the brutal grammar of totalitarianism." While he praises Pinter's use of silence, a characteristic device in his plays, Kennedy concludes that *Mountain Language* is an unsettling mix of artistry and politics "and the result leaves one wondering whether Pinter wasn't a far more effective political writer when he left you baffled, but unnerved."

Spencer, in his review for the *Daily Telegraph* insists that the play is "sketchy, paranoid and self-righteous." Spencer also concludes that "the characters are types, not people, meaning that audience reaction is one of generalized concern rather than specific sympathy." He also criticizes the play's

political themes, concluding that Pinter tries to create parallels between the play's totalitarianism and the current government in Britain. He writes that Pinter's "suggestion that Britain is indistinguishable from more oppressive regimes seems shrill and impertinent, not least to those who have suffered under real state tyranny."

CRITICISM

Wendy Perkins

Perkins is an associate professor of English at Prince George's Community College in Maryland.

In this essay, she examines Pinter's effective mix of realism and the absurd in Mountain Language.

Harold Pinter has admitted that *Mountain Language* is based on the long history of oppression the Kurds have suffered as a minority group under Turkish rule. Critics have praised the play for its realistic depiction of the victims and oppressors in a totalitarian state. In an overview of Pinter and his work in *Contemporary Dramatists,* Lois Gordon applauds the play's "frightening images" of oppression. Douglas Kennedy, in his review of the play in *New Statesman & Society* writes that *Mountain Language* is "a highly condensed guided tour through state tyranny" presented through "a series of stark . . . images of political repression." Yet, Pinter's dramatic structure is not purely realistic. He combines realism with elements of the absurd in an effort to highlight and reinforce the reality of totalitarianism and the meaninglessness at its core. The result is a compelling and shocking portrait of political terrorization.

The play presents a real and quite menacing situation. In an unnamed country at an unnamed prison, women wait all day in the freezing cold for the chance of seeing their men, who are incarcerated in the prison. Vicious guard dogs surround them, taunted by the guards, until one lunges forward and almost severs the thumb of an elderly woman. The inmates, held as "enemies of the state," are beaten and tortured as their women are prevented from offering them solace. This narrative could represent an accurate depiction of the horror of any totalitarian state, a point Pinter illustrates by refusing to name the country, the prison, or any of the officials. As the narrative unfolds, Pinter adds elements of absurdity to heighten, for his audience, the nightmare of totalitarian barbarism.

Tish Dace, in her overview of Pinter for the *Reference Guide to English Literature,* explains the playwright's motive for his unique structural devices that contain elements associated with plays of the Theatre of the Absurd. She notes that traditionally writers "feel obliged to explain their characters' behavior." The structure of one of Pinter's plays, however, "suggest[s] further exposure to the situation will merely compound the conundrum, heighten the obscurity, elaborate the elusive hints at sources for his characters' anxiety." She continues, "Where most playwrights bring clarity, shape, and order to what they dramatize, Pinter delights in slyly selecting what will appear most cryptic, vague,

> "BY DENYING A COMMUNITY ITS LANGUAGE AND THEREFORE A CRUCIAL PART OF ITS CULTURAL EXPRESSION, A TOTALITARIAN GOVERNMENT CAN EFFECTIVELY REMOVE THAT COMMUNITY'S IDENTITY AND THEREFORE ANY THREAT TO THE SYSTEM."

or even contradictory" as he substitutes "hints for exposition and intangible menace for explicit confrontation."

One of the main ways Pinter subverts "clarity, shape, and order" in *Mountain Language* is to present fragmented vignettes, offering only snapshots of the prisoners and the women who come to see them. The effect of these brief scenes, with no chronological or expository clues to help the audience piece together a coherent narrative, is to illustrate the sense of isolation and alienation that the characters experience. Throughout the entire first act, the women are separated from the men and are tormented by the prison officials. The remaining three acts present brief, truncated portraits of the women's visits with the men, characterized by broken communications, suggesting no possibility of permanent reunification.

Pinter explains his use of theatrical economy in a speech originally delivered in 1970 in Hamburg, and published in the fourth volume of his *Complete Works*: "The image must be pursued with the greatest vigilance, calmly, and once found, must be sharpened, graded, accurately focused and maintained." He notes that in his plays "the key word is economy, economy of movement and gesture, of emotion and its expression . . . so there is no wastage and no mess."

As Pinter constructs his economical scenes, he inserts elements of the absurd to reinforce the sense of meaninglessness and barbarity. The absurdity emerges in the dialogues between the prison officials and the inmates and the women who come to see them. The language in these scenes operates principally on a subtextual level; meaning lies not in the words themselves, which are often nonsensical, but in how and why the characters use language. Pinter's incorporation of scenes of miscommunication also reinforces the sense of isolation and alienation experienced by the characters.

In the opening conversation, Pinter creates verbal plays that point to the absurd situation in which the women find themselves. The sergeant appears and demands the names of the women, which they have already provided. This fact, however, makes no difference to the sergeant, who continually repeats the order, suggesting that he does not regard them as individuals, only as a group that needs to be controlled.

The second inane conversation in the play relates to the elderly woman who has been severely bitten by one of the guard dogs. When Sara asks the officers to help the woman, they become incensed, not by the seriousness of the injury but by the fact that the dog did not give his name before he bit her. This irrational response provides the first example of the problems inherent in the totalitarian system. The officials' treatment of the women and the prisoners has no logical cause, and, therefore, they can offer no logical defense for their actions.

The officer, however, tries to appear official in his explanation of the "formal procedure" dogs must follow when they bite someone. He also attempts to suggest an orderly system of rules and regulations when he insists that he will shoot the dog if the dog did not give his name before he bit the woman. The absurdity of his stance reinforces the sense that the officials in this system follow no logical plan as they carry out their duties.

One of the official decrees, the censure of the mountain people's language, is a tactic that many oppressive regimes have used on their victims. By denying a community its language, and therefore a crucial part of its cultural expression, a totalitarian government can effectively remove that community's identity and therefore any threat to the system. Yet, when Sara confirms that she is not a mountain person, nor is her husband, the officers prove the arbitrary nature of the decree, deciding her husband is still guilty of being "an enemy of the state" but offering no evidence of the specificity of his crimes.

The final absurd confrontation between Sara and the officials in this act comes at the end of the scene when they recognize that she is not a moun- tain woman. In order to reassert his power over her, the sergeant objectifies her sexually, placing his hands on her, asking "what language do you speak with your a——?" and claiming that she fairly "bounces" with sin. Noting that she comes from a higher social class than do the other women and prisoners, the sergeant determines that she is a "f—— intellectual" and that "intellectual a——s wob- ble the best." As a result of this sexual objectification, the sergeant successfully removes her identity and therefore does not need to treat her humanely.

The absurdity of the ban on mountain language becomes apparent in the second act when the guard jabs the elderly woman as she tries to communicate with her son. The ban causes a breakdown in communications not only between the woman and her son but also between the woman and the guard. When the guard tells her that her language has become officially "dead," she cannot understand what he is saying to her and so continues to speak her language as the guard persists in beating her.

Pinter uses the technique of silence in this scene, as he does in others, as a form of language that reflects the characters' interaction with each other. Pinter often uses silences in his plays as verbal acts of aggression, defense, and acquies- cence that often speak more loudly than words. In the first act, Sara shows her defiance and points to the absurdity of the officials' questions when she refuses to answer the sergeant's questions about the dog. In act II, the guard meets the prisoner's decla- ration of his mother's inability to understand the official language with silence, as an act of defense. If he does not acknowledge what the prisoner is saying, he will not have to admit the absurdity of the decree, and he can keep on abusing the elderly woman. An example of silence as acquiescence occurs at the end of the play when the elderly woman does not respond to her son's questions. At this point she has given in to the system, either due to her fear of being beaten or her despair over her son's condition.

Pinter uses a different form of silence in an absurd way. He explains this technique in a speech delivered at the 1962 National Student Drama Festi- val in Bristol and published as the introduction to *Complete Works One*. Pinter explains that there are two types of silences, one when nothing is said and the other "when perhaps a torrent of language is being employed. This speech is speaking of a lan- guage locked beneath it. That is its continual reference.'' He notes the subtext of this type of silence when he comments, ''the speech we hear is an indication of that which we don't hear. It is a necessary avoidance, a violent, sly, anguished or mocking smoke screen which keeps the other in its place.''

One example of this type of verbal subterfuge occurs during the third act when Sara accidentally stumbles upon her husband in a corridor. He shows clear signs of having been tortured. Flustered, the sergeant ejects a barrage of nonsense in an attempt to distract Sara from the reality of the situation. He tells her that she has come in the wrong door, due to the computer's ''double hernia.'' He then assures her that if she wants any ''information on any aspect of life in this place, we've got a bloke comes into the office every Tuesday week, except when it rains.''

Pinter allows no closure or resolution at the end of the play. The last image he leaves with the audience is an absurd one: the sergeant is complaining about the prisoners' failure to respond positively to an arbitrary change in the rules. Pinter's creative interweaving of realistic and absurd narrative elements throughout the structure of *Mountain Language* creates a gripping narrative of the workings and consequences of the tyranny of political systems.

Source: Wendy Perkins, Critical Essay on *Mountain Language,* in *Drama for Students,* The Gale Group, 2002.

Ronald Knowles

In the following overview, the author discusses Pinter's Mountain Language *and the devices he is known for using in his plays, particularly name- and language-play.*

Mountain Language concerns a group of women who have been waiting all day outside a prison in the hope of seeing their menfolk inside. They have to endure abuse from an intimidating sergeant, and in one case an elderly woman has almost had a thumb severed by a guard dog. On admission to the prisoners ''mountain language'' is forbidden, and prisoners and visitors must use the language of the capital. It was assumed that Pinter had written a barely veiled critique of Turkey's suppression of the Kurds and their language, but he resisted the identification, suggesting that the play has a certain significance for an English audience. Pinter's very short work of less than a thousand words can be seen in both a literal and metaphorical way.

> "IN CONTRAST TO THE NAMES IN *ONE FOR THE ROAD,* THIS COMES AS A SHOCK IF IT IS AUTOMATICALLY ASSUMED THAT SUCH ABUSES COULD ONLY HAPPEN IN PLACES LIKE TURKEY."

From a literal point of view an audience is likely to make the connection with the plight of the Kurds, though Brian Friel's play of 1980, *Translations,* reminded a British audience of the English encroachment on the Irish language in the nineteenth century. Friel's play was well attended in Wales, where it is not forgotten that England attempted to prohibit the speaking of Welsh in the last century. Throughout the performance of *Mountain Language* Pinter, as director, created a particular uneasiness in the audience by exploiting a specific condition of audience reception. The soldiers are dressed in regular battle fatigues, and the foulmouthed sergeant spoke with a strong London accent. British television screens have made British audiences long familiar with such images—in the Northern Ireland of the ''H'' blocks, no-go areas, proscription on broadcasting interviews with representatives of the IRA. By having political and geographical reference undetermined, but suggested, Pinter creates a polemical space in which the question arises just how far the United Kingdom could be said to have taken such a direction.

Pinter signals this in a fashion that is peculiarly his own. No British dramatist has used names and naming so consistently throughout a whole career as Pinter has. Let one example stand for many. In *Betrayal* the only time that the married name and titles of Robert and Emma are mentioned is precisely when Robert comes across Jerry's letter to Emma in the American Express office in Venice and intuitively realizes the nature of the contents: ''I mean, just because my name is Downs and your name is Downs doesn't mean that we're the Mr. and Mrs. Downs that they, in their laughing Mediterranean way, assume we are.'' Approximately halfway through *Mountain Language* one of the women reveals that her name is the very English ''Sara

Johnson.'' In contrast to the names in *One for the Road*, this comes as a shock if it is automatically assumed that such abuses could only happen in places like Turkey.

The first word of *Mountain Language* is ''Name?'' and this aspect of bureaucratic officialdom is cruelly parodied when one of the women complains of the older woman's injury from the dog. The officer in charge insists that he can only initiate disciplinary procedures if he is given the name of the animal: ''Every dog has a *name*! They answer to their name. They are given a name by their parents and that is their name, that is their *name*. Before they bite they *state* their name. It's a formal procedure.'' Beyond this overt bullying there is a certain kind of profundity.

The old woman is forbidden to speak her mountain language, and, unlike her prisoner son, she does not speak the language of the capital. Then the decision is reversed, and mountain language is allowed. But now the old woman is traumatized by the sight of blood on her son's face and her own pain and is speechless. At this the son is reduced to a voiceless shuddering. The logic of totalitarianism always seeks to suppress speech—by book-burning, torture, murder, or exile—because speech is itself symbolic of freedom. To speak is to name things like truth and tyranny, to speak is to give one's voice in a vote, in antiquity, or to mark a ballot paper in modern democracies. The final tableau of mother and son indicates the end of democracy— the body politic made speechless. Thankfully, after sound mountains echo; that is their ''language.''

The sketch ''New World Order'' appeared as a curtain raiser for Ariel Dorfman's acclaimed play *Death and the Maiden*. Set in post-Pinochet Chile, Dorfman's work concerns a woman's revenge against her past torturer. In Pinter's sketch two interrogators gloat over their blindfolded victim, swapping obscenities, until the almost sexual sadistic climax with one sobbing and the other congratulating him for ''keeping the world clean for democracy.'' These words were those used by the youthful Pinter and friends in ironic response to the dropping of atom bombs on Japan. As in *Mountain Language*, the victim is rendered literally and symbolically speechless: ''Before he came in here he was a big shot, he never stopped shooting his mouth off, he never stopped questioning received ideas. Now— because he's apprehensive about what's about to happen to him—he's stopped all that, he's got

nothing more to say.'' Similarly, upon Victor's second entrance in *One for the Road* he has difficulty speaking because his torturers have mutilated his tongue.

Source: Ronald Knowles, ''*Mountain Language* (1988) and 'New World Order' (1991),'' in *Understanding Harold Pinter*, University of South Carolina Press, 1995, pp. 192–95.

Penelope Prentice

In the following essay, the author discusses Pinter's use of the power of love, the opposite of love, and language in portraying questions of human nature and brutality in Mountain Language.

After *One for the Road* there might seem little more to say about the brutalities of torture. But *Mountain Language*, which continues to explore the conflict between Eros and Thanatos, offers further insights into the causes for such brutality and strengthens insights into further links between love and violence. Love or its opposite, fractally referenced and infused in each moment, drives the play's conflict. Love, devalued and deployed in brutal language and acts of the torturers as one weapon in the arsenal to destroy, is also a bond which can sustain the tortured and their families. Inspired by the plight of the Kurds who were forbidden to speak their language, *Mountain Language* is the bleakest, most pitiless, and remorseless of Pinter's plays.

The action in the play alternates between women in line waiting outside to see their men being held prisoner inside and the brief visits they are permitted: between a mother and son, a husband and wife, a woman and her lover.

The initial focus on the waiting women throws a spotlight upon their men being held prisoner and tortured. The play levels distinctions between age, education, and class: the young intellectual wife who has come to see her husband and the old peasant mother, to see her son. Both are equally humiliated, both, equally courageous. The near hopelessness of the women's plight, their stoical defiance of authority to support their men dramatizes a courage informed by love.

That love, which sustains the men and women through some of the worst outrages remains, however, impotent to save the men. Love without power is not enough.

As the play opens the Young Woman at the head of the line exhibits defiance as soon the Sergeant demands ''Name?'' She repeats her reply, ''We've given our names,'' each time he asks. Her refusal to comply with his senseless demands prompts the Officer who enters to engage in the familiar ''good cop/bad cop'' ploy by turning upon the Sergeant with, ''Stop this s———.'' He then asks the Young Woman, ''Any complaints?'' Momentarily releasing tension and raising hope, he notices the Elderly Woman's wounded hand and asks, ''Has someone bitten your hand?'' The term ''someone,'' one of the few grimly humorous turns in the play, both relieves and heightens tension. When the old peasant woman fails to answer his repeated question, the Young Woman finally says, ''A Doberman pinscher.''

Full dread begins to dawn when the Officer observes, ''I think the thumb is going to come off,'' as he again asks the Elderly Woman (whom we will only later learn does not understand his language), ''Who did this?'' Her failure to answer his question again prompts the Young Woman to reply, ''A big dog.'' He instantly demands, ''What was his name?'' and with another desolate trace of humor lights into the Young Woman with a lengthy diatribe:

> Every dog has a *name!* They answer to their name. They are given a name by their parents and that is their name, that is their *name!* Before they bite, they *state* their name. It's a formal procedure. They state their name and then they bite.

In contrast to the dogs who have names, the men being tortured and women waiting in line to see them remain nameless. The point of the Sergeant's repeatedly requesting the women's names serves only to remind them that they have none.

The Sergeant, with permission to speak, pronounces the men they have been waiting to see ''s———houses'' and ''enemies of the State.'' The Officer reminds the line of waiting women that by ''military decree'' and by ''law'' they are forbidden to speak their language: ''Your language is dead.''

The Young Woman tries to identify herself as apart from the others: ''I do not speak the mountain language.'' The Officer levels any distancing she attempts even in his ''good cop'' role; when he reminds his subordinate, ''These women, Sergeant, have as yet committed no crime,'' he allows himself to be corrected by his Sergeant who says, ''Sir! But you're not saying they're without sin?''

Their denying the equation of ''crime'' and ''sin'' only melds the values of church and state for the persecutors. The Officer agrees and the Sergeant further concurs, ''This one's full of it. She bounces

''LOVE, DEVALUED AND DEPLOYED IN BRUTAL LANGUAGE AND ACTS OF THE TORTURERS AS ONE WEAPON IN THE ARSENAL TO DESTROY, IS ALSO A BOND WHICH CAN SUSTAIN THE TORTURED AND THEIR FAMILIES.''

with it.'' When the Young Woman declares, ''My name is Sara Johnson. I have come to see my husband. It is my right,'' the word ''right'' is stripped of all meaning as she is asked for her papers, then informed, ''He's in the wrong batch.'' The Sergeant remarks, ''So is she. She looks like a f———ing intellectual to me,'' adding, ''Intellectual a———s wobble the best.'' His remark, which cuts at her softer life, also reduces her to a slab of meat, reminding her that she is without distinction from the other women in line and that neither her mind, education, nor knowledge of the law can privilege her above the other women. This enforced leveling of hierarchy by those in command does not destroy hierarchy but distills it to the simple dichotomy of an us vs them duality.

The introduction of her Anglo name, which must garner greater sympathy from an Anglo- or Eurocentric audience, also functions to ambush the audience, reroute and subvert any distancing belief, ''This could never happen to me.'' Her name all by itself also gives weight to her individuality to enhance audience sympathy. (But would a name such as Gingra Razzu serve the same function as Sara Johnson?) This second central Sara in Pinter's plays (though a variant spelling on Sarah of *The Lover*) serves to emphasize the biblical connotations not only of Sarah's lost children, but here, Sara's lost husband, and through his death, of their lost children.

The Elderly Woman with the wounded hand, now in the visitor's room with her son, is twice jabbed by a guard and forbidden to speak her language when once she says, ''I have bread—'' and another time, ''I have apples—'' Only then does the Guard realize she does not understand him. Nevertheless his message has been effectively conveyed—she does not speak again.

Pinter departs from his customary realism, transmitting to the audience the thoughts of the prisoners and visitors which they have been forbidden to speak. We hear in the Elderly Woman's thought/voice attempts to encourage her son as she sits mutely across from him to "tell" him in her mind that the baby is waiting, that everyone looks forward to his homecoming. The Prisoner's thought/voice also conveys love and concern as he notices that his mother's hand has been bitten. This invention conveys the depth of feeling the characters bear one another and the significance of their meeting—of her having made the visit and his having survived despite all odds. Their acts of love that sustain them endure to stand in stark contrast to the lack of any human kindness from those in authority.

But beneath their different exteriors and opposing circumstances, Pinter links the prisoners and the guards by a common thread of humanity: family. When the Guard remarks, "I've got a wife and three kids," the Prisoner volunteers the information that he does, too. Even though the prisoner's attempt to form a human connection only prompts the Guard to telephone in the complaint, "I think I've got a joker in here," and though The Guard refuses to recognize any commonality between himself and the man he holds prisoner (as, to continue his work, he must), the link has been forged for the audience.

In the penultimate scene, "Voice in the Darkness," when a Young Woman enters, the Sergeant barks "Who's that f——ing woman?" conveying anti-erotic sexual overtones which nevertheless parallel the thought/voice erotic communion between the Young Woman and her lover, who stands before her supported by two guards and with a bag over his head. The Young Man's and Young Woman's intertwining "voices" recall making love. Even here at the edge of the abyss their love sustains them as his thoughts import their past lovemaking into the present, sustaining him to withstand this intolerable situation and transforming it: "I watch you sleep. And then your eyes open. You look up at me about you and smile." The Young Woman's voice in perfect consort responds: "You smile. When my eyes open I see you above me and smile." Even though the hooded Young Man collapses without seeing his young lover, this scene of awakening to love transmits the larger point of the play.

The Sergeant terminates her visit: "Yes, you've come in the wrong door. It must be the computer. The computer's got a double hernia." The horror of that mistake, the irreversible human damage perpetuated upon a man wrongly imprisoned, resonates on the larger scale with the horror of the irrevocable human error in the whole situation: the imprisonment and torture of people who have committed no crime.

The Sergeant tells the Young Woman to come back in a week to see a man who comes in to answer questions. "His name is Dokes. Joseph Dokes." The authority, masked by a protected John Doe identity, reminds us that the only names the guards and officers bear in this play are their anonymous titles: Guard, Officer. Torturers and tortured alike are equally stripped of identity.

The brief moment of love between the young woman and man is quickly supplanted by the Sergeant's returning to his opening level of discourse: addressing love only as f——ing. Sex further reduces merely to an animal act to be bartered. When the Young Woman asks of Dokes, "Can I f—— him? If I f—— him, will everything be all right?" Though the Sergeant replies, "Sure," the audience knows that no human currency these women tender can release their men from their suffering.

The final scene, image, action, and language all conspire to reinforce the split between the destructive animality of the term "f——" as the authorities deploy it and the love between those linked by mutual affection, family bonds, and marriage. The mother and son are brought back together and this time told that the law has been changed, that they are now free to speak their language: "New Rules. Until further notice."

But when the son, now with blood on his face, tries to translate this news to his elderly, wounded, silent mother, she no longer speaks. The earlier action of the guard to prohibit speech speaks more forcefully than any words.

The son finally collapses to the floor in his effort to make his mother understand as the play closes with the Sergeant's, "Look at this. You go out of your way to give them a helping hand and they f—— it up." The double cliché "helping hand" and "f—— it up" seal into a single image the love/violence connection—referring focus both to the mother's wounded hand and to all the violence perpetuated in the name of love for a cause. The word "f——" here, stripped of all sexual and erotic connotation, any connection to love, reduces it to its function as an intensifying epithet in the weaponry of language and finally means almost nothing at all.

The violence in Pinter's plays, as entertainment, raises ethical questions. Pinter's admission that he opens himself to that charge and that at some level the audience takes some pleasure in the absolute power of the authorities does not divert the charge. Drama as a voyeuristic medium even encourages that, and some argue it provides an escape valve for real aggression. But Pinter's aim is obviously other. The responsibility, since it cannot be claimed or borne by the innocent victims, again transfers to the audience. But how? By raising consciousness.

At the very least these plays serve to raise conscious awareness of the plight of a great many innocent people worldwide. But the insight they offer into the impulse to violence and torture raises even larger questions about human nature which is portrayed as so easily brutalized to become brute. Pinter does that here by fairly conventional means. Nowhere else in Pinter's work are dominant characters drawn with so few or without any redeeming qualities, nor are the characters forced into submission, so wholly pure.

The question of responsibility thrown at the audience requires examination. It is not enough merely to *know* that such things happen. Pinter's recent plays are a call to action. But what action? What direction do I offer students when I teach, audiences, when I direct Pinter's plays? What ought I call upon myself to do in my writing and life? No doubt some classicists will ask of his work, but is this art? Is any call to action art? I would have to wait until *Moonlight* to fully answer these questions. *One for the Road* and *Mountain Language* cannot be lumped with and dismissed as mere diatribe.

In the subtext and the thematic connections between love and justice, the issues Pinter is raising are much larger: his plays provoke in audiences not merely specific emotional and intellectual responses to the injustice in the specific acts of torture but an attitude of sympathy, an empathy, a regard for the other as the self—even the torturer in the self. Without that perspective, humans who hold radically different views can be encouraged to continue to regard themselves as superior to all others who hold different religious or political views and can treat those others as vermin, lice to be smudged out and erased. Interestingly, such an attitude must also extend to the torturers. By extension, a happy ending to the torture plays would hardly be to see the torturers merely dead or themselves tortured but to see them awakened; the extermination of a torturer, even all those in such positions of power, resolves little beyond the moment.

Consistently Pinter's work reveals that how one regards the other remains a measure of how one regards the self. But again in this play we see that love is not enough. Love must assert itself in taking power necessary to defend itself or else the death-loving forces ''triumph.'' Because power is not something asked for, given, or granted, it must be seized. But before it can be exercised to promote the life-enhancing forces of growth and development rather than death and destruction, it must develop at that private level where awakening begins in self-knowledge.

What enhances the power of Pinter's work is that he acknowledges the dark, destructive but passionate Dionysian powers and weds them to the Apollonian, coolly rational quest for order and authority. He gives them equal play, blurring the traditional boundaries of each so that in the end, except for the torture plays, the two forces end in a stand-off. But brute physical power will always claim victory over mere love until love can develop its own sources of power and reclaim that power of attraction that death has appropriated as its own.

Pinter's portrayal of his authority figures' claims of doing good raises the ultimate issue, What does it mean to be good? What are the qualities necessary?

Pinter offers no easy answers. The virtues portrayed as admirable, when inner awareness and lesser strengths remain undeveloped and informed only by insecurity and fear, turn, in excess, to destructive forces loosed upon others that also turn inwardly against the self and outwardly on, the society it seeks to preserve and promote.

Death does not promote life, but the destructors in these plays remain blind to that and to what is mutilated, destroyed, and dead in themselves. Yet love remains powerless to contain, restrain or counter the forces of destruction. Like Good Deeds in *Everyman*, love's power seems nearly extinguished. What is necessary to reawaken love as a life-enhancing power which is justice? Perhaps the simple awareness that Pinter's work evokes and with that awareness action may follow.

Source: Penelope Prentice, ''*Mountain Language:* Torture Revisited,'' in *The Pinter Ethic*, Garland Publishing, Inc., 1994, pp. 285–91.

Ann C. Hall

In the following essay, the author discusses Pinter's use of the "voice-over" technique in his play Mountain Language *to articulate the political elements of "communicating beyond language through language."*

Inspired and appalled by his visit to Turkey in 1985, Harold Pinter in *Mountain Language* (1988) attempts to re-create the linguistic oppression he witnessed. Like the Turkish government which considers the language of Kurdistan subversive and so prohibits its usage, Pinter's torturers outlaw the "mountain language" of their victims. Clearly such a situation presents a difficult dilemma for a playwright. How can one represent the absence of language through language? Specifically, how can Pinter represent the effects of such oppression when the means for that representation, the convention of dramatic dialogue, is denied by the real-life situation which gave rise to the dramatic idea?

Pinter has made a career out of dramatizing such absences. His casts are filled with the verbally inept: characters pause, stop, stutter, and remain silent. As a matter of fact, Pinter often leads us down the garden path in terms of signification: just when we think his characters will say something—anything—to explain their unusual situations, their speeches become filled with elliptical interruptions. The people of Kurdistan, as well as many postmodern theorists, who argue that language is non-referential—that words do not "mean," they "signify"—could not ask for a better dramatist to illustrate their positions.

Despite his linguistic gymnastics, however, Pinter has resolutely remained a worker of words, a playwright and screenwriter. Unlike his mentor, Samuel Beckett, Pinter has not resorted to pantomime as Beckett did in, for example, *Act Without Words* (1957). Pinter's previous attitude toward language, then, can be best described as ambivalent: clearly aware of language's limits, the fact that what is left unsaid is often more important than what is actually articulated, Pinter continues to write, thereby implying a faith in language despite its weaknesses.

Mountain Language, however, presents a new situation for and from Pinter, and perhaps even marks a crisis in his career, a crisis brought about by the tension between his recent political interests and his prior aesthetic. As many have noted and Pinter himself admits, his dramatic concerns and even his readings of his earlier plays have shifted from the apolitical to the political. Such a shift may also imply a change in Pinter's attitude toward language. That is, given the fact that the victims in this play do not even have the opportunity to miscommunicate, that their lack of their own language is cause for concern, can Pinter avoid a sentimental or nostalgic view of language, a view he has spent his entire career subverting? In this play, Pinter attempts to reconcile these contradictory forces through a variation on the cinematic technique known as the "voice-over."

The relationship between cinematic sound and image is characterized by oppression; the image is privileged over the soundtrack. One reason for this relationship is based on the history of film itself. In the beginning, film did not have sound. When compared to the theatre, which clearly synchronized image and voice through dramatic dialogue, and radio, which relied on sound alone, motion pictures were defective. When sound did appear, the image was subordinate to the sound. Films were called "talkies." Even the logo of a major movie studio, RKO, boldly proclaimed that it now offered not "movies," but "radio pictures." Film, then, suffered and continues to suffer from an inferiority complex. Today, Rick Altman argues, film still attempts to repress the scandal of its defect by privileging the image over the voice.

While some historians psychoanalyze the history of the film medium, Mary Ann Doane and Stephen Heath psychoanalyze the effects that such privileging has upon the audience. According to Doane, the filmic image presents a "fantasmic body," a completely unified and uncomplicated representation of human existence to its audiences. Using the work of Jacques Lacan, particularly his formulations on the "mirror stage" and the "gaze," Stephen Heath argues that spectators gain a sense of mastery when they view the filmic image: the eye literally captures the object, whereas the ear cannot master sounds as effectively. For both the historians and the psychoanalytic critics, the image represents an uncomplicated view of reality; spectators need not question their ideologies, political beliefs, biases, etc. In effect, the filmic image is neatly framed. Sound, on the other hand, violates such framing devices and thereby violates the certainty the "fantasmic body" image provides. Consequently, all the recent technological developments in film soundtracks have been toward enhancing sound's ability to uphold the image. In Doane's words, such innovations elide the "material heterogeneity of film", the fact that film is not an uncomplicated "reality" but, instead, an illusory construct.

Traditional theater privileges the image similarly. The proscenium arch even mimics a picture frame. Like contemporary films, however, recent drama has experimented with the acoustic in order to challenge both the image's status and the existential security it provides through acoustical experiments, most notably Samuel Beckett's *Krapp's Last Tape* (1958) and *Rockaby* (1981). Pinter's interest in the auditory, perhaps influenced by Beckett or his own work in BBC radio during his early career as an actor, has, in fact, become his trademark: vituperative speeches, manic monologues, and commonplace queries are all punctuated by his notorious silences and pauses.

The following speech by Ruth in *The Homecoming* exemplifies Pinter's skill at accentuating both sound and image, as well as language's limitations. In the scene, Teddy and Lenny have been arguing about philosophy while Ruth remained silent. Suddenly she interrupts, saying:

> You've forgotten something. Look at me. I . . . move my leg.
> That's all it is. But I wear . . . underwear . . . which moves with me . . . it . . . captures your attention. Perhaps you misinterpret. The action is simple. It's a leg . . . moving. My lips move. Why don't you restrict . . . your observation to that? Perhaps the fact that they move is more significant . . . than the words which come through them. You must bear that . . . possibility . . . in mind.
> *Silence.*
> *Teddy stands.*
> I was born quite near here.
> *Pause.*
> Then . . . six year ago, I went to America.
> *Pause.*
> It's all rock and sand. It stretches . . . so far . . . everywhere you look. And there's lots of insects there.
> *Pause.*
> And there's lots of insects there.
> *Silence. She is still.*

Clearly, Ruth makes herself the object of both the audience's gaze and that of her male counterparts. She is the object to be viewed, the image. As Joan Navarre notes, Ruth is a film, a "moving picture." It would appear, then, that Ruth's physical positioning, as well as her reminder to Lenny and Teddy regarding the limits of words, privilege the image, transferring their search for philosophical certitude from language to her, the image. If, how-

> " FREQUENTLY USED IN DOCUMENTARY FILMS, THE 'VOICE-OVER' IS A DISEMBODIED VOICE WHICH RARELY UNITES THE IMAGE WITH THE SPEAKER . . . . AND YET, DURING THESE MOMENTS OF THE 'VOICE-OVER,' PINTER DOES INDICATE THAT WHILE LANGUAGE MAY NOT PROVIDE THE MEANS FOR SOCIAL CHANGE, IT DOES CREATE THE POSSIBILITY FOR SUCH SUBVERSION."

ever, Ruth is a "moving picture," the soundtrack is faulty, the dictum being that sound must prevail uninterrupted in order to uphold the image's status throughout a film. Here, however, frequent pauses and silences subvert the image's powerful position. Further, it is the sound of her voice which first captures and then retains the men's attention. Sound—both its presence and its absence—punctures the privileged but illusory status of the image.

Pinter's more recent work, moreover, highlights the importance of the voice even further. *Family Voices* (1981), for example, is a "radio play" which, to borrow Beckett's phrase, gives the audience the experience of "a text written to come out of the dark", a description which bears a close resemblance to the titles of two of Pinter's scenes in *Mountain Language*. As Stephen Gale notes, the play is "a series of disembodied voices." And, in *One For the Road* (1985), though we see the effects of physical torture on the victims, we never see the act of physical abuse; we only hear the insidious taunting of their oppressor and the victims' often muffled responses. Pinter's clear fascination with cinema, then, may not be restricted to the visual elements; instead, it may prompt him to reevaluate such emphasis.

The cinematic techniques of the "voice-off" and the "voice-over" threaten to undercut the filmic image's supremacy, as well. Simply, the "voice-off'' is the moment when a character's voice is separated from his or her image. In most films, however, the voice and body are united during prior or subsequent scenes. Similarly in theater, the off-stage voice is frequently followed or preceded by the appearance of the character whose voice we heard. In both instances, sound and image are neatly reunited, so no disruption occurs. As Doane argues, there is no interruption of the ''fantasmic body'' in such films; on the contrary, the technique actually expands ''the affirmation of the depicted unity and homogeneity of depicted space.''

Frequently used in documentary films, the ''voice-over'' is a disembodied voice which rarely unites the image with the speaker. Though sound and image remain separated, in traditional documentaries ''this voice has been for the most part that of the male, and its power resides in the possession of knowledge and in the privileged, unquestioned activity of interpretation.'' In this way, though the image is momentarily deprived of its status, the faith in a fantasmic body is unquestioned, since the voice-over leads the audience to presume that there is some ''body'' out there who represents the certitude the spectators seek.

In *Mountain Language*, Pinter offers a variation on these two cinematic techniques, a variation which privileges neither sound nor image but does highlight its disjunction in order to challenge his audience's position of authority. In effect, Pinter ''voices-over'' the ''voice-off'' by transmitting the characters' thoughts over the theater's sound system while they are still present on stage. The title of the two scenes in which this method is employed underscores Pinter's ability to balance the position of the image and sound, thereby producing a grim depiction of such oppression's effects: ''voices in the darkness.''

To some extent the technique resembles traditional dramatic conventions such as monologues, soliloquies, and asides: we are presented with the characters' inner thoughts. Such conventions, however, imply that the subversion of political oppression may be possible; the victims, after all, would speak in their ''mountain language,'' even if it is only to the audience. Hence, the audience's quest for comfort would not be threatened. By using this technique, Pinter apparently resolves the paradox created by his recent political interests and his prior attitudes towards language. By broadcasting his characters' speeches over their physical presence, Pinter shows us that the torturers disembody their

victims in more than physical ways. We see that the victims' voices are not in their possession; they are above and beyond them. Through this disjunction, this rupture between word and image, actor and dramatic dialogue, we see that the victims' bodies and voices have been as effectively severed as the Old Woman's thumb was torn from her hand.

The speeches themselves, moreover, are not filled with revolutionary fervor, nor do the victims even express a coherent understanding of their imprisoned state. Instead, their speeches contain memories and commonplace desires which highlight the pain of political oppression in personal terms. By the end of the play, moreover, even these disembodied voices are absent. When, for example, the elderly woman is finally permitted to speak in her own language, she cannot or will not. Whether the guards have literally taken her tongue is unclear, but Pinter, in any case, does not provide us with the reassurance a reunion of the body and voice would create. In this way, it would appear that Pinter succeeds in representing language's absence through language, without conjoining political power upon language through its absence.

And yet, during these moments of the ''voice-over,'' Pinter does indicate that while language may not provide the means for social change, it does create the possibility for such subversion. In the scene, for example, between the young woman and man, the characters may not talk about revolution, but they do seem to be able to construct an almost psychic connection which transcends their imprisonment and linguistic restrictions. Like Ruth in *The Homecoming*, they express a means of communicating beyond language through language. They, for instance, coincidentally remember the same comforting memory from their past:

> Man's voice: I watch you sleep. And then your eyes
> open. You look up at me and smile.
> Woman's voice: You smile. When my eyes open I see
> you above me and smile.
> Man's voice: We are out on a lake.
> Woman's voice: It is spring.
> Man's voice: I hold you. I warm you.

Despite their oppression, their silence does ''speak,'' just as the elderly woman's silence at the end of the play speaks of the cruel and arbitrary nature of political oppression.

In this way, Pinter does not entirely avoid idealizing the possibility of change through language. Pinter cannot exorcise from the play a spectral faith in linguistic power. Pinter's decision to write the play in the first place indicates that his political interests cannot allow him to remain silent. He may not know exactly what to say, but he must convey the heinousness of such oppression.

An interview with Pinter upon his return from Turkey may further illustrate this point. He says:

> I believe there's no chance of the world coming to other than a very grisly end in the next twenty-five years at the outside. Unless, God, as it were, finally speaks. Because reason is not going to do anything. Me writing *One For the Road*, documentaries, articles, lucid analyses, Avrell Harriman writing in the *New York Times,* voices here and there, people walking down the road and demonstrating. Finally it's hopeless. There's nothing one can achieve. Because the modes of thinking of those in power are worn out, threadbare, atrophied. Their minds are a brick wall. But still one can't stop attempting to try to think and see things as clearly as possible.

Here, too, Pinter cannot resolve his political concerns with his ambivalence towards language: the situation is hopeless, yet he continues to write. In *Mountain Language*, then, we not only witness an oppressed people in crisis but a playwright in crisis as well, who even identifies with his victims' separation from linguistic power. Language cannot communicate or bring about political change, yet something must be said. We are headed for self-destruction, and Pinter clearly doubts the written word's ability to stop such an end. As in the play, during this interview, Pinter invokes the ''voice-over'' through his parenthetical reference to the divine, the ultimate ''voice-over,'' the supreme ''disembodied voice,'' which he hopes will speak, like his characters, out of the darkness.

Source: Ann C. Hall, ''Voices in the Dark: The Disembodied Voice in Harold Pinter's *Mountain Language*,'' in *Pinter Review: Annual Essays 1991,* 1991, pp. 17–22.

SOURCES

Dace, Tish, ''Pinter, Harold,'' in *Reference Guide to English Literature,* 2nd ed., edited by D. L. Kirkpatrick, Vol. 2, St. James Press, 1991, pp. 1080–84.

Gordon, Lois, ''Harold Pinter: Overview,'' in *Contemporary Dramatists,* 5th ed., edited by K. A. Berney, St. James Press, 1993.

Kennedy, Douglas, ''Breaking the Silence,'' in *New Statesman & Society,* Vol. 1, No. 21, October 28, 1988, pp. 38–39.

Pinter, Harold, ''Introduction,'' in *The Complete Works One,* Grove Press, 1990.

Pinter, Harold, ''Introduction,'' in *The Complete Works Four,* Grove Press, 1990.

Spencer, Charles, ''An Interminable Slog through Pinter's Politics,'' in *Daily Telegraph,* June 28, 2001.

FURTHER READING

Armstrong, Raymond, *Kafka and Pinter Shadow-Boxing: The Struggle between Father and Son,* Palgrave, 1999.
    Armstrong provides a fascinating look at Kafka's influence on Pinter's plays.

Gale, Steven H., ed., *The Films of Harold Pinter,* SUNY Series, Cultural Studies in Cinema/Video, State University of New York Press, 2001.
    This volume contains essays by ten film scholars on Pinter's screenplays, including *Lolita, The Remains of the Day,* and *The French Lieutenant's Woman.*

Gussow, Mel, *Conversations With Pinter,* Grove Press, 1996.
    Gussow, a *New York Times* drama critic, collects a series of interviews he conducted with Pinter between 1971 and 1993 on the nature of Pinter's work.

Taylor, John Russell, ''Harold Pinter,'' in *British Writers:* Supplement I, edited by Ian Scott-Kilvert, Charles Scribner's Sons, 1987, pp. 367–82.
    Taylor presents a thematic study of Pinter's earlier plays.

Watch on the Rhine

LILLIAN HELLMAN

1941

After a critically acclaimed opening at the Martin Beck Theatre in New York in 1941, *Watch on the Rhine* ran for 378 performances. Pamela Monaco, in her article on Lillian Hellman for the *Dictionary of Literary Biography,* notes that the play's appearance at this historical moment, eight months before the Japanese attack on Pearl Harbor, responded to "the political climate of the day," entering into "the continuing debate on American neutrality." She concludes that Americans were already familiar with the Nazi threat but had never before imagined "an antifascist message within a domestic situation." Monaco argues that through her skillful dramatic crafting, Hellman warns that all "who chose to ignore the international crisis were helping to perpetuate it and that no one [could] count himself or herself free of danger." Katherine Lederer, in her article on Hellman for *Twayne's United States Authors Series Online* stated that it was the "right time—for Hellman, for the critics, and for the public. The reviews were glowing, and President Roosevelt ordered a command performance at the National Theater in Washington." In its depiction of a family who struggles to combat the menace of fascism in Europe during the Second World War, *Watch on the Rhine* emerges as a tribute to those who are willing to sacrifice their lives for a noble cause.

AUTHOR BIOGRAPHY

Lillian Hellman was born in New Orleans on June 20, 1906, to businessman Max Bernard and Julia Hellman. Carol MacNicholas, in her article on Hellman in the *Dictionary of Literary Biography,* notes that while she and her mother had opposite personalities, Hellman's ties to her mother were quite strong and became a focus of some of her work. After her college years at New York University and Columbia University in the early 1920s, Hellman began her literary career as a manuscript reader for Horace Liveright, Inc., a New York City publishing firm. There she met and married press agent Arthur Kober, with whom she moved to Europe, where she wrote short stories. While traveling to Germany, she observed the beginnings of the Nazi movement and its increasingly vocal anti-Semitism, subjects that she would later explore in her plays. In the 1930s, the couple moved to Hollywood, where Hellman read film scripts for Metro-Goldwyn-Mayer and started a long-term friendship with novelist and screenwriter Dashiell Hammett. With his encouragement, Hellman completed her first play, *The Children's Hour*, produced in 1934. The play, which focuses on the disastrous effects of vicious gossip, earned high praise for its courageous and compelling portrait of homosexual themes.

Throughout the 1930s and 1940s, with the production of several of her plays, including *Watch on the Rhine* in 1941, Hellman earned a reputation as one of America's finest playwrights. She also became a social activist during this period through her support of Spanish loyalists against dictator Generalissimo Francisco Franco and of Communist causes.

Her literary focus later turned to autobiographical works, including the critically acclaimed memoirs *An Unfinished Woman* (1969), *Pentimento* (1973), and *Scoundrel Time* (1976). One of the stories in *Pentimento* is ''Julia,'' which focuses on an American woman's work in the European underground during World War II, was adapted in 1977 into a successful film by the same name. *Scoundrel Time* includes a chronicle of Hellman's refusal to testify in front of the House Un-American Activities Committee in the 1950s.

During her literary career, Hellman won several awards, including the New York Drama Critics Circle Award in 1941 for *Watch on the Rhine* and in 1960 for *Toys in the Attic*, along with Academy Award nominations for the screenplays of *The Little Foxes* in 1941 and *The North Star* in 1943. In 1964

Lillian Hellman

she was awarded the Gold Medal for drama from the National Institute of Arts and Letters, and in 1969 she won the National Book Award in Arts and Letters for *An Unfinished Woman.* Hellman died of cardiac arrest on June 30, 1984, in Martha's Vineyard, Massachusetts. In his article on her for the *New York Times,* William Wright concludes that Lillian Hellman ''remains fascinating'' to the public because ''as a dramatist, author, screenwriter and activist, [she] was a commanding presence in America's cultural life for half a century.''

PLOT SUMMARY

Act 1

The play opens in the late spring of 1940 in the living room of the Farrelly home outside of Washington, D.C. Fanny Farrelly, the family matriarch, appears, insisting that her son David be awakened so he will have plenty of time to pick up his sister and her family at the train station. She expresses nervousness about whether everything has been perfectly prepared for her daughter's arrival.

She and Anise, her maid, discuss the bills rung up by their houseguests for the past six weeks, the

Count and Countess de Brancovis, and the interest David has taken in the Countess. Fanny explains that she took in Teck and Marthe, her houseguests, because she "felt sorry" for Marthe and was "rather amused" by Teck. However, as she senses the growing attraction between Marthe and her son, she concludes that Marthe and Teck should soon leave.

At breakfast, David and Marthe discuss his sister Sara's marriage to Kurt Müller and his mother's subsequent snubbing of Sara after Sara would not allow her mother to arrange the wedding. When Teck appears, David leaves, and Teck and Marthe discuss their meager finances. Teck tells her that he will be joining a poker game run by an old friend of his in the German Embassy. He explains that his friend may be useful when he wants to leave the country. Marthe responds angrily to the news, chiding, "you can't leave them alone" and insists that his old friends will ignore him. She warns him against being seen at the embassy. Teck changes the direction of their conversation to Marthe's relationship with David. He tells her he suspects her involvement with him and warns "it is unwise to calculate" Teck as a fool.

Later that morning, Sara appears with her family, all shabbily dressed. Sara becomes wistful about her comfortable childhood in that house and admits to her family that she always wanted a nice house for them. When she quickly assumes she has hurt Kurt, her husband, she quickly dismisses her notion, calling herself "foolish" and "sentimental."

When Fanny discovers Sara and her family, she welcomes them all affectionately but nervously. Fanny questions Kurt's health, noting that he was injured while fighting in Spain. Nine-year-old Bodo, clearly taken with his father and his devotion to the antifascist cause, declares him to be a great hero. He and Fanny begin to develop an affection for each other. When David appears, he greets his sister lovingly. Later Fanny criticizes David's taste in women and insists that he has been flirting with Marthe. She then admits she was wrong to disapprove of Sara's marriage to Kurt and suggests that they move in with her.

Fanny begins to ask Kurt about his past, which makes Sara visibly nervous. Kurt reveals he gave up a career in engineering to devote himself to the antifacist cause. Sara expresses her devotion to the cause as well and gets defensive about her life with Kurt, explaining to her mother that she has had a happy life despite its hardships. Fanny asks forgiveness for her bad manners.

When Teck is introduced, he insists he and Kurt have met before, but Kurt denies it. Later Marthe tells her husband to mind his own business in response to his questions about Kurt. Teck, however, responds, "anything might be my business now." He then abruptly asks her if she and David are having an affair. Marthe admits that she has feelings for David but that they have not consummated their relationship and insists that the subject is none of Teck's business. In a veiled threat, Teck tells her to stay away from David, warning, "you will go with me, when I am ready to go."

Act 2

Fanny reveals to the others that she has heard that Teck won a lot of money at the embassy poker game, which Kurt responds to uneasily. David criticizes Teck for associating with the Nazis. Tensions arise between Teck and Kurt.

Teck later confronts David about his feelings for Marthe when he discovers David has bought her some jewelry. When David, directed by Marthe, tells him their relationship is not his business, Teck warns Marthe that he will not forgive her for that and insists that she go upstairs and pack her things so she can leave with him. Marthe refuses, declaring that she will not "go with him now or ever." She admits that she has never liked him and that she is in love with David. Upset by the emotional scene, Fanny tells them to discuss their situation privately.

Marthe explains her plans to live in Washington, D.C. by herself. She reveals that when she was seventeen, her mother, who controlled and frightened her, forced her into marrying Teck. She then berates Fanny for trying to dominate her children in a similar way. Fanny promptly denies the charges.

After Kurt leaves the room to take a phone call, he returns agitated and tells Sara he has to go to California for a few weeks. Teck shows Kurt the newspaper that reports the capture of Colonel Max Friedank, the chief of the anti-Nazi underground movement. He admits that at the embassy the previous night his associates told him about the incident. They also revealed that they captured two men named Ebber and Triste but are still looking for a man called Gotter. Teck then declares that he would like to have ten thousand dollars before he leaves. Kurt explains that Teck intends to blackmail him.

Kurt concludes that Teck knows he is the hunted man named Gotter and reveals "I am an outlaw." He explains that he has worked in the underground for seven years. The scene closes with Kurt's vow to buy his three comrades' passage out of Germany, where they are being held, with the several thousand dollars he has been carrying around in his bag. Sara supports his decision and tells him not to be afraid.

Act 3

A half-hour later, Teck appears, carrying Kurt's briefcase. He warns David and Fanny to stay out of his negotiations with Kurt. Teck says he knows that Kurt is the Gotter the Nazis have been looking for and reads a statement provided by his acquaintances at the German Embassy about Gotter's activities. He then warns Kurt that if he tells the Nazis where Kurt is, Kurt will not get back to Germany. However, if Kurt gives him ten thousand dollars, Teck will keep silent. When Kurt refuses to be blackmailed, Fanny tells Teck that she will give him the money.

After Kurt determines that Teck will reveal Kurt's identity with or without the money, he kills him. Sara and Joshua, Kurt and Sara's son, cover up the crime. Sara admits ''it's the way it had to be.'' After explaining that his motives for the murder were to save the lives of others, Kurt asks Fanny and David to give him two days to get away. After their initial shock, both David and Fanny accept what has just happened. Fanny tells Kurt to go with her blessing and gives him the money she was going to give Teck so that he can use it for the cause.

Kurt has a difficult time saying goodbye to his children who are quite upset. He admits to them that he has done ''a bad thing,'' but tells them to think about the future and to fight ''to make a good world.'' Sara and Kurt express their love for each other and their hopes to be reunited soon. Fanny admits they have been ''shaken out of the magnolias'' and David agrees. She tells David, ''tomorrow will be a hard day,'' but tries to put a good face on it. The play ends with mother and son each admiring the other's strength in this difficult moment.

CHARACTERS

Anise

Anise, a sixty-year-old French woman, is the Farrelly's maid, who, as the play opens, is seen

MEDIA ADAPTATIONS

- *Watch on the Rhine,* a Warner Brothers film, was produced in 1943 by Hal Wallis and directed by Herman Shumlin. It starred Bette Davis as Sara and Paul Lukas as Kurt. Dashiell Hammett and Lillian Hellman wrote the screenplay.

---

sorting the family's mail. She is a very proud woman who stands up to Fanny Farrelly's overbearing nature. Often, when Fanny gets nervous or excited, Anise tells her to ''compose'' or to ''contain'' herself. Anise also often concerns herself with the family business. Fanny notes that she's a ''snooper,'' which Fanny claims ''shows an interest in life.''

Countess Marthe de Brancovis

Marthe de Brancovis, in her early thirties, is the daughter of a friend of Fanny's. She and her husband, Count Teck de Brancovis, have been staying with the Farrelly family. Marthe has a strained relationship with her domineering husband and admits during the course of the play that she is in love with David Farrelly. In an attempt to justify her marriage to a man she claims she never loved, she explains to the family that when she was seventeen, her mother forced her into marrying him. She admits that she obeyed her mother's wishes because her mother frightened her. Noting her own timid character, Marthe concludes, ''maybe I've always been frightened. All my life.''

Marthe gains courage, however, through her relationship with David, which prompts her to stand up to her husband, Teck. When Teck asks her questions about her feelings for David, initially she tells him that that information is none of his business. After Teck presses her, she admits that she is in love with David. Her growing defiance of her husband emerges after Teck tells her he plans on playing poker at the German Embassy. When he tells her that he wants to reestablish connections with the Nazis there, Marthe chides, "Your favorite dream, isn't it . . . that they will let you play with them again." She begins to find her own voice when Teck asks whether she has developed political convictions, responding that she is not sure, but she is certain that she does not like the Nazis. Her newly found courage also prompts her to stand up to Fanny, who, she concludes, has dominated David's life and has tried to force him to be a replacement for his father.

Count Teck de Brancovis

Count Teck de Brancovis is a handsome forty-five-year-old Romanian, married to Marthe. Fanny notes that Teck was "fancy" when Marthe married him but is no longer, "although still chic and tired . . . the way they are in Europe." Hellman provides only sketchy details of his past. Apparently he has had past associations with the Nazis, as Marthe points out when she berates him for wanting to establish connections with the Germans at the Embassy. Marthe concludes that he should not waste his time with them, warning "they seem to have had enough of you. . . . It would be just as well to admit they are smarter than you are and let them alone."

Teck, like Kurt, is an expatriate, but for different reasons. Kurt hints at the reasons Teck has left his homeland when he notes that Teck wants to return, "but they do not much want" him. Teck uses this connection between them to help him convince Kurt to give him money when he claims, "we are both men in trouble. The world, ungratefully, seems to like your kind even less than it does mine."

Teck, however, is Kurt's moral opposite. He bullies his wife and tries to sell another's life to gain money and a passage back to his home. He appears to have some conscience, but it does not deter his blackmailing scheme. When Fanny confronts him, declaring that she is sickened by his demands, Teck admits the situation "is very ugly. . . . I do not do it without some shame, and therefore I must sink my shame in money."

He reveals his clever nature as he plans to blackmail Kurt by prying open the lock on the suitcase full of money and discovering Kurt's real identity. He also tries to enlist the aid of Kurt's unsuspecting children. When Teck asks Bodo if his father is an expert electrician and "as good with

radio," Kurt understands that he is trying to ferret out damaging information and so tells Teck sharply to direct his questions to him.

David Farrelly

David Farrelly is a thirty-nine-year-old lawyer working at his deceased father's firm. For most of the play, he appears affable but weak. He admits, "Mama thinks of me only as a monument to Papa and a not very well made monument at that. I am not the man Papa was." He allows his mother to dominate his life. However, his love for Marthe and his confrontation with the realities of Kurt's dire situation force him to find his own voice.

He begins to stand his own ground with his mother, who criticizes him over his attentions to Marthe. He refuses to break off his relationship with her. His feelings for Marthe also prompt him to face Teck. After Teck asks David about his relationship with Marthe, David tells him that the subject is none of his business. The tension between the two men escalates when Teck reveals his plan to blackmail Kurt. When Teck offers an analysis of the German character, David angrily replies, "Oh, for God's sake, spare us *your* moral judgments." As Teck lays out his blackmailing scheme, David approaches him threateningly, insisting "I'm sick of your talk. We'll get this over with now, without any more fancy talk from you. I can't take much more of you at any cost."

David's greatest challenge, however, comes when he must respond to Kurt's murder of Teck. Initially, he is shocked, as is his mother. Yet when Kurt offers David and his mother two choices—to turn him in immediately or to give him two days to escape—David quickly reassures him, "Don't worry about things here. I'll take care of it. You'll have your two days." By the end of the play, David has developed into a self-confident man who has come out from under the shadow of his father.

Fanny Farrelly

Fanny is the sixty-three-year-old matriarch of the Farrelly family. The high-strung Fanny, although essentially good-natured, tries to control all in her sphere. Her need for control has alienated her from her daughter. When Sara first married Kurt, Fanny broke off ties with her daughter because, as David says, "they didn't let her arrange it." Fanny has been more successful exercising her control over her son. She continually reminds him that he has not lived up to the image she has of her beloved late husband, and, throughout most of his life, David has allowed her this power over him. Marthe confronts Fanny about her overbearing attitude toward David when she declares, "I am sick of watching you try to make him into his father." She forces Fanny to recognize the detrimental effects of her treatment of her son when she compares Fanny to her own mother, who forced her into a marriage with a man she did not love. Marthe concludes that while Sara "got away," David has suffered under his mother's control. She tells Fanny, "I don't think you even know you do it and I don't think he knows it, either. And that's what's most dangerous about it."

Joshua, Sara's son, points out Fanny's naivete about the hardships that her daughter and her family have suffered, when he notes that his grandmother "has not seen much of the world." She admits to this ignorance at the end of the play and attests to her awakening to the harsh realities of the family's situation when she tells David, "We are shaken out of the magnolias, eh?"

Fanny's strength of character, like David's, emerges most clearly at the end of the play when Teck tries to blackmail Kurt. First, she offers to give Teck money so that he will leave Kurt alone. Later, like her son, she must face the fact that Kurt has just committed murder. Initially shocked, she soon composes herself and tells Kurt that he has her blessing. She also gives him the money she had planned to give Teck and tells him to use it for the cause. Her show of courage, along with the recognition of the same quality in her son, helps strengthen the bond she has with David. After the two have made a commitment to help Kurt, David warns her, "We are going to be in for trouble." Fanny, however, insists, "We will manage. I'm not put together with flour paste. And neither are you—I am happy to learn."

Joseph

The Farrelly family's middle-aged black butler, who, like Anise, is not afraid to stand up to Fanny's overbearing personality.

Babette Müller

Babette is Sara and Kurt's twelve-year-old daughter. Despite the family's nomadic existence, the children appear to be well educated and can speak several languages. Babette and her brother Bodo become extremely upset at the news that their father will have to go to Germany without them.

Bodo Müller

Bodo is Sara and Kurt's nine-year-old son. He is devoted to his father's cause, as revealed when he explains to his grandmother, "if we are to fight for the good of all men, it is to be accepted that we must be among the most advanced." Bodo exhibits his philosophical nature when his mother and grandmother begin to argue. He tells them not to get angry with each other; instead they must channel their anger into something important, "for the good of other men." He forms a special bond with Fanny, who recognizes their similarities. They both have strong opinions and are good at heart.

Joshua Müller

Joshua, fourteen, is the Müller's oldest and most practical child. After his father knocks out Teck, Joshua keeps a cool head as he helps his father drag the body out onto the terrace where Kurt kills him.

Kurt Müller

Kurt, a "large, powerful," forty-seven-year-old German, is Sara's husband. For the past seven years, he has been working for the anti-fascist underground, risking his life. The bullet scars on his face and the broken bones in his hands attest to the suffering that he has endured fighting for the cause. He explains that he became politically active in Germany when he saw his people suffer and watched twenty-seven men murdered in a Nazi street fight. At that point he determined not to "stay by now and watch."

He shows great love and concern for his family; yet makes his devotion to the cause his highest commitment. He has put his family's welfare as well as his own in jeopardy as illustrated when he refuses to be blackmailed by Teck. Kurt explains that the money was given to him not to save his life or for the comfort of his family, even when it could have helped him feed them. He reveals his stoic nature when Fanny asks him why he must take the responsibility to fight the Nazis since he has a family, and he claims that everyone could find a reason not to commit himself to the cause.

What is most important to him is "to save the lives and further the work" of the others who fight against the Nazis. To this end, he will commit murder, even though it causes him and his family great pain. In an effort to explain his actions, he asks

Fanny and David, "does one understand a killing?" He then compares what he did to the necessity of killing in a war. Yet, he also admits, "I have a great hate for the violent. They are the sick of the world. Maybe I am sick now too." Bernard F. Dick, in his article for *American Writers Supplement,* notes that when Kurt apologizes to his children for committing the murder, he refers to Jean Valjean in *Les Miserables* and so invites a comparison "between the theft of bread and the murder of a fascist." In this way, Dick claims, Kurt "indicts himself and pardons himself at the same time."

Sara Müller

Sara Müller, Fanny's daughter and Kurt's wife, proves her independent nature when she ignores her mother's wish for her not to marry Kurt. Even though when she returns to the Farrelly home she becomes wistful for the comforts she enjoyed while growing up, she declares to her family that she has led a happy and fulfilled life despite its hardships. She fully supports Kurt's dangerous activities and keeps a cool head after he kills Teck, fixing up the room as if she has had this responsibility in the past.

THEMES

Heroism

One of the dominant themes in *Watch on the Rhine* is heroism exhibited in a dangerous situation. All of the characters in the play, except the villain Teck, display varying degrees of heroism as they face difficult decisions. The most clearly defined hero is Kurt, who has suffered bullet wounds and broken bones at the hands of the fascists, yet who refuses to give up the fight to overthrow them. When he realizes that he must go back to Germany to free his comrades, he is afraid he will be captured, tortured, and most likely killed, but his fears never deter his devotion to his cause or his decision to leave. Sara and the children also show their heroic nature when they must endure separation from the husband and father they dearly love, and give Kurt their unconditional support.

Fanny and David find themselves acting heroically at the end of the play, which surprises them a bit. After the initial shock at Kurt's murder of Teck,

they risk getting in trouble with the authorities, and possibly the fascists who are searching for Kurt, because they too have come to believe in Kurt's cause. They agree to help cover his tracks and give him money to free his comrades.

While not called on to act heroically, Marthe does display courage, especially given the fact, as she admits, that she has been "frightened" all of her life. She stands up to Teck, seemingly for the first time, demanding that he leave Kurt alone. Later in the play, she finds the courage to leave Teck, who has dominated her life since she was a teenager.

Duty and Responsibility

The courageous actions of several of the characters in the play stem from their devotion to duty and responsibility. Kurt feels that he has a duty to his countrymen, whom he has seen murdered by the Nazis, and to all who suffer under fascism. When Fanny implores him to let someone else take the dangerous responsibility of carrying on the fight, someone without a family, he tells her that anyone could find a reason not to commit oneself to the cause. He decided long ago that he could not "stay by now and watch" the fascists destroy others' lives. Sara and the children are devoted to the cause and especially to supporting Kurt, even to the point where they participate in covering up Teck's murder. David and Fanny display a sense of duty and responsibility to Sara and her family when they take them in, help Kurt escape, and determine that they will face the consequences of their actions.

Ignorance

The theme of ignorance takes the form of naïveté as Fanny gradually learns what it is like outside of her sheltered walls. After Fanny is shocked listening to the details of the hardships Sara and her family have endured, Joshua notes her naïveté when he tells her that she "has not seen much of the world." She admits this fact when, by the end of the play she has learned of the harsh reality of the outside world and acknowledges to David, "we are shaken out of the magnolias, eh?"

Fanny's ignorance can be seen as a metaphor for the ignorance of most Americans in the late 1930s who did not want to get involved in what they considered to be a European conflict. Americans knew of the Nazi threat but could never imagine it would touch their lives in any way. Through

Hellman's creative crafting of the play's themes, she warns that all people have the potential of being affected by the menace of fascism and that a continued avoidance of the facts could help enable those in power.

STYLE

Structure

Watch on the Rhine contains melodramatic elements. The melodrama is a type of narrative that incorporates threatening situations into the plot as well as a happy ending. Characters in melodramas tend to be stock figures, for example the long-suffering wife or the virtuous hero.

Hellman structures *Watch on the Rhine* around the threatening situation Kurt experiences when Teck discovers Kurt's identity and tries to blackmail him. Also, some of Hellman's characters appear stereotypical in the play. Sara provides a good example of the long-suffering wife and Joshua serves as the devoted son. Yet Hellman departs from the melodramatic structure through her revelation of the complexity of the play's theme and her depiction of other characters.

Hellman's departure from the traditions of the melodrama provides the play with its originality, which helps maintain the audience's interest. The solution to the threatening situation is Kurt's murder of Teck, which presents thorny moral questions. Even Kurt expresses doubt about his own character after committing the act. Hellman also creates a complex character in Fanny, as she struggles with her need to dominate her family and critique their actions. In addition, the play's ending does not follow the traditional melodramatic format. Kurt does escape Teck's threats, but his future is far from certain. Sara has noted the danger that will await him when he tries to help his comrades escape. She and her children understand that they may never see him again.

HISTORICAL CONTEXT

Fascism

Fascism is a totalitarian system of government that directs the state to take absolute control of the lives of its people. The term was first used by

TOPICS FOR FURTHER STUDY

- Look up the history of the underground movement in Germany. Were there any members who appear to be similar to the characters in the play? What kind of failures and successes did they have?

- Research one fascist regime that exists today and compare and contrast it to that of Nazi Germany.

- Compose a story about what happened to Kurt after he left the Farrelly house.

- Read the ''Julia'' section in Hellman's *Pentimento*. Julia was a friend of Lillian Hellman's who worked for the underground during World War II. Compare and contrast Julia's character to that of Kurt.

supporters of Benito Mussolini, Italy's dictator from 1922 until his capture and execution during World War II. Other countries that have established fascist regimes include Spain under the rule of Francisco Franco and Germany under the rule of Adolph Hitler.

Fascism emerged as a counter force to the egalitarianism of socialism and democracy, which frightened many conservative Europeans at the end of the nineteenth century and the beginning of the twentieth century. They feared that the lower classes would take power away from the bourgeoisie (middle) class. These conservatives also feared the chaos and general anarchy that inevitably ensued after political revolutions. Fascists played on these concerns, appealing to the people's nationalistic sentiments and promising a return to law and order and Christian morality.

The doctrine of fascism includes the glorification of the state and the complete subordination of the people to it. The state creates its own absolute law. A second principle, that of survival of the fittest, is borrowed from social Darwinism and applied to the state. Fascists use this as a justification for aggressive imperialism, claiming that weaker countries will inevitably fall to more powerful ones. This elitist dogma extends to the fascist concept of

COMPARE & CONTRAST

- **1939:** Germany invades Poland and World War II begins.

  Today: The conflict between the Israelis and Palestinians heightens tensions in the Middle East.

- **1941:** On December 7, Japan attacks Pearl Harbor and the United States enters World War II.

  Today: Terrorist attacks on the World Trade Center towers in New York City and the Pentagon in Washington, D.C., on September 11,

2001, are the first large scale attacks on U.S. soil since the attack on Pearl Harbor.

- **1939:** During the war years a strong underground movement emerges that helps stop Nazi aggression through sneak attacks, sabotage, and espionage.

  Today: Espionage activities continue between the former Soviet Union and the United States, even after the Soviet Union abolishes its communist government. In recent years, spies have been caught and prosecuted in the United States, in Russia, and in China.

---

an authoritarian leader, a superman with superior moral and intellectual powers, borrowed from the theories of philosopher Friedrich Nietzsche, who would unite his people and carry on the vision of the totalitarian state.

World War II

The world experienced a decade of aggression in the 1930s that would culminate in World War II. This war resulted from the rise of totalitarian regimes in Germany, Italy, and Japan, which gained control as a result of the depression experienced by most of the world in the early 1930s, and from the conditions created by the peace settlements following World War I. The dictatorships established in each of these countries encouraged expansion into neighboring countries. In Germany, Hitler strengthened the army during the 1930s. In 1936 Benito Mussolini's Italian troops took Ethiopia. From 1936 to 1939 Spain was engaged in civil war involving Francisco Franco's fascist army, aided by Germany and Italy. In March 1938 Germany annexed Austria and in March 1939 occupied Czechoslovakia. Italy took Albania in April 1939. One week after Nazi Germany and (the former) U.S.S.R. signed the Treaty of Nonaggression, on September 1, 1939, Germany invaded Poland, and World War II began. On September 3, 1939, Britain and France declared

war on Germany after a German submarine sank the British ship *Athenia* off the coast of Ireland. Another British ship, *Courageous,* was sunk on September 19, 1939. All the members of the British Commonwealth, except Ireland, soon joined Britain and France in their declaration of war.

The Underground Movement

During World War II an underground movement emerged in Western Europe organized by the Allies. In France, Norway, Denmark, Holland, Belgium, Italy, and Greece, fighting forces trained in guerrilla warfare were created and supported through airdrops and radio communications from London. These resistance forces, led for the most part by American- and British-trained officers, conducted sneak attacks against the enemy, industrial sabotage, espionage, propaganda campaigns, and organized escape routes for Allied prisoners of war. Their activities were one of the major factors that led to the defeat of Germany and the end of World War II.

CRITICAL OVERVIEW

Watch on the Rhine won the Drama Critics Circle Award in 1941. The citation for the award praised Lillian Hellman for creating "a vital, eloquent and passionate play about an American family, suddenly awakened to the danger threatening its liberty.'' The critical reception for *Watch on the Rhine* during its run on Broadway was quite positive. Although that initial acclaim has been tempered over the years, many critics still admire the play's compelling themes and finely-crafted structure.

Scholars have noted the timely and historically significant material in *Watch on the Rhine*. Pat Skantze, in an article on Hellman for *Modern American Women Writers,* notes in a discussion of Kurt's decision to kill Teck that ''the question of culpability is exactly what Hellman would be faced with when she appeared before HUAC [the House Un-American Activities Committee].'' Brooks Atkinson in a review in the *New York Times* argues that, due to Hellman's adept characterizations, *Watch on the Rhine* ''ought to be full of meaning a quarter of a century from now when people are beginning to wonder what life was like in America when the Nazi evil began to creep across the sea.''

Some critics, however, find the play dated. Kimball King, in his overview of Hellman for *Contemporary American Dramatists,* claims that *Watch on the Rhine* ''contains some witty repartee and suspenseful moments''; however ''its solutions to the international crisis are simplistic, and it is better described as an adventure story than a thesis play.''

Others have noted the play's effective dialogue. Skantze insists that a synopsis of the plot ''does not do justice to the subtlety and liveliness of the dialogue.'' Singling out a few key characters, Skantze writes, ''Fanny's caustic repartee is funny and loving and irritating. The children are the stiff grown-ups they should be in light of their past, while Teck is smarmy but charming.''

Skantze finds that the characters' actions follow a logical thread, noting ''the decision to kill Teck is all Kurt's, but the desire to support him comes thoughtfully and naturally from David and Fanny.'' Lederer, in her article on Hellman for *Twayne's United States Authors Series Online,* claims that Hellman wrote the character of Kurt ''with passion and admiration,'' and ''because he acts with decision and courage,'' he is Hellman's ''most eloquent spokesman for human rights and liberty.''

Some critics find fault with the play's structure. George Freedley in his review for the *Morning Telegraph* writes that Hellman ''cluttered her play with sub-plots and extraneous action to such an extent to obscure what might have been her best play.'' Bernard F. Dick, in his article for *American Writers Supplement,* deems the play a ''melodrama of the monochromatic school where the villain is unspeakably black and the hero angelically white. Written in 1940 and produced eight months before Pearl Harbor, the play was understandably more patriotic than eloquent.'' He finds little difference between the play and ''all the espionage films of the 1940's that portrayed an America infected with Nazi spies and fifth columnists, secrets being exchanged at embassy balls, and revolvers being whipped out of trenchcoat pockets'' but acknowledges that it was based in part on autobiographical experiences. He concludes, ''One can respect Hellman's sincerity without liking her play.''

Even though many modern scholars criticize its melodramatic elements, most admit that *Watch on the Rhine,* as noted by Skantze, ''combines the best of Hellman's strengths.''

CRITICISM

Wendy Perkins

Perkins is an associate professor of English at Prince George's Community College in Maryland and has written several articles on British and American authors. In this essay she examines the theme of aggression and resistance in Lillian Hellman's Watch on the Rhine.

Monaco, in her article on Lillian Hellman for the *Dictionary of Literary Biography,* notes that the appearance of *Watch on the Rhine* on Broadway in 1941, eight months before the Japanese attack on Pearl Harbor, responded to ''the political climate of the day,'' entering into ''the continuing debate on American neutrality.'' She concludes that Americans were already familiar with the Nazi threat but had never before imagined ''an antifascist message within a domestic situation.''

In 1941 fascism, a totalitarian system of government that takes absolute control of the lives of its people, emerged as the dominant political force in war-torn Europe as Nazi aggression continued to spread over the continent. During this period an underground movement surfaced in Western Europe, organized by the Allies, to fight against fascist control. In *Watch on the Rhine* Hellman creates a microcosm of this pattern of aggression and resist-

Bette Davis, as Sara Müller, and Paul Lukas, as Kurt Müller, in a scene from the 1943 film production of Watch on the Rhine

ance in the personal lives of her characters. As she documents the dynamics of the power struggles that occur among the members of the Farrelly family and their houseguests during the early days of World War II, Hellman raises important questions about the nature of ethical responsibility.

The first character Hellman introduces who engages in power plays is Fanny, the domineering matriarch of the Farrelly family. When Fanny first appears, she barks an order to her butler Joseph to ring the breakfast bell, insisting ''Breakfast is at nine o'clock in this house and will be until the day

after I die.'' When Joseph informs her that it is only eight-thirty, Fanny instructs him to turn the clocks ahead to nine and ring the bell.

Fanny has tried to dominate the lives of all in the Farrelly household. Besides bullying her servants, she has tried to exert her control over her daughter, Sara, and son, David. Sara escaped her mother's dominion through her marriage to Kurt, but David has put up with her harassment all of his life. Fanny dominates him through attacks on his self worth, continually reminding him that he has not lived up to the image she has of her beloved late husband. David has allowed her this power over him as she tries to shape him into her vision of his father. At one point, he admits to his sister, "Mama thinks of me only as a monument to Papa and a not very well-made monument at that. I am not the man Papa was."

Marthe points out the damaging effects of Fanny's exercise of power over her son, insisting that he is suffering under her control. She tells Fanny, "I don't think you even know you do it and I don't think he knows it, either. And that's what's most dangerous about it."

Fanny, however, has not set up a totalitarian regime in her household. Her basic humanity allows those she tries to dominate to resist her authority. For example, both of her servants practice resistance to her aggressive tendencies. Skantze, in his article on Hellman for *Modern American Women Writers,* criticizes Hellman's depiction of Anise as well as Joseph, insisting that her characterization of them presents a prejudicial, "two-dimensional ignorance of the lives of blacks and a lack of courage on the part of the playwright to allow the characters a life and story of their own." Skantze fails to recognize, however, that neither Anise nor Joseph, the Farrelly's servants, is afraid to stand up to Fanny's overbearing personality. When the play opens, the viewer sees Anise riffling through the family's mail, openly defying the traditional hierarchy of the master-servant relationship. Fanny responds to this overt challenge to her privacy by concluding that Anise is a "snooper," a quality Anise says "shows an interest in life."

Anise continues this defiance throughout the play by constantly upbraiding Fanny when her emotions get out of control, instructing her employer to "compose" or to "contain" herself. Joseph resists Fanny's authority in more subtle ways. Besides informing Fanny that she is planning breakfast too early, he reminds her after one of her outbursts, "you told me the next time you screamed to remind you to ask my pardon," and Fanny complies.

Fanny has also accepted Sara's challenge to her authority. She welcomes her daughter back into her home with open arms, willing to ignore the fact that Sara had refused to allow Fanny the planning of her wedding. As Fanny presses Sara and Kurt about their life together, Sara angrily remonstrates her mother for her critical views. Yet when Kurt explains the cause his family has been fighting for and

> BY THE END OF THE PLAY, MOTHER AND SON ACKNOWLEDGE THEIR PREVIOUS IGNORANCE OF THE REALITY OF THE EFFECTS OF FASCISM AND THE FACT THEY HAVE BEEN 'SHAKEN OUT OF THE MAGNOLIAS.' THEY PREPARE TO FACE TOGETHER, ON EQUAL FOOTING, THE 'TROUBLE' THAT LIES AHEAD OF THEM."

tells of the hardships they have endured, Fanny admits, "I am old. And made of dry cork. And bad-mannered," and asks for their forgiveness. Fanny's willingness to accept challenges to her power reveals her inherent morality, a quality that will emerge more fully by the end of the play when she becomes involved in Kurt's antifascist activities.

Eventually Fanny also accepts David's challenge to her authority. When David enters into a relationship with Marthe, Fanny disapproves and warns him to stay away from her. However, David's love for Marthe, coupled with his recognition of Teck's evil nature, gives him the courage to ignore his mother's wishes.

The most intense power struggle emerges between Teck, Fanny's Romanian houseguest, and Kurt. When Teck, a Nazi sympathizer, discovers Kurt's true identity, he tries to blackmail him. Teck determines he will enforce a fascist control over the situation, seemingly giving Kurt no choice but to acquiesce to his demands. Teck insists that he will inform his acquaintances at the German Embassy of Kurt's whereabouts if Kurt does not give him the money that he has collected for his antifascist cause.

Teck successfully exercises a similar type of rigid control over Marthe, whom he married when she was a teenager. This control is illustrated when Teck confronts Marthe about her relationship with David and warns, "Do not make plans with David. You will not be able to carry them out. You will go with me, when I am ready to go." Yet when Marthe suspects Teck's campaign to cause trouble for Kurt, she finds the courage to stand up to him and finally leave him. Her newfound strength also enables her to upbraid Fanny for her treatment of her son.

Marthe's decision to leave Teck, however, has no influence over his determination to blackmail Kurt. His brutal plan emerges from his desire to restore his reputation and so return to his homeland. Teck feels confident that by turning Kurt over to the Nazis, he will gain important allies. In addition, the power exhibited by the Nazis intrigues Teck, a fact Marthe notes when Teck tells her of his plans to play poker with them. At this point, Marthe chides, ''your favorite dream, isn't it . . . that they will let you play with them again.''

Faced with Teck's absolute control over his life and the lives of his comrades, Kurt makes a decision to resist, which raises complex moral questions. When he murders Teck so that he and his comrades may escape and continue the fight against fascism, he tries to justify his actions to the Farrelly family. He likens his situation to that of a war, explaining to them that if he had spared Teck's life, he would be ''pampering'' himself and risking the lives of others. Yet he also declares that he has ''a great hate for the violent,'' because ''they are the sick of the world,'' and then adds, ''Maybe I am sick now, too.''

At the end of the play, Kurt places his life in Fanny's and David's hands, when he asks that they give him two days to escape before they talk to the authorities. Neither Fanny nor David abuses the power he has given them. Hellman suggests that in their decision to support Kurt and aid in his escape, David and Fanny exhibit ethical responsibility. Their actions during this crisis have proved their inherent morality and have forced them to recognize each other's strengths. By the end of the play, mother and son acknowledge their previous ignorance of the reality of the effects of fascism and the fact they have been ''shaken out of the magnolias.'' They prepare to face together, on equal footing, the ''trouble'' that lies ahead of them.

In the stirring account of a family's battle against the menace of fascism during the first half of the twentieth century, Hellman explores the desire for power and its often devastating consequences. In its recreation of a historically significant moment, *Watch on the Rhine* raises compelling ethical questions in its complex study of the politics of aggression and resistance on a national as well as a personal front.

Source: Wendy Perkins, Critical Essay on *Watch on the Rhine,* in *Drama for Students,* The Gale Group, 2002.

Alice Griffin

In the following essay, the author discusses Hellman's Watch on the Rhine *as a mature depiction of an historical era, detailing the threat of war and larger ethical questions through its focus on one family.*

Watch on the Rhine, which opened 1 April 1941, was a call to arms to the American public, who, Hellman felt, were too complacent about the menace of Fascism, which she had experienced first-hand in the Spanish civil war. Like Bertolt Brecht, Mark Estrin notes, Hellman ''expects her audience to be enraged enough by the injustice she dramatizes to leave the theatre and take social action.'' As might be expected, the play did not generate an immediate reversal of American political policy, but it did have an impact on American thinking as an influential work rallying support for the allies. In October 1941 the Free World Association broadcast the play in German via shortwave to Germany in a special performance from backstage, with Mady Christians repeating her role as Sara and Otto Preminger as Kurt.

Eight months after *Watch on the Rhine* opened, the Japanese bombed Pearl Harbor, precipitating America's entry into World War II. From its opening night to its closing 378 performances later in February 1942, audiences responded enthusiastically. Critic Stark Young was more reserved: ''some of the first act appears to lose time or wander too amiably—for one instance, perhaps with the scene of the children in which so many lines are given to Bodo, the comical, pedantic little boy'' (*The New Republic,* 14 April 1941). Wolcott Gibbs of *The New Yorker* judged it ''a fine honest and necessary play in which the fundamental issue of our time has been treated with dignity, insight, and sound theatrical intelligence.'' The play earned the New York Drama Critics' ''best play'' award and in January appeared in a command performance at the White House, for ''the first public appearance of President Roosevelt since war had been declared.'' London and Moscow performances followed, and in 1942 and 1943, after the Broadway production closed, *Watch on the Rhine* was staged in regional theaters across America.

Feeling that ''her writing had to spring from a completely realized world, the kind a novelist presents,'' Hellman researched the play carefully, amassing material on every aspect of German life. Margaret Case Harriman was so impressed with Hellman's careful, voluminous notes that she believed they "could be expanded . . . into a detailed and accurate history of a period covering 25 years." The actual writing of the play went smoothly, says Hellman: "The only play I have ever written that came out in one piece, as if I had seen a landscape and never altered the trees or the seasons of their colors."

For her approach, Hellman used Henry James's contrast in *The American* and *The Europeans* between worldly wise Europeans and naive, well-meaning Americans. The play is family oriented, centering upon the Americans, the Farrellys, and set in their spacious, well-appointed home in the suburbs of Washington, D.C. Matriarch Fanny presides over the household; her son David, an attorney, lives with her. The action begins when her daughter Sara, who has left home to marry German anti-Fascist Kurt Muller, arrives from Europe with him and their three children. Another American is Marthe, forced into a loveless marriage to a Rumanian count by her mother, dazzled by his title. The Farrellys have not inquired into the background of the count, who, with Marthe, has been their houseguest for six weeks. Count Teck de Brancovis and Kurt are immediately suspicious of each other. A friend of the Nazi officials at the German embassy in Washington, Teck is down on his luck and nearly penniless. He suspects there is a price on Kurt's head as an anti-Fascist leader, whom he could betray to the Nazis, and further learns that Kurt is carrying $23,000, "gathered from the pennies of the poor," to finance the resistance. Their conflict forms the basis of the action, with a romantic subplot involving David Farrelly and Marthe. As the tension increases, it becomes clear it is a conflict that can be resolved only by the death of one of the men.

Teck de Brancovis is a man of no substance, neither material nor moral. His quest for money and power has long since eroded any scruples he ever had, and he is perfectly willing to play cards with Nazis and Americans who sell illegal armaments. Hellman based his character on Rumanian Prince Antoine Bibesco, a practiced cardsharp who fleeced her of some six hundred dollars at the London home of Lady Margot Asquith in 1936. Teck too is a cardsharp who relies on the game as a major source of income and looks to be useful to his unsavory associates in the hopes of regaining access to power.

The Muller family no sooner arrives in act 1 than Teck senses there is profit to be made from learning as much as possible about Kurt, Fanny's unlikely son-in-law, "a German who has bullet scars on his face and broken bones in his hands"

> HELLMAN'S INTENTION IS TO SHOW THAT AN EVIL OF SUCH MAGNITUDE COMPRISES A BROAD SPECTRUM OF HUMAN FRAILTIES, WHICH MAKES IT EVEN MORE DANGEROUS."

and whose luggage is unlocked, while a shabby briefcase is carefully locked. Sure that he is on the scent of someone the Nazis would pay to know about, Teck investigates the Muller baggage at the first opportunity. News of the capture of other important resistance leaders jogs Teck's memory. He realizes that Kurt is now at the top of the Nazis' most wanted list and attempts to blackmail him, offering him, in return for ten thousand dollars, a month of silence in which to try to return to Germany to rescue his comrades. Kurt, however, knows, as Fanny and David do not, of Teck's unsavory background in Europe and that his offer of silence is purest sham. He is a deadly threat to Kurt and Kurt's colleagues, and before he can betray them to their deaths, he must be killed. Through Teck, the audience sees that the charm, the culture, the polish of some European aristocracy masks a rotten core. Whatever last tatters of decency Teck displays in his farewell to Marthe and his excuses to the Farrellys, he remains a man who will sell anyone and anything for personal advantage, a dangerous enemy who must be eliminated.

Unlike Marthe and Teck, Sara and Kurt are an American/European combination that embodies that which is best in both worlds. They respect each other, their love is as fresh as when they first met twenty years ago, and their children are warm and courteous. The heroic figure of Kurt Muller is based, Hellman says, on her beloved friend Julia, who devoted her wealth, her intelligence, and even her life to fight Fascism. The choice to make Kurt a German indicates Hellman's acknowledgment that not all Germans slavishly followed Hitler. She further avoids a simplistic view of Germany and even of Fascists through Kurt's continuing pride in his country "for that which is good" and the hope he expresses of bringing the Farrellys to Europe after the war to "show them what Germany can be like."

In response to Teck's observation in act 3 that "there is a deep sickness in the German character . . . a pain-love, a death-love," Kurt offers an analysis that recognizes gradations among Fascists: "There are those who give the orders, those who carry out the orders, those who watch the orders being carried out . . . Frequently they come in high places and wish now only to survive. They came late: some because they did not jump in time, some because they were stupid, some because they were shocked at the crudity of the German evil, and preferred their own evils, and some because they were fastidious men." For the last group, he says, "we may well someday have pity."

In speaking of Hellman's "mature realism," Timothy Wiles points out that she "avoids a doctrinaire explanation for the Nazi's evil ascendancy based simply on economics, and dramatizes social forces like the authoritarian personality and ideas like the banality of evil." She recognizes Fascism as "a psychological force that could be unleashed in the mass mind by its proponents' conscious manipulation of racial hatred." At no point does Hellman underestimate the evil the Nazis represent, and Kurt's speech is not intended to mitigate that evil. In fact, when Teck tells Kurt, "You have an understanding heart," Kurt rejoins, "I will watch it." Hellman's intention is to show that an evil of such magnitude comprises a broad spectrum of human frailties, which makes it even more dangerous.

On a personal level, Kurt Muller is a charming, mature, acutely intelligent man who can hold his own with a forceful personality like Fanny Farrelly. His love for his family is profound, and he is very much aware that his work to guarantee their future has entailed the sacrifice of his children's childhood. By this revelation in act 3, the audience is aware that no such option as a normal childhood exists under the circumstances, and the life they have had is at least one of honor, decency, and hope.

One of Kurt's most appealing qualities is his love for his wife: he encourages her to enjoy the pleasures of her family home without fear of offending him; he respects and praises all her contributions to their partnership, and his love for her is both tender and yet still charged with sexual ardor. In act 2, when he knows he must return to Germany because of the capture of his colleagues, he draws Sara to him, saying, "How many years have I loved that face?" and then "kisses her, as if it were important," unheeding of the others in the room. It is a powerful display of lasting romantic love.

The major hallmarks of Kurt's heroism are his honesty and personal integrity. Hellman deliberately avoids affiliating him with any particular party, thereby removing the audience's option to disassociate from him on the basis of political prejudices, and it seems fair to assume that this was also the reason she includes no reference to anti-Semitism. Instead, Kurt is an Everyman, representing the potential in each person to respond to the call of conscience. He speaks movingly of the Spanish civil war, where he fought as a member of the German brigade. For Kurt, August 1931, when he saw "twenty-seven men murdered in a Nazi street fight" in his hometown, marked the end of passive hope and the beginning of action. He concludes the story, saying, "I remember Luther, 'Here I stand. I can do nothing else. God help me. Amen.'"

Repeatedly, Kurt brings the issue down to personal responsibility, a recurrent theme in Hellman's plays. When Fanny and David try to dissuade him from returning to almost certain death by citing his family as a reason to stay, Kurt points out that each man has a reason not to fight, yet each must sleep with his conscience. The fact that he is a vulnerable man whose hands, broken by torture, shake when he is afraid, and who admits to the fear he feels, only underscores his heroism. Kurt's courage and determination send the message, as David says in act 2, that "it's the way all of us should feel." And Kurt, who hates violence, makes sure there is no glossing over his murder of Teck, that his children know this is not the way their world should be. His leave-taking ends on an optimistic yet uncertain note, for the prospects for survival are dismal for so likable and courageous a man.

Sara Muller is the ideal wife and mother of the forties. In direct contrast to Marthe, Sara is the American girl of independent spirit who defied her mother and chose her husband for love, not status and wealth. Her mother is shocked to learn that Sara worked to support her family, enabling Kurt to pursue his anti-Fascist work, and says the Farrellys would gladly have sent money had it been requested. Yet Sara's convictions are Kurt's; her passionate espousal of his ideals is indistinguishable from her profound love for him. There is a satellite quality to both Sara's opinions and her status in her family. She explains to Fanny and David, "I wanted it the way Kurt wanted it," a combination of political and moral ideals and deep love for her husband. She may indeed be as Kurt describes her, "brave and good . . . handsome and gay"; nonetheless, she is still only a "good girl," as her brother so approvingly remarks when she says she wants Kurt to go, to save the people so important to him and to their cause.

Although their parts are minor, the children make important contributions to the play. They represent the most powerful motive of all for mounting the fight against Fascism, the future of the world's children. They serve less lofty purposes as well. In their innocence they remark on the wonders of American life, simultaneously flattering an American audience on their standard of living and revealing the harsh circumstances under which the Mullers have been existing. Babette's shy request for an egg for breakfast, "if an egg is not too rare or too expensive," makes their deprivations vividly real. The eldest, Joshua, invites Fanny to practice her languages with them as they "speak ignorantly, but much, in German, Italian, Spanish—." These pieces of information from the children picture the life the Mullers have been forced to live under Hitler and relieve Kurt of having to do so.

Individually, they are stereotypically fine young people. Joshua intends to carry on his father's fight against Fascism. Babette, like her mother, puts a brave face on hardships. Bodo, the youngest, is a funny little boy, self-confident, enchanted with grand words, and thoroughly convinced that his father is the greatest hero on earth. His age makes it appropriate for him to inadvertently reveal important information, and also allows him to sing his father's praises freely. His main function, however, is to transmit Kurt's philosophical and political beliefs in such a way as to make them accessible without the sententiousness they might have were an older person to deliver them. He makes pompous little speeches that are obvious echoes of his father's views, but Bodo's stilted English, filled with big words, often mispronounced, gives them a lighter, slightly comical flavor. Hellman thus gets across important ideological messages without diminishing their significance or boring the audience. If anything, Kurt's beliefs are enhanced by Bodo's endearing delivery of them.

Described as "a handsome woman of about sixty-three," Fanny Farrelly is a woman of strong, vivid personality who has enjoyed wealth and status all her life. Her father had been an ambassador and her husband, the late "famous Joshua Farrelly," was ambassador to France in addition to founding a distinguished law firm. Her life has been as rich in experience as in material comforts, and the deep love she and her husband had for one another is a source of happy memories and a point of pride with her. He remains the yardstick by which all men, especially her son David, are to be measured.

Since traditional ideals of romantic love, marriage, and family, and women's place in relation to them underpin the structure of this play, it is appropriate that Fanny Farrelly adored her husband while he was alive and cherishes his memory after his death. She represents a certain idea of the feminine that audiences at that time found particularly sympathetic, that of a woman who, while very much a distinctive personality in her own right, is yet quite happy to defer to her husband and to play a subordinate role. As Vivian Patraka points out, the appeal of romantic love surviving intact would divert most women today from the realities such a relationship implies. Fanny's frequent references to Joshua Farrelly make him an almost palpable presence in the play. Although Fanny may be a widow, she is not alone; the husband who was the source of her status still validates that status and attenuates her authority as matriarch. Fanny is free to speak as she pleases because she does not violate traditional ideas of womanly behavior and woman's place within the family.

Much of the humor of the play derives from Fanny's outspokenness and her capricious behavior. She expresses her opinions freely, even bluntly, as when she surveys her grandchildren for the first time. She compliments Joshua on bearing the name and looks of his grandfather, praises Babette, and then to nine-year-old Bodo remarks, "You look like nobody." Fanny and her son David embody characteristics generally recognized as American, and most of these are flattering to the national image. Fanny's candor and individuality, her self-confidence, and her generosity are such. However, Hellman's intention in *Watch on the Rhine* is not simply to mirror that which is admirable in the American character but to move Americans from a stance she considers dangerously naive.

This naïveté is displayed by both Fanny and David. Fanny has invited the count and Marthe as houseguests because, she explains to David in act 1, "I felt sorry for Marthe, and Teck rather amused me. He plays good cribbage and tells good jokes." Despite her years as an ambassador's wife, Fanny remains naive in her judgment of Europeans, and her superficial assessment of Teck proves a dangerous mistake. When she rebukes Kurt for carelessness in leaving thousands lying around, he points out that the money was in a locked briefcase, concluding, ''It was careless of you to have in your house a man who opens baggage and blackmails.'' Her carelessness is of a piece with her role in life. Political convictions were her husband's province. Her job was to be charming, to garner gossip, ''wit it up,'' and pass it along entertainingly. Fanny's antics do double, even triple, service. They are comic relief to the play's more serious theme, they mitigate Fanny's status as an authority figure so that she remains sympathetic, and they indicate an area where change and growth are needed. For Fanny will be capable of mature behavior when the need arises. As act 3 draws to a close, she rallies behind Kurt and his cause, signaling her support of him with that highest of accolades, a quotation from husband Joshua. She also stands prepared to take responsibility for helping Kurt hide the murdered Teck and to escape the country.

Her son David has not been able to assert himself because of his flawed self-esteem. The source of his difficulty may lie in Fanny's habitually comparing him to his father and his choosing to believe her judgments of him. His love for and defense of Marthe strengthens his resolve, as he does not permit Teck to bully her nor does he allow Fanny to interfere, as she has in the past, with his relationships. By the play's end he understands the dangers Kurt faces and is prepared to aid him. David has become a strong, mature, independent adult. When Fanny says to David at the end of act 3, ''Well, here we are. We are shaken out of the magnolias, eh?'' it is clear that they are now aware of the dangerous realities that lurk just beneath the surface of life as they have previously known it. When David warns her that trouble lies ahead, she replies that she understands: ''We will manage. I'm not put together with flour paste. And neither are you—I am happy to learn.''

Structurally, *Watch on the Rhine* is an interweaving of contrasts; the lighter comedic threads of Fanny's outbursts and sharp humor and Bodo's grandiose speeches provide relief from, and at the same time intensify the effect of, the darker strands of menace. The opening act is predominantly light, with the warmth of the reunion, yet darker notes sound with the threat posed by Teck's curiosity. Act 2, set ten days later, when relationships have developed, opens in a light, comic vein but darkens midway with the news of the capture of Kurt's comrades and Teck's attempt at blackmail. The final act reverses the first and is a crescendo of darkness relieved briefly by one or two comic

touches and by the warmth of Kurt's love for his family, and finally by the resolve of all to fight Fascism, despite the cost.

In 1942 the movie of *Watch on the Rhine* was scripted by Dashiell Hammett, with additional scenes by Hellman. Paul Lucas repeated his Broadway role of Kurt, and Bette Davis played Sara. One last hurdle Hellman had to overcome was the Breen Office stipulation that murder be punished, that Kurt be assassinated in retaliation for his killing Teck. Her letter to the censors, whom she complained to the producer were ''not only as unintelligent as they were in the old days, but . . . growing downright immoral,'' was characteristically caustic: the country was at war with the Nazis. Should American soldiers who killed Nazis also pay with their lives? The film still stands as a classic example of American cinematography. Although its revival in 1979 was considered ''dated'' by the critics, the play represents one of the best of the pro-war dramas, one which translated the panorama of ''historical events and emotions connected to them'' into the smaller, more accessible frame of the family, so that the spectator can ''internalize and internationalize what [is] now recreated as a domestic crisis.'' Much as *The Diary of Anne Frank* made the fate of millions a palpable reality through a single girl, *Watch on the Rhine*, through its focus on a family in early 1941, made Americans aware of the threat to their security.

Source: Alice Griffin, ''*Watch on the Rhine,*'' in *Understanding Lillian Hellman,* University of South Carolina Press, 1999, pp. 63–75.

Katherine Lederer

In the following article, the author examines Hellman's Watch on the Rhine *as a lasting drama which articulates the ethical choices of well-developed characters in a specific historical context.*

The time is late in the spring of 1940. The place is a spacious home twenty miles from Washington, D.C., where dowager Fanny Farrelly lives with her bachelor son David. Refugee Roumanian Count Teck De Brancovis and his wife Marthe (daughter of a girlhood friend of Fanny's) are house guests. The count, a decadent aristocrat who has always lived by his wits, is a hanger-on at the German embassy. Fanny's daughter Sara arrives from Europe with her children and her husband Kurt Müller, a member of the underground resistance movement. Kurt is carrying $23,000 in a briefcase, money to be used to help rescue political prisoners from the Nazis.

The count discovers the money, figures out Kurt's identity, and tries to blackmail him by threatening to reveal that identity to the Germans. Kurt is forced to kill him, and Fanny and David, stripped of their American naiveté decide to keep quiet about the murder long enough for Kurt to leave the country and return to Germany, where he will attempt to free the prisoners and will almost certainly be killed.

Kurt makes a moving farewell speech to his children in which he tells them that killing is always wrong and that he is fighting for a world where all men, women, and children can live in peace.

"There are plays that, whatever their worth, come along at the right time," says Hellman of *Watch on the Rhine*. It was the right time—for Hellman, for the critics, and for the public. The reviews were glowing, and President Roosevelt ordered a command performance at the National Theater in Washington.

Although many critics felt at the time that *Watch on the Rhine* was Hellman's best play, it has received little critical attention in subsequent years. In discussions of her work it is usually dismissed in a sentence or two as the best anti-Nazi play of the war years, although in 1941 it received the Drama Critics' award for the best play of the season. The Critics' award was presented for a "vital, eloquent and compassionate play about an American family suddenly awakened to the danger threatening their liberty." Herman Shumlin said he was not surprised that *Watch on the Rhine* won: "I have always thought from the day I read it that it was a great play and fine dramatic literature."

On opening night Shumlin stood in the lobby, hissing imprecations at people arriving late. Hellman had not been as sure of the play's success as Shumlin. Several reviewers commented on the bronchial opening night audience. Hellman sat through the first act, then went to Shumlin and told him, "It's no use, Herman. Make up your mind to it. This isn't going to go."

"Get out of here," Shumlin answered. "Get out and stay out. Don't you remember you said the same thing about *The Little Foxes*?"

The command performance requested by Roosevelt was for the benefit of the Infantile Paralysis Fund. At a supper following the performance the President asked Hellman several times when she had written the play. Hellman says, "When I told him I started it a year and a half before the war, he shook his head and said in that case he didn't

Peggy Ashcroft, as Fanny Farrelly, in a scene from the 1980 theatrical production of Watch on the Rhine, *performed at the National Theatre in London*

understand why Morris Ernst, the lawyer, had told him that I was so opposed to the war that I had paid for the 'Communist' war protesters who kept a continuous picket line around the White House before Germany attacked the Soviet Union. I said I didn't know Mr. Ernst's reasons for that nonsense story, but Ernst's family had been in business with my Alabama family long ago and that wasn't a good mark on any man."

She continues, "But the story about my connection with the picket line was there to stay, often repeated when the red-baiting days reached hurricane force. But by that time, some of the pleasant memories of *Watch on the Rhine* had also disappeared: Lukas, once so loud in gratitude for the play, put in his frightened, blunted knife for a newspaper interviewer."

But in 1941 there was mostly only praise for a fine, patriotic play. Except for Grenville Vernon's review, the strongest dissenting note came from the *New Masses* and the *Daily Worker*.

Authors of books about "radical theater" occasionally mention *Watch on the Rhine* as an exam-

> HELLMAN'S CONCERN WITH ETHICAL CHOICES HAS CAUSED HER TO STUDY THE BEHAVIOR OF THE WELL-TO-DO BECAUSE THEIR MONEY GIVES THEM THE FREEDOM TO MAKE MORAL CHOICES, TO DEAL WITH MORAL RESPONSIBILITIES."

ple of a "leftist" play. The writer of such a work never deals with Hellman extensively, using such reasons as Hellman's not having written enough plays in the 1930s for adequate analysis, although three plays would seem to be ample. The writers then use Odets, Lawson, *et al.* A more likely reason for Hellman's exclusion from such treatments is that her plays do not fit the writers' theses. She wrote *The Little Foxes*, not "*Waiting for Horace.*" As Hellman told Roosevelt, she had been working on *Watch on the Rhine* since 1939, and the play opened while the Nazi-Soviet Non-Aggression pact was still in effect.

Aside from the anti-fascist content of the play, the character of Kurt Müller, the resistance fighter, received the most attention. Critics praised Hellman for making the protagonist, as they so regarded him, German. Müller is described by reviewers as the protagonist, the central figure, the principal character, "her hero." If one feels that there is a single protagonist, then other criticisms follow. George Freedley, for example, complained that Hellman had "cluttered her play with sub-plots and extraneous action to such an extent to obscure what might have been her best play."

Let us assume for the moment that *Watch on the Rhine* is not solely about Kurt Müller, but is also the story of Fanny Farrelly, a matriarch from another time (her husband knew Henry Adams, and in Adams's day Washington was a relatively small, sleepy Southern town); of her son David, who has never asserted himself, but who has allowed his mother to attempt to make him into his father's image (Joshua's portrait watches over the living room, and Fanny refers to him often); of Marthe, an American who was forced by her mother to marry a title; and of the Roumanian count, European like Kurt Müller, but of the type who let Hitler happen, whose only interest is self-aggrandizement and survival.

In other words, let us assume that *Watch on the Rhine* is like *Days to Come, The Little Foxes, The Searching Wind, Another Part of the Forest, The Autumn Garden,* and *Toys in the Attic*—a multiple-character play. What, then, is the play about? "What it contrasts are two ways of life—ours with its unawakened innocence and Europe's with its tragic necessities." The contrast is presented in a sunny, spacious living room, a setting completely alien to the horrors occurring in Europe. But the watch on the Rhine comes to the Potomac, causing the Americans to be "shaken out of the magnolias." They learn what Alexandra learned in *The Little Foxes,* "that the fundamental clash in civilization is between those bent on self-aggrandizement and those who are not and that 'it doesn't pay in money to fight for that in which we believe'." There are those who eat the earth and those who stand around and watch them eat it.

We meet the Americans and their house guests at breakfast, and their characters are firmly established before the arrival of the Müllers. As Richard Watts said, Hellman provides the "comfortable feeling that the play you are watching is a living, breathing thing, with people in it who have a life of their own outside the narrow confines of the theater's walls, and thus are engaging in activities that have significance about them. All good plays obviously give some sense of this, but not all of them have the three-dimensional quality in so complete a fashion as 'Watch on the Rhine,' and for this I think the much-criticized first act . . . is in great part responsible."

The contrast, not only between Europeans and Americans but between two European-American marriages, may remind one of Henry James. (James Agee, reviewing the movie version, said he wished James had written it.) This resemblance is not coincidental, although Hellman says today that only diaries of the time "could convince [her] now that *Watch on the Rhine* came out of Henry James." At the time of the original production Hellman told an interviewer, "When I was working on 'The Little Foxes' I hit on the idea—well, there's a small, Midwestern American town, average or perhaps a little more isolated than average, and into that town Europe walks in the form of a titled couple—a pair of titled Europeans—pausing on their way to the West Coast . . . .

"Later I had another idea. What would be the reactions of some sensitive people who had spent much of their lives starving in Europe and found themselves as house guests in the home of some very wealthy Americans? What would they make out of all the furious rushing around, the sleeping tablets taken when there is no time to sleep them off, the wonderful dinners ordered and never eaten . . .? . . . That play didn't work either. I kept worrying at it, and the earlier people, the titled couple, returned continually. It would take all afternoon and probably a lot of tomorrow to trail all the steps that made those two plays into 'Watch on the Rhine.' The titled couple are still in, but as minor characters. The Americans are nice people, and so on. It all is changed, but the new play grew out of the other two."

In *Pentimento* Hellman says that she dreamed one night of the poker party in London at which she met the man who suggested the Roumanian count in *Watch on the Rhine*. Wanting to "write a play about nice, liberal Americans whose lives would be shaken up by Europeans, by a world the new Fascists had won because the old values had long been dead," she used the setting of an Ohio town. Waking from the dream, she knew that she "had stubbornly returned to the people and the place of *Days to Come*." She changed the setting to Washington, introduced the character of Kurt Müller, who "was, of course, a form of Julia," Hellman's girlhood friend killed by the Nazis. (Hellman eventually used her notion about European reaction to affluent Americans in *The Autumn Garden*. The profession of Fanny Farrelly's husband, diplomacy, is used in *The Searching Wind*.) *Watch on the Rhine* is, in a sense, her tribute to Julia, and also to the men "willing to die for what they believed in" whom she had seen in the Spanish Civil War.

Perhaps Kurt Müller seems the lone protagonist not only because Hellman wrote the role with passion and admiration, but because he acts with decision and courage and is Hellman's most eloquent spokesman for human rights and liberty. But the other characters are faced with ethical choices because of his arrival. At the end of the first act Marthe warns Teck against harming Kurt. She tells him she will leave him if he makes trouble. At the end of the second act, Teck asks her to leave with him. She refuses, saying, "You won't believe it, because you can't believe anything that hasn't got tricks to it, but David hasn't much to do with this. I told you I would leave someday, and I remember where I said it—and why I said it."

Kurt tells Fanny and David that Teck has discovered the $23,000 Kurt is carrying, "gathered from the pennies of the poor who do not like Fascism." When Fanny asks whether it wasn't careless of him to "leave twenty-three thousand dollars lying around to be seen," Kurt answers, "No, it was not careless of me. . . . It was careless of you to have in your house a man who opens baggage and blackmails." David and Fanny take the first step toward joining Kurt's side when they offer to pay Teck themselves. But they still don't understand completely. David tells Kurt he will be safe: "You're in this country. They can't do anything to you. They wouldn't be crazy enough to try it. Is your passport all right?" When Kurt says it isn't quite, Fanny asks why it isn't. Kurt says, "Because people like me are not given visas with such ease. . . . Madame Fanny, you must come to understand it is no longer the world you once knew."

Still failing to understand, David tells Kurt, "It doesn't matter. You're a political refugee. We don't turn back people like you." Sara says, "You don't understand, David," and explains that Kurt has to go back to Germany.

In Act III Teck reads from a German embassy list of wanted men a description of Kurt's underground activities. When Fanny says she is sickened by Teck, Kurt makes a key speech: "Fanny and David are Americans and they do not understand our world—as yet. (*Turns to David and Fanny*) All Fascists are not of one mind, one stripe. There are those who give the orders, those who carry out the orders, those who watch the orders being carried out. Then there are those who are half in, half hoping to come in. . . Frequently they come in high places and wish now only to survive. They came late: some because they did not jump in time, some because they were stupid, some because they were shocked at the crudity of the *German* evil, and preferred their own evils, and some because they were fastidious men. For those last, we may well someday have pity. They are lost men, their spoils are small, their day is gone. (*To Teck*) Yes?" And Teck replies, "Yes. You have the understanding heart."

When Fanny and David leave the room to get the money, Teck says, "The new world has left the room. . . We are Europeans, born to trouble and understanding it. . . . They are young. The world has gone well for most of them. For us—we are like peasants watching the big frost. Work, trouble, ruin—But no need to call curses at the frost. There it is, it will be again, always—for us.'' Teck is almost pitiable. Sara counters his effectiveness, however, by speaking up and saying, ''We know how many there are of you. They don't, yet. My mother and brother feel shocked that you are in their house. For us—we have seen you in so many houses.''

After Kurt kills Teck, he says, ''I have a great hate for the violent. They are the sick of the world. Maybe I am sick now, too.'' A gentle man, a man of peace, driven to murder to protect the cause he is fighting for, he says to his children as he prepares to leave them, ''Do you remember when we read *Les Misérables*? . . . He stole bread. The world is out of shape we said, when there are hungry men. And until it gets in shape, men will steal and lie and—and—kill. But for whatever reason it is done, and whoever does it—you understand me—it is all bad. I want you to remember that. Whoever does it, it is bad.''

Fanny and David make their decision when Kurt tells them they can either phone the police or wait two days to give him a head start, making themselves, in effect, accessories to murder. Fanny, agreeing to help him, makes another key speech. A critic once complained that we know what Hellman is against, but we don't know what she is *for*. Fanny's speech tells us. ''I was thinking about Joshua. I was thinking that a few months before he died, we were sitting out there.'' She points to the terrace. ''He said, 'Fanny, the complete American is dying.' I said what do you mean, although I knew what he meant, I always knew. 'A complete man,' he said, 'is a man who wants to know. He wants to know how fast a bird can fly, how thick is the crust of the earth, what made Iago evil, how to plow a field. He knows there is no dignity to a mountain, if there is no dignity to man. You can't put that in a man, but when it's there, put your trust in him!'''

At the end of the play, left alone on stage with David, Fanny says, ''We are shaken out of the magnolias, eh?'' David asks her if she understands that they are going to be in for trouble. Fanny replies, in a line reminiscent of *The Little Foxes* but spoken to a much different purpose, ''I understand it very well. We will manage. I'm not put together with flour paste. And neither are you—I am happy to learn.''

Hellman is not an ironist in this play inasmuch as the tone of the whole play is not ironic. Kurt and Sara are presented as admirable characters; Fanny and David are likable, though naive, and rise to the

moral occasion. Marthe is treated sympathetically. Even Teck is not presented with the ironic scorn one feels in *The Little Foxes*.

The title is ironic, coming from a German patriotic song, as the Americans learn that they must keep watch on the Potomac. There is ironic dialogue as Teck and Kurt talk over the heads of Fanny and the children in the second act. Fanny makes humorously ironic comments about other people, as does David.

We find an example of ''boomerang irony'' in Teck's blackmail threat, which causes his death, and again Hellman employs dramatic irony, letting the audience know Teck's plans, Kurt's work as a member of the resistance movement, Fanny's misgivings about David and Marthe. Again we have the tranquil moment before the climax, as Act II opens ten days after the Muellers' arrival, with Joshua playing baseball with Joseph, the butler; Babette sewing; and Bodo repairing the maid's heating pad, while Kurt plays the piano. Into this warm setting comes Teck, with his barbed remarks; and, as background to his probing questions, we hear the piano, played by a man with broken hands, broken by the Nazis.

Hellman's character development has been so thorough, almost novelistic, that we are prepared to accept Fanny's decision to help Kurt and David's love for Marthe. We have seen Fanny as the autocrat of the breakfast table, but we have also seen that, though a strong woman, given to raising her voice when she doesn't get her way, she is generous, loving, an old-fashioned liberal, of a day when the word meant something. And, before the climactic scene, David has been led to assert himself because of his love for Marthe.

We have seen, as so often we see in a Hellman play, the clash of generations. This time, the conflict is resolved. As Sara says, she comes of good stock, and both generations, shaken out of the magnolias, join to face the danger threatening their family and their country.

By the end of the play each character has committed a definitive act. In a strange essay, Elizabeth Hardwick says that ''in most of [Hellman's] plays there are servants, attractive people, money, expensive settings, agreeable surroundings and situations for stars. It is typical of her practice that when she writes in *Watch on the Rhine* of a German refugee coming to America in 1940, he goes not to the Bronx or Queens or even to Fort Washington Avenue, but to a charming country house near Washington.''

In a delightful response, Richard Poirier pointed out that, if Hardwick had used her own definition of melodrama, ''it might have kept her, too, from complaining that the German refugees in *Watch on the Rhine* did not go to Fort Washington Avenue instead of to a country house near Washington, D.C., where, freed of commuting, they could spend more time in the kind of environment to which Hellman wanted to expose them.''

Like Henry James, Hellman is a humanist, not a determinist; she believes in free will and personal responsibility for one's actions or failure to act. Hellman's concern with ethical choices has caused her to study the behavior of the well-to-do because their money gives them the freedom to make moral choices, to deal with moral responsibilities. To send the refugees to the Bronx would have destroyed the theme of the play.

In *Watch on the Rhine* we see a theme with which we are already familiar and which we shall see again in *The Searching Wind*; our world is the sum of our personal acts. Perhaps this concern with ethical responsibility led Bette Davis to accept the relatively minor role of Sara Müller in the screen version. Miss Davis said that she took the part because she believed *Watch on the Rhine* ''had something important to say at a time when it could do the most good.''

The film script was included in John Gassner's *Best Film Plays of 1943–1944,* and the film itself was voted the best movie of the year by the New York film critics. The play was successful on tour, as were productions in Europe and London. It was done after the war in Moscow, and in Germany, where it was called *On the Other Side.*

How would the play fare today? How much of the critical fervor was caused by the topicality? How would it strike a ''turned-off'' generation? In the 1960s Edward Albee announced plans to produce the play, but it was never done. Perhaps Hellman felt that audiences might view *Watch on the Rhine* as support for the war in Vietnam, which she opposed. She said at the time of the Broadway production, ''In 'Watch on the Rhine,' I find the play so variously interpreted on every hand that I have decided it is so fluid a script anybody can bring to it any meaning they want to.''

Viewed solely as a melodrama, solely as the story of Kurt Müller, the play may be dated. But, if it is the story of some nice, naive, liberal Americans put to the test; if it is a character drama, like *The Autumn Garden,* then it still should have validity. Until, however, a revival allows us to judge for ourselves, we can view it as probably the best of the World War II anti-Nazi plays, or we can agree with Brooks Atkinson that ''since Miss Hellman has communicated her thoughts dramatically in terms of articulate human beings, 'Watch on the Rhine' ought to be full of meaning a quarter of a century from now when people are beginning to wonder what life was like in America when the Nazi evil began to creep across the sea.''

Source: Katherine Lederer, ''The Plays of the 1940s: *Watch on the Rhine,*'' in *Lillian Hellman,* Twayne Publishers, 1979, pp. 50–58.

SOURCES

Atkinson, Brooks, Review in the *New York Times,* August 24, 1941.

Dick, Bernard F., Review in the *Morning Telegraph,* April 3, 1941.

Freedley, George, ''Lillian Hellman,'' in *American Writers: Supplement 1, Part 1,* edited by Leonard Unger, Charles Scribner's Sons, 1979, pp. 276–98.

King, Kimball, ''Hellman, Lillian (Florence),'' in *Contemporary American Dramatists,* edited by K. A. Berney, St. James Press, 1994, pp. 255–58.

Lederer, Katherine, ''Lillian Hellman: Chapter 3,'' in *Twayne's United States Authors Series Online,* G. K. Hall & Co., 1999.

Monaco, Pamela, ''Lillian Hellman,'' in *Dictionary of Literary Biography,* Volume 228: *Twentieth-Century American Dramatists, Second Series,* edited by Christopher J. Wheatley, The Gale Group, 2000, pp. 96–115.

Skantze, Pat, ''Lillian Hellman,'' in *Modern American Women Writers,* Charles Scribner's Sons, 1991, pp. 207–20.

FURTHER READING

Bryer, Jackson, *Conversations with Lillian Hellman,* Literary Conversations Series, University Press of Mississippi, 1986.
    Hellman sheds light on her writing process and the themes of her plays.

Griffin, Alice, and Geraldine Thorsten, *Understanding Lillian Hellman,* Understanding Contemporary American Literature Series, University of South Carolina Press, 1999.

Griffin and Thorsten place Hellman's work into historical context.

Podhoretz, Norman, *Ex-Friends: Falling Out with Allen Ginsberg, Lionel & Diana Trilling, Lillian Hellman, Hannah Arendt, and Norman Mailer,* Free Press, 1999.
Podhoretz presents entertaining and insightful snapshots of Hellman's life and those of her contemporaries in the literary scene.

Rollyson, Carl, *Lillian Hellman: Her Legend and Her Legacy,* http://www.iUniverse.com (1999; last accessed September, 2001).
In an examination of newly discovered diaries, letters, and interviews, Rollyson offers insight into Hellman's life and work.

Wine in the Wilderness

ALICE CHILDRESS

1969

Wine in the Wilderness (1969), by Alice Childress, was first performed on WGBH-TV in Boston, Massachusetts, as part of the series, ''On Being Black.''

Wine in the Wilderness takes place during a race riot in Harlem, New York City. Bill Jameson, an artist, is working on a ''triptych'' entitled ''Wine in the Wilderness.'' This series of three paintings is meant to express Bill's ''statement'' about ''black womanhood.'' The first painting, of a young black girl, is meant to represent the innocence of childhood. The middle painting is of a beautiful African-American woman in African clothing, meant to represent Bill's ideal black woman, whom he refers to as an ''African queen,'' or ''the wine in the wilderness.'' For the third painting, which he hasn't yet started, Bill is looking for a down-and-out woman to model for his image of ''what society has made of our women.''

Bill's friends introduce him to Tommy, a woman they've met at a bar, whom they think represents the ''hopeless'' type of woman he has in mind for his third painting. Tommy, however, discovers Bill's true intention to paint her as representative of a woman who is ''ignorant, unfeminine, coarse, rude, vulgar, poor,'' and ''dumb.'' She angrily criticizes Bill and his friends for thinking that they are better than she is and for looking down on the ''masses'' of the African-American community who are less educated and less privileged than they. Bill comes to realize that Tommy herself is his true ''African

queen,'' a woman like many in her community. He convinces Tommy to stay so he can paint her portrait as his new vision of African-American womanhood, the ''wine in the wilderness.''

In this play, Childress addresses the theme of perceptions of African-American women within the African-American community. Bill and his friends feel that African-American women have dominated African-American men in the past and should learn to be more subservient to the men in their lives. Tommy, on the other hand, argues that women like herself—strong, energetic, yet vulnerable—should not be criticized but should be embraced and celebrated by African-American men and the community as a whole.

AUTHOR BIOGRAPHY

Alice Childress was born October 12, 1920, in Charleston, South Carolina. She grew up in Harlem, New York City, where she was raised by her grandmother, the daughter of a former slave. Childress was inspired to write at an early age by her grandmother, who would sit with her at the window and encourage her to make up stories about the people who walked by. Childress attended two years of high school but left before receiving a degree.

In 1941, Childress joined the American Negro Theater, in Harlem, where she worked as an actress, playwright, and director for the next twelve years. *Florence* (1949), her first play to be produced, centers on a discussion between an African-American woman and a white woman who happen to meet in a railroad station in the South. Her *Gold Through the Trees* (1952) was the first play by an African-American woman to be professionally produced on the American stage. Her play *Trouble in Mind* (1955), about the difficulties faced by black actors, won the 1956 Obie Award for the Best Original Off-Broadway Play, making Childress the first female playwright ever to have won an Obie. *Wedding Band* (1966), her play about interracial marriage, set in South Carolina in 1918, was controversial, and the television broadcast was banned by a number of stations. *Wine in the Wilderness* (1969), also a controversial work, addresses issues of socioeconomic and gender conflict within the African-American community.

Childress is most widely known for her 1973 novel, *A Hero Ain't Nothin' but a Sandwich*, written for a young adult readership, about a young drug addict. The novel was widely acclaimed for its power and realism and was named one of the Outstanding Books of the Year by the *New York Times Book Review*. But it was also controversial and was banned by the Long Island school district as obscene. In 1978, a movie adaptation of *Hero*, the screenplay written by Childress, was released by New World Pictures. Her last published work, *Those Other People* (1989), is a young adult novel about a boy coming to terms with his homosexuality.

In 1957, Childress married Nathan Woodward, her second husband, a musician who composed music for many of her plays. She had one daughter from her first marriage. Childress died of cancer August 14, 1994, in New York City.

PLOT SUMMARY

Wine in the Wilderness opens during the tail end of a race riot in Harlem. Bill Jameson, an African-American painter, sits in his studio apartment, crouched down below the windows to avoid being hit by stray bullets. His friends, Cynthia and Sonny-man, have called him on the phone from a bar. Because of the riot, they were unable to return home. They have called Bill because, while at the bar, they met a woman they think will be perfect as a model for a painting Bill is planning.

Oldtimer, a man in his sixties, enters Bill's apartment, carrying a bundle of loot he has taken during the chaos of the riot. The police are looking around the building, and Oldtimer is afraid of being arrested for theft. One of the things he has taken is a bottle of whisky, which he shares with Bill. Bill explains that he is working on a ''triptych,'' a series of three paintings entitled, ''Wine in the Wilderness.'' The first painting, ''Black Girlhood,'' is of ''a charming little girl in Sunday dress and hair ribbon.'' The second, ''Wine in the Wilderness,'' is of his idealized vision of ''Mother Africa,'' a beautiful African-American ''queen,'' dressed in African fabrics. The third canvas, which he has not yet painted, is to be of an African-American woman Bill considers to be ''lost,'' down-and-out, what, according to him, ''society has made of our women.'' Although he hasn't yet found the model for this third painting, he describes to Oldtimer the type of woman he wants to represent: ''She's as far from my African queen as a woman can get and still be female, she's as close to the bottom as you can get without crackin' up . . . she's ignorant, unfeminine, coarse, rude . . . vulgar . . . a poor, dumb chick that's had her behind kicked until it's numb." Bill adds that "there is no hope" for this type of woman.

Bill helps Oldtimer to hide his bundle of loot by attaching it to a rope and dangling it outside of the window. Cynthia and Sonny-man enter the apartment with Tommy, a thirty-year-old factory worker whom they met at the bar. They introduce Tommy to Oldtimer and Bill. Tommy thinks that Cynthia and Sonny-man have brought her there because they think Bill will be interested in dating her. She hasn't been informed that they identified her as Bill's vision of the down-and-out woman for the third painting of his triptych. But Tommy immediately likes Bill and continues to think that he is interested in asking her out. Tommy is clearly less educated and not as financially comfortable as Bill, Cynthia, and Sonny-man. She explains that she was unable to return to her apartment because it was burned down in the riot. She is wearing a mismatched outfit of a skirt and sneakers because most of her clothes have been destroyed. Bill tells her that he is interested in painting her, allowing her to think that he wants to do so because he thinks she's pretty and is interested in dating her. Tommy makes it clear that she is looking for a husband and thinks Bill would be a good man for her. Bill, however, is not at all attracted to Tommy but goes along with this idea because he wants to paint her.

Tommy agrees to sit for Bill's painting, but only if he goes out to get her a large order of Chinese food, first. While the men are gone getting the food, Cynthia tries to let Tommy down easily, suggesting that Bill really isn't her type. Cynthia also tells Tommy that she should act more "feminine," and less hard and assertive, in order to attract a man. The men return and Bill orders everyone except Tommy to leave the apartment. He explains that the Chinese restaurant was destroyed in the riot and he has brought her a hotdog instead. Tommy complains at first but eats the hot dog. When she spills orange soda on her clothing, Bill gives her an African throw-cloth to wrap around herself as a make-shift dress. While she is changing into the throw-cloth, Bill's art dealer calls, and he discusses his "triptych," describing the "finest black woman in the world," which he has painted as "Wine in the Wilderness." Tommy, meanwhile, thinks that he is describing *her*. She is happy because she thinks that Bill thinks she is beautiful. But, once she is wearing the African wrap and has removed her wig, Bill for the first time is overcome by how beautiful he finds her. However, he is frustrated because she no

Alice Childress

longer looks like the down-and-out image he had planned on painting. He gives up trying to draw her, and kisses her instead. They embrace and the lights go down.

The next morning, Bill is taking a bath while Tommy makes coffee in his apartment. They both seem happy. While Bill is still in the bathroom, Oldtimer comes in. Before realizing what he is saying, Oldtimer explains to Tommy about Bill's triptych. After explaining the first two paintings, he tells Tommy that she will be modeling for the painting of "the worst gale in town . . . A messed-up chick." Cynthia and Sonny-man walk in, just as Tommy realizes what has been going on. Tommy becomes angry and criticizes Cynthia and Sonny-man for pretending to care about her when they were actually just using her. Bill comes out of the bathroom, and Tommy angrily criticizes him, along with his friends, for their treatment of her. She points out many of the ways in which they are disrespectful to African Americans who have less education and less money than they do. In expressing these things, Tommy comes to see that she herself is the true "African queen," or "Wine in the Wilderness," because she is more authentic in her approach to life, while Bill and Cynthia and Sonny-man are hypocritical in their attitudes toward the

African-American community. In the midst of these angry words, Tommy blurts out that she loves Bill. It finally dawns on Bill that Tommy really is his ideal "Wine in the Wilderness" African queen. Oldtimer, Cynthia, Sonny-man, and Tommy agree to pose for a new painting, based on Bill's new vision of his community and the African-American woman.

CHARACTERS

Cynthia

Cynthia is a twenty-five-year-old social worker. She is married to Sonny-man. Cynthia is a middle-class, educated, African-American woman, whose attitude toward Tommy, like that of Bill and Sonny-man, is arrogant and patronizing. She and Sonny-man meet Tommy in a bar, where they recognize her as the image of a down-and-out woman Bill is looking to paint. They take Tommy to Bill's apartment without explaining why and allow her to believe that she is being set up with Bill as a romantic interest. Thus, although she and Tommy are both African-American women, Cynthia demonstrates a lack of respect for Tommy, allowing her to be used by a man whose attitude toward her is insulting.

When the men leave, Cynthia and Tommy have a discussion that demonstrates Cynthia's ideas about how African-American women should behave in their relationships with men. She tells Tommy that she is too coarse and unfeminine and that she should allow men to have the upper hand in her relationships with them. Cynthia also criticizes Tommy for wearing a wig, instead of showing her natural hair. But, as Tommy later points out, the reason she wears a wig is that women like Cynthia make her feel ashamed of being her "natural" self. Cynthia also tells Tommy, "You have to let the black man have his manhood again," to which Tommy responds, "I didn't take it from him, how I'm gonna give it back?" Cynthia represents Childress's vision of the attitude of some educated, middle-class African-American women toward African-American women who are less educated and less privileged than they.

Bill Jameson

Bill Jameson is a thirty-three-year-old artist. He lives in an apartment in Harlem. Bill is working on a "triptych," or series of three paintings, to represent his "statement" on "black womanhood": "Black girlhood," an image of innocence and sweetness; "Wine in the Wilderness," his vision of an idealized "African queen"; and a third image, not yet painted, which represents his perception of "what society has done to our women." For this third picture, which he envisions as a down-and-out African-American woman who is "ignorant, unfeminine, coarse, rude . . . vulgar . . . a poor, dumb chick that's had her behind kicked until it's numb," and for whom "there's no hope."

Bill has been looking for a woman to model for this picture, and during a race riot in Harlem, Bill's friends bring to his apartment a woman they see as an embodiment of this third image. Bill quickly sees in Tommy this down-and-out, "hopeless chick" he had in mind. He convinces her to allow him to paint her only because she believes he is interested in her for romantic reasons. The next morning, however, Tommy discovers Bill's true intentions and becomes enraged. She realizes that Bill looks down on her for being less educated and less privileged than he and accuses him of looking down upon the "masses" of the African-American community, although he claims to represent the community through his art. Bill is defensive at first, but, when Tommy blurts out that she loves him, he is moved by this revelation to gain new insight into his art and his vision of African-American womanhood. He realizes that he has been misguided in his approach to art and his attitude toward the African-American community, that he has been "painting in the dark, all head and no heart." Bill finally understands that Tommy herself represents his ideal vision of the African-American woman, his "Wine in the Wilderness." He convinces her to stay and pose for a painting to represent her in this new light.

Tommorrow Marie
See Tommy

Edmond Lorenzo Matthews
See Oldtimer

Oldtimer

Oldtimer, in his sixties, is described as "an old roustabout character." He seems to be an alcoholic without much money, who often mooches off of his neighbors, although he is also friends with them. In the midst of the riot, Oldtimer enters Bill's apartment with a bundle of loot he claims to have picked up from the street after it was dropped by the rioters.

His bundle includes a bottle of whiskey, some salami, and a new suit. He is anxious because the police are looking around in the building, and he is afraid of getting arrested for stealing. Bill reluctantly helps him to hide the bundle, and the two share the bottle of whiskey. Oldtimer is a warm-hearted, good-humored man who is clearly much less educated than Bill. Bill explains his series of paintings to Oldtimer as they drink.

When Tommy is brought into the apartment and introduced to Oldtimer, she surprises everyone by asking his real name. Bill, Cynthia, and Sonny-man realize that they don't even know their friend's name. He tells them his name is Edmond Lorenzo Matthews. The fact that they didn't know his name, although they've clearly known him for some time, indicates the lack of respect these middle-class, educated people have for one of their elders. Tommy later criticizes them for not showing him more respect. Oldtimer likes Tommy right away and is flattered when she flirts with him. The next day, Oldtimer comes into the apartment and, without thinking about what he is saying, reveals to Tommy that Bill wants to paint her as an image of "the worst gal in town." He is immediately sorry for saying it, but Tommy is glad to have been told the truth about what Bill thinks of her.

By the end of the play, Tommy helps Bill to gain more respect for Oldtimer as representative of a different generation of African-American men who were given little opportunity for education or financial gain. Bill points out, "Now there's Oldtimer, the guy who was here before there were scholarships and grants and stuff like that, the guy they kept outta the schools, the man the factories wouldn't hire, the union wouldn't let him join."

Sonny-man

Sonny-man is a twenty-seven-year-old writer. He is married to Cynthia. Sonny-man wears a dashiki, an African-style shirt, in style during the 1960s and 1970s, which represents a celebration of African heritage. During the riot, he and Cynthia meet Tommy at a bar and recognize her as the image of a down-and-out woman Bill envisions for his third painting. They bring Tommy to Bill's apartment without explaining to her what Bill has in mind.

Like Cynthia and Bill, Sonny-man represents the arrogant and condescending attitude some middle-class, educated people hold for those less privileged than they. Like Bill, Sonny-man sees himself

MEDIA ADAPTATIONS

- *Wine in the Wilderness* was first performed on WGBH-TV in Boston, Massachusetts, in 1969, as part of the series "On Being Black." The state of Alabama banned the broadcast due to the controversial nature of the racial issues it addresses.

as a creative person working for the good of the African-American community as a whole; he intends to "write the revolution into a novel nine hundred pages long." But his attitude toward Tommy and Oldtimer betrays the fact that he looks down on the "masses" of the African-American community.

Tommy

Tommy is a thirty-year-old woman who works in a dress factory. She lives in an apartment over a store that has been burned in the riot. She has not been allowed back into her apartment and has lost most of her clothing and the money she was saving. Cynthia and Sonny-man meet her in a bar during the riot and bring her up to Bill's apartment because they have identified her as the type of woman he wants to paint for the third part of his "triptych." Tommy thinks they are trying to set her up with Bill as a romantic interest and has no idea how they really see her. She likes Bill right away and continues to believe that he has taken a romantic interest in her. Tommy is very intelligent, articulate, and witty but is much less educated than Bill and his friends. She finally agrees to sit for Bill's painting if he will buy her something to eat. While eating, she accidentally spills soda on her clothing, and he gives her an African throw-cloth to wear as a makeshift dress. While she is changing, she overhears Bill on the telephone talking to an art dealer about his picture of "Mother Africa"—Tommy does not see that he is talking about a painting and thinks that he is talking about how beautiful he thinks she is. When Bill sees Tommy in the African wrap without her wig, he is mesmerized by how beautiful she now looks to him. He and Tommy kiss.

The next morning, Tommy is happily making coffee while Bill takes a bath. Oldtimer comes in and reveals to Tommy that Bill intends to paint her as an image of "the worst chick in town." Tommy, hurt and angry, criticizes Bill and his friends (not including Oldtimer) for looking down on her and the "masses" of the African-American community, who are not as educated or privileged as they. Through her anger, Tommy comes to appreciate herself for the woman that she is, in spite of their degrading attitude toward her. However, she blurts out that she loves Bill, which moves him to realize that she is right in her criticisms. He realizes that Tommy in fact represents his ideal African-American woman, his "Wine in the Wilderness." He convinces Tommy to stay and pose for his new painting.

THEMES

Classism within the African-American Community

A central theme of *Wine in the Wilderness* is the issue of socioeconomic class divisions within the African-American community. Bill, Cynthia, and Sonny-man are educated, middle-class professionals; Cynthia is a social worker, Bill is an artist, and Sonny-man is a writer. Oldtimer and Tommy, on the other hand, are underprivileged and not well-educated; Tommy works in a factory, while Oldtimer seems to be unemployed. One of the primary tensions of the play is that caused by the class divisions between these two sets of characters. The middle-class characters look down on the working-class characters, pretending to befriend them while showing them little respect. They do not even have enough respect for Oldtimer, their elder, to ever have asked his real name. The entire plot revolves around their plan to use Tommy as a model for Bill's painting of "the worst chick in town."

Bill is generally condescending toward Tommy, holding his higher education and bookish knowledge of history and literature over her. He corrects her manner of speaking and treats her as if she were completely ignorant. Tommy becomes slightly aware of this class tension when she asks Cynthia if she is not good enough for Bill. However, it is not until Tommy learns of Bill's real perception of her as "the worst gal in town" that she finally sees clearly how much he and his friends look down on her. Tommy accurately accuses them of looking down on the "masses" of African-Americans, who are not as educated or as privileged as they. Tommy even points out that Bill looks down on his own parents, who worked hard in order to own a home and provide him with greater opportunities. Tommy further accuses Bill of claiming to "love" African-American culture, while he in fact despises the actual African-American people he sees on the street every day. By the end of the play, Bill learns from Tommy to overcome his attitude of class snobbery toward other members of his community.

African-American Womanhood

Another central theme of *Wine in the Wilderness* is African-American womanhood. Bill intends his series of three paintings to represent his "statement" on "black womanhood." Through his first painting, "Black girlhood," Bill expresses his view of African-American girls as innocent and pure. In the second painting, "Wine in the Wilderness," he depicts his idealized image of "perfect black womanhood," as a stylish, physically beautiful woman in Afro-centric clothing and accessories. This image betrays Bill's idealized vision of "black womanhood" as a sexual fantasy resembling an image in a fashion magazine, rather than a real woman engaging in the struggles and joys of everyday life.

Bill's unpainted third image represents a view of the average African-American woman as down-and-out and "hopeless." At this point, Bill's view of "black womanhood" is very insulting toward African-American women in general, as he expresses disdain for women who work and struggle and live and love on a day-to-day basis, mostly without the benefit of financial comfort or opportunity for higher education. Bill is critical of the "masses" of African-American women like Tommy, whom he views as "ignorant, unfeminine, coarse," and "rude." He perceives these women as dominating African-American men, and tells Tommy, "the Matriarchy gotta go." Cynthia, too, although an African-American woman, expresses a similar attitude toward women like Tommy. She instructs Tommy to be more subservient toward men and advises her to allow men to have the upper hand. Cynthia expresses the opinion that African-American women have somehow robbed African-American men of their masculinity. She tells Tommy, "You have to let the black man have his manhood again," to which Tommy responds, "I didn't take it from him, how I'm gonna give it back?"

TOPICS FOR FURTHER STUDY

- In this play, Childress refers to a number of different African-American leaders in politics and culture. Pick one of these figures and learn more about her or him. Write a biographical sketch of this figure. What contribution did she or he make to African-American history and culture? What obstacles did he or she overcome in order to accomplish her/his goals? In what ways can you consider this person a role model for your own life? The figures mentioned in the play include: Martin Luther King, Jr.; Frederick Douglass; Harriet Tubman; Malcolm X; Muhammad Ali; Paul Laurence Dunbar; LeRoi Jones (also known as Amiri Baraka); and Margaret Walker.

- *Wine in the Wilderness* takes place in Harlem during a race riot. There have been a number of race riots in the United States, such as: the riots in Memphis and New Orleans in 1866; Springfield, Illinois in 1908; East St. Louis, Illinois, in 1917; Chicago in 1919; and Detroit in 1943. Learn more about the history of one of these riots. What immediate events sparked the riot? How did it get started? How did the police and government forces respond to the riot? What was the outcome of the riot (How long did it last? How many people were killed? How many injured? What was the extent of property damage? etc.)? What broader political and social concerns were being protested or expressed by the riot? How could these concerns have been addressed through effective, nonviolent action? What, if any, social or political changes took place in the aftermath of the riot?

- Pick a five to ten page segment from *Wine in the Wilderness* to perform as a group. In what ways does your performance of this scene help you to gain a better understanding of the character you are performing and her or his motivation? How does this insight help you to gain a better under-

standing of the major themes of the play? In what ways is the message of the play more effective when acted out as a dramatic scene?

- In this play, an artist paints a "triptych" (series of three paintings unified by a common theme) in order to express a social and political vision of the status of African-American women. Draw or paint your "triptych," expressive of your own concerns about a particular social or political issue. In what ways is this series of images an effective means of communicating your ideas, thoughts, and feelings about this issue?

- This play addresses the issue of relations between African-American men and women, touching on specific tensions, concerns, and points of harmony in male-female relationships. Write a theatrical scene expressing your own ideas and concerns about romantic relationships in your community or peer-group. With a group of students, act out the scene you have written. Discuss the ideas expressed through this dramatic expression of your concerns.

- In *Wine in the Wilderness*, Childress addresses the issue of how African-American women are represented in art. These concerns can also be addressed in terms of other forms of visual media, such as film, television, and fashion magazines. Pick a film, television show, or magazine that includes images of African-American women. You may also find a painting representing African-American women in a museum near you, or in an art book. How does this visual representation fit into the artist's conception of African-American women as described in the play? In what ways is this image a positive representation of African-American women? In what ways is it a negative or stereotyped representation of African-American women? Write an essay or report based on your observations; if possible, include the images you are discussing with your project.

By the end of the play, Bill realizes that he has been misguided in perceiving the ''masses'' of African-American women in such a negative light. He realizes that everyday women like Tommy are ''the real beautiful people.'' Through the character of Tommy, Childress criticizes those African-American men who blame African-American women for the oppression they suffer in a white-dominated society. By contrast, Childress celebrates women like Tommy, who work and struggle through everyday life, as an ideal image of ''black womanhood.''

STYLE

Dialogue

The contrast in the speech patterns of the less educated characters with that of the more educated characters is a significant element of the dialogue in this play. The three middle-class characters, Bill, Cynthia, and Sonny-man, demonstrate their higher level of education through their use of vocabulary and their speech patterns. Tommy and Oldtimer, who are not well-educated, have somewhat different vocabulary and speech patterns. Childress ultimately uses this contrast in speech patterns throughout the dialogue to point out the tensions which arise from class differences within the African-American community. However, Childress is particularly concerned with demonstrating that those who are less educated are equally intelligent and articulate, although their vocabulary and frame of reference may be different from those with degrees. Tommy, for instance, is very intelligent and articulate, despite her lack of education, while Bill, Cynthia, and Sonny-man are ignorant in many ways, despite their education. Specific points of vocabulary throughout the dialogue are used to demonstrate this contrast and these points. For example, Bill tells Oldtimer that he intends to paint a ''triptych,'' which is a series of three paintings meant to be viewed together as a series or single unified work. Oldtimer, who does not know what a ''triptych'' is, asks, ''A what tick?''

Differences in vocabulary are also demonstrated by the terms used to refer to African Americans. Bill corrects Tommy's terminology in telling her to use the term *Afro-American,* which was considered to be the most respectful term among many African Americans during the period in which the play was written. Childress, however, introduces the term as a way of pointing out the hypocrisy among Bill and his friends, who use the proper terminology and yet do not demonstrate actual respect for the ''masses'' of African Americans, whom they look down on as ignorant and uncultured. Tommy thus uses the term *Afro-American* ironically, as a means of demonstrating their hypocrisy. Tommy points out that using this term of solidarity covers over various divisions within the African-American community. When Bill corrects her, Tommy responds, ironically, ''Well . . . the Afro-Americans burnt down my house.'' Childress thus uses differences in vocabulary to point out various internal divisions within the African-American community and the hypocrisy of those who try to deny those divisions simply by using the proper vocabulary.

Symbolism

Throughout the play, Childress makes use of symbolism in order to express her thematic concerns. The central symbol of *Wine in the Wilderness* is captured in the play's title, which is also the title of Bill's ''triptych,'' as well as the title of the central painting in the triptych. Bill's image of ''Wine in the Wilderness'' represents his idealized vision of ''black womanhood.'' He explains to Oldtimer the origin of this title: ''Once, a long time ago, a poet named Omar told us what a paradise life could be if a man had a loaf of bread, a jug of wine and . . . a woman singing to him in the wilderness.'' He states that his image of ''perfect black womanhood'' is ''the woman, she is the bread, she is the wine, she is the singing.'' In other words, she is ''paradise.''

Throughout the play, the phrase ''wine in the wilderness'' refers to an ideal image of ''black womanhood.'' However, by the end, Tommy comes to recognize within herself an ideal of black womanhood, not an outward ideal of physical beauty or perfection, but a real African-American woman facing everyday life with courage and hope. She explains: ''The real thing is takin' place on the inside . . . that's where the action is. That's 'Wine in the Wilderness,' . . . a woman that's a real one and a good one.'' By the end of the play, Bill, influenced by Tommy's words and love and energy, learns to reconceptualize his image of African-American women and his definition of the ''wine in the wilderness.'' He reconceptualizes the ''wilderness'' as a metaphor for the harsh conditions faced by African-American women throughout history, particularly slavery and the legacy of slavery. He understands the ''wine'' as a metaphor for the internal beauty of the countless African-American women who have survived such harsh conditions with courage and hope.

HISTORICAL CONTEXT

The Civil Rights Era

Wine in the Wilderness was written and takes place during the period of American history known as the Civil Rights era. During this period, spanning roughly from the mid-1950s through the mid-1970s, a number of African-American political leaders rose to prominence, working in various ways to create greater opportunities for African Americans. The characters in Childress's play discuss several of these leaders, such as Martin Luther King, Jr., Malcolm X, and the politician Adam Clayton Powell.

Martin Luther King, Jr. became the leader of the Civil Rights Movement and was active in organizing nonviolent protests and speaking out against segregation in the South. Inspired by the non-violent methods put forth by Indian nationalist leader Mahatma Gandhi, King worked through an organization known as the Southern Christian Leadership Conference to stage such events as the famous March on Washington, in 1963. King's leadership was effective in seeing through important civil rights legislation, such as the comprehensive 1964 Civil Rights Act and the 1965 Voting Rights Act. He was awarded the Nobel Prize for Peace in 1964. King was assassinated in 1968.

Malcolm X was a leader in the movement for black nationalism during the early 1960s. Born Malcolm Little, he converted to the Nation of Islam faith of Black Muslims and changed his name to Malcolm X. Malcolm X became known as a powerful speaker and effective leader in the Nation of Islam movement and was eventually assigned to be the minister at a mosque in Harlem. Malcolm X was critical of the Civil Rights Movement of Martin Luther King, Jr., advocating black separatism instead of integration and self-defense through violence rather than nonviolent protest. He was assassinated in 1965 during a rally in Harlem. His life and political views are captured in the much celebrated book, *The Autobiography of Malcolm X* (1965), written by Alex Haley, and Malcolm X.

A lesser known African-American political activist mentioned in Childress's play is Adam Clay-ton Powell, Jr., a pastor based in Harlem who worked as an elected public official from the 1940s through the 1960s. In 1941, Powell was the first African American to be elected to the New York City Council. In 1945, he was elected to the U.S. House of Representatives, to which he was reelected for eleven terms. Powell was active in working for the passage of some fifty separate liberal legislative acts and bills to support civil rights, end segregation, and promote education and fair labor practices. His political career stumbled in 1967, due to controversy over a private legal battle, and he retired from politics in 1971. He died a year later.

African-American Literature and the Arts

In *Wine in the Wilderness*, Childress makes reference to a number of prominent African-American writers from the late nineteenth century and throughout the twentieth century. One of the earliest writers mentioned in the play is the African-American author Paul Laurence Dunbar, who published successful collections of poetry and short stories, as well novels, during the 1890s.

Twentieth century African-American literature and the arts have been characterized by two important literary and aesthetic movements: The Harlem Renaissance and the Black Arts Movement. The Harlem Renaissance, also referred to as the New Negro Movement, designates a period during the 1920s in which African-American literature flourished among a group of writers concentrated in Harlem, New York. Childress mentions the prominent Harlem Renaissance poet Langston Hughes, known for the collection *The Weary Blues* (1926), among many other works. The period of incredible literary output known as the Harlem Renaissance diminished when the Depression of the 1930s affected the financial status of many African-American writers.

In *Wine in the Wilderness*, Bill mentions the author Margaret Walker, whose career spans both the Harlem Renaissance and the era of the Black Arts Movement. Walker was educated during the 1930s and became acquainted with writers of the Harlem Renaissance such as the novelist Richard Wright. She published a celebrated volume of poetry, *For My People,* in 1942. Her first novel, *Jubilee* (1966), was published during the era of the Black Arts Movement. *Jubilee,* based on the life of Walker's great-grandmother, has been contrasted with the novel *Gone With the Wind* (1936, by Margaret Mitchell) as a tale of nineteenth century

COMPARE & CONTRAST

- **1960s:** In 1965, a major race riot takes place over a period of six days in the Watts district of Los Angeles, California, leaving 34 dead and some 1000 injured. Over the next three years, race riots break out in most of the major cities of the United States. Some of the worst riots are in Newark, New Jersey, and Detroit, Michigan, in the summer of 1967. The last of this wave of riots occurs in the wake of the assassination of Martin Luther King Jr. in 1968.

  Today: A race riot takes place in south-central Los Angeles in 1992, resulting in 52 deaths. The rioting is sparked by a court ruling in favor of the white policemen accused of brutally beating African-American motorist Rodney King.

- **1960s:** The Black Arts Movement represents the cutting edge of African-American theater. *The Dutchman* (1964), by Amiri Baraka (also known as LeRoi Jones), is an early prominent theatrical production of the Black Arts Movement. Inspired by, and in part an initiator of, the Black Arts Movement, Baraka establishes the Black Repertory Theater in Harlem.

  Today: Numerous black theaters have been established throughout the United States, with many mainstream stages also featuring black theatrical productions. A new generation of African-American writers and artists are greatly influenced by

the legacy of the Black Arts Movement. *Ma Rainey's Black Bottom* (1985), by August Wilson, is the most celebrated play of the 1980s by an African-American writer.

- **1960s:** Prominent African-American political leaders include Martin Luther King, Jr., Malcolm X, and Adam Clayton Powell, as well as Huey Newton and Bobby Seale, who founds the revolutionary Black Panther Party in 1966.

  Today: Jesse Jackson, a Baptist minister, is one of the most prominent African-American civil rights leaders of the 1980s. Jackson's voter-registration drive during the 1980s helps lead to the election of Chicago's first African-American mayor, Harold Washington, in 1983. Louis Farrakhan, the African-American leader of his own sect of the Nation of Islam (also known as the Black Muslims) founded in 1978, also rises to prominence as an influential black leader in the 1980s and 1990s. Oprah Winfrey, although known primarily as a popular daytime TV talk show host and media personality, is arguably the most influential African-American woman in the United States. She is awarded the Woman of Achievement Award from the National Organization for Women in 1986, and the Image Award from the National Association for the Advancement of Colored People four years in a row (1989–1992).

Southern life, from the perspective of several generations of an African-American family which endured slavery.

During the 1960s and 1970s, The Black Arts Movement, also referred to as the Black Aesthetic Movement, emerged, embodying values derived from black nationalism and promoting politically and socially significant works, often written in Black English vernacular. Important writers of the Black Arts Movement include Imamu Amiri Baraka (also known as LeRoi Jones), who is referred to in

Childress's play familiarly as ''LeRoi.'' Other important writers of the Black Arts Movement include Eldridge Cleaver, Angela Davis, Alice Walker, and Toni Morrison.

CRITICAL OVERVIEW

Critics frequently discuss *Wine in the Wilderness* in terms of Childress's successful characterization of Tommy as an African-American heroine. Susan

Bennett, in the *International Dictionary of Theater,* notes that Childress's "creation of many major female characters" is "perhaps the most significant contribution" of her plays.

Elizabeth Brown-Guillory, in "Images of Blacks in Plays by Black Women," praises Childress as a creator of plausible heroines in her dramatic works, particularly *Wine in the Wilderness.* She asserts, "*Wine in the Wilderness* is the best illustration of Childress' superb handling of characterization," commenting, "Childress' heroines, in general, are at once courageous, discerning, vulnerable, insecure, and optimistic. In short, they are human, real." Brown-Guillory further observes, "Childress writes largely about poor women for whom the act of living is sheer heroism." She notes that the character of Tommy "epitomizes the typical heroine who peoples Childress' plays," in the sense that, "she steadily moves in the direction of wholeness." Tommy's triumph over her circumstances is celebrated by Brown-Guillory, who continues, "Regardless of the fact that her bourgeois acquaintances almost destroy her, Tommy moves to a state of completeness, i.e., develops a positive sense of self."

Victoria Sullivan and James Hatch, in their Introduction to *Plays by and about Women,* also praise Childress for creating a heroine in the character of Tommy:

> Tommy has neither money nor recognition, but she has a vitality and a knowledge of what human beings are and should be. She is a grass-roots woman who has survived the rats, the roaches, the riots, and the landlords of Harlem. With Tommy, Ms. Childress has created a strong new black woman character to contrast with the traditional strong "Mammy" type. Bill's self-serving notion that he is "better" than Tommy not only is defeated but he comes to recognize that her ability to survive is the wine in the wilderness that has enabled the whole black race to survive in America.

In "Black Women Playwrights: Exorcising Myths," Brown-Guillory compares *Wine in the Wilderness* to the much celebrated play, *for colored girls who have considered suicide, when the rainbow is enuf* (1977), by Ntozake Shange. She explains that the African-American women in both plays

> are preoccupied with themselves because they have been disappointed by the men who have come into their lives. These are women who have had their share of "deferred dreams" and are no longer willing to play the role of "woman-behind-her-man" to men who appreciate neither their submissiveness nor their docility. These women rebel and claim that no man is ever going to oppress them again. They are not

women who give up on men or feel that all men are insensitive beasts; instead, they are women who have become independent because of their fear of being abused physically and/or emotionally in subsequent relationships.

Brown-Guillory adds that, in both plays, "emphasis is placed on their ability to survive in a world where they are forced to care for themselves. The evolving black women in these plays fight back after they have been bruised, and they work toward improving their lifestyles."

Brown-Guillory, in "Images of Blacks in Plays by Black Women," opines, "Captivating drama that exhibits suspense, plausible conflicts, swift repartee, meaningful and well-developed dialogue, *Wine in the Wilderness* is perhaps Childress' finest play."

Other critics, however, have criticized Childress for using her characters as mouthpieces for putting forth her own political agenda. Some have also criticized her work as anti-male and anti-white.

CRITICISM

Liz Brent

Brent has a Ph.D. in American Culture, specializing in film studies, from the University of Michigan. She is a freelance writer and teaches courses in the history of American cinema. In the following essay, Brent discusses the use of humor in Childress's play.

Wine in the Wilderness is subtitled "A Comedy-Drama." Throughout the play, Childress utilizes the element of comedy to highlight her central thematic concerns, such as the nature of political and social action, male-female relationships, and class divisions within the African-American community. Although Childress is quite serious about these concerns, she makes use of humor both for its entertainment value and as a means of accenting these themes in a light-hearted manner.

One element of humor in *Wine in the Wilderness* centers around the characters' ironic commentary on the riot, which has been raging around them, and which has now abated. Bill, in particular, is presented as emotionally and mentally removed from the physical violence of the riot. In the opening

The Harlem race riots in the late 1960's provide the setting for Wine in the Wilderness

scene of the play, Bill is calmly sketching a picture while dodging the bullets that are flying all around him. The stage directions read:

> Bill is seated on the floor with his back to the wall, drawing on a large sketch pad with charcoal pencil. He is very absorbed in his task but flinches as he hears the bullet sound, ducks and shields his head with upraised hand, . . . then resumes sketching.

This scene demonstrates Bill's removed attitude toward the real struggles going on in his community—he prefers to retreat into the abstractness of his art, rather than to engage in the flesh-and-blood realities of life in Harlem. Bill is thus presented as disengaged from the physical reality of the riot and, symbolically, the community in which he lives and which he claims to represent through his art.

Bill makes light of the riot at several points throughout the play. This attitude of not taking the riot seriously is expressed when his friend Sonny-man calls from a bar. He answers the phone cautiously, so as to avoid being caught by a stray bullet and, when he learns that Sonny-man and Cynthia have not been killed in the riot, makes a lighthearted joke of the matter: ''Thought yall was dead. I'm sittin' here drawin' a picture in your memory. In a bar? Yall sittin' in a bar? See there, you done blew the picture that's in your memory.'' When his art dealer calls, Bill picks up the phone saying, ''Hello, survivor of a riot speaking.'' These comments indicate the extent to which Bill is unsympathetic to the real personal loss and tragedy that can occur as a result of a riot—such as Tommy losing her home, clothes, and money, and Richard Lee losing his restaurant.

Bill also provides ironic commentary on the dubious effectiveness of the riot as a means of bringing about social and political ''revolution.'' Tommy sends him out to buy Chinese food, but he comes back with a hotdog instead, explaining, ''No Chinese restaurant left, baby! It's wiped out. Gone with the revolution.'' Bill is clearly cynical about the effectiveness of such a ''revolution,'' which results only in such acts of destruction as the burning down of a neighborhood restaurant. Both Bill and Sonny-man share the attitude that social and political change, a.k.a., ''the revolution,'' is best enacted through art. Bill comments, ''The revolution is here. Whatta you do with her? You paint her!'' To which Sonny-man, a writer, adds, ''You write her . . . you write the revolution. I'm gonna write the revolution into a novel nine hundred pages long.''

Toward the end of the play, Tommy accuses Bill of celebrating the African-American community in the abstract, while actually despising the real, flesh-and-blood people among whom he lives.

> If a black somebody is in a history book, or printed on a pitcher, or drawed on a paintin' . . . or if they're a statue, . . . dead, and outtta the way, and can't talk back, then you dig 'em and full-a so much-a damn admiration and talk 'bout ''our'' history. But when you run into us livin' and breakin' ones, with the life's blood still pumpin' through us, . . . then you comin' on 'bout how we ain' never together. You hate us, that's what! You hate black me!

Tommy's point here echoes back to Bill's attitude in the opening of the play, in which he ironically expresses disappointment that his friends are still alive, rather than being killed in the riot, because, as he tells them, ''See there, you done blew the picture that's in your memory.'' Bill is more comfortable creating representations of people through his art than interacting with real, live people with ''life's blood still pumpin' through us.'' Bill's state of obliviousness to the reality of the riot is thus symbolic of his removed attitude toward the reality of the lives of the ''masses'' of African Americans,

> **"TOWARD THE END OF THE PLAY, TOMMY ACCUSES BILL OF CELEBRATING THE AFRICAN-AMERICAN COMMUNITY IN THE ABSTRACT, WHILE ACTUALLY DESPISING THE REAL, FLESH-AND-BLOOD PEOPLE AMONG WHOM HE LIVES."**

who are not as privileged as he. This contrast is made concrete by the idea of a riot as a form of protest against racial oppression that is expressed through physical violence, whereas Bill prefers the abstractness of art as a means of making a ''statement'' about African-American culture.

Childress also employs humor in fleshing out the character of Tommy. Tommy's sense of humor, which the other characters often appreciate, is important as an element of her personal charm—an indication of her lively, quick-witted mind, as well as being a part of what makes her a unique and attractive personality. Tommy's losses as a result of the riot have been much more serious than those of any other character in the play—her apartment has been burned with most of her clothing and all of her savings, as well as her other belongings. And yet, Tommy finds humor and joy in interacting with other people, despite the ''tragedy'' that the riot has visited upon her. Sonny-man tells Bill, ''She was breakin' up everybody in the bar . . . had us all laughin' . . . crackin' us up. In the middle of a riot . . . she's gassin' everybody!'' At Bill's apartment, Tommy, who is enjoying the company, comments, ''Ain't this a shame! That riot done wipe me out and I'm sittin' here havin' me a ball.'' Tommy's resilient spirit despite her recent loss is representative of the spirit of countless African-American women throughout history, who have survived harsh, tragic lives and yet maintained a zest for life. Only at the end of the play does Bill come to understand the ''beauty'' of African-American women such as Tommy, who ''came through the biggest riot of all . . . somethin' called 'Slavery,' and she's even comin' through the 'now' scene . . .''

Tommy's sense of humor, to some extent, is based on the very qualities which Bill claims to despise in women. Bill's description of ''the worst chick in town'' includes the idea that she is ''crude'' and ''vulgar.'' Yet Tommy causes ''general laughter'' among the other characters by talking about the ''corn'' on her foot—a topic some might consider ''crude'' or ''vulgar'' conversation material among mixed company that one has just met. When Old-timer gives her a chair to sit down, Tommy comments, ''Bet you can tell my feet hurt. I got one corn . . . and that one is enough.'' She adds, ''Oh, it'll ask you for somethin'.'' When she becomes suspicious that perhaps Bill has a wife or girlfriend lurking around, listening in on the conversation, Tommy intentionally speaks loudly to insist that she is not trying to steal anyone's man away from another woman. She pointedly states, ''I'm innocent. Don't wanta get shot at or jumped on. Cause I wasn't doin' a thing but mindin' my own business!''—the stage directions indicate that Tommy says this ''*in loud tone to be heard in other rooms.*'' Clearly, Tommy has been in situations before in which she found herself in the home of a man whose jealous wife or girlfriend threatened her with violence. Tommy's open expression of concern that she may be ''shot at or jumped on'' by another woman indicates her lack of social sophistication, in comparison to Bill, Cynthia, and Sonny-man.

Although some of Tommy's humor is intentional, some of her comments and questions that add a comic element to the play are based on her ignorance of Bill's cultural milieu. A number of humorous points in the dialogue of this play occur at moments in which Tommy misunderstands Bill's meaning, particularly when it comes to aspects of his educated, intellectual, privileged lifestyle. After being introduced to Tommy, Bill offers her a drink. When she asks for wine, Bill assumes that Tommy is a ''wine-o,'' an alcoholic. Bill's assumption betrays his attitude toward Tommy as a woman who is hopeless and at the bottom of the social ladder. Tommy, however, immediately points out that he is the one who keeps wine in his house. Bill then explains that he only uses the wine for cooking, to which Tommy responds, ''You like to get loaded while you cook?'' Bill of course meant that he keeps the wine to use as an ingredient in some recipes, but Tommy, it seems, is unfamiliar with the type of gourmet cooking that may call for wine. Thus, while Bill looks down on Tommy and assumes that she is a ''wine-o,'' Tommy turns the tables on him, suggesting that he is the ''wine-o.''

Tommy also makes a humorous commentary on Bill's half-finished attempt at remodeling his apartment, originally a low-income tenement, to look like a stylish studio space. The set directions explain that Bill has ''broken out walls and is half finished with a redecorating job. The place is now only partly reminiscent of its past tawdry days, plaster broken away and lathing exposed right next to a new brick-faced portion of wall.'' Tommy is clearly not familiar with the stylish type of redecorating done by professional, privileged people such as Bill, who move into formerly low-rent districts in order to transform them into classy living quarters. To Tommy, it looks like Bill's apartment has merely been torn apart in the riot. After pointing out that her own apartment was burned by rioters from within her own community—''the Afro-Americans burnt down my house''—Tommy looks around Bill's apartment, commenting, ''Looks like the Afro-Americans got to you too.'' Tommy's comment ironically points out to Bill that his abstract ideas about the black community as a unified group (the ''Afro-Americans'') are far from accurate, since it was ''the Afro-Americans'' who have destroyed her home and her belongings—as well as those of many others within the community.

Tommy also makes humorous comments to point out Cynthia's class snobbery toward women who have less money and education than she. When the men leave, Cynthia criticizes Tommy for wearing a wig, insisting that Tommy's ''natural'' hair must be ''just as nice or nicer'' than the wig. Tommy retorts, ''It oughta be. I only paid nineteen ninety five for this.'' Tommy later mocks Cynthia's criticism of the wig, bitterly pointing out that women like Cynthia only make things worse for women like Tommy: '''Do you have to wear a wig?' Yes! To soften the blow when y'all go up side-a my head with a baseball bat.''

Childress makes use of humor in this play to emphasize specific themes. In depicting Bill's disengaged and critical attitude about the riot, she raises the issue of the relative merit of artistic expression in comparison to violent action in struggling against racial oppression. Through the character of Tommy—whose sense of humor demonstrates her resilient spirit (despite her tragic circumstances), her intelligence (despite a lack of education), her charm (despite her lack of refinement or sophistication), and her biting commentary on the divisiveness which exists within the African-American community—Childress offers a critical assessment of relationships between African-American men and women, class divisions within the African-American community, and the effectiveness of either violence or art as a means of political action.

Source: Liz Brent, Critical Essay on *Wine in the Wilderness,* in *Drama for Students,* The Gale Group, 2002.

La Vinia Delois Jennings

In the following essay on Wine in the Wilderness, *the author discusses the idea of the play's protagonist as the ''true Africentrist'' in the midst of the intersections of class, race, and gender.*

In *Wine in the Wilderness*, Childress makes the point that the intersections of ''sexism, racism, and classism are immutably connected to black women's oppression while making it crystal clear that black women triumph because of a strong spirit of survival inextricably linked to an African heritage.'' Enlisting the background of a Harlem riot as a controlling metaphor for communal and intraracial fragmentation, Childress foregrounds the underclass, undereducated heroine of *Wine in the Wilderness* as the true Africentrist, proud of blacks and her blackness. She stands in stark relief to bourgeois, intellectual blacks whose white assimilationist and classist values expose their racial disingenuousness. Espousing the in-vogue black power rhetoric of brotherhood, liberation, and nationalism, the middle-class antagonists of the play accessorize themselves with the trappings of African culture—the dashiki, the Afro hairstyle, and African objets d'art. But they relegate the black woman in the black movement to the same position assigned her by real-life activists like Stokely Carmichael: ''prone.''

The play's gender conflict exposes the black consciousness movement's ambition to establish a black male hegemony that replicated the gender and class biases of white patriarchy. The female protagonist of *Wine in the Wilderness* refutes the accusation that she is the product of a matriarchal society that has appropriated the manhood of the black male. Resistant to exploitation by pretentious middle-class blacks, she rejects the sexist prescriptions of passivity submissiveness, voicelessness, and domesticity. An African ancestral connectedness, which the other black characters have failed to cultivate or have lost, enables her to resurrect a guiding, affirming blackness in the middle-class blacks she encounters. As Elizabeth Brown-Guillory posits, the female protagonist of *Wine in the Wilderness* is ''a

> " ... THE MIDDLE-CLASS ANTAGONISTS OF THE PLAY ACCESSORIZE THEMSELVES WITH THE TRAPPINGS OF AFRICAN CULTURE—THE DASHIKI, THE AFRO HAIRSTYLE, AND AFRICAN OBJETS D'ART. BUT THEY RELEGATE THE BLACK WOMAN IN THE BLACK MOVEMENT TO THE SAME POSITION ASSIGNED HER BY REAL-LIFE ACTIVISTS LIKE STOKELY CARMICHAEL: 'PRONE.'"

very spiritual and spirited woman,'' who ''rises to serve as a healer to her wounded community whose psyche is in need of re-Africanization.''

Childress situates the action of *Wine in the Wilderness* at the conclusion of a Harlem riot during the summer of 1964. Waiting out the storm of street violence in his apartment, Bill Jameson, a 33-year-old painter, receives a telephone call from his neighbors Sonny-man, a writer, and Sonny-man's wife, Cynthia, a social worker. They announce that they have found the perfect model for Bill's work-in-progress, the third panel of a triptych dedicated to the theme of black womanhood.

Before they arrive, Bill describes the triptych to Oldtimer, a homeless man, who drops by with loot picked up off the street. The first panel, titled ''Black Girlhood,'' depicts innocence—''a charming little girl in Sunday dress and hair ribbon.'' The second reveals ''a beautiful woman'' with ''deep mahogany complexion'' who is ''cold but utter perfection, draped in startling colors of African material.'' She is, Bill states, '''Wine in the Wilderness' . . . Mother Africa, regal, black womanhood in her noblest form.'' He explains that the third canvas, now blank, will contain the image of ''the kinda chick that is grass roots, . . . no, . . . underneath the grass. The lost woman, . . . what the society has made out of our women. She's as far from my African queen as a woman can get and still be

female. She's ignorant, unfeminine, coarse, rude
...vulgar...there's no hope for her.... If you had
to sum her up in one word it would be nothin'!''

Wearing a wig and mismatched skirt and
sweater, 30-year-old Tomorrow Marie Fields, called
Tommy, arrives with Sonny-man and Cynthia under
the impression that the two are trying to match her
up romantically with Bill. Lacking the sophistication and college education of the others, Tommy, an
eighth-grade dropout, is unpretentious, good-natured, and polite. When the men leave to get the
Chinese food Bill promises Tommy in exchange for
posing, Tommy shares with Cynthia her attraction
to Bill. Cynthia attempts to discourage Tommy's
affection, warning that Bill's art comes first and that
she should not put her trust in men. Tommy, however, understands Cynthia's true message, that she
is ''aimin' too high by looking at Bill.''

Seeking honesty, she asks Cynthia to tell her
why men like Bill fail to find her attractive. Cynthia
explains, stating ''You're too brash. You're too
used to looking out for yourself. It makes us lose our
femininity.... It makes us hard.... You have to let
the black man have his manhood again. You have to
give it back, Tommy.... Don't chase him.... Let
him pursue you.... Let him do the talking. Learn to
listen. Stay in the background a little. Ask his
opinion ... 'What do you think, Bill?'... What we
need is a little more sex appeal.'' Wearing an Afro
herself, she recommends that Tommy not wear a
wig. The conversation between the women terminates with the return of the men. Oldtimer, Cynthia,
and Sonny-man leave so that Bill can commence
painting.

Admitting her ignorance about books, Tommy
encourages Bill to share his knowledge of black
history. In between his elaborations on Frederick
Douglass and Monroe Trotter, he criticizes black
women in general and Tommy in particular. Uncomfortable about her shabby clothing, Tommy suggests that he paint her another time. His insistence
that she keep on the wig for the portrait vexes her,
and she accidentally spills orange drink on herself.
Perturbed by her clumsiness, Bill gives her an
African wrap in which to change while he talks on
the phone.

Tommy overhears Bill describing to the caller
the ebony queen of the ''Wine in the Wilderness''
panel and mistakenly thinks he is describing her.
''You just make sure your exhibition room is big
enough to hold the crowds that's gonna congregate
to see this fine chick I got here.... an ebony queen

of the universe.... but best of all and most important.... She's tomorrow ... she's my tomorrow,''
he states. Feeling valued and possibly loved, Tommy,
sans wig, emerges relaxed, confident, and beautifully draped. She sits on the model stand, reciting
bits of her family history as conversation. Astonished by her radical physical transformation, Bill is
strongly attracted to this Tommy. Unable to reconcile her present appearance with the earlier one, he
loses his incentive to paint. The two grow closer,
embrace, kiss, and ultimately spend the night together.

The next morning, an elated Tommy is deflated
and angered when Oldtimer returns and inadvertently reveals that she is not the African queen but
the ''messed-up chick'' of the triptych. Sonny-man
and Cynthia arrive shortly thereafter, and Tommy
denounces them all, accusing them of spouting pro-
black rhetoric when in actuality they obviously
despise ''flesh and blood niggers,'' as evidenced by
their classist, sexist, and deceptive treatment of her.
Bill's consciousness is slow to be raised, but her
insight takes the artist beyond his limited perception, inspiring him to begin the triptych anew. The
''chick'' of the old triptych, ''a dream I drummed
up outta the junk room of my mind,'' was painted
''in the dark'' with ''all head and no heart. I
couldn't see until you came,'' Bill pleads.

The first panel of the re-visioned triptych will
depict Oldtimer as emblematic of the black man's
past, when he was denied access to education,
unions, and factory work. The second panel will
contain Sonny-man and Cynthia, representative of
the ''Young Man and Woman working together to
do our thing.'' Bill persuades Tommy to pose for
the center panel, the woman of the future, the
''Wine in the Wilderness'' woman, who has come
''through the biggest riot of all, ... somethin'
called 'Slavery,' and she's even comin' through the
'now' scene.'' As the black woman whose identity is clearly etched as survivor, Tommy will be
the inspiration for the black men and women of
tomorrow.

Cultural Symbol versus Cultural Substance

The setting of the play, Bill Jameson's partially
renovated Harlem apartment, is conspicuously dominated by cultural iconography. African sculpture,
wall hangings, paintings, and books on African
American history signify the occupant's fashionable but vacuous preoccupation with African artifacts. An array of multicultural icons—a Chinese
Buddha incense-burner, a Native American feather

war helmet, a West Indian travel poster, a Mexican serape, and a Japanese fan—further objectifies Bill's vapid efforts to proclaim a political kinship with other oppressed people of color. He cannot sympathetically or psychically relate to those other cultures represented in his apartment, however, because he has failed to connect wholly with his own.

A creation of elitist, black, middle-class culture in imitation of white patriarchy, Bill is more concerned with cultural symbols than with cultural substance. The most telling indicator of his cultural insubstantiality is the exotic cluster of African symbols and associations he attaches to his vision of ''Wine in the Wilderness,'' perfect black womanhood. The exotic ''cold'' image of the ebony queen of the universe, of the ''Sudan, the Congo River, the Egyptian Pyramids,'' in essence Mother Africa who ''has come through everything that has been put on her,'' bears no resemblance to flesh and blood African and African American women who have actually withstood the trials and tribulations of daily struggle and survival. His ''gorgeous satin chick,'' whom every man would ''most like to meet on a desert island, or around the corner from anywhere,'' panders to male fantasy.

Bill's misguided vision of ''Wine in the Wilderness'' is the Madison Avenue paradigm of physical female beauty, only in blackface. His queen is the slick, air-brushed, glamorized, ornamental woman who mutely stares from billboards and magazine advertisements. With her blackness defamiliarized in a traditional white imaging of beauty, she propagates the ideology of whiteness, not blackness. Antithetical to the struggling black woman in America, the woman on the canvas is nothing but accessories—''startling colors of African material'' and ''golden headdress sparkling with brilliants and sequins . . . [s]omethin' you add on or take off.'' Flawless in appearance and conceptualization, Bill's ''Wine in the Wilderness'' has no grounding in reality.

Mainstream Assimilation

Because of their assimilation of mainstream values, Bill and his neighbors, Sonny-man and Cynthia, more concerned with black symbols, black discourse, and blackness in the abstract than in the concrete, disassociate themselves from blacks of lower socioeconomic status. Their classist disrespect for Oldtimer, who represents age, experience, and their ancestral past, exemplifies their detachment. In all the time they have known Oldtimer, never have they been genuinely interested enough to ask him his real name. His serving as their court fool and as an up-close example of how politically untogether poor, uneducated blacks can be, has militated against their recognition of his personhood. Similarly, the trio is interested in Tommy for her symbolic value, not for her real self. Voicing both class and regional bias, they view her as ''the kinda woman that grates on your damn nerves . . . back-country . . . right outta the wilds of Mississippi,'' though she was born and reared in Harlem. Since she ''ain't fit for nothin''' and ''there's no hope for her,'' political enlightenment and social empowerment are, theoretically, wasted on her. The only sensible response from privileged, enlightened blacks like themselves is ''to . . . just pass her by.''

Living in Harlem, a mecca of blackness, yet not identifying with their black sisters and brothers on the street, has severed the middle-class blacks of the play from their racial roots. Tommy forces them to face their intraracial bigotry and their illusion that they are different from ''the black masses'' when she comprehends that they see her as inferior:

> Sonny-Man: The sister is upset.
> Tommy: And you stop callin' me ''the'' sister, . . . if you feelin' so brotherly why don't you say ''my'' sister? Ain't no we-ness in your talk. ''The'' Afro-American, ''the'' black man, there's no we-ness in you. Who you think you are?
> Sonny-Man: I was talkin' in general er . . . my sister, 'bout the masses.
> Tommy: There he go again. ''The'' masses. Tryin' to make out like we pitiful and you got it made. You the masses your damn self and don't even know it.

Tommy reminds them that the white definition of ''nigger'' extends equally to them: ''When they say 'nigger', just dry-long so, they mean educated you and uneducated me.'' Her words startle Bill into a psychological journey toward black affirmation. Shocked, he discovers that counter to what he has been taught, the dictionary definition of ''nigger'' does not mean ''a low, degraded person'' but ''A Negro . . . A member of any dark-skinned people.'' Tommy's definition of ''nigger''—by which she designates both the rioters who have burned her out of her apartment and Bill, once she discovers he has misrepresented his intentions in painting her—applies to those blacks who hurt and exploit other blacks to fuel their own self-esteem and to satisfy their own egocentric aims.

The racial denial, divisiveness, and do-nothing politics of Bill and other bourgeois blacks are just as destructive to black advancement and self-acceptance as the looting and burning done by those who destroy their own people's businesses and homes in the name of revolution or as the scavenging of those who profit from the leavings. The rioters, as Tommy points out, holler ''whitey, whitey . . . but who they burn out? Me.'' Their violence is not unleashed on those they regard as the enemy but internalized, deflected onto the black community.

Contemptuous of black Harlemites, Bill, like the rioters, ironically abuses his own people, thereby revealing his unrecognized self-hatred and self-devaluation. Quick to sermonize but lacking a plan of his own, Bill is critical of both black factionalism—the rioters and looters—and black unity the leaderships of Malcolm X and Martin Luther King, Jr. Nothing blacks do seems to please him. Even his suburban upbringing in Jamaica, Long Island, where everyone in his family worked for the post office and every house on his block had ''an aluminum screen door with a duck on it,'' receives his disdain. Tommy plainly points all this out to him, perceiving that his rejection of her symbolizes his rejection of his mother, his family, the ''flesh and blood'' black community:

> Ain't a-one-a us you like that's alive and walkin' by you on the street . . . you don't like flesh and blood niggers. . . . If a black somebody is in a history book, or printed on a pitcher, or drawed on a paintin' . . . or if they're a statue, . . . dead, and outta the way, and can't talk back, then you dig 'em and full-a so much-a damn admiration and talk 'bout ''our'' history. But when you run into us livin' and breathin' ones, with the life's blood still pumpin' through us, . . . then you comin' on 'bout we ain' never together. You hate us, that's what! You hate black me! . . .
>
> Maybe I look too much like the mother that give birth to you. Like the Ma and Pa that worked in the post office to buy you a house and a screen door with a damn duck on it. And you so ungrateful you didn't even like it . . . You didn't like who was livin' behind them screen doors. Phoney Nigger!

Even with limited education and social exposure, Tommy knows that identity and self-worth do not come from acting out prescriptive black roles, reading black history, surrounding oneself with African art, or holding one's familial roots in contempt.

A Guiding Africentrism

Essential to the sustenance of a positive black national culture, Childress argues, is the possession of a guiding respectful Africentrism. The nurturing racial attitudes that Tommy embraces serve as the essential ingredients for the propagation of that culture. Unlike Bill and his bourgeois neighbors, Tommy responds to Oldtimer, her elder and a survivor of past black oppression, as an equal. Her caring acknowledgment of his identity as Edmond L. Matthews recovers his personhood and reclaims his rightful membership in the social framework from which the others have consistently excluded him.

Tommy does not assume she ''knows'' Oldtimer by reading his physical appearance as a sociopsychological text. She respectfully tells him, ''I'll call you Oldtimer like the rest but I like to know who I'm meetin'.'' The others have narrowly defined Matthews by what he is, not by who he is, while the who of his identity, as Tommy intuitively comprehends, is more important than the what. Her humanity toward Oldtimer is again demonstrated near the end of the play when he debases himself because of his intellectual deficiency. Tommy, gently rebuking his self-deprecation, remarks, ''Hush that talk . . . You know lotsa things, everybody does.''

Tommy's respectful regard for the intimate relationships between black men and women is apparent from the moment she enters Bill's apartment. Thirty and unmarried, she desires male intimacy and commitment; nevertheless, she is unwilling to sabotage the committed relationship of another black woman with a man in her own pursuit of love and companionship. For the benefit of any significant other possibly present in Bill's apartment, Tommy makes it clear that she will have nothing to do with a married or attached man. Speaking loudly, she asserts, ''Let's get somethin' straight. I didn't come bustin' in on the party, . . . I was asked. If you married and any wives or girl-friends round here . . . I'm innocent.'' Later, when she concerns herself more with the benefits that marriage and a family will confer on her individually rather than on the race as a whole, she seems uncomfortable. Implicit in her apology to Bill that both ''might be good; for your people as a race, but I was thinkin' 'bout myself a little,'' is the belief that considering herself first is a bit selfish.

Her familial and ancestral pasts empower Tommy. Unlike Bill, who is contemptuous of his parents and suburban upbringing, Tommy uses her now-deceased mother, a victim of spousal abandonment and its all too often ensuing cycle of poverty, as a major motivation for taking control of her life. Observing her mother ''tyin' up her stockin's with strips-a rag 'cause she didn't have no garters'' and having herself had ''[n]othin' much'' to eat when she returned home from school induced Tommy to seek employment and self-determination. She is not resentful that she had to terminate her schooling and does not blame her mother for their impoverished circumstances.

Tommy's account of her family history further demonstrates her racial groundedness. In contrast to Bill's detachment from the black community and black history, Tommy is closely attached to her hometown's ordinary, local people, often members of her own family, and their small but real accomplishments—winning a scholarship in a speech contest, for instance, or tracing the family history back to slaves from Sweetwater Springs, Virginia. Reciting the geneses of The Improved Benevolent Protective Order of Elks of the World and the African Methodist Episcopal Zion Church in which she taught for two years identifies her as an active bearer of oral tradition and preserver of her cultural heritage.

Directing no hatred toward whites, Tommy's Africentrism is not predicated on racism; she simply prefers the company of blacks. Presented with the choice of a live-in domestic job on Park Avenue with her own private bath and television and work in a Harlem dress factory among her friends, she chooses the latter. In contrast to Cynthia, who attempted to date white men but gave up when she realized that her education would not ensure her passage into the "so called 'integrated' world," Tommy affirms that she has never been interested in white men and doesn't find them physically attractive. "When I look at 'em," she tell Cynthia, "nothin' happens. . . . I don't hate 'em, don't love 'em . . . just nothin' shakes a-tall."

The Matriarchal Society

Cynthia, who is unable to shrug off the oppressive patriarchy of the movement and defines herself in contrast to the image of the black matriarch, perceives herself as the responsible black woman who willingly subjugates her autonomy, spirit, and vision to help establish a black patriarchal world order. Accepting the commands and chastisement of her husband, she is at his beck and call. Sonny-man's directive that she run down to their apartment and perform the gender-specific activity of cooking eggs for Bill's model draws from her a "weary look" but a complacent verbal response: "Oh, Sonny, that's such a lovely idea." Later, she is rendered mute by Sonny-man's childlike chiding of her for apologizing to Tommy for their role in Bill's deception. "Cynthia, I tell you all the time, keep outta other people's business. What the hell you got to do with who's gonna get what outta what?" Though she has not been totally deluded by the male rhetoric of the black consciousness movement, she has certainly accepted female subservience and the proselytizing of other women for the male cause.

The sociosexual hierarchy in which man is "mounter" and woman is "mounted" is not the acknowledged norm of the black society of *Wine in the Wilderness* but rather it is the ideal toward which Cynthia believes it should strive. Cynthia shares the view of Bill and Sonny-man that "the problem with the black subculture . . . is that it is a matriarchy in which woman is mounter, thereby depriving black men of their masculine role." She counsels Tommy that her lack of attractiveness to Bill emanates from her excessive brashness, independence, and dominance. The only way Tommy can rectify her masculinized behavior is by returning the black man's manhood, by staying in the background and allowing him to pursue her. Cynthia enumerates ways that black women can empower black men to counter the debilitating "Matriarchal Society," but suggests no course for female empowerment.

According to Cynthia, Tommy's domineering nature has been formed in a matriarchal society, a society "in which the women rule . . . the women have the power . . . the women head the house." Tommy's refutation of the charge that she was reared in a matriarchal environment once her "papa picked hisself up and ran off with some finger-poppin' woman" makes profound sense and deflates Cynthia's fraudulent appraisal of her upbringing in a single sentence: "We didn't have nothin' to rule over, not a pot nor a window." Her statement succinctly dramatizes the fact that women who survive in the absence of men do not constitute a power structure and that their survival tactics are not emblematic of man hating. Furthermore, Tommy's blunt pronouncement regarding her and her mother's powerlessness exposes the myth of black matriarchy: that it means social, economic, political, and personal power, yet power in any form has been the primary feature of life to which black women have had little or no access. Iterating her powerlessness, Tommy refuses to assume any responsibility for the loss of black manhood. "I didn't take it from him, how I'm gonna give it back," she rhetorically questions Cynthia.

Cynthia's wry parting utterance to Bill, that his portrait of "Wine in the Wilderness" is "exploitation," supports the inclusion of the earlier scene where the women converse in the absence of the men and points to the possibility of women's exchange functioning as a vehicle for consciousness raising, leading to in turn to sisterly honesty and solidarity. Gayle Austin draws the following conclusion from the construction of a "women only" scene in *Wine in the Wilderness*:

> There is in this play, unlike so many by male authors, a scene between women, between Tommy and Cynthia, in which Cynthia realizes long before Bill does that the actual Tommy is not of the image they had preconstructed of her. Tommy raises Cynthia's consciousness by sharing her experiences, which strike a note of recognition in Cynthia. This scene points out that race and gender liberation are separate but related pursuits for black women. The scene is permeated by a sense of honesty possible between women when they are not looked at by men. Such a scene is almost nonexistent in plays that do not portray women as active subjects. There is a power in women getting together that is dangerous to male dominance.

A truthful reconstructed image of Tommy, an outgrowth of the women's dialogue, raises Cynthia's consciousness and her caution. Hesitant to protest more aggressively the use of Tommy as the matriarchal messed-up chick and thereby be categorized as domineering herself, Cynthia stifles a desire to repudiate the slick glamorized image of black womanhood that bears no resemblance to her either.

Tommy's Anger

Counter to the ineffectual anger of the street riot, the liberating forces of anger and self-reliance empower Tommy not "to wait for anybody's by-your-leave to be a 'Wine in the Wilderness' woman." Tommy fights for herself because no one else will, and her strong sense of values and self steer her clear of "take low" politics based on class and privilege. "There's something inside-a me that says I ain' suppose to let nobody play me cheap. Don't care how much they know!" she avows to Bill. Recognition of her own self-worth allows Tommy to discount the false ideology that blames the matriarchal black woman for a legion of cultural, familial, and social ills. Rejecting educated black culture's view of her, she contends that "the real thing is takin' place on the inside . . . that's where the action is. That's 'Wine in the Wilderness,' . . . a woman that's a real one and a good one. And y'all just better believe I'm it." True liberation, Tommy discovers, is an internal phenomenon.

Not "cold but utter perfection," not "messed-up chick," not "bitch," not "*the* sister" but her own inscription of self sets Tommy up as "creator; she becomes the true artist etching the complexity of what it means to be a poor woman of color." Her outbursts of spirit and anger against the prescriptive roles that men attempt to impose on her resonate with the message that "women must begin to name themselves, to express their totality, to fill up the blank page with recognizable images of women".

Source: La Vinia Delois Jennings, "Blacks in the Abstract versus 'Flesh and Blood Niggers'," in *Alice Childress*, Twayne Publishers, 1995, pp. 65–75.

Janet Brown

In the following essay, the author discusses the protagonist's feminism and how her individual spirit overcomes the cultural limitations of patriarchy and race that surround her.

Wine in the Wilderness by Alice Childress shows a black woman's assertion of her autonomy in an "educated" black culture striving to imitate the white patriarchy. The associational clusters in the play reveal a false ideal of subservient, glamorous black womanhood, opposed to another false picture of contemporary black women as domineering matriarchs. The associational cluster surrounding Tommy, the protagonist, opposes both of these with an image of the self-reliant black woman seeking equality with men. Tommy's symbolic actions are assertions of her autonomy, at first unconscious expressions of her character, and finally, in the climactic scene, a conscious rejection of the false ideals held by the other characters.

Because the white hierarchical structure has not been fully adopted by the black culture in the play, it is possible for Tommy to transcend the limitations of such a hierarchy herself, and to convert the society around her to an ideal of equality and mutual respect. The philosophic conclusions of the play are idealistic. Tommy's individual spirit overcomes the societal determinants in the play, making it an optimistic statement of the feminist impulse. . . .

In the first scene of *Wine in the Wilderness*, two of the important clusters of associations in the play make their first appearances. Bill establishes the cluster of associations defining his ideal black woman, and the one defining her opposite, the "nothing" black woman, in this scene.

Before a word is spoken, the audience can tell from the setting that Bill has a taste for the exotic.

According to the stage directions, "The room is obviously *black* dominated, pieces of sculpture, wall hangings, paintings." It also "reflects an interest in other darker peoples of the world. . . . A Chinese incense-burner Buddha, an American Indian feathered war helmet, a Mexican serape, a Japanese fan, a West Indian travel poster." Bill's ideal woman, the "Wine in the Wilderness" painting, shares the exotic quality of his furnishings:

> Mother Africa, regal, black womanhood in her noblest form. . . . This Abyssinian maiden is paradise, . . . She's the Sudan, the Congo River, the Egyptian Pyramids . . . Her thighs are African Mahogany . . . she speaks and her words pour forth sparkling clear as the waters . . . Victoria Falls.

These images, with the set decorations, form a cluster of associations around exotic, foreign beauty.

The second cluster of associations in this scene forms around the opposite of this ideal, the "lost woman." Her associations are with "grass roots." She is "a back country chick right outta the wilds of Mississippi, . . . but she ain' never been near there. Born in Harlem, raised right here in Harlem, . . . but back country." She is "ignorant, unfeminine, coarse, rude . . . vulgar." This cluster of associations is the opposite of the first, negative rather than positive, and familiar rather than exotic.

Oldtimer, hearing the first cluster of associations, comments that Victoria Falls is a pretty name for a woman. So foreign are the associations clustering around Bill's ideal black woman that they are laughably unfamiliar to an uneducated American black like Oldtimer. In contrast, when Oldtimer hears the description of "the lost woman" later in this scene, he recognizes it at once, and says, "Oh, man, you talkin' 'bout my first wife." The positive qualities in Bill's triptych are unrecognizable to a black man off the street, but the negative qualities are a completely familiar critique of black women. Although this is evident to the audience from Oldtimer's reactions in the first scene, it takes Bill the rest of the play to reach this awareness.

In the last scene, Tommy tells him:

> If a black somebody is in a history book, or printed on a pitcher, or drawed on a paintin', . . . or if they're a statue, . . . dead, and outta the way, and can't talk back, then you dig 'em and full-a so much-a damn admiration and talk 'bout "*our*" history. But when you run into us livin' and breathin' ones, with the life's blood still pumpin' through us, . . . then you comin' on 'bout how we ain' never together. You hate us, that's what."

DESCRIBING HER DREAM TO CYNTHIA, TOMMY SAYS THAT SHE IS LOOKING FOR A MAN 'TO MEET ME HALFWAY.' SHE DOES NOT EXPECT HIM TO SUPPORT HER; RATHER 'THE BOTH OF YOU GOTTA PULL TOGETHER. THAT WAY YOU ACCOMPLISH.'"

And the stage directions tell us that Bill is "stung to the heart" by this distinction between the associations surrounding his ideal, and those surrounding his view of real black women.

When Tommy and Cynthia discuss Bill, the cluster of associations around his ideal grows. Cynthia says that in order to please Bill, Tommy should stop wearing her wig. She should also "let him do the talking. Learn to listen. Stay in the background a little. Ask his opinion . . . 'What do *you* think, Bill?'" This description fits very well with Bill's analysis of what is wrong with black women in a later scene. "Our women don't know a damn thing 'bout bein' feminine. *Give in* sometime." The ideal black woman, he says, should "throw them suppers together, keep your husband happy, raise the kids."

The cluster surrounding Bill's ideal of womanhood, then, includes not only exotic beauty but subservience to men. Cynthia and Bill envision a socio-sexual hierarchy in which men are dominant. Tommy, however, when she hears Cynthia's suggestions, says, "Mmmmm. 'Oh, hooty, hooty, hoo'," a comment she has made a few lines earlier in reference to white men. "The dullest people in the world. The way they talk . . . 'Oh, hooty, hooty, hoo' . . . break it down for me to A, B, C's." Tommy is correct in associating Cynthia's description with white men. The behavior that Cynthia says will please Bill is the behavior demanded of women in the white patriarchal society.

According to Cynthia, Tommy's problem is having been raised in a matriarchal society which has robbed black men of their manhood. In other words, Cynthia is describing a reversal of the socio-sexual hierarchy in which women are dominant.

Tommy rejects this idea, saying that women did not rule in her family because: "We didn't have nothin' to rule over, not a pot nor a window." When Cynthia tells Tommy to give the black man his manhood, Tommy answers, "I didn't take it from him, how I'm gonna give it back?"

To these two choices, the cluster of associations surrounding a subservient role for women in imitation of white patriarchy or the cluster surrounding a black matriarchy of "lost women," Tommy adds a third alternative: equal roles for women and men. Describing her dream to Cynthia, Tommy says that she is looking for a man "to meet me halfway." She does not expect him to support her; rather "the both of you gotta pull together. That way you accomplish." She hopes for companionship: "Somebody in my corner. Not to wake up by myself in the mornin' and face this world all alone." The third cluster of associations, defining Tommy's ideal, begins to form in this scene.

The three clusters of associations—around Bill's exotic ideal, around the "lost," matriarchal, black woman, and around Tommy, the woman seeking an equal relationship—continue to develop in subsequent scenes. In Tommy's next scene with Bill, the cluster of associations surrounding his ideal grows to include Afro-American history. He has pictures on his wall of Frederick Douglass and John Brown, and tells Tommy about other figures in black history with whom she is not familiar. But he discourages her questions about them, saying, "Trouble with our women, . . . they all wanta be great brains. Leave somethin' for a man to do." Although his ideal includes heroic men and women in history, it also includes ignorant women in the present day, allowing their men intellectual superiority.

Tommy also finds a picture on his wall of a blonde, blue-eyed model who, Bill says, could sit on her long, silky hair. Tommy responds bitterly, saying that it is this attitude that forces her to wear a wig, "'cause you and those like you go for long, silky hair, and this is the only way I can have some without burnin' my mother-grabbin' brains out." Although Bill claims that his ideal is black, it is in fact an imitation of the white ideal of womanhood symbolized by the blonde model: an ornamental, subservient woman without intellectual independence.

Tommy counters this false ideal when, later in the same scene, she overhears Bill describing his painting and believes that he is in love with her. Confident of his appreciation, she appears without the wig symbolic of the false ideal of beauty. In an effective reversal of Bill's history lesson, Tommy reveals her own local history, more personal and touching than Bill's version, and showing honest pride:

> I had a uncle who was an "Elk," . . . a member of "The Improved Benevolent Protective Order of Elks of the World": "The Henry Lincoln Johnson Lodge." You know, the white "Elks" are called "The Benevolent Protective Order of Elks" but the black "Elks are called "The *Improved* Benevolent Protective Order of Elks of *the World*." That's because the black "Elks" got the copyright first but the white "Elks" took us to court about it to keep us from usin' the name. Over fifteen hundred black folk went to jail for wearin' the "Elk" emblem on their coat lapel. Years ago, . . . that's what you call history."

Tommy's history, in contrast to Bill's, is filled with "real" people, often members of her own family, and their small but real accomplishments—winning a scholarship in a speech contest, for instance, or tracing the family history back to slaves from Sweetwater Springs, Virginia. She reveals her personality in her history and in preferences such as pink roses for corsages and four o'clocks for bush flowers.

Bill's negative associations with this kind of local, recent history, part of the cluster surrounding the "lost woman," appear in his description of his own family:

> Everybody in my family worked for the Post Office. They bought a house in Jamaica, Long Island. Everybody on that block bought an aluminum screen door with a duck on it, . . . or was it a swan? I guess that makes my favorite flower crab grass and hedges."

In Bill's mind, only the exotic is positive; the familiar is always vulgar, not "together."

The three clusters of associations finally conflict directly in the last scene when Tommy discovers that she is not "Wine in the Wilderness" to Bill, but a model for the "messed-up chick" in his triptych. Her wig figures symbolically once more, when Tommy tells Cynthia that Tommy does, indeed, have to wear a wig: "To soften the blow when yall go upside-a my head with a baseball bat." In other words, Tommy needs the wig, which she had felt safe in removing, as a defense against the false ideal of beauty.

Tommy makes the distinction between Bill's positive, exotic ideal and his negative view of real black women explicit in this final scene: "Ain't a-one-a us you like that's alive and walkin' by you on the street . . . you don't like flesh and blood niggers." It is not the screen doors with ducks on them that offended him in his childhood, she says: "You didn't like who was livin' behind them screen doors. Phoney Nigger!"

Bill's ideal is false not only because it is unrealistically exotic and based on white values, but also because it objectifies the black woman—makes an "other" of her just as the white society does of white women. In the final scene, Tommy asserts her autonomy, her ability to be subject rather than object, to be a "real," contemporary black woman who is admirable:

> Bill, I don't have to wait for anybody's by- your-leave to be a "Wine in the Wilderness" woman. I can be it if I wanta, . . . and I am. I am. I am. I'm not the one you made up and painted, the very pretty lady who can't talk back, . . . but I'm "Wine in the Wilderness" . . . alive and kickin' me . . . Tomorrow Marie, cussin' and fightin' and lookin' out for my damn self 'cause ain' nobody else 'round to do it, dontcha know.

The falsity of Bill's ideal finally becomes clear to him. He rejects the exotic "other," the black queen he has imagined. "She's not it at all, Tommy, This chick on the canvas, . . . nothin' but accessories, a dream I dreamed up outta the junk of my mind. *You* are . . . the real beautiful people." The painting, and Tommy, are explicitly identified as representative at the end of the play.

In fact, each of the associational clusters has elements on each of the three levels distinguished by Burke: the sensory, the familial, and the abstract. On the sensory level are the physical descriptions of the "Wine in the Wilderness" painting, of the planned painting of the "lost woman," and of Tommy when she appears as her natural self in an African throw, without her wig. On the familial level, the "Wine in the Wilderness" woman is "Mother Africa" and the "lost woman" is the domineering matriarch destroying her family. Tommy is associated with the positive, familial images of her family history.

On the abstract level, all three clusters operate as symbolic representations of black womanhood. The "Wine in the Wilderness" painting represents the false ideal of exotic beauty and subservience in imitation of the white socio-sexual hierarchy. The "lost woman" represents the black matriarchy, a reversed socio-sexual hierarchy supposedly

destroying black society. And Tommy represents the true societal ideal, autonomous and equal women and men.

Pattern of Symbolic Action

Tommy's assertions of her own autonomy and pride in her race make up the pattern of symbolic action of the play. From the beginning, Tommy displays these qualities unconsciously in her behavior. By asking Oldtimer's real name, something his friends have never bothered to do, she shows respect for another black person. "I'll call you Oldtimer like the rest but I like to know who I'm meetin'," she says. Later in this scene, Tommy explains that, although she could keep house for a white family on Park Avenue, she prefers to work in a factory and live among her black friends in Harlem. In her scene with Cynthia, Tommy says that she never gave up dating white men as Cynthia did. "I never had none to give up," she says. "I'm not soundin' on you. White folks, nothin' happens when I look at 'em. I don't hate 'em, don't love 'em, . . . just nothin' shakes a-tall. The dullest people in the world." Throughout the play, Tommy shows more respect and love for her own race than the others do, just as she shows respect for herself.

Tommy tells Cynthia that she would like to marry because she is lonely, but "I don't want any and everybody. What I want with a no-good piece-a nothin'?" Tommy has too much self-respect to marry someone she does not love and admire. Later in the play, she demonstrates this attitude again, when Bill brings her a frankfurter instead of Chinese food. She likes Bill very much, as she has just told Cynthia. But her liking and her hopes of marriage don't stop her from objecting to this supper. "You brought me a frank-footer? That's what you think a-me, a frank-footer?" Bill says that kings and queens eat frankfurters, but Tommy is not put off. "If a queen sent you out to buy her a bucket-a Foo-yung, you wouldn't come back with no lonely-ass frank-footer," she says.

Tommy's account of her family history further demonstrates her respect for herself and her race. And she consistently rejects Cynthia's and Bill's suggestions that she be more subservient, usually on grounds of common sense. When Cynthia suggests that she not chase Bill, "at least don't let it look that way. Let him pursue you," Tommy answers, "What if he won't? Men don't chase me much, not the kind I like." When Cynthia tells Tommy that black women "do for ourselves too much," Tommy answers, "If I don't, who's gonna do for me?" But to Bill's suggestion that she should "keep your husband happy, raise the kids," she responds, "Bein' married and havin' a family might be good for your people as a race, but I was thinkin' 'bout myself a little."

This statement demonstrates the unconscious quality of Tommy's assertions of autonomy. She seems to suggest that assertiveness and "thinking about herself" might be wrong, and that the subservient, objectified ideal held up by Cynthia and Bill might be more beneficial to her race. The turning point in the pattern of symbolic action comes when Tommy decides that she is right in asserting her autonomy.

Up until the point of her decision, the other characters have attempted to reprimand and correct Tommy's assertions of her autonomy. Tommy, while she has not backed down, has admitted that the others probably know more about correct behavior than she does. When Bill tells her to say "Afro-Americans," not "niggers," she does, at least for a while. She tells Cynthia: "If there's somethin' wrong that I can change, I'm ready to do it. Eighth grade, that's all I had of school. You a social worker, I know that mean college." Examining Bill's books and pictures on black history, Tommy says, "This room is full-a things I don't know nothin' about. How'll I get to know?" All of these comments indicate Tommy's acceptance of her own inferiority, and the unconscious quality of her own attitude of self-respect.

The turning point in the pattern of symbolic action comes when Tommy discovers that she was to model for the "messed-up chick" in the triptych. All of Tommy's former assertions of autonomy and all of the reproofs she accepted from Cynthia and Bill appear in a new light to her at that point. She throws Cynthia's advice on wigs back in her face in this scene. She corrects Sonny-man for calling her "the sister": "If you feelin' so brotherly why don't you say '*my*' sister? Ain't no we-ness in your talk. 'The' Afro-American, 'the' black man, there's no we-ness in you. Who you think *you* are?" She tells Oldtimer: "You their fool too. 'Til I got here they didn't even know your damn name." She rejects Bill's knowledge of Afro-American history, knocking his books to the floor and saying, "There's something inside-a me that says I ain' suppose to let *nobody* play me cheap. Don't care how much they know!" And she insists on calling Bill a nigger over

his protests that she is using the word incorrectly because, he says, "A nigger is a low, degraded person, *any* low degraded person." He looks it up in the dictionary to prove his point, and discovers that the definition is: "A Negro . . . a member of any dark-skinned people."

All of this only re-affirms what has already become clear to the audience: that Tommy is the truly autonomous individual, and Bill, Sonny-man and Cynthia are striving for a false ideal imitative of the white patriarchy, despite their education and sophistication. But the scene is important because it is the point in the play at which this distinction finally reaches Tommy's consciousness.

Tommy's earlier belief in the others' superior education and her fear that her assertiveness is not for the good of the race are laid to rest in this scene. She regrets her previous assumption of her own inferiority: "Trouble is I was Tommin' to you, to all of you, . . . 'Oh, maybe they gon' like me.' . . . I was your fool, thinkin' writers and painters know more'n me, that maybe a little bit of you would rub off on me."

Seeing the falsity of their ideal—the cluster of associations surrounding the "Wine in the Wilderness" painting—she asserts that the elements of this ideal are just "accessories": "Somethin' you add on or take off. The real thing is takin' place on the inside . . . that's where the action is. That's 'Wine in the Wilderness,' . . . a woman that's a real one and a good one. And yall just better believe I'm it." And she starts for the door, having become fully aware of her own autonomy.

This new awareness is the significant change in motivation in the play. Tommy realizes that it is a change, and tells the others, "I hate to do it but I have to thank you 'cause I'm walkin' out with much more than I brought in." She is walking out with a new awareness of her own strength, of her own power to assert her autonomy, something she has done unconsciously throughout the play.

Agent:Scene Ratio

Because *Wine in the Wilderness* shows a female protagonist, Tommy, asserting her autonomy in opposition to an unjust socio-sexual hierarchy, the play can be considered a feminist drama. Analysis of the agent-scene ratio reveals the play's affinity to a particular philosophic school: idealism. Because Tommy's achievement of autonomy is emphasized, the play is idealistic, showing the triumph of the individual spirit.

The depiction of scene, the unjust socio-sexual hierarchy, is unusual in *Wine in the Wilderness*. The socio-sexual hierarchy in which man is ''mounter'' and woman is ''mounted'' is not the norm in the society of the play, but rather is the ideal toward which the characters believe they should strive. The problem with the black sub-culture, Bill and Cynthia believe, is that it is a matriarchy in which woman is mounter, thereby depriving black men of their masculine role.

But Tommy disagrees with this depiction of her society. Women do not rule in the black society; rather, they are the most oppressed members of the oppressed black caste. Her own mother ''ruled'' in the home only because her father deserted the family: ''My pappa picked hisself up and run off with some finger-poppin' woman and we never hear another word 'til ten, twelve years later when a undertaker call up and ask if Mama wanta claim his body.'' If black women are strong, Tommy maintains that it is because they have had to be self-sufficient.

Because black women have been forced to be self-sufficient, and because black men have been oppressed, the black culture has not succeeded in imitating thoroughly the socio-sexual hierarchy of white society. As a result, it is possible for Tommy to assert her autonomy within this sub-culture, and to seek a relationship of equality outside of either a patriarchal or a matriarchal structure.

In doing so, she is at first opposed by the scene, the ''educated'' element of black society which maintains that a patriarchy is the race's hope of the future, and which holds up as ideal the glamorous but subservient, objectified ''Wine in the Wilderness'' woman. Finally, however, Tommy's assertion of her own individuality is revealed as a more sincere black pride, a more perfect ideal than Bill's painting or Cynthia's image of the patriarchal society.

According to Burke, if the agent's achievement is featured in a play, the play is idealistic. In an idealistic play, spirit triumphs over matter; the individual transcends societal limitations. In *Wine in the Wilderness*, Tommy's individual spirit transcends the hierarchical view of society formerly held by the other characters.

In the last scene of the play, Bill replaces the ''Wine in the Wilderness'' painting with a picture of Tommy, thus symbolically replacing the objectified, subservient image of black womanhood with Tommy, the autonomous subject. By speaking up for herself, Tommy has not only gained a new consciousness of her own individual spirit, but she has converted the society around her to a new ideal. Bill summarizes what her self-reliance and pride represent as an ideal for their race:

> Look at Tomorrow. She came through the biggest riot of all, . . . somethin' called ''Slavery,'' and she's even comin' through the ''now'' scene, . . . folks laughin' at her, even her own folks laughin' at her. And look *how* . . . with her head high up like she's poppin' her fingers at the world. (*Takes up charcoal pencil and tears old page off sketch pad so he can make a fresh drawing*) Aw, let me put it down, Tommy. ''Wine in the Wilderness,'' you gotta let me put it down so all the little boys and girls can look up and see you on the wall. And you know what they're gonna say? ''Hey, don't she look like somebody we know?''

Tommy is ''somebody we know,'' an individual whose spirit triumphs over matter, making the play an idealistic, feminist drama.

Conclusion

Because *Wine in the Wilderness* depicts a female protagonist asserting her autonomy in opposition to an unjust socio-sexual hierarchy, it is a feminist drama. The associational clusters in the play show a false ideal of subservient black womanhood, a negative cluster describing the supposed black matriarch, and a cluster describing the truly autonomous, individual black woman seeking equality. The pattern of symbolic action is one of Tommy's repeated assertions of her autonomy, at first unconscious and made from an assumption of inferiority. At the turning point in the play's motivation, Tommy becomes aware of her own self-worth, and converts the society of the play to her values. Agent dominates in this drama, in which Tommy's individual spirit transcends the false ideal of a patriarchal socio-sexual hierarchy. The play is an idealistic, optimistic statement of the feminist impulse.

Source: Janet Brown, ''*Wine in the Wilderness,*'' in *Feminist Drama,* Scarecrow Press, Inc., 1979, pp. 56–70.

SOURCES

Bennett, Susan, ''Alice Childress,'' in the *International Dictionary of Theatre–2: Playwrights,* edited by Mark Hawkins-Dady and Helen Ottaway, St. James Press, 1993, pp. 191–93.

Brown-Guillory, Elizabeth, ''Black Women Playwrights: Exorcising Myths,'' in *Phylon,* Vol. XLVIII, No. 3, Fall 1987, pp. 229–39.

———, ''Images of Blacks in Plays by Black Women,'' in *Phylon,* Vol. XLVII, No. 3, September, 1986, pp. 230–37.

Childress, Alice, *Wine in the Wilderness,* in *Plays by and about Women,* edited by Victoria Sullivan and James Hatch, Random House, 1973, pp. 381–421.

Sullivan, Victoria, and James Hatch, eds., ''Introduction,'' in *Plays by and about Women: An Anthology,* Random House, 1973, p. xv.

FURTHER READING

Andrews, Bert, and Paul Carter Harrison, *In the Shadow of the Great White Way: Images from the Black Theatre,* Thunder's Mouth Press, 1989.
    This photographic history of Black Theater in the United States is comprised of photographs by Andrews and text by Harrison.

Branch, William B., ed., *Black Thunder: An Anthology of Contemporary African American Drama,* Penguin Books, 1992.
    Branch provides a collection of plays by contemporary African-American writers, such as Amiri Baraka and August Wilson.

Brown-Guillory, Elizabeth, *Their Place on the Stage: Black Women Playwrights in America,* Greenwood Press, 1988.
    Brown-Guillory offers a historical and critical overview of the role of African-American women playwrights in the history of African-American theater.

———, ed., *Wines in the Wilderness: Plays by African-American Women from the Harlem Renaissance to the Present,* Greenwood Press, 1990.
    Brown-Guillory has compiled an anthology of plays by African-American women, including Marita Bonner, Georgia Douglass Camp, Sonia Sanchez, and Alice Childress.

Jennings, La Vinia Delois, *Alice Childress,* Twayne, 1995.
    Jennings offers criticism and interpretation of Childress's major works.

Lewis, Samella S., *African-American Art and Artists,* University of California Press, 1994.
    Lewis provides a historical overview of African-American art, with biographical information on key artists.

McElroy, Guy C., Richard J. Powell, and Sharon F. Patton, *African-American Artists, 1880–1987: Selections from the Evans-Tibbs Collection,* University of Washington Press, 1989.
    This book of reprints of African-American art in the twentieth century is drawn from collections of the Smithsonian Institution.

Schoener, Allon, ed., *Harlem on My Mind: Cultural Capital of Black America, 1900–1968,* New Press, 1995.
    Schoener provides a pictorial history of the arts in Harlem, drawn from collections of the Metropolitan Museum of Art in New York City.

Williams, Mance, *Black Theater in the 1960s and 1970s: A Historical-Critical Analysis of the Movement,* Greenwood Press, 1985 (originally published in 1969).
    Williams provides a historical overview of African-American theater during the period in which Childress's play was first performed.

Y2K

ARTHUR KOPIT

1999

Like some of Kopit's other plays, *Y2K* is a social commentary with a hint of darkness. Through a computer, a man and wife, with a perhaps not highly moral sexual history, are thrown into another reality where everything they do or don't do is blown out of proportion. The main action of the play is interrupted by the memory sequences of Costa Astrakhan, a self-centered teenager who, if not insane, is delighted by the power a computer can give him. While these sequences seem more like a sexual fantasy than reality, Astrakhan translates them into digital fact. The devastation to the married couple that follows is sudden and complete; while the Secret Service is aware of Astrakhan's actions, Astrakhan himself seems to have escaped capture at the end of the play.

While *Y2K* does touch on the horror of identity theft and the dangers of privacy invasion in the digital age, the main theme is how revenge (in this case, Astrakhan's revenge upon Joseph, who has kicked Astrakhan out of his class) can take on a new form through technology. From his depiction of unscrupulous federal agents to his portrayal of an implacable computer hacker, Kopit shows that power corrupts. He places the focus on the abuse of authority, which happens simply because it is possible.

Arthur Kopit

AUTHOR BIOGRAPHY

Born May 10, 1937, in New York City, New York, Arthur Kopit is a contemporary American playwright who is sensitive to the honor and the humiliation of the human condition. His first successful play, *Oh Dad, Poor Dad, Mama's Hung You in the Closet and I'm Feelin' So Sad,* debuted in 1960.

Kopit is the son of George and Maxine (Dubin) Kopit; his father was a jeweler in Long Island, New York. When Kopit enrolled in Harvard University, he was interested in engineering, but he soon found that he had a talent for the arts. During his college years, Kopit won two playwriting contests. He directed six of his seven plays that were produced at Harvard.

The Questioning of Nick, Kopit's first one-act drama, was a serious play about teenage rebellion written during the spring of 1957 for Dunster House Drama Workshop at Harvard University. *Don Juan in Texas,* Kopit's witty turn on the American Western, was also written in 1957. In 1958, Kopit wrote *On the Runway of Life, You Never Know What's Coming Off Next,* which features a fifteen-year-old boy seeking adventure in a carnival. In 1958 Kopit

also wrote *Across the River and into the Jungle,* a parody of Ernest Hemingway's 1950 novel *Across the River and into the Trees.*

Other Kopit plays include *Gemini* (1957), *Aubad* (1959), *Sing to Me through Open Windows* (1959), *To Dwell in a Place of Strangers* (1959), *Asylum: or What the Gentlemen Are Up To, and As for the Ladies* (1963), *The Day the Whores Came Out to Play Tennis* (1965), *Indians* (1968), *Wings* (1978), *End of the World with Symposium to Follow* (1984), and *Road to Nirvana* (1991). For his musical *Nine,* Kopit won the Best Musical Tony award in 1982.

At the close of the twentieth century, Kopit wrote *Y2K,* which deals with the threat the Internet poses to personal privacy. According to the preface he wrote for the play, Kopit was inspired in 1999 by the investigation into then-president Bill Clinton's affair with Monica Lewinsky. The play conveys the fear of having one's reality suddenly changed by outside forces.

Ranging from explorations of serious issues to satire, Kopit's plays expose the elements of daily life, whether they are cruel, whimsical, or threatening.

Kopit is married to Leslie Ann Garis and has three children: Alex, Ben, and Kathleen. He graduated cum laude with a bachelor's degree from Harvard University in 1959 and is a member of Phi Beta Kappa. He is also a member of the Writer's Guild of America, the Dramatists Guild, the Hasty Pudding Society, and the Signet Society.

PLOT SUMMARY

Astrakhan Enters
Y2K begins with Astrakhan in the spotlight on stage, stating that he is everywhere and on the hunt. Like the Greek chorus, Astrakhan introduces the play, explains the action, and concludes the drama.

Warehouse Scene
Secret Service agents Orin Slake and Dennis McAlvane have taken Joseph Elliot to an abandoned warehouse that smells of dead meat in New York City's Soho neighborhood. Just as in classic spy thrillers when the person being interrogated is under a bright light, Joseph is sitting under a single bulb.

The two agents allow Joseph to call his lawyer but refuse to give him their names. Slake and

McAlvane ask Joseph apparently nonsensical questions about names and whether he has had any contact with someone who calls himself ISeeU. Joseph says that neither he nor his wife Joanne is acquainted with anyone who has identified himself in that way.

Living Room Scene 1

Astrakhan declares that he can see everything and that no one can hide from him.

The spotlight moves to the Elliots. Joseph tries to tell Joanne about his interrogation, but she tells him about his daughter Emma's receiving a crank call, which sounded as though it were in Joseph's voice.

The lights return to Astrakhan. With increasing arrogance, Astrakhan states that he is a "Master of Downloading." He admits to toying with others through his knowledge of computers.

As the action returns to the Elliots, Joseph explains his interrogation. Joanne reveals why she was unable to listen to Joseph earlier: she has had a run-in with her ex-husband, Francis Summerhays. An indication of Joseph's mistrust of his wife surfaces as he questions her as to whether she is still in love with Francis. After Joanne reassures him, the couple embraces.

Astrakhan returns to the spotlight and gives details on Joanne's history, including her supposed affair with Joseph while Joseph's wife was dying of cancer.

Office Interrogation

Slake and McAlvane appear in Joseph's office, and their questions about his computer use turn into threats of arrest. An interesting fact in this scene is that Joseph apparently publishes books that might attract the attention of the authorities. The book *Mapplethorpe* (an apparent reference to the controversial artist Robert Mapplethorpe, known for his homoerotic photographs) is one McAlvane thinks that Joseph should not be proud of. This gives possible support to Astrakhan's later claim that Joseph loved the plagiarized pornographic story that Astrakhan submitted in class as his own work.

During this second interrogation, Astrakhan interrupts from time to time to explain how he targets someone through a computer. At the end of the scene, he claims that he had a lurid affair with Joseph's wife after becoming one of Joseph's stu-

dents in a writing class. His memory, Astrakhan says, becomes "clearer" each time he goes over the details, which is a hint that perhaps he is embellishing.

Astrakhan Sequence

This sequence is presented as a memory, but it is presented by Astrakhan; therefore, it is very likely that what actually happened is very different from what is presented.

Astrakhan arrives in the Elliots's living room. He claims that he is fifteen but that drug use has made him seem older. Instead of finding this alarming, Joseph is flattered into thinking that he has been responsible for stopping Astrakhan's drug use. Both Joseph and Joanne have read and are impressed by the pornographic story Astrakhan wrote for Joseph's class, and Joanne is particularly delighted by its filthiness. Soon she is seducing Astrakhan by displaying herself unclothed in front of him. Joanne says that Joseph tells his students, "Everything you invent is true," which seems to be something Astrakhan has adopted as his mantra. The sequence ends with Joanne's rejection of Astrakhan.

Living Room Scene 2

Joseph is even more suspicious of his wife, for he questions her about a trip she took to see her mother. He explains how he unintentionally gave Astrakhan access to their identities. When Joseph talks about connecting to Joanne's computer, it seems to be an allusion to his sexual possession of his wife, because he says that he found it stimulating.

In between drinks, Joseph tells Joanne that Astrakhan has usurped their identities and made her into a porno star and him into a child molester. Joanne immediately says that allegations of molestation against Joseph are ridiculous, but it is evident that Joseph half-believes the allegations against her. He produces photos, which she tries, unconvincingly, to discredit. Then Joseph tells her that Astrakhan has falsified records to make it look like he is the son of Joseph and his first wife.

Admitting that there is some truth in some of the things that Astrakhan has invented about him, Joseph tells Joanne he is sure that the situation is similar for her. Because they are penniless (Astrakhan has stolen all their money after stealing their identities), Joseph says that they are unable to follow Joanne's suggestion that they hire a private detective to find Astrakhan. Instead, he suggests that she resign from her job as he did from his. His mistrust of her is evident.

Astrakhan ends the scene as the spotlight moves to him. He is triumphant that things will be as he remembers them.

CHARACTERS

Costa Astrakhan

Astrakhan is a teenager who is obsessed with asserting his own importance. He associates nearly everything with sexuality, including his need to control others. As he strives to bolster his ego, Astrakhan is, in his own words, "as relentless as the wrath of God." But unlike God, Astrakhan does not care what the truth is; he would rather make up his own version of events. In Astrakhan, there is no recognition of factual reality, because whatever he says is "honest," according to him, whether it is completely contrived or partially accurate.

Astrakhan is nineteen, but he is so wasted and haunted that he looks more like he's in his middle twenties. His hair is neon blue; some actors, however, have chosen to portray him with hair sticking on up on end or wearing a peaked cap. His shoes are of electric green suede and his sunglasses are almond-shaped. He wears a T-shirt that says "Nemesis." His leather pants and leather jacket are reminiscent of those worn by Mel Gibson in *Road Warrior.*

Astrakhan provides many of the details about the Elliots, the main characters. As an unreliable source, he cannot be trusted to be giving completely accurate information, although Joseph recognizes that some of the details are factual.

A student in Joseph's writing class who was kicked out for plagiarism, Astrakhan does not seem to have a grasp on what is real and what is not. He makes up information, blending it with bits of truth until fact and fiction are almost indistinguishable. Joanne says that Astrakhan is obviously insane; if so, he is also very clever, for he is able to completely obliterate the Elliots's real identities as well as their bank accounts.

Astrakhan goes by several aliases. He has attracted the attention of the Secret Service by his ability to hack into computers and create digital identities. He creates identities for the Elliots that make them seem more despicable than they perhaps really are. He also makes it seem as if he is Joseph's son by his first wife.

BcuzICan

See Costa Astrakhan

Joanne Summerhays Elliot

Joanne is an enigmatic woman who wishes to be "tethered" to the one she loves. Her idea of love is of being "sheltered" by the strength of her lover. She seems to be constantly trying to reassure her husband that she is true to him while at the same time being a bit defiant about it. Although she explains to Joseph that she loves him, she admits that at one time she loved her ex-husband.

Joanne is in her late thirties. Her maiden name is Joanne Elizabeth Simpson. Both her parents were university professors: her father taught moral philosophy and her mother taught the flute. There may be some irony in Joanne's background because it is so seemingly innocent and wholesome, yet Joanne displays a knowledge of coarse behavior that scarcely matches this picture.

If played by an American actress, Joanne is supposed to have been born October 15, 1961, in Ann Arbor, Michigan, and to have graduated in 1983 from Princeton. If played by a British actress, she is supposed to have been born in a small town not far from the University of Manchester and to have graduated from Oxford. Her major was art history; she works at Sotheby's auction house as an administrative assistant specializing in jade and Chinese porcelain.

Joanne's first husband, Francis Summerhays, has been harassing her. He is a venture capitalist whom she met at an Asian art auction. The marriage lasted less than a year, and even though Francis supposedly has been calling Joanne incessantly and leaving disgusting messages, she still believes he is capable of acting like a perfect gentleman. Whether Francis is actually doing everything Joanne says he is, is difficult to determine. How much Joanne can be trusted is questionable since she admits to lying at least once in the play.

Joanne supposedly met and pursued Joseph while she and he were still married to their first partners. Information about her moral character is contradictory, so it seems possible, although not definite, that this is true. While she calls Joseph her rock and chastises him for blasphemy, she herself uses crass language. All in all, it is possible that her behavior may not be as pure as she would like Joseph to think.

According to Astrakhan, Joanne had an affair with him after she married Joseph. He says that she had eight encounters just to satisfy her lust and then told Astrakhan it was over. Also according to Astrakhan, Joanne loves filthy books; however, she shows a definite distaste for pornography.

Whether Joanne is without any moral scruples is hard to determine; that she is capable of committing adultery seems somewhat likely since she was willing to get into a limousine with her ex-husband and to lie to Joseph about it. Like Joseph, she seems to turn to vodka throughout the play. Also like Joseph, she seems fixated on sexual topics and crude language.

Joseph Elliot

Joseph is an editor at Random House. He seems concerned about whether his wife is faithful to him. Although he seems to want to believe that she is not capable of immoral behavior, he has his doubts. He tries to convince a Secret Service agent that his wife is not the kind of woman to use foul language, but he obviously knows this is not necessarily the case, since at the same time he adds, ''Who can say how her youth was spent?'' Even though he is extremely defensive when the agent suggests that ISeeU (Astrakhan) knows his wife, Joseph's suspicions that Joanne is capable of cheating on him frequently surface. While he exhibits jealousy and questions his wife's actions, Joseph does not examine his own behaviors very closely.

Joseph is in his early fifties. He drinks quite a bit throughout the play, starting with a vodka and tonic and apparently ending with straight vodka. He also refers to having been drinking Bloody Marys on the day he inadvertently gave Astrakhan access to his computer. He seems to urge drinks on his wife throughout the play.

Joseph's first wife, Annabel, died of cancer. While she was undergoing chemotherapy, Annabel became pregnant and chose to have an abortion in Paris. Astrakhan claims the child was actually delivered; he has falsified documents to show that he is the child.

Joseph's daughter, Emma, is Annabel's daughter. She is in Paris when the play starts and tells Joanne that she has received an obscene phone call that sounded like her father's voice. At the age of twelve, Emma supposedly refused to attend her father's second wedding, which, if true, may indicate that Joseph's behavior to his first wife was less than exemplary.

Just how much Joseph tells the truth is somewhat obscured. When questioned by federal agents, he claims that he does not have much use for his computer; yet he not only has a computer, he also bought one for his wife. When talking to Joanne, he calls his computer a ''lovely new machine'' and admits that he likes visiting Web sites. Yet he tells Slake and McAlvane that he doesn't have difficulty resisting the urge to go online.

FlowBare

See Costa Astrakhan

ISeeU

See Costa Astrakhan

Dennis McAlvane

McAlvane is in the Secret Service and seems intent upon pleasing his superior, Slake. He is quick to speak in Slake's direction and quick to act at Slake's request. Without really showing a personality of his own, McAlvane is eager to display a knowledge of Slake's methods and desires. Slake calls him ''Mac'' and seems to look upon him as a promising protégé.

McAlvane is a bit younger than Slake, which would put him in his thirties. He is the junior federal agent investigating Astrakhan's activities. Described by Kopit as a trainee trying to emulate Slake, McAlvane does not take the initiative in the two sessions in which he and Slake question Joseph. He is like an echo, repeating what Slake says and reinforcing his arguments. When he does take the lead in talking about sending the Elliots to jail, he receives a mild reproof from Slake. Immediately, McAlvane takes his cue, agreeing with Slake's adjustment to his statement about Joanne being the most likely one to be imprisoned as long as Joseph cooperates.

Orin Slake

Slake is supposed to look as if he is in his forties. Dressed in a dark, undistinguished suit and tie, he has an open, friendly face and easy smile. He even pretends that he would be willing to conduct the interview with Joseph in a restaurant. This demeanor is deceptive, however. Slake is very serious about his job, which is to investigate the computer fraud perpetrated by Astrakhan, otherwise known as ''ISeeU'' or ''BCuzICan.''

Like Astrakhan, Slake is not above snooping and knows that Joseph has a lunch appointment at the Gramercy Tavern in an hour. He also indicates that he has records as to exactly how much time Joseph spends on the Internet. His name, ''Slake,'' may suggest that he must satisfy his desire to know all about the case.

Displaying a veneer of geniality that thinly masks his zeal for closing in on his prey, Slake tells Joseph to stop ''pretending'' and to admit the truth. He insinuates that Joanne is involved in something illegal and will be arrested even if Joseph is not. Slake's main role seems to be that of interrogator, the kind who assumes guilt whether it is present or not.

THEMES

Appearances

Illusion is something magicians make a living creating, and Astrakhan makes a life of it. To himself, he appears bigger than life, almost godlike. In reality, he is a criminal whom federal agents are trying to apprehend. He toys with them, keeping up the appearance of power and control.

In Shakespeare's *As You Like It,* the heroine, Rosalind, poses as a man and hides her true appearance from the man she loves. So too does Joanne keep back her true nature from her husband. She may have a scandalous past, as the pictures Joseph shows her seem to indicate, but she never admits to it. Although she complains to Joseph that she is ''staggered at how little'' he understands her, Joanne seems to prefer to maintain appearances that make it impossible for him to truly know her. Joseph also is interested in maintaining appearances. He is elusive about his computer use, claiming that he prefers to write things out by hand. It seems likely that he publishes works of dubious merit.

Infidelity

The question of faithfulness is key in the Elliots' marriage. They were not faithful to their first spouses, so how can they be sure they are faithful to each other? Joanne does seem to have a little more contact with her ex-husband, Francis, than is normal, and Joseph is fixated on whether she is cheating on him. He even asks her if she gets a charge from the indecent way Francis talks to her.

Jealousy is already Joseph's weak point, but Astrakhan adds fuel to the fire when he manufactures evidence (if it is manufactured) of a sexual

liaison between himself and Joanne. Like Iago, who stirs up Othello's mistrust of Desdemona in Shakespeare's play *Othello,* Astrakhan incites Joseph's suspicions of his wife. These suspicions seem to be confirmed by the photos that Astrakhan has made available, though Joseph knows that Astrakhan has invented some incorrect information about his own fidelity.

Identity Theft

At the core of every human being is identity. People spend years defining who they are. They decide where to go to college, what to choose as a career, and whom to marry. They build reputations, assets, and credit histories. All that the Elliots have built is wiped out with Astrakhan's computer hacking. In changing their identities, Astrakhan is usurping them.

Troubled by a lack of self-esteem and recognition, Astrakhan decides that he is not satisfied with his parents. His mother, Glenda, was a dental hygienist and sometime prostitute killed by her former husband, a tap dancer with Tourette's Syndrome (an inherited, neurological disorder characterized by repeated involuntary movements and uncontrollable vocal sounds, often including profanity). Astrakhan decides that they are not his real parents, so he rewrites history to become Joseph's son. He promises to take care of his new ''parents'' with the financial resources he has stolen from them. The Elliots lose their identities, and Astrakhan gains a new one.

Privacy and the Internet

Computer technology is a useful tool in *Y2K.* Joanne keeps a journal on the computer. Joseph uses it to research material he is about to publish. But as they go about using the technology, they become vulnerable. Their innermost thoughts and feelings are exposed for someone else to use against them.

As home computers become networked to global servers, society in the twenty-first century becomes increasingly threatened by privacy invasion. As Keith Regan points out in *E-Commerce Times,* if a person has an e-mail address, someone is selling information about that person to the highest bidder. People prefer to think that their information remains in one place. The Elliots apparently believed that until it was too late.

Though a company may assure customers that their personal data will not be sold to others, the fact is that when a company changes hands, most likely the information, too, will be sold. There is no telling exactly where the information will end up, as Joseph learns.

According to the Federal Trade Commission, although computer technology makes it easier for companies to share information, it also makes it easier for law enforcement to track down criminals and prevent fraud. It advises, however, that people take precautions as to how much information they submit online. Perhaps such a warning is too late for most people. In Kopit's *Y2K,* the damage was done quickly, and it was apparently irreversible.

Sexual Impropriety

A distrusting couple, the Elliots have both been married before and seem a little uncomfortable in their second marriage. Perhaps that is because they committed adultery together while they were married to their previous spouses. Or perhaps it is because neither one can resist sexual impropriety.

Joseph and Joanne accuse each other of sexual liaisons with other people. They use very coarse terms to communicate. Elyse Sommer points out in *CurtainUp* that the way Joseph and Joanne talk to each other is not the way people normally talk to each other.

Charles McNulty notes in *Village Voice* that *Y2K* is "erotically charged." Demonstrations of affection and love between Joseph and Joanne almost seem out of place, because the language they use with each other is lewd rather than respectful. Whether the sexual impropriety is mostly just talk or whether there is substance behind it is not certain, but it is a prevalent theme that drives the play.

STYLE

Narrator

Y2K is a contemporary drama narrated by Astrakhan, a teenager with the ability to hack into computers but apparently with little else in the way of accomplishments. He invents a number of events and details, so he is not a reliable narrator. Since he is also the villain of the piece, his purpose seems to be to create the story as well as to tell it.

The play proceeds in a disjointed style, with past and present blending together. Astrakhan's version of reality becomes dominant, so that it is

TOPICS FOR FURTHER STUDY

- At the end of the play, Astrakhan seems to get away with his crimes. Write a different ending in which he somehow has to pay for what he has done. Imitate Kopit's style so that your ending blends with the rest of the play and seems plausible.

- Research Internet privacy. What kinds of security software solutions are available? Are they effective? What kinds of regulations govern the Internet? Are they sufficient? Write a one-page summary of your findings.

- One of the themes in *Y2K* is revenge. The preface quotes Stalin's statement on the sweetness of vengeance, "To choose one's victims, to prepare one's plan minutely, to slake an implacable vengeance, and then to go to bed . . . there is nothing sweeter in the world." Is revenge sweet or is it bitter? Write an answer that draws on Kopit's play and on your own experience.

- In the play, Costa Astrakhan repeatedly says that he is honest. Do you think that he is aware or unaware that he is dishonest? Explain why or why not.

difficult to determine if he invented most of the events, especially those that are explicitly sexual. At the end of the drama, Astrakhan's version of what happened has become a digital reality that the Elliots must cope with.

Setting

Set at the end of 1999, *Y2K* takes place just before the new millennium. There is considerable concern that computers not programmed to function in years with dates beyond 1999 will disrupt many of the normal functions of society. A book Joseph is about to publish, *Crisis,* predicts doom. Joseph questions whether this prediction is accurate. The physical settings vary from the ordinary to the eerie. For the most part, the play takes place in the Elliots's living room or in Joseph's office. But the play starts in an abandoned warehouse, a setting in which the Secret Service agents seem comfortable but in which Joseph is not.

Subject

Y2K deals with sexual indiscretions and how destructive they can be when made public. Joseph Elliot discovers that the computer age makes both discovering and using such information easier; he compares the situation to a house of cards that is "ready to come toppling at the slightest wind." One of Astrakhan's aliases is "BCuzICan." Kopit shows that once this kind of ammunition exists, it will be used, simply because it can be. The subject matter of the play was inspired by Kenneth Starr's investigation into Bill Clinton's sexual indiscretions and his later testimony about them, according to Kopit's preface.

HISTORICAL CONTEXT

The Monica Lewinsky Scandal

In June 1995, Monica Lewinsky began an internship at the White House. In mid-January 1998, FBI agents questioned Lewinsky about whether she had had a sexual relationship with then-president Bill Clinton. The next day, in a deposition he gave in another case involving allegations of sexual misconduct with Paula Jones, Clinton denied that he had had sexual relations with Lewinsky. The story of a possible affair with Lewinsky, and lying to cover it up, broke to the media just four days later, and the scandal escalated from there.

Federal independent counsel Kenneth Starr expanded his investigation of the Paula Jones suit to include Lewinsky. He filed a motion on April 14, 1998, to compel testimony about Lewinsky's relationship with Clinton from Secret Service agents. Starr also wanted to question Lewinsky, and she agreed to answer Starr's questions in return for immunity from prosecution. She testified before a grand jury on August 6, 1998, that she had had a sexual relationship with Clinton.

After a lengthy and expensive investigation into his relationship with Lewinsky and into statements he had made under oath about that relationship, Clinton was impeached. On December 19, 1998, the House of Representatives passed two articles of impeachment against him, with eleven counts of perjury, obstruction of justice, and abuse of power. Clinton was the second president of the United States to be impeached while in office. (Andrew Johnson was impeached in 1868.)

Impeachment is one step in the process that may lead to a public official being removed from office, if the official is also convicted of the crimes for which he or she is impeached. Because Clinton was not convicted, he was not removed from office. As he finished his term in January 2001, Clinton avoided indictment for lying under oath by agreeing to pay $25,000 in fines and accepting a five-year suspension of his license to practice law.

Y2K Fears

Y2K stands for Year 2000. (*K* is an abbreviation for thousand.) In the late 1990s, there was growing fear that computers whose built-in, two-digit calendars were not programmed to recognize *00* as signifying the year 2000 would fail to operate beginning at midnight on January 1 of that year. Since computers are involved in providing most services necessary to modern cities, businesses, and residences, there was a great deal of concern about what systems would fail and what the results might be. Some of the concerns included loss of computer data, loss of utilities and power, loss of telephone services, breakdowns in transportation (including air-control systems), and the resulting social and economic chaos.

In *Time Bomb 2000,* written to help people prepare for the possible disruption in their lives, Edward and Jennifer Yourdon advised people to "spend the remaining months until the new millennium paring down and simplifying your life, so that you can face it with as much flexibility as possible." And they were among the more moderate voices. The anticipated problems did not develop, however. Virtually all computer systems were upgraded to recognize *00* as the year 2000 before the date changed. The new millennium was celebrated around the world with no major disruptions in services.

CRITICAL OVERVIEW

Many reviewers regarded *Y2K* as inferior to Kopit's other notable works, such as *Oh Dad, Poor Dad,*

Mama's Hung You in the Closet and I'm Feelin' So Sad, Wings, and *Indians.* John Simon wrote in *New York Magazine* that *Y2K* is not a believable story and not of the same quality as Kopit's respected works. McNulty observed in *Village Voice,* "Kopit makes things somewhat more confusing than he needs to." Sommer in *CurtainUp* called *Y2K* "a thriller that fails to thrill" and compared it unfavorably to John Guare's *Six Degrees of Separation* and Craig Lucas's *Dying Gaul,* complaining that Kopit's play "has none of the complexity and depth of either." She concluded, "Presumably the resolution that never comes is intended to leave you pondering the issue of our eroding privacy. . . . In point of fact, you're simply left feeling you've had an unsatisfying meal that didn't even offer a dessert."

Writing in *Variety,* Charles Isherwood allowed, "The play turns on authentically disturbing questions. "He added, though, "Kopit doesn't deeply explore these issues. He's content to tell a scary story, without examining the larger issues it raises." Isherwood concluded by agreeing with Sommer that "the play seems slight indeed, and even a little half-baked."

On the other hand, some critics welcomed *Y2K* as an exploration of the moral risks of the information age. Jeffrey Eric Jenkins, writing in *Seattle Post-Intelligencer,* called the play "riveting, paranoic, and plausible." Martin F. Kohn of the *Detroit Free Press* described it as "a chilling play that taps into whatever millennial angst is floating nearby."

CRITICISM

April Schulthies

Schulthies is an editor who holds a master's degree in English literature and teaches English at the community college level. In the following essay, she examines surrealistic evil and its harmful effects in Kopit's play.

Arthur Kopit's contemporary drama *Y2K* creates a feeling of lurking evil in a surrealistic setting. Kopit suggests an ominous unreality that hints at, rather than shouts of, potential danger. The evil feels close at hand because it "lives" in personal computers,

Playbill cover from the 1999 theatrical production of Y2K, *directed by Bob Balaban*

which people keep in their private homes. As people use their computers, they reveal personal information in e-mails and in their Internet use. In *Y2K,* Kopit poses the question, what if the most personal details of people's lives could be tapped into and used against them?

Computers "talk" to one another at high speeds, networks record messages sent and received, and information of all kinds is submitted and accepted. But, as Kopit points out, information is also being tracked. Personal profiles are collected and saved. "Cookies" store strings of text on a user's computer in order to monitor the user's activities. Servers record the Internet Protocol address of the user and sometimes link it to personal information. As his drama progresses, Kopit shows that as people are served by the computer, the computer is serving others who may be evil.

Kopit's *Y2K* shows the disastrous effects of privacy invasion in the technological age. When Joseph Elliot uses his computer, he is unaware of the lurking presence of someone bent on revenge. But other eyes can monitor his progress through a Web site and keep track of his preferences and personal data. Later Joseph is shocked to find out that using

> IN *Y2K,* KOPIT POSES THE QUESTION, WHAT IF THE MOST PERSONAL DETAILS OF PEOPLE'S LIVES COULD BE TAPPED INTO AND USED AGAINST THEM?''

his computer opened the door to prying eyes, because, as he relates to his wife, he thought the computer was his ''FRIEND.''

Joseph and his wife learn that there are eyes eagerly compiling all the personal data they can. As their daily lives crumble like so many bits of scrambled data, the Elliots enter a surrealistic world, haunted by the fact that their personal identities are not their own.

Among the billions of people on the earth, many use computers on a daily basis. The scope for privacy invasion is vast and frightening. In *Y2K,* Kopit skims the surface of such a possibility, using a villain who respects no one and who recognizes no limits. Inspired by the way Kenneth Starr pursued Monica Lewinsky after her affair with President Clinton, Kopit displays a personal vendetta that destroys the lives of others.

In his preface to the drama, Kopit writes that he was impressed by what he called Starr's ''fascism.'' Webster's dictionary defines fascism as ''a strongly nationalistic regime characterized by regimentation, rigid censorship, and suppression of opposition.'' Kopit sees these qualities in the political environment that allowed Kenneth Starr to examine the most intimate details of Lewinsky's life.

Y2K starts off in an abandoned warehouse, where Joseph is being questioned by two Secret Service men. It is an unbelievable setting and an unbelievable circumstance; Joseph is being interrogated, but interrogated with unlikely, nonsensical questions that he does not appear to understand. This is followed by a scene in which Joseph learns that his daughter has called his apartment and said that she received an obscene phone call from someone who sounded like him.

Unreality follows unreality in such a tangle that it is hard to make sense of the facts. Most of the play takes place in the living room of Joseph and Joanne, who are both in their second marriage. In what is supposedly a private domain, the two are watched by the play's villain, the young and vindictive Costa Astrakhan.

Suffering from an apparent God complex, Astrakhan is an outrageous figure with neon hair and neon shoes. He has a taste for power that he is only able to satisfy through the computer. ''And though you cannot see where I really am, I can see all of you,'' Astrakhan gloats.

Astrakhan is infuriated over being accused of cheating, though he admits to the audience he has cheated. Expelled from Joseph Elliot's class for plagiarism, Astrakhan decides that no one can hide from him. Through technology, he has the power to slake his desire for revenge.

As Kopit notes in his preface, the pursuit of Monica Lewinsky by Kenneth Starr was something Kopit found alarming. With his penchant for prying, Astrakhan seems to represent Kenneth Starr. If so, then Astrakhan's evil madness would reflect a kind of diabolical insanity that Kopit saw in Starr. Just as Starr based his investigation on actual events that were nonetheless denied, so too does Astrakhan base his attack on recorded facts.

Astrakhan is a demented figure of malice. His grasp of reality is so minimal that it is impossible to tell whether there is any real reason for his act of revenge or whether he invented it. Certainly he seems to have no conscience. Kopit seems to indicate that therein lies the danger: if someone has the ability to spy on others, he probably will, whether there is justification for it or not. Evil will take command.

The setting for the play feels unreal partly because what happens and what doesn't happen is unclear. The audience sees things that one character remembers but another does not. One moment the Elliots seem like a devoted couple, and the next they are insulting each other. At times there is warmth and understanding between them, and at others there is animosity. It is difficult to determine whether they are to be pitied; they almost seem to become part of the evil that is haunting them.

Kopit shows that reality is a fragile thing. Joanne admits to Joseph that she got into a limousine with her ex-husband, Francis Summerhays, because it was raining. Her husband finds his wife's behavior extraordinary and questions her on it.

After all, she had just been comparing Francis to a vampire. Does Joanne really despise her ex-husband? Or is she fascinated by him? As for Joseph, he seems overly adamant about how little he uses a computer. Does he really only turn on his computer only every once in awhile, or does he use it for something that might be embarrassing? What is true?

Unreal circumstances plague *Y2K*. Bits of reality mix with complete fiction in such a way that the real story is unclear. Both Joanne and Joseph are unsure of events, but so, too, is the audience. Did Joanne have an affair with Joseph's male student? She certainly seems to think it more likely that Joseph would have an affair with one of his female students. Do either of the Elliots know with certainty that the other is a moral, decent person? After all, they supposedly had an affair together while Joseph's first wife was dying of cancer.

Kopit seems to be saying that perhaps no one's life should be scrutinized too closely. Joseph and Joanne feel the impact on their personal relationships as they focus on how little they trust each other rather than on how they can start reclaiming their lives. Misery fills them, as neither knows how many of the lies Astrakhan invents have a basis in truth.

Joanne tells her husband that they can explain that all of the information is false—information on the computer that indicates that she is practically a prostitute and that he is a sex offender. But her husband replies, ''But all of it is *not* fake. . . . Is it?''

All this doubt is substantiated by the slipperiness of *Y2K*'s characters. There is no real reason to believe that Joanne and Joseph would not do any of the lewd things that are hinted at. After all, both of them use language that indicates a lack of sensitivity to each other, so it is not difficult to believe that they are inured to what is decent and what is not. On the other hand, there is quite a bit of evidence that the two genuinely care about each other, as when Joanne goes to comfort her husband when he is remembering his first wife's pregnancy during her chemotherapy. It seems unlikely that either would behave in a way calculated to hurt the other.

But the suspicion is there; evil has entered. When the incriminating photos make an appearance, Joanne at first denies they are real and then recalls that at least one of them may be. When she is asked if she really did make advances to Astrakhan, Joanne denies it, saying, ''It's the sort of thing I generally remember. Joseph, have you lost your mind?''

Astrakhan is the supreme figure of evil in the play. He goes by a number of aliases, including ''ISeeU.'' While he is watching others, Astrakhan clearly is not very much aware of himself. He invents a whole history in which he is the son of Joseph's first wife, Annabel. He plagiarizes a pornographic story and then claims it is an autobiography. He ''remembers'' having an affair with Joanne, who says she scarcely recalls meeting him. The question of how much of what he remembers is invention and how much is based on truth is never answered.

Strange as the circumstances are, the characters are stranger yet. They seem intent on sexual encounters, whether imagined or real, in a manner that seems to mirror the Starr investigation. The lines between what actually occurred and what didn't are blurred. Joanne either went to see her mother or made up the trip as a cover for an illicit encounter; Joseph either used his computer as a paperweight or used it for something far less serviceable; Astrakhan either invented his encounters with, and dismissal by, Joanne or was simply recalling something Joanne preferred to forget.

If there was any clarity to the Elliots' lives to begin with, there certainly is none by the end of the play. The two become a mere invention, victims of the kind of abuse perpetrated by computer hackers. ''We are nothing but abstractions now—strings of digits, signifying anything you want, floating in the ether,'' Joseph tells his wife.

Purposely playing on the fear of having identities recreated by someone with malignant intent, Kopit blends the known and the unknown so that the truth is impossible to detect. Unreality pervades, and evil is a felt but ill-defined presence. Reputation, finances, and trust vanish before the victims understand what is happening. The computer—the trusted and seemingly benign servant—has become a corrupt master.

Source: April Schulthies, Critical Essay on *Y2K,* in *Drama for Students,* The Gale Group, 2002.

Ryan D. Poquette

Poquette has a bachelor of arts degree in English and specializes in writing drama and film. In the following essay, Poquette explores Kopit's manipulation of truth and reality.

Today, as never before, ordinary people can acquire the power to reshape the reality of a person's life— by becoming computer hackers. In Kopit's *Y2K,* the playwright elevates hacking to an art form, in the process challenging the audience's definition of truth in the digital age.

The nineteen-year-old computer hacker in *Y2K*, Costa Astrakhan, who is also the play's narrator, addresses the audience early in the play: "With what I know, I can go anywhere, and you can too."

For the duration of the play, Astrakhan demonstrates to the audience exactly how to alter a person's life in cyberspace, using Joseph and Joanne Elliot as his real-life tutorial. By the end of the play, Astrakhan has revised the Elliots' respective lives so that Joseph, a Random House book editor and teacher, is a child pornographer, while Joanne, who works at Sotheby's, the famous art auction house, is "a kind of porno star." Says Joseph to his wife: "And now it seems he has revised my life. No, rewritten it. I've got a whole new history, Joanne."

It is an ironic twist of events for Joseph, a man who has made much of his fortune editing others' stories. He says as much to his wife:

If I could just step back, I would admire it. Because what he's done of course is written a kind of novel. Only not in the old fashioned linear one-sentence-follows-the-other sort of way, but, somehow, in all dimensions, simultaneously. A novel built of zeroes and ones. And we are its characters.

Through his computer hacking, Kopit arms Astrakhan with a new-age model for storytelling, a real-life story on a grand scale that surpasses the impact of any other medium. Books, plays, films—all of these artistic creations require the reader or viewer to transport themselves inside the world of the story. But in Astrakhan's digital story, the audience is the entire world, and the characters are real-life people who face real-life consequences—not figments of an author's imagination.

"We are nothing but abstractions now—strings of digits, signifying anything you want, floating in the ether," Joseph says to Joanne.

In this era of modern drama, where the boundaries of realism have been tested for more than a hundred years, Kopit breaks through into new territory, creating an art form for the new millennium—the scripting of reality itself. In the beginning, however, the audience watching Kopit's play doesn't suspect that this is what Astrakhan is doing, in part due to his style of keep-no-secrets narration. As Katie Hafner of the *New York Times* notes to Kopit in an e-mail interview, "[Astrakhan is] a classic unreliable narrator."

Throughout the play, Astrakhan seems to be upfront and honest, telling people both bad and good things about himself, when in fact he is a liar. As Kopit says in his e-mail interview, "Generally, we assume that when someone says something in a seemingly honest way, it's true—or at least what that person thinks is true." Astrakhan's forthright and direct manner is put in an even better light when contrasted with the Elliots, who aren't always truthful with each other. This helps to sway the audience into believing that Astrakhan's narration of current and past events—which the audience is seeing brought to life on stage—is in fact correct. For a large portion of the play, the audience assumes that Joanne has had an affair with Astrakhan, who describes the sordid details of their affair in vivid and specific detail. Says Astrakhan, "Am I being indiscreet? I'm sorry but there's no avoiding it. Not if honesty is to be our policy. And truth to be told."

It is a complete shock to the audience to find out that Joanne doesn't even recall meeting Astrakhan. Up until this point, the audience thinks they are getting more accurate information than the Elliots since Astrakhan confides in the audience constantly. This final, long scene, in which Joseph describes the particulars of how Astrakhan has ruined their lives, is the turning point in the play, where both the Elliots and the audience realize that they've been had. "Strategically, Kopit wants to challenge the solidity of both the Elliots' and the audience's sense of reality," said John Lahr in his review in the *New Yorker*.

Astrakhan's tendency to have false memories is particularly interesting since he is so adamant about telling the truth. The play is saturated with references to honesty and truth, and many of them are from Astrakhan, emphasizing to the audience that he is an honest person. Astrakhan addresses the audience: "I only tell the truth. That's because lying is obscene." And yet Astrakhan lies to himself and the audience, even when he is reenacting fake events from his past, such as when Joanne asks how old he is in a false memory. "Sixteen," he replies, having just told Joseph a few minutes ago that he is fifteen. When describing another event from his false past with the Elliots, Astrakhan hints at the narrative process that he uses to rewrite both his own history and that of the Elliots: "not a day passes that I don't bring it back to mind, with, somehow, each time, some new detail emerging, until now it seems even clearer than it was back then. Funny, how memory works."

The idea of real versus fictionalized memories is familiar territory for Kopit. Says Lahr, "*Y2K* . . . is another of Kopit's brilliant speculations informed by fact, an unnerving hall of mirrors that adds a new perspective to his obsession with memory and identity." Astrakhan takes his cue from a Flaubert quote that Joseph likes to quote to his writing class: "Everything you invent is true." This is certainly the case with Astrakhan's new brand of digital fiction, although it needs a kernel of truth upon which to support the digital narrative. In the case of the Elliots, this seed of truth is never disclosed to the audience. Although Joseph reveals one secret to Joanne, the fact that he and his ex-wife aborted their child during its last trimester when she was undergoing chemotherapy, this is not the other secret to which both he and Astrakhan refer. One suspects that the secret is most likely some dabbling in pornography since this is the major crime that Astrakhan pins on Joseph in the hacker's digital story. Says Joseph to Joanne: "Speaking for myself, there are things he has found—about me—and which he's tucked in with all of the really dreadful 'invented' stuff—which is going to come out." Joseph suggests that Joanne has dark secrets as well, especially after seeing lurid photos of her with other men, some of which don't look fake. Whether Joanne is telling the truth to Joseph doesn't matter. In the digital age, the hacker's reality is the only one that anybody else will believe. "Astrakhan has the power to re-create the virtual universe at will in his own demented image," says Lahr.

So what is Astrakhan's image? What is the idea that he develops so carefully when he revises the Elliots' lives and his own memories? He wishes to be a part of the Elliots' family. And by manipulating their lives and scripting new histories for them, Astrakhan writes himself into their lives for good. Astrakhan tells the audience that Joseph was "his way in," then corrects himself: "No, let's be honest: to me he is far more than that. In fact, always has been. I just hadn't discovered it yet." Astrakhan's "discovery," is the aborted baby, and through the hacker's manipulation of hospital records, he brings the baby back to life and becomes that baby. Astrakhan foreshadows this turn of events at several points throughout the play, especially when he refers to Joseph as a kind of father figure. "If only someone like you had entered my life earlier, my life would be entirely different now," Astrakhan tells Joseph in a false memory.

In another false memory of his first visit to the Elliots' apartment, Astrakhan tells Joseph: "When I

> " . . . KOPIT BREAKS THROUGH INTO NEW TERRITORY, CREATING AN ART FORM FOR THE NEW MILLENNIUM—THE SCRIPTING OF REALITY ITSELF."

publish my first novel, I tell you *this* is where I'm gonna live." Astrakhan goes on to clarify that he didn't mean live with "you and your wife . . . nice as that might be!" Astrakhan does in fact publish his novel, at least in the digital sense, by creating the new life stories of the Elliots. And in the end, he does end up living with the Elliots, or at least the audience suspects that he will, based on the last few lines of the play:

> Like any homecoming, it will be difficult at first. For all of us. So much to get used to! But we will. In time. And then . . . Yes . . . It will all be, once again, as I remember it. . . . And I will take care of them, forever and ever.

"The villain of Mr. Kopit's slender play is, in fact, quite a twisted piece of humanity," says Peter Marks in his *New York Times* review, and by the end of the play, the audience agrees. Joseph could try to fight the hacker by proving his innocence, but the tools at the hacker's disposal are too massive. Astrakhan has created such a large, intricate, digital history that it is almost impossible to disprove. Furthermore, to mount such a massive campaign would require funds that Joseph and Joanne no longer have because Astrakhan has made their bank accounts unattainable, as he himself is unattainable. As Joseph explains to Joanne: "Thompson says it's almost impossible to know where he actually is, his messages are all time-delayed and routed in a Byzantine way Thompson claims is like a work of art." For the Elliots, the unfortunate, unwilling characters in a hacker's digital story, reality is whatever their new puppetmaster says it is.

Source: Ryan D. Poquette, Critical Essay on *Y2K,* in *Drama for Students,* The Gale Group, 2002.

Chris Semansky

Semansky is an instructor of English literature and composition and writes regularly for literary

LUCILLE LORTEL THEATRE

MANHATTAN THEATRE CLUB
artistic director   executive producer
LYNNE MEADOW   BARRY GROVE
by special arrangement with
LUCILLE LORTEL THEATRE FOUNDATION
presents

Y 2 K
by
ARTHUR KOPIT

with
(in alphabetical order)

DAVID BROWN JR.   ERIK JENSEN   PATRICIA KALEMBER
JAMES NAUGHTON   ARMAND SCHULTZ

set design   costume design   lighting design
LOY ARCENAS   TOM BROECKER   KEVIN ADAMS
sound design   production stage manager
DARRON L. WEST   JAMES FITZSIMMONS

directed by
BOB BALABAN

casting   production manager   press representative
NANCY PICCIONE   MICHAEL R. MOODY   BONEAU/BRYAN-BROWN

associate artistic director   general manager
MICHAEL BUSH   VICTORIA BAILEY

Special funding for new American works is provided by The Harold and Mimi Steinberg Charitable Trust.

This production of Y2K is supported in part by a grant from the National Endowment for the Arts.
The world premiere of Y2K was at the 1999 Humana Festival of New American Plays at Actors Theatre of Louisville.
Manhattan Theatre Club productions are made possible in part with public funds from
the New York City Department of Cultural Affairs and the New York State Council on the Arts, a State Agency.

A 1999 playbill cast list of Y2K, *performed at the Lucille Lortel Theatre in New York City*

magazines and journals. In this essay, he considers the idea of representation in Kopit's play.

On the surface, Kopit's play, *Y2K*, is a cautionary tale about computer technology taking over peoples' lives. In positioning technology as the enemy, Kopit raises questions about the representative power of words and images, suggesting that they hold the key to human identity.

In his preface, Kopit writes that he was inspired to write the play after being outraged by Special Investigator Kenneth Starr's intrusion into the private life of Monica Lewinsky during his investigation of her relationship with former president Bill Clinton. Like the Clinton-Lewinsky story, Kopit's play releases information incrementally, by different players at key points, essentially reshaping what the audience (the audience for the Clinton-Lewinsky story being the media-consuming public) believes to be the truth. Both stories change the audience perception of the central characters by throwing private actions into public light. *Y2K*, however, suggests that what happens to Joseph Elliot and his wife, Joanne, can happen to anyone.

In foregrounding the power of technology to reconstitute human identity, Kopit begs certain questions about what makes people who they are. Assumptions about human identity that have guided thinking in the industrialized world include the notion that identity is universal and is based on features such as character and personality, which are intrinsic to a person. In contrast, Kopit's play emphasizes the notion that identity rests primarily upon the idea of narrative, rather than anything intrinsic or essential. That is, the story of a person's life, in fact, *is* that person's life. Kopit underscores this idea by manipulating readers' expectations of the truth, so that characters such as Joseph and Joanne, who once seemed to be certain types of people, turn out (possibly) to be other types entirely. By putting stories inside stories inside stories, Kopit blurs the distinction between reality and fiction, creating a hall of mirrors in which characters can no longer recognize characters and readers must construct their own theories for what happened and why. There is no single demonstrable truth against standing behind the many versions of events.

The play opens with punk hacker Costa Astrakhan bragging about his power and his ubiquity. Telling the audience he is everywhere, ''on the outskirts of your mind, in the ether, in the darkness,'' Astrakhan portrays himself as an arrogant and unreliable narrator. Astrakhan appears both as a realistic character in the play, interacting with Joanne and Joseph during a dinner at their apartment, and as a demonic presence, hovering over and commenting on the play's action. In the latter role, he is symbolic of technology's pervasive influence in peoples' lives. Astrakhan's speeches about his power, his hacking history, and his relationship with Joanne provide the explanation for much of what happens to Joanne and Joseph. In this way, the play is didactic, meaning that its purpose is to teach the audience something. What it teaches, however, is not so clear. Ostensibly, the play is about the evils of computer technology; but it is also about trust, marital and generational, and the relationship between private and public realities.

Without Astrakhan's speeches, the play would be more of a mystery. By using Astrakhan as a symbolic character, Kopit introduces nonrealistic elements in the play. Nonrealistic plays differ from realistic plays in that they often distort character and time and use symbolic as opposed to realistic settings. Samuel Beckett's plays, for example, are nonrealistic plays, as they usually ignore both clock time and historical time and have absurd settings, such as cartoon-like characters inhabiting trashcans. Other nonrealistic playwrights include Eugene Ionesco, Harold Pinter, and David J. LeMaster. By combining realistic elements such as believable settings and action with nonrealistic elements, Kopit further reinforces the idea that reality itself is an unstable phenomenon over which people often have little control.

Take the character of Joanne, for example. Kopit masterfully pits readers' knowledge of her, which they gain through seeing her interact with her husband, against Astrakhan's story of her life, which he puts together by hacking into computer systems, including her own and her husband's. At first, she appears to be a loving, if somewhat distracted, wife to Joseph, effervescent and with a dry sense of humor. The audience finds out through the couple's interaction that Joanne is fending off the advances of her ex-husband, Francis Summerhays, a wealthy and obsessive venture capitalist, whom Joseph despises. Astrakhan's representation of her mixes what appears to be fact—details of her birth, education, etc.—with a story of how they came to be lovers. However, even though readers have every reason to doubt Astrakhan's version of Joanne's life and especially of their ''affair''—after all, he is a proven liar, plagiarist, drug abuser, and self-confessed hacker—they have no credible alternative to what really happened. Joanne's credibility has already been compromised. Joseph distrusts her, partly because of his own jealousy of Francis and partly because she was reluctant to provide complete information about her encounter with Francis. In addition, throughout most of the play, the characters drink heavily, causing the audience to question the truthfulness and motivation of their words.

As the audience re-evaluates the truthfulness of the various characters' versions of events in light of new information, they also begin to question the characters' motivation. This resembles the way in which the Clinton-Lewinsky affair unfolded and, indeed, the way in which many such situations unfold, where a secret is gradually brought to light by others not initially involved. In some ways, the play resembles a courtroom drama with evidence offered, stories presented and denied, intent and motivation probed, and a jury voting to believe one side's version of events versus another side's.

One of the primary theories that viewers and readers of *Y2K* must consider is the possibility that the entire play is a construct of Astrakhan's mind. His words frame the action, and his god-like pres-

> **"ONE EXPLANATION IS THAT ASTRAKHAN'S STORY REPRESENTS THE VENGEANCE OF A YOUNGER GENERATION UPON AN OLDER ONE."**

ence during the course of events suggests that he controls what gets said and done. Although Astrakhan has claimed that he initially became interested in Joseph because he wanted to sleep with a girl in Joseph's writing class, readers are later told that his ''true'' motivation is to reunite with the Elliots, whom he believes are his biological parents. But even this motivation for ruining their lives is questionable, given Astrakhan's previous explanations.

If readers consider the play as the machinations of Astrakhan's mind, complete with the invention of characters, self-referentiality, and stories inside stories, they must ask themselves what larger symbolic meaning this hacker fantasy holds. One explanation is that Astrakhan's story represents the vengeance of a younger generation upon an older one. As someone barely out of his teens (or so he says at the beginning of the play), Astrakhan stands in for what marketing demographers sometime refer to as Generation Y, those born between 1979 and 1994. The children of baby boomers, they are also sometimes referred to as Echo Boomers, or the Millennium Generation. Even more so than Generation X, which preceded them, Generation Y has something to prove. Often raised by parents who espouse the idealistic values of the 1960s, but with all the material privilege that the bull market of the 1980s and 1990s have given them, Generation Y'ers are the literal embodiment of deeply rooted contradictions.

Carving out their own identities, then, means grappling with the identity of their parents. Astrakhan, then, as hacker and playwright, ''solves'' this problem by first creating his parents, the Elliots, then destroying them, and then, in the play's final image, holding himself out as their possible salvation. As a Generation Y son of boomers, he creates the family he never had, and on his own terms. The fact that it is a virtual family is apropos for a generation raised on the (for Kopit, ironic) promise of computer technology to improve the quality of human life.

Source: Chris Semansky, Critical Essay on *Y2K,* in *Drama for Students,* The Gale Group, 2002.

Katie Hafner

In the following interview, based on e-mail exchanges, Arthur Kopit discusses the ideas behind, research for, and technological context of his play Y2K.

KATIE HAFNER. How did you get the idea for ''*Y2K*''?

ARTHUR KOPIT. From thinking about the way Kenneth Starr was pursuing Monica Lewinsky. Which is to say, I was not thinking about computers at all but invasion of privacy. And I was feeling outrage. And that outrage went completely off the charts when Starr tried to subpoena records showing what books Monica Lewinsky had bought. I thought, my God, there's no stopping him! If you're looking for a real threat to our country, this is it. And that led me to thinking about the ways all of us were vulnerable to such an assault in the future and right now. And those thoughts led to this play.

Q. The technical language spewed by Astrakhan, the hacker, is very impressive. Did you interview hackers?

A. Didn't need to. I found so much material on the Net—interviews with hackers, articles written by hackers, profiles of hackers, that getting the vocabulary right was not hard.

Q. And why the rather unusual name of Astrakhan for the hacker?

A. I modeled Astrakhan's renegade character, at least somewhat, on a wildly unpredictable, deeply gifted student I once had in a playwriting workshop I was giving. He was Armenian, or claimed he was. After a while, I began to suspect he was also a terrorist. He was a good reference point. I chose Astrakhan because my wife had just bought an Astrakhan hat, and the word jumped out at me. By the way, Astrakhan is not his real name. I'm not sure what his real name is. In the world he inhabits, no one knows his real name.

Q. He's the narrator in the play, which is intriguing because he's a classic unreliable narrator.

A. The question of ''what is reliable information and what is not'' is at the heart of the story. Generally, we assume that when someone says something in a seemingly honest way, it's true—or at least what that person thinks is true. I wanted to play with that idea to such a degree that the audience would suddenly understand that what they had been accepting as true was in fact totally in question. Because that's what happens to Joseph at the end, isn't it? Almost overnight, his whole world has become unreliable. And I wanted my audience to experience his state of shock.

Q. Have you had any experiences like this yourself, especially when it comes to electronic information?

A. Fortunately, no. I did get a virus though, and inadvertently sent it on. Then I realized I was ''infected'' and had to tell everyone I had been in contact with. And found it a bit embarrassing. I mean, this really is sexual. Not literally, of course, but close. So, in that trivial way—my virus was the equivalent of a minor cold—I saw how easily one's entire life could be undone, the way a common cold can turn into pneumonia. And kill you.

Q. The play is erotic, from beginning to end. Why did you infuse it with so much eroticism?

A. I wanted the audience to be not only Joseph, watching his world collapse, but Astrakhan, on the hunt, powerful, almost invulnerable, and that meant having them experience the erotic thrill Astrakhan gets from invading Joseph's privacy. It's really a rape, isn't it? For which, by the way, he'll never get punished, even if he's caught. Because the National Security Agency will hire him. Or Microsoft. Because he's that good at this.

Q. I noticed that the Y2K computer glitch itself is hardly mentioned at all in the play. Why the title?

A. I'm using Y2K metaphorically, hoping it will suggest the deeper, more profound Year 2000 Problem: our potential loss of personal and political freedom through technology. We depend on these machines now for almost everything and are therefore vulnerable in ways we have never been. Our view of what is real and what is not, and what is inviolable and what is not, is going to have to change. So will the way we see ourselves. In a very short time, you'll be able to find out pretty much anything you want to know about anyone.

Q. Has this play made you less sanguine about the future?

A. Actually, I don't think I look at it any one way. It's a story isn't it—what we're living? So I'm mostly curious. To see how it's all going to play out. It's like a great epic drama. The next act is about to begin. We're coming back from intermission all abuzz. And we have no idea what we are going to see. Scary thought. Exciting thought.

Q. Speaking of intermissions, there isn't one in this play. Why is that?

A. The play's intentions don't allow for one. I was in an earthquake once, in Mexico, and it's startling how, instantly, what you had always believed was solid turns out not to be. That's why my play is so quick, and doesn't so much end as stop. It's about the suddenness of it all.

Q. In the end, Astrakhan's motive for ruining these two people's lives seems completely unclear.

A. I'm not sure he has a motive other than gratification. Anyway, I'm not sure how much we ever understand about motives. In any case, a motive would have let us off the hook. But for those who need motives, Astrakhan does give one. He says, "I do it because I can." It's one of the few places I think he's telling the truth.

Q. What do you think of the Internet? When did you first go online?

A. I went online in a serious way at the end of the summer before last, when I got the idea for this play. So I was a bit like Joseph with computers. Which was good for the play, because my inevitable mistakes I knew would be like his mistakes. I did crash my system during that time, which threw me no end, because I had only a narrow window of time to write the play. I spent three whole days talking to tech support people at I.B.M. and Microsoft, trying to figure out what I had done wrong so I could get my computer working again. In the end, I had to reformat my hard disk, erase everything and basically start over.

And then I saw how I could turn those three terrible lost days into three invaluable days of research. I simply used this incident in the play. And what happened to me happens now to Joseph, and is the pivotal event that allows Astrakhan to get in. That accident speeded things along. So, at the moment, I'm happy with the Internet. But that could end. I mean, it's not a solid relationship.

Source: Katie Hafner and Arthur Kopit, "Going Online and Finding a Window on the Times," in the *New York Times,* December 5, 1999, p. 7, section 2.

 I'M USING Y2K METAPHORICALLY, HOPING IT WILL SUGGEST THE DEEPER, MORE PROFOUND YEAR 2000 PROBLEM: OUR POTENTIAL LOSS OF PERSONAL AND POLITICAL FREEDOM THROUGH TECHNOLOGY."

SOURCES

Hafner, Katie and Arthur Kopit, "Going Online and Finding a Window on the Times," in the *New York Times,* December 5, 1999, p. 7 section 2.

Hoover, Calvin B., *Dictators and Democracies,* Macmillan, 1937.

Isherwood, Charles, Review of *Y2K,* in *Variety,* December 13, 1999.

Jenkins, Jeffrey Eric, "Humana Fest Puts Its Stamp on a Fresh Crop of Plays," in the *Seattle Post-Intelligencer,* March 25, 1999.

Kohn, Martin F., "Next Stop: Detroit," in the *Detroit Free Press,* April 4, 1999.

Lahr, John, "Open Secrets," in the *New Yorker,* Vol. 75, No. 39, December 20, 1999, pp. 100–101.

Marks, Peter, "He's Mad, He's Bad and He's Got Their Passwords," in the *New York Times,* December 8, 1999, p. 7.

McNulty, Charles, "On the Verge," in the *Village Voice,* March 31–April 6, 1999.

Regan, Keith, "Is Internet Privacy an Oxymoron," in *E-Commerce Times* (http://www.newsfactor.com/perl/story/9318.html), April 27, 2001.

Simon, John, "Mystery Science Theatre 2000," in *New York Magazine,* December 20, 1999.

Sommer, Elyse, "A CurtainUp Review: *Y2K,*" in *CurtainUp,* July 27, 2000.

Yourdon, Edward, and Jennifer Yourdon, *Time Bomb 2000,* Macmillan, 1997, pp. 506.

FURTHER READING

Berlant, Lauren, and Lisa Duggan, eds., *Our Monica, Ourselves: The Clinton Affair and the Public Interest (Sexual Cultures),* New York University Press, 2001.

This anthology criticizes the relationship between politics and sensationalism.

Eatwell, Roger, *Fascism: A History,* Allen Lane, 1996. Eatwell shows how fascist ideology succeeded in Italy and Germany and failed in France and England. He suggests that the preconditions for the future rise of fascism exist.

McLean, Deckle, *Privacy and Its Invasion,* Praeger, 1995.

McLean uses his background in communications to look at the erosion of privacy in the United States by corporations and institutions.

Peterson, Chris, *I Love the Internet, but I Want My Privacy, Too!,* Prima Publishing, 1998. The author explores the advantages and disadvantages of shared information and looks at steps government and corporations are taking to ensure privacy.

Glossary of Literary Terms

A

Abstract: Used as a noun, the term refers to a short summary or outline of a longer work. As an adjective applied to writing or literary works, abstract refers to words or phrases that name things not knowable through the five senses. Examples of abstracts include the *Cliffs Notes* summaries of major literary works. Examples of abstract terms or concepts include ''idea,'' ''guilt'' ''honesty,'' and ''loyalty.''

Absurd, Theater of the: See *Theater of the Absurd*

Absurdism: See *Theater of the Absurd*

Act: A major section of a play. Acts are divided into varying numbers of shorter scenes. From ancient times to the nineteenth century plays were generally constructed of five acts, but modern works typically consist of one, two, or three acts. Examples of five-act plays include the works of Sophocles and Shakespeare, while the plays of Arthur Miller commonly have a three-act structure.

Acto: A one-act Chicano theater piece developed out of collective improvisation. *Actos* were performed by members of Luis Valdez's Teatro Campesino in California during the mid-1960s.

Aestheticism: A literary and artistic movement of the nineteenth century. Followers of the movement believed that art should not be mixed with social, political, or moral teaching. The statement ''art for art's sake'' is a good summary of aestheticism. The movement had its roots in France, but it gained widespread importance in England in the last half of the nineteenth century, where it helped change the Victorian practice of including moral lessons in literature. Oscar Wilde is one of the best-known ''aesthetes'' of the late nineteenth century.

Age of Johnson: The period in English literature between 1750 and 1798, named after the most prominent literary figure of the age, Samuel Johnson. Works written during this time are noted for their emphasis on ''sensibility,'' or emotional quality. These works formed a transition between the rational works of the Age of Reason, or Neoclassical period, and the emphasis on individual feelings and responses of the Romantic period. Significant writers during the Age of Johnson included the novelists Ann Radcliffe and Henry Mackenzie, dramatists Richard Sheridan and Oliver Goldsmith, and poets William Collins and Thomas Gray. Also known as Age of Sensibility

Age of Reason: See *Neoclassicism*

Age of Sensibility: See *Age of Johnson*

Alexandrine Meter: See *Meter*

Allegory: A narrative technique in which characters representing things or abstract ideas are used to convey a message or teach a lesson. Allegory is typically used to teach moral, ethical, or religious lessons but is sometimes used for satiric or political purposes. Examples of allegorical works include Edmund Spenser's *The Faerie Queene* and John Bunyan's *The Pilgrim's Progress.*

Allusion: A reference to a familiar literary or historical person or event, used to make an idea more easily understood. For example, describing someone as a ''Romeo'' makes an allusion to William Shakespeare's famous young lover in *Romeo and Juliet.*

Amerind Literature: The writing and oral traditions of Native Americans. Native American literature was originally passed on by word of mouth, so it consisted largely of stories and events that were easily memorized. Amerind prose is often rhythmic like poetry because it was recited to the beat of a ceremonial drum. Examples of Amerind literature include the autobiographical *Black Elk Speaks,* the works of N. Scott Momaday, James Welch, and Craig Lee Strete, and the poetry of Luci Tapahonso.

Analogy: A comparison of two things made to explain something unfamiliar through its similarities to something familiar, or to prove one point based on the acceptedness of another. Similes and metaphors are types of analogies. Analogies often take the form of an extended simile, as in William Blake's aphorism: ''As the caterpillar chooses the fairest leaves to lay her eggs on, so the priest lays his curse on the fairest joys.''

Angry Young Men: A group of British writers of the 1950s whose work expressed bitterness and disillusionment with society. Common to their work is an anti-hero who rebels against a corrupt social order and strives for personal integrity. The term has been used to describe Kingsley Amis, John Osborne, Colin Wilson, John Wain, and others.

Antagonist: The major character in a narrative or drama who works against the hero or protagonist. An example of an evil antagonist is Richard Lovelace in Samuel Richardson's *Clarissa,* while a virtuous antagonist is Macduff in William Shakespeare's *Macbeth.*

Anthropomorphism: The presentation of animals or objects in human shape or with human characteristics. The term is derived from the Greek word for ''human form.'' The fables of Aesop, the animated films of Walt Disney, and Richard Adams's *Watership Down* feature anthropomorphic characters.

Anti-hero: A central character in a work of literature who lacks traditional heroic qualities such as courage, physical prowess, and fortitude. Anti-heros

typically distrust conventional values and are unable to commit themselves to any ideals. They generally feel helpless in a world over which they have no control. Anti-heroes usually accept, and often celebrate, their positions as social outcasts. A well-known anti-hero is Yossarian in Joseph Heller's novel *Catch-22.*

Antimasque: See *Masque*

Antithesis: The antithesis of something is its direct opposite. In literature, the use of antithesis as a figure of speech results in two statements that show a contrast through the balancing of two opposite ideas. Technically, it is the second portion of the statement that is defined as the ''antithesis''; the first portion is the ''thesis.'' An example of antithesis is found in the following portion of Abraham Lincoln's ''Gettysburg Address''; notice the opposition between the verbs ''remember'' and ''forget'' and the phrases ''what we say'' and ''what they did'': ''The world will little note nor long remember what we say here, but it can never forget what they did here.''

Apocrypha: Writings tentatively attributed to an author but not proven or universally accepted to be their works. The term was originally applied to certain books of the Bible that were not considered inspired and so were not included in the ''sacred canon.'' Geoffrey Chaucer, William Shakespeare, Thomas Kyd, Thomas Middleton, and John Marston all have apocrypha. Apocryphal books of the Bible include the Old Testament's Book of Enoch and New Testament's Gospel of Peter.

Apollonian and Dionysian: The two impulses believed to guide authors of dramatic tragedy. The Apollonian impulse is named after Apollo, the Greek god of light and beauty and the symbol of intellectual order. The Dionysian impulse is named after Dionysus, the Greek god of wine and the symbol of the unrestrained forces of nature. The Apollonian impulse is to create a rational, harmonious world, while the Dionysian is to express the irrational forces of personality. Friedrich Nietzche uses these terms in *The Birth of Tragedy* to designate contrasting elements in Greek tragedy.

Apostrophe: A statement, question, or request addressed to an inanimate object or concept or to a nonexistent or absent person. Requests for inspiration from the muses in poetry are examples of apostrophe, as is Marc Antony's address to Caesar's corpse in William Shakespeare's *Julius Caesar:* ''O, pardon me, thou bleeding piece of earth, That I am meek and gentle with these butchers!... Woe to the hand that shed this costly blood!..."

Archetype: The word archetype is commonly used to describe an original pattern or model from which all other things of the same kind are made. This term was introduced to literary criticism from the psychology of Carl Jung. It expresses Jung's theory that behind every person's "unconscious," or repressed memories of the past, lies the "collective unconscious" of the human race: memories of the countless typical experiences of our ancestors. These memories are said to prompt illogical associations that trigger powerful emotions in the reader. Often, the emotional process is primitive, even primordial. Archetypes are the literary images that grow out of the "collective unconscious." They appear in literature as incidents and plots that repeat basic patterns of life. They may also appear as stereotyped characters. Examples of literary archetypes include themes such as birth and death and characters such as the Earth Mother.

Argument: The argument of a work is the author's subject matter or principal idea. Examples of defined "argument" portions of works include John Milton's *Arguments* to each of the books of *Paradise Lost* and the "Argument" to Robert Herrick's *Hesperides*.

Aristotelian Criticism: Specifically, the method of evaluating and analyzing tragedy formulated by the Greek philosopher Aristotle in his *Poetics*. More generally, the term indicates any form of criticism that follows Aristotle's views. Aristotelian criticism focuses on the form and logical structure of a work, apart from its historical or social context, in contrast to "Platonic Criticism," which stresses the usefulness of art. Adherents of New Criticism including John Crowe Ransom and Cleanth Brooks utilize and value the basic ideas of Aristotelian criticism for textual analysis.

Art for Art's Sake: See *Aestheticism*

Aside: A comment made by a stage performer that is intended to be heard by the audience but supposedly not by other characters. Eugene O'Neill's *Strange Interlude* is an extended use of the aside in modern theater.

Audience: The people for whom a piece of literature is written. Authors usually write with a certain audience in mind, for example, children, members of a religious or ethnic group, or colleagues in a professional field. The term "audience" also applies to the people who gather to see or hear any performance, including plays, poetry readings, speeches, and concerts. Jane Austen's parody of the gothic novel, *Northanger Abbey*, was originally intended for (and also pokes fun at) an audience of young and avid female gothic novel readers.

Avant-garde: A French term meaning "vanguard." It is used in literary criticism to describe new writing that rejects traditional approaches to literature in favor of innovations in style or content. Twentieth-century examples of the literary *avant-garde* include the Black Mountain School of poets, the Bloomsbury Group, and the Beat Movement.

B

Ballad: A short poem that tells a simple story and has a repeated refrain. Ballads were originally intended to be sung. Early ballads, known as folk ballads, were passed down through generations, so their authors are often unknown. Later ballads composed by known authors are called literary ballads. An example of an anonymous folk ballad is "Edward," which dates from the Middle Ages. Samuel Taylor Coleridge's "The Rime of the Ancient Mariner" and John Keats's "La Belle Dame sans Merci" are examples of literary ballads.

Baroque: A term used in literary criticism to describe literature that is complex or ornate in style or diction. Baroque works typically express tension, anxiety, and violent emotion. The term "Baroque Age" designates a period in Western European literature beginning in the late sixteenth century and ending about one hundred years later. Works of this period often mirror the qualities of works more generally associated with the label "baroque" and sometimes feature elaborate conceits. Examples of Baroque works include John Lyly's *Euphues: The Anatomy of Wit*, Luis de Gongora's *Soledads*, and William Shakespeare's *As You Like It*.

Baroque Age: See *Baroque*

Baroque Period: See *Baroque*

Beat Generation: See *Beat Movement*

Beat Movement: A period featuring a group of American poets and novelists of the 1950s and 1960s—including Jack Kerouac, Allen Ginsberg, Gregory Corso, William S. Burroughs, and Lawrence Ferlinghetti—who rejected established social and literary values. Using such techniques as stream of consciousness writing and jazz-influenced free verse and focusing on unusual or abnormal states of mind—generated by religious ecstasy or the use of drugs—the Beat writers aimed to create works that were unconventional in both form and subject matter. Kerouac's *On the Road* is perhaps the best-known example of a Beat Generation novel, and Ginsberg's *Howl* is a famous collection of Beat poetry.

Black Aesthetic Movement: A period of artistic and literary development among African Americans in the 1960s and early 1970s. This was the first major African-American artistic movement since the Harlem Renaissance and was closely paralleled by the civil rights and black power movements. The black aesthetic writers attempted to produce works of art that would be meaningful to the black masses. Key figures in black aesthetics included one of its founders, poet and playwright Amiri Baraka, formerly known as LeRoi Jones; poet and essayist Haki R. Madhubuti, formerly Don L. Lee; poet and playwright Sonia Sanchez; and dramatist Ed Bullins. Works representative of the Black Aesthetic Movement include Amiri Baraka's play *Dutchman,* a 1964 Obie award-winner; *Black Fire: An Anthology of Afro-American Writing,* edited by Baraka and playwright Larry Neal and published in 1968; and Sonia Sanchez's poetry collection *We a BadDDD People,* published in 1970. Also known as Black Arts Movement.

Black Arts Movement: See *Black Aesthetic Movement*

Black Comedy: See *Black Humor*

Black Humor: Writing that places grotesque elements side by side with humorous ones in an attempt to shock the reader, forcing him or her to laugh at the horrifying reality of a disordered world. Joseph Heller's novel *Catch-22* is considered a superb example of the use of black humor. Other well-known authors who use black humor include Kurt Vonnegut, Edward Albee, Eugene Ionesco, and Harold Pinter. Also known as Black Comedy.

Blank Verse: Loosely, any unrhymed poetry, but more generally, unrhymed iambic pentameter verse (composed of lines of five two-syllable feet with the first syllable accented, the second unaccented). Blank verse has been used by poets since the Renaissance for its flexibility and its graceful, dignified tone. John Milton's *Paradise Lost* is in blank verse, as are most of William Shakespeare's plays.

Bloomsbury Group: A group of English writers, artists, and intellectuals who held informal artistic and philosophical discussions in Bloomsbury, a district of London, from around 1907 to the early 1930s. The Bloomsbury Group held no uniform philosophical beliefs but did commonly express an aversion to moral prudery and a desire for greater social tolerance. At various times the circle included Virginia Woolf, E. M. Forster, Clive Bell, Lytton Strachey, and John Maynard Keynes.

Bon Mot: A French term meaning "good word." A *bon mot* is a witty remark or clever observation. Charles Lamb and Oscar Wilde are celebrated for their witty *bon mots.* Two examples by Oscar Wilde stand out: (1) "All women become their mothers. That is their tragedy. No man does. That's his." (2) "A man cannot be too careful in the choice of his enemies."

Breath Verse: See *Projective Verse*

Burlesque: Any literary work that uses exaggeration to make its subject appear ridiculous, either by treating a trivial subject with profound seriousness or by treating a dignified subject frivolously. The word "burlesque" may also be used as an adjective, as in "burlesque show," to mean "striptease act." Examples of literary burlesque include the comedies of Aristophanes, Miguel de Cervantes's *Don Quixote,*, Samuel Butler's poem "Hudibras," and John Gay's play *The Beggar's Opera.*

C

Cadence: The natural rhythm of language caused by the alternation of accented and unaccented syllables. Much modern poetry—notably free verse—deliberately manipulates cadence to create complex rhythmic effects. James Macpherson's "Ossian poems" are richly cadenced, as is the poetry of the Symbolists, Walt Whitman, and Amy Lowell.

Caesura: A pause in a line of poetry, usually occurring near the middle. It typically corresponds to a break in the natural rhythm or sense of the line but is sometimes shifted to create special meanings or rhythmic effects. The opening line of Edgar Allan Poe's "The Raven" contains a caesura following "dreary": "Once upon a midnight dreary, while I pondered weak and weary. . . ."

Canzone: A short Italian or Provencal lyric poem, commonly about love and often set to music. The *canzone* has no set form but typically contains five or six stanzas made up of seven to twenty lines of eleven syllables each. A shorter, five- to ten-line "envoy," or concluding stanza, completes the poem. Masters of the *canzone* form include

Petrarch, Dante Alighieri, Torquato Tasso, and Guido Cavalcanti.

Carpe Diem: A Latin term meaning "seize the day." This is a traditional theme of poetry, especially lyrics. A *carpe diem* poem advises the reader or the person it addresses to live for today and enjoy the pleasures of the moment. Two celebrated *carpe diem* poems are Andrew Marvell's "To His Coy Mistress" and Robert Herrick's poem beginning "Gather ye rosebuds while ye may. . . ."

Catharsis: The release or purging of unwanted emotions— specifically fear and pity—brought about by exposure to art. The term was first used by the Greek philosopher Aristotle in his *Poetics* to refer to the desired effect of tragedy on spectators. A famous example of catharsis is realized in Sophocles' *Oedipus Rex,* when Oedipus discovers that his wife, Jacosta, is his own mother and that the stranger he killed on the road was his own father.

Celtic Renaissance: A period of Irish literary and cultural history at the end of the nineteenth century. Followers of the movement aimed to create a romantic vision of Celtic myth and legend. The most significant works of the Celtic Renaissance typically present a dreamy, unreal world, usually in reaction against the reality of contemporary problems. William Butler Yeats's *The Wanderings of Oisin* is among the most significant works of the Celtic Renaissance. Also known as Celtic Twilight.

Celtic Twilight: See *Celtic Renaissance*

Character: Broadly speaking, a person in a literary work. The actions of characters are what constitute the plot of a story, novel, or poem. There are numerous types of characters, ranging from simple, stereotypical figures to intricate, multifaceted ones. In the techniques of anthropomorphism and personification, animals—and even places or things—can assume aspects of character. "Characterization" is the process by which an author creates vivid, believable characters in a work of art. This may be done in a variety of ways, including (1) direct description of the character by the narrator; (2) the direct presentation of the speech, thoughts, or actions of the character; and (3) the responses of other characters to the character. The term "character" also refers to a form originated by the ancient Greek writer Theophrastus that later became popular in the seventeenth and eighteenth centuries. It is a short essay or sketch of a person who prominently displays a specific attribute or quality, such as miserliness or ambition. Notable characters in lit-

erature include Oedipus Rex, Don Quixote de la Mancha, Macbeth, Candide, Hester Prynne, Ebenezer Scrooge, Huckleberry Finn, Jay Gatsby, Scarlett O'Hara, James Bond, and Kunta Kinte.

Characterization: See *Character*

Chorus: In ancient Greek drama, a group of actors who commented on and interpreted the unfolding action on the stage. Initially the chorus was a major component of the presentation, but over time it became less significant, with its numbers reduced and its role eventually limited to commentary between acts. By the sixteenth century the chorus—if employed at all—was typically a single person who provided a prologue and an epilogue and occasionally appeared between acts to introduce or underscore an important event. The chorus in William Shakespeare's *Henry V* functions in this way. Modern dramas rarely feature a chorus, but T. S. Eliot's *Murder in the Cathedral* and Arthur Miller's *A View from the Bridge* are notable exceptions. The Stage Manager in Thornton Wilder's *Our Town* performs a role similar to that of the chorus.

Chronicle: A record of events presented in chronological order. Although the scope and level of detail provided varies greatly among the chronicles surviving from ancient times, some, such as the *Anglo-Saxon Chronicle,* feature vivid descriptions and a lively recounting of events. During the Elizabethan Age, many dramas— appropriately called "chronicle plays"—were based on material from chronicles. Many of William Shakespeare's dramas of English history as well as Christopher Marlowe's *Edward II* are based in part on Raphael Holinshead's *Chronicles of England, Scotland, and Ireland.*

Classical: In its strictest definition in literary criticism, classicism refers to works of ancient Greek or Roman literature. The term may also be used to describe a literary work of recognized importance (a "classic") from any time period or literature that exhibits the traits of classicism. Classical authors from ancient Greek and Roman times include Juvenal and Homer. Examples of later works and authors now described as classical include French literature of the seventeenth century, Western novels of the nineteenth century, and American fiction of the mid-nineteenth century such as that written by James Fenimore Cooper and Mark Twain.

Classicism: A term used in literary criticism to describe critical doctrines that have their roots in ancient Greek and Roman literature, philosophy, and art. Works associated with classicism typically exhibit restraint on the part of the author, unity of design and purpose, clarity, simplicity, logical organization, and respect for tradition. Examples of literary classicism include Cicero's prose, the dramas of Pierre Corneille and Jean Racine, the poetry of John Dryden and Alexander Pope, and the writings of J. W. von Goethe, G. E. Lessing, and T. S. Eliot.

Climax: The turning point in a narrative, the moment when the conflict is at its most intense. Typically, the structure of stories, novels, and plays is one of rising action, in which tension builds to the climax, followed by falling action, in which tension lessens as the story moves to its conclusion. The climax in James Fenimore Cooper's *The Last of the Mohicans* occurs when Magua and his captive Cora are pursued to the edge of a cliff by Uncas. Magua kills Uncas but is subsequently killed by Hawkeye.

Colloquialism: A word, phrase, or form of pronunciation that is acceptable in casual conversation but not in formal, written communication. It is considered more acceptable than slang. An example of colloquialism can be found in Rudyard Kipling's *Barrack-room Ballads:* When 'Omer smote 'is bloomin' lyre He'd 'eard men sing by land and sea; An' what he thought 'e might require 'E went an' took—the same as me!

Comedy: One of two major types of drama, the other being tragedy. Its aim is to amuse, and it typically ends happily. Comedy assumes many forms, such as farce and burlesque, and uses a variety of techniques, from parody to satire. In a restricted sense the term comedy refers only to dramatic presentations, but in general usage it is commonly applied to nondramatic works as well. Examples of comedies range from the plays of Aristophanes, Terrence, and Plautus, Dante Alighieri's *The Divine Comedy,* Francois Rabelais's *Pantagruel* and *Gargantua,* and some of Geoffrey Chaucer's tales and William Shakespeare's plays to Noel Coward's play *Private Lives* and James Thurber's short story ''The Secret Life of Walter Mitty.''

Comedy of Manners: A play about the manners and conventions of an aristocratic, highly sophisticated society. The characters are usually types rather than individualized personalities, and plot is less important than atmosphere. Such plays were an important aspect of late seventeenth-century English comedy. The comedy of manners was revived in the eighteenth century by Oliver Goldsmith and Richard Brinsley Sheridan, enjoyed a second revival in the late nineteenth century, and has endured into the twentieth century. Examples of comedies of manners include William Congreve's *The Way of the World* in the late seventeenth century, Oliver Goldsmith's *She Stoops to Conquer* and Richard Brinsley Sheridan's *The School for Scandal* in the eighteenth century, Oscar Wilde's *The Importance of Being Earnest* in the nineteenth century, and W. Somerset Maugham's *The Circle* in the twentieth century.

Comic Relief: The use of humor to lighten the mood of a serious or tragic story, especially in plays. The technique is very common in Elizabethan works, and can be an integral part of the plot or simply a brief event designed to break the tension of the scene. The Gravediggers' scene in William Shakespeare's *Hamlet* is a frequently cited example of comic relief.

Commedia dell'arte: An Italian term meaning ''the comedy of guilds'' or ''the comedy of professional actors.'' This form of dramatic comedy was popular in Italy during the sixteenth century. Actors were assigned stock roles (such as Pulcinella, the stupid servant, or Pantalone, the old merchant) and given a basic plot to follow, but all dialogue was improvised. The roles were rigidly typed and the plots were formulaic, usually revolving around young lovers who thwarted their elders and attained wealth and happiness. A rigid convention of the *commedia dell'arte* is the periodic intrusion of Harlequin, who interrupts the play with low buffoonery. Peppino de Filippo's *Metamorphoses of a Wandering Minstrel* gave modern audiences an idea of what *commedia dell'arte* may have been like. Various scenarios for *commedia dell'arte* were compiled in Petraccone's *La commedia dell'arte, storia, technica, scenari,* published in 1927.

Complaint: A lyric poem, popular in the Renaissance, in which the speaker expresses sorrow about his or her condition. Typically, the speaker's sadness is caused by an unresponsive lover, but some complaints cite other sources of unhappiness, such as poverty or fate. A commonly cited example is ''A Complaint by Night of the Lover Not Beloved'' by Henry Howard, Earl of Surrey. Thomas Sackville's ''Complaint of Henry, Duke of Buckingham'' traces the duke's unhappiness to his ruthless ambition.

Conceit: A clever and fanciful metaphor, usually expressed through elaborate and extended comparison, that presents a striking parallel between two seemingly dissimilar things—for example, elaborately comparing a beautiful woman to an object like a garden or the sun. The conceit was a popular device throughout the Elizabethan Age and Baroque Age and was the principal technique of the seventeenth-century English metaphysical poets. This usage of the word conceit is unrelated to the best-known definition of conceit as an arrogant attitude or behavior. The conceit figures prominently in the works of John Donne, Emily Dickinson, and T. S. Eliot.

Concrete: Concrete is the opposite of abstract, and refers to a thing that actually exists or a description that allows the reader to experience an object or concept with the senses. Henry David Thoreau's *Walden* contains much concrete description of nature and wildlife.

Concrete Poetry: Poetry in which visual elements play a large part in the poetic effect. Punctuation marks, letters, or words are arranged on a page to form a visual design: a cross, for example, or a bumblebee. Max Bill and Eugene Gomringer were among the early practitioners of concrete poetry; Haroldo de Campos and Augusto de Campos are among contemporary authors of concrete poetry.

Confessional Poetry: A form of poetry in which the poet reveals very personal, intimate, sometimes shocking information about himself or herself. Anne Sexton, Sylvia Plath, Robert Lowell, and John Berryman wrote poetry in the confessional vein.

Conflict: The conflict in a work of fiction is the issue to be resolved in the story. It usually occurs between two characters, the protagonist and the antagonist, or between the protagonist and society or the protagonist and himself or herself. Conflict in Theodore Dreiser's novel *Sister Carrie* comes as a result of urban society, while Jack London's short story "To Build a Fire" concerns the protagonist's battle against the cold and himself.

Connotation: The impression that a word gives beyond its defined meaning. Connotations may be universally understood or may be significant only to a certain group. Both "horse" and "steed" denote the same animal, but "steed" has a different connotation, deriving from the chivalrous or romantic narratives in which the word was once often used.

Consonance: Consonance occurs in poetry when words appearing at the ends of two or more verses have similar final consonant sounds but have final vowel sounds that differ, as with "stuff" and "off." Consonance is found in "The curfew tolls the knells of parting day" from Thomas Grey's "An Elegy Written in a Country Church Yard." Also known as Half Rhyme or Slant Rhyme.

Convention: Any widely accepted literary device, style, or form. A soliloquy, in which a character reveals to the audience his or her private thoughts, is an example of a dramatic convention.

Corrido: A Mexican ballad. Examples of *corridos* include "Muerte del afamado Bilito," "La voz de mi conciencia," "Lucio Perez," "La juida," and "Los presos."

Couplet: Two lines of poetry with the same rhyme and meter, often expressing a complete and self-contained thought. The following couplet is from Alexander Pope's "Elegy to the Memory of an Unfortunate Lady": 'Tis Use alone that sanctifies Expense, And Splendour borrows all her rays from Sense.

Criticism: The systematic study and evaluation of literary works, usually based on a specific method or set of principles. An important part of literary studies since ancient times, the practice of criticism has given rise to numerous theories, methods, and "schools," sometimes producing conflicting, even contradictory, interpretations of literature in general as well as of individual works. Even such basic issues as what constitutes a poem or a novel have been the subject of much criticism over the centuries. Seminal texts of literary criticism include Plato's *Republic,* Aristotle's *Poetics,* Sir Philip Sidney's *The Defence of Poesie,* John Dryden's *Of Dramatic Poesie,* and William Wordsworth's "Preface" to the second edition of his *Lyrical Ballads.* Contemporary schools of criticism include deconstruction, feminist, psychoanalytic, poststructuralist, new historicist, postcolonialist, and reader-response.

D

Dactyl: See *Foot*

Dadaism: A protest movement in art and literature founded by Tristan Tzara in 1916. Followers of the movement expressed their outrage at the destruction brought about by World War I by revolting against numerous forms of social convention. The Dadaists presented works marked by calculated madness and flamboyant nonsense. They stressed total freedom of expression, commonly through primitive displays of emotion and illogical, often senseless, poetry. The movement ended shortly after the war, when it was replaced by surrealism. Proponents of Dadaism include Andre Breton, Louis Aragon, Philippe Soupault, and Paul Eluard.

Decadent: See *Decadents*

Decadents: The followers of a nineteenth-century literary movement that had its beginnings in French aestheticism. Decadent literature displays a fascination with perverse and morbid states; a search for novelty and sensation—the ''new thrill''; a preoccupation with mysticism; and a belief in the senselessness of human existence. The movement is closely associated with the doctrine Art for Art's Sake. The term ''decadence'' is sometimes used to denote a decline in the quality of art or literature following a period of greatness. Major French decadents are Charles Baudelaire and Arthur Rimbaud. English decadents include Oscar Wilde, Ernest Dowson, and Frank Harris.

Deconstruction: A method of literary criticism developed by Jacques Derrida and characterized by multiple conflicting interpretations of a given work. Deconstructionists consider the impact of the language of a work and suggest that the true meaning of the work is not necessarily the meaning that the author intended. Jacques Derrida's *De la grammatologie* is the seminal text on deconstructive strategies; among American practitioners of this method of criticism are Paul de Man and J. Hillis Miller.

Deduction: The process of reaching a conclusion through reasoning from general premises to a specific premise. An example of deduction is present in the following syllogism: Premise: All mammals are animals. Premise: All whales are mammals. Conclusion: Therefore, all whales are animals.

Denotation: The definition of a word, apart from the impressions or feelings it creates in the reader. The word ''apartheid'' denotes a political and economic policy of segregation by race, but its connotations— oppression, slavery, inequality—are numerous.

Denouement: A French word meaning ''the unknotting.'' In literary criticism, it denotes the resolution of conflict in fiction or drama. The *denouement* follows the climax and provides an outcome to the primary plot situation as well as an explanation of secondary plot complications. The *denouement* often involves a character's recognition of his or her state of mind or moral condition. A well-known example of *denouement* is the last scene of the play *As You Like It* by William Shakespeare, in which couples are married, an evildoer repents, the identities of two disguised characters are revealed, and a ruler is restored to power. Also known as Falling Action.

Description: Descriptive writing is intended to allow a reader to picture the scene or setting in which the action of a story takes place. The form this description takes often evokes an intended emotional response—a dark, spooky graveyard will evoke fear, and a peaceful, sunny meadow will evoke calmness. An example of a descriptive story is Edgar Allan Poe's *Landor's Cottage,* which offers a detailed depiction of a New York country estate.

Detective Story: A narrative about the solution of a mystery or the identification of a criminal. The conventions of the detective story include the detective's scrupulous use of logic in solving the mystery; incompetent or ineffectual police; a suspect who appears guilty at first but is later proved innocent; and the detective's friend or confidant— often the narrator—whose slowness in interpreting clues emphasizes by contrast the detective's brilliance. Edgar Allan Poe's ''Murders in the Rue Morgue'' is commonly regarded as the earliest example of this type of story. With this work, Poe established many of the conventions of the detective story genre, which are still in practice. Other practitioners of this vast and extremely popular genre include Arthur Conan Doyle, Dashiell Hammett, and Agatha Christie.

Deus ex machina: A Latin term meaning ''god out of a machine.'' In Greek drama, a god was often lowered onto the stage by a mechanism of some kind to rescue the hero or untangle the plot. By extension, the term refers to any artificial device or coincidence used to bring about a convenient and simple solution to a plot. This is a common device in melodramas and includes such fortunate circumstances as the sudden receipt of a legacy to save the family farm or a last-minute stay of execution. The *deus ex machina* invariably rewards the virtuous and punishes evildoers. Examples of *deus ex machina* include King Louis XIV in Jean-Baptiste Moliere's *Tartuffe* and Queen Victoria in *The Pirates of Penzance* by William Gilbert and Arthur Sullivan. Bertolt Brecht parodies the abuse of such devices in the conclusion of his *Threepenny Opera.*

Dialogue: In its widest sense, dialogue is simply conversation between people in a literary work; in its most restricted sense, it refers specifically to the speech of characters in a drama. As a specific literary genre, a ''dialogue'' is a composition in which characters debate an issue or idea. The Greek philosopher Plato frequently expounded his theories in the form of dialogues.

Diction: The selection and arrangement of words in a literary work. Either or both may vary depending on the desired effect. There are four general types of diction: ''formal,'' used in scholarly or lofty writing; ''informal,'' used in relaxed but educated conversation; ''colloquial,'' used in everyday speech; and ''slang,'' containing newly coined words and other terms not accepted in formal usage.

Didactic: A term used to describe works of literature that aim to teach some moral, religious, political, or practical lesson. Although didactic elements are often found in artistically pleasing works, the term ''didactic'' usually refers to literature in which the message is more important than the form. The term may also be used to criticize a work that the critic finds ''overly didactic,'' that is, heavy-handed in its delivery of a lesson. Examples of didactic literature include John Bunyan's *Pilgrim's Progress,* Alexander Pope's *Essay on Criticism,* Jean-Jacques Rousseau's *Emile,* and Elizabeth Inchbald's *Simple Story.*

Dimeter: See *Meter*

Dionysian: See *Apollonian and Dionysian*

Discordia concours: A Latin phrase meaning ''discord in harmony.'' The term was coined by the eighteenth-century English writer Samuel Johnson to describe ''a combination of dissimilar images or discovery of occult resemblances in things apparently unlike.'' Johnson created the expression by reversing a phrase by the Latin poet Horace. The metaphysical poetry of John Donne, Richard Crashaw, Abraham Cowley, George Herbert, and Edward Taylor among others, contains many examples of *discordia concours.* In Donne's ''A Valediction: Forbidding Mourning,'' the poet compares the union of himself with his lover to a draftsman's compass: If they be two, they are two so, As stiff twin compasses are two: Thy soul, the fixed foot, makes no show To move, but doth, if the other do; And though it in the center sit, Yet when the other far doth roam, It leans, and hearkens after it, And grows erect, as that comes home.

Dissonance: A combination of harsh or jarring sounds, especially in poetry. Although such combinations may be accidental, poets sometimes intentionally make them to achieve particular effects. Dissonance is also sometimes used to refer to close but not identical rhymes. When this is the case, the word functions as a synonym for consonance. Robert Browning, Gerard Manley Hopkins, and many other poets have made deliberate use of dissonance.

Doppelganger: A literary technique by which a character is duplicated (usually in the form of an alter ego, though sometimes as a ghostly counterpart) or divided into two distinct, usually opposite personalities. The use of this character device is widespread in nineteenth- and twentieth- century literature, and indicates a growing awareness among authors that the ''self'' is really a composite of many ''selves.'' A well-known story containing a *doppelganger* character is Robert Louis Stevenson's *Dr. Jekyll and Mr. Hyde,* which dramatizes an internal struggle between good and evil. Also known as The Double.

Double Entendre: A corruption of a French phrase meaning ''double meaning.'' The term is used to indicate a word or phrase that is deliberately ambiguous, especially when one of the meanings is risque or improper. An example of a *double entendre* is the Elizabethan usage of the verb ''die,'' which refers both to death and to orgasm.

Double, The: See *Doppelganger*

Draft: Any preliminary version of a written work. An author may write dozens of drafts which are revised to form the final work, or he or she may write only one, with few or no revisions. Dorothy Parker's observation that ''I can't write five words but that I change seven'' humorously indicates the purpose of the draft.

Drama: In its widest sense, a drama is any work designed to be presented by actors on a stage. Similarly, ''drama'' denotes a broad literary genre that includes a variety of forms, from pageant and spectacle to tragedy and comedy, as well as countless types and subtypes. More commonly in modern usage, however, a drama is a work that treats serious subjects and themes but does not aim at the grandeur of tragedy. This use of the term originated with the eighteenth-century French writer Denis Diderot, who used the word *drame* to designate his plays about middle- class life; thus ''drama'' typically features characters of a less exalted stature than those of tragedy. Examples of classical dramas include Menander's comedy *Dyscolus* and Sophocles' tragedy *Oedipus Rex.* Contemporary dramas include Eugene O'Neill's *The Iceman Cometh,* Lillian Hellman's *Little Foxes,* and August Wilson's *Ma Rainey's Black Bottom.*

Dramatic Irony: Occurs when the audience of a play or the reader of a work of literature knows something that a character in the work itself does not know. The irony is in the contrast between the intended meaning of the statements or actions of a character and the additional information understood by the audience. A celebrated example of dramatic irony is in Act V of William Shakespeare's *Romeo and Juliet,* where two young lovers meet their end as a result of a tragic misunderstanding. Here, the audience has full knowledge that Juliet's apparent ''death'' is merely temporary; she will regain her senses when the mysterious ''sleeping potion'' she has taken wears off. But Romeo, mistaking Juliet's drug-induced trance for true death, kills himself in grief. Upon awakening, Juliet discovers Romeo's corpse and, in despair, slays herself.

Dramatic Monologue: See *Monologue*

Dramatic Poetry: Any lyric work that employs elements of drama such as dialogue, conflict, or characterization, but excluding works that are intended for stage presentation. A monologue is a form of dramatic poetry.

Dramatis Personae: The characters in a work of literature, particularly a drama. The list of characters printed before the main text of a play or in the program is the *dramatis personae.*

Dream Allegory: See *Dream Vision*

Dream Vision: A literary convention, chiefly of the Middle Ages. In a dream vision a story is presented as a literal dream of the narrator. This device was commonly used to teach moral and religious lessons. Important works of this type are *The Divine Comedy* by Dante Alighieri, *Piers Plowman* by William Langland, and *The Pilgrim's Progress* by John Bunyan. Also known as Dream Allegory.

Dystopia: An imaginary place in a work of fiction where the characters lead dehumanized, fearful lives. Jack London's *The Iron Heel,* Yevgeny Zamyatin's *My,* Aldous Huxley's *Brave New World,* George Orwell's *Nineteen Eighty-four,* and Margaret Atwood's *Handmaid's Tale* portray versions of dystopia.

E

Eclogue: In classical literature, a poem featuring rural themes and structured as a dialogue among shepherds. Eclogues often took specific poetic forms, such as elegies or love poems. Some were written as the soliloquy of a shepherd. In later centuries, ''eclogue'' came to refer to any poem that was in the pastoral tradition or that had a dialogue or mono-

logue structure. A classical example of an eclogue is Virgil's *Eclogues,* also known as *Bucolics.* Giovanni Boccaccio, Edmund Spenser, Andrew Marvell, Jonathan Swift, and Louis MacNeice also wrote eclogues.

Edwardian: Describes cultural conventions identified with the period of the reign of Edward VII of England (1901-1910). Writers of the Edwardian Age typically displayed a strong reaction against the propriety and conservatism of the Victorian Age. Their work often exhibits distrust of authority in religion, politics, and art and expresses strong doubts about the soundness of conventional values. Writers of this era include George Bernard Shaw, H. G. Wells, and Joseph Conrad.

Edwardian Age: See *Edwardian*

Electra Complex: A daughter's amorous obsession with her father. The term Electra complex comes from the plays of Euripides and Sophocles entitled *Electra,* in which the character Electra drives her brother Orestes to kill their mother and her lover in revenge for the murder of their father.

Elegy: A lyric poem that laments the death of a person or the eventual death of all people. In a conventional elegy, set in a classical world, the poet and subject are spoken of as shepherds. In modern criticism, the word elegy is often used to refer to a poem that is melancholy or mournfully contemplative. John Milton's ''Lycidas'' and Percy Bysshe Shelley's ''Adonais'' are two examples of this form.

Elizabethan Age: A period of great economic growth, religious controversy, and nationalism closely associated with the reign of Elizabeth I of England (1558-1603). The Elizabethan Age is considered a part of the general renaissance—that is, the flowering of arts and literature—that took place in Europe during the fourteenth through sixteenth centuries. The era is considered the golden age of English literature. The most important dramas in English and a great deal of lyric poetry were produced during this period, and modern English criticism began around this time. The notable authors of the period—Philip Sidney, Edmund Spenser, Christopher Marlowe, William Shakespeare, Ben Jonson, Francis Bacon, and John Donne—are among the best in all of English literature.

Elizabethan Drama: English comic and tragic plays produced during the Renaissance, or more narrowly, those plays written during the last years of and few years after Queen Elizabeth's reign. William Shakespeare is considered an Elizabethan dramatist in the broader sense, although most of his work was produced during the reign of James I. Examples of Elizabethan comedies include John Lyly's *The Woman in the Moone,* Thomas Dekker's *The Roaring Girl, or, Moll Cut Purse,* and William Shakespeare's *Twelfth Night.* Examples of Elizabethan tragedies include William Shakespeare's *Antony and Cleopatra,* Thomas Kyd's *The Spanish Tragedy,* and John Webster's *The Tragedy of the Duchess of Malfi.*

Empathy: A sense of shared experience, including emotional and physical feelings, with someone or something other than oneself. Empathy is often used to describe the response of a reader to a literary character. An example of an empathic passage is William Shakespeare's description in his narrative poem *Venus and Adonis* of: the snail, whose tender horns being hit, Shrinks backward in his shelly cave with pain. Readers of Gerard Manley Hopkins's *The Windhover* may experience some of the physical sensations evoked in the description of the movement of the falcon.

English Sonnet: See *Sonnet*

Enjambment: The running over of the sense and structure of a line of verse or a couplet into the following verse or couplet. Andrew Marvell's "To His Coy Mistress" is structured as a series of enjambments, as in lines 11-12: "My vegetable love should grow/Vaster than empires and more slow."

Enlightenment, The: An eighteenth-century philosophical movement. It began in France but had a wide impact throughout Europe and America. Thinkers of the Enlightenment valued reason and believed that both the individual and society could achieve a state of perfection. Corresponding to this essentially humanist vision was a resistance to religious authority. Important figures of the Enlightenment were Denis Diderot and Voltaire in France, Edward Gibbon and David Hume in England, and Thomas Paine and Thomas Jefferson in the United States.

Epic: A long narrative poem about the adventures of a hero of great historic or legendary importance. The setting is vast and the action is often given cosmic significance through the intervention of supernatural forces such as gods, angels, or demons. Epics are typically written in a classical style of grand simplicity with elaborate metaphors and allusions that enhance the symbolic importance of a hero's adventures. Some well-known epics are Homer's *Iliad* and *Odyssey,* Virgil's *Aeneid,* and John Milton's *Paradise Lost.*

Epic Simile: See *Homeric Simile*

Epic Theater: A theory of theatrical presentation developed by twentieth-century German playwright Bertolt Brecht. Brecht created a type of drama that the audience could view with complete detachment. He used what he termed "alienation effects" to create an emotional distance between the audience and the action on stage. Among these effects are: short, self-contained scenes that keep the play from building to a cathartic climax; songs that comment on the action; and techniques of acting that prevent the actor from developing an emotional identity with his role. Besides the plays of Bertolt Brecht, other plays that utilize epic theater conventions include those of Georg Buchner, Frank Wedekind, Erwin Piscator, and Leopold Jessner.

Epigram: A saying that makes the speaker's point quickly and concisely. Samuel Taylor Coleridge wrote an epigram that neatly sums up the form: What is an Epigram? A Dwarfish whole, Its body brevity, and wit its soul.

Epilogue: A concluding statement or section of a literary work. In dramas, particularly those of the seventeenth and eighteenth centuries, the epilogue is a closing speech, often in verse, delivered by an actor at the end of a play and spoken directly to the audience. A famous epilogue is Puck's speech at the end of William Shakespeare's *A Midsummer Night's Dream.*

Epiphany: A sudden revelation of truth inspired by a seemingly trivial incident. The term was widely used by James Joyce in his critical writings, and the stories in Joyce's *Dubliners* are commonly called "epiphanies."

Episode: An incident that forms part of a story and is significantly related to it. Episodes may be either self-contained narratives or events that depend on a larger context for their sense and importance. Examples of episodes include the founding of Wilmington, Delaware in Charles Reade's *The Disinherited Heir* and the individual events comprising the picaresque novels and medieval romances.

Episodic Plot: See *Plot*

Epitaph: An inscription on a tomb or tombstone, or a verse written on the occasion of a person's death. Epitaphs may be serious or humorous. Dorothy Parker's epitaph reads, "I told you I was sick."

Epithalamion: A song or poem written to honor and commemorate a marriage ceremony. Famous examples include Edmund Spenser's

"Epithalamion" and e. e. cummings's "Epithalamion." Also spelled Epithalamium.

Epithalamium: See *Epithalamion*

Epithet: A word or phrase, often disparaging or abusive, that expresses a character trait of someone or something. "The Napoleon of crime" is an epithet applied to Professor Moriarty, arch-rival of Sherlock Holmes in Arthur Conan Doyle's series of detective stories.

Exempla: See *Exemplum*

Exemplum: A tale with a moral message. This form of literary sermonizing flourished during the Middle Ages, when *exempla* appeared in collections known as "example-books." The works of Geoffrey Chaucer are full of *exempla*.

Existentialism: A predominantly twentieth-century philosophy concerned with the nature and perception of human existence. There are two major strains of existentialist thought: atheistic and Christian. Followers of atheistic existentialism believe that the individual is alone in a godless universe and that the basic human condition is one of suffering and loneliness. Nevertheless, because there are no fixed values, individuals can create their own characters—indeed, they can shape themselves—through the exercise of free will. The atheistic strain culminates in and is popularly associated with the works of Jean-Paul Sartre. The Christian existentialists, on the other hand, believe that only in God may people find freedom from life's anguish. The two strains hold certain beliefs in common: that existence cannot be fully understood or described through empirical effort; that anguish is a universal element of life; that individuals must bear responsibility for their actions; and that there is no common standard of behavior or perception for religious and ethical matters. Existentialist thought figures prominently in the works of such authors as Eugene Ionesco, Franz Kafka, Fyodor Dostoyevsky, Simone de Beauvoir, Samuel Beckett, and Albert Camus.

Expatriates: See *Expatriatism*

Expatriatism: The practice of leaving one's country to live for an extended period in another country. Literary expatriates include English poets Percy Bysshe Shelley and John Keats in Italy, Polish novelist Joseph Conrad in England, American writers Richard Wright, James Baldwin, Gertrude Stein, and Ernest Hemingway in France, and Trinidadian author Neil Bissondath in Canada.

Exposition: Writing intended to explain the nature of an idea, thing, or theme. Expository writing is often combined with description, narration, or argument. In dramatic writing, the exposition is the introductory material which presents the characters, setting, and tone of the play. An example of dramatic exposition occurs in many nineteenth-century drawing-room comedies in which the butler and the maid open the play with relevant talk about their master and mistress; in composition, exposition relays factual information, as in encyclopedia entries.

Expressionism: An indistinct literary term, originally used to describe an early twentieth-century school of German painting. The term applies to almost any mode of unconventional, highly subjective writing that distorts reality in some way. Advocates of Expressionism include dramatists George Kaiser, Ernst Toller, Luigi Pirandello, Federico Garcia Lorca, Eugene O'Neill, and Elmer Rice; poets George Heym, Ernst Stadler, August Stramm, Gottfried Benn, and Georg Trakl; and novelists Franz Kafka and James Joyce.

Extended Monologue: See *Monologue*

F

Fable: A prose or verse narrative intended to convey a moral. Animals or inanimate objects with human characteristics often serve as characters in fables. A famous fable is Aesop's "The Tortoise and the Hare."

Fairy Tales: Short narratives featuring mythical beings such as fairies, elves, and sprites. These tales originally belonged to the folklore of a particular nation or region, such as those collected in Germany by Jacob and Wilhelm Grimm. Two other celebrated writers of fairy tales are Hans Christian Andersen and Rudyard Kipling.

Falling Action: See *Denouement*

Fantasy: A literary form related to mythology and folklore. Fantasy literature is typically set in nonexistent realms and features supernatural beings. Notable examples of fantasy literature are *The Lord of the Rings* by J. R. R. Tolkien and the Gormenghast trilogy by Mervyn Peake.

Farce: A type of comedy characterized by broad humor, outlandish incidents, and often vulgar subject matter. Much of the "comedy" in film and television could more accurately be described as farce.

Feet: See *Foot*

Feminine Rhyme: See *Rhyme*

Femme fatale: A French phrase with the literal translation ''fatal woman.'' A *femme fatale* is a sensuous, alluring woman who often leads men into danger or trouble. A classic example of the *femme fatale* is the nameless character in Billy Wilder's *The Seven Year Itch,* portrayed by Marilyn Monroe in the film adaptation.

Fiction: Any story that is the product of imagination rather than a documentation of fact. characters and events in such narratives may be based in real life but their ultimate form and configuration is a creation of the author. Geoffrey Chaucer's *The Canterbury Tales,* Laurence Sterne's *Tristram Shandy,* and Margaret Mitchell's *Gone with the Wind* are examples of fiction.

Figurative Language: A technique in writing in which the author temporarily interrupts the order, construction, or meaning of the writing for a particular effect. This interruption takes the form of one or more figures of speech such as hyperbole, irony, or simile. Figurative language is the opposite of literal language, in which every word is truthful, accurate, and free of exaggeration or embellishment. Examples of figurative language are tropes such as metaphor and rhetorical figures such as apostrophe.

Figures of Speech: Writing that differs from customary conventions for construction, meaning, order, or significance for the purpose of a special meaning or effect. There are two major types of figures of speech: rhetorical figures, which do not make changes in the meaning of the words, and tropes, which do. Types of figures of speech include simile, hyperbole, alliteration, and pun, among many others.

Fin de siecle: A French term meaning ''end of the century.'' The term is used to denote the last decade of the nineteenth century, a transition period when writers and other artists abandoned old conventions and looked for new techniques and objectives. Two writers commonly associated with the *fin de siecle* mindset are Oscar Wilde and George Bernard Shaw.

First Person: See *Point of View*

Flashback: A device used in literature to present action that occurred before the beginning of the story. Flashbacks are often introduced as the dreams or recollections of one or more characters. Flashback techniques are often used in films, where they are typically set off by a gradual changing of one picture to another.

Foil: A character in a work of literature whose physical or psychological qualities contrast strongly with, and therefore highlight, the corresponding qualities of another character. In his Sherlock Holmes stories, Arthur Conan Doyle portrayed Dr. Watson as a man of normal habits and intelligence, making him a foil for the eccentric and wonderfully perceptive Sherlock Holmes.

Folk Ballad: See *Ballad*

Folklore: Traditions and myths preserved in a culture or group of people. Typically, these are passed on by word of mouth in various forms—such as legends, songs, and proverbs— or preserved in customs and ceremonies. This term was first used by W. J. Thoms in 1846. Sir James Frazer's *The Golden Bough* is the record of English folklore; myths about the frontier and the Old South exemplify American folklore.

Folktale: A story originating in oral tradition. Folktales fall into a variety of categories, including legends, ghost stories, fairy tales, fables, and anecdotes based on historical figures and events. Examples of folktales include Giambattista Basile's *The Pentamerone,* which contains the tales of Puss in Boots, Rapunzel, Cinderella, and Beauty and the Beast, and Joel Chandler Harris's Uncle Remus stories, which represent transplanted African folktales and American tales about the characters Mike Fink, Johnny Appleseed, Paul Bunyan, and Pecos Bill.

Foot: The smallest unit of rhythm in a line of poetry. In English-language poetry, a foot is typically one accented syllable combined with one or two unaccented syllables. There are many different types of feet. When the accent is on the second syllable of a two syllable word (con- *tort*), the foot is an ''iamb''; the reverse accentual pattern (*tor* -ture) is a ''trochee.'' Other feet that commonly occur in poetry in English are ''anapest'', two unaccented syllables followed by an accented syllable as in inter-*cept*, and ''dactyl'', an accented syllable followed by two unaccented syllables as in *su*-i- cide.

Foreshadowing: A device used in literature to create expectation or to set up an explanation of later developments. In Charles Dickens's *Great Expectations,* the graveyard encounter at the beginning of the novel between Pip and the escaped convict Magwitch foreshadows the baleful atmosphere and events that comprise much of the narrative.

Form: The pattern or construction of a work which identifies its genre and distinguishes it from other genres. Examples of forms include the different genres, such as the lyric form or the short story form, and various patterns for poetry, such as the verse form or the stanza form.

Formalism: In literary criticism, the belief that literature should follow prescribed rules of construction, such as those that govern the sonnet form. Examples of formalism are found in the work of the New Critics and structuralists.

Fourteener Meter: See *Meter*

Free Verse: Poetry that lacks regular metrical and rhyme patterns but that tries to capture the cadences of everyday speech. The form allows a poet to exploit a variety of rhythmical effects within a single poem. Free-verse techniques have been widely used in the twentieth century by such writers as Ezra Pound, T. S. Eliot, Carl Sandburg, and William Carlos Williams. Also known as *Vers libre.*

Futurism: A flamboyant literary and artistic movement that developed in France, Italy, and Russia from 1908 through the 1920s. Futurist theater and poetry abandoned traditional literary forms. In their place, followers of the movement attempted to achieve total freedom of expression through bizarre imagery and deformed or newly invented words. The Futurists were self-consciously modern artists who attempted to incorporate the appearances and sounds of modern life into their work. Futurist writers include Filippo Tommaso Marinetti, Wyndham Lewis, Guillaume Apollinaire, Velimir Khlebnikov, and Vladimir Mayakovsky.

G

Genre: A category of literary work. In critical theory, genre may refer to both the content of a given work—tragedy, comedy, pastoral—and to its form, such as poetry, novel, or drama. This term also refers to types of popular literature, as in the genres of science fiction or the detective story.

Genteel Tradition: A term coined by critic George Santayana to describe the literary practice of certain late nineteenth- century American writers, especially New Englanders. Followers of the Genteel Tradition emphasized conventionality in social, religious, moral, and literary standards. Some of the best-known writers of the Genteel Tradition are R. H. Stoddard and Bayard Taylor.

Gilded Age: A period in American history during the 1870s characterized by political corruption and materialism. A number of important novels of social and political criticism were written during this time. Examples of Gilded Age literature include Henry Adams's *Democracy* and F. Marion Crawford's *An American Politician.*

Gothic: See *Gothicism*

Gothicism: In literary criticism, works characterized by a taste for the medieval or morbidly attractive. A gothic novel prominently features elements of horror, the supernatural, gloom, and violence: clanking chains, terror, charnel houses, ghosts, medieval castles, and mysteriously slamming doors. The term ''gothic novel'' is also applied to novels that lack elements of the traditional Gothic setting but that create a similar atmosphere of terror or dread. Mary Shelley's *Frankenstein* is perhaps the best-known English work of this kind.

Gothic Novel: See *Gothicism*

Great Chain of Being: The belief that all things and creatures in nature are organized in a hierarchy from inanimate objects at the bottom to God at the top. This system of belief was popular in the seventeenth and eighteenth centuries. A summary of the concept of the great chain of being can be found in the first epistle of Alexander Pope's *An Essay on Man,* and more recently in Arthur O. Lovejoy's *The Great Chain of Being: A Study of the History of an Idea.*

Grotesque: In literary criticism, the subject matter of a work or a style of expression characterized by exaggeration, deformity, freakishness, and disorder. The grotesque often includes an element of comic absurdity. Early examples of literary grotesque include Francois Rabelais's *Pantagruel* and *Gargantua* and Thomas Nashe's *The Unfortunate Traveller,* while more recent examples can be found in the works of Edgar Allan Poe, Evelyn Waugh, Eudora Welty, Flannery O'Connor, Eugene Ionesco, Gunter Grass, Thomas Mann, Mervyn Peake, and Joseph Heller, among many others.

H

Haiku: The shortest form of Japanese poetry, constructed in three lines of five, seven, and five syllables respectively. The message of a *haiku* poem usually centers on some aspect of spirituality and provokes an emotional response in the reader. Early masters of *haiku* include Basho, Buson,

Kobayashi Issa, and Masaoka Shiki. English writers of *haiku* include the Imagists, notably Ezra Pound, H. D., Amy Lowell, Carl Sandburg, and William Carlos Williams. Also known as *Hokku.*

Half Rhyme: See *Consonance*

Hamartia: In tragedy, the event or act that leads to the hero's or heroine's downfall. This term is often incorrectly used as a synonym for tragic flaw. In Richard Wright's *Native Son,* the act that seals Bigger Thomas's fate is his first impulsive murder.

Harlem Renaissance: The Harlem Renaissance of the 1920s is generally considered the first significant movement of black writers and artists in the United States. During this period, new and established black writers published more fiction and poetry than ever before, the first influential black literary journals were established, and black authors and artists received their first widespread recognition and serious critical appraisal. Among the major writers associated with this period are Claude McKay, Jean Toomer, Countee Cullen, Langston Hughes, Arna Bontemps, Nella Larsen, and Zora Neale Hurston. Works representative of the Harlem Renaissance include Arna Bontemps's poems "The Return" and "Golgotha Is a Mountain," Claude McKay's novel *Home to Harlem,* Nella Larsen's novel *Passing,* Langston Hughes's poem "The Negro Speaks of Rivers," and the journals *Crisis* and *Opportunity,* both founded during this period. Also known as Negro Renaissance and New Negro Movement.

Harlequin: A stock character of the *commedia dell'arte* who occasionally interrupted the action with silly antics. Harlequin first appeared on the English stage in John Day's *The Travailes of the Three English Brothers.* The San Francisco Mime Troupe is one of the few modern groups to adapt Harlequin to the needs of contemporary satire.

Hellenism: Imitation of ancient Greek thought or styles. Also, an approach to life that focuses on the growth and development of the intellect. "Hellenism" is sometimes used to refer to the belief that reason can be applied to examine all human experience. A cogent discussion of Hellenism can be found in Matthew Arnold's *Culture and Anarchy.*

Heptameter: See *Meter*

Hero/Heroine: The principal sympathetic character (male or female) in a literary work. Heroes and heroines typically exhibit admirable traits: ideal-

ism, courage, and integrity, for example. Famous heroes and heroines include Pip in Charles Dickens's *Great Expectations,* the anonymous narrator in Ralph Ellison's *Invisible Man,* and Sethe in Toni Morrison's *Beloved.*

Heroic Couplet: A rhyming couplet written in iambic pentameter (a verse with five iambic feet). The following lines by Alexander Pope are an example: "Truth guards the Poet, sanctifies the line,/ And makes Immortal, Verse as mean as mine."

Heroic Line: The meter and length of a line of verse in epic or heroic poetry. This varies by language and time period. For example, in English poetry, the heroic line is iambic pentameter (a verse with five iambic feet); in French, the alexandrine (a verse with six iambic feet); in classical literature, dactylic hexameter (a verse with six dactylic feet).

Heroine: See *Hero/Heroine*

Hexameter: See *Meter*

Historical Criticism: The study of a work based on its impact on the world of the time period in which it was written. Examples of postmodern historical criticism can be found in the work of Michel Foucault, Hayden White, Stephen Greenblatt, and Jonathan Goldberg.

Hokku: See *Haiku*

Holocaust: See *Holocaust Literature*

Holocaust Literature: Literature influenced by or written about the Holocaust of World War II. Such literature includes true stories of survival in concentration camps, escape, and life after the war, as well as fictional works and poetry. Representative works of Holocaust literature include Saul Bellow's *Mr. Sammler's Planet,* Anne Frank's *The Diary of a Young Girl,* Jerzy Kosinski's *The Painted Bird,* Arthur Miller's *Incident at Vichy,* Czeslaw Milosz's *Collected Poems,* William Styron's *Sophie's Choice,* and Art Spiegelman's *Maus.*

Homeric Simile: An elaborate, detailed comparison written as a simile many lines in length. An example of an epic simile from John Milton's *Paradise Lost* follows: Angel Forms, who lay entranced Thick as autumnal leaves that strow the brooks In Vallombrosa, where the Etrurian shades High over-arched embower; or scattered sedge Afloat, when with fierce winds Orion armed Hath vexed the Red-Sea coast, whose waves o'erthrew Busiris and his Memphian chivalry, While with perfidious hatred they pursued The sojourners of

Goshen, who beheld From the safe shore their floating carcasses And broken chariot-wheels. Also known as Epic Simile.

Horatian Satire: See *Satire*

Humanism: A philosophy that places faith in the dignity of humankind and rejects the medieval perception of the individual as a weak, fallen creature. "Humanists" typically believe in the perfectibility of human nature and view reason and education as the means to that end. Humanist thought is represented in the works of Marsilio Ficino, Ludovico Castelvetro, Edmund Spenser, John Milton, Dean John Colet, Desiderius Erasmus, John Dryden, Alexander Pope, Matthew Arnold, and Irving Babbitt.

Humors: Mentions of the humors refer to the ancient Greek theory that a person's health and personality were determined by the balance of four basic fluids in the body: blood, phlegm, yellow bile, and black bile. A dominance of any fluid would cause extremes in behavior. An excess of blood created a sanguine person who was joyful, aggressive, and passionate; a phlegmatic person was shy, fearful, and sluggish; too much yellow bile led to a choleric temperament characterized by impatience, anger, bitterness, and stubbornness; and excessive black bile created melancholy, a state of laziness, gluttony, and lack of motivation. Literary treatment of the humors is exemplified by several characters in Ben Jonson's plays *Every Man in His Humour* and *Every Man out of His Humour.* Also spelled Humours.

Humours: See *Humors*

Hyperbole: In literary criticism, deliberate exaggeration used to achieve an effect. In William Shakespeare's *Macbeth,* Lady Macbeth hyperbolizes when she says, "All the perfumes of Arabia could not sweeten this little hand."

I

Iamb: See *Foot*

Idiom: A word construction or verbal expression closely associated with a given language. For example, in colloquial English the construction "how come" can be used instead of "why" to introduce a question. Similarly, "a piece of cake" is sometimes used to describe a task that is easily done.

Image: A concrete representation of an object or sensory experience. Typically, such a representation helps evoke the feelings associated with the object or experience itself. Images are either "literal" or "figurative." Literal images are especially concrete and involve little or no extension of the obvious meaning of the words used to express them. Figurative images do not follow the literal meaning of the words exactly. Images in literature are usually visual, but the term "image" can also refer to the representation of any sensory experience. In his poem "The Shepherd's Hour," Paul Verlaine presents the following image: "The Moon is red through horizon's fog;/ In a dancing mist the hazy meadow sleeps." The first line is broadly literal, while the second line involves turns of meaning associated with dancing and sleeping.

Imagery: The array of images in a literary work. Also, figurative language. William Butler Yeats's "The Second Coming" offers a powerful image of encroaching anarchy: Turning and turning in the widening gyre The falcon cannot hear the falconer; Things fall apart. . . .

Imagism: An English and American poetry movement that flourished between 1908 and 1917. The Imagists used precise, clearly presented images in their works. They also used common, everyday speech and aimed for conciseness, concrete imagery, and the creation of new rhythms. Participants in the Imagist movement included Ezra Pound, H. D. (Hilda Doolittle), and Amy Lowell, among others.

In medias res: A Latin term meaning "in the middle of things." It refers to the technique of beginning a story at its midpoint and then using various flashback devices to reveal previous action. This technique originated in such epics as Virgil's *Aeneid.*

Induction: The process of reaching a conclusion by reasoning from specific premises to form a general premise. Also, an introductory portion of a work of literature, especially a play. Geoffrey Chaucer's "Prologue" to the *Canterbury Tales,* Thomas Sackville's "Induction" to *The Mirror of Magistrates,* and the opening scene in William Shakespeare's *The Taming of the Shrew* are examples of inductions to literary works.

Intentional Fallacy: The belief that judgments of a literary work based solely on an author's stated or implied intentions are false and misleading. Critics who believe in the concept of the intentional fallacy typically argue that the work itself is sufficient matter for interpretation, even though they may concede that an author's statement of purpose can be useful. Analysis of William Wordsworth's *Lyri-*

cal Ballads based on the observations about poetry he makes in his ''Preface'' to the second edition of that work is an example of the intentional fallacy.

Interior Monologue: A narrative technique in which characters' thoughts are revealed in a way that appears to be uncontrolled by the author. The interior monologue typically aims to reveal the inner self of a character. It portrays emotional experiences as they occur at both a conscious and unconscious level. images are often used to represent sensations or emotions. One of the best-known interior monologues in English is the Molly Bloom section at the close of James Joyce's *Ulysses.* The interior monologue is also common in the works of Virginia Woolf.

Internal Rhyme: Rhyme that occurs within a single line of verse. An example is in the opening line of Edgar Allan Poe's ''The Raven'': ''Once upon a midnight dreary, while I pondered weak and weary.'' Here, ''dreary'' and ''weary'' make an internal rhyme.

Irish Literary Renaissance: A late nineteenth- and early twentieth-century movement in Irish literature. Members of the movement aimed to reduce the influence of British culture in Ireland and create an Irish national literature. William Butler Yeats, George Moore, and Sean O'Casey are three of the best-known figures of the movement.

Irony: In literary criticism, the effect of language in which the intended meaning is the opposite of what is stated. The title of Jonathan Swift's ''A Modest Proposal'' is ironic because what Swift proposes in this essay is cannibalism—hardly ''modest.''

Italian Sonnet: See *Sonnet*

J

Jacobean Age: The period of the reign of James I of England (1603-1625). The early literature of this period reflected the worldview of the Elizabethan Age, but a darker, more cynical attitude steadily grew in the art and literature of the Jacobean Age. This was an important time for English drama and poetry. Milestones include William Shakespeare's tragedies, tragi-comedies, and sonnets; Ben Jonson's various dramas; and John Donne's metaphysical poetry.

Jargon: Language that is used or understood only by a select group of people. Jargon may refer to terminology used in a certain profession, such as computer jargon, or it may refer to any nonsensical language that is not understood by most people. Literary examples of jargon are Francois Villon's *Ballades en jargon,* which is composed in the secret language of the *coquillards,* and Anthony Burgess's *A Clockwork Orange,* narrated in the fictional characters' language of ''Nadsat.''

Juvenalian Satire: See *Satire*

K

Knickerbocker Group: A somewhat indistinct group of New York writers of the first half of the nineteenth century. Members of the group were linked only by location and a common theme: New York life. Two famous members of the Knickerbocker Group were Washington Irving and William Cullen Bryant. The group's name derives from Irving's *Knickerbocker's History of New York.*

L

Lais: See *Lay*

Lay: A song or simple narrative poem. The form originated in medieval France. Early French *lais* were often based on the Celtic legends and other tales sung by Breton minstrels—thus the name of the ''Breton lay.'' In fourteenth-century England, the term ''lay'' was used to describe short narratives written in imitation of the Breton lays. The most notable of these is Geoffrey Chaucer's ''The Minstrel's Tale.''

Leitmotiv: See *Motif*

Literal Language: An author uses literal language when he or she writes without exaggerating or embellishing the subject matter and without any tools of figurative language. To say ''He ran very quickly down the street'' is to use literal language, whereas to say ''He ran like a hare down the street'' would be using figurative language.

Literary Ballad: See *Ballad*

Literature: Literature is broadly defined as any written or spoken material, but the term most often refers to creative works. Literature includes poetry, drama, fiction, and many kinds of nonfiction writing, as well as oral, dramatic, and broadcast compositions not necessarily preserved in a written format, such as films and television programs.

Lost Generation: A term first used by Gertrude Stein to describe the post-World War I generation of American writers: men and women haunted by a sense of betrayal and emptiness brought about by the destructiveness of the war. The term is commonly applied to Hart Crane, Ernest Hemingway, F. Scott Fitzgerald, and others.

Lyric Poetry: A poem expressing the subjective feelings and personal emotions of the poet. Such poetry is melodic, since it was originally accompanied by a lyre in recitals. Most Western poetry in the twentieth century may be classified as lyrical. Examples of lyric poetry include A. E. Housman's elegy "To an Athlete Dying Young," the odes of Pindar and Horace, Thomas Gray and William Collins, the sonnets of Sir Thomas Wyatt and Sir Philip Sidney, Elizabeth Barrett Browning and Rainer Maria Rilke, and a host of other forms in the poetry of William Blake and Christina Rossetti, among many others.

M

Mannerism: Exaggerated, artificial adherence to a literary manner or style. Also, a popular style of the visual arts of late sixteenth-century Europe that was marked by elongation of the human form and by intentional spatial distortion. Literary works that are self-consciously high-toned and artistic are often said to be "mannered." Authors of such works include Henry James and Gertrude Stein.

Masculine Rhyme: See *Rhyme*

Masque: A lavish and elaborate form of entertainment, often performed in royal courts, that emphasizes song, dance, and costumery. The Renaissance form of the masque grew out of the spectacles of masked figures common in medieval England and Europe. The masque reached its peak of popularity and development in seventeenth-century England, during the reigns of James I and, especially, of Charles I. Ben Jonson, the most significant masque writer, also created the "antimasque," which incorporates elements of humor and the grotesque into the traditional masque and achieved greater dramatic quality. Masque-like interludes appear in Edmund Spenser's *The Faerie Queene* and in William Shakespeare's *The Tempest.* One of the best-known English masques is John Milton's *Comus.*

Measure: The foot, verse, or time sequence used in a literary work, especially a poem. Measure is often used somewhat incorrectly as a synonym for meter.

Melodrama: A play in which the typical plot is a conflict between characters who personify extreme good and evil. Melodramas usually end happily and

emphasize sensationalism. Other literary forms that use the same techniques are often labeled "melodramatic." The term was formerly used to describe a combination of drama and music; as such, it was synonymous with "opera." Augustin Daly's *Under the Gaslight* and Dion Boucicault's *The Octoroon, The Colleen Bawn,* and *The Poor of New York* are examples of melodramas. The most popular media for twentieth-century melodramas are motion pictures and television.

Metaphor: A figure of speech that expresses an idea through the image of another object. Metaphors suggest the essence of the first object by identifying it with certain qualities of the second object. An example is "But soft, what light through yonder window breaks?/ It is the east, and Juliet is the sun" in William Shakespeare's *Romeo and Juliet.* Here, Juliet, the first object, is identified with qualities of the second object, the sun.

Metaphysical Conceit: See *Conceit*

Metaphysical Poetry: The body of poetry produced by a group of seventeenth-century English writers called the "Metaphysical Poets." The group includes John Donne and Andrew Marvell. The Metaphysical Poets made use of everyday speech, intellectual analysis, and unique imagery. They aimed to portray the ordinary conflicts and contradictions of life. Their poems often took the form of an argument, and many of them emphasize physical and religious love as well as the fleeting nature of life. Elaborate conceits are typical in metaphysical poetry. Marvell's "To His Coy Mistress" is a well-known example of a metaphysical poem.

Metaphysical Poets: See *Metaphysical Poetry*

Meter: In literary criticism, the repetition of sound patterns that creates a rhythm in poetry. The patterns are based on the number of syllables and the presence and absence of accents. The unit of rhythm in a line is called a foot. Types of meter are classified according to the number of feet in a line. These are the standard English lines: Monometer, one foot; Dimeter, two feet; Trimeter, three feet; Tetrameter, four feet; Pentameter, five feet; Hexameter, six feet (also called the Alexandrine); Heptameter, seven feet (also called the "Fourteener" when the feet are iambic). The most common English meter is the iambic pentameter, in which each line contains ten syllables, or five iambic feet, which individually are composed of an unstressed syllable followed by an accented syllable. Both of the following lines from Alfred, Lord Tennyson's

"Ulysses" are written in iambic pentameter: Made weak by time and fate, but strong in will To strive, to seek, to find, and not to yield.

Mise en scene: The costumes, scenery, and other properties of a drama. Herbert Beerbohm Tree was renowned for the elaborate *mises en scene* of his lavish Shakespearean productions at His Majesty's Theatre between 1897 and 1915.

Modernism: Modern literary practices. Also, the principles of a literary school that lasted from roughly the beginning of the twentieth century until the end of World War II. Modernism is defined by its rejection of the literary conventions of the nineteenth century and by its opposition to conventional morality, taste, traditions, and economic values. Many writers are associated with the concepts of Modernism, including Albert Camus, Marcel Proust, D. H. Lawrence, W. H. Auden, Ernest Hemingway, William Faulkner, William Butler Yeats, Thomas Mann, Tennessee Williams, Eugene O'Neill, and James Joyce.

Monologue: A composition, written or oral, by a single individual. More specifically, a speech given by a single individual in a drama or other public entertainment. It has no set length, although it is usually several or more lines long. An example of an "extended monologue"—that is, a monologue of great length and seriousness—occurs in the one-act, one-character play *The Stronger* by August Strindberg.

Monometer: See *Meter*

Mood: The prevailing emotions of a work or of the author in his or her creation of the work. The mood of a work is not always what might be expected based on its subject matter. The poem "Dover Beach" by Matthew Arnold offers examples of two different moods originating from the same experience: watching the ocean at night. The mood of the first three lines— The sea is calm tonight The tide is full, the moon lies fair Upon the straights. . . . is in sharp contrast to the mood of the last three lines— And we are here as on a darkling plain Swept with confused alarms of struggle and flight, Where ignorant armies clash by night.

Motif: A theme, character type, image, metaphor, or other verbal element that recurs throughout a single work of literature or occurs in a number of different works over a period of time. For example, the various manifestations of the color white in Herman

Melville's *Moby Dick* is a "specific" *motif,* while the trials of star-crossed lovers is a "conventional" *motif* from the literature of all periods. Also known as *Motiv* or *Leitmotiv.*

Motiv: See *Motif*

Muckrakers: An early twentieth-century group of American writers. Typically, their works exposed the wrongdoings of big business and government in the United States. Upton Sinclair's *The Jungle* exemplifies the muckraking novel.

Muses: Nine Greek mythological goddesses, the daughters of Zeus and Mnemosyne (Memory). Each muse patronized a specific area of the liberal arts and sciences. Calliope presided over epic poetry, Clio over history, Erato over love poetry, Euterpe over music or lyric poetry, Melpomene over tragedy, Polyhymnia over hymns to the gods, Terpsichore over dance, Thalia over comedy, and Urania over astronomy. Poets and writers traditionally made appeals to the Muses for inspiration in their work. John Milton invokes the aid of a muse at the beginning of the first book of his *Paradise Lost:* Of Man's First disobedience, and the Fruit of the Forbidden Tree, whose mortal taste Brought Death into the World, and all our woe, With loss of Eden, till one greater Man Restore us, and regain the blissful Seat, Sing Heav'nly Muse, that on the secret top of Oreb, or of Sinai, didst inspire That Shepherd, who first taught the chosen Seed, In the Beginning how the Heav'ns and Earth Rose out of Chaos. . . .

Mystery: See *Suspense*

Myth: An anonymous tale emerging from the traditional beliefs of a culture or social unit. Myths use supernatural explanations for natural phenomena. They may also explain cosmic issues like creation and death. Collections of myths, known as mythologies, are common to all cultures and nations, but the best-known myths belong to the Norse, Roman, and Greek mythologies. A famous myth is the story of Arachne, an arrogant young girl who challenged a goddess, Athena, to a weaving contest; when the girl won, Athena was enraged and turned Arachne into a spider, thus explaining the existence of spiders.

N

Narration: The telling of a series of events, real or invented. A narration may be either a simple narrative, in which the events are recounted chronologically, or a narrative with a plot, in which the account is given in a style reflecting the author's artistic concept of the story. Narration is sometimes used as a synonym for "storyline." The recounting of scary stories around a campfire is a form of narration.

Narrative: A verse or prose accounting of an event or sequence of events, real or invented. The term is also used as an adjective in the sense "method of narration." For example, in literary criticism, the expression "narrative technique" usually refers to the way the author structures and presents his or her story. Narratives range from the shortest accounts of events, as in Julius Caesar's remark, "I came, I saw, I conquered," to the longest historical or biographical works, as in Edward Gibbon's *The Decline and Fall of the Roman Empire,* as well as diaries, travelogues, novels, ballads, epics, short stories, and other fictional forms.

Narrative Poetry: A nondramatic poem in which the author tells a story. Such poems may be of any length or level of complexity. Epics such as *Beowulf* and ballads are forms of narrative poetry.

Narrator: The teller of a story. The narrator may be the author or a character in the story through whom the author speaks. Huckleberry Finn is the narrator of Mark Twain's *The Adventures of Huckleberry Finn.*

Naturalism: A literary movement of the late nineteenth and early twentieth centuries. The movement's major theorist, French novelist Emile Zola, envisioned a type of fiction that would examine human life with the objectivity of scientific inquiry. The Naturalists typically viewed human beings as either the products of "biological determinism," ruled by hereditary instincts and engaged in an endless struggle for survival, or as the products of "socioeconomic determinism," ruled by social and economic forces beyond their control. In their works, the Naturalists generally ignored the highest levels of society and focused on degradation: poverty, alcoholism, prostitution, insanity, and disease. Naturalism influenced authors throughout the world, including Henrik Ibsen and Thomas Hardy. In the United States, in particular, Naturalism had a profound impact. Among the authors who embraced its principles are Theodore Dreiser, Eugene O'Neill, Stephen Crane, Jack London, and Frank Norris.

Negritude: A literary movement based on the concept of a shared cultural bond on the part of black Africans, wherever they may be in the world. It traces its origins to the former French colonies of Africa and the Caribbean. Negritude poets, novelists, and essayists generally stress four points in their writings: One, black alienation from traditional African culture can lead to feelings of inferiority. Two, European colonialism and Western education should be resisted. Three, black Africans should seek to affirm and define their own identity. Four, African culture can and should be reclaimed. Many Negritude writers also claim that blacks can make unique contributions to the world, based on a heightened appreciation of nature, rhythm, and human emotions—aspects of life they say are not so highly valued in the materialistic and rationalistic West. Examples of Negritude literature include the poetry of both Senegalese Leopold Senghor in *Hosties noires* and Martiniquais Aime-Fernand Cesaire in *Return to My Native Land.*

Negro Renaissance: See *Harlem Renaissance*

Neoclassical Period: See *Neoclassicism*

Neoclassicism: In literary criticism, this term refers to the revival of the attitudes and styles of expression of classical literature. It is generally used to describe a period in European history beginning in the late seventeenth century and lasting until about 1800. In its purest form, Neoclassicism marked a return to order, proportion, restraint, logic, accuracy, and decorum. In England, where Neoclassicism perhaps was most popular, it reflected the influence of seventeenth- century French writers, especially dramatists. Neoclassical writers typically reacted against the intensity and enthusiasm of the Renaissance period. They wrote works that appealed to the intellect, using elevated language and classical literary forms such as satire and the ode. Neoclassical works were often governed by the classical goal of instruction. English neoclassicists included Alexander Pope, Jonathan Swift, Joseph Addison, Sir Richard Steele, John Gay, and Matthew Prior; French neoclassicists included Pierre Corneille and Jean-Baptiste Moliere. Also known as Age of Reason.

Neoclassicists: See *Neoclassicism*

New Criticism: A movement in literary criticism, dating from the late 1920s, that stressed close textual analysis in the interpretation of works of literature. The New Critics saw little merit in historical and biographical analysis. Rather, they aimed to examine the text alone, free from the question of how external events—biographical or otherwise—may have helped shape it. This predominantly American school was named "New Criticism" by one of its practitioners, John Crowe Ransom. Other important New Critics included Allen Tate, R. P. Blackmur, Robert Penn Warren, and Cleanth Brooks.

New Negro Movement: See *Harlem Renaissance*

Noble Savage: The idea that primitive man is noble and good but becomes evil and corrupted as he becomes civilized. The concept of the noble savage originated in the Renaissance period but is more closely identified with such later writers as Jean-Jacques Rousseau and Aphra Behn. First described in John Dryden's play *The Conquest of Granada,* the noble savage is portrayed by the various Native Americans in James Fenimore Cooper's "Leatherstocking Tales," by Queequeg, Daggoo, and Tashtego in Herman Melville's *Moby Dick,* and by John the Savage in Aldous Huxley's *Brave New World.*

O

Objective Correlative: An outward set of objects, a situation, or a chain of events corresponding to an inward experience and evoking this experience in the reader. The term frequently appears in modern criticism in discussions of authors' intended effects on the emotional responses of readers. This term was originally used by T. S. Eliot in his 1919 essay "Hamlet."

Objectivity: A quality in writing characterized by the absence of the author's opinion or feeling about the subject matter. Objectivity is an important factor in criticism. The novels of Henry James and, to a certain extent, the poems of John Larkin demonstrate objectivity, and it is central to John Keats's concept of "negative capability." Critical and journalistic writing usually are or attempt to be objective.

Occasional Verse: poetry written on the occasion of a significant historical or personal event. *Vers de societe* is sometimes called occasional verse although it is of a less serious nature. Famous examples of occasional verse include Andrew Marvell's "Horatian Ode upon Cromwell's Return from England," Walt Whitman's "When Lilacs Last in the Dooryard Bloom'd"— written upon the death of Abraham Lincoln—and Edmund Spenser's commemoration of his wedding, "Epithalamion."

Octave: A poem or stanza composed of eight lines. The term octave most often represents the first eight lines of a Petrarchan sonnet. An example of an octave is taken from a translation of a Petrarchan sonnet by Sir Thomas Wyatt: The pillar perisht is whereto I leant, The strongest stay of mine unquiet mind; The like of it no man again can find, From East to West Still seeking though he went. To mind unhap! for hap away hath rent Of all my joy the very

bark and rind; And I, alas, by chance am thus assigned Daily to mourn till death do it relent.

Ode: Name given to an extended lyric poem characterized by exalted emotion and dignified style. An ode usually concerns a single, serious theme. Most odes, but not all, are addressed to an object or individual. Odes are distinguished from other lyric poetic forms by their complex rhythmic and stanzaic patterns. An example of this form is John Keats's "Ode to a Nightingale."

Oedipus Complex: A son's amorous obsession with his mother. The phrase is derived from the story of the ancient Theban hero Oedipus, who unknowingly killed his father and married his mother. Literary occurrences of the Oedipus complex include Andre Gide's *Oedipe* and Jean Cocteau's *La Machine infernale,* as well as the most famous, Sophocles' *Oedipus Rex.*

Omniscience: See *Point of View*

Onomatopoeia: The use of words whose sounds express or suggest their meaning. In its simplest sense, onomatopoeia may be represented by words that mimic the sounds they denote such as "hiss" or "meow." At a more subtle level, the pattern and rhythm of sounds and rhymes of a line or poem may be onomatopoeic. A celebrated example of onomatopoeia is the repetition of the word "bells" in Edgar Allan Poe's poem "The Bells."

Opera: A type of stage performance, usually a drama, in which the dialogue is sung. Classic examples of opera include Giuseppi Verdi's *La traviata,* Giacomo Puccini's *La Boheme,* and Richard Wagner's *Tristan und Isolde.* Major twentieth- century contributors to the form include Richard Strauss and Alban Berg.

Operetta: A usually romantic comic opera. John Gay's *The Beggar's Opera,* Richard Sheridan's *The Duenna,* and numerous works by William Gilbert and Arthur Sullivan are examples of operettas.

Oral Tradition: See *Oral Transmission*

Oral Transmission: A process by which songs, ballads, folklore, and other material are transmitted by word of mouth. The tradition of oral transmission predates the written record systems of literate society. Oral transmission preserves material sometimes over generations, although often with variations. Memory plays a large part in the recitation and preservation of orally transmitted material. Breton lays, French *fabliaux,* national epics (including the Anglo- Saxon *Beowulf,* the Spanish *El Cid,* and the Finnish *Kalevala*), Native American myths and legends, and African folktales told by plantation slaves are examples of orally transmitted literature.

Oration: Formal speaking intended to motivate the listeners to some action or feeling. Such public speaking was much more common before the development of timely printed communication such as newspapers. Famous examples of oration include Abraham Lincoln's ''Gettysburg Address'' and Dr. Martin Luther King Jr.'s ''I Have a Dream'' speech.

Ottava Rima: An eight-line stanza of poetry composed in iambic pentameter (a five-foot line in which each foot consists of an unaccented syllable followed by an accented syllable), following the abababcc rhyme scheme. This form has been prominently used by such important English writers as Lord Byron, Henry Wadsworth Longfellow, and W. B. Yeats.

Oxymoron: A phrase combining two contradictory terms. Oxymorons may be intentional or unintentional. The following speech from William Shakespeare's *Romeo and Juliet* uses several oxymorons: Why, then, O brawling love! O loving hate! O anything, of nothing first create! O heavy lightness! serious vanity! Mis-shapen chaos of well-seeming forms! Feather of lead, bright smoke, cold fire, sick health! This love feel I, that feel no love in this.

P

Pantheism: The idea that all things are both a manifestation or revelation of God and a part of God at the same time. Pantheism was a common attitude in the early societies of Egypt, India, and Greece—the term derives from the Greek *pan* meaning ''all'' and *theos* meaning ''deity.'' It later became a significant part of the Christian faith. William Wordsworth and Ralph Waldo Emerson are among the many writers who have expressed the pantheistic attitude in their works.

Parable: A story intended to teach a moral lesson or answer an ethical question. In the West, the best examples of parables are those of Jesus Christ in the New Testament, notably ''The Prodigal Son,'' but parables also are used in Sufism, rabbinic literature, Hasidism, and Zen Buddhism.

Paradox: A statement that appears illogical or contradictory at first, but may actually point to an underlying truth. ''Less is more'' is an example of a paradox. Literary examples include Francis Ba-

con's statement, ''The most corrected copies are commonly the least correct,'' and ''All animals are equal, but some animals are more equal than others'' from George Orwell's *Animal Farm.*

Parallelism: A method of comparison of two ideas in which each is developed in the same grammatical structure. Ralph Waldo Emerson's ''Civilization'' contains this example of parallelism: Raphael paints wisdom; Handel sings it, Phidias carves it, Shakespeare writes it, Wren builds it, Columbus sails it, Luther preaches it, Washington arms it, Watt mechanizes it.

Parnassianism: A mid nineteenth-century movement in French literature. Followers of the movement stressed adherence to well-defined artistic forms as a reaction against the often chaotic expression of the artist's ego that dominated the work of the Romantics. The Parnassians also rejected the moral, ethical, and social themes exhibited in the works of French Romantics such as Victor Hugo. The aesthetic doctrines of the Parnassians strongly influenced the later symbolist and decadent movements. Members of the Parnassian school include Leconte de Lisle, Sully Prudhomme, Albert Glatigny, Francois Coppee, and Theodore de Banville.

Parody: In literary criticism, this term refers to an imitation of a serious literary work or the signature style of a particular author in a ridiculous manner. A typical parody adopts the style of the original and applies it to an inappropriate subject for humorous effect. Parody is a form of satire and could be considered the literary equivalent of a caricature or cartoon. Henry Fielding's *Shamela* is a parody of Samuel Richardson's *Pamela.*

Pastoral: A term derived from the Latin word ''pastor,'' meaning shepherd. A pastoral is a literary composition on a rural theme. The conventions of the pastoral were originated by the third-century Greek poet Theocritus, who wrote about the experiences, love affairs, and pastimes of Sicilian shepherds. In a pastoral, characters and language of a courtly nature are often placed in a simple setting. The term pastoral is also used to classify dramas, elegies, and lyrics that exhibit the use of country settings and shepherd characters. Percy Bysshe Shelley's ''Adonais'' and John Milton's ''Lycidas'' are two famous examples of pastorals.

Pastorela: The Spanish name for the shepherds play, a folk drama reenacted during the Christmas season. Examples of *pastorelas* include Gomez

Manrique's *Representacion del nacimiento* and the dramas of Lucas Fernandez and Juan del Encina.

Pathetic Fallacy: A term coined by English critic John Ruskin to identify writing that falsely endows nonhuman things with human intentions and feelings, such as "angry clouds" and "sad trees." The pathetic fallacy is a required convention in the classical poetic form of the pastoral elegy, and it is used in the modern poetry of T. S. Eliot, Ezra Pound, and the Imagists. Also known as Poetic Fallacy.

Pelado: Literally the "skinned one" or shirtless one, he was the stock underdog, sharp-witted picaresque character of Mexican vaudeville and tent shows. The *pelado* is found in such works as Don Catarino's *Los effectos de la crisis* and *Regreso a mi tierra.*

Pen Name: See *Pseudonym*

Pentameter: See *Meter*

Persona: A Latin term meaning "mask." *Personae* are the characters in a fictional work of literature. The *persona* generally functions as a mask through which the author tells a story in a voice other than his or her own. A *persona* is usually either a character in a story who acts as a narrator or an "implied author," a voice created by the author to act as the narrator for himself or herself. *Personae* include the narrator of Geoffrey Chaucer's *Canterbury Tales* and Marlow in Joseph Conrad's *Heart of Darkness.*

Personae: See *Persona*

Personal Point of View: See *Point of View*

Personification: A figure of speech that gives human qualities to abstract ideas, animals, and inanimate objects. William Shakespeare used personification in *Romeo and Juliet* in the lines "Arise, fair sun, and kill the envious moon,/ Who is already sick and pale with grief." Here, the moon is portrayed as being envious, sick, and pale with grief—all markedly human qualities. Also known as *Prosopopoeia.*

Petrarchan Sonnet: See *Sonnet*

Phenomenology: A method of literary criticism based on the belief that things have no existence outside of human consciousness or awareness. Proponents of this theory believe that art is a process that takes place in the mind of the observer as he or she contemplates an object rather than a quality of the object itself. Among phenomenological critics

are Edmund Husserl, George Poulet, Marcel Raymond, and Roman Ingarden.

Picaresque Novel: Episodic fiction depicting the adventures of a roguish central character ("picaro" is Spanish for "rogue"). The picaresque hero is commonly a low-born but clever individual who wanders into and out of various affairs of love, danger, and farcical intrigue. These involvements may take place at all social levels and typically present a humorous and wide-ranging satire of a given society. Prominent examples of the picaresque novel are *Don Quixote* by Miguel de Cervantes, *Tom Jones* by Henry Fielding, and *Moll Flanders* by Daniel Defoe.

Plagiarism: Claiming another person's written material as one's own. Plagiarism can take the form of direct, word-for- word copying or the theft of the substance or idea of the work. A student who copies an encyclopedia entry and turns it in as a report for school is guilty of plagiarism.

Platonic Criticism: A form of criticism that stresses an artistic work's usefulness as an agent of social engineering rather than any quality or value of the work itself. Platonic criticism takes as its starting point the ancient Greek philosopher Plato's comments on art in his *Republic.*

Platonism: The embracing of the doctrines of the philosopher Plato, popular among the poets of the Renaissance and the Romantic period. Platonism is more flexible than Aristotelian Criticism and places more emphasis on the supernatural and unknown aspects of life. Platonism is expressed in the love poetry of the Renaissance, the fourth book of Baldassare Castiglione's *The Book of the Courtier,* and the poetry of William Blake, William Wordsworth, Percy Bysshe Shelley, Friedrich Holderlin, William Butler Yeats, and Wallace Stevens.

Play: See *Drama*

Plot: In literary criticism, this term refers to the pattern of events in a narrative or drama. In its simplest sense, the plot guides the author in composing the work and helps the reader follow the work. Typically, plots exhibit causality and unity and have a beginning, a middle, and an end. Sometimes, however, a plot may consist of a series of disconnected events, in which case it is known as an "episodic plot." In his *Aspects of the Novel,* E. M. Forster distinguishes between a story, defined as a "narrative of events arranged in their time- sequence," and plot, which organizes the events to a "sense of causality." This definition closely mirrors Aristotle's discussion of plot in his *Poetics.*

Poem: In its broadest sense, a composition utilizing rhyme, meter, concrete detail, and expressive language to create a literary experience with emotional and aesthetic appeal. Typical poems include sonnets, odes, elegies, *haiku,* ballads, and free verse.

Poet: An author who writes poetry or verse. The term is also used to refer to an artist or writer who has an exceptional gift for expression, imagination, and energy in the making of art in any form. Well-known poets include Horace, Basho, Sir Philip Sidney, Sir Edmund Spenser, John Donne, Andrew Marvell, Alexander Pope, Jonathan Swift, George Gordon, Lord Byron, John Keats, Christina Rossetti, W. H. Auden, Stevie Smith, and Sylvia Plath.

Poetic Fallacy: See *Pathetic Fallacy*

Poetic Justice: An outcome in a literary work, not necessarily a poem, in which the good are rewarded and the evil are punished, especially in ways that particularly fit their virtues or crimes. For example, a murderer may himself be murdered, or a thief will find himself penniless.

Poetic License: Distortions of fact and literary convention made by a writer—not always a poet—for the sake of the effect gained. Poetic license is closely related to the concept of "artistic freedom." An author exercises poetic license by saying that a pile of money "reaches as high as a mountain" when the pile is actually only a foot or two high.

Poetics: This term has two closely related meanings. It denotes (1) an aesthetic theory in literary criticism about the essence of poetry or (2) rules prescribing the proper methods, content, style, or diction of poetry. The term poetics may also refer to theories about literature in general, not just poetry.

Poetry: In its broadest sense, writing that aims to present ideas and evoke an emotional experience in the reader through the use of meter, imagery, connotative and concrete words, and a carefully constructed structure based on rhythmic patterns. Poetry typically relies on words and expressions that have several layers of meaning. It also makes use of the effects of regular rhythm on the ear and may make a strong appeal to the senses through the use of imagery. Edgar Allan Poe's "Annabel Lee" and Walt Whitman's *Leaves of Grass* are famous examples of poetry.

Point of View: The narrative perspective from which a literary work is presented to the reader.

There are four traditional points of view. The "third person omniscient" gives the reader a "godlike" perspective, unrestricted by time or place, from which to see actions and look into the minds of characters. This allows the author to comment openly on characters and events in the work. The "third person" point of view presents the events of the story from outside of any single character's perception, much like the omniscient point of view, but the reader must understand the action as it takes place and without any special insight into characters' minds or motivations. The "first person" or "personal" point of view relates events as they are perceived by a single character. The main character "tells" the story and may offer opinions about the action and characters which differ from those of the author. Much less common than omniscient, third person, and first person is the "second person" point of view, wherein the author tells the story as if it is happening to the reader. James Thurber employs the omniscient point of view in his short story "The Secret Life of Walter Mitty." Ernest Hemingway's "A Clean, Well-Lighted Place" is a short story told from the third person point of view. Mark Twain's novel *Huck Finn* is presented from the first person viewpoint. Jay McInerney's *Bright Lights, Big City* is an example of a novel which uses the second person point of view.

Polemic: A work in which the author takes a stand on a controversial subject, such as abortion or religion. Such works are often extremely argumentative or provocative. Classic examples of polemics include John Milton's *Aeropagitica* and Thomas Paine's *The American Crisis.*

Pornography: Writing intended to provoke feelings of lust in the reader. Such works are often condemned by critics and teachers, but those which can be shown to have literary value are viewed less harshly. Literary works that have been described as pornographic include Ovid's *The Art of Love,* Margaret of Angouleme's *Heptameron,* John Cleland's *Memoirs of a Woman of Pleasure; or, the Life of Fanny Hill,* the anonymous *My Secret Life,* D. H. Lawrence's *Lady Chatterley's Lover,* and Vladimir Nabokov's *Lolita.*

Post-Aesthetic Movement: An artistic response made by African Americans to the black aesthetic movement of the 1960s and early '70s. Writers since that time have adopted a somewhat different tone in their work, with less emphasis placed on the disparity between black and white in the United States. In the words of post-aesthetic authors such as Toni Morrison, John Edgar Wideman, and Kristin Hunter, African Americans are portrayed as looking inward for answers to their own questions, rather than always looking to the outside world. Two well-known examples of works produced as part of the post-aesthetic movement are the Pulitzer Prize-winning novels *The Color Purple* by Alice Walker and *Beloved* by Toni Morrison.

Postmodernism: Writing from the 1960s forward characterized by experimentation and continuing to apply some of the fundamentals of modernism, which included existentialism and alienation. Postmodernists have gone a step further in the rejection of tradition begun with the modernists by also rejecting traditional forms, preferring the anti-novel over the novel and the anti-hero over the hero. Postmodern writers include Alain Robbe-Grillet, Thomas Pynchon, Margaret Drabble, John Fowles, Adolfo Bioy-Casares, and Gabriel Garcia Marquez.

Pre-Raphaelites: A circle of writers and artists in mid nineteenth-century England. Valuing the pre-Renaissance artistic qualities of religious symbolism, lavish pictorialism, and natural sensuousness, the Pre-Raphaelites cultivated a sense of mystery and melancholy that influenced later writers associated with the Symbolist and Decadent movements. The major members of the group include Dante Gabriel Rossetti, Christina Rossetti, Algernon Swinburne, and Walter Pater.

Primitivism: The belief that primitive peoples were nobler and less flawed than civilized peoples because they had not been subjected to the tainting influence of society. Examples of literature espousing primitivism include Aphra Behn's *Oroonoko: Or, The History of the Royal Slave,* Jean-Jacques Rousseau's *Julie ou la Nouvelle Heloise,* Oliver Goldsmith's *The Deserted Village,* the poems of Robert Burns, Herman Melville's stories *Typee, Omoo,* and *Mardi,* many poems of William Butler Yeats and Robert Frost, and William Golding's novel *Lord of the Flies.*

Projective Verse: A form of free verse in which the poet's breathing pattern determines the lines of the poem. Poets who advocate projective verse are against all formal structures in writing, including meter and form. Besides its creators, Robert Creeley, Robert Duncan, and Charles Olson, two other well-known projective verse poets are Denise Levertov and LeRoi Jones (Amiri Baraka). Also known as Breath Verse.

Prologue: An introductory section of a literary work. It often contains information establishing the situation of the characters or presents information about the setting, time period, or action. In drama, the prologue is spoken by a chorus or by one of the principal characters. In the "General Prologue" of *The Canterbury Tales,* Geoffrey Chaucer describes the main characters and establishes the setting and purpose of the work.

Prose: A literary medium that attempts to mirror the language of everyday speech. It is distinguished from poetry by its use of unmetered, unrhymed language consisting of logically related sentences. Prose is usually grouped into paragraphs that form a cohesive whole such as an essay or a novel. Recognized masters of English prose writing include Sir Thomas Malory, William Caxton, Raphael Holinshed, Joseph Addison, Mark Twain, and Ernest Hemingway.

Prosopopoeia: See *Personification*

Protagonist: The central character of a story who serves as a focus for its themes and incidents and as the principal rationale for its development. The protagonist is sometimes referred to in discussions of modern literature as the hero or anti-hero. Well-known protagonists are Hamlet in William Shakespeare's *Hamlet* and Jay Gatsby in F. Scott Fitzgerald's *The Great Gatsby.*

Protest Fiction: Protest fiction has as its primary purpose the protesting of some social injustice, such as racism or discrimination. One example of protest fiction is a series of five novels by Chester Himes, beginning in 1945 with *If He Hollers Let Him Go* and ending in 1955 with *The Primitive.* These works depict the destructive effects of race and gender stereotyping in the context of interracial relationships. Another African American author whose works often revolve around themes of social protest is John Oliver Killens. James Baldwin's essay "Everybody's Protest Novel" generated controversy by attacking the authors of protest fiction.

Proverb: A brief, sage saying that expresses a truth about life in a striking manner. "They are not all cooks who carry long knives" is an example of a proverb.

Pseudonym: A name assumed by a writer, most often intended to prevent his or her identification as the author of a work. Two or more authors may work together under one pseudonym, or an author may use a different name for each genre he or she publishes in. Some publishing companies maintain "house pseudonyms," under which any number of authors may write installations in a series. Some authors also choose a pseudonym over their real names the way an actor may use a stage name. Examples of pseudonyms (with the author's real name in parentheses) include Voltaire (Francois-Marie Arouet), Novalis (Friedrich von Hardenberg), Currer Bell (Charlotte Bronte), Ellis Bell (Emily Bronte), George Eliot (Maryann Evans), Honorio Bustos Donmecq (Adolfo Bioy-Casares and Jorge Luis Borges), and Richard Bachman (Stephen King).

Pun: A play on words that have similar sounds but different meanings. A serious example of the pun is from John Donne's "A Hymne to God the Father": Sweare by thyself, that at my death thy sonne Shall shine as he shines now, and hereto fore; And, having done that, Thou haste done; I fear no more.

Pure Poetry: poetry written without instructional intent or moral purpose that aims only to please a reader by its imagery or musical flow. The term pure poetry is used as the antonym of the term "didacticism." The poetry of Edgar Allan Poe, Stephane Mallarme, Paul Verlaine, Paul Valery, Juan Ramoz Jimenez, and Jorge Guillen offer examples of pure poetry.

Q

Quatrain: A four-line stanza of a poem or an entire poem consisting of four lines. The following quatrain is from Robert Herrick's "To Live Merrily, and to Trust to Good Verses": Round, round, the root do's run; And being ravisht thus, Come, I will drink a Tun To my *Propertius.*

R

Raisonneur: A character in a drama who functions as a spokesperson for the dramatist's views. The *raisonneur* typically observes the play without becoming central to its action. *Raisonneurs* were very common in plays of the nineteenth century.

Realism: A nineteenth-century European literary movement that sought to portray familiar characters, situations, and settings in a realistic manner. This was done primarily by using an objective narrative point of view and through the buildup of accurate detail. The standard for success of any realistic work depends on how faithfully it transfers common experience into fictional forms. The realistic method may be altered or extended, as in stream of consciousness writing, to record highly subjec-

tive experience. Seminal authors in the tradition of Realism include Honore de Balzac, Gustave Flaubert, and Henry James.

Refrain: A phrase repeated at intervals throughout a poem. A refrain may appear at the end of each stanza or at less regular intervals. It may be altered slightly at each appearance. Some refrains are nonsense expressions—as with "Nevermore" in Edgar Allan Poe's "The Raven"—that seem to take on a different significance with each use.

Renaissance: The period in European history that marked the end of the Middle Ages. It began in Italy in the late fourteenth century. In broad terms, it is usually seen as spanning the fourteenth, fifteenth, and sixteenth centuries, although it did not reach Great Britain, for example, until the 1480s or so. The Renaissance saw an awakening in almost every sphere of human activity, especially science, philosophy, and the arts. The period is best defined by the emergence of a general philosophy that emphasized the importance of the intellect, the individual, and world affairs. It contrasts strongly with the medieval worldview, characterized by the dominant concerns of faith, the social collective, and spiritual salvation. Prominent writers during the Renaissance include Niccolo Machiavelli and Baldassare Castiglione in Italy, Miguel de Cervantes and Lope de Vega in Spain, Jean Froissart and Francois Rabelais in France, Sir Thomas More and Sir Philip Sidney in England, and Desiderius Erasmus in Holland.

Repartee: Conversation featuring snappy retorts and witticisms. Masters of *repartee* include Sydney Smith, Charles Lamb, and Oscar Wilde. An example is recorded in the meeting of "Beau" Nash and John Wesley: Nash said, "I never make way for a fool," to which Wesley responded, "Don't you? I always do," and stepped aside.

Resolution: The portion of a story following the climax, in which the conflict is resolved. The resolution of Jane Austen's *Northanger Abbey* is neatly summed up in the following sentence: "Henry and Catherine were married, the bells rang and everybody smiled."

Restoration: See *Restoration Age*

Restoration Age: A period in English literature beginning with the crowning of Charles II in 1660 and running to about 1700. The era, which was characterized by a reaction against Puritanism, was the first great age of the comedy of manners. The finest literature of the era is typically witty and urbane, and often lewd. Prominent Restoration Age writers include William Congreve, Samuel Pepys, John Dryden, and John Milton.

Revenge Tragedy: A dramatic form popular during the Elizabethan Age, in which the protagonist, directed by the ghost of his murdered father or son, inflicts retaliation upon a powerful villain. Notable features of the revenge tragedy include violence, bizarre criminal acts, intrigue, insanity, a hesitant protagonist, and the use of soliloquy. Thomas Kyd's *Spanish Tragedy* is the first example of revenge tragedy in English, and William Shakespeare's *Hamlet* is perhaps the best. Extreme examples of revenge tragedy, such as John Webster's *The Duchess of Malfi,* are labeled "tragedies of blood." Also known as Tragedy of Blood.

Revista: The Spanish term for a vaudeville musical revue. Examples of *revistas* include Antonio Guzman Aguilera's *Mexico para los mexicanos,* Daniel Vanegas's *Maldito jazz,* and Don Catarino's *Whiskey, morfina y marihuana* and *El desterrado.*

Rhetoric: In literary criticism, this term denotes the art of ethical persuasion. In its strictest sense, rhetoric adheres to various principles developed since classical times for arranging facts and ideas in a clear, persuasive, appealing manner. The term is also used to refer to effective prose in general and theories of or methods for composing effective prose. Classical examples of rhetorics include *The Rhetoric of Aristotle,* Quintillian's *Institutio Oratoria,* and Cicero's *Ad Herennium.*

Rhetorical Question: A question intended to provoke thought, but not an expressed answer, in the reader. It is most commonly used in oratory and other persuasive genres. The following lines from Thomas Gray's "Elegy Written in a Country Churchyard" ask rhetorical questions: Can storied urn or animated bust Back to its mansion call the fleeting breath? Can Honour's voice provoke the silent dust, Or Flattery soothe the dull cold ear of Death?

Rhyme: When used as a noun in literary criticism, this term generally refers to a poem in which words sound identical or very similar and appear in parallel positions in two or more lines. Rhymes are classified into different types according to where they fall in a line or stanza or according to the degree of similarity they exhibit in their spellings and sounds. Some major types of rhyme are "masculine" rhyme, "feminine" rhyme, and "triple" rhyme. In a masculine rhyme, the rhyming sound falls in a single accented syllable, as with "heat" and "eat." Feminine rhyme is a rhyme of two syllables, one stressed and one unstressed, as with "merry" and "tarry." Triple rhyme matches the sound of the accented syllable and the two unaccented syllables that follow: "narrative" and "declarative." Robert Browning alternates feminine and masculine rhymes in his "Soliloquy of the Spanish Cloister": Gr-r-r—there go, my heart's abhorrence! Water your damned flower-pots, do! If hate killed men, Brother Lawrence, God's blood, would not mine kill you! What? Your myrtle-bush wants trimming? Oh, that rose has prior claims— Needs its leaden vase filled brimming? Hell dry you up with flames! Triple rhymes can be found in Thomas Hood's "Bridge of Sighs," George Gordon Byron's satirical verse, and Ogden Nash's comic poems.

Rhyme Royal: A stanza of seven lines composed in iambic pentameter and rhymed *ababbcc.* The name is said to be a tribute to King James I of Scotland, who made much use of the form in his poetry. Examples of rhyme royal include Geoffrey Chaucer's *The Parlement of Foules,* William Shakespeare's *The Rape of Lucrece,* William Morris's *The Early Paradise,* and John Masefield's *The Widow in the Bye Street.*

Rhyme Scheme: See *Rhyme*

Rhythm: A regular pattern of sound, time intervals, or events occurring in writing, most often and most discernably in poetry. Regular, reliable rhythm is known to be soothing to humans, while interrupted, unpredictable, or rapidly changing rhythm is disturbing. These effects are known to authors, who use them to produce a desired reaction in the reader. An example of a form of irregular rhythm is sprung rhythm poetry; quantitative verse, on the other hand, is very regular in its rhythm.

Rising Action: The part of a drama where the plot becomes increasingly complicated. Rising action leads up to the climax, or turning point, of a drama. The final "chase scene" of an action film is generally the rising action which culminates in the film's climax.

Rococo: A style of European architecture that flourished in the eighteenth century, especially in France. The most notable features of *rococo* are its extensive use of ornamentation and its themes of lightness, gaiety, and intimacy. In literary criticism, the term is often used disparagingly to refer to a decadent or over-ornamental style. Alexander Pope's "The Rape of the Lock" is an example of literary *rococo.*

Roman a clef: A French phrase meaning ''novel with a key.'' It refers to a narrative in which real persons are portrayed under fictitious names. Jack Kerouac, for example, portrayed various real-life beat generation figures under fictitious names in his *On the Road.*

Romance: A broad term, usually denoting a narrative with exotic, exaggerated, often idealized characters, scenes, and themes. Nathaniel Hawthorne called his *The House of the Seven Gables* and *The Marble Faun* romances in order to distinguish them from clearly realistic works.

Romantic Age: See *Romanticism*

Romanticism: This term has two widely accepted meanings. In historical criticism, it refers to a European intellectual and artistic movement of the late eighteenth and early nineteenth centuries that sought greater freedom of personal expression than that allowed by the strict rules of literary form and logic of the eighteenth-century neoclassicists. The Romantics preferred emotional and imaginative expression to rational analysis. They considered the individual to be at the center of all experience and so placed him or her at the center of their art. The Romantics believed that the creative imagination reveals nobler truths—unique feelings and attitudes—than those that could be discovered by logic or by scientific examination. Both the natural world and the state of childhood were important sources for revelations of ''eternal truths.'' ''Romanticism'' is also used as a general term to refer to a type of sensibility found in all periods of literary history and usually considered to be in opposition to the principles of classicism. In this sense, Romanticism signifies any work or philosophy in which the exotic or dreamlike figure strongly, or that is devoted to individualistic expression, self-analysis, or a pursuit of a higher realm of knowledge than can be discovered by human reason. Prominent Romantics include Jean-Jacques Rousseau, William Wordsworth, John Keats, Lord Byron, and Johann Wolfgang von Goethe.

Romantics: See *Romanticism*

Russian Symbolism: A Russian poetic movement, derived from French symbolism, that flourished between 1894 and 1910. While some Russian Symbolists continued in the French tradition, stressing aestheticism and the importance of suggestion above didactic intent, others saw their craft as a form of mystical worship, and themselves as mediators between the supernatural and the mundane. Russian symbolists include Aleksandr Blok, Vyacheslav Ivanovich Ivanov, Fyodor Sologub, Andrey Bely, Nikolay Gumilyov, and Vladimir Sergeyevich Solovyov.

S

Satire: A work that uses ridicule, humor, and wit to criticize and provoke change in human nature and institutions. There are two major types of satire: ''formal'' or ''direct'' satire speaks directly to the reader or to a character in the work; ''indirect'' satire relies upon the ridiculous behavior of its characters to make its point. Formal satire is further divided into two manners: the ''Horatian,'' which ridicules gently, and the ''Juvenalian,'' which derides its subjects harshly and bitterly. Voltaire's novella *Candide* is an indirect satire. Jonathan Swift's essay ''A Modest Proposal'' is a Juvenalian satire.

Scansion: The analysis or ''scanning'' of a poem to determine its meter and often its rhyme scheme. The most common system of scansion uses accents (slanted lines drawn above syllables) to show stressed syllables, breves (curved lines drawn above syllables) to show unstressed syllables, and vertical lines to separate each foot. In the first line of John Keats's *Endymion,* ''A thing of beauty is a joy forever:'' the word ''thing,'' the first syllable of ''beauty,'' the word ''joy,'' and the second syllable of ''forever'' are stressed, while the words ''A'' and ''of,'' the second syllable of ''beauty,'' the word ''a,'' and the first and third syllables of ''forever'' are unstressed. In the second line: ''Its loveliness increases; it will never'' a pair of vertical lines separate the foot ending with ''increases'' and the one beginning with ''it.''

Scene: A subdivision of an act of a drama, consisting of continuous action taking place at a single time and in a single location. The beginnings and endings of scenes may be indicated by clearing the stage of actors and props or by the entrances and exits of important characters. The first act of William Shakespeare's *Winter's Tale* is comprised of two scenes.

Science Fiction: A type of narrative about or based upon real or imagined scientific theories and technology. Science fiction is often peopled with alien creatures and set on other planets or in different dimensions. Karel Capek's *R.U.R.* is a major work of science fiction.

Second Person: See *Point of View*

Semiotics: The study of how literary forms and conventions affect the meaning of language. Semioticians include Ferdinand de Saussure, Charles Sanders Pierce, Claude Levi-Strauss, Jacques Lacan, Michel Foucault, Jacques Derrida, Roland Barthes, and Julia Kristeva.

Sestet: Any six-line poem or stanza. Examples of the sestet include the last six lines of the Petrarchan sonnet form, the stanza form of Robert Burns's "A Poet's Welcome to his love-begotten Daughter," and the sestina form in W. H. Auden's "Paysage Moralise."

Setting: The time, place, and culture in which the action of a narrative takes place. The elements of setting may include geographic location, characters' physical and mental environments, prevailing cultural attitudes, or the historical time in which the action takes place. Examples of settings include the romanticized Scotland in Sir Walter Scott's "Waverley" novels, the French provincial setting in Gustave Flaubert's *Madame Bovary,* the fictional Wessex country of Thomas Hardy's novels, and the small towns of southern Ontario in Alice Munro's short stories.

Shakespearean Sonnet: See *Sonnet*

Signifying Monkey: A popular trickster figure in black folklore, with hundreds of tales about this character documented since the 19th century. Henry Louis Gates Jr. examines the history of the signifying monkey in *The Signifying Monkey: Towards a Theory of Afro-American Literary Criticism,* published in 1988.

Simile: A comparison, usually using "like" or "as", of two essentially dissimilar things, as in "coffee as cold as ice" or "He sounded like a broken record." The title of Ernest Hemingway's "Hills Like White Elephants" contains a simile.

Slang: A type of informal verbal communication that is generally unacceptable for formal writing. Slang words and phrases are often colorful exaggerations used to emphasize the speaker's point; they may also be shortened versions of an often-used word or phrase. Examples of American slang from the 1990s include "yuppie" (an acronym for Young Urban Professional), "awesome" (for "excellent"), wired (for "nervous" or "excited"), and "chill out" (for relax).

Slant Rhyme: See *Consonance*

Slave Narrative: Autobiographical accounts of American slave life as told by escaped slaves. These works first appeared during the abolition movement of the 1830s through the 1850s. Olaudah Equiano's *The Interesting Narrative of Olaudah Equiano, or Gustavus Vassa, The African* and Harriet Ann Jacobs's *Incidents in the Life of a Slave Girl* are examples of the slave narrative.

Social Realism: See *Socialist Realism*

Socialist Realism: The Socialist Realism school of literary theory was proposed by Maxim Gorky and established as a dogma by the first Soviet Congress of Writers. It demanded adherence to a communist worldview in works of literature. Its doctrines required an objective viewpoint comprehensible to the working classes and themes of social struggle featuring strong proletarian heroes. A successful work of socialist realism is Nikolay Ostrovsky's *Kak zakalyalas stal (How the Steel Was Tempered).* Also known as Social Realism.

Soliloquy: A monologue in a drama used to give the audience information and to develop the speaker's character. It is typically a projection of the speaker's innermost thoughts. Usually delivered while the speaker is alone on stage, a soliloquy is intended to present an illusion of unspoken reflection. A celebrated soliloquy is Hamlet's "To be or not to be" speech in William Shakespeare's *Hamlet.*

Sonnet: A fourteen-line poem, usually composed in iambic pentameter, employing one of several rhyme schemes. There are three major types of sonnets, upon which all other variations of the form are based: the "Petrarchan" or "Italian" sonnet, the "Shakespearean" or "English" sonnet, and the "Spenserian" sonnet. A Petrarchan sonnet consists of an octave rhymed *abbaabba* and a "sestet" rhymed either *cdecde, cdccdc,* or *cdedce.* The octave poses a question or problem, relates a narrative, or puts forth a proposition; the sestet presents a solution to the problem, comments upon the narrative, or applies the proposition put forth in the octave. The Shakespearean sonnet is divided into three quatrains and a couplet rhymed *abab cdcd efef gg.* The couplet provides an epigrammatic comment on the narrative or problem put forth in the quatrains. The Spenserian sonnet uses three quatrains and a couplet like the Shakespearean, but links their three rhyme schemes in this way: *abab bcbc cdcd ee.* The Spenserian sonnet develops its theme in two parts like the Petrarchan, its final six lines resolving a problem, analyzing a narrative, or applying a proposition put forth in its first eight lines. Examples of sonnets can be found in Petrarch's *Canzoniere,* Edmund Spenser's *Amoretti,* Elizabeth Barrett

Browning's *Sonnets from the Portuguese,* Rainer Maria Rilke's *Sonnets to Orpheus,* and Adrienne Rich's poem ''The Insusceptibles.''

Spenserian Sonnet: See *Sonnet*

Spenserian Stanza: A nine-line stanza having eight verses in iambic pentameter, its ninth verse in iambic hexameter, and the rhyme scheme ababbcbcc. This stanza form was first used by Edmund Spenser in his allegorical poem *The Faerie Queene.*

Spondee: In poetry meter, a foot consisting of two long or stressed syllables occurring together. This form is quite rare in English verse, and is usually composed of two monosyllabic words. The first foot in the following line from Robert Burns's ''Green Grow the Rashes'' is an example of a spondee: Green grow the rashes, O

Sprung Rhythm: Versification using a specific number of accented syllables per line but disregarding the number of unaccented syllables that fall in each line, producing an irregular rhythm in the poem. Gerard Manley Hopkins, who coined the term ''sprung rhythm,'' is the most notable practitioner of this technique.

Stanza: A subdivision of a poem consisting of lines grouped together, often in recurring patterns of rhyme, line length, and meter. Stanzas may also serve as units of thought in a poem much like paragraphs in prose. Examples of stanza forms include the quatrain, *terza rima, ottava rima,* Spenserian, and the so-called *In Memoriam* stanza from Alfred, Lord Tennyson's poem by that title. The following is an example of the latter form: Love is and was my lord and king, And in his presence I attend To hear the tidings of my friend, Which every hour his couriers bring.

Stereotype: A stereotype was originally the name for a duplication made during the printing process; this led to its modern definition as a person or thing that is (or is assumed to be) the same as all others of its type. Common stereotypical characters include the absent- minded professor, the nagging wife, the troublemaking teenager, and the kindhearted grandmother.

Stream of Consciousness: A narrative technique for rendering the inward experience of a character. This technique is designed to give the impression of an ever-changing series of thoughts, emotions, images, and memories in the spontaneous and seemingly illogical order that they occur in life. The

textbook example of stream of consciousness is the last section of James Joyce's *Ulysses.*

Structuralism: A twentieth-century movement in literary criticism that examines how literary texts arrive at their meanings, rather than the meanings themselves. There are two major types of structuralist analysis: one examines the way patterns of linguistic structures unify a specific text and emphasize certain elements of that text, and the other interprets the way literary forms and conventions affect the meaning of language itself. Prominent structuralists include Michel Foucault, Roman Jakobson, and Roland Barthes.

Structure: The form taken by a piece of literature. The structure may be made obvious for ease of understanding, as in nonfiction works, or may obscured for artistic purposes, as in some poetry or seemingly ''unstructured'' prose. Examples of common literary structures include the plot of a narrative, the acts and scenes of a drama, and such poetic forms as the Shakespearean sonnet and the Pindaric ode.

Sturm und Drang: A German term meaning ''storm and stress.'' It refers to a German literary movement of the 1770s and 1780s that reacted against the order and rationalism of the enlightenment, focusing instead on the intense experience of extraordinary individuals. Highly romantic, works of this movement, such as Johann Wolfgang von Goethe's *Gotz von Berlichingen,* are typified by realism, rebelliousness, and intense emotionalism.

Style: A writer's distinctive manner of arranging words to suit his or her ideas and purpose in writing. The unique imprint of the author's personality upon his or her writing, style is the product of an author's way of arranging ideas and his or her use of diction, different sentence structures, rhythm, figures of speech, rhetorical principles, and other elements of composition. Styles may be classified according to period (Metaphysical, Augustan, Georgian), individual authors (Chaucerian, Miltonic, Jamesian), level (grand, middle, low, plain), or language (scientific, expository, poetic, journalistic).

Subject: The person, event, or theme at the center of a work of literature. A work may have one or more subjects of each type, with shorter works tending to have fewer and longer works tending to have more. The subjects of James Baldwin's novel *Go Tell It on the Mountain* include the themes of father-son relationships, religious conversion, black life, and sexuality. The subjects of Anne Frank's

Diary of a Young Girl include Anne and her family members as well as World War II, the Holocaust, and the themes of war, isolation, injustice, and racism.

Subjectivity: Writing that expresses the author's personal feelings about his subject, and which may or may not include factual information about the subject. Subjectivity is demonstrated in James Joyce's *Portrait of the Artist as a Young Man,* Samuel Butler's *The Way of All Flesh,* and Thomas Wolfe's *Look Homeward, Angel.*

Subplot: A secondary story in a narrative. A subplot may serve as a motivating or complicating force for the main plot of the work, or it may provide emphasis for, or relief from, the main plot. The conflict between the Capulets and the Montagues in William Shakespeare's *Romeo and Juliet* is an example of a subplot.

Surrealism: A term introduced to criticism by Guillaume Apollinaire and later adopted by Andre Breton. It refers to a French literary and artistic movement founded in the 1920s. The Surrealists sought to express unconscious thoughts and feelings in their works. The best-known technique used for achieving this aim was automatic writing—transcriptions of spontaneous outpourings from the unconscious. The Surrealists proposed to unify the contrary levels of conscious and unconscious, dream and reality, objectivity and subjectivity into a new level of ''super-realism.'' Surrealism can be found in the poetry of Paul Eluard, Pierre Reverdy, and Louis Aragon, among others.

Suspense: A literary device in which the author maintains the audience's attention through the build-up of events, the outcome of which will soon be revealed. Suspense in William Shakespeare's *Hamlet* is sustained throughout by the question of whether or not the Prince will achieve what he has been instructed to do and of what he intends to do.

Syllogism: A method of presenting a logical argument. In its most basic form, the syllogism consists of a major premise, a minor premise, and a conclusion. An example of a syllogism is: Major premise: When it snows, the streets get wet. Minor premise: It is snowing. Conclusion: The streets are wet.

Symbol: Something that suggests or stands for something else without losing its original identity. In literature, symbols combine their literal meaning with the suggestion of an abstract concept. Literary symbols are of two types: those that carry complex associations of meaning no matter what their con-

texts, and those that derive their suggestive meaning from their functions in specific literary works. Examples of symbols are sunshine suggesting happiness, rain suggesting sorrow, and storm clouds suggesting despair.

Symbolism: This term has two widely accepted meanings. In historical criticism, it denotes an early modernist literary movement initiated in France during the nineteenth century that reacted against the prevailing standards of realism. Writers in this movement aimed to evoke, indirectly and symbolically, an order of being beyond the material world of the five senses. Poetic expression of personal emotion figured strongly in the movement, typically by means of a private set of symbols uniquely identifiable with the individual poet. The principal aim of the Symbolists was to express in words the highly complex feelings that grew out of everyday contact with the world. In a broader sense, the term ''symbolism'' refers to the use of one object to represent another. Early members of the Symbolist movement included the French authors Charles Baudelaire and Arthur Rimbaud; William Butler Yeats, James Joyce, and T. S. Eliot were influenced as the movement moved to Ireland, England, and the United States. Examples of the concept of symbolism include a flag that stands for a nation or movement, or an empty cupboard used to suggest hopelessness, poverty, and despair.

Symbolist: See *Symbolism*

Symbolist Movement: See *Symbolism*

Sympathetic Fallacy: See *Affective Fallacy*

T

Tale: A story told by a narrator with a simple plot and little character development. Tales are usually relatively short and often carry a simple message. Examples of tales can be found in the work of Rudyard Kipling, Somerset Maugham, Saki, Anton Chekhov, Guy de Maupassant, and Armistead Maupin.

Tall Tale: A humorous tale told in a straightforward, credible tone but relating absolutely impossible events or feats of the characters. Such tales were commonly told of frontier adventures during the settlement of the west in the United States. Tall tales have been spun around such legendary heroes as Mike Fink, Paul Bunyan, Davy Crockett, Johnny Appleseed, and Captain Stormalong as well as the real-life William F. Cody and Annie Oakley. Literary use of tall tales can be found in Washington Irving's *History of New York,* Mark Twain's *Life on the Mississippi,* and in the German R. F. Raspe's *Baron Munchausen's Narratives of His Marvellous Travels and Campaigns in Russia.*

Tanka: A form of Japanese poetry similar to *haiku.* A *tanka* is five lines long, with the lines containing five, seven, five, seven, and seven syllables respectively. Skilled *tanka* authors include Ishikawa Takuboku, Masaoka Shiki, Amy Lowell, and Adelaide Crapsey.

Teatro Grottesco: See *Theater of the Grotesque*

Terza Rima: A three-line stanza form in poetry in which the rhymes are made on the last word of each line in the following manner: the first and third lines of the first stanza, then the second line of the first stanza and the first and third lines of the second stanza, and so on with the middle line of any stanza rhyming with the first and third lines of the following stanza. An example of *terza rima* is Percy Bysshe Shelley's ''The Triumph of Love'': As in that trance of wondrous thought I lay This was the tenour of my waking dream. Methought I sate beside a public way Thick strewn with summer dust, and a great stream Of people there was hurrying to and fro Numerous as gnats upon the evening gleam,. . .

Tetrameter: See *Meter*

Textual Criticism: A branch of literary criticism that seeks to establish the authoritative text of a literary work. Textual critics typically compare all known manuscripts or printings of a single work in order to assess the meanings of differences and revisions. This procedure allows them to arrive at a definitive version that (supposedly) corresponds to the author's original intention. Textual criticism was applied during the Renaissance to salvage the classical texts of Greece and Rome, and modern works have been studied, for instance, to undo deliberate correction or censorship, as in the case of novels by Stephen Crane and Theodore Dreiser.

Theater of Cruelty: Term used to denote a group of theatrical techniques designed to eliminate the psychological and emotional distance between actors and audience. This concept, introduced in the 1930s in France, was intended to inspire a more intense theatrical experience than conventional theater allowed. The ''cruelty'' of this dramatic theory signified not sadism but heightened actor/audience involvement in the dramatic event. The theater of cruelty was theorized by Antonin Artaud in his *Le Theatre et son double* (*The Theatre and Its Double*), and also appears in the work of Jerzy Grotowski, Jean Genet, Jean Vilar, and Arthur Adamov, among others.

Theater of the Absurd: A post-World War II dramatic trend characterized by radical theatrical innovations. In works influenced by the Theater of the absurd, nontraditional, sometimes grotesque characterizations, plots, and stage sets reveal a meaningless universe in which human values are irrelevant. Existentialist themes of estrangement, absurdity, and futility link many of the works of this movement. The principal writers of the Theater of the Absurd are Samuel Beckett, Eugene Ionesco, Jean Genet, and Harold Pinter.

Theater of the Grotesque: An Italian theatrical movement characterized by plays written around the ironic and macabre aspects of daily life in the World War I era. Theater of the Grotesque was named after the play *The Mask and the Face* by Luigi Chiarelli, which was described as ''a grotesque in three acts.'' The movement influenced the work of Italian dramatist Luigi Pirandello, author of *Right You Are, If You Think You Are.* Also known as *Teatro Grottesco.*

Theme: The main point of a work of literature. The term is used interchangeably with thesis. The theme of William Shakespeare's *Othello*—jealousy—is a common one.

Thesis: A thesis is both an essay and the point argued in the essay. Thesis novels and thesis plays share the quality of containing a thesis which is supported through the action of the story. A master's thesis and a doctoral dissertation are two theses required of graduate students.

Thesis Play: See *Thesis*

Three Unities: See *Unities*

Tone: The author's attitude toward his or her audience may be deduced from the tone of the work. A formal tone may create distance or convey politeness, while an informal tone may encourage a friendly, intimate, or intrusive feeling in the reader. The author's attitude toward his or her subject matter may also be deduced from the tone of the words he or she uses in discussing it. The tone of John F. Kennedy's speech which included the appeal to ''ask not what your country can do for you'' was intended to instill feelings of camaraderie and national pride in listeners.

Tragedy: A drama in prose or poetry about a noble, courageous hero of excellent character who, because of some tragic character flaw or *hamartia*, brings ruin upon him- or herself. Tragedy treats its subjects in a dignified and serious manner, using poetic language to help evoke pity and fear and bring about catharsis, a purging of these emotions. The tragic form was practiced extensively by the ancient Greeks. In the Middle Ages, when classical works were virtually unknown, tragedy came to denote any works about the fall of persons from exalted to low conditions due to any reason: fate, vice, weakness, etc. According to the classical definition of tragedy, such works present the ''pathetic''—that which evokes pity—rather than the tragic. The classical form of tragedy was revived in the sixteenth century; it flourished especially on the Elizabethan stage. In modern times, dramatists have attempted to adapt the form to the needs of modern society by drawing their heroes from the ranks of ordinary men and women and defining the nobility of these heroes in terms of spirit rather than exalted social standing. The greatest classical example of tragedy is Sophocles' *Oedipus Rex*. The ''pathetic'' derivation is exemplified in ''The Monk's Tale'' in Geoffrey Chaucer's *Canterbury Tales.* Notable works produced during the sixteenth century revival include William Shakespeare's *Hamlet, Othello,* and *King Lear.* Modern dramatists working in the tragic tradition include Henrik Ibsen, Arthur Miller, and Eugene O'Neill.

Tragedy of Blood: See *Revenge Tragedy*

Tragic Flaw: In a tragedy, the quality within the hero or heroine which leads to his or her downfall. Examples of the tragic flaw include Othello's jealousy and Hamlet's indecisiveness, although most great tragedies defy such simple interpretation.

Transcendentalism: An American philosophical and religious movement, based in New England from around 1835 until the Civil War. Transcendentalism was a form of American romanticism that had its roots abroad in the works of Thomas Carlyle, Samuel Coleridge, and Johann Wolfgang von Goethe. The Transcendentalists stressed the importance of intuition and subjective experience in communication with God. They rejected religious dogma and texts in favor of mysticism and scientific naturalism. They pursued truths that lie beyond the ''colorless'' realms perceived by reason and the senses and were active social reformers in public education,

women's rights, and the abolition of slavery. Prominent members of the group include Ralph Waldo Emerson and Henry David Thoreau.

Trickster: A character or figure common in Native American and African literature who uses his ingenuity to defeat enemies and escape difficult situations. Tricksters are most often animals, such as the spider, hare, or coyote, although they may take the form of humans as well. Examples of trickster tales include Thomas King's *A Coyote Columbus Story,* Ashley F. Bryan's *The Dancing Granny* and Ishmael Reed's *The Last Days of Louisiana Red.*

Trimeter: See *Meter*

Triple Rhyme: See *Rhyme*

Trochee: See *Foot*

U

Understatement: See *Irony*

Unities: Strict rules of dramatic structure, formulated by Italian and French critics of the Renaissance and based loosely on the principles of drama discussed by Aristotle in his *Poetics.* Foremost among these rules were the three unities of action, time, and place that compelled a dramatist to: (1) construct a single plot with a beginning, middle, and end that details the causal relationships of action and character; (2) restrict the action to the events of a single day; and (3) limit the scene to a single place or city. The unities were observed faithfully by continental European writers until the Romantic Age, but they were never regularly observed in English drama. Modern dramatists are typically more concerned with a unity of impression or emotional effect than with any of the classical unities. The unities are observed in Pierre Corneille's tragedy *Polyeuctes* and Jean-Baptiste Racine's *Phedre.* Also known as Three Unities.

Urban Realism: A branch of realist writing that attempts to accurately reflect the often harsh facts of modern urban existence. Some works by Stephen Crane, Theodore Dreiser, Charles Dickens, Fyodor Dostoyevsky, Emile Zola, Abraham Cahan, and Henry Fuller feature urban realism. Modern examples include Claude Brown's *Manchild in the Promised Land* and Ron Milner's *What the Wine Sellers Buy.*

Utopia: A fictional perfect place, such as ''paradise'' or ''heaven.'' Early literary utopias were included in Plato's *Republic* and Sir Thomas More's

Utopia, while more modern utopias can be found in Samuel Butler's *Erewhon,* Theodor Herzka's *A Visit to Freeland,* and H. G. Wells' *A Modern Utopia.*

Utopian: See *Utopia*

Utopianism: See *Utopia*

V

Verisimilitude: Literally, the appearance of truth. In literary criticism, the term refers to aspects of a work of literature that seem true to the reader. Verisimilitude is achieved in the work of Honore de Balzac, Gustave Flaubert, and Henry James, among other late nineteenth-century realist writers.

Vers de societe: See *Occasional Verse*

Vers libre: See *Free Verse*

Verse: A line of metered language, a line of a poem, or any work written in verse. The following line of verse is from the epic poem *Don Juan* by Lord Byron: ''My way is to begin with the beginning.''

Versification: The writing of verse. Versification may also refer to the meter, rhyme, and other mechanical components of a poem. Composition of a ''Roses are red, violets are blue'' poem to suit an occasion is a common form of versification practiced by students.

Victorian: Refers broadly to the reign of Queen Victoria of England (1837-1901) and to anything with qualities typical of that era. For example, the qualities of smug narrowmindedness, bourgeois materialism, faith in social progress, and priggish morality are often considered Victorian. This stereotype is contradicted by such dramatic intellectual developments as the theories of Charles Darwin, Karl Marx, and Sigmund Freud (which stirred strong debates in England) and the critical attitudes of serious Victorian writers like Charles Dickens and George Eliot. In literature, the Victorian Period was the great age of the English novel, and the latter part of the era saw the rise of movements such as decadence and symbolism. Works of Victorian lit-

erature include the poetry of Robert Browning and Alfred, Lord Tennyson, the criticism of Matthew Arnold and John Ruskin, and the novels of Emily Bronte, William Makepeace Thackeray, and Thomas Hardy. Also known as Victorian Age and Victorian Period.

Victorian Age: See *Victorian*

Victorian Period: See *Victorian*

W

Weltanschauung: A German term referring to a person's worldview or philosophy. Examples of *weltanschauung* include Thomas Hardy's view of the human being as the victim of fate, destiny, or impersonal forces and circumstances, and the disillusioned and laconic cynicism expressed by such poets of the 1930s as W. H. Auden, Sir Stephen Spender, and Sir William Empson.

Weltschmerz: A German term meaning ''world pain.'' It describes a sense of anguish about the nature of existence, usually associated with a melancholy, pessimistic attitude. *Weltschmerz* was expressed in England by George Gordon, Lord Byron in his *Manfred* and *Childe Harold's Pilgrimage,* in France by Viscount de Chateaubriand, Alfred de Vigny, and Alfred de Musset, in Russia by Aleksandr Pushkin and Mikhail Lermontov, in Poland by Juliusz Slowacki, and in America by Nathaniel Hawthorne.

Z

Zarzuela: A type of Spanish operetta. Writers of *zarzuelas* include Lope de Vega and Pedro Calderon.

Zeitgeist: A German term meaning ''spirit of the time.'' It refers to the moral and intellectual trends of a given era. Examples of *zeitgeist* include the preoccupation with the more morbid aspects of dying and death in some Jacobean literature, especially in the works of dramatists Cyril Tourneur and John Webster, and the decadence of the French Symbolists.

Cumulative Author/Title Index

Nationality/Ethnicity Index

Subject/Theme Index